Doing What Comes Naturally

Doing What Comes Naturally

Change, Rhetoric, and the Practice of Theory in Literary and Legal Studies

Stanley Fish

CLARENDON PRESS   OXFORD   1989

Oxford University Press, Walton Street, Oxford OX2 6DP
Oxford New York Toronto
Delhi Bombay Calcutta Madras Karachi
Petaling Jaya Singapore Hong Kong Tokyo
Nairobi Dar es Salaam Cape Town
Melbourne Auckland

and associated companies in
Berlin Ibadan

Oxford is a trade mark of Oxford University Press

© Duke University Press 1989

British Library Cataloging in Publication Data
(data available)
ISBN 0-19-812998-X
ISBN 0-19-812999-8 (Pbk.)

Printed in the United States of America

This book is for
Kenneth Abraham
Michael Fried
Walter Michaels
and
Baltimore, Maryland

Contents

Preface

I can imagine at least two objections to the following pages. Some might complain that they do not comprise a book, but rather present a collection of essays on diverse topics: Milton, Freud, the law, professionalism, formalism, the teaching of composition, irony, literary history, speech acts, change, rhetoric, blind submission, the uses of theory, literary history. Others might voice the opposite complaint: every essay in this book is the same; no matter what its putative topic each chapter finally reduces to an argument in which the troubles and benefits of interpretive theory are made to disappear in the solvent of an enriched notion of practice. This second group would be right.

In the course of this book, I say very little about its title, *Doing What Comes Naturally*. I intend it to refer to the unreflective actions that follow from being embedded in a context of practice. This kind of action—and in my argument there is no other—is anything but natural in the sense of proceeding independently of historical and social formations; but once those formations are in place (and they always are), what you think to do will not be calculated in relation to a higher law or an overarching theory but will issue from you as naturally as breathing. In the words of John Milton, "from a sincere heart"—that is, a heart embedded in a structure of conviction—"unimpos'd expressions" will come "unbidden into the outward gesture" (*Apology, Complete Prose Works of John Milton,* ed. Don M. Wolfe, New Haven, 1953, p. 941).

A number of chapters have been previously published, often in shorter forms. Chapters 2, 10, and 14 were published in *Critical Inquiry;* Chapter 3 first appeared in *Diacritics*. Chapter 4 first appeared both in *Critical Inquiry* and the *Texas Law Review;* Chapter 5 appeared in the *Texas Law Review*. Chapter 6 was first published in the *Stan-*

ford Law Review. Chapter 7 first appeared in the *South Atlantic Quarterly.* Chapter 8 first appeared in *PMLA.* Chapter 9 was published in *Daedalus.* Chapter 11 appeared both in the *Cardozo Law Review* and in *New Literary History.* Chapter 12 appeared in a much briefer form in *Literature and History* (ed. G. S. Morson, Stanford, 1986). Chapters 13 and 17 appeared in the *Yale Law Journal.* Chapter 15 appeared in *The Current Criticism* (ed. C. Koelb and V. Lokke, Lafayette, Indiana, 1987). Chapter 16 appeared in *Law and Philosophy.* Chapter 18 appeared in two successive issues of the *Raritan Review* and in the *Duke Law Journal.* Chapter 22 has appeared in various shorter versions in the *Times Literary Supplement, Trial(s) of Psychoanalysis* (ed. Françoise Meltzer, Chicago, 1988), and *The Linguistics of Writing* (ed. N. Fabb, D. Attridge, A. Durant, and C. MacCabe, Manchester, 1987). Chapter 21 has been published in the *Washington and Lee Law Review.* Chapters 1, 19, and 20 are published here for the first time. I am grateful for permission to reprint.

This book could not have been produced had it not been for Sandy Vinson, who prepared the manuscript with infinite patience, and Stanley Blair, who proofread it and made a wonderful index.

1. Introduction: Going Down the Anti-Formalist Road

I It is one of the theses of this book that many of the issues in interpretive theory can be reduced to a few basic questions in the philosophy of language. Consider, for example, the discussion of "presupposition" in Ruth Kempson's *Presupposition and the Delimitation of Semantics* (Cambridge, 1975). Kempson begins by observing that presupposition can be defined "in one of two ways—either as a relation between statements (parallel to entailment, synonymy, etc.) or as a property of the speaker's belief in uttering a sentence" (p. 2). The difference is between a *formal* notion of presupposition in which it is a feature of sentences as they exist in the abstract apart from any particular occasion of use, and presupposition as a fact about what is in a speaker's mind—his understanding of the world and of the situation in which he now finds himself—at the moment of utterance. As Kempson observes, the possibility of deriving meaning from the formal properties of sentences cannot survive the serious assertion of a speaker-based theory of presupposition, for "if presuppositions in terms of speaker-belief are considered to be a part of the semantic interpretation of sentences, then it seems that the meaning of sentences must be in terms of speaker-hearer relations and not . . . in terms of the relation between a symbol or set of symbols and the object or state described" (pp. 2–3). And if that is so, "one must give up the standard claim that the meaning of a sentence is a function of the meaning of its constituent parts" (p. 60). This follows because if the presuppositions of an utterance vary with the beliefs of speakers and hearers—that is, if no sentence has "a unique set of presuppositions"—then "every sentence can be analyzed with . . . as many different sets of presuppositions" as there are different possible contextualizations and there is no regular and predictable way to assign a meaning, or even a range of possible meanings, to a particular sentence. Meaning, in short, becomes entirely contextual and "cannot be determined independent of the speaker of a sentence in a particular situation" (p. 60). Once this conclusion has been reached, others immediately follow:

> One is thus faced with an analysis of meaning which claims that every sentence has an indeterminate number of indeterminable meaning representations. And if the meanings of sentences are indeterminable, then meaning relations between sentences such as entailment, contradiction, by definition cannot be predicted. Moreover . . . it would follow that the grammaticality of sentences cannot be determined either, independent of the situation in which they are uttered. But this has the immediate consequence that one's grammar would not be predictive.

By producing this sequence of entailments, Kempson (however inadvertently and even reluctantly) makes a very important point: once you start down the anti-formalist road, there is no place to stop; remove the connection between observable features and the specification of meaning, and you also remove everything else that is supposedly independent of context; entailment, contradiction, grammaticality itself, all become as variable and contingent as presupposition. This, however, is not the conclusion Kempson reaches; and indeed it is the specter of reaching it that drives her in the opposite direction:

> We are thus faced with the conclusion that a theory which incorporates a speaker relative concept of presupposition as part of its semantic representation is in principle unable to fulfill any of the four conditions I set up initially (1.1) as a prerequisite for any semantic theory and therefore must be relinquished. (p. 60)

Those conditions include "a systematic relation between the meaning of lexical items and the syntactic structure of the sentence," a "finite set of predictive rules," the mechanical separation of non-deviant from anomalous sentences, and predictability of meaning relations between sentences. Kempson is quite right to observe that a speaker-relative concept of presupposition and therefore of meaning makes the fulfilling of those conditions impossible since the variability of speakers and the difficulty of determining what is in their minds precludes generality and makes every speech situation unique. The surprise is in the last phrase: "and therefore must be relinquished." Her reasoning is that since speaker-relative presupposition, if taken seriously, would create grave (indeed, insurmountable) difficulties for a semantic theory, we cannot take it seriously. The conclusion is not reached because the evidence for speaker-relative presupposition is weak or because the connection between speaker-relative presupposition and meaning is specious, but because to pursue this line of thought would be to give up the pursuit of theory. In short, for Kempson this line of thought is unthinkable in the sense that her deepest assumptions mark it as obviously absurd. Surely any thesis that is incompatible with the assumed goal of linguistics—the goal of building a theoretical model of language—must be rejected out of hand; after all, the "four demands" that speaker-relative presupposition fails to satisfy "are agreed in principle by all linguists" (p. 2). If Kempson were to give credence to this thesis, she would be denying her membership in the community of linguists and (in effect) denying the most significant aspect of her being.

I would not be misunderstood. I am not criticizing Kempson for rejecting arguments that are stigmatized in advance by the beliefs she necessarily holds as a practicing linguist. She has no choice, if by choice one means a judgment reached independently of any predispositions or biases. It is just those predispositions and biases—those assumptions concerning what must be the case in the matter of language—that fill her judgment, and one would be making if not an impossible at least a Herculean demand if one were to ask her to set them aside.

Again, I would not be misunderstood. I am not saying that Kempson is beyond criticism simply because the context of which she is an extension prevents her from seeing certain arguments as respectable or even makable. In my very strong opinion the arguments she clings to, the arguments that underwrite the project of formal linguistics, are wrong. And it is part of *my* argument that I can say that despite the sympathetic analysis I make of her "epistemological condition." This does not mean that I am not in the same condition—embedded in conviction—but that precisely because I am embedded in conviction, my sense of the rightness of my arguments is no less strong than hers and is in no way diminished by my ability to give an account of its source. That at least is the burden of several of the essays in this volume, especially of those that assert the inconsequentiality (in certain terms) of theory.

This, however, is to get ahead of my story, and for the time being I would like to linger a little longer on the issues Kempson raises, for

much of what I want to say builds on the thesis from which she draws
back in horror, the thesis that the meaning of a sentence is *not* a function of the meaning of its constituent parts; or to put it another way,
that meaning cannot be formally calculated, derived from the shape of
marks on a page; or to put it in the most direct way possible, that there
is no such thing as literal meaning, if by literal meaning one means a
meaning that is perspicuous no matter what the context and no matter
what is in the speaker's or hearer's mind, a meaning that because it is
prior to interpretation can serve as a constraint on interpretation. It
might seem that the thesis that there is no such thing as literal meaning is a limited one, of interest largely to linguists and philosophers of
language; but in fact it is a thesis whose implications are almost bound-
less, for they extend to the very underpinnings of the universe as it is
understood by persons of a certain cast of mind. It is a cast of mind
Kempson displays when she concludes that if a unit of meaning cannot
be identified independently of the beliefs of speakers and hearers, the
entire enterprise of formal linguistics falls apart, since the first principle
of that enterprise demands what the speaker-relative account of presupposition denies.

The far-reaching effects of the unavailability of literal meaning
are even more evident in the decision of a Minnesota court in a case
argued in 1924. The point at issue is the "parol evidence rule," a rule
that prohibits the introduction of oral evidence in order to alter or vary
the meaning of a contract that is deemed to be complete in itself. Obviously it is a rule designed to hold interpretation in check by insisting
that it respect a self-sufficient and self-declaring (literal) meaning. The
alternative, as the court sees it, is chaos:

> Were it otherwise, written contracts would be enforced not accord-
> ing to the plain effect of their language, but pursuant to the story
> of their negotiation as told by the litigant having at the time being
> the greater power of persuading the trier of fact. So far as con-
> tracts are concerned the rule of law would give way to the mere
> notions of men as to who should win law suits. Without that [the
> parol evidence] rule there would be no assurance of the enforce-
> ability of a written contract. If such assurance were removed today
> from our law, general disaster would result . . . (*Cargill Com-
> mission Co. v. Swartwood,* 198 N.W. 538 [1924]).

What is remarkable about this passage is the short time it takes to move from the focus on the "plain effect" of language to the conclusion that if that focus is abandoned, *general* disaster—not just disaster for those with a professional interest in notions like "plain meaning"—will result. The reasoning behind this conclusion is not drawn out, but it is worth drawing out because it is writ large in many of the essays that follow. It is first and last a question of *power* in relation to the putting in place of *constraints*. What the Cargill court sees is that if there is no public way of setting down marks that stand firm against interpretive manipulation, the rule of law—of perfectly explicit and impersonal utterances—is replaced by the rule of *persuasion,* the rule of "the litigant having at the time being the greater power of persuading the trier of fact." As a result, authority becomes structurally unstable, embodied not in some abiding core (what H. L. A. Hart calls an "authoritative mark"[1]) but in the words of whatever person or persons happens to have sway "at the time being." This last phrase connects the court's fear with an ancient tension between a notion of truth as something independent of local, partial perspectives and a notion of truth as whatever seems perspicuous and obvious to those embedded in some local, partial perspective. It is the difference between a truth that judges human achievements and a truth that *is* a human achievement, inseparable finally from "the mere notions of men," and it is the court's contention that only the first kind of truth—the truth whose availability makes plain language at once possible and essential—will assure order that is *principled,* based not on the accidents of history and culture, but on the essence of enduring values.

By making its cases in these terms, the Cargill court illustrates the intimate relationship between formalism as a thesis in the philosophy of language and foundationalism as a thesis about the core constituents of human life. Formalism as a doctrine has been under attack for a long time now and few will acknowledge subscribing to it, but as Roberto Unger has observed, "Those who dismiss formalism as a naive illusion . . . do not know what they are in for . . . they fail to understand what the classic liberal thinkers saw earlier: the destruction of formalism brings in its wake the ruin of all other liberal doctrines of adjudication."[2] Here and in other places Unger issues a double warning: don't think that formalism is a simple position, easily identified and easily avoided, and don't think that you avoid formalism by acknowledging context, or proclaiming the inescapability of politics, or any other of the gestures by which the anti-foundationalist insight is embraced at a general level without any strong awareness of the implications of that insight for assumptions and practices that remain unexamined. Formalism, as Unger correctly sees, is not merely a linguistic doctrine, but a doctrine that implies, in addition to a theory of language, a theory of the self, of community, of rationality, of practice, of politics. A formalist believes that words have clear meanings, and in order to believe that (or because he believes that) he must also believe (1) that minds see those clear meanings clearly; (2) that clarity is a condition that persists through changes in context; (3) that nothing in the self interferes with the perception of clarity, or, that if it does, it can be controlled by something else in the mind; (4) that meanings are a property of language; (5) that language is an abstract system that is prior to any occasion of use; (6) that occasions of use are underwritten by that system; (7) that the meanings words have in that system (as opposed to the meanings they acquire in situations) are or should be the basis of "general" discourses like the law; (8) that because they are general rather than local, such discourses can serve (in the form of rules or statutes) as constraints on interpretive desires; (9) that interpretive desires must (and can) be set aside when there is serious public business afoot; (10) that the fashioning of a just political system requires such a setting aside, the submission of the individual will to impersonal and public norms (encoded in an impersonal and public language); (11) that this submission would be a rational act, chosen by the very will that is to be held in check; (12) that rationality, like meaning, is an abstract system that stands apart from the contexts in which its standard is to be consulted; (13) that the standard of rationality is available for the settling of disputes between agents situated in different contexts; (14) that the mark of a civilized (lawful) community is the acknowledgment of that standard as a referee or judge; (15) that communities whose members fail to acknowledge that standard are, by definition, *ir*rational; and (16) that irrationality is the state of being ruled by desire and force—that is, by persuasion—rather than by a norm that reflects the desires of no one, but protects the desires of everyone. All of these beliefs and more follow from and give support to the belief that words have clear meanings, and many of the essays in this book begin by challenging the linguistic thesis and end by challenging everything else.

II

Often the challenge is made in the name of *intention,* a much debated topic in literary studies since the late 1940s and one that has been increasingly the center of controversy in legal studies. To some it seems curious that such a minor topic should receive so much attention, and from several quarters there has been an almost incredulous response to Steven Knapp's and Walter Michaels' assertion that "what a text means is what its author intends."[3] Knapp and Michaels have been misread as urging a methodology in order to assure that interpretation will proceed "objectively"; but in fact their identification of intention with meaning removes the possibility of objectivity in interpretation by making its object something the interpreter constructs. It is only if meaning is embedded in texts—is a *formal* fact—that one could devise a method for "reading it off"; but if meaning is a matter of what a speaker situated in a particular situation has in mind (precisely the thesis of speaker-relative presupposition), one can only determine it by going behind the words to the intentional circumstances of production in the light of which they acquire significance. Nor is it the case that these circumstances can themselves be regarded as a new (and higher) set of formal facts, a new text whose meaning can now be read off; for if it is by means of the intentional context and not directly that a reader imputes meaning to a text, that context must itself be imputed—given an interpreted form—since the evidence one might cite in specifying it—the evidence of words, marks, gestures—will only be evidence, have a certain shape rather than another, if its own shape has already (and interpretively) been assumed. Once words have been dislodged as the repository of meaning in favor of intention, no amount of them will suffice to establish an intention since the value they have will always depend on that which they presume to establish. In Unger's words, "as soon as it is necessary to engage in a discussion of purpose [another word for intention] to determine what an utterance means formalism has been abandoned" (p. 93); and it is my contention in the essays that follow that the abandonment of formalism—of the derivation of meaning from mechanically enumerable features—has always and already occurred.

This is a hard conclusion for many linguists and philosophers to reach for reasons that are nicely articulated by John Searle. Commenting on H. P. Grice's theory of meaning, a theory in which meaning is the effect of having recognized another's intention, Searle points out that "on Grice's account it would seem that any sentence can be uttered with any meaning whatever, given that the circumstances make possible the appropriate intentions."[4] This is, of course, precisely Kempson's objection to speaker-relative presupposition when she rejects "an analysis of meaning which claims that every sentence has an indeterminate number of . . . meaning representations"; and Searle anticipates Kempson when he adds, "but that has the consequence that the meaning of the sentence then becomes just another circumstance." In fact, the case is worse than that: under this analysis, a sentence doesn't *have* a meaning if by "have a meaning" you refer to its meaning in the abstract, apart from an occasion of use; any meaning a sentence might be seen to have would be the product of a moment of situated interpretive labor, and that labor would not be constrained by any meanings the words themselves (now a nonsense phrase) contain. It is at this point that we see the full implications of the shift by which meaning is disengaged from language and relocated in the (interpreted) intentions of speakers: there are no longer any constraints on interpretation that are not themselves interpretive. Since intentions themselves can be known only interpretively, the meanings that follow upon the specification of intention will always be vulnerable to the challenge of an alternative specification. It is just as the Cargill court feared; a contract or anything else will be enforced not by its plain language (something that simply does not exist) but by the litigant or interpreter "having at the time being the great power of persuading the trier of fact" or any other socially situated agent who is captured by his "story."

As an example of how interpretation works under this analysis, consider the case of John Milton as he argues in 1643 for the relaxing of the constraints on divorce. In 1643 both sides must support their positions from Scripture, and one of the crucial proof texts cited by Milton's opponents is this verse from Matthew: "Whosoever shall put away his wife, except it be for fornication . . . committeth adultery" (19:9). In the course of his *Doctrine and Discipline of Divorce* Milton labors at what might seem an impossible task, to read that text as saying that a man may put away his wife for any reason he likes. He does it (or tries to do it) by arguing from intention. He points out that when Christ uttered these words he was speaking to the Pharisees in a context in which they were tempting him to a lax pronouncement concerning the law. It is, says Milton, in response to their provocations that Christ delivers a judgment even more severe than they themselves would have delivered, thus simultaneously escaping their net and undercutting their strictness by overgoing it: "So heer he may be justly thought to have giv'n this rigid sentence against divorce, not to cut off all remedy from a good man who finds himself consuming away in a disconsolate and uninjoy'd matrimony, but to lay a bridle upon the bold abuses of those overweening Rabbies."[5] In other words, since this stricture was intended only for those of pharisaic temper, the freedom of men who are not Pharisees cannot properly be abrogated by invoking a prohibition that was not addressed to them. While Christ might say to the Pharisees, "*You* can divorce only for reason of adultery," he says to us, "to *you* divorce is permitted if, in your judgment, your marriage is not a true spiritual union"; and since true spirituality does not show itself, but is a matter of interpretation, there is no principled way of ruling out of court the judgment of one who claims a spiritual lack in his marriage. Therefore, by Christ's own words, a man may put his wife away for any reason he likes.

It is an open question as to whether this argument works, but its success or failure is less important than the illustration it provides for the point I am making. Meanings that seem perspicuous and literal are rendered so by forceful interpretive acts and not by the properties of language. In the event that Milton is persuasive, it is not because he has moved the words from their "normal" setting to the setting of a special intention, but because he has dislodged the words from one special setting (all intentional settings are special), where their meaning was obvious, and placed them in another where their meaning is also obvious, but different. It is not a matter of doing something willful as opposed to doing something else, but of one willful action supplanting another. Those who read Christ's words as plainly prohibiting divorce (except in one well-defined circumstance) are not submitting their interpretive wills to the "words themselves"; for they, no less than Milton, are hearing those words within some intentional context (i.e., of a God who would hold his creatures to strict, even mechanical strictures, as opposed to a God whose stance toward his creatures' weaknesses is charitable) to which they have been persuaded in the same way and by the same means that Milton would now persuade us.

The result is a world aptly described by Bishop Hoadly's observation that "whoever hath an absolute authority to interpret any written or spoken laws it is he who is the lawgiver to all intents and purposes and not the person who first wrote or spake them."[6] Hoadly is cited by H. L. A. Hart as an illustration of the conclusion he wants us *not* to reach, for were we to reach it, he points out, the law would rest on grounds no different from those assumed by the gunman who demands your money or your life, the grounds of force.[7] The fear is of a world without principle, a world where might makes right, and personal preferences run roughshod over the rules and laws intended to constrain them. Does might make right? In a sense the answer I must give is yes, since in the absence of a perspective independent of interpretation some interpretive perspective will always rule by virtue of having won out over its competitors. This at any rate is explicitly the argument of "Force," "Fish v. Fiss," and "Still Wrong After All These Years." But at the same time in these and other essays the identification of might or force as the bottom-line category of interpretive and deliberative activity is followed by an assertion that the situation—that is, our situation—is not as bad as it might seem. Here the reasoning depends on challenging the picture of the self and of the decision-making process in relation to which the ascendancy of force is a disaster. In that picture the self is a quantity of desire that must be constrained by something independent of it so that its actions might have a social or public direction rather than a merely personal one. Constraints are found in rules or laws or principles that hold the self's natural impulses (desires, biases, prejudices) in check. Responsible persons accept these constraints and defer to them in the course of reaching a conclusion; irresponsible persons ignore them and give reign to their "mere preferences." It is this picture that underwrites much of the thinking in legal circles about the activity of judging. What judges do, at least when they are doing their jobs properly, is set their personal feelings aside and come to their decisions by consulting the rule (of law) they have accepted as a bridle on their wills. Thus Kenney Hegland cites a famous contract case (*Mills v. Wyman*) in which Chief Justice Parker of the Massachusetts Supreme Court, finding himself faced with a defendant whose actions he abhors, nevertheless rules for him because the law he has sworn faithfully to execute bids him do so. Hegland takes this as a particularly perspicuous example of the operation of independent constraints on "personal predilections," an example which, he claims, refutes the "deconstructionist position that legal doctrine does not constrain judicial decision."[8]

As Hegland sees it, the opposition is clear: "personal predilections" versus the constraint of doctrine, and equally clear is the larger opposition of which this one is an instance: civilization and order versus the anarchy of the individual will. But is it really so clear as that? Not if one interrogates the opposition at a basic level and asks, as a starter, what exactly is a "personal predilection"? Where does it come from? In order for the opposition to work with the force (a nice word) Hegland intends, personal predilections or preferences must come from nowhere, must originate in the self in a way unrelated to social and public norms; otherwise, the opposition would be blurred. But how could such a preference even form apart from some conventional system of thought or mores in relation to which it was possible and thinkable? In the case Hegland cites, although Judge Parker is repelled by a man who breaks a promise to someone who cared for his dying son, he decides that since the promise was not supported by "consideration" (the Good Samaritan did not bargain for payment), it is not legally binding. But it hardly makes any sense to say that Parker's distaste for this ingrate is a "personal predilection"; rather it is a sentiment that forms part of a conventionally established system of obligation which Parker has internalized just as he has internalized the legal doctrine that now trumps his conventional sentiment. The conflict he feels is not between a normative obligation and "mere preference," but between two normative obligations, one of which carries the day because it is central to the role he is now playing. Indeed, there is no such thing as a "mere preference" in the sense that makes it a threat to communal norms, for anything that could be experienced as a preference will derive from the norms inherent in some community.

The conclusion only appears to be paradoxical: all preferences are principled, that is, they are intelligible and doable only by virtue of some principled articulation of the world and its possibilities; but by the same token all principles are preferences, because every principle is an extension of a particular and *contestable* articulation of the world and none proceeds from a universal perspective (a contradiction in terms). When Judge Parker holds for the defendant because no consideration attached to his promise, he speaks from a vision of public life that is anything but neutral and impersonal. In that vision contracting parties begin in what has been called an "equality of distrust" and are presumed to be bargaining for advantage; actions of altruism and simple faith are not recognized except as aberrations that the law will neither respect nor protect. In the eyes of some, these "principles" of contract are obviously *un*principled, although for others (including, presumably, Judge Parker) they are necessary to the healthy functioning of a free market. In short, one person's principles are another person's illegitimate ("mere") preferences, and any characterization of a dispute or a choice that puts the principles on one side and the "personal predilections" on the other is itself interested and (in the sense defined above) personal. In the (certain) event that some characterization will prevail (at least for a time) over its rivals, it will do so because some interested assertion of principle has managed to *forcefully* dislodge other (equally interested) assertions of principle. It is in this sense that force is the sole determinant of outcomes, but the sting is removed from this conclusion when force is understood not as "pure" or "mere" force (phenomena never encountered) but as the urging (perhaps in the softest terms) of some point of view, of some vision of the world complete with purposes, goals, standards, reasons—in short, with everything to which force is usually opposed in the name of principle.

Once the opposition between principle and force has been deconstructed, any number of issues begin to look very different, including the issue of constraints. Constraints, you will recall, are what is supposedly required to prevent a self composed of desire from going its own (unprincipled) way; but if desires (or preferences) cannot have shape independently of some normative vision, the self that is composed of desires is, ipso facto, composed of constraints, and no *additional* constraints are needed to give it a direction it already has. This is perhaps the most surprising and counterintuitive consequence of the denial of independent constraints (which is one and the same with the denial of literal meaning): rather than leaving us in a world where the brakes are off, it situates us in a world where the brakes—in the form of the imperatives, urgencies, and prohibitions that come along with any point of view (and being in a point of view is not something one can avoid)—are always and already on. When Judge Parker sits down to consider *Mills v. Wyman,* he is in no sense "free" to see the facts in any way he pleases; rather his very first look is informed (constrained) by the ways of thinking that now fill his consciousness as a result of his initiation into the professional community of jurists. That is to say, he looks with judicially informed eyes, eyes from whose perspective he cannot distance himself for a single second except to slip into another way of seeing, no less conventional, no less involuntary. At no time is he free to go his "own way," for he is always going in a way marked out by the practice or set of practices of whose defining principles (goals, purposes, interdictions) he is a moving extension, and therefore it would be superfluous of him to submit his behavior to principles other than the ones that already, and *necessarily,* constrain him.

But, someone might object, there are principles and principles, constraints and constraints. What Parker is in the grip of, by virtue of his membership in the legal community, are the "weak constraints of practice," constraints that flow from local and historically limited modes of thought and action. Isn't it the essence of truly responsible behavior—legal or any other—always to be looking beyond the horizons of the local and contingent to more *general* principles (of logic, ethics, reason), principles that would add a level of constraint *higher* than that already built into practice? The answer is "no," and the reason is that there are no higher or more general constraints, only constraints that are *different,* constraints built into practices other than the one whose reform is now being contemplated. It is simply not possible even to conceive of a constraint (or rule or law or principle) without already having assumed a context of practice in relation to which it is intelligible (this is the argument against literal meaning all over again; everything proceeds from it), and whenever a so-called outside or external or independent constraint is invoked, what is really being invoked is the interested agenda (complete with norms, evidentiary criteria, etc.) of a project already in (some other) place. Whether or not the invocation takes, whether it is heeded or dismissed as beside the discipline's point, will depend on the extent to which the discipline's sense of itself (precisely the content of its principles and constraints) is already (potentially) responsible to news from other precincts, and that will be a political question to which the answer will be different at different times. As things stand now, legal practitioners are responsive to the news from economics and invoke it as a constraint on their own activities. It was, of course, not always thus (despite the revisionist histories of some "law and economics" advocates), and it may not be so in the future, especially if those in the profession who are now looking to literary models for guidance are successful. But whether they succeed or not, whatever "principles" legal actors have recourse to as constraints on their own practice will be (1) principles the practice legitimizes in advance, and (2) principles of no higher order than the principles the practice already declares.

III

The general conclusion that follows from this is that the model in which a practice is altered or reformed by constraints brought in from the outside (the commonsense model by which change is understood) never in fact operates, and the conclusion that follows from that conclusion is the most controversial one to be found in these essays, the conclusion that theory has no consequences. It follows because theory, as I define it, is a name for a set of principles or rules or procedures that is attached to (in the sense of being derived from) no particular field of activity, but is of sufficient generality to be thought of as a constraint on (and an explanation of) all fields of activity. Since there are no such principles—no constraints that are more than the content of a practice from which they are indistinguishable—there can be no such thing as theory, and something that does not exist cannot have consequences. (I am aware that others would define theory more generously and include in the category any high-level generalization or heuristic, but for reasons given below in "Consequences" [chapter 14] I find such a liberalization of the notion self-defeating.)

This does not mean, however, that theory, or more properly, "theory talk," cannot do work and, in doing work, have consequences of a nontheoretical (and *therefore* real) kind. The distinction between theory and theory-talk is a distinction between a discourse that stands apart from all practices (and no such discourse exists) and a discourse that is itself a practice and is therefore consequential to the extent that it is influential or respected or widespread. It is a distinction between the claims often made for theory—that it stands in a relationship of governance or independence to practice—and the force that making those claims (which are uncashable) may have acquired as the result of conditions existing in an institution. That is, it may be the case that in a particular discipline engaging in theory-talk and asserting its impossible claims are efficacious and even obligatory strategies, and in that discipline the presence of "theory" will certainly have consequences, but they will be no different from, or more predictable than, the consequences of any form of talk that has acquired cachet and prestige. In short, when theory has consequences, they will be rhetorical, not theoretical; a point of theory successfully (i.e., persuasively) urged will never have the effect of altering or revolutionizing the basic structure of thought, making it more firmly centered or more determinedly decentered (the dreams of the right and left, respectively), but it can have the effect of altering the resources with which thought pursues its contingent (but orderly) course.

Consider, for example, the Senate hearings on the candidacy for the Supreme Court of Robert Bork. In those hearings Senator Arlen Specter pursued a point of theory in his debate with the nominee. Specter argued that, contrary to what Bork was claiming, a resolution to adhere to the intentions of the framers when interpreting the Constitution does not constrain interpretation; for since the framers' intentions are not self-declaring, but must be constructed from evidence that is itself controversial, the avowed intentionalist is in no better position than anyone else and therefore cannot claim the moral/linguistic high ground.[9] Now let us suppose that Specter's argument (which I believe to be correct) becomes widely accepted, at least in those circles where such matters are debated. What difference would it make? Well, one important difference would be that if you were a participant in those debates you would no longer be able to claim with any particular advantage that you were following the path of original intention, for it would now be generally understood that to be on that path is not to distinguish yourself in the way once claimed (as a passive and self-effacing rather than an activist interpreter). It could then be said that here is an instance in which the structure of legal *practice* has been altered by a theoretical argument—and, in fact, that would be true—for as a result of that argument certain pieces of polemical currency will have lost their blue-chip status and will no longer be so readily invoked. But what will *not* have been altered is your interpretive relation to intention; for if you are persuaded by Specter you will still be in the same relation to intention as you always were, trying to figure it out with the help of whatever evidence you can gather. The change in your interpretive theory will not have changed your interpretive abilities; all that will have changed (and it is no small thing) is the stock of arguments to which you can have recourse in the presentation and defense of your interpretations.

Nor will that change depend on the fact that the argument you will have been persuaded to is right (as Specter's argument is in my opinion). What is required is that it be established so strongly that it exists as a resource, and even as an obligatory checkpoint, for anyone who would operate successfully in a particular arena. In some corners of the world of feminist theory, for example, there is an accepted distinction between male and female thinking or between thought that is assertive, exclusionary, and totalizing and thought that is tentative, generous, and flexible. That distinction is one I argue against repeatedly because it seems to me that all thought is totalizing in that its successive incarnations always deliver a fully articulated world, a world without gaps or spots of unintelligibility. (This doesn't mean that everything is understood, but that even what is puzzling and mysterious is so in ways specific to some elaborated system of thought.) It follows then that the differences between ways of thinking (forms of belief) can never be characterized as the difference between closed and open structures, but between structures that are differently (if temporarily) closed; and it follows further that one cannot be meaningfully urged to become more flexible or generous in one's thinking; flexibility or openness is not a possible mode of cognitive performance for human beings (male or female); although flexibility or openness may well be the pattern human cognitive performance traces out, it cannot be a program a human performer might self-consciously enact.

In short, those feminists who rely in their arguments on a distinction between male and female epistemologies are wrong, but, nevertheless, it may not be wrong (in the sense of unproductive) for them to rely on it. Take the case of Catherine MacKinnon who, in a series of powerful essays, has attempted to alter our thinking about pornography and rape. As Paul Brest and Ann Vandenberg put it in a review of the efforts of MacKinnon and her colleague Andrea Dworkin to pass an anti-pornography ordinance in Minneapolis: "MacKinnon and Dworkin pressed the citizens of Minneapolis to view familiar events and phenomena in unfamiliar ways."[10] Brest and Vandenberg also correctly identify the cornerstone of the MacKinnon-Dworkin strategy, a transformation in *vocabulary,* a change in ways of talking that effects a change in what is being talked about. In an appearance before the city's zoning and planning committee, Dworkin attacked the "euphemisms" the committee members trafficked in: "I think you should say . . . that you, the City Council, are going to permit the dissemination of materials that uphold the inferior status of women . . . I think you should say that you are going to permit the exploitation of live women, the sadomasochistic use of live women, the binding and torture of real women" and MacKinnon followed by urging the council to "consider that pornography, as it subordinates women to men, is a form of discrimination on the basis of sex" (Brest-Vandenberg, p. 615). There is a double effort here: the council members are to be made uncomfortable in their support of views that have effects they have never confronted; and the confrontation of those effects is itself supposed to have the effect of removing pornography from the category of speech protected by the First Amendment where it has been so firmly placed in the thoughts of even the most socially concerned and liberal. No wonder one participant in that meeting described the testimony as "mind-boggling" (p. 616); habits of thought so basic that a challenge to them seemed unthinkable are being relentlessly questioned, and in the event the challenge proves successful, the worldview, and therefore the world, of many persons will have been changed.

In MacKinnon's essays the strategy of change is brilliantly on display. What she does is employ a vocabulary that departs from ordinary (or as she might say "ideologically frozen") usage in ways that cannot be ignored. Often she will drop in a provocative phrase without announcing or even appearing to notice its provocativeness; and then she will surround the "oddness" of the phrase with neighboring oddnesses until at a certain point (presumably a different point for different readers) what was once odd is suddenly ordinary. One such phrase is "rape in ordinary circumstances."[11] The phrase is provocative because in the way of thinking MacKinnon wishes to dislodge, rape is defined as an exceptional and statistically deviant act against a background of mutually agreed upon sexual transactions. It is this conception of rape that informs current rape law and determines the criteria of evidence, the assigning of responsibility, the burden of proof, and every other aspect of investigation and trial. If rape is *re*conceived as a constitutive ingredient of everyday heterosexual intercourse, including intercourse in marriage, an entire legal structure (and much else) will have to be dismantled and replaced by another. Once the notion of rape in ordinary circumstances is introduced, it serves as a gloss on, and is itself glossed in return by, MacKinnon's basic thesis that as society now is structured sexuality is "a social sphere of male power of which forced sex is paradigmatic." Of course, this is once again a challenge to the distinction between "natural" heterosexuality and violent sex, and as MacKinnon now says with a self-reflexive resonance, "the problem remains what it has always been: telling the difference." She has been doing just that, in a double sense; she has been telling us that the difference has been "told," that our assumption of a distinction flows from the words and phrases that furnish our thought, and that the difference can be retold or untold by the forceful institution of new words and phrases.

The power of MacKinnon's discourse is obvious, I think, even in this small sample, and it is a power that is supremely rhetorical. MacKinnon, however, doesn't see it that way; she thinks the power derives from a theoretical insight into the nature of epistemology. Like many other feminists she posits two distinct ways of knowing, male and female. The male way of knowing is universalizing and committed to objectivity; it "does not comprehend its own perspectivity, does not recognize . . . that the way it apprehends its world is a form of its [the world's] subjugation."[12] As I understand it, what this means is (1) that males typically see the world from the point of view of their interests and concerns and therefore turn objects and persons into reflections of their own desires and agendas ("what is sexual about a woman is what the male point of view requires for its excitement" [p. 19]); and (2) that this colonizing and subjugating act does not acknowledge itself for what it is, does not recognize itself as a perspective but identifies itself with the way things are and must be; "aperspectivity"—the claiming of universality for a partial point of view—is "a strategy of male hegemony" (p. 23). MacKinnon thinks that these two points go together, but I think they fall apart. It might be the case that some men *create the world from their point of view which then becomes the truth to be described,*" but it is not, and could not be, the case that these men might soften the imperialism of their ways of knowing by acknowledging them as merely ways, or that women (or at least some women) already and characteristically do this. The reason is that "aperspectivity," as MacKinnon defines it, is not a strategy, but a name for the condition of believing that what you believe is in fact true, and that is a condition one cannot transcend. (The full argument is given below in "Critical Self-Consciousness, Or Can We Know What We're Doing?," chapter 17.) This does not mean that beliefs (and therefore consciousness) cannot change, only that change will not be from a state of undoubted belief to a state in which the grip of belief has been relaxed, but from one state of not-at-the-moment-seen-around belief to another.

The enemy, in short, is not aperspectivity, but a perspectivity different from that which follows from the structure of conviction in which you are presently embedded. MacKinnon makes the point inadvertently when she criticizes Mary Daly's analysis of suttee, "a practice in which Indian widows are supposed to throw themselves upon their dead husband's funeral pyres in grief" (p. 25n). Daly observes that, despite claims to the contrary, women who practice suttee do not do so voluntarily, but "are drugged, pushed, browbeaten, or otherwise coerced by the dismal and frightening prospect of widowhood in Indian society." MacKinnon complains that by focusing on the surface coercions Daly misses an underlying level of coercion that leads some women who are not drugged or pushed to fling themselves on the pyre quite "freely." These, she says, "are suttee's deepest victims: women who *want* to die when their husband dies, who volunteer for self-immolation because they believe their life is over when his is."

Now much depends on what we take the object of this complaint to be: is it that these women are victims of the wrong beliefs, or is it that they are so captivated by their beliefs that they are unable to see around them or through them to the reality they obscure? The first is a complaint about the kind of beliefs by which one is held; the second is a complaint that one is held by beliefs at all. In this footnote and elsewhere, MacKinnon seems to be taking the second tack: the very *"reality"* of Indian women, she says, has been created "by male epistemology" which has earlier been glossed as the *"power to create the world from one's point of view, . . . power in its male form"* (p. 23). But the "power to create the world from one's point of view" is not male and is not a matter of epistemology, of the producing of accounts of how we know what we know. Rather it is a power that attends successful persuasion (either of oneself or of others) whether effected by men or by women, a power whose effects are always and necessarily objectifying since to be under its sway (and everyone is at every moment of his or her life) is to see the world from a point of view in relation to which other points of view are objectively (obviously) false. What is wrong with Indian women from the feminist point of view is not that they are willing (in a precisely nonvoluntarist sense) to die for the beliefs that have captured them, but that they have not been captured—constituted, formed, made into what they are—by the right beliefs. Were they to be captured by the right (feminist) beliefs, they would still be willing to die for them, and in doing so they would be the recipients, not of MacKinnon's pitying scorn (too bad their consciousnesses weren't sufficiently raised), but of the same praise she earlier bestows on women who know the "difference between a society in which sexism is expressed in the form of female infanticide and a society in which sexism takes the form of unequal representation on the Central Committee," and who know too that "the difference is worth dying for" (p. 8). The words are Barbara Ehrenreich's, but they are invoked by MacKinnon with obvious approval, and they make clear (although apparently not to her) that the issue is not the removal of objectivity, but the determination of the point of view from which objectivity (what is real, perspicuous, undoubted, worth dying for) will reveal itself.

What I am saying is that there is a lack of fit between what Mac-Kinnon is doing in these essays and her account of what she's doing (although as we shall see that account is also a part of what she is doing). What she is doing, as Brest and Vandenberg observe, is effecting "transformations of language" (p. 659) and thereby transforming not only the field of discourse—the ways of talk that are authorized in the sense of being taken for granted—but the very objects of that field (rape, pornography, marital sex, etc.) which will no longer have the shape they had before the transformation. She is, in short, exercising power; but in her account of what she's doing, power is dismissed as a male strategy "combining . . . legitimation with force" (p. 25), as something ultimately unreal and yet consequential so long as its status as an "illusion" is not exposed. She claims, that is, to be undoing the effects of power and force even as she works new effects by means of a rhetorical skill that could not be more force-fully power-full. There is (dare I say it) a double standard operating in her text: she quite properly excoriates as "one-sided" "male readings" of the rape scene in which even cries of "no, no" are interpreted as consent ("I know you really want it") but does not see that her own re-reading of the same scene in which consent ceases to be "a meaningful concept" (p. 650) is equally, albeit differently (and blamelessly), one-sided. *All* readings are one-sided: there is a difference to be sure between a reading in which women are *always* consenting no matter what they say and a reading in which women are *never* consenting no matter what they say (or think), but it is not a difference between an inflexible point of view and one more generous (less one-sided), but between points of view displaying and urging differing shapes of inflexibility. I am not saying that MacKinnon should acknowledge that her view of the matter is on a par with that of her opponents; according to her lights (which in this case are also mine), they are wrong and she is right, but her rightness does not result from having been released from the grip of objectivity, but from having exchanged one form of objectivity for another, the same exchange she now urges on her readers.

Of course, there are distinctions between the ways in which the objective knowledge that flows from one's beliefs might be urged on others, styles of self-presentation that are often thought of wrongly as styles of knowing. I might say to you, for example, "what you have just said is obviously false for the following indisputable reasons" (this is, in fact, my style), or I might say, "I see your point, and it is certainly an important one, but I wonder if we might make room for this other perspective," and, depending on your sense of decorum and on the conventions in place in the arena of our discussion, the conversation between us would unfold differently. But whichever style of discussion I adopt, that style will always be grounded firmly in the beliefs that ground me, the beliefs from the vantage point of which your assumptions present the only aspect they could possibly have, the aspect of beliefs that are not mine and are therefore not right. There is no end to the ways in which you can assert your beliefs—no end to styles of self-presentation—but none of them involve the loosening of the hold they have on you.

All of which is to say that MacKinnon is not, despite her own pronouncements, exhorting us to a new way of knowing, but to know different things than we currently know (about rape, pornography, etc.) in the same (and only) way we know anything, by having been convinced of it. Once convinced, we will not exhibit or enact a new epistemology; indeed, we will not be enacting any epistemology because epistemologies are accounts of how we know what we know, not recipes for knowing. Of course, epistemology is one of the things you can know, and therefore one of the things about which you can be convinced. It is just that the effect of having been convinced by a new epistemological account does not extend beyond the arena where such accounts are offered and judged; there is no *general* relationship between the epistemology you might profess were you asked to profess one and the way you might think about problems that arise in some other (nonformally philosophical) area of your life; there is no general relationship, that is, between your epistemology and your politics.

There may, however, be a local contingent relationship between your epistemology and your politics and that is why, as I said earlier, although MacKinnon is wrong to think that her argument hangs on the issue of male vs. female epistemology (epistemology is not gendered, although ways of thinking about particular questions can be), she may be right to make that issue a part of her argument. It is a question finally of the political context in which she is operating. In this case the context is the (presumably) feminist readership of *Signs* and many in that readership will subscribe to some version of a distinction between a male reliance "on abstract laws and universal principles to adjudicate disputes" and a female preference "for an understanding of the context for . . . choice," for "dialogue and exchange of views" rather than impersonal procedure.[13] It would be my contention that this distinction will not hold up from either end: abstract laws are never abstract or universal but are always reflections of some (albeit unacknowledged) context; and an understanding of context will never be simply inductive, but will always be produced by principles (themselves contingent and transformable) already in place. (This is the argument against the distinction between principle and preference all over again.) The cogency of the distinction, however, has nothing to do with the advisability of invoking it, for its presence in an argument is itself an argument in the old rhetorical sense, a sign or indication of one's general allegiance that may well play a part in persuading one's hearers on a particular point. While MacKinnon's talk about male and female epistemology is not and could not be doing the work she claims for it—altering ways of knowing in the direction of more flexibility and openness—it is nevertheless doing work insofar as it contributes to the goal of changing her readers' minds; not of course changing them so that they are more capacious, but changing them from one narrow (insistent, one-sided, totalizing) vision to another.

The fact that epistemology talk can, on occasion, do such political work is a reflection of the prestige of theory in contemporary intellectual life (a prestige that is rapidly waning as I write and may have disappeared altogether by the time this sentence is read). In the first of her *Signs* essays (subtitled "An Agenda for Theory"), MacKinnon observes that feminism "has not been perceived as having a method . . . but as a loose collection of factors, complaints, and issues which, taken together, describe rather than explain the misfortunes of the female sex" (p. 14). In other words feminist practice is seen as local and occasional, a response to particular problems and opportunities rather than an enactment of "a feminist political theory" (p. 15). MacKinnon does not bother to explain why the perceived lack of a theory is so damaging to feminism; she merely assumes it and proceeds to take up "the challenge . . . to demonstrate that feminism systematically converges upon a central explanation" (p. 14). On its face, however, it is hard to see why the challenge is taken so seriously since feminism has flourished in the absence of a full-blown theory and there is no reason to think that the addition of one would make it more "systematic" than it now is. Indeed, it could well be that the "looseness" of feminist practice, its eclectic and even ramshackle character, is essential to its success, to its ability to intervene in situations linked only by the fact that in them women's interests are seen to be at stake. That ability might well be impeded if every action that an actor wished to identify as feminist first had to be accredited by referring it to the stringent and explicit demands of a theory (assuming for the sake of argument that there could be one). In another sense, however (the sense MacKinnon is presumably responding to), theory is crucial to feminism because in one of the worlds in which it must make its way—the world of the academy and of Marxist thought—having or being a theory is a mark of seriousness and respectability. To be sure, this is becoming less and less the case, but in the early 1980s when these essays were published the "theory requirement" was still in force and, as a strategy of self-presentation, MacKinnon was well advised to satisfy it. I am not suggesting that she doesn't believe in her "theory" or in the relationship between it and the power of her discourse (beliefs I would regard as mistaken), only that the claim of theory was an important and effective one to assert even if, as I would contend, it could never be made good.

The point finally is a simple one: theory is not what gives feminism its power, but in the course of exercising its power, theory or theory talk may well be one of the things feminism thinks to employ. This is what I mean when I say that theory cannot have the consequences of its claim—the claim to provide a perspective to the side of practice from the vantage of which practice might be guided or reformed—but that it can have any and all of the contingent consequences of a vocabulary that already commands attention and can therefore be invoked in the confidence that it will be an ornament to one's position. Indeed, a theory, like any other form of talk, can become so accepted in a community—so taken for granted as a minted currency—that almost every issue is presented, and even conceived of, in its terms; when this happens (as it did happen in certain post-structuralist circles in the heyday of the theory rage), the production of theory talk will be, for that community, an extension of "common sense."

It is here that the real power resides, in whatever vocabulary has so permeated the culture that it seems simply descriptive of independent realities; and it is in the succession of powerful vocabularies that one finds the answer to the question so often raised in these essays and in the critiques they have drawn: what is it that produces *change?* Change is produced when a vocabulary takes hold to the extent that its ways of elaborating the world become normative and are unreflectively asserted in everyday practices. Occasionally this can happen when a community self-consciously rejects one theory in favor of another, as when within two years of Noam Chomsky's *Syntactic Structures* almost every linguist was thinking in terms of transformations, kernel sentences, recursive functions, etc.; but change-by-theory (that is, by the officially declared victory of one mode of interrogation over its competitors) is the exception not the rule; more often change just creeps up on a community as a vocabulary makes its unsystematic way into its every corner. It is not the force of feminist theory or even of supposedly theoretical slogans ("the personal is the political," "gender is a social construction") that has made such an impression on everyone, but the impossibility of avoiding feminist ways of thinking even when you reject them. Indeed, rejecting them is in some sense what one cannot do: the man who refuses to substitute "he or she" for "he" and believes that in doing so he is remaining true to his prefeminist self, is self-deluding; for the fact that he feels obliged to refuse marks his act as different from the one he used to perform when he wrote "he" without any awareness that it was a choice. Feminism "has" him, in the sense of determining his behavior no matter what he does. And this is only one small instance of what is now a true revolution in our political and social life. Wherever one turns—the classroom, the workplace, the family, the grocery, the courts, the hospital, the factory, the boardroom, the bedroom—the pressure either to adopt a feminist perspective or to resist it (and by resisting it to testify to its power) cannot be avoided.

And how has this come about? In innumerable ways: by opportunities grasped, by accident, by vacuums into which feminists rushed, by changes in the demographics of professions, by the 1960s, by the sexual revolution, by the end of the sexual revolution, by the co-optation of feminist themes, by Madison Avenue, by presses that have filled their lists with feminist texts, by jokes, by resistances; in short, by more things than any feminist philosophy could dream of or plan for. All one can say finally is that the feminist vocabulary—incredibly diverse and unified only by its insistence on women's interests (themselves a matter of contest within that same vocabulary)—has spread everywhere and continues to spread as I write. That is power greater than any theory, and it is the power MacKinnon at once taps and extends in her essays. The fact that in these same essays she attributes that power to a theory (of male and female epistemologies) that is at most a component (a "bit player") in her rhetorical program is a tribute to the hold theory continues to have on the academic mentality; but while that hold is not a negligible fact and can itself be the basis of effective political action, it can never be strong enough to validate theory's strongest claim, the claim to be a special kind of activity in relation to which practice is, or should be, derivative and as a consequence of which practice can be transformed. As Thomas Heller has observed, that claim is essentially elitist: "The claim to a meta-status for theory may be seen as a claim to institutional power for the practitioners of theory." Heller adds that "to admit this does not delegitimate theory; it decenters it."[14] That is, theory becomes what it always was anyway, one among many rhetorical forms whose impact and sway are a function of contingencies (of institutional history, perceived needs, emergent crises, etc.) it can neither predict nor control.

IV

"Rhetorical" is, of course, a master-word in the essays that make up this book, and indeed the conclusion of the book (hardly a novel one) is finally that we live in a rhetorical world. It is a conclusion that is inevitable once one removes literal meaning as a constraint on interpretation; for this first step down the anti-formalist road contains all the others: (1) the relocation of interpretive constraint in intention; (2) the realization that intention must itself be interpretively established, and that it can be established only through persuasion ("by the litigant having at the time being the greater power of persuading the trier of fact"); (3) the characterization of persuasion as a matter en-

tirely contingent, rational only in relation to reasons that have themselves become reasons through the mechanisms of persuasion; (4) the
insight that contingency, if taken seriously, precludes the claims for
theory as they are usually made; (5) the demoting of theory to a practice no different from any other; (6) the elevation of practice to a
new, if ever-changing, universal in relation to which there is nothing
higher (more general, abstract, formal) that can be invoked. It might
seem that in traveling this road one is progressively emancipated from
all constraints, but, as we have seen, the removal of *independent* constraints to which the self might or might not conform does not leave
the self free but reveals the self to be always and already constrained
by the contexts of practice (interpretive communities) that confer on
it a shape and a direction.

It is instructive to observe that the myth of the self free from
constraints is necessary to the positions of both the intellectual right
and left; on the right the myth generates the fear that if public controls are not kept in place the self will go its own way; on the left the
myth generates the hope that if public controls can only be removed
the self will be able to go its own way. One side fears that anti-foundationalist thought—teaching as it does that all facts and values are
social and political constructs—will deprive us of our certainties; the
other side hopes that anti-foundationalist thought will deprive us of
our certainties. But anti-foundationalist thought deprives us of nothing;
all it offers is an alternative account of how the certainties that will
still grip us when we are persuaded to it came to be in place. I said at
the beginning of this introduction that once you start down the anti-
formalist road there is nowhere to stop (this insight is writ large in the
history of Reformation theology); what I am saying now is when you
get to the end of the anti-formalist road nothing will have changed except the answers you might give to some traditional questions in philosophy and literary theory.

Moreover, nothing will have changed by virtue of the realization
that nothing will have changed. Those who listen to the argument
against theory often resist it because they feel that they are losing
something; that is, they attribute a consequence to the thesis that theory
has no consequences. But that is to make the mistake of thinking that
by telling people that there is something that they have never been
able to do—leave the realm of practice for a realm more general and
abstract—you take something away from them; but of course you

can't take away a capacity no one has ever had, and therefore the argument that theory has no consequences is no more consequential than theory itself.

Then why make it? What's the point? There is no point if by "point" one means a conclusion that implies a call to action. But, on the other hand, that *is* the point, that there is no further point to be made: the thesis that theory goes nowhere (except in the wholly contingent ways of all rhetorics) is itself a thesis that can go nowhere—to no program or agenda—lest it contradict itself. So that while the point, insofar as there is one, is very small—does not imply or demand anything—its smallness is itself something large in relation to the expectation of something bigger. The smallness of the point is what makes people who have hopes for theory (and fears for anti-theory) unhappy, and therefore it is a point worth making and a point worth diminishing.

The chief hopes and fears for theory have been political, and it is for their political deficiencies that the essays collected here have been most vigorously attacked. The foundationalist right worries that if people hearken to me and my kind they will be moved to divest themselves of all standards and restraints; the anti-foundationalist left worries that if people are persuaded by the "no consequences argument" they will leave off trying to divest themselves of standards and constraints. I reply that constraints are not something one can either embrace or throw off because they are constitutive of the self and of its possible actions. On the one hand, the condition of being without constraints is quite literally unimaginable and therefore need not be feared; but on the other, the constraints that are always in place are not fixed but interpretive—forever being altered by the actions they make possible—and there is no danger that they will forever hold us in the same position.

Not surprisingly, these answers have not satisfied: the right complains that the constraints and standards I admit to are local and temporary, and therefore are not really constraints at all; the left complains that the changes and adjustments I admit to are entirely internal to the discipline or enterprise that always survives them and that the only kind of change that matters—radical change—is ruled out in my account. ("Fish's theory discredits the power and energy of radicalism.")[15] This is not quite true; I do not argue against radical change, but against the possibility that radical change, of either a feared or desired kind, will be brought about by theory. However, even this formulation must be qualified. In a context where what matters is the giving of theoretical accounts, the triumph of one theory over its competitors will indeed mark a radical change because it will entirely redo the lines of authority and power in that context. But in contexts where theory production is only one component among many, the impact of a theoretical argument will be mediated and attenuated and may sometimes barely be felt. It all depends on the extent to which, in the rhetorical structure of a situation, there is a direct line from changes in theory to social or political change; and even when such a direct line is in place the nature of the relationship between theory change and political/social change will vary. Although there are certainly situations in which theory is consequential, the direction and shape of its consequentiality will be a local, contingent matter. When Cornel West asks of Richard Rorty, "What are the ethical and political consequences of adopting his neo-pragmatism?,"[16] the answer is "none necessarily," although in certain circumstances the proclaiming of pragmatist views might have political effects of an unpredictable kind. West wonders how an argument like Rorty's can "kick the philosophical props from under bourgeois capitalist societies and require no change in our cultural practices." The explanation is simple: bourgeois capitalist societies are not propped up by philosophy, but by the material conditions of everyday life—by the means of production, by the patterns of domestic relations, by the control or dissemination of information, etc. It is when those conditions are altered or removed that the cultural practices of bourgeois capitalist society will tremble; all that will tremble when the hit parade of theory undergoes a change is the structure of philosophy departments.

Again, I am not denying that theory can have political consequences, merely insisting that those consequences do not belong by right or nature to theory, but are contingent upon the (rhetorical) role theory plays in the particular circumstances of a historical moment. Of course, this holds too for the pronouncements of anti-theory, which can also be consequential in relation to configurations of interest and power already in place. So that while it is true that the argument against theory's consequences does not itself have any necessary consequences, it may very well have consequences of a contingent, practical kind, and it may be that Frank Lentricchia is right when he declares that the expounding of the anti-theory position "at this juncture cannot help but bring comfort, energy and ideas to the enemies of change."[17] That is, even though the "no consequences" argument is in principle neutral between political agendas, in practice it is likely to further one rather than another, and therefore those who make it may have something political to answer for. The point is a nice one and difficult to gainsay, but I feel uneasy at the suggestion that before putting an argument into the world we should calculate the effects of its falling into the wrong hands. Such calculations can certainly be made, but, given the infinite appropriability of what we say, it would seem that predicting in the direction of possible harm is no less foolhardy than predicting in the direction of positive good.

Two more points and I will finally let these essays speak for themselves. The first is an answer to an argument often thought fatal to anti-foundationalist thought. It is that the anti-foundationalist position cannot itself be asserted without contradiction. The reasoning is as follows: either anti-foundationalism (or cultural relativism or radical skepticism) is asserted seriously, in which case it is asserted as a foundation and undoes the very position it supposedly proclaims, or it is asserted unseriously, that is, not urged on us as a statement of what is really the case, and therefore it has no claim on our serious attention. Philosophers of a certain kind love this argument, and one can almost hear them chortle as they make it. Here is a recent version by Hadley Arkes. Taking as a typical proposition of cultural relativism, "There are no truths of moral significance that hold across cultures," Arkes asks (triumphantly) "whether this proposition itself does not purport to state a truth of moral consequence that holds across cultures," and adds that, "if it does, then the doctrine of cultural relativism refutes itself," while if it does not, "then the 'truth' affirmed in cultural relativism might [itself] be nothing more than a 'local persuasion.' "[18] Obviously Arkes thinks that he has caught his anti-foundationalist opponent between pincers, and indeed this argument is always plunked down with the air of something that will permanently block the road, a point so irrefutable that no one can get around it.

Despite Arkes's smugness, however, it is a point easily gotten around. First of all, it mistakes the nature of the anti-foundationalist claim, which is not that there are no foundations, but that whatever foundations there are (and there always are some) have been established by persuasion, that is, in the course of argument and counter-argument on the basis of examples and evidence that are themselves cultural and contextual. Anti-foundationalism, then, is a thesis about how foundations emerge, and in contradistinction to the assumptions that foundations do not emerge but simply *are,* anchoring the universe and thought from a point above history and culture, it says that foundations are local and temporal phenomena, and are always vulnerable to challenges from other localities and other times. This vulnerability also extends, of course, to the anti-foundationalist thesis itself, and that is why its assertion does not involve a contradiction, as it would if what was being asserted was the impossibility of foundational assertion; but since what is being asserted is that assertions—about foundations or anything else—have to make their way against objections and counter-examples, anti-foundationalism can without contradiction include itself under its own scope and await the objections one might make to it; and so long as those objections are successfully met and turned back by those who preach anti-foundationalism (a preaching and a turning back I am performing at this very moment), anti-foundationalism can be asserted as absolutely true since (at least for the time being) there is no argument that holds the field against it.

My second final point is more delicate and has to do with the (relative) crudeness of my argument with respect to the nuances one might want to introduce as qualifications and refinements. In this introduction and in the chapters that follow there are a number of key terms that are invoked as if they were monolithic and unproblematical: persuasion, interest, practice, interpretation, constraint, community, belief. It seems, for example, that when I invoke "belief" against foundationalists' claims for transcontextual rationalism on the one hand, and against (mistaken) anti-foundationalist claims for critical self-consciousness on the other, I am invoking some seamless totality, a structure without tensions or incongruities, that operates in the manner of a perfectly calibrated machine. This is, of course, a false picture of belief and of the mind furnished by it, if only because each of us is a member of not one but innumerable interpretive communities in relation to which different kinds of belief are operating with different weight and force. I am, among other things, white, male, a teacher, a literary critic, a student of interpretation, a member of a law faculty, a father, a son, an uncle, a husband (twice), a citizen, a (passionate) consumer, a member of the middle class, a Jew, the oldest of four children, a cousin, a brother, a brother-in-law, a son-in-law, a Democrat, short, balding, fifty, an easterner who has been a westerner and is now a southerner, a voter, a neighbor, an optimist, a department chairman. In each of these roles (and in the many I have not named) my performance flows from some deeply embedded (I don't have to consult or apply it) sense of an enterprise, some conviction by which I am (quite literally) grasped concerning the point and purpose of being a member of the enterprise, a conviction that is not additional or supplemental to, but constitutive of, what I am doing. But, of course, that conviction or sense of the enterprise is not "pure"; I am never merely a teacher or a parent or a homeowner, for when I am playing any one of these roles I am registering to some extent the obligations and urgencies that attend the playing of the others; no doubt my way of being a parent is all mixed with my way of being a teacher; and I can never contemplate decisions about my house without at the same time taking into account the obligations of fatherhood.

All of this is obvious as is the possibility of *conflict* between the various roles I am called on to play. I am old enough to remember when it was not a simple matter to be both an academic and a Jew (now almost an identification), when the academic culture, especially in literary studies, was so insistently, if unself-consciously (precisely the measure of the insistence) Protestant that one was faced with a choice between assimilating—imitating one's senior colleagues down to the patches on their elbows—and various forms of "acting out," a choice even more sharply posed today to those blacks who are simultaneously being recruited by the academy *as* blacks and required to comport themselves just like everyone else, that is, according to academic "standards" that are supposedly indifferent to race, sex, ethnic origin, etc. What sense does it make to speak in such situations of being constrained by belief, when one's beliefs, rather than cohering, pull one in different directions? It makes perfect sense so long as constraints are not required to be monolithic. One is often "conflictually" constrained, that is, held in place by a sense of a situation as requiring negotiation between conflicting demands that seem equally legitimate. One may be constrained, for example, both by one's understanding of what it means to be an academic and one's understanding of what it means to be a feminist. But even here we must be careful not to overdramatize the conflict by speaking of it as creating a "split-consciousness." An academic who is also a feminist is not two persons, but one—an academic-who-is-also-a-feminist. That is, when her feminism weighs upon her, it takes the form specific to her situation; it is feminism-as-an-academic-might-be-concerned-with-it. Being a feminist is a state no less complex than being an academic, and when they come together, they do not do so as sovereign and separate obligations, but as obligations that have already been defined by their relationship to one another. Nor is that relationship itself stable: a feminist-academic may have worked out a modus vivendi that allows her to satisfy and even make capital of her "divided" loyalties, only to find in a moment of crisis that the two loyalties cannot both be satisfied and that, for the present at least, she must shut herself off from considerations to which she would otherwise be attuned. But even in that moment she will be constrained by her beliefs, by some already-in-place understanding that tells her that this is a crisis and that it is one she cannot avoid. Those who object to my specification of belief as a constraint assume that if I were to acknowledge the complexity and instability of belief I would see that its constraints are continually being relaxed as beliefs jostle one another; but, in fact, that acknowledgment in no way lessens the hold of constraint; it only asks us to remember that constraints are themselves relational and shifting and that (as I put it in "Change," chapter 7) in the act of organizing and assimilating contingent experience constraints are forever bringing about their own modification. Still, the fact that there is nothing monolithic about constraint (or belief, or community, or practice) does not mean that they can be thought of as more or less loose, as possibly "leaking" and opening up at the seams or at points of pressure where the possibility of actions or thoughts *not* constrained is waiting to be seized. However nuanced one's talk about constraint and belief and community may get to be, the nuances will never add up to a moment or a place where consciousness becomes transparent to itself and can at last act freely. Being embedded means just that, being embedded *always,* and one does not escape embeddedness by acknowledging, as I do, that it is itself a fractured, fissured, volatile condition.

But why, one might ask, is there so little of that acknowledgment in your work? Why are these key terms almost always employed in a way that implies the seamlessness and closure you now repudiate? The answer to this (really) final question is that everything in discourse depends on what I call the "angle of lean," the direction you are facing as you begin your discursive task. In these essays there are characteristically two: either I am facing those who wish to identify a rationality to which beliefs or community practices would be submitted for judgment, or I am facing those who find in the deconstruction of that rationality the possibility of throwing off those beliefs and practices that now define us. When I argue against the first group, beliefs are forever escaping the constraints that rationality would impose; when I argue against the second group, beliefs are themselves constraints that cannot be escaped. Neither stance delivers a finely tuned picture of the operations of belief (or community or practice) because that is not my task, and indeed it is a task which, if taken seriously (as it certainly should be), would prevent me from doing what I have here tried to do. Whether I have done it and whether it is worth doing are questions that are happily not mine either to ask or to answer.

Meaning and Constraint

2. With the Compliments of the Author:
Reflections on
Austin and Derrida

The most important thing in acting is honesty; once you learn to fake that, you're in.—Sam Goldwyn

I In the summer of 1977, as I was preparing to teach Jacques Derrida's *Of Grammatology* to a class at the School of Criticism and Theory in Irvine, a card floated out of the text and presented itself for interpretation. It read:

WITH THE COMPLIMENTS OF THE AUTHOR

Immediately I was faced with an interpretive problem, not only in the ordinary and everyday sense of having to determine the meaning and the intention (they are the same thing) of the utterance, but in the special sense (or so it might seem) occasioned by the fact that I didn't know who the author named or, rather, not named by the card was. It might have been Derrida himself, whom I had met, but only in passing. Or it might have been Derrida's translator, Gayatri Spivak, whom I had known for some time and who might well have put me on the publisher's list. Or it might have been the publisher, in this case the Johns Hopkins University Press, of whose editorial board I was then a member. In the absence (a key word) of any explicit identification, I found myself a very emblem of the difficulties or infelicities that attend distanced or etiolated communication: unable to proceed because the words were cut off from their anchoring source in a unique and clearly present intention. That is to say, I seemed, in the very moment of my perplexity, to be proving on my pulse the superiority of face-to-face communication, where one can know intentions directly, to communication mediated by the marks of writing and in this case by a writing that materialized without any clues as to its context of origin. It may not have been a message found in a bottle, but it certainly was a message found in a book.

Philosophers and literary critics have long had a way of talking about such situations by contrasting them with others in which questions of meaning and intention are less indeterminate. The principle underlying this exercise has often been formulated but nowhere more succinctly than in this pronouncement by Jonathan Culler: "Some texts are more orphaned than others."[1] Given such a principle, it might seem reasonable to construct a taxonomy of contexts of communication, arranged in a hierarchy from the least to the most orphaned. The elaboration of such a taxonomy is not my purpose here, but a sketch might afford us a perspective on some crucial issues in philosophy and literary theory.

One would begin, of course, with the optimal context, a face-to-face exchange of utterances between two people who know each other and who are able, in the event of confusion or discontinuity or obscurity, to put questions to one another. A less certain but still relatively risk-free form of communication would occur between persons who know each other but who are separated either by time or by space and are therefore reduced to the medium of letter or telegram or telephone; such persons would be hearing or reading one another against the background of a history of shared experiences and common concerns, and that background would operate in the absence of physical proximity as a constraint on interpretation. Constraints of another kind are operative when communication is between persons who don't know each other but who speak from within a context that stabilizes the direction and shape of their understandings: clerks and customers in a department store, teachers and students on the first day of class, waiters and patrons in a restaurant, and so on. Serious difficulties begin to set in when that kind of stabilizing context is absent. A coincidence of concerns is serendipitous rather than probable because one party is speaking or writing to a heterogeneous audience and hoping that the right-minded listener or reader is tuning in; television commentators, direct-mail advertisers, and newspaper columnists are in this situation and are always in danger of being misunderstood because of miscalculation, special vocabularies, and unanticipated responses. As we continue down the scale, things go from bad to worse as the incommensurabilities of other times and other cultures are added to the difficulties occasioned by physical distance. Finally, at the outermost reaches of this declination from sure and transparent verbal encounters we arrive at literature, and especially at fiction; here interpretive hazards seem to be everywhere and without a check as we attempt to fix the meanings and intentions of long-dead authors whose words have reference not to a world that has passed from the earth but to a world that never was except in the interior reaches of their imaginations. In other cases the interpretive efforts of readers and listeners are tied, even if in some attenuated way, to specifiable empirical conditions, but in the case of fiction and drama those conditions are a construct of the author and in turn must be reconstructed, without the aid of extramental entities, by readers and listeners.

The picture I have just drawn is commonsensical and powerful, and something like it underlies the pronouncements of many of our most influential theorists. Culler assumes it when he says that words in a poem "do not refer us to an external context but force us to construct a fictional situation of utterance" because poems are by definition removed "from an ordinary circuit of communication" (p. 166); the same reasoning leads John Ellis to declare that once something is identified as literature "we do not generally concern ourselves with whether what it says is true or false, or regard it as relevant to any specific practical purpose," because it is not perceived "as part of the immediate context we live in."[2] Indeed, Barbara Herrnstein Smith concludes in the same vein: "A poem does not reflect but *creates* the context in which its meanings are located"; like a letter a poem "will be read in a context both temporally and spatially remote from that in which it was composed," but the limitations under which poets and their readers must operate are even more severe because a poet "must convey to his readers not only a context remote from space and time, but one that may have never existed in history or nature."[3] Wolfgang Iser is even more explicit and categorical: "Fictional texts constitute their own objects and do not copy something already in existence"; "everyday pragmatic language . . . presupposes reference to a given object," and therefore the "multiplicity of possible meanings [is] narrowed down"; fictional language on the other hand "opens up an increasing number of possibilities," which entail decisions and acts of construction on the part of the reader.[4] For Iser, this increased reader activity is characteristic of literary experience as opposed, for example, to the experience of a scientific text where acts of construction are not required because the object—that is, the world—is already given. The same point is made somewhat more elegantly by Richard Ohmann: in ordinary discourse, Ohmann asserts, "we assume the real world and judge the felicity of the speech acts"; but in fictional discourse "we assume the felicity of the speech acts and infer a world."[5] The mechanics of how we do this are explained by John Searle. Fictional discourse is made possible, according to Searle, by "a set of conventions which suspend the normal operation of the rules relating illocutionary acts to the world."[6] In place of this normal operation, in which language is tied to an already existing referent, a writer of fiction, Searle explains, *pretends* to refer to real characters and events and by so pretending creates fictional characters and events (pp. 71–72); as readers we fall in with this pretense, we share in it, and thus share in the construction of the fictional world and its meanings (p. 73).

It may seem that in the course of this brief survey the focus has shifted from the question of distanced or orphaned speech to the question of fictional language; but the survey shows that the two questions are one. Both orphaned speech and fictional speech are regarded by these and other theorists as deviations from the full presence and normative contextuality of face-to-face communication; and in both cases the consequences are the same, an increase in the interpretive work required of readers and listeners (here there is an implicit formula: the more distance, the more work) which means, in turn, an increase in the risks and hazards attendant on any effort to fix and determine meanings. Indeed, it is remarkable how many issues in philosophy and critical theory finally resolve to the basic issue raised by the privileging of proximate or anchored speech. There are any number of paired terms that line up with orphaned versus full speech and ordinary versus fictional language to form a related and interdependent set of oppositions. The few theorists I have already cited yield the following list of examples, which is by no means exhaustive:

literal language	vs.	metaphorical language
determinate	vs.	indeterminate
brute facts	vs.	institutional facts
objective discourse	vs.	subjective discourse
real people	vs.	fictional characters
direct speech acts	vs.	indirect speech acts
real objects	vs.	fictional objects
scientific language	vs.	expressive language
explicit performative	vs.	implicit performative
locutionary	vs.	illocutionary

meaning	vs.	significance
perception	vs.	interpretation
real experience	vs.	aesthetic experience
constative	vs.	performative

What makes these oppositions transformations of one another is the epistemological premise underlying each of them: that the first or left-hand term stands for a mode of knowing that is, at least relatively if not purely, direct, transparent, without difficulties, unmediated, independently verifiable, unproblematic, preinterpretive, and sure; and, conversely, that the mode of knowing named by the right-hand term is indirect, opaque, context-dependent, unconstrained, derivative, and full of risk. One reason for the extraordinary appeal of this distinction in its many forms is the support it seems to derive from the evidence of common sense. Here, we can say (imitating Dr. Johnson), is a stone; it is more available for inspection and description than a rock in France or a rock in a novel by Dickens. Or, alternatively, here am I, standing before you; you know me and you know what I mean by what I say, and if you don't, you can just ask me, something you couldn't do if I were in China or dead or alive only in the pages of an epic poem. The appeal, in short, is to the experience of *immediacy* in contrast to the experience of objects and persons that can only be apprehended at a remove, and it is a contrast that seems confirmed by the anecdote with which I began. Presumably, if in 1977 I had been in possession of more precise information and had been able to meet my benefactor face-to-face, the uncertainty and indeterminancy that characterized my efforts to construe WITH THE COMPLIMENTS OF THE AUTHOR would have been lessened and perhaps eliminated entirely.[7]

Let us, for the sake of argument, test this presumption by imagining the happy or felicitous circumstances in which this particular speech act would have been more certain of success. First of all, let us assume that I had been able to determine that the gift and therefore the card announcing it were sent to me by Derrida. Would my position with respect to interpretive certainty be improved? Well, in some sense, the answer is, "Of course"; I would no longer be attempting to interpret a message from Spivak or the Johns Hopkins University Press; but I would still be left with the problem of interpreting a message from Derrida, and the fact that I now knew his name would not in and of itself be decisive, for what I would *want* to know are his intentions, his purposes, his reasons. That is, I would want to know in what *spirit* Derrida had sent me his book. It could be that mine is only one name on a very long list submitted by an editor or a publicist and that in response to its suggestion Derrida replied, "Stanley Who?" Nor would my perplexity necessarily be removed if the message were to be delivered in person, if Derrida were to walk into my office and say, "Aha, here is Stanley Fish, let me present this to you, with the compliments of the author." I might still suspect that he was being ironic rather than complimentary and that he was really saying, "With the compliments of *the* author," in which case the way would be open to hearing his utterance as an assertion both of precedence and superiority.

Of course, in the event of such a suspicion, I could simply ask. That is, I could put to Derrida any number of direct and piercing questions, like "What did you mean by that?" or "How am I to take it?" or "Do you expect something in return?" It is entirely possible that the answer to one or more of these questions would satisfy me, perhaps because it invoked a formula that was for me a particularly powerful marker of sincerity, or perhaps because it was accompanied by information about some past action of Derrida's that appeared to me to be strong evidence of his goodwill. However, it is also possible that my suspicions would not be allayed at all because they were deeply rooted in some professional insecurity—an insecurity which, rather than being removed by verbal (or other) assurances, simply made them into its renewed occasion. The point is not that I could never be certain about the meaning of WITH THE COMPLIMENTS OF THE AUTHOR but that neither the achievement of certainty nor the failure to achieve it will have a necessary relationship to the fact of physical proximity. The evidence that might convince me of Derrida's goodwill could have its effect on me even if it were relayed to me in a letter or by some third person; for its status as evidence does not depend only or even chiefly on my ability to eyeball it but on my holding a belief about the relationship of certain acts and formulas to the presence of goodwill. And, conversely, the physical proximity of such evidence, in the form of Derrida's words or gestures, might still fail to be convincing if my professional anxiety (which is also a belief that can also function at long distance as well as "close up") were strong enough to override it.

The fact of a face-to-face exchange, then, is no assurance that communication will be certain or even relatively trouble-free. The point is illustrated nicely by a cartoon that appeared some years ago in the *New*

Yorker. It shows a man sitting in front of a television set, his eyes locked on the picture; standing above him is a woman, presumably his wife, who is obviously angry. The caption reads, "You look sorry, you act sorry, you say you're sorry, but you're not sorry." The supposed advantage of face-to-face communication is that it allows us to deduce the meaning of an utterance from the direct inspection of the speaker's words and actions; but the cartoon seems to be reminding us that the direction of inference is often the other way around: the woman knows in advance what will be meant by what her husband says because she knows, and knows with the passion of belief, what kind of person he is; and therefore she is able to hear whatever words issue from him as confirmation of what she already knows. He could present witnessed affidavits; he could secure testimonials from his minister, his doctor, or her mother, and she might still continue to interpret his words and all supporting documents as evidence of his insincerity.[8]

The juxtaposition of the cartoon with my anecdote is illuminating in part because at first they seem to be illustrative of quite different situations—of a particularly attenuated speech act, on the one hand, and a speech act tied firmly to its context, on the other. But in fact the two situations are finally very much alike because in both of them the crucial role in the attempt to fix meaning is played by assumptions and beliefs. In one case, a wife's tenaciously held assumption about the kind of man her husband is generates a single and unswerving interpretation of his words; in the other, my inability to believe wholeheartedly in Derrida's sincerity leaves me in doubt as to the right interpretation of his message. In both cases the shape of belief (either about another or about oneself) is responsible for the shape of interpretation, irrespective of whether those beliefs operate at a remove or in a proximate encounter. My "reading" of Derrida's intention would not necessarily be stabilized by his presence; and if the husband were to leave his wife a note saying he was sorry, her reception of it would be as sure as her reception of his spoken words. What this means is that the difference between the two cases (and differences remain) cannot be explained as the difference between direct and mediated communication; and, indeed, if we are to generalize from these examples, there is no epistemological difference between direct and mediated communications because, in a fundamental sense, all communications are mediated. That is, communications of every kind are characterized by exactly the same conditions—the necessity of interpretive work, the unavoidability of perspective, and the construction by acts of interpretation of that which supposedly grounds interpretation, intentions, characters, and pieces of the world.

It would seem that rather than confirming "Culler's law," our analysis has led us to its reversal, to the conclusion that all texts are equally and radically orphaned in the sense that no one of them is securely fastened to an independently specifiable state of affairs. With this assertion I at last approach Derrida's critique of J. L. Austin, for the issue between them (or so it would seem) is the possibility of identifying a kind of speech act that is not orphaned, that is "tethered to [its] origin" (*HT*, p. 61). In "Signature Event Context," Derrida questions that possibility when he reaches "a paradoxical but unavoidable conclusion—a successful performative is necessarily an 'impure' performative" ("SEC," p. 191). A pure performative would be one that was *assured* of success because a combination of verbal explicitness, a clear-cut context, and a transparency of intention so constrained its reception that there was no room for doubt and therefore no need for interpretation. Derrida's argument is that the optimal conditions that would be required for such a success do not exist because the risk attending the so-called impure cases—cases in which illocutionary force must be inferred through a screen of assumptions rather than read out directly—is constitutive of *all* cases. Derrida is struck by the fact that while Austin spends more than a little time on the "doctrine of the infelicities," or "the doctrine of the things that can be and go wrong," he remains committed to the ideal of a speech situation in which everything goes right (*HT*, p. 14). That is, Austin acknowledges the pervasiveness of infelicity but continues to think of infelicity as "accidental," as an unfortunate deviation from the norm "of an exhaustively definable context, of a free consciousness present to the totality of the operation, and of absolutely meaningful speech" ("SEC," p. 188). Derrida, on the other hand, regards infelicity not as accidental but as structural and founding, and he makes his case in part by posing a series of questions:

> Is this general possibility necessarily one of a failure or trap into which language may *fall* or lose itself as in an abyss situated outside of or in front of itself? . . . In other words, does the quality of risk admitted by Austin *surround* language like a kind of *ditch* or external place of perdition which speech could never hope to leave, but which it can escape by remaining "at home?" . . . Or, on the contrary, is this risk rather its internal and positive condi-

tion of possibility? Is that outside its inside, the very force and law of its emergence? ("SEC," p. 190)

By "general possibility" Derrida means the possibility that language may fall prey to interpretation rather than being anchored to an originating and constraining center; interpretation, with all its hazards and uncertainties, is the source of infelicity; it *is* the "risk." In the traditional or classical view the risk of interpretation is only incurred when the conditions of communication are characterized by distance and etiolation; ordinary or basic communication takes place in a space of grounded or tethered security where meanings cannot go astray. Given such a view, it makes sense to proceed as Austin does in the early chapters of his book—by first isolating normative and clear-cut cases and then building up to difficult and derivative cases. But as Derrida observes, such a procedure, however methodologically innocent it may seem, conceals behind its reasonableness an entire metaphysics, the metaphysics of presence, of objects and/or intentions that possess a purity which can either be preserved or compromised in the act of communication.

In the first part of "Signature Event Context," Derrida offers as an example of that metaphysics Condillac's account of the origin of writing: " 'Men in a state of communicating their thoughts by means of sounds, felt the necessity of imagining new signs capable of perpetuating those thoughts and of making them *known* to persons who are *absent*' " ("SEC," p. 176). This account is exemplary in the tradition because it assumes and, by assuming, fixes the secondary status of writing, which is here a means of conveying something prior to it, something that was in its moment of occurrence immediate and transparent, something once *present*. As a conveyer, the responsibility of writing is to transmit that presence with as little alteration as possible: "The same content, formerly communicated by gestures and sounds, will henceforth be transmitted by writing" ("SEC," p. 176). Writing so conceived is thus not a break in presence but a modification of presence, a modification made necessary by the unhappy fact of distance (absence), and yet a modification that is always connected to its originating source and is therefore always "at home." The situation becomes dangerous only when writing loses contact with this origin and is therefore no longer subordinated, as it should be, to a more substantial reality, to the reality of independent objects and intentions.

Derrida's challenge to this comfortable picture begins with an apparently trivial observation: "To be what it is, all writing . . . must be capable of functioning in the radical absence of every empirically determined receiver" ("SEC," p. 180). That is to say, writing is such that even someone who has no relationship whatsoever to the original receiver or sender will be able to construe it, to make something of it. If this were not so, if a piece of writing or speech could only function in the context of its original production, it would not be a representation of that context but a part of it; it would be a piece of presence. "A writing that is not structurally readable—iterable—beyond the death of the addressee would not be writing" ("SEC," p. 180). In this characterization, writing and language in general become too powerful for assimilation by the classical view in which writing "stands in" for an absent presence of which it is a mere representation; for if writing is readable even by those who know nothing of its original source or of its intended recipient, then it is doing its "standing in" without the anchoring presence, even at a remove, of anything to stand in for. As Derrida puts it, "The mark can do without the referent" ("SEC," p. 183); that is, the mark can be construed as referring to persons or objects or intentions to which readers have no independent or extralinguistic access either in person or in memory.

To put the matter this way, however, is to invite misunderstanding by suggesting that such construings are necessary only in the case of an empirical absence, that is, when the intended receiver or the object referred to are "actually" not there. It is a misunderstanding that is also courted when Derrida observes of the marks that he produces that their functioning will not be hindered by "my future disappearance." As it stands, this allows a reading in which at one time, in the original context of its production, the mark was stabilized by his "appearance"; but this reading, which has been deliberately encouraged, is immediately blocked by a qualifying statement:

> When I say "my future disappearance," it is in order to render this proposition more immediately acceptable. I ought to be able to say my disappearance, pure and simple, my non-presence in general, for instance the non-presence of my intention of saying something meaningful. ("SEC," pp. 180–81)

By this Derrida means that, even in the original moment of production, his is an interpreted presence, a presence that comes into view in the act of construing performed *necessarily* by those who hear him even in a face-to-face situation. Moreover, this is as true for him as it is for others, since in order to "know" his own intention he must consult himself and interrogate his motives with categories of interrogation that limit in advance the image he can have of himself.[9] Even when he is physically present, he will not be an unmediated entity either in his own eyes (or ears) or in the eyes of his interlocutors. (The same can be said of the nonpresent presence, the disappearance in general, of the husband in the *New Yorker* cartoon or of Derrida in my anecdote.) So that when Derrida declares that "the sign possesses the characteristic of being readable even if the moment of its production is irrevocably lost" ("SEC," p. 182), we must understand that the moment of production is *itself* a moment of loss, in that its components—including sender, receiver, referents, and message—are never transparently present but must be interpreted or "read" into being. Thus, Derrida's argument in this section moves from the assertion that utterances are readable even in the special conditions of empirical absence to the assertion that utterances are *only* readable (as opposed to being deciphered or seen through) even in the supposedly optimal condition of physical proximity.

It is this insight that informs Derrida's vexing use of the term "iterability." To say that something is iterable is usually understood to mean that after an original use it can be used *again* (iter); but for Derrida, iterability is a *general* condition that applies to the original use, which is therefore not original in the sense of being known or experienced without reference to anything but itself. This becomes clear when we consider what would have to be the case for there to be something like what Derrida says there could not be, the "non-iteration of an event" ("SEC," p. 192). The noniteration of an event would be an event that was apprehended not by a relationship of sameness or difference to something else (something prior) but directly, simply as itself; but if the components of an event—however simple or complex, near or far—come into view only in the act of reading, then there can be no such instance of a noniteration, and every event is always and already a representation or a repetition. To this someone like Searle would reply, not unreasonably, "Repetition or representation of what?" The answer is repetition or representation of itself, which seems a contradiction until we understand that the assertion is precisely that "itself" (the event, its agents, its objects, its meanings) is never apprehended except in an interpreted—hence repeated or represented—form. That is what Derrida means when he speaks of "the logic that ties repetition to alterity" ("SEC," p. 180). The repetition or representation of something is different from that something, which becomes its other; but since the repetition or representation is all one can have, it will always be "other" than itself. In Samuel Weber's words, "If something must be iterable in order to become an object of consciousness, then it can never be entirely grasped, having already been split in and by its being-repeated (or more precisely: by its *repeated being*)."[10] Iterability, then, stands for the general condition of having-to-be-read, and noniterability stands for the condition of availability-independent-of-reading, a condition which in Derrida's argument we can never enjoy. Noniterability, in short, is another word for full and unmediated presence, and iterability is another word for readability, not as a possibility but as a necessity. It is a necessity that has already been demonstrated by the example of the *New Yorker* cartoon: even in the most favorable of circumstances, when the woman is within earshot of her husband, his appearance (a word nicely hesitating between substance and surface), his intentions, and his meaning only emerge in the act of construing for which they are supposedly the ground; they are all iterated, repeated, represented, or, in a word, "read," entities. The moment of face-to-face exchange that founds Condillac's account of communication is the moment of the production within reading of that which is thought anterior to reading. In Derridean terms, the interpretive gesture which threatens to infect the center (that is, presence) is responsible for the very form of the center and of everything it contains, including persons, their messages, and their very worlds. That outside is its inside, the very force and law of its emergence.

II

One effect of this account of everyday or face-to-face communication is to raise in an immediate and urgent form the question of fictional language: for it is fictional language, in the traditional characterization, that brings worlds, complete with objects, persons, events, and intentions, into being, while ordinary or serious language is said to be responsible to the world of empirical fact. It is this distinction that underlies Austin's decision to exclude from his account of speech acts fictional and dramatic utterances, and it is that decision which is more or less the occasion of Derrida's critique. This key passage occurs in Austin's second chapter:

A performative utterance will, for example, be *in a peculiar way* hollow or void if said by an actor on the stage, or if introduced in a poem, or spoken in soliloquy. This applies in a similar manner to any and every utterance—a sea-change in special circumstances. Language in such circumstances is in special ways . . . used not seriously, but in ways *parasitic* upon its normal uses—ways which fall under the doctrine of the *etiolations* of language. (*HT*, p. 22)

The reasoning behind this declaration is clear enough: a speaker in a poem or an actor on a stage does not produce his utterance with a full and present intention but with the intention of someone behind him, a poet or a playwright; his is a *stage utterance,* and in order to get at its true meaning we have to go behind the stage to its originating source in the consciousness of an author. In construing the illocutionary force of stage utterances, we are, in short, at a remove.

Derrida's reply is that we are always and already at such a remove, and it is a reply that is implicit in the examples with which this essay began. If Derrida were to stand before me with his book and his message and his "presence," I would still be in the position of a playgoer, inferring his intention and his meaning not directly from his words but through the screen, already in place, of what I assumed to be his purposes, goals, concerns, and so on. I would be proceeding, that is, on the basis of the role I conceived him to be playing in relation to his "real" or interior or "offstage" intention; and the wife in the *New Yorker* cartoon proceeds in the same way when she hears her husband say that he is sorry, but she decides, because she knows what kind of person he "really" is, that he isn't sorry at all, that he is only acting. And even if I immediately accepted Derrida's words at face value, or if the wife never for a moment doubted her husband's sincerity, she and I would still be operating from within a prior construction of the character of our interlocutors. If by "stage utterances" one understands utterances whose illocutionary force must be inferred or constructed, then all utterances are stage utterances, and one cannot mark them off from utterances that are "serious."[11]

There is, however, another way to maintain the position that stage or literary utterances are not "used seriously"; one can point to their perlocutionary effects or, rather, as Austin does, to the absence of those effects: "There are parasitic uses of language, which are 'not serious,' not the 'full normal use.' The normal conditions of reference may be suspended, or no attempt made at a standard perlocutionary act, no attempt to make you do anything, as Walt Whitman does not seriously incite the eagle of liberty to soar" (*HT*, p. 104). Here the argument turns on the word "seriously," which seems to mean straightforwardly or nonmetaphorically and *therefore* productive of action in the world. The claim, in short, is that only when the words of an utterance refer to empirically specifiable conditions can it be called serious. But such a rigorous definition of serious would exclude many of the perlocutionary acts we perform daily. Surely, for example, the politician who incites the eagle of liberty to soar would be doing so seriously, in part because he would be attempting to make his hearers *do* something by making them think of themselves as extensions of the eagle of liberty. Someone intent on saving the difference between the serious and the literary might argue from "use" and point out that the politician would simply be saying one (metaphorical) thing while meaning another (real-world) thing; but the same observation could be made of a poet or a dramatist who uses an allegorical fable to urge a political action. However the relationship between perlocutionary effect and metaphor is characterized, that characterization cannot be turned into a distinction between serious and literary utterances, since perlocutions and metaphors will be found indifferently in both. The point would not even have to be made in relation to pre-Romantic aesthetics which were frankly didactic and hortatory (one cannot imagine telling Milton or Herbert or Jonson that they of course did not expect their readers to do anything in response to their works); and while some modernist aesthetics tell us that literature must be rigorously divorced from action of any kind, the reading or hearing of any play or poem involves the making of judgments, the reaching of decisions, the forming of attitudes, the registering of approval and disapproval, the feeling of empathy or distaste, and a hundred other things that are as much perlocutionary effects as the most overt of physical movements. The most one can say finally is that the kinds of perlocutionary effects produced by literary and nonliterary discourse are sometimes, but not always or necessarily, different, and this is not enough to warrant the distinctions Austin wants to make between ordinary and special circumstances, between normal and parasitic usage, between real-world utterances and stage or fictional utterances; at every point the conditions that supposedly mark off the lesser or derivative case can be shown to be defining of the normative case as well. In Derrida's words, "What Austin excludes as anomaly, exception, 'non-serious,' *citation* (on stage, in a poem, or a soliloquy) is the determined modification of a general citationality," that is, a highlighted instance of a general condition ("SEC," p. 191).

There are two obvious objections to this line of reasoning. The first one is posed by Derrida himself: If all utterances, serious as well as fictional, are detached from a centering origin and abandoned to an "essential drift" ("SEC," p. 182), then how is it that any of the world's verbal business gets satisfactorily done? One cannot deny, acknowledges Derrida, "that there are also performatives that succeed, and one has to account for them: meetings are called to order, . . . people say: 'I pose a question'; they bet, challenge, christen ships, and sometimes even marry. It would seem that such events have occurred. And even if only one had taken place only once, we would still be obliged to account for it" ("SEC," p. 191).

Derrida responds to his own objection first by saying "perhaps," and then by proceeding to inquire more closely into the notion of "occurrence." If by occurrence is meant an event whose certainty can be verified by independent evidence from the *outside,* then such events do not occur, because there is no "totally saturated context," no context so perspicuous that its interpretive cues can be read off by anyone no matter what his position; no context that precludes interpretation because it wears its meaning on its face. But if by occurrence is meant the conviction on the part of two or more contextually linked speakers that a particular speech act has taken place, then such events occur all the time, although independently of that conviction no external evidence could verify the communication. (Of course, speakers often subsequently *act* on the conviction that communication has occurred, and that continuing action is a kind of verification; but it *springs* from the conviction and does not stand outside it.)

Derrida offers as an example the context in which he originally delivered—orally, of course—the text of "Signature Event Context," a colloquium on philosophy in the French language whose theme was communication. Derrida calls this colloquium a "conventional context—produced by a kind of consensus that is implicit but structurally vague" ("SEC," p. 174). That is, while it is certainly in force, the consensus cannot be identified with an explicit statement of it because that statement itself would be "consensually" readable only by those whose consciousnesses were already informed by the goals and assumptions that give the colloquium its identity. The point is made by one of Derrida's typical jokes when he offers his own account—formal and written—of that consensus. It is understood, he explains, that at this colloquium one is to "propose 'communications' concerning communication, communications in a discursive form, colloquial communications, oral communications destined to be listened to, and to engage or to pursue dialogues within the horizon of an intelligibility and truth that is meaningful" ("SEC," p. 174). But all of this, he says, is "evident; and those who doubt it need only consult our program to be convinced" ("SEC," p. 174). The joke is that it will be evident only to those who are *able* to consult the program or who know what it is to consult the program of a philosophical colloquium, and they will *already* be convinced since their ability to consult is coextensive with the knowledge of why they are there. Someone who was without that ability—a passerby who happened to wander into the meeting room—might be convinced only that he didn't belong.

This, then, is how successful performatives occur, by means of the shared assumptions which enable speakers and hearers to make the same kind of sense of the words they exchange. And this also explains why the occurrence of successful performatives is not assured, because those who hear within different assumptions will be making a different kind of sense. One way to resist this argument, while appearing to assent to it, is to make the body of assumptions into an object by making a project of its description. Derrida believes that this is the project Austin pursues in the name of "context" when he declares in a famous passage that "what we have to study is *not* the sentence but the issuing of an utterance in a speech situation" (*HT,* p. 138). This dislodgment of the freestanding sentence from its traditional position of privilege is usually regarded as Austin's most powerful move; but Derrida sees that the move will have made very little difference if speech situations or contexts are conceived of as self-identifying; for then all that will have happened is that one self-interpreting entity will have been replaced by another; rather than sentences that declare their own meaning, we will now have contexts that declare their own meaning.

The issue here is between two notions of context: traditionally a context has been defined as a collection of features and therefore as something that can be identified by any clear-eyed observer; but Derrida thinks of a context as a structure of assumptions, and it is only by those who hold those assumptions or are held by them that the features in question can first be picked out and then identified as belonging to a context. It is the difference between thinking of a context as something *in* the world and thinking of a context as a construction *of* the world, a construction that is itself performed under contextualized conditions. Under the latter understanding one can no longer have any simple (that is, noninterpretive) recourse to context in order to settle disputes or resolve doubts about meaning, because contexts, while they are productive of interpretation, are also the products of interpretation. It would be useless, for example, to adjudicate the quarrel between the husband and wife in the *New Yorker* cartoon by appealing to the context, since it is precisely because they conceive the contextual conditions of their conversation differently that there is a quarrel at all. Of course, it is still the case, as Derrida acknowledges, that apologies are successfully offered and accepted ("there are also performatives that succeed"), but when that happens it is because the parties share or are shared by the same contextual assumptions and not because each can check what the other says against the independently available features of an empirical context. The contextual features of a simple exchange are no less "read" and therefore no more "absolutely" constraining than the contextual features of a stage performance or of a conversation reported in a poem.

This brings me directly to the second of the objections to this line of argument, that it denies the obvious differences between fiction and real life. But in fact it denies nothing. It simply asserts that the differences, whatever they are (and they are not always the same), do not arrange themselves around a basic or underlying difference between unmediated experience and experience that is the product of interpretive activity. If it is true, as Searle, Ohmann, and others contend, that we build up the world of a novel by reading it within a set of shaping conventions or interpretive strategies, it is no less true of the emergence into palpable form of the equally conventional worlds within which we experience real life. The "facts" of a baseball game, of a classroom situation, of a family reunion, of a trip to the grocery store, of a philosophical colloquium on the French language are only facts for those who are proceeding within a prior knowledge of the purposes, goals, and practices that underlie those activities. Again, this does not mean that there is no difference between them, only that they are all conventional as are the facts they entail.

The result is not to deny distinctions but to recharacterize them as distinctions between different kinds of interpretive practice. Thus, one might contrast the law, where interpretive practice is such that it demands a single reading (verdict), with the practice of literary criticism, where the pressure is for multiple readings (so much so that a text for which only one reading seemed available would be in danger of losing the designation "literary"). And if the contrast were extended to "ordinary conversation," that interpretive practice would be found to be more like the law than literary criticism in that a single reading is the understood norm; but, unlike the law, it is a reading for which one is not supposed to work, since it is a tacit rule of ordinary conversation that you accept things at their (contextually determined) face value and don't try to penetrate below the surface (again contextually determined) of an utterance. (Austin makes this into an ethical principle on pages 10 and 11 of *How to Do Things with Words.*) The violation of this rule is what makes the *New Yorker* cartoon funny; you're not supposed to question the surface currency of sincerity in everyday exchanges, and when you do, the resulting dislocation is at once irritating (as it is to the husband in the cartoon) and humorous (as it is to the readers of the *New Yorker*). One might say, then, that ordinary or everyday discourse is characterized by interpretive confidence and consequently by a minimum of self-conscious interpretive work; but this should not be understood to mean that the empirical conditions of ordinary discourse *compel* interpretive confidence: rather, interpretive confidence, as an assumption that produces behavior, also produces the empirical conditions it assumes.

Of course, this could be said of all conventional activities, each of which is carried on in a setting that it also elaborates and each of which is constitutive of the facts in its field of reference. This suggests the possibility of a new project or a new metaphysics, a taxonomic account of conventional activities and of the different kinds of fact they make available. Such an account, however, would itself be a conventional activity and thus could not escape the "interestedness" it claimed to describe. Moreover, such an account would never be able to catch up with the ability of conventional practices to modify themselves, to shrink or expand so that the boundaries between them, along with the facts marked off by those boundaries, are continually changing. In short, conventional differences are themselves a matter of convention and are no more available for direct inspection than the facts they entail. That is why the determination both of whether or not something is a fact and of what kind of fact it is can be a matter of dispute, as different criteria of difference are put into operation; and that is also why such disputes can only be adjudicated by invoking evidentiary procedures that will be no less conventional than the facts they are called on to establish. My morning newspaper reports that a plaque has been set up in Annapolis to commemorate the landing in America of Kunta Kinte, a displaced African. At the same time the Dublin city fathers are resisting efforts by a committee of Joyceans to have a plaque placed on the door of the house where Leopold Bloom was born on the grounds that he was only a fictional character. The two cases seem clear-cut until one begins to examine them. The primary documentary evidence of Kunta Kinte's independent existence is Alex Haley's *Roots,* a work whose integrity as a piece of research is very much in question; while, as Hugh Kenner has recently commented, Bloom is a personage more fully documented than the Irish national hero Cuchulain, whose statue stands in a Dublin post office. Nor can a fact/fiction boundary be definitively drawn by saying that, however imperfectly documented, there really was once a Kunta Kinte or a slave by a similar name of whom Haley's character is a representation; for the same thing can be said of Bloom who is a representation, many scholars believe, of a man named Hunter, a Dubliner who had himself changed his name (perhaps from Bloom) because it marked him as Jewish. It is not that these boundaries can't be settled but that when they are settled it will be by interpretive or institutional acts and not by evidence that is available independently of such acts. If Kunta Kinte has a plaque commemorating him in Annapolis, it is not because he has been objectively certified as a real person; rather his certification as a real person, when and if it is complete, will be the cumulative product of acts like the setting up of a plaque to commemorate him, and the force of *that* act depends upon a convention linking the setting up of plaques and the validation of historical persons.

The point again is not that there are no such things as historical persons but that the category is no less a conventional one (with a membership conventionally established) than the category of fictional persons. The fact that it is a conventional category doesn't mean that the distinction is itself conventional; either Kunta Kinte was real or he was not. But the procedures for establishing the *fact* of his reality will always be conventional; that is, the fact will always have the status of something determined within a system of intelligibility and will never have the status of something determined outside of any system whatsoever. Nevertheless, since there always is a system, complete with evidentiary procedures and rules for applying them, the determination can always be made (although, given the claims of other systems, it can always be challenged).

That is why Derrida ostentatiously *refuses* to conclude that there "is no performative effect, no effect of ordinary language, no effect of presence or of discursive event (speech act). It is simply," he says, "that those effects do not exclude what is generally opposed to them, term by term; on the contrary, they presuppose it . . . as the general space of their possibility" ("SEC," p. 193). That is to say, there *are* differences in the experienced world of discourse that correspond to the differences traditionally posited between face-to-face and etiolated communication, between historical and fictional persons. It is just that those differences, rather than deriving from a *basic* difference between unmediated and mediated experience, mark off varieties of mediation. It is true that those varieties can be ordered with respect to their distance from an ideal or normative case, the case of ordinary circumstances, but that case, as we have seen, is nothing more than a set of interpretive practices (such as the practice of assuming sincerity) that produces what supposedly underlies the practices. Distance is not a special condition in relation to which interpretation becomes necessary; it is a general condition ("the general space of . . . possibility") that is productive of everything, including the circumstances—ordinary or presence-full circumstances—from which it is supposedly a falling away. Whatever hierarchy of communication situations may be in force, it is not a natural hierarchy, although within the space made available by the institutional and the conventional—finally the only available space—it will be received as natural, at least until it is challenged and reconstituted in another, equally institutional, form.[12] While there is no pure performative in the sense that authorizes Austin's exclusion of stage utterances, there is, as Derrida explains, a "relative purity" of performatives; but, he continues, "this relative purity does not emerge *in opposition* to citationality or iterability [Derrida's words in "Signature Event Context" for the institutional], but in opposition to other kinds of iteration within a general iterability" ("SEC," p. 192). That iterability—the condition of having-to-be-read—covers the field and can never be opposed to the "singular and original event-utterance," the transparent and simple speech act for which *How to Do Things with Words* is an extended but unsuccessful search.

III

The Derrida who emerges in the preceding pages may strike some readers as not at all like the apostle of "free play" they have learned either to fear or admire. While he is certainly not a believer in determinate meaning in a way that would give comfort to, say, M. H. Abrams or Frederick Crews, he does believe that communications between two or more persons regularly occur and occur with a "relative" certainty that ensures the continuity of everyday life. Rather than a subverter of common sense, this Derrida is very much a philosopher of common sense, that is, of the underlying assumptions and conventions within which the shape of common sense is specified and acquires its powerful force. One might even say, with the proper qualifications, that he is a philosopher of ordinary language. In so saying I am suggesting that Derrida and Austin may not be so far apart as some have thought. Searle begins his reply to Derrida by asserting that the confrontation between the two philosophers "never quite takes place" because the gulf that separates them is so wide and is made even wider by Derrida's "mistakes."[13] I want to argue, on the contrary, that the confrontation never quite takes place because there finally is not enough space between them for there to be a confrontation; and in the remainder of this essay I want to make that argument from the opposite direction by focusing on the process by which, at the conclusion of *How to Do Things with Words,* the supposedly normative class of constatives is shown to be a member of the supposedly exceptional class of performatives. Once that reversal has been effected, everything that Derrida says follows, including his challenge to the exclusion of stage or fictional utterances.

As it is first offered, the original distinction contrasts utterances that are responsible to the facts of an independent world with utterances that bring facts, of a certain kind, into being. Utterances of the first type are constatives, and the business of a constative is to " 'describe' some state of affairs, or to 'state some fact', which it must do either truly or falsely" (*HT,* p. 1). Performatives, on the other hand, are actions in the sense that, rather than reporting on a state of affairs, they produce and create states of affairs. If I say, "I promise (to do X)," the effect of that "speech action" is to establish a future obligation (that is what a promise, by definition, is); that obligation was not a prior fact on whose existence I was reporting by saying "I promise" but a fact that came into the world by virtue of my saying "I promise." Of course, the creation of an obligation depends not simply on the words but on the uttering of the words within appropriate circumstances; if I promise to do something that I have already done or something that would not be of benefit to the promisee or something that I was obviously about to do anyway, the promise will be hollow or void or infelicitous for a variety of reasons analyzed by Searle in *Speech Acts*. Appropriateness, then, stands to performatives as truth and falsehood stand to constatives. The difference is that appropriateness as a standard varies with circumstances—it is a social or institutional judgment—while truth and falsehood as a standard refer to a relationship (between word and world) that *always* obtains.

Although Austin makes this distinction very firmly in the opening pages, much of the book is devoted to blurring it. The blurring begins with the last sentence of the first chapter: " 'False' is not necessarily used of statements only" (*HT*, p. 11). By the end of chapter 4, we are being told that "in order to explain what can go wrong with statements we cannot just concentrate on the proposition involved (whatever that is) as has been done traditionally" (*HT*, p. 52). The parenthesis tells its own story: if you can't isolate a proposition, it is going to be hard to isolate the properties of statements. At the beginning of chapter 5 Austin admits that "there is danger of our initial . . . distinction between constative and performative breaking down," and chapter 6 opens by suggesting that "the performative is not altogether so obviously distinct from the constative" (*HT*, pp. 54, 67). In chapter 7 Austin pauses to "consider where we stand" and reports that we have now "found sufficient indications that unhappiness nevertheless seems to characterize both kinds of utterance . . . and that the requirement of conforming or bearing some relation to the facts . . . seems to characterize performatives . . . similarly to the way which is characterized of supposed constatives" (*HT*, p. 91).

The fact that constatives are now being referred to as "supposed" alerts us to the significance of what has been happening; terms are not merely blurring but a hierarchy is becoming undone. That is, the drawing together of performative and constative is finally to the benefit of performatives which under the traditional model were a subsidiary and inferior class because they were dependent on circumstances and not on judgments of truth and falsehood; but now judgments on truth and falsehood have been shown to be just as circumstantial as judgments of felicity (which themselves have been shown to be inseparable from questions of "fact"), with the result that constatives can no longer be defined as having a transparent relationship to the facts. Indeed, the notion of "fact" has been destabilized by the very same process; for since facts are established by means of true-false judgments (is it the case or is it not?) the circumstantialization of those judgments is also the circumstantialization of fact; that is, the question of whether something is or is not a fact will receive a different answer in different circumstances.

Austin makes this explicit in his last chapter when he declares that "truth and falsity are . . . not names for relations, qualities, or what not but for a dimension of assessment" (HT, p. 148). By "dimension of assessment," he means "a general dimension of being a right or proper thing to say as opposed to a wrong thing, in these circumstances, to this audience, for these purposes and with these intentions" (HT, p. 144). His example, "France is hexagonal," is surely a constative if anything is (HT, p. 142). Is it true or false? he asks. Well, perhaps, for certain intents and purposes, it might be true, if uttered in a military dimension of assessment by a general; but it might well be thought false if uttered in another dimension of assessment at a convention of geographers. It is not only that the terms within which the judgment is made change; the object of fact in relation to which one judges changes too. In one dimension France is conceived of as a military objective, in the other as a shape that must be reduced to a mapmaker's scale. One is tempted to say that underlying these different perspectives is a single factual entity, the "real" France, but that phrase can only stand for a France conceived within no dimension of assessment whatsoever, and that is precisely what it is impossible to do. France can only be thought of or even *thought* within some dimension of assessment, and so it will always be thought of as having or not having the kind of shape that is appropriate to that dimension. The France you are talking about will always be the product of the kind of talk (military, geographical, culinary, economic, literary) you are engaging in and will never be available *outside* any kind of talk whatsoever where it could function as an objective point of verification.

The point is made even clearer by Austin's next example. "Lord Raglan won the battle of Alma." True or false? Well, it depends on, among other things, whether it appears in a schoolbook or in a work of historical research. In a schoolbook it might be accepted as true because of the in-force assumptions as to what a battle is, what constitutes winning, the relationship of a general to success or failure, and so on; in a work of historical research all of these assumptions may have been replaced by others with the result that the very notions "battle" and "won" have a different shape. The mistake would be to think that "battle of Alma" was or ever could be an interpretation-free fact. Like France it is the product of the interpretive context—dimension of assessment—within which it has been conceived.

These accounts of France and the battle of Alma retroactively complicate the examples Austin had earlier offered to illustrate his original distinction. In chapter 4 he had cited the utterance "He is running" as a model constative because its truth can be determined simply by checking it against "the fact that he is running" (*HT*, p. 47). But once we realize that facts are only facts within a dimension of assessment, the relationship of transparency between the constative and the state of affairs on which it "reports" is immediately compromised. One need only imagine someone saying to the speaker, "You call that running, it's barely jogging," to see that the fit between the description and the "fact" will only be obvious to those for whom the articulations of the language of description correspond to their beliefs about the articulations in nature. If two speakers conceive of the distinction between running and jogging differently (or if one doesn't hold to any distinction at all), then they will disagree about the accuracy of "He is running" because each will be checking the utterance against a different set of "dimension-of-assessment" specific facts. Of course, it is always possible that a third party will enter the dispute and say, somewhat smugly, "You two are arguing about semantics; what you want is a vocabulary uninvolved in any particular perspective. If you were to describe the activity in terms of force, ratio of distance to speed, resistance, angles, velocity, and so on, you would have a neutral account of it, and *then* you could argue about whether to call it running or jogging." There is no reason to doubt that this could succeed as a strategy, since one can always have recourse to a vocabulary at a higher level of generality (a higher level of shared assumptions) than the level at which there is a dispute. But while the vocabulary may rise above and include the differing perspectives of the disputants, it will itself proceed from, and refer to the facts of, some or other perspective, and therefore the account it produces, while persuasive and convincing to all parties, will have no epistemological priority over the accounts it transcends. Talk of angles and ratios and velocities may have more cachet in the game of "accurate" description than talk of running and jogging, but it is still talk made possible in its intelligibility by a dimension of assessment; and therefore the accuracy such talk achieves will be relative to the facts as they are within that dimension.

On this analysis there is still a line of business for constatives to be in: but that business can no longer be thought of as involving a privileged relationship to reality. Whereas in the opening chapters of *How to Do Things with Words,* constatives are responsible to the world "as it is," by chapter 11 a constative is responsible to the world *as it is given within a dimension of assessment.* Rather than occupying a position of centrality in relation to which other uses of language are derivative and parasitic, constative speech acts are like all others in that the condition of their possibility (the condition of always operating within a dimension of assessment or interpretive community) forever removes them from any contact with an unmediated presence. By Austin's own argument, then, the exclusion of stage and other etiolated utterances as deviations from ordinary circumstances loses its warrant; for ordinary circumstances, circumstances in which objects, events, and intentions are transparently accessible, are shown to be an impossible ideal the moment the absolute (as opposed to conventional) distinction between constatives and performatives can no longer be made.

It would seem, then, that Derrida is right when he finds a contradiction at the heart of Austin's enterprise between his acknowledgment of the risk or infelicity inherent in all speech acts and his attempt to regulate that risk by excluding from consideration one class of speech acts because they are infected by risk. Derrida finds this strategy "curious," but he himself has directed us to a more generous reading of Austin's text when he characterizes it as "patient, open, aporetical, in constant transformation, often more fruitful in the acknowledgment of its impasses than in its positions" ("SEC," p. 187). That seems to me to be exactly right; the one thing that remains constant in *How to*

Do Things with Words is that nothing remains constant: no term, no definition, no distinction survives the length of the argument, and many do not survive the paragraph or sentence in which they are first presented. The overturning of the distinction with which the book begins is of course the most dramatic instance of the pattern, but smaller and related instances abound, and they are all alike in that they simultaneously advance and retard the argument. Quite early on, Austin provides us with an account of his "method" when he remarks on the tendency of philosophy to begin by getting things wrong and says, cheerfully, "We must learn to run before we can walk" (*HT*, p. 12). By inverting the traditional proverb, Austin lets us know in advance that progress in this book will be a matter of declaring definitions that one must then take back, and moving forward will mean moving less quickly and perhaps, if we think of our goal as the achieving of undoubted rigor and clarity, not moving at all. Something of the feel of this experience is communicated in a remarkable series of sentences at the opening of the second chapter: "So far then we have merely felt the firm ground of prejudice slide away beneath our feet. But now how, as philosophers, are we to proceed? One thing we might go on to do, of course, is to take it all back: another would be to bog, by logical stages, down. But all this must take time" (*HT*, p. 13). The first sentence leaves us uncomfortable with either the past on which it reports or the future it promises. No one wants to feel that he is grounded in prejudice; but still less do we like to think that we may not be grounded at all. This Hobson's choice is immediately reproduced in the two alternative courses of action, taking everything back or bogging, by logical stages, down. When Austin then says, "But all this must take time," it is not at all clear what "all this" is or whether, at the end of it, we will once again have something under our feet.

Once Austin gets started (if that is the word), he regularly imitates God by first giving and then taking away. Later in chapter 3 he makes a distinction between those failures in communication that result from "botched procedures" and those failures that result when the procedures have been correctly executed but improperly invoked. He calls the first "misfires" and the second "abuses" and then admonishes the reader, one-half second too late, "Do not stress the normal connotations of these names" (*HT*, p. 16). The effect of this is complex: the names are on record and the distinction is in force, but at the same time the names are under a cloud, and the distinctions, as Austin almost immediately says, are "not hard and fast." Of course, hard and fast distinctions are not to be expected from an author who warns you that any new keys he puts in your hand will also be two skids under your feet (*HT*, p. 25). If one were to label this kind of writing, one might very well term it writing "under erasure," that is, writing which simultaneously uses and calls into question a vocabulary and a set of concepts. Of course, writing "under erasure" is a phrase that is associated with Derrida (who borrows it from Heidegger), and by invoking it I am easing into a claim that might at first seem counterintuitive: when all is said and done Derrida and Austin are very much alike. They are alike in writing a prose that complicates its initial assertions and obfuscates the oppositions on which it supposedly turns; and they are alike in the use to which that prose is put, a simultaneous proffering and withdrawing of procedural tests for determining the force and significance of utterances.

This has always been recognized in the case of Derrida, in part because the notorious difficulty of his prose, even at the surface level, flags the degree to which this discourse is concerned, not to say obsessed, with its own status. In Austin's case, however, it has been possible to overlook the fact of his style, either because it was thought irrelevant to the content of his philosophy or because it was regarded as a mannerism appropriate to a professor at Oxford. But in fact it is not a mannerism at all but a self-consciously employed strategy that is intended to produce, among other things, impatience and irritation. At one point Austin says as much. "Many of you will be getting impatient at this approach—and to some extent quite justifiably. You will say, 'Why not cut the cackle? . . . Why not get down to discussing the thing bang off in terms of linguistics and psychology in a straightforward fashion? Why be so devious?'" (*HT*, p. 122). To discuss the thing in terms of linguistics would be to produce criteria by which performatives could be marked off from constatives, and illocutionary acts distinguished from perlocutionary; and to discuss the thing in terms of psychology would be to correlate internal states with a list of verbs. In the course of his book Austin attempts more than once to do exactly that, but in each instance the formulas he considers turn out to be unworkable. Here on page 122 the address to the reader follows a chapter-long discussion of the prepositions "in" and "by" as possible ways of identifying different kinds of speech acts. He now asks, "Will these . . . formulas provide us with a test for distinguishing illocutionary from perlocutionary acts?" That is, will they do what we have been assuming all along that they could do? The answer is brief and crushing: "They will not." At times it seems that the only point of the book is to devise tests that will *not* work. In chapter 5 a succession of "absolute" criteria for picking out performatives is offered and rejected: the first person singular, the present indicative, tense, and mood—each of them is passed in review and of each of them Austin finally says, this "will not do." We are, he admits, at an "impasse over any *single simple* criterion of grammar or vocabulary" (*HT*, p. 59); but perhaps, he speculates, it may not be impossible to "produce a complex criterion" or "at least a set of criteria"; perhaps, for example, "one of the criteria might be that everything with the verb in the imperative mood is performative." But this proposal is no sooner made than it is threatened by an infinite regress: "This leads, however, to many troubles over . . . when a verb is in the imperative mood and when it is not, into which I do not propose to go" (*HT*, pp. 59–60). Presumably, if he did go into it, he would encounter the same difficulty he encounters here: the test for whether or not a verb was in the imperative mood would turn out to be no less vulnerable to exceptions and counterexamples than the tests that have already failed.

As his argument unfolds (exactly the wrong word), Austin continues to pursue this double strategy: he searches for a criterion of which it can be said, "it is only to be used in circumstances which make it unambiguously clear that it is being used," but the search yields only the repeated demonstration that such a criterion is unavailable because, as he immediately declares, it rests on "a counsel of perfection" (*HT*, p. 34). That counsel impels his enterprise forward and draws us on with its promise—the promise of a pure performative, of a mechanical procedure for distinguishing one kind of speech act from another, of a point of transparency—but the promise is never redeemed as Austin teases out his examples until the distinctions they supposedly illustrate are blurred and even reversed. The pattern is particularly clear in the extended discussion through several chapters of the so-called explicit performative. An explicit performative is a verb that serves "the special purpose of *making explicit* . . . what precise action it is that is being performed by the issuing of the utterance" (*HT*, p. 61). In other words, the illocutionary force is named in the utterance itself by a performative verb, as in "I *promise* to pay you five dollars," or "I *order* you to leave the room." The position occupied by the explicit performative in the theory is thus a familiar one in philosophy: it stands for a core or paradigm case in relation to which other more doubtful cases are to be evaluated and understood. The explicit performative, in short, centers or anchors a system that at its outermost edges is characterized by uncertainty. The presence of an explicit performative affords a clear indication of the intention with which an utterance is issued; whereas in its absence the way in which an utterance can be taken is "open" (*HT*, p. 33).

Almost immediately, however, Austin complicates this picture by presenting an example in which the presence of an explicit performative does not in and of itself determine the force of an utterance. "Suppose I say 'I promise to send you to a nunnery'—when I think, but you do not, that this will be for your good, or again when you think it will but I do not, or even when we both think it will, but in fact, as may transpire, it will not?" (*HT*, pp. 37–38). Have I promised? Or "have I invoked a non-existent convention in inappropriate circumstances?" Austin does not answer his own questions but merely points out that "there can be no satisfactory choice between these alternatives, which are too un-subtle to fit subtle cases" (*HT*, p. 38). There is no "short-cut": no mechanical procedure for making these decisions; instead, one must expound "the full complexity of the situation which does not exactly fit any common classification" (*HT*, p. 38). But what this and other examples suggest is that *all* cases may be similarly subtle and that the situation which would fit the common classification—the situation in which illocutionary force is perfectly explicit—will never be encountered.

Whenever the explicit performative reappears, it is in contexts like this one, contexts that take away the interpretive comfort it promises to provide. In chapter 6 Austin offers a speculative genealogy in which the explicit performative and the "pure" statement emerge not before but *after* "certain more primary utterances, many of which are already implicit performatives" (*HT*, p. 71). In this account vagueness and indeterminacy, rather than being a departure from a more basic condition of precision, are in fact primitive, and we are very close to Derrida's assertion that "the quality of risk" is internal to the very structure of language and not something that infects only peripheral and nonnormative cases. In the same chapter the strong claim for the explicit performative is made once again when Austin says "the explicit performative rules out equivocation and keeps the performance fixed," but he then softens the claim almost to nothing by adding to his sentence a single word, "relatively" (*HT*, p. 76). On the very next page he declares explicitly what his examples have been all the while implying: "The existence and even the use of explicit performative does not remove all our troubles" (*HT*, p. 77). By troubles Austin means the "uncertainty of sure reception," and the reason that the explicit performative does not remove that uncertainty is because it is uncertain—that is, a matter of interpretation—as to whether or not a particular locution is in fact explicit in the way required. Rather than resolving an interpretive dispute, the citing of an explicit performative merely adds another component to the dispute. The final judgment on the explicit performative is delivered in chapter 9, and it is a judgment that renders the term incapable of performing the function it was introduced to serve: "We have found . . . that it is often not easy to be sure that, even when it is apparently in explicit form, an utterance is performative or that it is not" (*HT*, p. 91). "Apparently" is a master word here; it carries with it all the force of the critique Derrida will later make of this same book. "It is time," Austin declares in the very next sentence, "to make a fresh start on the problem." Of course by now making a fresh start means that the problem has itself been reconceived in a way so radical that even its outlines are no longer what they were when it was initially posed.

"It is difficult," Austin says at the end of chapter 9, "to say where conventions begin and end" (*HT*, p. 118). At times in the book this seems to be a difficulty that, once acknowledged, can be overcome, but in fact that difficulty, with all its implications for the possibility of certain formal projects, is finally triumphant in *How to Do Things with Words*. The rhetoric of the book's opening pages suggests a modest proposal: a type of utterance that had not been sufficiently attended to, and was in danger of escaping serious attention altogether, was to be brought into the circle that had been drawn around language by traditional philosophy; but, once in, the attempt to provide an account of that type begins to undermine the assumptions that allow the circle to be drawn in the first place, and in the end we have the revolution so elegantly reported by Searle: the special cases swallow the general case.[14] It is important to see that this is not a mere reversal in which two terms change places within a system whose structural shape remains the same. The revisionary effect of this discourse is much more wholesale; it challenges and dislodges the picture of things that at once gave the terms their shape and made conceivable the project of formally relating them. That project (of getting things straight "bang off") is what gives the book its apparent structure, but the true structure is its gradual dissolution as the distinctions with which it begins are blurred and finally collapsed. It is this double structure that is responsible for the fact that the book has given rise to two versions of speech-act theory, one committed to reabsorbing illocutionary force into a formal theory of the Chomsky type (here representative figures are John Ross, Jerrold Katz, and Jerrold Saddock)[15] and the other committed to making illocutionary force a function of pragmatic—that is, unformalizable—circumstances (here one might cite the work of H. P. Grice and Mary Pratt).[16] In a third version, represented at times by Searle and more recently by Kent Bach and Robert Harnisch, there is an attempt to reconcile the formal and the pragmatic, but this usually involves granting them an independence that the pragmatic view, if taken seriously, inherently destabilizes.[17] For Austin, the formal and the pragmatic are neither alternatives to be chosen nor simple opposites to be reconciled but the components of a dialectic that works itself out in his argument, a tacking back and forth between the commitment to intelligibility and the realization that intelligibility, although always possible, can never be reduced to the operation of a formal mechanism. That is why Derrida's reading of Austin is finally not a critique but a tribute to the radical provisionality of a text that has too often been domesticated, and it is a reading that is more faithful than many that have been offered by the master's disciples. Indeed, had he thought of it, Derrida might well have dedicated "Signature Event Context" to Austin; and it is pleasant to think that in some philosopher's heaven he will be able to present it to him, WITH THE COMPLIMENTS OF THE AUTHOR.

3. Why No One's Afraid of Wolfgang Iser

At a time when we are warned daily against the sirens of literary theory, Wolfgang Iser is notable because he does not appear on anyone's list. He is not included among those (Derrida, de Man, Bloom, Miller, Fish) who are thought of as subverting standards, values, and the rule of common sense; nor do we find him cited as one of those (Abrams, Hirsch, Booth, Graff, Crews, Shattuck) who are fighting the good fight against the forces of deconstructive nihilism. His absence from the field of pitched battle does not mean that he goes unread; on the contrary, his two major works, *The Implied Reader* and *The Act of Reading,* outsell all other books on the prestigious list of the Johns Hopkins University Press with the exception of Derrida's *Of Grammatology* (a book that is, I suspect, more purchased than read). Iser is, in short, a phenomenon: he is influential without being controversial, and at a moment when everyone is choosing up sides, he seems to be on no side at all or (it amounts to the same thing) on every side at once.

How does he do it? (I might have asked, "how does he get away with it?" but that would have been to tip my hand.) The answer lies, I think, in the terms in which he conceives of his project which is no less than to free the literary text from the demand that it yield or contain a referential meaning, an embodied truth. Such a demand, Iser complains, reduces literary texts "to the level of documents," and thus robs them "of that very dimension that sets them apart from the document, merely the opportunity they offer us to experience for ourselves the spirit of the age, social conditions, the author's neuroses, etc."[1] The emphasis here is on the word "experience," for what is left out of the traditional or classical account is the actualizing role played by the reader in the production—as opposed to the mere perception or uncovering—of literary meaning. "How can the meaning possibly be experienced if—as is always assumed by the classical norm of interpretation—it is already there, namely waiting for a referential exposition?" (p. 18.) Meaning in a literary text does not simply lie there, it must be brought out in an act of concretization (p. 21). It follows then that the critic's "object should . . . be not to explain a work, but to reveal the conditions that bring about its various possible effects," effects that require the participation of a reader in whose experience "the text comes to life" (p. 19).

As Iser sees it, the advantage of his theory is that it avoids identifying the aesthetic object either with the text, in its formal and objective self-sufficiency, or with the idiosyncratic experience of individual readers. The literary work "cannot be identical with the text or with the concretization, but must be situated somewhere between the two. It must inevitably be virtual in character, as it cannot be reduced to the reality of the text or to the subjectivity of the reader" (p. 21). To the question informing much of contemporary literary theory—what is the source of interpretive authority, the text or the reader—Iser answers "both." He does not, however, conceive of the relationship between them as a partnership in which each brings a portion of the meaning which is then added to the portion brought by the other; for in his theory meaning is something neither of them *has* (it is not an embodied object); rather it is something that is produced or built up or assembled by a *process* of interaction in which the two parties play quite different, but interdependent, roles. The role of the text is to "designate *instructions* for the *production* of the signified" (p. 65), which in the case of literature is the aesthetic object; the role of the reader is to follow these directions and so to produce it. "It" in this last sentence does not stand for a thing but for an event, a happening; the emphasis of the model is finally temporal rather than spatial (although, as we shall see, it contains spatial elements), and the literary work is not to be identified with any one point in the "dyadic interaction" but with the entire process. "The text can never be grasped as a whole—only as a series of changing viewpoints, each one restricted in itself and so necessitating further perspectives. This is the process by which the reader 'realizes' an overall situation" (p. 68).

The relationship, then, is one of script to performer, but in literary texts, Iser explains, the script is not explicit in an exhaustive way, and therefore the reader's activities are not wholly constrained by its directions. Indeed, the literary text is distinguished from the nonliterary, and especially from the texts of science (p. 87), by the presence (actually an absence) in it of "gaps" or "indeterminacies" or "blanks" which are then filled in by a reader according to his "individual disposition" (p. 123). That is, the "structure of the text allows for different ways" of fulfilling its "potential" (p. 37). The different perspectives embedded in the text are set alongside one another in ways that demand that they be organized, and it is the reader who must "build up" the connections, "the syntheses which eventually individualize the aesthetic object" (p. 118). So that "while the meaning of the literary work remains related to what the printed text says, . . . it requires the creative imagination of the reader to put it all together" (p. 142).

It is statements like these (which are found everywhere in the book) that account in part for the attractiveness of Iser's theory: it seems able to accommodate emphases that have often been perceived as contradictory in the writings of other theorists. It is at once spatial—in that it conceives of the text as an object with a particular shape (the shape of the "designated instructions")—and temporal—in that the production of literary meaning is a process that the text only sets in motion; it is for the same reason a theory that can claim a measure of objectivity—its operations begin with something that is "given"—and yet at the same time it requires the subjective contribution of the reader who must do his individual part; it is therefore a theory that sets limits to interpretation—as Iser repeatedly says the subjective element is not "arbitrary" (pp. 23–24) because it is "guided" or "prestructured" (p. 21) or "moulded" (p. 122) by the structures the text contains (p. 21)—and yet within these limits it allows, and indeed demands, the exercise of interpretive freedom.

It is in sum a capacious and liberal theory that in its generosity seems particularly well suited to the pluralism of most American literary criticism. Pluralism is by and large an attempt to steer a middle way between the poles of objectivity and subjectivity. That is, pluralists wish neither to embrace a theory in which literary texts have one and only one correct reading (because that would be as they see it to violate the essence of literature), nor to embrace a theory in which a literary text can receive as many correct or legitimate readings as there are readers (because then words like "correct" and "legitimate" would lose their force). It is their contention, therefore, that while a literary text is distinguished by its openness to a number of readings, it is not open to any and all readings; there may be a plurality of significances that can legitimately be specified for a literary work, but that plurality is not an infinity. It follows, then, that what pluralist practice requires is a theory that can accommodate the diversity of interpretation and yet at the same time identify the constraints that prevent interpretation from being arbitrary.

Iser's is obviously such a theory, and moreover it has the additional advantage of answering to the demand of recent criticism that the reader be given his due. Pluralism is not necessarily a reader-oriented doctrine. In its new critical manifestation it is rather a testimony to the richness of the literary text which is said to contain the multiple meanings that a competent reader will discern. Since these meanings are particularly complex and many-leveled, it is not surprising, the argument goes, that no one critical approach or perspective can do justice to them. The (limited) tolerance of diverse views that characterizes this brand of pluralism is a concession not to the reader's creative imagination, but to the difficulty of his task (a task that is by definition incapable of completion). In Iser's theory, however, the reader is given a more prominent role because what the text contains is not a meaning, however complex, but a set of directions for assembling a meaning, directions he will carry out in his own way. "Thus, the meaning of a literary text is not a definable entity but, if anything, a dynamic happening" (p. 22).

At times, however, Iser reserves the word "meaning" for the "intersubjective structure" that provokes the reader's activities, while referring to the product of those activities—the building up of the aesthetic object—as "significance." "The intersubjective structure of meaning assembly can have many forms of significance, according to the social and cultural code or the individual norms which underlie the formation of this significance" (p. 151). This is another point at which Iser touches base with a familiar critical formula, but redefines it in such a way as to remove some of the difficulties it has seemed to offer. The distinction (derived from Frege) between meaning and significance is associated in Anglo-American criticism with E. D. Hirsch, for whom it is a distinction between intended or authorial meaning and the meanings that might be educed by readers who are "pursuing their own interests unchecked by intentions."[2] It is thus not an innocent distinction, but one heavily weighted in the direction of authorial or historical meaning to which, Hirsch believes, we have an *ethical* obligation. (Would we want others to ignore or distort *our* intentions?) In Iser's formulation, however, we are relieved of the necessity to choose between an intended meaning and the meanings that issue from our subjectivities because the intended meaning is not a referential statement or an encoded attitude or a representation of a state of affairs, but a script for performance, and therefore it lives only in its manifestations and in every one of its manifestations. Every time a reader builds his own structure of significance, he is simultaneously being faithful to authorial meaning, and, indeed, he can be faithful only in that way. Rather than being opposed to authorial meaning, interpreter's meaning is necessary to its actualization. In the same way Iser avoids the hard choice, also implicit in Hirsch's distinction, between historical and ahistorical interpretation. The readers contemporary to an author are in no more a privileged position than the readers of later generations; for both sets of readers are provoked to an act of construction rather than an act of retrieval; and since the blueprint for construction is significantly incomplete—it displays gaps and blanks and indeterminacies—no instance of construction is more accurate, in the sense of being truer to an historically embodied meaning, than any other. Even the first reader of a work is called upon to complete the connections left unspecified in the text according to his "individual disposition." This does not mean, as Iser is quick to point out, that the history of successive constructions or assemblings or actualizations is of no interest; it is just that it is an empirical rather than a theoretical question—it is a study of the individual realizations of a literary work rather than what makes those realizations possible in the first place—and it is therefore a question that belongs properly to the "aesthetics of reception" (p. x), a branch of inquiry identified with the work of H. R. Jauss and others. Iser thus manages the considerable feat of operating at a level that escapes historical contingency while at the same time acknowledging the legitimacy of historically conditioned readings both as a phenomenon and as an object of study.

In addition, his theory boasts an historical component of its own. It is his contention that in the nineteenth and twentieth centuries literary texts became more and more indeterminate, and as a result "the reader's viewpoint became less clearly oriented, which meant correspondingly greater demands on his own structuring activity" (p. 205). Moreover, as the reader's activity becomes more strenuous he receives to a greater degree the chief benefit of literary experience, which is, according to Iser, the opportunity to "take a fresh look at the forces which guide and orient him, and which he may hitherto have accepted without question" (p. 74). These "forces" are the "thought systems" or "prevailing norms" that have provided the reader with "a framework for the social action"

(p. 71) and a basis for the conduct of human relations (p. 73). In the literary text these systems and norms are arranged in such a way as to provoke the reader to an examination of their limitations and distortions. Thus while "the literary work arises out of the reader's own social or philosophical background, it will serve to detach prevailing norms from their functional context, thus enabling the reader to observe how such social regulators function, and what effect they have on the people subject to them" (p. 74). In the case of works written long ago the reader will be doubly enabled: "he will be able not only to reconstruct . . . the historical situation that provided the framework for the text but also to experience for himself the specific deficiencies brought about by [its] historical norms" (p. 74).

Again, Iser is impressive in his ability to affirm both sides of a traditional opposition, in this case the opposition between literature and life. On the one hand, literature is not mimetic or representational ("it is no mere copy of life"), for rather than reproducing or mirroring or urging the thought system of an age (as one might do in a journalistic essay or political speech), it "almost invariably tends to take as its dominant 'meaning' those possibilities that have been neutralized or negated by that system" (p. 72); but, on the other hand, literature is valuable because of the perspective it affords on life; it is the means by which we achieve a distance on our "habitual dispositions," a distance that enables us to recognize and supply their deficiencies. This is even truer when the work is built up out of the systems of an earlier age; for in the act of grasping a reality that is not our own (p. 74) we are moved to rethink and revise the conceptual framework that underlies "the ordinary process of day-to-day living" (p. 74). In short, not only does literature "call into question" (p. 61) conventional notions of validity and coherence; in doing so it promotes change and growth in the individual:

> The significance of the work . . . does not lie in the meaning sealed within the text, but in the fact that the meaning brings out what had previously been sealed within us. When the subject is separated from himself, the resultant spontaneity is guided and shaped by the text in such a way that it is transformed into a new and real consciousness. Thus each text constitutes its own reader. . . . This structure pinpoints the reciprocity between the constituting of meaning and the heightening of self awareness which develops in the reading process. (pp. 157–59)

In other words, as the reader puts the work together, he is himself put together; as the text "begins to exist as a gestalt in the reader's consciousness" (p. 121), the gestalt that *is* the reader's consciousness is in the process of being altered by the structure it is building; in response to an indeterminate set of directions, the reader is moved to assemble the virtual object in his own way, but as that object takes shape it begins to have a reciprocal effect on the way that the reader considers his own; the reader may be following his individual disposition in the act of construction, but that disposition is itself changed in an interaction with what it has constructed: "Hence, the constitution of meaning not only implies the creation of a totality emerging from interacting textual perspectives . . . but also, through formulating this totality, it enables us to formulate ourselves, and thus discover an inner world of which we had hitherto not been conscious" (p. 158).

As the claims for literature expand to include the fostering of self-consciousness, so do the claims for Iser's theory which is now not only an aesthetic, an ontology, and a history, but a psychology and an epistemology as well. Indeed, the range of problems that Iser apparently solves is remarkable; but even more remarkable is the fact that he achieves his solutions without sacrificing any of the interests that might be urged by one or another of the traditional theoretical positions. His theory is mounted on behalf of the reader, but it honors the intentions of the authors; the aesthetic object is constructed in time, but the blueprint for its construction is spatially embodied; each realization of the blueprint is historical and unique; but it itself is given once and for all; literature is freed from the tyranny of referential meaning, but nevertheless contains a meaning in the directions that trigger the reader's activities; those activities are determined by a reader's "stock of experience" (p. 38), but in the course of their unfolding, that stock is transformed. The theory, in short, has something for everyone, and denies legitimacy to no one.

And yet, in the end it falls apart, and it falls apart because the distinction on which it finally depends—the distinction between the determinate and the indeterminate—will not hold. The distinction is crucial because it provides both the stability and flexibility of Iser's formulations. Without it he would not be able to say that the reader's activities are constrained by something they do not produce; he would not be able at once to honor and to bypass history by stabilizing the set of directions the text contains; he would not be able to define the aesthetic object in opposition to the world of fact, but tie its production securely to that world; he would have no basis (independent of interpretation) for the thesis that since the end of the eighteenth century literature has been characterized by more and more gaps; he would not be able to free the text from the constraints of referential meaning and yet say that the meanings produced by innumerable readers are part of its potential.

It is important to realize how "firm" the determinacy/indeterminacy distinction is for Iser. When he is at his most phenomenological (pp. 114, 118, 151–54, 202–3) it sometimes seems that the very features of the text emerge into being in a reciprocal relationship with the reader's activities; but in his more characteristic moments Iser insists on the brute-fact status of the text, at least insofar as it provides directions for the assembling of the "virtual object." Thus he declares in one place, "the stars in a literary text are fixed; the lines that join them are variable"; and in another, "the structure of the text sets off a sequence of mental images which lead to the text translating itself into the reader's consciousness"; and in still another, "the text itself . . . offers 'schematized aspects' through which the actual subject matter of the work can be produced." Each of these statements (and there are countless others) is a version of the basic distinction, reaffirmed unequivocally by Iser in the *Diacritics* interview (June 1980), "between a significance which is to be supplied, and a significance which *has* been supplied" (p. 72) or, in other words, between what is already given and what must be brought into being by interpretive activity.

Iser is able to maintain this position because he regards the text as a *part of the world* (even though the process it sets in motion is not), and because he regards the world, or external reality, as itself determinate, something that is given rather than supplied. It is the objective status of the world that accounts for the difference between literary and nonliterary mental activity. In ordinary experience "the given empirical object" acts as a constraint on any characterization of it; whereas in literary experiences objects are produced by the mental images we form, images that endow the "nongiven . . . with presence" (p. 137). Sentences uttered in everyday life are assessed in terms of their fidelity to empirical facts, but "for the literary text there can be no such 'facts'; instead we have a sequence of schemata which have the function of stimulating the reader himself into establishing the 'facts' " (p. 141). The point is that these "schemata" are themselves facts of a determinate kind and are therefore ontologically (rather than merely temporally) prior to the (literary) facts whose production they guide.

Iser's most developed example of this process concerns the presentation of Allworthy in Fielding's *Tom Jones:*

> Allworthy is introduced to us as a perfect man, but he is at once brought face to face with a hypocrite, Captain Blifil, and is completely taken in by the latter's feigned piety. Clearly, then, the signifiers are not meant solely to designate perfection. On the contrary, they denote instructions to the reader to build up the signified which presents not a quality of perfection, but in fact a vital defect, Allworthy's lack of judgment. (p. 65)

This is an instance, in Iser's vocabulary, of the "changing perspectives" (p. 114) that are juxtaposed in such a way as to stimulate the reader's search for consistency (p. 120). Thus two "character perspectives," that of Allworthy as *homo perfectus* and Blifil as apparent saint, "confront one another" (p. 121), and the reader is led to reject the simple designation of perfection and to formulate for himself a revised conception of Allworthy's character. It is a perfect illustration of what distinguishes a literary from a nonliterary text. In a nonliterary text the connections are all supplied (by the structure of empirical reality), and as a result the reader is left with nothing to do; but in the literary text "textual segments" are presented without explicit indications of the relationships between them, and as a result "gaps" open up which it is the responsibility of the reader to close and fill.

It is all very neat until one begins to examine the textual segments that constitute the category of the "given." Consider the characterization of Allworthy as a perfect or all-worthy man. In order for Iser's account to be persuasive, perfection in humankind must be understood (at least at first) to be incompatible with being taken in by a hypocrite; for only then will the "Allworthy perspective" and the "Blifil perspective" be perceived as discontinuous. But one can easily imagine a reader for whom perfection is inseparable from the vulnerability displayed by Allworthy, and for such a reader there would be no disparity between the original description of Allworthy and his subsequent behavior. That is, the text would display "good continuation" (a characteristic, according to Iser, of nonliterary texts) and would not, at least at this point, present a gap or blank for the reader to fill up. I am not urging this reading against Iser's, but merely pointing out that it is a possible one, and that its possibility irreparably blurs the supposedly hard lines of his theory: for if the "textual signs" do not announce their shape but appear in a variety of shapes according to the differing expectations and assumptions of different readers, and if gaps are not built into the text, but appear (or do not appear) as a consequence of particular interpretive strategies, then there is no distinction between what the text gives and what the reader supplies; he supplies *everything;* the stars in a literary text are not fixed; they are just as variable as the lines that join them.

Let me make clear what I am *not* saying. I am *not* saying that it is impossible to give an account of *Tom Jones* which depends on a distinction between what is in the text and what the reader is moved, by gaps in the text, to supply; it is just that the distinction itself is an assumption which, when it informs an act of literary description, will *produce* the phenomena it purports to describe. That is to say, every component in such an account—the determinacies or textual segments, the indeterminacies or gaps, and the adventures of the reader's "wandering viewpoint"—will be the products of an interpretive strategy that demands them, and therefore no one of those components can constitute the independent given which serves to ground the interpretive process.

The point can be made again with another of Iser's examples, a chapter in *Vanity Fair* entitled "Arcadian Simplicity." The "textual segment" is, according to Iser, a "signal from the author," a "pointer" that "ensures that the reader will never lose sight of the narrator's views on the social ambitions" (p. 114) of Becky Sharpe. As a signal or pointer, the title is, says Iser, "explicitly ironic" (p. 117) and therefore establishes the perspective of the narrator which can then interact with the perspective of the character. This interaction then "spurs the reader on to build up the syntheses which eventually individualize the aesthetic object" (p. 118). But the irony of "Arcadian Simplicity" is not explicit in the sense that it announces itself before interpretation begins; it will be ironic only in the light of an interpretation—a specification of the author's purpose—already assumed. In the light of another interpretation, of another specification of Thackeray's purpose, it will not be explicitly ironic at all; it will be explicitly something else, and the reader's "building up" will follow a course other than the course described by Iser. Indeed, the reader's building up begins with the characterization of "Arcadian Simplicity" as ironic or as nonironic or as anything at all. Again the textual segment that initiates the process of construction in

Iser's sequence is itself a construction, and is not, at least in the way that Iser would claim, "given."

To this Iser might reply (and does reply in the *Diacritics* interview) that whatever one makes of "Arcadian Simplicity" the words are, after all, there and do constitute a determinate textual feature. ("In the Thackeray example, we have the given textual segments of chapter heading and chapter.") But this assumes that the words (these or any others) are "pointable to" apart from some or other interpretive perspective. That is, it assumes there is a level of observation, a place for a reader to stand, where "Arcadian Simplicity" can be seen *before* it receives an interpretation. But even to see it as a chapter heading is already to have assigned it an interpretation according to a system of intelligibility in which chapter headings are things that it is possible to see; and, moreover, the assigning of that interpretation is not something one does *after* seeing; it is the shape of seeing, and if seeing does not have this (interpretive) shape, it will have some other. Perception is never innocent of assumptions, and the assumptions within which it occurs will be responsible for the contours of what is perceived. The conclusion is the one I have reached before: there can be no category of the "given" if by given one means what is there before interpretation begins. (And if Iser doesn't mean that, it is hard to see what he does mean.)

It is a conclusion that must be extended to the larger theory that stands behind Iser's pronouncements on merely literary matters, the theory by which the world itself is "given" in a way that the world of literary (read fictional) works are not. It is only if the world—or "reality"—is itself a determinate object, an object without gaps that can be grasped immediately, an object that can be perceived rather than read, that *in*determinacy can be specified as a special feature of literary experience. Once, however, that move is made, it brings with it a set of interrelated assumptions: the assumption that looking at real objects is different from *ima*gining objects in a poem or novel; the assumption that in the one activity the viewer simply and passively takes in an already formed reality, while in the other he must participate in the construction of a reality; the assumption that knowledge of real people is more direct and immediate than knowledge of characters or lyric speakers; and, finally, the assumption that these two kinds of experience come to us in two kinds of language, one that requires only that we check its structure against the already constituted structure it reproduces or describes, and the other that requires us to produce the objects, events, and persons to which it (in a curious, even mysterious, literary way) refers.

Underlying these assumptions, of course, is the familiar distinction between the determinate or given and the indeterminate or supplied; and they fall by the same reasoning which makes that distinction finally untenable: what must be supplied in literary experience must *also* be supplied in the "real life" experience to which it is, point for point, opposed. Consider, for example, Iser's characterization of the difference between "dyadic interaction" (that is, conversation between two people) as it is presented in the novels of Ivy Compton-Burnett and as it occurs in everyday life. In Compton-Burnett, Iser asserts, "the pragmatically oriented speech act of everyday dialogue is . . . replaced by the imponderability out of which speech arises" (p. 193). By this Iser intends a contrast between fictional dialogue and a *"face-to-face situation"* in which "the partners in dyadic interaction can ask each other questions in order to ascertain how far their views have controlled contingency, or their images have bridged the gap of inexperienceability of one another's experience" (p. 166). That is, in face-to-face dialogue communication is facilitated by the presence of a real object (the other person) which acts as an empirical check on the turns and twists of the conversation. Conversation is thus a particular instance of the general constraint on ordinary (as opposed to fictional) language: "it presupposes reference to a given object [which] in turn demands a continuous individualization of the developing speech act so that utterance may gain its intended precision" (p. 184). The absence of this constraint in Compton-Burnett's novels is indicated by the fact that, despite the characters' willingness to ask each other questions "in order to ensure that they have grasped what has been said," "the various speech acts do not serve to promote understanding as regards facts and intentions, but instead they uncover more and more implications arising from every utterance" (p. 193). As the dialogue unfolds, the partners grow further and further apart as each response to the question "what do you mean?" is received as evidence of a meaning to which the other will not admit, and in the end "the characters' images of each other become more and more monstrous" (p. 193). The dialogue is thus "endless" (i.e., not ended by a clear and unambiguous achievement of understanding), and it is endless because, "in Hilary Corke's words, the dialogue is 'not a transcript

of what he or she would have said in "real life" but rather of what
would have been said plus what would have been implied but not spoken
plus what would have been understood though not implied.' "

One's response to this can only be, as opposed to what? That is,
however accurate this is as an account of conversation in Compton-
Burnett, it is a perfectly accurate account of conversation in everyday
life. Iser and Corke seem to believe that in everyday life we are in the
position of being able to attend to what has been said independently of
what is implied or of what is understood because it goes without saying.
That is, they think that the pragmatic conditions of face-to-face discourse serve to fix the meanings of words, whereas in fictional discourse
meanings are the products of a structure of assumptions and hypotheses,
a structure which we, as readers, build. But, in fact, it is just such a
structure that is responsible for the shape that meanings have in everyday life and even for the shape of the "pragmatic conditions" in the context of which those meanings are received. Consider as an illustration a
cartoon that appeared some time ago in the *New Yorker*. It shows a
man seated in a chair, staring morosely at a television set. Above him
stands a woman, presumably his wife, and she is obviously speaking to
him with some force and conviction. The caption reads, "You look
sorry, you act sorry, you say you're sorry, but you're not sorry." So much
for the ensured precision of face-to-face dyadic interaction! What the
woman is able to hear depends on her assumption of the kind of man
her husband is; she constructs an image of him (has been constructing
it for a long time), and that image controls her sense of his intentions
and produces what is for her the obvious literal meaning of his utterance, and also of his facial expression and physical gesture. (What that
literal meaning is, we aren't told, but it might be something like, "O.K.,
I'm sorry. Now leave me alone.'") Moreover, it is that image that defines for her the "pragmatic conditions" of the interaction, the "real
life" situation as she sees it, no doubt in opposition to the situation as it
is seen by him. At one point Iser says "we must distinguish between perception and ideation as two different means of access to the world"
(p. 137). But, as this example shows, that is precisely the distinction
we cannot make because perception itself *is* an act of ideation; if by
ideation we mean the inferring of a world from a set of assumptions
(antecedently held) about what it must be like. To put it another way,
mediated access to the world is the only access we ever have; in face to
face situations or in the act of reading a novel, the properties of objects,

persons, and situations emerge as a consequence of acts of construction that follow (and because they follow they are not, in any simple sense, free) from a prestructured understanding of the shapes any meaningful item could possibly have. What this means is that we know "real people" no more directly than we know the characters in a novel; that "real life" objects are no less "ideated" than fictional objects; that ordinary language is no more in touch with an unmediated reality than the language of literature.

The obvious objection to this line of reasoning is that it flies in the face of differences we all feel. As Iser puts it in the *Diacritics* interview:

> My interpretation of the world may well be as much a product of linguistic acts as my interpretation of a literary text, but I maintain that there are substantial differences between the things being interpreted. First, the real world is perceivable through the senses, whereas the literary text is perceivable only through the imagination—unless one believes that reading the words sunset, music, silk, wine, and scent is the same as seeing, hearing, touching, tasting, and smelling the real things. Secondly, all known experience suggests that the real world (uninterpreted) lives and functions independently of the individual observer, whereas the literary text does not. Thirdly, our contact with the real world has immediate physical or social consequences, whereas our contact with the literary text need not, and indeed rarely does have any such consequences. (p. 72)

One should note first of all that in making his argument Iser is continually shifting his terms in order to make his different points. In the first sentence the literary text is itself an object, a part of the world, as indeed it must be if the directions or "schemata" or "textual segments" are to occupy the position of "given" in relation to what must be supplied. But in the second sentence the literary text is suddenly not perceivable through the senses and is thus as far as one can tell no longer an object at all. I suppose that what Iser means is that the things, persons, and events to which a literary text refers are not perceivable through the senses, but that the literary text itself is. The text and the world, then, are both "things," but they are different things and therefore they are interpreted differently. But this is to assume precisely what is in dispute, the objectivity of either the text or the world. The issue is not whether there are differences between them (or more properly between the material world and the world in the text) but whether those differences are equivalent to the distinction between what is given and what is supplied; and it is my contention that they are not, and that rather than being different objects of interpretation the world and the world of the text are different interpreted—that is, made—objects. To put it another way, one can agree with Iser that reading about sunsets, wine, and silk is not the same as seeing, tasting, and touching them without agreeing that seeing, touching, and tasting are natural rather than conventional activities. What can be seen will be a function of the categories of vision that already inform perception, and those categories will be social and conventional and not imposed upon us by an independent world. One can see a hand raised in a classroom *as* a hand raised in a classroom only because one is already implicated in, and acting as an extending agent of, a conventional system of purposes, goals, and understood practices; if one didn't see it as a hand raised in a classroom, one would see it as something else, and that something else would similarly be pick-outable only within some set of conventional categories or other; and even if one had recourse to a supposedly neutral vocabulary and described the action in terms of angles, movements, tendons, and joints, that description would itself be possible only under a *theory* of movement, ligatures, etc., and therefore would be descriptive only of what the theory (that is, the interpretation) prestipulates as available for description. Again, the point is not that seeing (or tasting or touching) something is the same as reading about it, but that the two activities are alike conventional and mediated, and, therefore, whatever differences they might be said to have, they would not be differences between an activity that was in touch with (and therefore constrained by) the "real world" and one that was not.

Does this mean, then, that everything, even the objects, events, and persons of everyday life, is indeterminate? The question is an inevitable one in the context of the task Iser's theory sets for itself, the *control* of arbitrary (a word he uses often) subjectivities by fixed or determinate points of reference. He sees this as a problem peculiar to the reading of literature, since in the "reading" of the world our "individual dispositions" are constrained by its objects. But if the world and the objects in it are no less the product of human invention than the world of literary experience, the brakes are off everywhere and communication—ordinary and literary—would seem to be deprived of its ground. However, the conclusion I would draw from my argument is exactly the reverse. The brakes are *on* everywhere because in order for them to be off readers would have to be in a position to specify significance in a random or irresponsible way; but it is just the point of my examples—literary and nonliterary—that there could be no such position because perception (and reading is an instance of perception) always occurs within a set of assumptions that preconstrains what could possibly be perceived (or heard, or tasted, or touched). It is only if it were possible to perceive independently of assumptions, of interpretive categories, that irresponsible or arbitrary perception would be a danger. If perception is always conventional—prestructured by categories (like the classroom or some notion of genre) that are public and communal rather than individual and unique—then perception can never be arbitrary, and the project, Iser's project, of explaining how arbitrariness or subjectivity is to be controlled loses its urgency.

For the same reason, the question "is everything then indeterminate?" loses its force because it would make just as much sense to say that everything is determinate. Indeterminacy in Iser's theory refers to "the subjectivist element of reading" (p. 24), that which is supplied by the "individual observer" out of his private experience. What I have been saying is that there is no subjectivist element of reading because the observer is never individual in the sense of unique or private, but is always the product of the categories of understanding that are his by virtue of his membership in a community of interpretation. It follows, then, that what that experience in turn produces is not open or free, but determinate, constrained by the possibilities that are built into a conventional system of intelligibility. Earlier I concluded that the distinction between what is given and what is supplied won't hold up because everything is supplied, both the determinate and the indeterminate poles of the "aesthetic object"; now I am arguing that the same distinction won't hold because everything is given. There is no paradox here. It is just that "supplied" and "given" will only make sense as fundamental categories of classification if the entities to which they refer are pure, if, at some level, we can speak meaningfully of a text that is simply there, waiting for a reader who is, at least potentially, wholly free. But it is precisely that purity I have been calling into question by pointing out on the one hand that perception is always mediated (and therefore objects are never available directly), and on the other that perception is always conventional (and therefore readers are never free). In the absence of that purity one can say either that everything is determinate, because nothing proceeds from an unfettered imagination, or that everything is indeterminate, because everything is produced by the activities of the reader (but by a reader who is, like what he produces, community property). The only thing that you can't say is that there is a distinction, at least insofar as it is an *absolute* distinction, between a world that "lives and functions independently" of interpretive activity and a world that is produced by interpretive activity.

This is not to say that such a distinction cannot be operative as a *consequence* of an overarching interpretive assumption. That is, if determinate and indeterminate (or given and supplied) are conventional categories *within* a system of intelligibility, then those who are implicated in the system will "see," in the sense of producing, determinacies and indeterminacies, but everything they see will be at once constructed (as opposed to being simply "found") and constrained (as opposed to being simply invented).

One sees this clearly in Iser's readings of Fielding and others, where the specification of "textual segments" and "blanks" is an interpretive gesture—grounded in an already assumed view of literary history and literary value—in relation to which the activities of individual readers are severely constrained. That is, Iser never gives any examples of readers going their own way (even in the modified sense allowed by his theory) because the reader he can imagine is always the creature of the machine he has already set in motion; in every analysis the reader is described as being "guided," "controlled," "induced," and even "jerked" (p. 130), and what he is guided or jerked by are textual elements that are themselves the product of interpretation. Again, there are two ways of seeing this, either as demonstrating that both text and reader are determinate, in that their respective shapes are in no sense free, or that both text and reader are indeterminate, in that the shape each has is the product of interpretive activity. In short, Iser's own analyses are continually pointing to the unavailability of the two acontextual entities—the free-standing text and the free-standing reader—whose relationship he promises to describe.

A reader sympathetic to Iser might argue that he himself knows that his basic categories are conventional rather than natural. He does, after all, say at one point that "pure perception is quite impossible" (p. 166). But when he says that, what he means is that perception is a compound of the object (purely perceived) *plus* the subjective perspective of the reader; otherwise, he could not claim that "textual seg-ments" are given and determinate. In other words, Iser doesn't take his own pronouncement seriously (if he did, he'd have to give up his theory), but nevertheless he receives the credit for having made it. In-deed, this is a pattern in his work which has the effect of putting him on both sides of almost every issue. He criticizes theories "which give the impression that texts automatically imprint themselves on the read-er's mind" (p. 107), but his theory cannot get off the ground unless it claims exactly that for the set of directions that guide the reader's "meaning assembly." He argues that we are never able to experience one another directly (p. 165), but then he privileges face-to-face en-counters as a form of communication that bridges "the gap of inexpe-rienceability" (p. 164). He claims to have rid himself of the subject/object dichotomy (p. 25), but he spends the entire book talking about their interaction, and acting as if the term "intersubjectivity" could hide the fact that the distinction between them remains as firm as ever. The theory is finally nothing more than a loosely constructed network of pasted-together contradictions; push it hard at any point, and it im-mediately falls apart. Ask it a hard question—if one can argue about where the gaps are (or about whether or not there are any), how can they be distinguished from the givens? what authorizes the assumption that everyday life is characterized by continuity and determinacy? if gaps have increased in the nineteenth and twentieth centuries, and if literature is defined by the presence (strange word) of gaps, does this mean that literature is becoming more literary or that pre-nineteenth-century literature wasn't literature?—and it can only respond by re-hearsing its basic distinctions.

But the asking of hard questions is not something the theory encourages, and indeed its weaknesses from one point of view are its strengths from another. By defining his key terms in a number of ways, Iser provides himself in advance with a storehouse of defensive strate-gies. A theory that characterizes reality in one place as a set of de-terminate objects, and in another place as the product of "thought systems," and in a third place as a heterogeneous flux will not be em-barrassed by any question you might put to it. It is a marvelous machine whose very loose-jointedness makes it invulnerable to a frontal assault (including, no doubt, the assault I am now mounting). It is in fact not a theory at all, but a piece of literature that satisfies Iser's own criteria for an "aesthetic object": it is full of gaps, and the reader is invited to fill them in his own way. For that reason, no reader will ever feel threatened by the theory; no one will ever be afraid of Wolfgang Iser. Who could be anything but comfortable with someone who declares, in the first part of a sentence, that "I have endeavored to suspend my own tastes and my own beliefs," and concludes the same sentence by asserting "that all our beliefs have theoretical presuppositions"? (*Diacritics* interview, pp. 73–74). The late Joan Webber once characterized Thomas Browne's ability to embrace contradictions cheerfully (like Tertullian he professed to believe things *because* they were impossible) by saying that he "pulls the sting from pain." Wolfgang Iser is the Thomas Browne of literary theory.

4. Working on the Chain Gang:
Interpretation in Law and Literature

In his essay *Law as Interpretation*[1] Ronald Dworkin is concerned to characterize legal practice in such a way as to avoid claiming either that in deciding a case judges find the plain meaning of the law "just 'there'" or, alternatively, that they make up the meaning "wholesale" in accordance with personal preference or whim. It is Dworkin's thesis that neither of these accounts is adequate because interpretation is something different from both.[2] Dworkin is right, I think, to link his argument about legal practice to an argument about the practice of literary criticism, not only because in both disciplines the central question is, "What is the source of interpretative authority?," but also because in both disciplines answers to that question typically take the form of the two positions Dworkin rejects. Just as there are those in the legal community who have insisted on construing statutes and decisions "strictly" (that is, by attending only to the words themselves), so there are those in the literary community who have insisted that interpretation is, or should be, constrained by what is "in the text"; and just as the opposing doctrine of legal realism holds that judges' "readings" are always rationalizations of their political or personal desires, so do proponents of critical subjectivity hold that what a reader sees is merely a reflection of his predispositions and biases. The field is divided, in short, between those who believe that interpretation is grounded in objectivity and those who believe that interpreters are, for all intents and purposes, free. Dworkin moves to outflank both of these positions by characterizing legal and critical practice as "chain enterprises," enterprises in which interpretation is an extension of an institutional history made up of "innumerable decisions, structures, conventions and practices."[3] Interpretation so conceived is not purely objective since its results will not "wring assent from a stone" (there is still "room for disagreement"), but neither is it wholly subjective, since the interpreter does not proceed independently of what others in the institution have done or said.

In general, I find this account of interpretation and its constraints attractive, in part because I find it similar in important ways to the account I have offered under the rubric of "interpretive communities" in *Is There a Text in This Class?*[4] There are, however, crucial differences between the two accounts, and in the course of explicating those differences I will argue that Dworkin repeatedly falls away from his own best insights into a version of the fallacies (of pure objectivity and pure subjectivity) he so forcefully challenges.

We can begin by focusing on the most extended example in his essay of a "chain enterprise," the imagined literary example of a novel written not by a single author but by a group of coauthors, each of whom is responsible for a separate chapter. The members of the group draw lots and the

> lowest number writes the opening chapter of a novel, which he or she then sends to the next number who adds a chapter, with the understanding that he is adding a chapter to that novel rather than beginning a new one, and then sends the two chapters to the next number, and so on. Now every novelist but the first has the dual responsibilities of interpreting and creating, because each must read all that has gone before in order to establish, in the interpretivist sense, what the novel so far created is. He or she must decide what the characters are "really" like; what motives in fact guide them; what the point or theme of the developing novel is; how far some literary device or figure, consciously or unconsciously used, contributes to these, and whether it should be extended or refined or trimmed or dropped in order to send the novel further in one direction rather than another.[5]

In its deliberate exaggeration this formulation of a chain enterprise is helpful and illuminating, but it is also mistaken in several important respects. First of all, it assumes that the first person in the chain is in a position different in kind from those who follow him because he is only creating while his fellow authors must both create and interpret. In an earlier draft of the essay Dworkin had suggested that as the chain extends itself the freedom enjoyed by the initiator of the sequence is more and more constrained, until at some point the history against which "late novelists" must work may become so dense "as to admit only one good-faith interpretation"; and indeed that interpretation will not be an interpretation in the usual sense because it will have been *demanded* by what has already been written. Dworkin has now withdrawn this suggestion (which he had qualified with words like "probably"), but the claim underlying it—the claim that constraints thicken as the chain lengthens—remains as long as the distinction between the first author and all the others is maintained. The idea is that the first author is free because he is not obliged "to read all that has gone before" and therefore doesn't have to decide what the characters are "really" like and what motives guide them, and so on. But, in fact, the first author has surrendered his freedom (although, as we shall see, surrender is exactly the wrong word) as soon as he commits himself to writing a novel, for he makes his decision under the same constraints that rule the decisions of his collaborators. He must decide, for example, how to begin the novel, but the decision is not "free" because the very notion "beginning a novel" exists only in the context of a set of practices that at once enable and limit the act of beginning. One cannot think of beginning a novel without thinking within, as opposed to thinking "of," these established practices, and even if one "decides" to "ignore" them or "violate" them or "set them aside," the actions of ignoring and violating and setting aside will themselves have a shape that is constrained by the preexisting shape of those practices. This does not mean that the decisions of the first author are wholly determined, but that the choices available to him are "novel-writing choices," choices that depend on a prior understanding of what it means to write a novel, even when he "chooses" to alter that understanding.[6] In short, he is neither free nor constrained (if those words are understood as referring to absolute states), but free *and* constrained. He is free to begin whatever kind of novel he decides to write, but he is constrained by the finite (although not unchanging) possibilities that are subsumed in the notions "kind of novel" and "beginning a novel."

Moreover, those who follow him are free and constrained in exactly the same way. When a later novelist decides to "send the novel further in one direction rather than in another," that decision must follow upon a decision as to what direction has already been taken; and *that* decision will be an interpretive one in the sense that it will not be determined by the independent and perspicuous shape of the words, but will be the means by which the words are given a shape. Later novelists do not read directly from the words to a decision about the point or theme of the novel, but from a prior understanding (which may take a number of forms) of the points or themes novels can possibly have to a novelistic construction of the words. Just as the first novelist "creates" within the constraints of "novel practice" in general, so do his successors on the chain interpret him (and each other) within those same constraints. Not only are those constraints controlling, but they are uniformly so; they do not relax or tighten in relation to the position an author happens to occupy on the chain. The last author is as free, within those constraints, to determine what "the characters are really like" as is the first. It is tempting to think that the more information one has (the more history) the more directed will be one's interpretation; but information only comes in an interpreted form (it does not announce itself). No matter how much or how little you have, it cannot be a check against interpretation because even when you first "see" it, interpretation has already done its work. So that rather than altering the conditions of interpretation, the accumulation of chapters merely extends the scope of its operation.

If this seems counterintuitive, imagine the very real possibility of two (or more) "later" novelists who have different views of the direction the novel has taken and are therefore in disagreement as to what would constitute a continuation of "that" novel as opposed to "beginning a new one." To make the example more specific, let us further imagine that one says to another, "Don't you see that it's ironic, a social satire?," and the second replies, "Not at all, at most it's a comedy of manners," while a third chimes in, "You're both wrong; it's obviously a perfectly straightforward piece of realism." If Dworkin's argument is to hold, that is, if the decisions he talks about are to be constrained in a strong sense by an already-in-place text, it must be possible to settle this disagreement by appealing to that text. But it is precisely because the text appears differently in the light of different assumptions as to what is its mode that there is a disagreement in the first place. Or, to put it another way, "social satire," "comedy of manners," and "piece of realism" are not labels applied mechanically to perspicuous instances; rather, they are names for ways of reading, ways which when put into operation make available for picking out the "facts" which those who are proceeding within them can then cite. It is entirely possible that the parties to our imagined dispute might find themselves pointing to the same "stretch of language" (no longer the same, since each would be characterizing it differently) and claiming it as a "fact" in support of opposing interpretations. (The history of literary criticism abounds in such scenarios.) Each would then believe, and be able to provide reasons for his belief, that only he is continuing the novel in the direction it has taken so far and that the others are striking out in a new and unauthorized direction.

Again, this does not mean that a later novelist is free to decide anything he likes (or that there is no possibility of adjudicating a disagreement), but that within the general parameters of novel-reading practice, he is as free as anyone else, which means that he is as constrained as anyone else. He is constrained in that he can only continue in ways that are recognizable novel ways (and the same must be said of the first novelist's act of "beginning"), and he is free in that no amount of textual accumulation can make his choice of one of those ways inescapable. Although the parameters of novel practice mark the limits of what anyone who is thinking within them can think to do, within those limits they do not *direct* anyone to do this rather than that. (They are not a "higher" text.) Every decision a later novelist makes will rest on his assessment of the situation as it has developed; but that assessment will itself be an act of interpretation which will in turn rest on an interpreted understanding of the enterprise in general.

This, then, is my first criticism of Dworkin's example: the distinction it is supposed to illustrate—the distinction between the first and later novelists—will not hold up because everyone in the enterprise is equally constrained. (By "equally" I mean equally with respect to the condition of freedom; I am making no claims about the number or identity of the constraints.) My second criticism is that in his effort to elaborate the distinction Dworkin embraces both of the positions he criticizes. He posits for the first novelist a freedom that is equivalent to the freedom assumed by those who believe that judges (and other interpreters) are bound only by their personal preferences and desires; and he thinks of later novelists as bound by a previous history in a way that would be possible only if the shape and significance of that history were self-evident. Rather than avoiding the Scylla of legal realism ("making it up wholesale") and the Charybdis of strict constructionism ("finding the law just 'there' "), he commits himself to both. His reason for doing so becomes clear when he extends the example to an analysis of the law:

Deciding hard cases at law is rather like this strange literary exercise. The similarity is most evident when judges consider and decide "common-law" cases; that is, when no statute figures centrally in the legal issue, and the argument turns on which rules or principles of law "underlie" the related decisions of other judges in the past. Each judge is then like a novelist in the chain. He or she must read through what other judges in the past have written not simply to discover what these judges have said, or their state of mind when they said it, but to reach an opinion about what these other judges have collectively *done,* in the way that each of our novelists formed an opinion about the collective novel so far written. Any judge forced to decide any law suit will find, if he looks in the appropriate books, records of many arguably similar cases decided over decades or even centuries past by many other judges of different styles and judicial and political philosophies, in periods of different orthodoxies of procedure and judicial convention. Each judge must regard himself, in deciding the case before him, as a partner in a complex chain enterprise of which these innumerable decisions, structures, conventions and practices are the history; it is his job to continue that history into the future through what he does. He *must* interpret what has gone before because he has a responsibility to advance the enterprise in hand rather than strike out in some new direction of his own.[7]

The emphasis on the word *"must"* alerts us to what is at stake for Dworkin in the notion of a chain enterprise. It is a way of explaining how judges are kept from striking out in a new direction, much as later novelists are kept by the terms of their original agreement from beginning a new novel. Just as it is the duty of a later novelist to continue the work of his predecessors, so it is the duty of a judge to "advance the enterprise in hand." Presumably, the judge who is tempted to strike out in "some new direction of his own" will be checked by his awareness of his responsibility to the corporate enterprise; he will then comport himself as a partner in the chain rather than as a free and independent agent.

The force of the account, in other words, depends on the possibility of judges comporting themselves in ways other than the "chain-enterprise" way. But is there in fact any such possibility? What would it mean for a judge to strike out in a new direction? Dworkin doesn't tell us, but presumably it would mean deciding a case in such a way as to have no relationship to the history of previous decisions. It is hard to imagine what such a decision would be like since any decision, to be recognized as a decision by a judge, would have to be made in recognizably judicial terms. A judge who decided a case on the basis of whether or not the defendant had red hair would not be striking out in a new direction; he would simply not be acting as a judge, because he could give no reasons for his decision that would be seen *as* reasons by competent members of the legal community. (Even in so extreme a case it would not be accurate to describe the judge as striking out in a new direction; rather he would be continuing the direction of an enterprise—perhaps a bizarre one—*other* than the judicial.) And conversely, if in deciding a case a judge *is* able to give such reasons, then the direction he strikes out in will not be new because it will have been implicit in the enterprise as a direction one could conceive of and argue for. This does not mean that his decision will be above criticism, but that it will be criticized, if it is criticized, for having gone in one judicial direction rather than another, neither direction being "new" in a sense that would give substance to Dworkin's fears.

Those fears are equally groundless with respect to the other alternative Dworkin imagines, the judge who looks at the chain of previous decisions and decides to see in it "whatever he thinks should have been there."[8] Here the danger is not so much arbitrary action (striking out in a new direction) as it is the willful imposition of a personal perspective on materials that have their own proper shape. "A judge's duty," Dworkin asserts, "is to interpret the legal history he finds and not to invent a better history."[9] Interpretation that is constrained by the history one finds will be responsible, whereas interpretation informed by the private preferences of the judge will be wayward and subjective. The opposition is one to which Dworkin repeatedly returns in a variety of forms, but in whatever form it is always vulnerable to the same objection: neither the self-declaring or "found" entity nor the dangerously free or "inventing" agent is a possible feature of the enterprise.

First of all, one doesn't just find a history; rather one views a body of materials with the assumption that it is organized by judicial concerns. It is that assumption which gives a shape to the materials, a shape that can *then* be described as having been "found." Moreover, not everyone will find the same shape because not everyone will be proceeding within the same notion of what constitutes a proper judicial concern, either in general or in particular cases. One sees this clearly in Dworkin's own account of what is involved in legal decisionmaking. A judge, he explains, will look in the "appropriate books" for cases "arguably similar" to the one before him. Notice that the similarity is "arguable," which means that it must be argued *for;* similarity is not something one finds, but something one must establish, and when one establishes it one establishes the configurations of the cited cases as well as of the case that is to be decided. Similarity, in short, is not a property of texts (similarities do not announce themselves), but a property conferred by a relational argument in which the statement *A* is like *B* is a characterization (one open to challenge) of *both A* and *B*. To see a present-day case as similar to a chain of earlier ones is to reconceive that chain by finding it in an applicability that has not always been apparent. Paradoxically, one can be faithful to legal history only by revising it, by redescribing it in such a way as to accommodate and render manageable the issues raised by the present.[10] This is a function of the law's conservatism, which will not allow a case to remain unrelated to the past, and so assures that the past, in the form of the history of decisions, will be continually rewritten. In fact, it is the *duty* of a judge to rewrite it (which is to say no more than that it is the duty of a judge to decide), and therefore there can be no simply "found" history in relation to which some other history could be said to be "invented." All histories are invented in the weak sense that they are not simply "discovered," but assembled under the pressure of some present urgency; no history is invented in the strong sense that the urgency that led to its assembly was unrelated to any generally acknowledged legal concern.

To put it another way, there could be no such strongly invented history because there could be no such strong inventor, no judge whose characterization of legal history displayed none of the terms, distinctions, and arguments that would identify it (for competent members) as a *legal* history. Of course, someone who stood apart from the enterprise, someone who was not performing as a judge, might offer such a history (a history, for example, in which the observed patterns were ethnic or geographical), but to accuse such a historian of striking out in a new direction or inventing a better history would be beside the point since whatever he did or didn't do would have no legal (as opposed to sociological or political) significance. And, conversely, someone who was in fact standing within the enterprise, thinking in enterprise ways, could only put forward a history that was enterprise-specific, and that history could not be an invented one. It is true, of course, that jurists can and do accuse each other of inventing a history, but that is a charge you level at someone who has "found" a history different from yours. It should not be confused with the possibility (or the danger) of "really" inventing one. The distinction between a "found" history and an "invented" one is finally nothing more than a distinction between a persuasive interpretation and one that has failed to convince. One man's "found" history will be another man's invented history, but neither will ever be, because it could not be, either purely found or purely invented.

As one reads Dworkin's essay, the basic pattern of his mistakes becomes more and more obvious. He repeatedly makes two related and mutually reinforcing assumptions: he assumes that history in the form of a chain of decisions has, at some level, the status of a brute fact; and he assumes that wayward or arbitrary behavior in relation to that fact is an institutional possibility. Together these two assumptions give him his project, the project of explaining how a free and potentially irresponsible agent is held in check by the self-executing constraints of an independent text. Of course, by conceiving his project in this way—that is, by reifying the mind in its freedom and the text in its independence—he commits himself to the very alternatives he sets out to avoid, the alternatives of legal realism on the one hand and positivism on the other. As a result, these alternatives rule his argument, at once determining its form and emerging, again and again, as its content.

An example, early in the essay, involves the possibility of reading an Agatha Christie mystery as a philosophical novel. Such a reading, Dworkin asserts, would be an instance of "changing" the text rather than "explaining" it because the text *as it is* will not yield to it without obvious strain or distortion. "All but one or two sentences would be irrelevant to the supposed theme, and the organization, style and figures would be appropriate not to a philosophical novel but to an entirely different genre."[11] The assumption is that sentences, figures, and styles announce their own generic affiliation, and that a reader who would claim them for an inappropriate genre would be imposing his will on nature. It is exactly the same argument by which judges are supposedly constrained by the obvious properties of the history they are to continue, and it falls by the same analysis. First of all, generic identification, like continuity between cases, is not something one finds, but something one establishes, and one establishes it for a reason. Readers don't just "decide" to recharacterize a text; there has to be some reason why it would occur to someone to treat a work identified as a member of one genre as a possible member of another. There must already be in place ways of thinking that will enable the recharacterization to become a project, and there must be conditions in the institution such that the prosecution of that project seems attractive and potentially rewarding. With respect to the project Dworkin deems impossible, those ways and conditions already exist. It has long been recognized that authors of the first rank—Poe, Dickens, Dostoyevski—have written novels of detection, and the fact that these novels have been treated seriously means that the work of less obviously canonical authors—Wilkie Collins, Conan Doyle, among others—are possible candidates for the same kind of attention. Once this happens, and it has already happened, any novel of detection can, at least provisionally, be considered as a "serious" work without a critic or his audience thinking that he is doing something bizarre or irresponsible; and in recent years just such consideration has been given to the work of Hammet, Chandler (whom Dworkin mentions), Highsmith, Sayers, Simenon, Freeling, John D. MacDonald, and Ross Macdonald. In addition, the emergence of semiotic and structural analysis has meant that it is no longer necessarily a criticism to say of something that it is "formulaic"; a term of description, which under a previous understanding of literary value would have been invoked in a gesture of dismissal, can now be invoked as a preliminary to a study of "signifying systems." The result has been the proliferation of serious (not to say somber) formalist readings of works like Fleming's *Goldfinger*.[12] Whatever one might think of this phenomenon, it is now a recognized and respectable part of the academic literary scene. At the same time the advocates of "popular culture" have been pressing their claim with a new insistence and a new rigor (prompted in part by the developments I have already mentioned), and a measure of their success is the number of courses in detective fiction now offered in colleges and universities at all levels.

Given these circumstances (and others that could be enumerated), it would be strange if a sociological or anthropological or philosophical interpretation of Agatha Christie had *not* been put forward (in fact, here we have an embarrassment of riches),[13] and as a longtime reader of her novels it has occurred to me to put one forward myself. I have noticed that Christie's villains are often presented as persons so quintessentially evil that they have no moral sense whatsoever and can only simulate moral behavior by miming, without understanding, the actions and attitudes of others. It is typical of these villains also to be chameleons, capable almost at will of changing their appearance, and one can see why: since they have no human attachments or concerns, they can clothe themselves in whatever attachment or concern suits their nefarious and often unmotivated ends. (The parallel with Shakespeare's Iago and Milton's Satan is obvious.) It would seem, then, that Christie has a theory of evil in relation to personal identity that accounts for (in the sense of generating a description of) many of the characteristics of her novels: their plots, the emphasis on disguise, the tolerance for human weakness even as it is being exposed, etc. Now, were I to extend this general hypothesis about Christie into a reading of one or more of her works, I would not be proceeding as Dworkin's pronouncement suggests I would. I would not, that is, be changing the novel by riding roughshod over sentences bearing obvious and inescapable meanings; rather, I would be reading those sentences within the assumption that they were related to what I assumed to be Christie's intention (if not this one, then some other), and as a result they would appear to me in an already related form. Sentences describing the weaknesses of characters other than the villain would be seen as pointing to the paradoxical strength of human fraility; sentences detailing the topography and geography of crucial scenes would be read as symbolic renderings of deeper issues, and so on. This interpretive action, or any other that could be imagined, would not be performed in violation of the facts of the text, but would be an effort to establish those facts. If in the course of that effort I were to dislodge another set of facts, they would be facts that had emerged within the assumption of another intention, and they would therefore be no less interpretive than the facts I was putting in their place. Of course, my efforts might very well fail in that no one else would be persuaded of my reading, but neither success nor failure would prove anything about what the text does or does not allow; it would only attest to the degree to which I had mastered or failed to master the rules of argument and evidence as they are understood (tacitly, to be sure) by members of the professional community.

The point is one that I have made before: it is neither the case that interpretation is constrained by what is obviously and unproblematically "there," nor the case that interpreters, in the absence of such constraints, are free to read into a text whatever they like (once again Dworkin has put himself in a corner with these unhappy alternatives).

Interpreters are constrained by their tacit awareness of what is possible and not possible to do, what is and is not a reasonable thing to say, what will and will not be heard as evidence, in a given enterprise; and it is within those same constraints that they see and bring others to see the shape of the documents to whose interpretation they are committed.

Dworkin's failure to see this is an instance of a general failure to understand the nature of interpretation. The distinction between explaining a text and changing it can no more be maintained than the others of which it is a version (finding vs. inventing, continuing vs. striking out in a new direction, interpreting vs. creating). To explain a work is to point out something about it that had not been attributed to it before and therefore to change it by challenging other explanations that were once changes in their turn. Explaining and changing cannot be opposed activities (although they can be the names of claims and counterclaims) because they are the same activities. Dworkin opposes them because he thinks that interpretation is itself an activity in need of constraints, but what I have been trying to show is that interpretation is a *structure* of constraints, a structure which, because it is always and already in place, renders unavailable the independent or uninterpreted text and renders unimaginable the independent and freely interpreting reader. In searching for a way to protect against arbitrary readings (judicial and literary), Dworkin is searching for something he already has and could not possibly be without. He conducts his search by projecting as dangers and fears possibilities that could never be realized and by imagining as discrete concepts entities that are already filled with the concerns of the enterprise they supposedly threaten.

One of those entities is intention. Dworkin spends a great deal of time refuting the view that interpretation in law and in literature must here concern itself with the intentions of the author. He argues, first, that the intention of a novelist or legislator is "complex" and therefore difficult to know. Second, he argues that even if the intention were known, it would be only a piece of "psychological data,"[14] and therefore would be irrelevant to the determination of a meaning that was not psychological but institutional. In short, he argues that to make intention the key to interpretation is to bypass the proper interpretive context—the history of practices and conventions—and substitute for it an interior motion of the mind. This argument would make perfect sense if intentions were, as Dworkin seems to believe them to be, private property and more or less equivalent with individual purpose or even whim. But it is hard to think of intentions formed in the course of judicial or literary activity as "one's own," since any intention one could have will have been stipulated in advance by the understanding of what activities are possible to someone working in the enterprise. One could no more come up with a unique intention with respect to the presentation of a character or the marshaling of legal evidence than one could come up with a new way of beginning a novel or continuing a chain of decisions. Simply to do something in the context of a chain enterprise is ipso facto to "have" an enterprise-specific intention, and to read something identified as part of a chain enterprise is ipso facto to be in the act of specifying that same intention. That is to say, the act of reading itself is at once the asking and answering of the question, "What is it that is meant by these words?," a question asked not in a vacuum, but in the context of an already-in-place understanding of the various things someone writing a novel or a decision (or anything else) might mean (i.e., intend).

In Dworkin's analysis, on the other hand, reading is simply the construing of sense and neither depends nor should depend on the identification of intention. He cites as evidence the fact that authors themselves have been known to reinterpret their own works. This, Dworkin asserts, shows that "[a]n author is capable of detaching what he has written from his earlier intentions . . . of treating it as an object in itself."[15] But in fact this only shows that an author is capable of becoming his own reader and deciding that he meant something other by his words than he had previously thought. Such an author-reader is not ignoring intention, but recharacterizing it; he is not interpreting in a "non-intention-bound style,"[16] but interpreting in a way that leads to a new understanding of his intention. Nor is there anything mysterious about this; it is no more than what we all do when sometime after having produced an utterance (it could be in less than a second) we ask ourselves, "What did I mean by that?" This will seem curious if intentions are thought of as unique psychological events, but if intentions are thought of as forms of possible conventional behavior that are to be conventionally "read," then one can just as well reread his own intentions as he can reread the intentions of another.

The crucial point is that one cannot read *or* reread independently of intention, independently, that is, of the assumption that one is dealing with marks or sounds produced by an intentional being, a being situated in some enterprise in relation to which he has a purpose or a point of view. This is not an assumption that one adds to an already construed sense in order to stabilize it, but an assumption without which the construing of sense could not occur. One cannot understand an utterance without *at the same time* hearing or reading it as the utterance of someone with more or less specific concerns, interests, and desires, someone with an intention. So that when Dworkin talks, as he does, of the attempt to "discover" what a judge or a novelist intended, he treats as discrete operations that are inseparable. He thinks that interpretation is one thing and the assigning of intention is another, and he thinks that because he thinks that to discover intention is to plumb psychological depths unrelated to the meaning of chain-enterprise texts. In fact, to specify the meaning of a chain-enterprise text is exactly equivalent to specifying the intention of its author, an intention which is not private, but a form of conventional behavior made possible by the general structure of the enterprise. This, of course, does not mean that intention anchors interpretation in the sense that it stands outside and guides the process; intention like anything else is an interpretive fact; that is, it must be construed; it is just that it is impossible *not* to construe it and therefore impossible to oppose it either to the production or the determination of meaning.

The fact that Dworkin does so oppose it is of a piece with everything else in the essay and is one more instance of its basic pattern. Once again he has imagined a free-floating and individualistic threat to interpretation—in this case it is called "intention"—and once again he has moved to protect interpretation by locating its constraints in a free-standing and self-declaring object—in this case "the work itself," detached from the antecedent designs of its author. And this means that once again he has committed himself in a single stroke to the extremes he set out to avoid, the objectivity of meanings that are "just there" and the subjectivity of meanings that have been "made up" by an unconstrained agent.

I cannot conclude without calling attention to what is perhaps the most curious feature of Dworkin's essay, the extent to which it contains its own critique. Indeed, a reader sympathetic to Dworkin might well argue that he anticipates everything I have said in the preceding pages. He himself says that "the artist can create nothing without interpreting as he creates, since . . . he must have at least a tacit theory of why what he produces is art,"[17] and he also points out that the facts of legal history do not announce themselves but will vary with the beliefs of particular judges concerning the general function of the law.[18] In another place he admits that the constraint imposed by the words of a text "is not inevitable," in part because any theory of identity (i.e., any theory of what is the same and what is different, of what constitutes a departure from the same) "will be controversial."[19] And after arguing that the "constraint of integrity" (the constraint imposed by a work's coherence with itself) sets limits to interpretation, he acknowledges that there is much disagreement "about what counts as integration"; he acknowledges in other words that the constraint is itself interpretive.

Even more curious than the fact of these reservations and qualifications is Dworkin's failure to see how much they undercut his argument. Early in the essay he distinguishes between simple cases in which the words of a statute bear a transparent relationship to the actions they authorize or exclude (his sample statute is "No will shall be valid without three witnesses"), and more difficult cases in which reasonable and knowledgeable men disagree as to whether some action or proposed action is lawful. But immediately after making the distinction he undermines it by saying (in a parenthesis), "I am doubtful that the positivists' analysis holds even in the simple case of the will; but that is a different matter I shall not argue here."[20] It is hard to see how this is a different matter, especially since so much in the essay hangs on the distinction. One doesn't know what form the argument Dworkin decides *not* to make would take, but it might take the form of pointing out that even in a simple case the ease and immediacy with which one can apply the statute to the facts is the result of the same kind of interpretive work that is more obviously required in the difficult cases. In order for a case to appear readable independently of some interpretive strategy consciously employed, one must already be reading within the assumption of that strategy and employing, without being aware of them, its stipulated (and potentially controversial) definitions, terms, modes of inference, etc. This, at any rate, would be the argument I would make, and in making it I would be denying the distinction between hard and easy cases, not as an empirical fact (as something one might experience), but as a fact that reflected a basic difference between cases that are self-settling and cases that can be settled only by referring them to the history of procedures, practices, and conventions. All cases are so referred (not after reading but in the act of reading), and they could not be anything but so referred and still be seen as cases.[21] The point is an important one because Dworkin later says that his account of chain enterprises is offered as an explanation of how we decide "hard cases at law";[22] that is, his entire paper depends on a distinction that he himself suggests may not hold, and therefore, as we have seen, his entire paper depends on the "positivist analysis" he rejects in the parenthesis.[23]

One can only speculate as to what Dworkin intends by these qualifications, but whether they appear in a parenthesis or in an aside or in the form of quotation marks around a key word, their effect is the same: to place him on both sides of the question at issue and to blur the supposedly hard lines of his argument. As a result, we are left with two ways of reading the essay, neither of which is comforting. If we take the subtext of reservation and disclaimer seriously, it so much weakens what he has to say that he seems finally not to have a position at all; and if we disregard the subtext and grant his thesis its strongest form, he will certainly have a position, but it will be, in every possible way, wrong.

5. Wrong Again

I Before turning to Ronald Dworkin's response to my critique, I would like to disavow in advance one form of argument to which he has frequent recourse. That argument surfaces as an expression of dismay at what Dworkin takes to be my willful misreading of his original essay. He could not, he complains, be assuming the availability, at some level, of a brute or uninterpreted fact because he nowhere announces such an assumption and indeed asserts its contrary in the very pages under discussion. The general line of reasoning behind this complaint is as follows: "I could not possibly hold that position you attribute to me because I repeatedly say I do not."

I find this line of reasoning less than compelling, first, because it is nothing more than an assertion, and, second, because it begs the question, which is whether or not one's general claims or self-descriptions are consistent with one's particular assertions and arguments. I, for example, would be begging the question in the same way were I to respond to Dworkin's charge that I and my (unnamed) colleagues are skeptics by pointing to the many places where I declare that I am not a skeptic and to argue (very much as Dworkin does in section III of his essay) that skepticism of a certain kind is incoherent. I will not so respond because what is at issue are not my declarations but the extent to which my repudiation of skepticism squares with the account I give of the interpretive process. Dworkin, therefore, is quite right to put to me questions of the form, "how can you maintain X and yet say Y," and it is that form which I will myself employ in what follows.

Let me begin by returning to the case of Agatha Christie, whose books, whatever they may have been, are now a fair way to becoming contested texts in contemporary interpretative theory. Christie enters Dworkin's argument in the context of an effort to shore up his "aesthetic hypothesis": "an interpretation of a piece of literature attempts to show which way of reading . . . the text reveals it as the best work of art."[1] Dworkin is concerned lest this hypothesis be understood as legitimating any interpretation whatsoever, since, as he points out, there exist "different normative theories about what literature is and what it is for and about what makes one work of literature better than another."[2] He therefore amends the hypothesis by declaring that no interpretation can be legitimate if it *changes* rather than *explains* the work, and he identifies the text itself as the constraint that enforces the distinction between changing and explaining: "The text provides one severe constraint in the name of identity: all the words must be taken account of and none may be changed to make 'it' a putatively better work of art."[3]

To illustrate the constraint, Dworkin offers two examples. Perhaps, he speculates, Shakespeare might have written a better *Hamlet* if he made the hero "a more forceful man of action." But it does not follow, he continues, that one should substitute the play one might have preferred for the play Shakespeare wrote; one should refrain, that is, from acting as if the *Hamlet* we actually have "really is like that after all."[4] Now, it is not clear which of two possible arguments Dworkin is making here. He might be saying that someone who is convinced that Hamlet is not a man of forceful action, but who also thinks that the play would be better if he were, would not be justified in setting aside the play he believes Shakespeare to have written in favor of the play he would have liked him to write. Or, alternatively, he might be saying that given the *Hamlet* Shakespeare *really* wrote, no one could responsibly offer a reading in which the hero was a man of forceful action, and that anyone who did would not be *explaining* the work, but *changing* it.

The two arguments are very different, even though they are both concerned with constraints and texts. In the first argument the constraint is the interpreter's belief about what the text means, and what he is constrained from doing (at least from the perspective of a certain morality) is attributing to the text a meaning he doesn't believe it to have. In the second argument the constraint is the text as it is, independent of anyone's belief, and what it constrains are the beliefs one might legitimately have about it. The first argument is directed against those who, for whatever reason, fail to tell what they take to be the truth about a text. The second argument is directed against those who tell a truth that the text—irrespective of what anyone takes it to be—simply does not allow. The first argument has nothing to say about the ontological status of texts and seeks only to prescribe the moral behavior of believing agents. The second argument is precisely a claim about the ontological status of texts, and the claim is that texts constrain their own interpretations.

Any doubt as to which argument Dworkin is making is resolved by his discussion of Agatha Christie. Again, the intention is to ward off an understanding of the "aesthetic hypothesis" that would allow absurd or impossible readings,[5] and the example (again hypothetical) is an interpretation of an Agatha Christie novel in which it is read as a philosophical treatise on death. "This interpretation fails," says Dworkin,

> not only because an Agatha Christie novel, taken to be a treatise on death, is a poor treatise less valuable than a good mystery, but because the interpretation makes the novel a shambles. All but one or two sentences would be irrelevant to the supposed theme; and the organization, style, and figures would be appropriate not to a philosophical novel but to an entirely different genre.[6]

Here it is clear, it seems to me, that Dworkin is saying that there is something about an Agatha Christie novel that renders inappropriate certain interpretations, and it was and is my contention that in saying this he makes the positivist assumption that at some level the novel is available in an uninterpreted shape; that is, in a shape that determines which interpretations of it will be appropriate. He does this in several ways. Most obviously, he assumes that the "organization, style, and figures" are "givens," specifiable apart from a theme that they will or will not support.[7] He assumes, in other words (and here I repeat a phrase that much offended him),[8] that organization, style, and figure announce themselves, are self-identifying, and therefore stand as a measure or check against which a proposed reading can be assessed either as an explanation or a change. Indeed, the distinction between explaining and changing, at least in the form Dworkin would have it, requires some such assumption, and it is not at all surprising that he makes it.

This assumption will not hold up, however, because organization, style, and figure are interpretive facts—facts which, rather than setting limits to the elaboration of a reading, emerge and become established in the course of that very elaboration. In short, that which is to be the measure of change is itself subject to change and is, therefore, not sufficiently stable to underwrite the distinction between changing and explaining.

Perhaps an example from literary history will make the point clearer. For a long time it was thought that Milton's *Paradise Lost,* in the words of Bernard Bergonzi, did not "possess the kind of coherence and psychological plausibility that we have come to expect from the novel."[9] This judgment was supported by the standard characterization of what was universally known as Milton's "grand style," a style appropriate to the scope and sweep of an epic, but inappropriate to the subtleties and nuances of lived psychological experience. Within four years of Bergonzi's pronouncement, however, the situation had entirely changed, in part as the result of the publication of Christopher Ricks's *Milton's Grand Style,*[10] in which passage after passage of *Paradise Lost* was read in a way that turned the verse into just the flexible instrument everyone had always known that it wasn't. Once this was done, and done in a way that many in the Milton community found persuasive, at least one bar to claiming for the poem "the kind of coherence and psychological plausibility that we have come to expect from the novel" was removed; in the years that followed, Milton was more and more celebrated as a penetrating psychologist and as a precursor of Henry James and other novelists who told their stories by masterfully varying point of view.

What is nice about the example is that it demonstrates the interdependence, and indeed the *interpretive* interdependence, of everything that Dworkin must keep separate. Thus the generic identification of *Paradise Lost,* the specification of its theme, and the description of its organization, style, and figure are not separate acts, but acts that support and subtend one another within assumed interpretive conditions. When those conditions change, when the shape of one "given" is altered, the way is open to altering the shape of others, and in some cases, over a number of years, the genre, theme, and style of a work may come to wear a completely different face.

My point is that what *has* happened to *Paradise Lost could* happen to Agatha Christie, and that if it did, if in the course of criticism and commentary, not only the theme, but the style, organization, and even genre of her novel were recharacterized, then it could not be said that interpretation will have made the novel a "shambles" because interpretation will have remade the novel. And my further point is that, once this is recognized as a possibility, the firm distinction between *changing* and *explaining* is undermined and cannot be invoked to shore up the "aesthetic hypothesis," and that someone who invokes the distinction can do so only by embracing the positivism Dworkin claims to reject.

This does not mean that the distinction has no force whatsoever, only that its force is felt from *within* interpretive conditions that give certain objects and shapes a real but constructed—and therefore unsettleable—stability. The reason that the example of Hamlet as a forceful man of action seems such a good one to Dworkin is that Hamlet's indecisiveness has been part of the interpretive tradition for so long that it is almost proverbial. For most, if not all, readers and viewers (and certainly, directors) of the play, it is a "given" and, to say the least, the burden of proof would be on anyone who thought to deny it or to offer a reading with which it was incompatible. In fact, no one does think to deny it. Therefore, Hamlet's indecisiveness often functions in readings as a piece of evidence in relation to which other, less settled, interpretive issues are posed. All of which is to say that one, at the present time, cannot describe Hamlet as a forceful man of action without provoking a charge that the text, rather than being explained, has been changed.

Of course, exactly the same situation once obtained with respect to *Paradise Lost* and with it the plausibility of attributing to it a novelistic subtlety. That situation has now changed, and it is not impossible (although neither is it inevitable) that there could come a time when because of an argument successfully prosecuted—perhaps one in which Hamlet is from the very first executing a predetermined plan—the hero of Shakespeare's play will be regarded as the very type of decisiveness. (It goes without saying that such an argument would not be made in isolation, but would involve a simultaneous recharacterization of many other of the "givens" that now make up our sense of what *Hamlet* is.)

If Hamlet were recharacterized in this way or if Agatha Christie's novels were routinely regarded as "philosophical," it would no longer be the case that to call Hamlet a forceful man of action or reading a Christie novel as a treatise on death would be instances of "changing" rather than "explaining," but it would still be the case that there would be many readings of both works that would legitimately provoke such a charge. In short, while the text of *Hamlet* or of a Christie novel will always have a generally accepted shape (in the sense that when one looks at it or thinks of it one will already have categorized and described it), that shape will itself be subject to change. Moreover, when that change occurs, a corresponding change in the content of the still relevant distinction between "changing" and "explaining" will have occurred. (Dworkin says repeatedly that I deny this distinction and thereby make all acts of interpretation the same;[11] but my point is only that "explaining" and "changing" are acts of interpretation and therefore that neither can serve—as Dworkin wants "explaining" to serve—as the noninterpretive pole of a binary opposition.)

Exactly the same argument holds for the distinction between "finding" and "inventing" (or as Dworkin sometimes puts it, between "continuing" and "beginning anew").[12] In Dworkin's argument this is a distinction between two different forms of judicial activity, and he illustrates it, as he did in the earlier essay, with the literary example of a novel written serially by different authors, each of whom accepts the obligation to continue what his predecessors have done as opposed to striking out in a new direction of his own.[13] Dworkin asks us to imagine that *A Christmas Carol* was written not by Dickens but by a chain of novelists. "Most chain novelists," he says, "would think that certain interpretations of Scrooge's character would be incompatible with the text of *A Christmas Carol* toward the end of that book, but not after the opening pages alone,"[14] and consequently, he asserts, "a novelist at the end of the *Christmas Carol* chain will have more difficulty seeing Scrooge as inherently evil than a novelist second in line."[15]

In essence, this is an argument about context. Dworkin is contending, for example, that a novelist who is provided with, say, seven-eighths of *A Christmas Carol* is constrained by that context in such a way as to make unavailable to him (assuming that he is operating in good faith) a characterization of Scrooge that would have seemed plausible, and perhaps even inevitable, to a novelist who had read only the first chapter. But while it is certainly true that context constrains interpretation, it is also true, as Dworkin fails to see, that context is a product of interpretation and as such is itself variable as a constraint. That is, what a later novelist does or does not have difficulty in seeing will depend on what he has already seen; but since what he has already seen will itself be a matter of interpretation, one can make no general or predictive statements about what a novelist who has been given seven-eights of *A Christmas Carol* will think about Scrooge.

Thus, two novelists or readers who are both given seven-eighths of

A Christmas Carol might still disagree about Scrooge's moral character because they disagreed about the configuration and facts of what they had already read. "Don't you see," one might remonstrate, "that Scrooge is already changed when he feels compassion for Tiny Tim?" "That's not real compassion at all," the other might reply, "but a calculated strategy in response to a precarious situation." Of course, both could then go on to cite even earlier sections of the novel in support of their respective positions. Yet the same pattern of disagreement, rooted in different convictions as to what the interpreted object was, might very well repeat itself at every point, even if the inquiry were pushed all the way back to the opening words of chapter one or to the title. (Think of all the disagreements that occur in situations, domestic and otherwise, in which no more than a sentence or two has been spoken; brevity no more guarantees agreement than prolixity guarantees difficulty.) Or, to reverse the scenario, two later novelists who are given different assignments—one to continue, the other to strike out in a new direction—might then come up with the *same* characterization of Scrooge because they are operating within diametrically opposed understandings of what they are supposed to maintain or abandon.

I say all this not to deny the distinction between continuing and inventing, but to point out that, as in the case of explaining versus changing, the distinction is interpretive and that because it is interpretive, one cannot determine whether a particular piece of behavior is one or the other by checking it against the text; for it is always possible (and indeed likely) that someone characterized as "inventing" will reply that his accuser is mistaken as to the nature of that which is to be continued. This holds true too when the distinction becomes a judicial one and marks the difference, according to Dworkin, between a judge who feels constrained in his actions by the "past record of statutes and decisions" and a judge who ignores legal history and decisions "to decide cases 'on a clean slate' instead."[16] Here the legal history is in the position of *A Christmas Carol* (or *Hamlet,* or any other literary work), and the judge is in the position of the novelist who is asked to continue the chain and enjoined from breaking it, and the point made in relation to the novelists applies *mutatis mutandis* to the judge: the question of whether the legal history is being ignored or consulted depends upon a prior decision as to what the legal history is, and that decision will be an interpretive one. Therefore, insofar as the distinction is a mechanism for distinguishing between two forms of judicial activity (and if it *is* not for that then it is hard to see what it is for), it won't work because there is no *independent* way of determining whether or not a particular judge is acting in one way as opposed to the other.

There is also a deeper point that relates to both the literary and the legal examples. Suppose that a later novelist in Dworkin's hypothetical chain were told not to continue the chain, but to strike out in a new direction. How would he go about it? First of all, he could only hear the assignment as an imperative of the following form: "Depart from this" where "this" is the shape of what already has been written by his predecessors. That is, in order to depart from the chain, however, he must first determine what it would mean to continue the chain by determining what patterns, themes, principles, and so forth, the chain displays. In other words, he is as constrained by the chain in the act of departing from it as he would be in the act of continuing it (although one must remember that in both instances the constraint—that is, the chain—is interpreted). Thus, paradoxically, but only in terms of the assumptions underlying the distinction, departing from the chain is one way of continuing it, and even more paradoxically, an agent cannot depart from the chain even if he wants to and believes that he is doing so. Thus, the judge in Dworkin's example who resolves to "ignore precedent or the statute" in favor of what he feels "would make the community better off on the whole"[17] is not in fact ignoring precedent but is deciding, by a judicial mechanism Dworkin explicates in his original essay,[18] that precedent is mistaken. Moreover, he arrives at his sense of what would make the community better off on the whole by rejecting the vision of community needs he finds (interpretively, of course) in the legal history. In short, Dworkin's judge is in exactly the position of the later novelist who departs from his predecessors' work, constrained by the very chain he supposedly breaks and striking out not in a "new direction of his own," but in a direction already implicit in the practice in which he continues to be engaged.

To this, Dworkin would reply (and does reply) that I have simply redefined words like "finding" and "inventing" and given them meanings "wholly alien"[19] to those they have in practice. In other words, by pitching my argument at so general and abstract a level that nothing could possibly count as "beginning anew" or "striking out in a direction of one's own," I elide and finesse the "crucial" and "critical difference between two assignments a judge might accept."[20] But it is only if the difference can be invoked at that level that it will be "crucial" in the sense that it will do the work Dworkin wants it to do—characterize judicial activity in a decisive and illuminating way. That at least was Dworkin's original claim, although he now seems to have modified it to an extent that leaves him with virtually nothing to say. In the essay that occasioned the present exchange, he was saying something like this: what judges do is operate as members of a chain enterprise (an enterprise in which their actions are constrained by a previous history), which means that they don't do something else like striking out in a new direction. But now Dworkin is saying that striking out in a new direction is just another "way of continuing the 'practice of judging.' "[21] He doesn't see that he can't say that and *also* say, as he does in the very same sentence, that continuing and striking out in a new direction "are radically different ways."[22] They can only be "radically" different if the difference they mark is between judging and something wholly apart from judging. But a difference *that* radical could tell us nothing about judging except that there is something it isn't, and it certainly could not tell a judge what it is that he ought to do.

Dworkin seems to have realized this, and he now has moved to relocate the difference *within* the practice of judging rather than *between* it and something else; but that won't work either because, by his own admission, continuing the chain and deciding "on a clean slate" are both names for "continuing." They are *not* names for obviously distinguishable forms of judicial practice, but are possible characterizations of a practice that is, with respect to the opposition chain/non-chain, uniform. To put it another way, there are no decisions that are on their face one or the other, but there are strategies for presenting or attacking a decision that amount to claiming or complaining that it is one or the other. Thus while there is, at the level of practice, a distinction between continuing the legal history and striking out in a new direction, it is a distinction between methods of justifying arguments and not between actions whose difference is perspicuous apart from any argument whatsoever. The difference, in short, is interpretive, and because it is interpretive, it can't be used to settle anything, for it is itself what is continually being settled. Dworkin is thus in a perfect bind: he can stick with the original or "hard" (chain versus nonchain) form of his distinction, in which case he fails to distinguish *meaningfully* (in a way that can be consulted or used) between judicial activity and anything else; or he can invoke it as a distinction within chain practice, in which case it has no prescriptive or normative force because it is a distinction between contestable modes of self-description or accusation.

II

Rather than saying that Dworkin is in a bind, one might say instead that he is running two arguments at once and that the two arguments, at least with respect to the issues in dispute between us, are incompatible. I said as much at the conclusion of my first critique,[23] but the point deserves more elaboration than it received there. It gets to the heart of what has been characterized as the vague and slippery nature of Dworkin's writing and thought,[24] the feeling, as one reads him, that the terms of the discussion and the levels on which it is proceeding are continually shifting, although no shift is ever announced.

Sometimes this happens in the course of a single sentence, as when Dworkin declares that to interpret a Christie mystery as "a novel about the meaning of death would be a mistake, because it would make the novel a shambles, and that is not because all novels announce their own genre but because her novels become wrecks if we try to read them in that particular way."[25] This is a nice sentence because the basic Dworkin move is performed twice. As I observed earlier, one can only claim that a particular reading would make a novel a shambles if the novel is assumed to have a core which, because it is independent of any reading whatsoever, can serve as a bench mark or reference point in relation to which the distorting or "shambles-making" potential of a reading can be measured. That is a "brute fact" or a positivist assumption, but it is also one that Dworkin doesn't want to make or doesn't want to think he makes. He, therefore, immediately disclaims it or thinks he disclaims it by denying that he believes that "novels announce their own genre." But then he immediately proceeds to demonstrate that he believes exactly that when he ends the sentence by simply reasserting its beginning with only the slight and inconsequential substitution of "wrecks" for "shambles." Thus in the same sentence we have a positivist assertion followed by a repudiation of positivism followed by another—virtually identical—positivist assertion.

Dworkin thinks that he escapes this characterization of his position when he disavows the belief "that everyone who sets out to interpret any particular work of literature will reach the same conclusion about its genre."[26] In his view it is only because I attribute to him such a belief that I am able to make his theory "seem ridiculous."[27] In fact, he declares, all he believes (and said) is that while Christie can be "interpreted in very different ways,"[28] a "certain way of reading [her] would be wrong."[29] But I do not have to saddle Dworkin with the thesis that a text demands a single reading or assignment of genre in order to convict him of textual positivism. So long as he believes that there are some ways, some generic identifications, that a work rules out—and he must believe that in order to declare that the style and figure of a Christie novel do not allow a philosophical reading because they are "appropriate . . . to an entirely different genre"[30]—then he is as much a positivist as anyone would want him or not want him to be, since he has once again (re)assumed the existence in the text of an uninterpreted core. To be sure, the core in this revised formulation acts liberally rather than tyrannically: it allows some readings instead of just one. But that just makes Dworkin a positivist of the pluralist variety, one who doesn't believe that a text constrains a single interpretation, but believes that the text constrains the range of interpretations it will receive without becoming a shambles. The important point, however, is that he assumes the constraint (however it operates) and that he assumes it to be in the text.[31]

I have lingered so long over this small moment in Dworkin's discourse because it illustrates so concisely the way in which he shifts back and forth between lines of argument that are finally contradictory. In this particular sequence the contradiction fairly leaps off the page (one might almost say that it announces itself). In other places it is less obvious and amounts to allowing two different understandings of what is being asserted to coexist in a manner that forces neither the author nor the reader to choose. We have already seen an example in the discussion of *Hamlet*.[32] Is Dworkin saying that the text of *Hamlet* constrains the beliefs one can hold about it, in which case he would be strongly asserting a positivist or "brute fact" position? Or is he merely saying that one's belief about *Hamlet* ought to constrain what one says about it, in which case he is promulgating an unexceptionable moral dictum that has no bearing on the status of the text whatsoever? Since it remains unclear which of these assertions Dworkin is making, he gets credit for both, and when he feels himself pressed on the one, he can always avail himself of the vocabulary (and therefore of the presuppositions) of the other.

This is not to suggest a conscious strategy on Dworkin's part. He does not embrace contradictory positions because he wants to gain an advantage over his readers (although that may be in fact what happens) but because he is confused. Nowhere is his confusion more spectacular and more revealing than in his lengthy discussion of "the actual practice of interpretation"[33] in section II.[34] At several points he articulates a view of that practice with which I have no quarrel whatsoever. Here is a particularly felicitous formulation from the beginning of his discussion of theory dependence:

> Any interpreter's beliefs about, for example, the genre and characterizations of a novel will reflect a great network of his aesthetic beliefs and attitudes. . . . These other beliefs will furnish, for him, whatever grounds he has for thinking his interpretation better than others. No feature of an interpretation is exempt from this description, not even the threshold question of what counts as the physical text—the canonical set of marks on paper—that identifies the work to be interpreted.[35]

However, just before he delivers this pronouncement Dworkin declares that the first question any theory of interpretation must answer is how people make the discriminations necessary to "think one interpretation . . . better than another."[36] But if an interpretation is grounded, as Dworkin is about to say, in the interpreter's beliefs, then it goes (or should go) without saying that the interpreter believes in his interpretation. If he believes in his interpretation, then he necessarily believes it to be better (for if he thought some other interpretation better he would believe in *it*). And if he believes it to be better, then one need seek no explanation of how it is possible for him to think this, for it is flatly impossible for him to think anything else.

How does Dworkin miss this? How can he at once identify interpretive judgment with belief and think that we require an account of how the interpreter comes to believe his interpretation? The answer is that despite having embedded the interpreter in a "network of beliefs," he repeatedly imagines him in a position outside that network, a position from which he must look for independent support for what he believes. And where will he find that support? Why, in some noninterpretive distinction between explaining and changing or (it amounts to the same thing) in some textual fact or configuration that establishes limits to what can be believed about it. Here the two facts of Dworkin's positivism meet, as they necessarily must. In my original critique I said that "[r]ather than avoiding the Scylla of legal realism ('making it up wholesale') and the Charybdis of strict constructionism ('finding the law just "there" '), [Dworkin] commits himself to both,"[37] and we can now see that the two commitments are inextricable. If one conceives of the interpreter as free to choose his beliefs and therefore to choose his interpretations, then one must always imagine a constraint on that choice so that it won't be irresponsible or whimsical. And, of course, the reverse holds: anyone who is in search of constraints, or thinks it crucial to identify them, must at the same time imagine an interpreter who needs the constraint because he stands apart from any tethering structure or gestalt. In the positivist picture of things the uninterpreted text (or rule or distinction) and the unsituated (or weakly situated) subject are constitutive of one another and of the questions theory must supposedly answer, such as: "How *do* we decide that one interpretation or one argument for an interpretation is better than another?";[38] "[H]ow [do] people who think one interpretation can be better than another make the discriminations necessary to hold on to that second-order belief?";[39] "[What must] an interpreter . . . believe in order to believe in his own interpretation?";[40] "What must an interpreter believe to believe that his interpretation of these rules is better than alternate interpretations of them?";[41] and, "[H]ow [can] an interpreter . . . come to think that his interpretation is superior to others[?]"[42]

These are the questions that Dworkin says I cannot answer, but it is my contention that they require no answer. They seem urgent only in the context of the very odd assumption that one can believe an interpretation and not be convinced of it. That is, Dworkin imagines a two-stage process in which one first has a belief and then must determine whether or not to believe it. To put it that way is immediately to see the dilemma: either that which will make the determination is itself a belief (a position Dworkin seems sometimes to hold), in which case the two-stage process is really a succession in which one belief gives way to another; or that which will make the determination is not a belief, but an independent piece of the world, in which case belief has become just another name for error. (This is the position of the positivist Dworkin.)

But the dilemma evaporates once one sees that to have a belief (or an interpretation) is to believe it, to believe it is to think that it is correct, and to think it correct is to prefer it to someone else's belief. In short, everything that Dworkin would secure in the name of the "right-wrong" picture—a ground for assuming "that interpretations may be sound or unsound, better or worse, more or less accurate"[43]—already is secured by the fact that the interpreter is embedded in a structure of beliefs of which his judgments are an extension. The entire project of explaining how "ordinary interpreters think" as they do—think that they are right and others are wrong and that what they believe is true— is unnecessary because they could not possibly think anything else. For the same reason, it is equally unnecessary to answer the questions that Dworkin rehearses so often and so urgently.

Of course, questions remain to be answered: How do beliefs about what is right and wrong change? How are beliefs acquired? What is the relationship between belief and the world? How do disputes between believing agents get adjudicated? This is not the place to consider these questions, but a full consideration (which I have attempted elsewhere)[44] would involve the specification (insofar as it is possible) of the conventions of description, argument, judgment, and persuasion as they operate in this or that profession or discipline or community. Dworkin several times dismisses these conventions as the "weak" constraints of practice.[45] The dismissal is revealing and characteristic, for if one rejects as "pale" and "wholly subjective"[46] the constraints "imposed by practice,"[47] one does so in the name of constraints that are independent of any practice whatsoever. Those independent constraints can only be of the abstract and preinterpretive kind that are perspicuous to anyone no matter what his situation. Once again Dworkin maneuvers himself into the familiar bind: either he acknowledges that the constraints imposed by practice are as strong as anyone could want or he commits himself to the existence of constraints so strongly transcontextual that they can only be positivist.

There remains only the matter of intention, a vexed topic that usually brings out the worst in everyone. Dworkin correctly reports my position when he says that I think that to report "an author's intention is just another way of reporting an interpretation of that author's work,"[48] but Dworkin then shows that he misunderstands what he has reported. He thinks that I am making a recommendation (i.e., let's call interpretations intentions), when in fact I am asserting an epistemological necessity. The argument is not one about what people should or should not do, but about what they cannot help doing: they cannot help positing an intention for an utterance if they are in the act of regarding it as meaningful. If this seems counterintuitive, you need only try to think of a meaningful utterance (even a one-word imperative like "go!") without *already* having imagined the circumstances (including an intending agent) in which it has the meaning you're thinking of. You will find that the experiment is impossible to perform, or (and it amounts to the same thing) you will find that if you succeed you will have succeeded in transforming what once was a stretch of language into a sequence of marks.

Now as Dworkin rightly observes, this account of intention renders it methodologically useless. One cannot use it (as some intentionalist critics want to) as a constraint on or key to interpretation because it is not distinguishable from that which it would constrain. But that does not mean, as Dworkin contends, that in my argument intention "is simply a phrase used to report interpretations already established in some other way,"[49] for "in some other way" can only mean in a way independent of intention. But it is precisely my thesis (with which, of course, one might quarrel) that in whatever way one establishes an interpretation, one will at the same time be assigning an intention.

Dworkin simply turns that thesis around and has me asserting an arbitrary relationship between actions whose inseparability is my entire point. He does this again when he says of the intention I attribute to Agatha Christie that "[Fish] offers no evidence for the intention he assumes beyond the evidence he says he has for the interpretation he favors."[50] Again, it is the very heart of my account that to offer evidence for the one is to offer evidence for the other. It goes without saying that this is not Dworkin's thesis. He believes that to specify intention and to interpret are different. Moreover, he shares this belief with the intentionalists, while disagreeing only with their methodological prescription that one should look to intention when doing interpretation. *His* prescription is that intention should be set aside. I, on the other hand, have no prescription whatsoever (at least not on this point), not because there is a fatal weakness in my position, but because that *is* my position.

Of that position (insofar as he understands it) Dworkin complains that it "cannot discriminate between assigning someone a literary intention and asking whether the text he has created succeeds in expressing that intention."[51] But the complaint would have force only if the text "he has created" can first be looked at and *then* compared with one or more assignments of its intention. If, as I maintain, to look at the text (in the sense of regarding it as meaningful) is already to have posited for it an intention (by assuming the intentional circumstances of its production), then what one would be doing is comparing one assignment of intention with another. Does this mean that we cannot say of an author that he failed to execute a declared intention? Not at all. It is just that when we say so we are not opposing a specification of intention to something else—to a text whose meaning has been determined independently of intention—but opposing one specification of intention—of what is meant by these words—to another. The fact that the first specification may have been made by the author only indicates that authors, like anyone else, must construe intention even when it is "their own." It also indicates that their construing can be disputed and that on occasion they can be persuaded that their intention was not what they had assumed it to be.

In his original essay Dworkin contrives to turn this commonplace occurrence into an aesthetic mystery when he moves from the observation that an author can change his mind about what he means to the conclusion that his new understanding has been produced by "detaching what he has written from his earlier intentions."[52] He then moves to the further conclusion that an author writing a work of art writes with the very particular intention of producing a work "capable of being treated that way," that is, as an "object in itself."[53] But Dworkin is simply confusing a fact about interpretation in general—that the construing of intention can always begin anew even when the intention is one's own—with a supposedly special fact about aesthetic intention—that it leads to the creation of texts that live untethered to any intention whatsoever. (It is interesting, but not at all surprising, that this account of artistic creation and of the properties peculiar to works of art simply reaffirms the New Critical doctrine of aesthetic autonomy, which is one more positivist assumption to which Dworkin is firmly, if unknowingly, committed.) The matter, however, is at once more simple and more complex. Neither artists nor anyone else can produce texts capable of being detached from intention; but since intention is an interpretive fact, there is nothing to prevent the intention of a text, including one you have yourself written, from being interpreted again.

To all of this Dworkin still might reply that I have still failed to explain how "[w]e can read *Hamlet* in a psychodynamic way without supposing that Shakespeare either did or could have intended that we do so."[54] He thinks that this ability (which we certainly have) proves the independence of meaning from intention, but it proves nothing of the kind. If we are convinced that the meaning of *Hamlet* is psychodynamic but that Shakespeare intended no such meaning, then we are attributing the meaning to an intentional agent other than Shakespeare, perhaps to the spirit of the age, to some transhistorical truth about human nature, or to the intentional structure of language. And if we are convinced both that Shakespeare intended no psychodynamic meaning and that the play displays no such meaning, but decide nevertheless to read it psychodynamically, then we have simply set aside what we know to be the play's meaning and Shakespeare's intention for something else. In neither case, however, will we have sundered meaning or interpretation from intention; we just will have demonstrated, first, that one can conceive of intention as something other than the possession of a "particular historical person,"[55] and, second, that there are things one can do with texts that are not interpretations of them.

That, I think, about covers it, and I will only add that in deference to Professor Dworkin's request,[56] I have not once used the word "objectivity," although I have now mentioned it.

6. Fish v. Fiss

I   The Rules of the Game

On the first page of his essay *Objectivity and Interpretation* Owen Fiss characterizes interpretation as "neither a wholly discretionary nor a wholly mechanical activity," but a "dynamic interaction between reader and text" of which meaning is the "product."[1] This middle way, he asserts, "affords a proper recognition of both the subjective and objective dimensions of human experience."[2] The alternatives Fiss rejects will be familiar to all students of both literary and legal interpretation. The "wholly mechanical" alternative is the view, often termed positivist, that meaning is a property of—is embedded in—texts and can therefore be read without interpretive effort or intervention by a judge or a literary critic. The "wholly discretionary" alternative is the opposite view, often termed subjectivist, that texts have either many meanings or no meanings, and the reader or judge is free to impose—create, legislate, make up, invent—whatever meanings he or she pleases, according to his or her own whims, desires, partisan purposes, etc. On the one view, the text places constraints on its own interpretation; on the other, the reader interprets independently of constraints. Fiss proposes to recognize the contributions of both text and reader to the determination of meaning by placing between the two a set of "disciplining rules" derived from the specific institutional setting of the interpretive activity. These rules "specify the relevance and weight to be assigned to the material" and define the "basic concepts and . . . procedural circumstances under which the interpretation must occur."[3] They thus act as constraints on the interpreter's freedom and direct him to those meanings in the text that are appropriate to a particular institutional context.

On its face this proposal seems reasonable enough, but ultimately it will not do, and it will not do because the hinge on which Fiss's account turns is not sufficiently fixed to provide the stability he needs.

That hinge is the notion of "disciplining rules" that will constrain read-ers or interpreters and mitigate (if not neutralize) the inherent am-biguity of texts.[4] The claim is that, given a particular situation, the rules tell you what to do and prevent you from simply doing whatever you like.

The trouble is that they don't. If the rules are to function as Fiss would have them function—to "constrain the interpreter"—they them-selves must be available or "readable" independently of interpretation; that is, they must directly declare their own signficance to any observer, no matter what his perspective. Otherwise, they would "constrain" individual interpreters differently, and you would be right back in the original dilemma of a variously interpretable text and an interpretively free reader. To put the matter another way, if the rules tell you what to do with texts, they cannot themselves be texts, but must be—in the strong sense assumed by an older historiography—documents.[5] Unfor-tunately, rules *are* texts. They are in need of interpretation and cannot themselves serve as constraints on interpretation.

That at least is my argument, and we can test it by trying to think of some rules. Fiss does not spend much time telling us what the dis-ciplining rules are like, but the general form they would take is clear from what he does say. They would be of at least two kinds, particular and general. A particular rule would be one that "specif[ied] the rele-vance and weight to be assigned to the material"[6] and would presum-ably take a form like: "If someone takes the property of another with-out his consent, count that as larceny." A general rule would be one that defined the "basic concepts and . . . procedural circumstances under which the interpretation must occur,"[7] and its form would be something like: "Always consult history" (one of Fiss's examples, in fact).[8] The problem with the particular rule is that there will always be disputes about whether the act is indeed a "taking" or even about what a "taking" is. And even where the fact of taking has been estab-lished to everyone's satisfaction, one can still argue that the result should be embezzlement or fraud rather than larceny. The same analy-sis holds for the more general rules. To say that one must always consult history does not prevent—but provokes—disagreements about exactly what history is, or about whether or not this piece of informa-tion counts as history, or (if it does count) about what its factual configurations are.

Fiss himself acknowledges the possibility of such disputes but says that they "pose only issues of application";[9] that is to say, they do not affect the "legitimacy of the disciplining rules," which are still doing their disciplining. "The authority of a particular rule can be maintained even when it is disputed. . . ."[10] But how can "it" be maintained *as a constraint* when the dispute is about what "it" is or about what "it" means? Fiss assumes that one first "has" a rule and then interprets it. But if the shape of the rule could be had without interpretation, then the interpretation would be superfluous.[11] And if interpretation is not superfluous to the "reading" of rules (Fiss would agree that it is not) then one only has rules in an interpreted shape. Thus we are back once again to my assertion that a so-called "disciplining rule" cannot be said to act as a constraint on interpretation because it is (in whatever form has been specified for it) the product of an interpretation.

This is true even in those cases where there are no disputes, where there is perfect agreement about what the rule is and what it means. There is a temptation (often irresistible to those on Fiss's side of the street) to assume that such cases of perfect agreement are normative and that interpretation and its troubles enter in only in special circumstances. But agreement is not a function of particularly clear and perspicuous rules; it is a function of the fact that interpretive assumptions and procedures are so widely shared in a community that the rule appears to all in the same (interpreted) shape. And if Fiss were to reply that I am not denying the existence—and authority—of disciplining rules, but merely suggesting a new candidate for them in the "persons" of interpretive assumptions and procedures, I would simply rehearse the argument of the previous paragraphs all over again, pointing out this time that interpretive assumptions and procedures can no more be grasped independently of interpretation than disciplining rules can; thus they cannot be thought of as constraints upon interpretation either.[12]

The difficulty, in short, cannot be merely patched over; it pervades the entire situation in which someone (a judge, a literary critic) faced with the necessity of acting (rendering a judgment, turning out a reading) looks to some rule or set of rules that will tell him what to do. The difficulty becomes clear when the sequence—here I am, I must act, I shall consult the rule—becomes problematic in a way that cannot be remedied. Let us imagine that the president of the United States or some other appropriate official appoints to the bench someone with no previous judicial or legal experience. This person is, however, intelligent, mature, and well-informed. As she arrives to take up her new position she is handed a booklet and told, "Here are the rules—go to it!" What would happen? The new judge would soon find that she was unable to read the rules without already having a working knowledge of the practices they were supposed to order, or, to put it somewhat more paradoxically, she would find that she could read the rules that are supposed to tell her what to do only when she already knew what to do. This is so because rules, in law or anywhere else, do not stand in an independent relationship to a field of action on which they can simply be imposed; rather, rules have a circular or mutually interdependent relationship to the field of action in that they make sense only in reference to the very regularities they are thought to bring about. The very ability to read the rules in an informed way presupposes an understanding of the questions that are likely to arise (should liability be shared or strictly assigned?), the kinds of decisions that will have to be made, the possible alternative courses of action (to dismiss, to render a summary judgment), the consequences (for future cases) of deciding one way or another, and the "deep" issues that underlie the issue of record (are we interested in retribution or prevention?). Someone who was without this understanding would immediately begin to ask questions about what a rule *meant,* and in answer would be told about this or that piece of practice in a way that would alert her to what was "going on" in some corner of the institutional field. She would then be able to read the rule because she would be seeing it as already embedded in the context of assumptions and practices that make it intelligible, a context that at once gives rise to it (in the sense that it is a response to needs that can be felt) and is governed by it.

Even that would not be the end of the matter. Practices are not fixed and finite—one could no more get out a list of them than one could get out a list of *the* rules. Sooner or later the new judge would find herself "misapplying" the rules she thought she had learned. In response to further questions she would discover that a situation previously mastered also intersected with a piece of the field of practice of which she had been ignorant; and in the light of this new knowledge she would see that the rule must be differently applied because in a sense it would be a different, though not wholly different, rule.

Let me clarify this somewhat abstract discussion by juxtaposing to it another example. Suppose you were a basketball coach and had taught someone how to shoot baskets and how to dribble the ball, but had imparted these skills without reference to the playing of an actual basketball game. Now you decide to insert your student into a game, and you equip him with some rules. You say to him, for instance, "Take only good shots." "What," he asks reasonably enough, "is a good shot?" "Well," you reply, "a good shot is an 'open shot,' a shot taken when you are close to the basket (so that the chances of success are good) and when your view is not obstructed by the harassing efforts of opposing players." Everything goes well until the last few seconds of the game; your team is behind by a single point; the novice player gets the ball in heavy traffic and holds it as the final buzzer rings. You run up to him and say, 'Why didn't you shoot?" and he answers, "It wasn't a good shot." Clearly, the rule must be amended, and accordingly you tell him that if time is running out, and your team is behind, and you have the ball, you should take the shot even if it isn't a good one, because it will then *be* a good one in the sense of being the best shot in the circumstances. (Notice how both the meaning of the rule and the entities it covers are changing shape as this "education" proceeds.) Now suppose there is another game, and the same situation develops. This time the player takes the shot, which under the circumstances is a very difficult one; he misses, and once again the final buzzer rings. You run up to him and say "Didn't you see that John (a teammate) had gone 'back door' and was perfectly positioned under the basket for an easy shot?" and he answers "But you said. . . ." Now obviously it would be possible once again to amend the rule, and just as obviously there would be no real end to the sequence and number of emendations that would be necessary. Of course, there will eventually come a time when the novice player (like the novice judge) will no longer have to ask questions; but it will not be because the rules have finally been made sufficiently explicit to cover all cases, but because explicitness will have been rendered unnecessary by a kind of knowledge that informs rules rather than follows from them.

Indeed, explicitness is a good notion to focus on in order to see why Fiss's disciplining rules won't do what he wants them to do (namely, provide directions for behavior). On the one hand, no set of rules could be made explicit enough to cover all the possible situations that might emerge within a field of practice; no matter how much was added to the instruction "Take only good shots," it could never be descriptive of all the actions it was supposed to direct, since every time the situation changes, what is or is not a "good" shot will change too. On the other hand, for someone already embedded in a field of practice, the briefest of instructions will be sufficient and perhaps even superfluous, since it will be taken as referring to courses of action that are already apparent to the agent; upon hearing or remembering the rule, "Take only good shots," a player will glance around a field already organized in terms of relevant pieces of possible behavior. A rule can never be made explicit in the sense of demarcating the field of reference independently of interpretation, but a rule can always be received as explicit by someone who hears it within an interpretive preunderstanding of what the field of reference could possibly be.[13]

The moral of the story, then, is not that you could never learn enough to know what to do in every circumstance, but that what you learn cannot finally be reduced to a set of rules. Or, to put the case another way (it amounts to the same thing), insofar as the requisite knowledge *can* be reduced to a set of rules ("Take only good shots," "Consult history"), it will be to rules whose very intelligibility depends on the practices they supposedly govern. Fiss believes that the rules must exist prior to practice, or else practice will be unprincipled; but as the examples of the judge and the basketball player have shown, practice is already principled, since at every moment it is ordered by an understanding of what it is practice *of* (the law, basketball), an understanding that can always be put into the form of rules—rules that will be opaque to the outsider—but is not produced by rules.

The point has been well made by Thomas Kuhn when he wrote that "scientists . . . never learn concepts, laws, and theories in the abstract and by themselves." "Instead," he adds, "these intellectual tools are from the start encountered in a historically and pedagogically prior unit that displays them with and through their applications."[14] As an illustration, Kuhn offers an example that is on all fours with the ones we have already considered. His text is an eighteenth-century law of rational mechanics: "Actual descent equals potential ascent."

Taken by itself, the verbal statement of the law . . . is virtually impotent. Present it to a contemporary student of physics, who knows the words and can do all these problems but now employs different means. Then imagine what the words, though all well known, can have said to a man who did not know even the problems. For him the generalization could begin to function only when he learned to recognize "actual descents" and "potential ascents" as ingredients of nature, and that is to learn something, prior to the law, about the situations that nature does and does not present. That sort of learning is not acquired by exclusively verbal means. Rather it comes as one is given words together with concrete examples of how they function in use. . . . To borrow . . . Michael Polanyi's useful phrase, what results from this process is "tacit knowledge" which is learned by doing science rather than by acquiring rules for doing it.[15]

In another place Kuhn characterizes this process as one "of learning by finger exercise" and identifies it with "the process of professional initiation."[16] The generality of this assertion can be seen immediately when one considers what happens in the first year of law school (or, for that matter, in the first year of graduate study in English). The student studies not rules but cases, pieces of practice, and what he or she acquires are not abstractions but something like "know-how" or "the ropes," the ability to identify (not upon reflection, but immediately) a crucial issue, to ask a relevant question, and to propose an appropriate answer from a range of appropriate answers. Somewhere along the way the student will also begin to formulate rules or, more properly, general principles, but will be able to produce and understand them only because he or she is deeply inside—indeed, is a part of—the context in which they become intelligible.

II   Independence and Constraint

To have said as much is already to have taken the next step in my argument. In the course of explaining why rules cannot serve as constraints on interpretation, I have explained why rules (in that strong sense) are not necessary; and in the course of explaining why rules are unnecessary, I also have explained why the fear of unbridled interpretation— of interpreters whose determinations of meaning are unconstrained—is baseless.[17] It is this fear that animates Fiss's entire enterprise, but it is a fear that assumes an interpreter who is at least theoretically free to determine meaning in any way he or she likes, and who therefore must be constrained by something *external,* by rules or laws. But on the analysis offered in the preceding paragraphs there can be no such interpreter. To be, as I have put it, "deeply inside" a context is to be already and always thinking (and perceiving) with and within the norms, standards, definitions, routines, and understood goals that both define and are defined by that context.

The point is an important one because it clarifies the relationship between my argument and Fiss's (which is not simply one of opposition, as it is, for example, in the dispute between Fiss and Sanford Levinson).[18] The notion of disciplining rules is crucial to Fiss's account because it represents for him the chief constraint on the process of adjudication; and by taking away the firmness and independence of those rules I may seem to have undermined the process altogether by leaving an undisciplined interpreter confronting a polysemous text, with nothing between them to assure that the assignment of meaning will proceed in one direction rather than another. But these consequences follow only if readers and texts are in need of the constraints that disciplining rules would provide, and the implication of what I have already said is that they are not.

To see why they are not, one must remember that Fiss's account takes the form it does because he begins by assuming two kinds of independence, one good and one bad. The bad kind of independence attaches to readers and texts: Readers are free to choose any meanings they like, and texts contain too many meanings to guarantee a principled choice. The good kind of independence attaches to rules: Because they stand outside of or are prior to a field of interpretive practice, they can guide and control it in appropriate ways. The good kind of independence controls and disciplines the bad. My contention is that by showing why the good kind of independence can never be achieved, I have shown at the same time why the bad kind is never a possibility. Just as rules can be read only in the context of the practice they supposedly order, so are those who have learned to read them constrained by the assumptions and categories of understanding embodied in that same practice. It is these assumptions and categories that have been internalized in the course of training, a process at the end of which the trainee is not only possessed *of* but possessed *by* a knowledge of the ropes, by a tacit knowledge that tells him not so much what to do, but already has him doing it as a condition of perception and even of thought. The person who looks about and sees, without reflection, a field already organized by problems, impending decisions, possible courses of action, goals, consequences, desiderata, etc., is not free to choose or originate his own meanings because a set of meanings has, in a sense, already chosen him and is working itself out in the actions of perception, interpretation, judgment, etc., he is even now performing. He is, in short, already filled with and constituted by the very meanings that on Fiss's account he is dangerously free to ignore. This amounts finally to no more, or less, than saying that the agent is always and already situated, and that to be situated is not to be looking about for constraints, or happily evading them (in the mode, supposedly, of nihilism), but to be already constrained. To be a judge or a basketball player is not to be able to consult the rules (or, alternatively, to be able to disregard them) but to have become an extension of the know-how that gives the rules (if there happen to be any) the meaning they will immediately and obviously have.[19]

Of course, what holds for the rules holds too for every other "text" encountered in a field of practice, including the text with which Fiss is most concerned, the Constitution. Fiss believes that texts present the same liabilities (the liabilities of independence) as interpreters. Interpreters have too many choices; texts have too many meanings. "[F]or any text," he says, "there are any number of possible meanings and the interpreter creates a meaning by choosing one."[20] I have tried to show why this is the wrong account of the position occupied by interpreters, and I shall now show why it is also (and for the same reasons) the wrong account of texts. Although Fiss says that any text has any number of possible meanings, we have already seen that for his system to work there must be at least some texts—that is, disciplining rules—that have only one meaning, and we have seen too that (1) there are no such texts, and (2) the fact that there are no such texts is not fatal to the goal of principled interpretive behavior. The reason that this fact is not fatal is that there are also no texts that have a plurality of meanings, so that there is never a necessity of having to choose between them.

Now I know that this will seem immediately paradoxical. How can there be at once no texts that have a single meaning and no texts that have many meanings, and how can this impossible state of affairs (even if it could exist) be seen as a *solution* to the problem of interpretation? The answer to this question will emerge once we are no longer in the grip of the assumption that gives rise to the paradox, the assumption that texts "have" properties before they are encountered in situations, which is also the assumption that it is possible to encounter texts in anything but an already situated—that is, interpreted—condition. It is this assumption that impels the project of formal linguistics, the project of specifying the properties of sentences as they exist in an acontextual state, so that one could finally distinguish in a principled way between sentences that were straightforward, ambiguous, multiply ambiguous, etc. But as I have argued elsewhere,[21] sentences never appear in any but an already contextualized form, and a sentence one hears as ambiguous (for example, "I like her cooking")[22] is simply a sentence for which one is imagining, at the moment of hearing, more than one set of contextual circumstances. Any sentence can be heard in that way, but there are conditions under which such imaginings are not being encouraged (although they are still possible), and under these conditions any sentence can be heard as having only a single obvious meaning. The point is that these conditions (of ambiguity and straightforwardness) are not linguistic, but contextual or institutional. That is to say, a sentence does not ask to be read in a particular way because it is a particular kind of sentence; rather, it is only in particular sets of circumstances that sentences are encountered at all, and the properties that sentences display are always a function of those circumstances. Since those circumstances (the conditions within which hearing and reading occur) can change, the properties that sentences display can also change; and it follows that when there is a disagreement about the shape or meaning of a sentence, it is a disagreement between persons who are reading or hearing (and therefore constituting) it according to the assumptions of different circumstances.

Everything that I have said about sentences applies equally, *mutatis mutandis,* to texts. If there are debates about what the Constitution means, it is not because the Constitution "provokes" debate, not because it is a certain *kind* of text, but because for persons reading (constituting) it within the assumption of different circumstances, different meanings will seem obvious and inescapable. By "circumstances" I mean, among other things, the very sense one has of what the Constitution is *for.* Is it an instrument for enforcing the intentions of the framers?[23] Is it a device for assuring the openness of the political process?[24] Is it a blueprint for the exfoliation of a continually evolving set of fundamental values?[25] Depending on the interpreter's view of what the Constitution is for, he will be inclined to ask different questions, to consider different bodies of information as sources of evidence, to regard different lines of inquiry as relevant or irrelevant, and, finally, to reach different determinations of what the Constitution "plainly" means. Notice, how-

ever, that these differences are not infinite; at any one time there are
only so many views as to what the Constitution is for;[26] and therefore
even those who are proceeding within different views and arguing for
different meanings are constrained in their proceedings by the shared
(if tacit) knowledge that (1) the number of such views is limited, and
(2) they are all views of the *Constitution,* a document whose centrality
is assumed by all parties to the debate. (Here is a way in which it does
make a kind of sense to say that the Constitution "provokes" debate—
not because of any properties it "has," but because the position it occupies in the enterprise is such that specification of its meaning is the
business everyone is necessarily in.) Even when the central text of the
enterprise is in dispute, all parties to the dispute are already situated
within the enterprise, and the ways of disputing and the versions of the
Constitution produced by those ways are "enterprise-specific." What this
means is that the Constitution is never in the condition that occasions
the urgency of Fiss's essay—it is never an object waiting around for interpretation; rather, it is always an already-interpreted object, even
though the interpretations it has received and the forms it has taken
are in conflict with one another.

How are these conflicts to be settled? The answer to this question
is that they are always in the process of being settled, and that no transcendent or algorithmic method of interpretation is required to settle
them. The means of settling them are political, social, and institutional,
in a mix that is itself subject to modification and change. This means, of
course, that the *arena* of settling is never purely internal; and, indeed,
the distinction between the internal and the external is in general less
firm and stable than Fiss assumes. He makes the point that judgments
concerning the law are sometimes made from an "external perspective"
by someone who is operating "on the basis of some religious or ethical
principle (such as denying the relevance of any racial distinction) or on
the grounds of some theory of politics (such as condemning the decision
because it will cause social unrest)."[27] In such instances, he concludes,
"the evaluation is not in terms of the law."[28] Well, yes and no. If Fiss
means by this that the evaluation originates from a source that is not
part of the "judicial system," narrowly conceived, then his statement is
both true and trivial; but if he means that an evaluation emanating from
some social, political, religious, or moral concern is not a legal one,
then he is propounding a notion of the law that is as positivistic as it is
impossible. Instead, one might say (to take up just one of Fiss's exam-

ples) that the desire to avoid social unrest is one of the enabling conditions of law; it is one of the tacitly assumed "goods" that dictates the shape of the law even when particular laws nowhere refer to it. For the most part the stated purpose of a statute is the regulation of some precisely defined set of activities in industry or public life (for instance, traffic laws); but it is some unstated general purpose on the order of "avoiding social unrest" that impels the very attempt at regulation and determines the details of the statute as it is finally written. The content of the law, even when its manifestation is a statute that seems to be concerned with only the most technical and mechanical of matters (taxes, for example), is always some social, moral, political, or religious vision; and when someone objects to a decision "on the basis of some ethical or religious principle," his objection is not "external" to the law (except in the narrow procedural sense acknowledged above), but represents an effort to alter the law, so that one's understanding of what was internal to it would be different. If that alteration were effected, it would not be because the structure of the law had been made to bend to the pressure of some moral or political perspective, but because a structure *already* moral and political had been given another moral and political shape.

How might that happen? Just as Fiss says it would, when he enumerates the courses of action available to the "external critic": "He may move to amend the Constitution or engage in any number of lesser and more problematic strategies designed to alter the legal standards, such as packing the court or enacting statutes that curtail jurisdiction."[29] However, in calling these latter strategies "lesser" and "more problematic," Fiss once again assumes a distinction that cannot be maintained. Presumably they are "lesser" and "more problematic" because they are more obviously political; but in fact the entire system is political, and the question at any moment is: From which point in the system is pressure being applied, and to what other points? It is no more illegitimate to enact statutes or to make appointments than it is to engage in the slower and less theatrical activity of amending the Constitution. The processes for executing any of these courses of action are already in place, and they have been put in place by political acts. The fact that one rather than another course is taken reflects the conditions obtaining in the entire system, not a bypassing of the system or an unwarranted intrusion on proper legal procedure.

Consider, for example, the course of "packing the Court." That phrase, now laden with pejorative connotations, refers to an attempt by

Franklin Delano Roosevelt to assure that the ethical and social philosophy informing the Court's decisions was similar to his own. Roosevelt made that attempt not as an anarchist or an outlaw but as a political agent whose actions were subject to the approval or disapproval of other political agents, all of whom were operating within a system of constraints that made it possible for him to do something but not everything. In other words, "packing the Court" is a possible legal strategy, but it can be successful only if other parts of the legal system assist it or fail to block it. The fact that Roosevelt was in fact blocked is not to be explained by saying that a "lesser" strategy was foiled by a legitimate one, but by saying that the political forces always at work in the system exist in ever-changing relationships of strength and influence. (It is not the case that because Roosevelt was unable to do it, it can never be done; but it is true that doing it has been made harder by the fact that he tried and failed.)

At times the disposition of the entire system will be such that the judiciary can settle constitutional questions by routine procedures and in accordance with principles that have been long articulated and accepted; at other times the legislature or the executive will feel called upon to intervene strongly in an attempt to alter those principles and institute new procedures. The mistake is to think that one state of affairs is normative and "legal" while the other is extraordinary and "external." Both are perfectly legal and normative; they simply represent different proportions of the mix of agencies that participate in the ongoing project of determining what the Constitution is. The same analysis holds for the oft-opposed policies of judicial restraint and judicial activism. It is often assumed that the one indicates a respect for the Constitution while the other is an unwarranted exercise of interpretive power, as influenced by social and political views; but, in fact, so-called judicial restraint is exercised by those judges who, for a variety of reasons, decide to leave in place the socially and politically based interpretations of the activists of an earlier generation.

III   Interpretive Authority and Power

It is time, I think, to take stock and look back at the argument as it has unfolded so far. The first thing to recall is that Fiss's account of adjudication is inspired by the fear that interpretation will be unprincipled, either because (1) the "interaction" between the reader and the text is not sufficiently constrained by rules that put limits on the freedom of the one and the polysemy of the other, or because (2) interpretive authority is simply a function of the power wielded by those who happen to occupy dominant positions in certain political or bureaucratic structures. I have argued against the first version of this fear by pointing out that readers and texts are never in a state of independence such that they would need to be "disciplined" by some external rule. Since readers are already and always thinking within the norms, standards, criteria of evidence, purposes, and goals of a shared enterprise, the meanings available to them have been preselected by their professional training; they are thus never in the position of confronting a text that has not already been "given" a meaning by the *interested* perceptions they have become. More generally, whereas Fiss thinks that readers and texts are in need of constraints, I would say that they are *structures* of constraint, at once components of and agents in the larger structure of a field of practices, practices that are the content of whatever "rules" one might identify as belonging to the enterprise. At every point, then, I am denying the independence (of both the "good" and "bad" kinds) that leads Fiss first to see a problem and then to propose its solution.

The second version of Fiss's fear—that the law may be nothing but "masked power"[30]—is merely a bogeyman reformulation of the first, and it can be disposed of in the same way. By "masked power" Fiss means authority that is not related to any true principle, but that instead represents a "mere" exercise of some official will. The opposition surfaces most revealingly when Fiss contrasts two claims that a judge might make in his efforts to secure obedience to a decision. In the best of circumstances the judge may base his claim "on a theory of virtue," but in some situations he "may have to assert the authoritativeness that proceeds from institutional power alone."[31] Once again the mistake is to imagine two pure entities—"institutional virtue" and "institutional power"[32]—which can then be further conceived of as alternative and mutually exclusive bases for action in a community. And, once again, the way to see past the mistake is to challenge the independence of *either* entity.

To begin with "institutional virtue": What exactly would that be? The answer is that it would be precisely *institutional,* virtue defined not in some abstract or asituational way, but in terms of the priorities, agreed-upon needs, and long- and short-term goals of an ongoing social and political project. It would, in short, be virtue in relation to the perspective of an enterprise, and an appeal to it would be compelling only to someone with a commitment to that enterprise. To that same someone the threat of a contempt proceeding or some other punitive action would be no less compelling, and for the same reason. That is to say, the person who on one occasion complies with a decision because he agrees with it and on another occasion because of a judicial threat is in each instance signifying his commitment to the legal institution and its principles. Adherence to the rule of law does not mean agreement with its decisions but a respect for its procedures and its power, including the power to fine, to cite, and to imprison. Such power is not, as Fiss believes, a matter of "brute force," even when its instruments are "rifles, clubs, and tear gas,"[33] but is instead an extension of the standards and norms—indeed, of the "theory of virtue"—that inform the decision in the first place. "Institutional power" is just another (and unflattering) name for an obligation, inherent in an office, to decide this or enforce that, and therefore it is not something extrinsic to a principled enterprise but is itself principled.

This is not to say that there are no differences between immediate compliance and compliance under threat, or compliance in the form of undergoing incarceration. The differences are real, but they cannot simply be characterized as the difference between obedience to a principle and obedience to brute force. Neither the principle, which is authoritative (i.e., *forceful*) only because of the political enactment (sometimes following upon revolution) of some vision or agenda, nor the force, which is an etiolated version of the authority vested in the principle, can be sufficiently distinguished in a way that would make the one a threat to the integrity of the other. Of course, force can be abused—I am not proposing anything as crude as "might makes right"—but the decision that it has been abused is itself an institutional one, and such a decision implicitly entails the recognition that under certain well-defined institutional circumstances force is legitimate and—in terms of the institution's assumed goals and purposes—even virtuous.

The opposition between legitimate (virtue-based) and illegitimate (power-based) authority is for Fiss part of a broader opposition between authority of any kind and interpretation:

It is important to note that the claim of authoritativeness, whether it be predicated on virtue or power, is extrinsic to the process of interpretation. It does not arise from the act of interpretation itself and is sufficient to distinguish the judge from the literary critic or moral philosopher who must rely on intellectual authority alone.[34]

Obviously there is a harmless (and trivial) sense in which what Fiss says is true: Arriving at a judicial decision and subsequently enforcing it are distinct processes, in the sense that the one precedes the other; but to say that one is *extrinsic* to the other is to attribute to both of them an independence and purity that neither could have. That is to say, neither "arises" from the other, since they both "arise" from the same set of institutional imperatives. Interpretation is not an abstract or contextless process, but one that elaborates itself in the service of a specific enterprise, in this case the enterprise of the law; the interpretive "moves" that occur to a judge, for example, occur to him in a shape already informed by a general sense of what the law is *for,* of what its operations are intended to promote and protect. Even when particulars are the subject of debate, it is that general sense that legitimizes interpretation, because it is the content of interpretation. As we have seen, it is that same general sense that legitimizes (because it is the content of) authority, whether of the virtue-based or power-based variety. To put the matter starkly, interpretation is a form of authority, since it is an extension of the prestige and power of an institution; and authority is a form of interpretation, since it is in its operations an application or "reading" of the principles embodied in that same institution. So while it is possible to distinguish between these two activities on a narrow procedural level (on the level, for example, of temporal precedence), it is not possible to distinguish between them as activities essentially different in kind.

Nor is it possible to distinguish between the law and literary criticism or philosophy by saying that practitioners of the latter "must rely on intellectual authority alone."[35] Again, there is a fairly low-level sense in which this is true: The decisions or interpretations of literary critics and philosophers are not backed up by the machinery of a court. But Fiss means more by "intellectual authority"; he means the authority exerted by arguments that make their way simply by virtue of a superior rationality and do not depend for their impact on the lines of power and influence operating in an institution.[36] That kind of authority, I submit, does not exist. In literary studies, for example, one possible reason for hearkening to an interpretation is the institutional position occupied by the man or woman who proposes it, the fact that he or she has a record of successfully made (that is, influential) arguments, or is known as the editor of a standard text, or is identified with an important "approach," or is highly placed in a professional organization (a department, a professional society), or all of the above. These and other institutional facts are not external to the issue of intellectual authority, because the very shape of intellectual authority—in the form of "powerful" arguments and "decisive" evidence and "compelling" reasons—has been established (not for all time, but for a season) by the same processes that have established these facts—by publications, public appearances, pedagogical influence, etc. When a Northrop Frye or a Jacques Derrida speaks, it is with all the considerable weight of past achievements, battles fought and won, constituencies created, agendas proposed and enacted; and that weight is inseparable from the "intellectual" decision to "comply" with what they have said. Of course, Frye and Derrida cannot call in the judiciary or the Congress or the president of the United States to implement their interpretations, but there are other means of implementation at their disposal and at the disposal of their adherents. They can influence decisions about tenure, promotion, publications, grants, leaves, appointments, prizes, teaching assignments, etc. Although the "compliance" secured by these and other means is more diffuse and less direct than the compliance secured by a judge, it is rooted in authority nevertheless, and this authority, like that wielded in the law, is *at once* intellectual and institutional. This is not to deny that literary and legal practice are importantly different, but their differences cannot be captured by drawing the kind of line Fiss draws.

It may seem that by collapsing so many distinctions—between the intellectual and the institutional, between authority and power, between virtue and authority—I am undermining the possibility of rational adjudication; but, in fact, everything I have said points to the conclusion that adjudication does not need these distinctions (any more than it needs "disciplining rules") to be rational. All it needs is an understanding, largely tacit, of the enterprise's general purpose; with that in place (and it could not help but be) everything else follows. Fiss knows this too, but not in a way that figures strongly in his analysis. He knows, for example, that "[a] judge quickly learns to read in a way that avoids crises,"[37] and that "[t]he judge must give a remedy";[38] but he does not recognize such facts for what they are: the very motor of adjudication and a guarantee of its orderliness. The judge who has learned to read in a way that avoids crises is a judge who has learned what it means to be a judge, and has learned that the maintenance of continuity is a prime judicial obligation because without continuity the rule of law cannot claim to be stable and rooted in durable principles. It is not simply that crisis would be disruptive of the process, but that crisis and disruption are precisely what the process is supposed to forestall. That is why the judge must give a remedy: not only because the state, defendant, and plaintiff have a right to one, but also because every time a remedy is given the message is repeated that there is always a remedy to be found, and that the law thereby underwrites and assures the ongoing and orderly operations of society.

The situation is exactly the reverse in literary studies, at least in the context of a modernist aesthetic where the rule is that a critic must learn to read in a way that *multiplies* crises, and must never give a remedy in the sense of a single and unequivocal answer to the question, "What does this poem or novel or play mean?" This rule is nowhere written down, and the ways of following it are nowhere enumerated. But it is a rule inherent in the discipline's deepest beliefs about the objects of its attention, in its deepest understanding of what literary works are for—for contemplation, for the reflective exploration of complexity, for the entertainment of many perspectives, for the *suspension of judgment*. Critics who hold these beliefs (and, for many, to hold them or be held by them is what it means to be a critic) interrogate texts assumed to be literary in such a way as to "reveal" the properties—ambiguity, irony, multivalence—a literary text is supposed to have. That is to say, the procedures of literary criticism—its methods of inquiry, notions of evidence, mechanisms for evaluation—flow naturally from a sense, already in place, of what literature is and should be; and it follows that these same procedures are not in need of any external or independent constraints to assure their orderliness. A literary critic faced with an interpretive task always knows in general what to do (find interpretive crises), although the ways of doing it will vary with the circumstances, with his commitment to this or that methodology, with the currently received wisdom about a text or a period, with the scope of the project (a teaching of a single poem, of an entire oeuvre, of a genre, of a period). And, by the same reasoning, a judge always knows in general what to do (avoid crises, give a remedy), although his ways of doing it will vary with the nature of the case, with the forces (political, social, legislative) pressing for this or that decision, with the (interpreted) history of previous decisions.[39]

In neither discipline, then, does rationality depend on the presence of "disciplining rules"; nor is the shape of rationality a function of different kinds of texts. Legal texts might be written in verse or take the form of narratives or parables (as they have in some cultures); but so long at the underlying rationales of the enterprise were in place, so long as it was understood (at a level too deep to require articulation) that judges give remedies and avoid crises, those texts would be explicated so as to yield the determinate or settled result the law requires. In both law and literature it is ways of reading, inseparable from the fact of the institution itself, and not rules or special kinds of texts that validate and justify the process of rational interpretation, whether it leads to the rendering of a clear-cut legal decision or to the demonstration that what is valuable about a poem is its resolute refusal to decide.

All of which is to say that, while I stand with Fiss in his desire to defend adjudication in the face of "nihilist" and "subjectivist" arguments, I do not believe that this defense need take the form of asserting a set of external constraints, because the necessary constraints are always already in place. Indeed, I would put the case even more strongly: It is not just that the dangers Fiss would guard against—the dangers of excessive interpretive freedom, of "masked power," of random or irresponsible activity—have been neutralized, but that they are *unrealizable,* because the conditions that would make them the basis of a reasonable fear—the condition of free subjectivity, of "naturally" indeterminate texts, of unprincipled authority—could never obtain; the "worst-case" scenario that Fiss calls up in his penultimate paragraph could never unfold:

> The great public text of modern America, the Constitution, would be drained of meaning. It would be debased. It would no longer be seen as embodying a public morality to be understood and expressed through rational processes like adjudication; it would be reduced to a mere instrument of political organization—distributing political power and establishing the modes by which that power will be exercised. Public values would be defined only as those held by the current winners in the processes prescribed by the Constitution; beyond that, there would be only individual morality, or even worse, only individual interests.[40]

Were I to attempt a full-fledged analysis of this paragraph, I would find myself repeating everything I have said thus far, for it has been the business of this essay to redefine and recharacterize every one of the concepts and entities Fiss here invokes. On my analysis the Constitution cannot be drained of meaning because it is not a repository of meaning; rather, meaning is always being conferred on it by the very political and institutional forces Fiss sees as threats. Nor can these forces be described as "mere," because their shape and exercise are constrained by the very principles they supposedly endanger. And, since the operation of these forces is indeed principled, the fact that they determine (for a time) what will be thought of as "public values" is not something to be lamented, but simply a reflection of the even more basic fact that values derive from the political and social visions that are always competing with one another for control of the state's machinery. Moreover, such values are never "individual," since they always have their source in some conventional system of purposes, goals, and standards; therefore, the very notion of "merely individual" interests is empty.[41] In short, if *these* are the fears that animate Fiss's efforts, then there is nothing for him to worry about.

Paradoxically, he need not even be worried by the possibility that his account of adjudication might be wrong. Fiss believes that it is important to get things right because, if we don't, nihilism might triumph. Nihilism must therefore be "combated" in "word and in deed" because it "calls into question the very point of constitutional adjudication."[42] But if I am right, nihilism is impossible; one simply cannot "exalt the . . . subjective dimension of interpretation"[43] or drain texts of meanings, and it is unnecessary to combat something that is not possible. Of course, there may be people who regard themselves as nihilists or subjectivists (whether these are the people who promote "deconstruction" is the subject of another essay), and who try to instruct others in nihilist ways, but the fact that they intend the impossible does not make them capable of doing it; they would simply be conferring meanings and urging courses of action on the basis of principles they had not fully comprehended. One could, of course, combat those principles and dispute those meanings; but in doing so one would simply be urging alternative courses of action, not combating nihilism.

Another way of putting this is to say that nothing turns on Fiss's account or, for that matter, on my account either. To be sure, one would rather be right than wrong, but in this case being right or wrong has no consequences for the process we are both trying to describe.[44] Fiss thinks otherwise; he thinks that there are consequences and that they are grave ones: "Viewing adjudication as interpretation helps to stop the slide toward nihilism. It makes law possible."[45] But if the slide toward nihilism is not a realizable danger, the urging of nihilist views cannot accelerate it, and, conversely, the refutation of nihilist views cannot retard it. From either direction, the account one has of adjudication is logically independent of one's ability to engage in it. Your account may be nihilist or (as it is for Fiss) objectivist or (as it is for me) conventionalist, and when all is said and done, adjudication is still either possible or it is not. The empirical evidence is very strong that it is; and it has been my argument that its possibility is a consequence of being situated in a field of practice, of having passed through a professional initiation or course of training and become what the sociologists term a "competent member." Owen Fiss has undergone that training, but I have not; and, therefore, even though I believe that his account of adjudication is wrong and mine is right, anyone who is entering the legal process would be well-advised to consult Fiss rather than Fish.

7. Change

The notion of "interpretive communities" was originally introduced as an answer to a question that had long seemed crucial to literary studies. What is the source of interpretive authority: the text or the reader? Those who answered "the text" were embarrassed by the fact of disagreement. Why, if the text contains its own meaning and constrains its own interpretation, do so many interpreters disagree about that meaning? Those who answered "the reader" were embarrassed by the fact of agreement. Why, if meaning is created by the individual reader from the perspective of his own experience and interpretive desires, is there so much that interpreters agree about? What was required was an explanation that could account for both agreement and disagreement, and that explanation was found in the idea of an interpretive community, not so much a group of individuals who shared a point of view, but a point of view or way of organizing experience that shared individuals in the sense that its assumed distinctions, categories of understanding, and stipulations of relevance and irrelevance were the content of the consciousness of community members who were therefore no longer individuals, but, insofar as they were embedded in the community's enterprise, community property. It followed that such community-constituted interpreters would, in their turn, constitute, more or less in agreement, the same text, although the sameness would not be attributable to the self-identity of the text, but to the communal nature of the interpretive act. Of course, if the same act were performed by members of another community—of some rival school of criticism informed by wholly different assumptions—the resulting text would be different, and there would be disagreement; not, however, a disagreement that could be settled by the text because what would be in dispute would be the interpretive "angle" from which the text was to be seen, and in being seen, made. In this new vision both texts and readers lose the independence that would be necessary for either of them to claim the honor of being the source of interpretive authority; both are absorbed by the interpretive community which, because it is responsible for all acts interpreters can possibly perform, is finally responsible for the texts those performances bring into the world.

In the years since *Is There a Text in This Class?* was published, this argument has been variously criticized, and one criticism frequently heard is that the privileging of the interpretive community leaves us without an adequate account of change. This objection takes different forms, according to the political disposition of the critic; from the right comes the complaint that an interpretive community, unconstrained by any responsibility to a determinate text, can simply declare a change without consulting anything but its own desires; this is the burden of an essay by Walter Davis entitled "The Fisher King: *Wille zur Macht* in Baltimore."[1] From the left comes the complaint that an interpretive community, enclosed in the armor of its own totalizing assumptions, is impervious to change and acts only to perpetuate itself and its interests; in this view the business of an interpretive community and of the theory that privileges it is the legitimization of the status quo. The two accusations, different as they are, articulate a fear that is based on the same assumption, the assumption that an interpretive community is monolithic and is therefore a new kind of object in relation to which the problem of interpretation is not resolved but merely reinscribed. It is that assumption, I think, that must be challenged, but before challenging it I would first like to look more closely at the process by which change has come to be seen as a problem, as something to be accounted for rather than as a simple and obvious fact of life.

The first thing to note is that under an older (and by no means entirely discredited) epistemology—which we may for convenience label essentialist or foundationalist—change is not a problem at all because it follows naturally from a certain picture of the scene of interpretation. In that picture the landscape is dominated by two discrete and independent entities—the world of objects, in all of its details, and the perceiving self—and mediating between them is some vocabulary or methodology by means of which what is perceived is given a discursive form. In literary terms this means a text, a reader, and a system of description that reflects a fully articulated universe, complete with genres, periods, styles, a canon, major and minor authors, questions, answers, projects, desiderata, unthinkable thoughts, etc. The goal of criticism under this picture is to give an accurate account of the text, and changes either mark progress toward that goal or (as it is determined later and by hindsight) a retrograde movement in the opposite direction. Progress is made when the machinery of description is refined, when its definitions, categories, levels, etc., have been brought into a closer correspondence with the facts of the text; progress is impeded when that machinery is informed by the bias of an individual observer or a partisan group. The check against interpretive bias is the text, which is therefore at once the object to be described and the judge of which of its descriptions is the more accurate. Change, then, is a function of a text's operation as a regulating and adjudicative principle, and in the best scenario, when the text has fully completed its judicial work, the correct description will have been achieved and change will have ceased.

The comfortable outlines of this picture are blurred, however, when one substitutes for this foundationalist epistemology an epistemology in which the object to be described cannot be sharply distinguished from the descriptive vocabulary that seems appropriate to it. This is the consequence of a number of arguments that have been made in the last twenty years with increasing success. One could cite Kuhn's contention in *The Structure of Scientific Revolutions*[2] that since "a paradigm is prerequisite to perception itself" and all descriptive languages are paradigm-specific, our inquiries always "presuppose a world already perceptually and conceptually divided in a certain way," and we are never in the position of being able to compare that way with a world apprehended independently of any paradigm whatsoever. Or one could refer to Nelson Goodman's assertion in *Ways of Worldmaking*[3] that if "I ask about the world, you can offer to tell me how it is under one or more frames of reference, but if I insist that you tell me how it is apart from all frames," there is nothing you can say, because our universe consists of "ways of describing . . . rather than of a world of worlds." Or one could listen to Richard Rorty as he declares with characteristic brusqueness in *The Consequences of Pragmatism*[4] that "there is no way to think about either the world or our purposes except by using our language," no way "of breaking out of language to compare it with something else." Or we could even attend to Stanley Fish when he argues in *Is There a Text in This Class?* and elsewhere[5] that we cannot check our interpretive accounts against the facts of the text because it is only within our accounts—that is, within an already assumed set of stipulative definitions and evidentiary criteria—that the text and its facts, or, rather, *a* text and its facts, emerge and become available for inspection. These are only representative formulations, and there are distinctions to be made between them, but I think it is fair to say that one consequence of following their general line is to make a problem out of change; for it is no longer possible to see change as occurring when the world or a piece of the world forces us to revise or correct our description of it; since descriptions of the world are all we have, changes can only be understood as change in description, and we are left with the task of explaining not only how they come about, but why they should ever come about in the first place.

Nor is that the worst of it. Not only is there insufficient distance in this newer model between the community and the object of its attention; there is also insufficient distance between the community and its methods. The traditional understanding of change assumes and requires not only the independence of entities from our representations of them, but the independence of our representations from the criteria by which they are judged; but if those criteria, those measures of adequacy and accuracy, are no less community- or paradigm-specific than the facts they are intended to measure, confirmation or validation would seem to be at once assured and empty. And since the procedures of validation, the description to be validated, and the object in relation to which validity is to be assessed are homologous, the analyst who uses the perspective of any one to get a purchase on the others is apparently engaged in a circular and futile exercise. Indeed, the very notion of the analyst as a discrete agent is called into question when he is seen not as an independent consciousness capable of turning a disinterested eye on the alternatives that vie for his attention, but as an already embedded practitioner whose standards of judgment, canons of evidence, or normative measures are extensions of the community or communities of which he is a member.

One begins to see that there are now not one, but several, problems of change. First, there is the problem of *what* changes if the world and its objects are not independent of the characterizations we make of them; then there is the problem of how change can be principled if nothing constrains the community except its own assumptions and procedures, and this leads directly to the puzzle of individual change: how can someone whose perceptions and judgments are delimited by the norms, criteria, and definitions of an interpretive community take note of anything that would lead him to revise those norms, criteria, and definitions? How can a mind that cannot see anything beyond its horizon change? It would seem that it must be the case either that: (1) the mind is, in fact, able to take into account something not already presupposed by its assumptions, or that (2) the mind remains forever confined within the circle of community assumptions. The first alternative has the disadvantage of enfeebling (and indeed emptying) the notion of an interpretive community, which loses its claim to authority if the shape of its own activity is constrained by independent facts. The second alternative has the disadvantage of forcing us to the (counterintuitive) conclusion that no one has ever changed his mind.

There is a way, I think, to escape these alternatives, and I will approach it by recalling an occasion on which just these questions were put, and put by someone whose behavior was at that very moment providing an answer. The questioner was a student in a graduate seminar in literary theory who acknowledged that in the course of the semester he had been persuaded to the conventionalist views I have been describing. What bothered him was the very fact that he had been persuaded, for. given those same views, he didn't see how his mind could have been changed. He had, after all, been a member of an interpretive community, and indeed of a *literary* interpretive community, when he entered my class. How is it that he was able to move out of that community and into another? A part of the explanation emerged when I asked him what would have happened if a student in one of his own classes—he was then teaching an introductory literature course in the same department—had challenged him with arguments like those I had been making. He responded by saying that in all likelihood he would have moved to disarm the student's objections either by invoking a distinction she had failed to take into account or by demonstrating that properly understood his own position already included hers or by some other strategy that had the effect of protecting and recuperating the assumptions underlying the routines and procedures of the class. What he would not have been inclined to do (although, as we shall see, there are conditions under which his inclinations would have been different) was consider his student's remarks as the occasion for a thoroughgoing rethinking of everything he believed about literature, the status of the text, the sources of interpretive authority, or the origins of genres. That, however, is exactly what he had done as a student in my course, and the reason, or at least one reason, for his having done so was that among his beliefs was the belief that challenges from some directions should be taken more seriously than challenges from others. I am not suggesting that the mere fact of my position as instructor was sufficient to make my assertions the stimulus to change; it is easy to imagine an instructor who did not command respect because he had not thought through the implications of his argument or, from the other side, a student whose performance had been so impressive that an instructor would feel obliged to come to terms with anything she said. But in any of these circumstances it would still be the case that change, in the form of the reconsideration of received opinion, would be prompted by a suggestion that came from a source assumed in advance to be, if not authoritative, at least weighty.

One could say, then, that in the course of the semester my student was induced by one belief—a belief in the likely authority of some members of the community relative to others—to change another belief, or in this case a set of beliefs, about the nature and shape of interpretation. Putting it this way allows us to see that beliefs are not all held at the same level or operative at the same time. Beliefs, if I may use a metaphor, are nested, and on occasion they may affect and even alter one another and so alter the entire system or network they comprise. Even though the mind is informed by assumptions that limit what it can even notice, among those is the assumption that one's assumptions are subject to challenge and possible revision under certain circumstances and according to certain procedures when they are set in motion by certain persons. What this means is that the mind is not a static structure, but an assemblage of related beliefs any one of which can exert pressure on any other in a motion that can lead to a self-transformation. In short, and this is a formulation to which I shall return, rather than being an object of which one might ask, "how does it change," the mind (and, by extension, the community) is an engine of change, an ongoing project whose operations are at once constrained and the means by which those same constraints can be altered.

Those operations are not limited to the formal institutional setting of the present example. Change does not require confrontation in a highly defined and hierarchical situation like the classroom. It can occur when no one else is present, in the privacy of one's room. Suppose, for example, that you were reading something that was, as far as you were consciously aware, unrelated to your professional views and concerns, an essay in another field or in an entirely different discipline or in no "discipline" whatsoever; and suppose further that it occurred to you suddenly that what you were reading had a direct bearing on your own work and even indicated to you the necessity of revising your understanding of what was involved in that work. This is an experience that most of us will have had, and on its face it would seem to be quite different from the experience of the student in my seminar; for rather than the interaction of two agents or elements in the same framework or community, it would seem that in this imagined situation someone operating from within a framework or a community had been moved to change by something wholly outside that framework or community.

But, in fact, that something would not have been noticed at all (at least not in this way) if there had not been already in place, as a part of the community's conception of itself, the assumption of a relationship between it and some neighboring body of knowledge. That is, in order for a formulation from economics or mathematics or anthropology to be seen as related to a problem or project in literary studies, literary studies would themselves have to be understood in such a way that the arguments and conclusions of economics or mathematics or anthropology were already seen by practitioners as at least potentially relevant. To put the matter in what only seems to be a paradox, when a community is provoked to change by something outside it, that something will already have been inside, in the sense that the angle of its notice— the angle from which it is related to the community's project even before it is seen—will determine its shape, not *after* it has been perceived, but *as* it is perceived. And all of this will follow from the community's understanding of itself as a mode of inquiry responsible to the facts and theorems of some, but not all, other modes of inquiry.

Consider, as a concrete and historical example, the case of linguistics. The period 1957–70 witnessed a remarkable growth in the amount of literary work informed by linguistic principles and models. That was also, not coincidentally, the period of the "Chomskian revolution" and one might think that the conceptual power of Chomsky's formulations, so much the center of discussion in the academy and elsewhere, is sufficient to explain the phenomenon; like so many other intellectuals, literary students simply felt compelled to reconsider their methods and assumptions in the light of something so perspicuously and undeniably far-reaching. In fact, however, that is not what happened at all. Only a small percentage of those working in literary studies was markedly affected by transformational grammar, which came and went without changing at all the way most literary business was done. (This is not to say, of course, that changes were not being brought about in some other way.) Those who did alter their ways of reading and writing did so because they were already committed to a view of criticism in which the close study of linguistic facts was central and obligatory; that is, they were in agreement with Harold Whitehall's declaration in 1951 that "no criticism can go beyond its linguistics,"[6] and therefore when linguistics underwent a profound and apparently authoritative change, they were obliged, by the principles they already held, to change too. Those whose principles and commitments were different, those for whom stylistics, Chomskian or any other, was an interesting but fringe activity, could feel free to continue on as before.

The example illustrates how misleading it is to think of change as the process by which something from the outside penetrates and alters the inside of a community or of a consciousness informed by community assumptions. It is misleading because it assumes that the distinction between outside and inside is empirical and absolute, whereas in fact it is an interpretive distinction between realms that are interdependent rather than discrete. For those who already think of themselves as stylisticians, Chomsky is inside even before he appears on the scene; for those who practiced literary history or some "soft" version of New Criticism, he was outside and has remained so. This does not mean that he was *absolutely* outside, but that he was outside in relation to a set of assumptions concerning what is and is not a piece of literary information. In other words, his status as something or someone outside is conferred by the very community from which he is supposedly distinct; he is an *interpreted* outside, and forms along with other items and persons a general background of irrelevance that defines and is defined by the sense of relevance that informs the community, telling it what it must pay attention to and what it can afford to ignore. When that sense of relevance changes—when the community is persuaded (by arguments that rely on assumptions not at the moment being challenged) that its project requires the taking into account of what had hitherto been considered beside the point or essential only to someone else's point—the boundaries of outside/inside will have been redrawn, and redrawn *from the inside.*

But how can that come about? Why should it come about? Why should someone convinced that the researches of formal linguistics were unrelated to his work ever change his mind, especially when conditions in the institution were such that he could do what he had always done without penalty? The answer lies in the nature of an interpretive community which is at once homogeneous with respect to some general sense of purpose and purview, and heterogeneous with respect to the variety of practices it can accommodate. Any one of those practices exists in some relationship of assumed justification to that general sense; both those who do and those who don't practice stylistics believe that they are engaged in the business of determining the meaning and value of literary texts, and if one wants to persuade the other to his point of view, he will do so by invoking the goal they both acknowledge and arguing that it cannot be reached except by the route he follows. The stylistician will question the possibility of even talking about meaning in the absence of a fully articulated semantics; the nonstylistician will reply that semantics is merely a formalization of what the sensitive and intelligent critic intuits. Each will have recourse to examples that would seem to challenge the other's assumptions, and so it would go until one persuaded the other. Of course, persuasion is not inevitable, but should it occur in either direction, one party will have changed his understanding of what is internal to his discipline, and that change will have come about by mechanisms that are themselves internal.

One could object that this explanation of change is still too narrowly institutional and says nothing, for example, about the changes that can follow upon some momentous political event, a war, a shift in federal policy, an economic crisis, etc. Surely events like these would be external to the literary community or to any other community narrowly conceived, and yet the members of that community would certainly be impelled by them to reconsider and revise their ways of doing business. Well, yes and no. It depends on the extent to which the members of the community see the event in question as one that has a direct bearing on their conception of what they do; and that will depend on whether or not their conception of what they do, their sense of the enterprise, is bound up in an essential way with political issues. Some of us changed our teaching methods and our research priorities markedly during the Vietnam War; others of us went on as before as if nothing were happening. Even the drying up of funds or the elimination from the university of literature departments might be received with equanimity by somone who believed (or thought he believed) that literary studies were best conducted in the privacy of one's study or in an informal colloquium on the model of Socrates, and who therefore might welcome the withering away of a structure and a bureaucracy that served only to overwhelm and subvert the true values of the literary experience. In principle, then, the impact on literary studies of a political revolution would be no different from the impact of a revolution in linguistic theory; both would vary with the extent to which the profession or part of the profession did or did not consider the phenomenon as, at some level, a literary one.

I am now in a position to return to what may have earlier seemed an enigmatic assertion: that an interpretive community, rather than being an object of which one might ask "how does it change?" is an engine of change. It is an engine of change because its assumptions are not a mechanism for shutting out the world but for organizing it, for seeing phenomena as already related to the interests and goals that make the community what it is. The community, in other words, is always engaged in doing work, the work of transforming the landscape into material for its own project; but that project is then itself transformed by the very work it does. The stylistician who reaches out to absorb Chomsky into the structure of his own concerns is at once extending those concerns and altering them in as much as they will wear a different aspect once Chomsky has been assimilated. In the words of the sociologist D. L. Weider, the enterprise, as a moving project or bundle of interests, is both "self and setting elaborative."

Weider's example is a community of ex-convicts who live in a halfway house but continue to abide by the convict code. The heart of that code, the task it at once directs and commands, is the obligation to show loyalty to the residents by displaying resistance to the staff. As an instance of the code at work Weider recalls an occasion when a resident, upon expressing interest in the formation of a house baseball team, was asked by the director to organize one himself. He replied, "You know I can't organize a baseball team" and was immediately understood by both the director and the sociologist to have said, "You know that the code forbids me to participate in your program that way, and you know that I'm not going to violate the code. So why ask me?"[7]

The exchange is illuminating and to my point because the question of organizing a baseball team had not arisen before. This shows that the code is not a list of specific maxims—a closed set of rules that can serve as a self-executing decision procedure—but is rather a general project whose implementation involves the continual discovery of its own content, a discovery that is at the same time the accomplishment of its own alteration. As soon as the resident says what he says and is understood as Weider and the director understand him, two things have happened: (1) the scope of the code has been extended to render intelligible an occurrence it could not have predicted; (2) the code, which is inseparable from the practices it enables (it cannot be reduced to a formal rule), has been augmented or modified and has therefore changed. The code, in short, has done its work of elaborating the setting, and at the same time it has elaborated itself. The code, then, is not a set of explicit directions or a prescriptive description; rather, as Weider points out, it is "part of life in the halfway house, and it [is] a part that [is] itself included within the scope of things over which it [has] jurisdiction." "In this sense," he concludes, "it is more appropriate to think of the code as a continuous, ongoing process, rather than as a set of stable elements of culture which endure through time."[8] In other words, and in terms that are crucial to my own argument, even though it is fully articulated and underwritten by a full-fledged philosophy of life complete with an ontology and an epistemology, the code is not monolithic and self-confirming; it is an entirely flexible instrument for organizing contingent experience in a way that does not preclude but renders inevitable its own modification.

It may seem, however, that this flexibility goes only in one direction, the direction of annexation and imperialism. The example suggests that the code as an interpretive strategy operates in the manner of an amoeba, simply surrounding and ingesting anything that comes its unstoppable way. This, however, is not the case, as we may see by imagining an alternate ending to the story Weider tells. Suppose the director of the halfway house, rather than accepting the resident's response—"You know I can't organize a baseball team"—had chosen to dispute it. What might he have said? Well, he might have argued that organizing a baseball team was an activity entirely independent of the staff and would have the effect of helping the residents; or he might have pointed out that the suggestion to organize a baseball team didn't come from him, but from a resident, and that he was simply refusing to do something which could then be done by someone else as a form of resistance. It is true that whatever then happened would still be happening under the aegis of the code (were it otherwise, the category of the absolute outside would have been revived), but the code will have shown itself to be not a single simple organism, but a set of interlocking assumptions one of which can always be brought into play as a check against the others and all of which are answerable to the complex social situation that is at once the code's mooring and its accomplishment. Admittedly, the circumstances of this example are special, but the analysis can easily be extended to situations that are not special at all. How often have we seen a presidential spokesman, or an attorney, or a journalist respond to a question by saying I can't answer that because it is a matter of national security or because the case is still under litigation or because it is privileged information? These are all instances of what Weider calls "telling the code" as a means of organizing and controlling experience, but they are all equally open to a challenge that proceeds from the very same concerns that are being invoked. (It is always possible to question the definition of privileged information or to dispute the scope of national security or to counter-invoke the public's right to know.)

The argument has now come full circle and taken a curious turn. I began, you will recall, by pointing out that change is not a problem if one posits independent agents who can check their accounts and descriptions against an equally independent reality; for then change is easily explained as a function of the constraints placed by reality on our interpretations of it. But the neatness of this picture is sacrificed if one conceives of persons not as free agents, but as extensions of interpretive communities, communities whose warranting assumptions delimit what can be seen and therefore what can be described; for then the describing agent, the object of description, and the descriptive vocabulary are all transformations of one another and there would not seem to be enough room between them to make change a possibility. In the preceding pages this impasse has been negotiated by a demonstration that neither interpretive communities nor the minds of community members are stable and fixed, but are, rather, moving projects—engines of change— whose work is at the same time assimilative and self-transforming. The conclusion, therefore, is that change is not a problem; and, indeed, to the extent that there is a problem, it would seem to be one of explaining how anything ever remains the same; or, even more precisely, how, given the vision of a system and of agents continually "on the move," can one even say that a change has occurred since the very notion of change requires, as Robert Nisbet has pointed out, "some object entity or being the identity of which persists through all the successive differences"?[9]

The answer to this question is that not everything changes at once. Interpretive communities are no more than sets of institutional practices; and while those practices are continually being transformed by the very work that they do, the transformed practice identifies itself and tells its story in relation to general purposes and goals that have survived and form the basis of a continuity. So that, for example, insofar as there has been for some time a practice of literary description, and insofar as there is something called *Paradise Lost* that has for some time been considered an object of that practice, it makes perfect and legitimate sense to regard the successive descriptions of *Paradise Lost* as a description of a persisting identity. Of course, it is an identity as conceived within a continuity of practice; but the alternative would be to reserve the idea of identity and the notion of change for an object that appeared to us under no practice whatsoever, an alternative that is as unimaginable as it is nonsensical. The fact that the objects we have are all objects that appear to us in the context of some practice, of work done by some interpretive community, doesn't mean that they are not objects or that we don't have them or that they exert no pressure on us. All it means is that they are interpreted objects and that since interpretations can change, the perceived shape of objects can change too.

But how does that change occur? That, after all, is the question we set out to answer, but with every turn of the argument an answer seems further away, especially if we expect it to take the form of something like a *theory* of change, complete with criteria and a predictive formula. It becomes increasingly obvious that there could be no such theory and that change is something that does or does not occur in particular institutional situations where this or that set of already-in-place concerns can (but not *must*) lead to the noticing and taking into account of an open-ended, although not infinite, range of phenomena. The answer to the question "what can cause change?" is "anything," although in a specific situation "anything" will be qualified by the structure of relevancy the situation displays: everything cannot be noticed at every moment, although what can be noticed can change (that word again) at every moment. It would seem that if change can be understood at all, it is only in the context of a historical reconstruction of its empirical conditions and not in the context of any (impossible) general account.

It follows, then, that there is nothing that is inherently—by right of its nature—an agent of change, although that is exactly the claim that has been routinely made for the operation of theory, and especially for that form of theory that supposedly enables us to distance ourselves from our practices. When Jonathan Culler declares in *On Deconstruction* that theoretical inquiry leads to "changes in assumptions, institutions, and practice," he articulates an article of faith held by theorists and antitheorists alike.[10] Thus the first respondent to a recent survey in *New Literary History* declares that "literary theory should contribute to the changing of social and professional institutions," while another asserts in a similar vein that "a basic function of literary theory consists in opening up new realms of investigation," and a third regards literary theory as, at least potentially, a "well-defined practice, of social critique and social redirection." These large claims are not disputed but are made the basis of a fear by those who see in theory the specter of frivolous and value-subverting change and hope, as one respondent put it, that when the rage for theory abates, "the study of literature can continue its uninterrupted course without having suffered any permanent damage."[11]

Both parties to the debate about theory agree that theory is something special, something that stands apart from the field of practice which is either reformed by theory or misled by its beguiling ways. But the granting to theory of such power is just one more version of the picture in which a community is provoked to revise its assumptions by an independent agency. On the analysis offered here, however, the agent of change must already be a component in the field it alters, and so it is with theory. No theory can compel a change that has not in some sense already occurred, although it may seem to both those who promote it and those who resist it that what has been proposed is entirely new. Not long ago an old friend rushed up to me brandishing a copy of *PMLA* and crying, "look at what you and your kind have done." The object of his ire was a reading of a novel to which he had devoted much of his career, yet he complained that this essay, published in the profession's leading journal, spoke to no concerns he could recognize and was written in a style he found impenetrable. This sad state of affairs, he was convinced, was directly attributable to the appearance on the scene of deconstruction. But in fact deconstruction is no more or less than a particularly arresting formulation of principles and procedures that have been constitutive of literary and other studies for some time.

Indeed, deconstruction would have been literally unthinkable were it not already an article of faith that literary texts are characterized by a plurality of meanings and were it not already the established methodology of literary studies to produce for a supposedly "great text" as many meanings as possible. Deconstruction takes the additional step of attributing these meanings not to the text as a special kind of object, but to signification as a force untethered to any grounding origin, but this step too can be seen to follow from the growing influence in this century of hermeneutical thought with its emphasis on contexts, cultural matrices, and gestalts. It goes without saying that I vastly oversimplify what in the full telling would be an immensely complex story, but even if that story were told, its point, I think, would turn out to be the same: rather than something new which in its newness gives rise to revolutionary practices, deconstruction is a programmatic and tendentious focusing of ways of thinking and working that have already come to be regarded as commonplace and orthodox. That is why, when deconstructionist doctrine began to be promulgated, one of the first things people did was to exclaim that so and so—usually Kenneth Burke—was a deconstructionist before there was a name for it, or that they themselves had been speaking deconstruction all their lives.

What is true of deconstruction is true of any theory, so-called. A theoretical pronouncement is always an articulation of a shift that has in large part already occurred; it announces a rationale for practices already in force; it provides a banner under which those who are already doing what it names can march; it provides a visible target for those who have long thought that things are going from bad to worse. In a sense, then, a theory does cause change since it will give rise to controversy and lead to the calling of symposia, and the founding of journals, and the funding of chairs, but these are the consequences of any practice that can be identified and imitated: they are not consequences that can be described as revolutionary or groundbreaking. Theory does not cause change on the level claimed by those who either see it as the means of salvation or fear it as the subverter of values. It does not even cause critical self-consciousness or make one aware of one's assumptions (these are the usual claims); first, because self-consciousness is a necessary condition of any activity even if one cannot produce its informing principles on demand; and second, because if one were to produce those principles—that is, make one's assumptions explicit—that activity would itself occur within assumptions of which one was not and could not be aware. All of which is to say that theory's project—the attempt to get above practice and lay bare the grounds of its possibility—is an impossible one. Theory is a form of practice, as rooted in particular historical and cultural conditions as any other, and, as in the case of any other, the extent to which its introduction will or will not give rise to changes, small and large, cannot be determined in advance.

This returns me to the question with which I began: what is the relationship between the theory of interpretive communities and change? In fact, it is three questions. First, one might ask, does an interpretive community encourage or license change by relieving its members of any responsibility to the world or to the text, or does it inhibit change by refusing to take into account anything that is contrary to its assumptions and interests? The bulk of this essay has been concerned with demonstrating that this question, in either its left or right versions, is misconceived: since an interpretive community is an engine of change, there is no status quo to protect, for its operations are inseparable from the transformation of both its assumptions and interests; and since the change that is inevitable is also orderly—constrained by evidentiary procedures and tacit understandings that at once enable change and are changed by what they enable—license and willful irresponsibility are never possibilities. A second question looks very much like the first, but is slightly different, for it is concerned not with the work interpretive communities do, but with the work done by the fact that the term "interpretive community" is available to practitioners as a mode of self-description. Does this fact give comfort to those who want to turn everything upside down, or is it ammunition for those who want everything to go on as before? The answer is the same. The desire of neither party is authorized by the notion of interpretive communities, which says to the left "anything you can do I can do better," and to the right "the more things stay the same, the more they change." There is, however, a third question. What is likely to be the effect of the intervention in the field of the theory of interpretive communities? Which of the parties now contending for control of the literary profession's machinery will turn the theory to most advantage? That question has an answer, although the answer I must now give is, "I don't know." The reason it has an answer is that it is an empirical question, directed not at the political implications built into the theory (there are none), but at the political consequences of having the theory as a resource. It is undoubtedly the case that the practice of professing interpretive communities will, like any other practice, participate in the ongoing modification of the enterprise, but the shape and the extent of that participation are not predictable because the relationship between the emergence of a theory and change is not theoretical.

I do not mean to say that in time the nature and extent of the changes brought about by the notion of interpretive communities will be obvious; for in so saying I would be making the *fact* of change into something that was or could be self-evident. But no fact is self-evident, and therefore it is a mistake to think of change or its absence as being verifiable by a simple (unmediated) act of empirical observation; rather it is only within the perspective of some interpretive descriptive system that change is or is not a feature. That is to say, the fact of change, like any other fact, is irremediably interpretive; its specification cannot be made independently of the way a community conceives of itself, of the story it tells about itself and lives out in the actions of its members. The enterprise of the law, for example, is by definition committed to the ahistoricity of its basic principles, and workers in the field have a stake in seeing the history of their own efforts as the application of those principles to circumstances that are only *apparently* new (i.e., changed). That is why a judge will do almost anything to avoid overturning a precedent, and why even those who hold to the doctrine of legal realism—the doctrine that the law is whatever the courts happen on that day to say it is—are uncomfortable with that doctrine and wish that they held to something else. In short, the very point of the legal enterprise requires that its practitioners see continuity where others, with less of a stake in the enterprise, might feel free to see change. The scientific community has an even greater stake in its own continuity, and I suspect that, despite the wide circulation of Kuhn's arguments, most scientists continue to think of themselves as constrained in their labors by an unchanging nature and continue to believe that what changes are the descriptions of herself that nature either confirms or rejects. (Indeed, were these not their beliefs, they would cease to be scientists.) The assumption of continuity is also necessary to anyone who would write the history of philosophy from its beginning to the present, an exercise which, as Richard Rorty has recently observed, depends on "the idea that philosophy is the name . . . of a discipline which in all ages and places, has managed to dig down to the same deep fundamental questions."[12] If someone with that idea sets out to write the history of philosophy, he will already have ruled out the possibility that what he will be writing is a history of changes. In literary history and the history of criticism the position occupied by the great philosophical questions is often occupied by the genres assumed to be major and by the approaches assumed to be basic; changes are explained (or explained away) as variations on a few persisting forms, and the story then told is a cyclical rather than a progressive one. But that is not the only story being currently told: for those who write under the influence of the new historiography as represented in the work of Foucault and others, the persistence of genres, either in literature or criticism, is a fiction, and the truth is that even when the vocabulary of an enterprise remains stable, its terms refer to radically different activities informed and enabled by radically different principles. In the resulting narrative, which assumes and produces *dis*continuities, change is at once inevitable and somewhat mysterious, since the assumptions impelling this kind of history forbid the discovery of a pattern too regular or too rational.

In all of these cases, and in any others that can be imagined, a theory of change is inscribed in the self-description that at once directs and renders intelligible the characteristic labors of workers in the community. The question of change is therefore one that cannot be posed independently of some such self-description which gives a shape to the very facts and events to which the question is put. Does this mean, then, that we can never say "what really happened" because we can only say what happened under some description or account? Not at all. Every description and account—including the descriptions and accounts that make up this paper—is an attempt to say what really happened. If the claim to be saying that is contested (as it often is), it will not be contested by some view of the event independent of description but by a competing description, and the competition will be adjudicated with reference to the norms, standards, and procedures understood by the community to be appropriate to the determination of empirical fact. The problem arises only when one thinks that by "what really happened" is meant "what really happened after all the competing descriptions have been discounted or set aside?" But it's hard even to give *that* question a sense, since the fact of what happened, like any other fact, can only be said to exist relative to some characterization or description. To ask "what really happened independently of any account or description whatsoever" is to ask for a description that is not a description; it is what no one could ever tell you, not because it remains hidden as the real truth behind all the partial ones, but because there is nothing to tell. What one does tell and tells continually is what really happened in the only sense that makes sense: one tells what happened as it seems manifest within some set of interpretive assumptions concerning what events are alike, what is necessary to establish their shape, what is evidence for their having occurred. It is in that sense and within assumptions of that kind that I have been speaking to you here, telling you, by way of examples, what really happened when this or that state of affairs underwent a change.

This brings me to a final question. Change in relation to what? Or, what's the point? That is, for many people, an intellectual enterprise—be it literary criticism or philosophy or science—is legitimized finally by its goal, and it is in relation to some goal that changes must be justified. Otherwise, it is often said, change would be "mere" change or meaningless change or change for change's sake. The idea is that change is intolerable unless it is perceived as progress and that the sense of progress must be underwritten by a belief in the achievability of some desired end. One can understand this in two ways. In the first and stronger way the word "end" is taken to refer to that time when a particular activity will cease, because, for example, all of the world's goods will have been equitably distributed or all of the world's texts correctly described. But while this may be a desire periodically voiced, it does not correspond, I think, to anything that a practitioner in the field really wants. Is it really the case that we do what we do so that there will come a day when we are not called upon any longer to do it? Should such a day ever seem to be approaching, in literary studies or any other, I venture to predict that there will suddenly be the discovery that the problem was more complicated than we had assumed, the discovery that the last word has not yet been explicated.

There is, however, another way to take the word "end" so that it refers not to an ultimate state of rest or closure but to a time when things will be better—"better" understood in relation to the perceived deficiencies of our present circumstances. This is Kuhn's understanding when he suggests that we think of progress not as teleological, but as "evolution from the community's state of knowledge at any given time."[13] And it is, I would contend, the understanding under which we all labor even when we speak as if the end we have in mind were transcendental. In short, there is no need to envision a point or a goal outside of practice because practice is at every moment organized in relation to goals already known, although it should now go without saying that the accomplishment of those goals will be inseparable from the emergence of others and therefore inseparable from the call for more practice. Perhaps the most persistent charge against the notion of interpretive communities is that it seems to make disciplinary and professional activity its own end. But since that end itself is continually changing, the charge can be cheerfully embraced because it says only that the members of a community will always believe in the ends for which they work, and that therefore their work will never be ended even though it will be ceaselessly transformed.

Professionalism

8. No Bias, No Merit:
The Case Against Blind Submission

I 1979

When members of an institution debate, it may seem that they are arguing about fundamental principles, but it is more often the case that the truly fundamental principle is the one that makes possible the terms of the disagreement and is therefore not in dispute at all. I am thinking in particular of the arguments recently marshaled for and against blind submission to the journal of the Modern Language Association. Blind submission is the practice whereby an author's name is not revealed to the reviewer who evaluates his or her work. It is an attempt, as William Schaefer explained in the *MLA Newsletter*, "to ensure that in making their evaluations readers are not influenced by factors other than the intrinsic merits of the article."[1] In his report to the members Schaefer, then executive director of the association, declared that he himself was opposed to blind submission because the impersonality of the practice would erode the humanistic values that are supposedly at the heart of our enterprise. Predictably, Schaefer's statement provoked a lively exchange in which the lines of battle were firmly, and, as I will argue, narrowly, drawn. On the one hand, those who agreed with Schaefer feared that a policy of anonymous review would involve a surrender "to the spurious notions about objectivity and absolute value that . . . scientists and social scientists banter about"; on the other hand, those whose primary concern was with the fairness of the procedure believed that "[j]ustice should be blind."[2] Each side concedes the force of the opposing argument—the proponents of anonymous review admit that impersonality brings its dangers, and the defenders of the status quo acknowledge that it is important to prevent "extraneous considerations" from interfering with the identification of true merit.[3]

It is in phrases like "true merit" and "extraneous considerations" that one finds the assumptions to which all parties subscribe. The respondent who declares that "the point at issue is how to avoid the bias of a reviewer upon grounds other than those intrinsic to the article under review"[4] is making an unexceptional statement. Everyone agrees that intrinsic merit should be protected; it is just a question of whether or not the price of protection—the possible erosion of the humanistic community—is too high. In what follows I would like not so much to enter the debate as to challenge its terms by arguing that merit is not in fact identifiable apart from the "extraneous considerations" that blind submission would supposedly eliminate. I want to argue, in short, that there is no such thing as intrinsic merit, and, indeed, if I may paraphrase James 1, "no bias, no merit."

We might begin by noting that while in the course of this debate everyone talks about intrinsic merit, no one bothers to define it, except negatively as everything apart from the distractions of rank, affiliation, professional status, past achievements, ideological identification, sex, "or anything that might be known about the author."[5] Now this is a list so inclusive that one might wonder what was left once the considerations it enumerates were eliminated. The answer would seem to be that what is left is the disinterested judgment as to whether or not an article does justice to the work or works it purports to characterize. But that answer will be satisfactory only if the notion "does justice to" can be related to a standard or set of standards that operates independently of the institutional circumstances that have been labeled extraneous. My thesis is, first of all, that there is no such standard (which is not the same thing as saying there is no standard) and, second, that while we may, as a point of piety, invoke it as an ideal, in fact we violate it all the time by practices that are at once routine and obligatory. Consider, for example, the practice of referring, at the beginning of an essay, or in the course of its unfolding, or in a succession of footnotes (the conditions under which it would be proper to do it one way rather than another could themselves be profitably studied) to the body of previous scholarship. This is a convention of the profession, and a failure to respect it will sometimes be grounds for rejecting an article. The reason is obvious. The convention is a way of acknowledging that we are engaged in a community activity in which the value of one's work is directly related to the work that has been done by others; that is, in this profession you earn the right to say something because it has not been said by anyone else, or because it is a reversal of what is usually said, or because while it has been said, its implications have not yet been spelled out. You do not offer something as the report of a communion between the individual critical sensibility and a work or its author; and if you did, if your articles were all written as if they were titled "What I Think about *Middlemarch*" or "The *Waste Land* and Me" they would not be given a hearing. (The fact that this is not true of some people does not disprove but makes my point.) Instead, they would be dismissed as being a waste of a colleague's time, or as beside the point, or as uninformed, or simply as unprofessional. This last judgment would not be a casual one; to be unprofessional is not simply to have violated some external rule or piece of decorum. It is to have ignored (and by ignoring flouted) the process by which the institution determines the conditions under which its rewards will be given or withheld. These conditions are nowhere written down, but they are understood by everyone who works in the field, and, indeed, any understanding one might have of the field is inseparable from (because it will have been produced by) an awareness, often tacit, of these conditions.

What are they? A full answer to the question would be out of place here, but a partial enumeration would include a canon of greater and lesser works and hence a stipulation as to what is or is not a major project, a set of authorized and unauthorized methodologies along with a recognized procedure by which members of one set can be moved into another, a list of the tasks that particularly need doing and of those that have already been well done, a specification of the arguments that are properly literary and of the kinds of evidence that will be heard as telling and/or conclusive (authorial statements, letters, manuscript revisions, etc.). Of course, these conditions can and do change—and the process by which they change is one of the things they themselves regulate—but they always have some shape or other, and one cannot, without risk, operate independently of them.

Everyone is aware of that risk, although it is usually not acknowledged with the explicitness that one finds in the opening sentence of Raymond Waddington's essay on books XI and XII of *Paradise Lost*. "Few of us today," Waddington writes, "could risk echoing C. S. Lewis's condemnation of the concluding books of *Paradise Lost* as an 'untransmuted lump of futurity.' "[6] The nature of the risk that Waddington is about *not* to take is made clear in the very next sentence, where we learn that a generation of critics has been busily demonstrating the subtlety and complexity of these books and establishing the fact that they are the product of a controlled poetic design. What this means is that the kind of thing that one can now say about them is constrained in advance, for, given the present state of the art, the critic who is concerned with maintaining his or her professional credentials is obliged to say something that makes them better. Indeed, the safest thing the critic can say (and Waddington proceeds in this essay to say it) is that, while there is now a general recognition of the excellence of these books, it is still the case that they are faulted for some deficiency that is in fact, if properly understood, a virtue. Of course, this rule (actually a rule of thumb) does not hold across the board. When Waddington observes that "few of us today could risk," he is acknowledging, ever so obliquely, that there are some of us who could. Who are they, and how did they achieve their special status? Well, obviously C. S. Lewis was once one (although it may not have been a risk for him, and if it wasn't, why wasn't it?), and if he had not already died in 1972, when Waddington was writing, presumably he could have been one again. That is, Lewis's status as an authority on Renaissance literature was such that he could offer readings without courting the risk facing others who might go against the professional grain, the risk of not being listened to, of remaining unpublished, of being unattended to, the risk of producing something that was by definition—a definition derived from prevailing institutional conditions—without merit.

With this observation we return to the notion of "intrinsic merit" as it relates to the issue of blind submission; for what the Waddington-Lewis example shows (among other things) is that merit, rather than being a quality that can be identified independently of professional or institutional conditions, is a product of those conditions; and, moreover, since those conditions are not stable but change continually, the shape of what will be recognized as meritorious is always in the process of changing too. So that while it is true that as critics we write with the goal of living up to a standard (of worth, illumination, etc.) it is a standard that had been made not in eternity by God or by Aristotle but in the profession by the men and women who have preceded us; and in the act of trying to live up to it, we are also, and necessarily, refashioning it. My use of "we" might suggest a communal effort in which everyone pulls an equal weight and exerts an equal influence. But, of course, this is not the case. Ours is a hierarchical profession in which some are more responsible for its products than others; and since one of those products is the standard of merit by which our labors will, for a time, be judged, there will always be those whose words are meritorious (that is, important, worth listening to, authoritative, illuminating) simply by virtue of the position they occupy in the institution. It is precisely this situation, of course, that the policy of blind submission is designed to remedy; the idea is to prevent a reviewer from being influenced in his or her judgment of merit by the professional status of the author; but on the analysis offered in this essay, merit is inseparable from the structure of the profession and therefore the fact that someone occupies a certain position in that structure cannot be irrelevant to the assessment of what he or she produces.

The point is made in passing by a respondent (anonymous, I am afraid) to the Executive Council's survey who asserts that "[i]f Northrop Frye should write an essay attacking archetypal criticism, the article would by definition be of much greater significance than an article by another scholar attacking the same approach."[7] The reason is that the approach is not something independent of what Northrop Frye has previously said about it; indeed, in large part archetypal criticism *is* what Northrop Frye has said about it, and therefore anything he now says about it is not so much to be measured against an independent truth as it is to be regarded, at least potentially, as a new pronouncement of what the truth will hereafter be said to be. Similarly, an article by Fredson Bowers on the principles of textual editing would automatically be of "general interest to the membership" because the sense the membership has of what the principles of textual editing could possibly be is inseparable from what Fredson Bowers has already written. However, it is not necessary to search for a hypothetical example. The fact that the judgment on *Paradise Lost* XI and XII was made by C. S. Lewis in a book that was immediately recognized as authoritative—a recognition that was itself produced in no small part by the prior authority of *The Allegory of Love*—was sufficient to ensure that it would be over fifteen years before a group of scholars could begin the rehabilitation of those books and another fifteen before Waddington could pronounce their effort successful by declaring that few of us today could risk echoing C. S. Lewis.

It could be argued that these are special cases, but they are special only in that Frye, Bowers, and Lewis are (or were) in the position of exerting a general authority over the entire discipline; but in the smaller precincts of subdisciplines and subsubdisciplines there are words that matter more than other words spoken by those who address a field that they themselves have in large part constituted. These are men and women who are identified with a subject (Frances Yates on arts of memory), with a period (M. H. Abrams on Romanticism), with a genre (Angus Fletcher on allegory), with a poet (Hugh Kenner on Pound), with a work (Stephen Booth on Shakespeare's *Sonnets*). When Geoffrey Hartman speaks on Wordsworth, is his just another voice, or is it the voice of someone who is in great measure responsible for the Wordsworth we now have, insofar as by that name we understand an array of concerns, formal properties, sources, influences, and so on? Of course, Geoffrey Hartman's Wordsworth is not everyone's, but everyone's Wordsworth is someone's; that is, everyone's Wordsworth is the product of some characterization of him that has been put forward (within constraints that are already in place) and has been found to be persuasive by a significant number of workers in the profession. The point is that whatever Wordsworth we have he will not be available independently of the institution's procedures; rather he will be the product of these procedures, and of the work of certain men and women, and therefore the identity of the men and women who propose to speak about him cannot be irrelevant to a judgment of the merit of what they have to say.

I make the point in order to anticipate an obvious objection to the preceding paragraphs: it may be the case that the merit of pieces of literary criticism is a function of conditions prevailing in the profession, but surely the merit of literary works themselves is another matter, for they precede the profession and are the occasion of its efforts and the justification of its machinery. This is a powerful objection because it is rooted in the most basic myth the profession tells itself, the myth that it is secondary in relation to literary works that are produced independently of its processes; but it is precisely my contention that literary works have the shape they do because of the questions that have been put to them, questions that emerge from the work of the profession and are understood by members of the profession to be the proper ones to ask. We often think of our task as the *description* of literary works, but description requires categories of description, and those categories, in the form of the questions we think to ask, will limit in advance the kinds of things that can be described, which in turn will limit the shapes that can even be seen. That is to say, the objects of our professional attention—texts, authors, genres, and so on—are as much the products of the institution as are the acceptable forms that attention can take. It follows then that the machinery of the institution does not grow up to accommodate needs that are independently perceived but that, rather, the institutional machinery comes first and the needs then follow, as do the ways of meeting them.

In short, the work to be done is not what the institution responds to but what it *creates,* and it was not long ago that this truth was brought home to me when I received the first of many mailings from the then fledgling Spenser Society of America. So fledgling was that society in 1977 that I hadn't yet heard of it, and I was therefore somewhat surprised to open a letter from its treasurer thanking me for my support. What became clear as the letter proceeded was that my ignorance of the society in no way exempted me from its operations. "We are almost two hundred strong," read the second sentence of the letter, and the suggestion of a military organization into which I had been conscripted was unmistakable. Moreover, that organization was already fully articulated. I was informed of the identity of "my" officers, who had arranged "our luncheon," for which I was urged to make an immediate reservation because my fellow members had already spoken for thirty of the fifty available seats. By the end of the second paragraph I was not only firmly placed in the rank and file of a marching army but informed that I was already behind in my dues. It was not until the third and final paragraph, however, that the true significance of the society's operation was revealed in the announcement of an annual volume to be called *Spenser Studies,* the first number of which was already scheduled by an editorial board that had already signed an agreement, in my name, I suppose, with a prominent university press. We would be happy, wrote my treasurer, "if you would inform colleagues and students that we Spenserians now have another possibility for publication." Here is the real message of the letter and the real rationale of the Spenser Society of America: to multiply the institutional contexts in which writing on Spenser will at once be demanded and published. It so happens that the letter was written before the society's first meeting, but as this sentence shows, the society need never have met at all, since its most important goal—the creation of a Spenser industry with all its attendant machinery—had already been achieved.

In later communications that machinery was further elaborated, first of all by the calling of an International Conference on Cooperation in the Study of Edmund Spenser. The scheduled panels indicate the directions the cooperative studies will take: "Cooperation in the Study of

Spenser's Medieval English Backgrounds," "Cooperation in the Study
of Spenser's Continental Backgrounds." What is emerging here is not
simply the shape of an organization but the shape of Edmund Spenser.
Nor will that shape be allowed to grow like Topsy. The topic of the
first panel is the *limits* of cooperative study; the same document at once
calls into being an activity and begins to regulate it. It is not long before both cooperation and regulation take on a more substantial form
in the promised production of a Spenser *Encyclopedia* (if a category or
subject is not in the encyclopedia, it will not be in Spenser), plans for
which, I was informed, were already "well advanced." It is a feature of
this correspondence that the world it declares is provided with a past
and a future that tend to obscure its purely documentary origin. Things
are always "well advanced" or "previously discussed" in a way that suggests events are being reported rather than made. But it takes only a
moment's reflection to see that in a paragraph like this one every event
is brought into being by a piece of paper that is underwritten by a bureaucracy that is itself created and sustained by other pieces of paper:

> Plans are now all advanced for the projected *Spenser Encyclope-
> dia,* which was discussed at conferences last October and Decem-
> ber. (See reports on these conferences in the latest issue of *Spenser
> Newsletter,* 10, no. 1.) An official announcement of the *Encyclo-
> pedia* will be made on 4th May 1979 at Kalamazoo, Michigan,
> where we hope to continue the cooperative spirit of the Interna-
> tional Conference at Duquesne.

It may seem that I am overestimating the power of a series of letters,
even if the first in the series was written on the 4th of July; and it is
true that this letter and subsequent ones did not create the society's machinery and the possibilities attendant upon it in a vacuum or ex nihilo:
there is, it turns out, an authority that legitimizes these documents and
accounts for their immediate force. The identity of that authority was
revealed in the reporting of a lack. The Spenser Society, it seems, was,
at the time of its birth, without a constitution, and therefore the framing
of a constitution was declared to be the first order of business at the first
meeting. Before that meeting was held, however, a second letter arrived,
written this time by "my" president, informing me that the constitution
was in fact already available in the form of the constitution, ready-
made as it were, of the Milton Society, which also, the letter went on to
say, was to provide the model for a banquet, a reception, an after-dinner

speaker, an honored scholar, and the publication of a membership book-let, the chief function of which was to be the listing of the publications, recent and forthcoming, of the members. The manner in which work on Spenser is to be recognized and honored will have its source not in a direct confrontation with the poet or his poem but in the apparatus of an organization devoted to another poet. Spenser studies will be imita-tive of Milton studies; the anxiety of influence, it would seem, can work backward. Moreover, it continues to work. The recent mail has brought me, and some of you, an announcement of a new publication, the *Sidney Newsletter,* to be organized, we are told, "along the lines of the well-established and highly successful *Spenser Newsletter,*" which was organized along the lines of the well-established and highly successful *Milton Newsletter.*

Now I wouldn't want to be understood as criticizing the Spenser Society for its colonizing activities or for having been colonized, in its turn, by the Milton Society. My account of these matters is offered with affection and, indeed, with gratitude, for were it not for the opportuni-ties made available by these organizations there would be nothing for us to do. As I have already said, the work to be done is not what the in-stitution responds to but what it *creates,* and it is the business of these societies first to create the work and second to make sure that it will never get done. I say this from a position of authority, as a past presi-dent of the Milton Society, an office whose only duty is to preside over an annual meeting. At the meeting over which I presided the members of the society heard reports on the *Milton Encyclopedia,* the *Variorum Commentary, The Complete Prose,* the friends of Milton's cottage, the Milton Society Archive and Library, the Milton Society awards, and "upcoming panels and conferences at which members of the society might speak." These were labeled as "progress reports," and to some extent the label was accurate; but the rate of progress was reassuringly slow, and there were signs that mechanisms were already in motion to ensure that it would never get too far. *The Complete Prose* was threat-ening to become, in fact, complete; but there was an announcement that the seventh volume would soon be reissued in a revised and improved version, and if the seventh volume, could the first, second, third, fourth, fifth, and sixth be far behind? The volumes of the *Variorum* have hardly begun to appear, but already there is talk that the *Paradise Regained* is inadequate and will have to be redone. I myself was aghast to discover that antinomianism was not even an entry in the *Milton Ency-*

clopedia and began to think that similar omissions might necessitate the issuing of a new and improved edition. In so thinking I was not being cynical or opportunistic; I was responding with an honest act of judgment to a project that was called into being by the needs of the field. The fact that those needs corresponded to the need of the workers in the field to have something to do is worth noting; to note it, however, is not to call into question the sincerity of their efforts but to point out that those efforts are first and foremost professional and that therefore the motives one might have for engaging in them are professional too. To say this is to say what should go without saying: we do not write articles in order to report to no one in particular in no context in particular our unmediated experience of a literary work; articles are written by men and women who have something to contribute as "contribution" is defined by the conditions prevailing in the institution, an institution that provides both the questions and acceptable ways of answering them and provides too the canon of works to which the questions can be put. Indeed, the very writing of an article only makes sense within an institutional framework, and when an article gets published it is not because some independent agency has validated its merit but because in the machinery of a *political* agency—the Milton Society, the Spenser Society, the MLA—there is already a place for it.

With the word *political* we come to the heart of the matter, for that word names everything that so many in the profession would like to deny. It is the mark of a profession to claim that its activities are not tied to any one set of economic or social circumstances but constitute a response to needs and values that transcend particular times and places.[8] The profession of literary criticism carries this claim to an extreme that is finally self-destructive by declaring that its activities finally have very little value at all. The explanation for this curious maneuver lies in the relationship between what literary critics do and the commodity that occupies the center of the enterprise—literature. It is an article of faith in the profession that this commodity precedes the profession's efforts, which are seen as merely exegetical; and that means that from the very first the profession has a sense of itself as something secondary and superfluous. If the work itself is all-sufficient (a cardinal principle of twentieth-century aesthetics), the work of the critic is ultimately unnecessary, and criticism would seem to have compromised its claim to be a profession, even before that claim has been made.

One sees this clearly, for example, in John Crowe Ransom's "Criticism Inc.," a manifesto in which the literary community is urged to become more self-consciously professional. "Criticism," Ransom declares, "must become more scientific, or precise and systematic, and this means that it must be developed by the collective and sustained effort of learned persons—which means that its proper seat is in the universities."[9] This is the very language of professionalism, and it is accompanied by a disdain for amateurs[10] and by a rejection of the notion that criticism "is something which anyone can do."[11] But when it comes time to describe this new profession, its principles turn out to be unlike any other in that they are directed *away* from the public. To the question "What is criticism?" Ransom answers with what it is not, and what it is not is anything that might recommend it to the community at large; it does not report on the "moral content" of literature; it is not concerned with the lives of authors, or with literature's relationship to science, politics, the law, or geography; it must not make claims that its commodity is "moving" or "exciting" or "entertaining" or "great"; and above all it must not suggest that "art comes into being because the artist . . . has designs upon the public, whether high moral designs or box-office ones."[12] In this last phrase, high moral designs (which might include the design to enlighten one's readers, or to make them better, or to enlist them in some social or religious cause) are tarred, by association, with the brush of vulgarity; they are just another version of box-office designs because the intention of those who have them is to move others to this or that action in relation to this or that quotidian concern. Poetry, by contrast, is an effort deliberately abstracted from such concerns; the poet, Ransom writes, "perpetuates in his poem an order of existence which in actual life is constantly crumbling beneath his touch";[13] and the critic must attend only to that order and avoid attending to anything that would deny or compromise "the autonomy of the work itself as existing for its own sake."[14] In practice this means an exclusive focus on technique as it exists apart from any social or moral end,[15] a focus that promotes rapt contemplation as the only attitude that can properly belong to an activity defined in opposition to the business of everyday life, or to the everyday life of business.

The result is a professionalism that is divided against itself. It claims for itself the exclusive possession of a certain skill (the skill of attending properly to poems), but then it defines that skill in such a way as to remove its exercise from the activities of the marketplace where professions compete for the public's support. Indeed, it is a skill

that can be exercised only if the conditions of the marketplace are reso-
lutely ignored in favor of the *eternal* conditions that obtain, or should
obtain, between poem and reader. So long as it is a first principle that
poetry must be studied "for its own sake," the profession of literary criticism will exist in a shamefaced relationship with professional machinery,
which will be regarded as a temporary and regrettable excrescence.

That is why the literary community teaches its members a contradictory lesson: literary criticism is a profession—it is not something that
anyone can do—but it is not professional—it is not done in response to
marketplace or political pressures. A policy of blind submission is an
extension of that lesson and is also the extension of a general practice
by which the profession hides from itself the true (political) nature of
its own activities. As we have seen, the case for blind submission is that
it protects the intrinsic from the extraneous; but what I have been trying to show, from a variety of perspectives, is that everything labeled
extraneous—considerations of rank, professional status, previous achievement, ideology, and so on—is essential to the process by which intrinsic
considerations are identified and put into place. I said at the beginning
of this essay that there is no such thing as the intrinsic, and I would say
it again if by "intrinsic" was meant a category of value that was in place
for all time; but if we think of the intrinsic as something the profession
determines, then there is always a category of the intrinsic, but it isn't
always the same one. It therefore cannot be defined in opposition to the
profession because it is a part of the profession's work to produce it, and
then, in the course of discussion and debate, to produce it again.

The intrinsic, in short, is a political rather than an essential category, and as such it will always reflect the interests—wholly legitimate
because without interest there would be no value—of those who have
had a hand in fashioning it. In the process the interests of others will
have been excluded or slighted, and those groups will, more often than
not, protest their exclusion in the name of intrinsic merit; but what they
will really be doing is attempting to replace someone else's notion of
intrinsic merit with their own; that is, they will be playing politics. This
is precisely what the proponents of blind submission are doing, whether
they know it or not, and therefore the one claim they cannot legitimately maintain, although they make it all the time, is that they are doing away with politics. There are certainly arguments that can be made
for blind submission, but they are frankly political arguments and if
they were presented as such they might even receive a more sympathetic

hearing. As things stand now, for example, I am against blind submission because the fact that my name is attached to an article greatly increases its chances of getting accepted. But that is just the condition we wish to change, someone might object, and to this I might reply that I have paid my dues and earned the benefit of the doubt I now enjoy and don't see why others shouldn't labor in the vineyards as I did. I would, that is, be responding in terms of my own self-interest, by which I don't mean *selfish* interests but interests that appear to me to be compelling given a sense of myself as a professional with a history and with a stake in the future of the profession.

A similar point is made by some of the participants in a discussion of peer review published in *The Behavorial and Brain Sciences: An International Journal of Current Research and Theory with Open Peer Commentary*.[16] The occasion was the report of research conducted by D. P. Peters and S. J. Ceci. Peters and Ceci had taken twelve articles published in twelve different journals, altered the titles, substituted for the names of the authors fictitious names identified as researchers at institutions no one had ever heard of (because they were made up), and resubmitted the articles to the journals that had originally accepted them. Three of the articles were recognized as resubmissions, and of the remaining nine eight were rejected. The response to these results ranged from horror ("It puts at risk the whole conceptual framework within which we are accustomed to make observations and construct theories"[17]) to "so what else is new." Almost all respondents, however, agreed with the researchers' call for the development of "fair" procedures, "fair . . . defined here as being judged on the merit of one's ideas, and not on the basis of academic rank, sex, place of work, publication record, and so on."[18] Nevertheless, there were a few who questioned that definition of fairness and challenged the assumption that it was wrong for reviewers to take institutional affiliation and history into consideration. "We consider a result from a scientist who has never before been wrong much more seriously than a similar report from a scientist who has never before been right. . . . It is neither unnatural nor wrong that the work of scientists who have achieved eminence through a long record of important and successful research is accepted with fewer reservations than the work of less eminent scientists."[19] "A reviewer may be justified in assuming at the outset that [well-known] people know what they are doing."[20] "Those of us who publish establish some kind of track record. If our papers stand the test of time . . .

it can be expected that we have acquired expertise in scientific methodology."[21] (This last respondent is a woman and a Nobel laureate.)
What this minority is saying is that a paper identified with a distinguished record is a better bet than a paper not so identified. I would go
even further and say that a paper so identified will be *a different paper.*
In a footnote to his *The Structure of Scientific Revolutions* Thomas Kuhn
reports that when Lord Rayleigh submitted a paper to the British Association, his name was "inadvertently omitted" and the paper was rejected "as the work of some 'paradoxer.' "[22] But when his name was subsequently restored the paper was accepted immediately. On its face this
might seem to be a realization of the worst fears of those who argue for
blind submission, but I would read the result differently: shorn of its institutional lineage the paper presented itself as without direction, and
whimsical; but once the reviewers were informed of its source they were
able to see it as the continuation of work—of lines of direction, routes
of inquiry—they already knew, and all at once the paper made a different kind of sense than it did when they were considering it "blindly."

Of course, they were not considering it blindly at all. Reviewers
who receive a paper from which the identifying marks have been removed will immediately put in place an (imagined) set of circumstances of exactly the kind they are supposedly ignoring. Indeed, in the
absence of such an imaginative and projective act, the paper could not be
read *as* a paper situated in a particular discipline. Strictly speaking, there
is no such thing as blind submission. The choice is not between a reading influenced by "extraneous" information and a reading uninflected
by "extraneous" information but between readings differently inflected.
The pure case of a reading without bias is never available, not because
we can never remove all our biases but because without them there
would be nothing either to see or to say. A law school colleague told
me the other day of a judge who was asked to disqualify himself from a
case involving a black plaintiff and a white defendant on the grounds
that since he himself was black he would be biased. The judge refused,
pointing out that "after all, he had to be one color or the other." The
moral is clear and it is my moral: bias is just another word for seeing
from a particular perspective as opposed to seeing from no perspective
at all, and since seeing from no perspective at all is not a possibility, bias
is a condition of consciousness and therefore of action. Of course, perspectives differ, as do the actions that follow from them, and one can
predict that a *PMLA* after blind submission will not be the same jour-

nal; but to the extent that it is different, that difference will be the result not of a process that has been depoliticized but of the passage from one political agenda to another.

II 1988

I wrote the preceding pages in 1979 and revised them slightly in 1982, and by one of those accidents that attend professional life the collection for which the piece was intended was never published. It is of course now out-of-date, but its out-of-dateness can be seen as extension of my point, that it is the conditions currently obtaining in the profession rather than any set of independent and abiding criteria that determine what is significant and meritorious. The point still holds, although many of the examples used to illustrate it will now strike readers as either obvious (and hence not worth elaborating) or simply wrong. The examples that are obvious will be so in part because of work subsequently done by me and by others. The reference to the status of books XI and XII of *Paradise Lost* has been expanded into a study of the critical history of that poem. The "professional anti-professionalism" of literary studies has been explored in a series of essays that show it to be a constituent of professional ideology. (To be a professional is to think of oneself as motivated by something larger than marketplace conditions— by, for instance, a regard for justice or for the sanctity of human life or for the best that has been thought and said—even as that larger something is itself given shape and being by the very market conditions it supposedly transcends.) These essays have been vigorously criticized by James Fanto, Drucilla Cornell, Bruce Robbins, Steven Mailloux, Samuel Weber, Martha Nussbaum, David Luban, Gerald Graff, Walter Davis, and others, and the resulting dialogue has done its part (along with the work of Michel Foucault, Pierre Bourdieu, Michel de Certeau, Terry Eagleton, Robert Scholes, Paul Bové, William Cain, John Fekete, Jonathan Arac, and Russell Jacoby) in making the question of professionalism a more familiar and respectable one than it was in 1979.

Other things have changed since 1979. Antinomianism is no longer absent from the *Milton Encyclopedia,* having been added as an entry in a special supplement to the final volume. The Spenser Society is fully established and its activities are ritualized no less than are the activities of the Milton Society, which of course goes on as it always has. (Some things never change.) Romanticism is no longer firmly identified with

M. H. Abrams or with anyone else. The canon of greater and lesser works is no longer firmly in place. Indeed, it never was except as an assumption continually belied by history; now the fact of the canon is no longer even assumed; new challenges emerge every day and have become as orthodox as the orthodoxy they indict.

But perhaps the greatest change is the one that renders the key opposition of the essay—between the timeless realm of literature and the pressures and exigencies of politics—inaccurate as a description of the assumptions prevailing in the profession. To be sure, there are those who still believe that literature is defined by its independence of social and political contexts (a "concrete universal" in Wimsatt's terms), but today the most influential and up-to-date voices are those that proclaim exactly the reverse and argue that the thesis of literary autonomy is itself a political one, part and parcel of an effort by the conservative forces in society to protect traditional values from oppositional discourse. Rather than reflecting, as Ransom would have it, an "order of existence" purer than that which one finds in "actual life," literature in this new (historicist) vision directly and vigorously "participates in historical processes and in the political management of reality."[23] Moreover, as Louis Montrose observes, if literature is reconceived as a social rather than a merely aesthetic practice, literary criticism, in order to be true to its object, must be rearticulated as a social practice too and no longer be regarded as a merely academic or professional exercise.[24]

It is with this turn in the argument that one begins to see something strange (or perhaps not so strange): in at least one of its aspects the new historicism is the old high formalism writ political. I say "in one of its aspects" because the kind of work produced by the two visions is markedly different in many important ways, in the questions asked, in the materials interrogated, in the structures revealed, and in the claims made for the revelation—on one hand the claim to have reaffirmed a distinct and abiding aesthetic realm, on the other the claim to have laid bare the contradictions and fissures that an ideology can never quite manage to contain. Within these differences, however, one thing remains the same: the true and proper view of literature and literary studies defines itself against academic politics, which are seen by the aestheticians as being too much like the politics of "actual life" and by the new historicists as being not enough like the politics of "actual life." The complaint is different, but its target—the procedures and urgencies of professional activity—is familiar, and so is the opposition underlying the different complaints, the opposition between an activity in touch with higher values and an activity that has abandoned those values for something base and philistine. Whether the values are generality, detachment, disembodied vision, and moral unity on the one hand or discontinuity, rupture, disintegration, and engagement on the other, the fear is that they will be compromised by the demands that issue from the pressures of careerism, the pressure to publish, to say something new, to get a job, to get promoted, to get recognized, to get famous, and so on. In the context of the aesthetic vision these pressures are destructive of everything that is truly intellectual; in the context of the historicist vision, they are destructive of everything that is truly (as opposed to merely institutionally) political. Not only do the two visions share an enemy, they share a vocabulary, the vocabulary of transcendence, for in the discourses of both we are urged to free ourselves from parochial imperatives, to realize the true nature of our calling, to participate in that which is *really* and abidingly important. It is just that in one case the important thing is the life of the poetic mind, while in the other it is the struggle against repression and totalization; but that is finally only the difference between two differently pure acts, both of which are pure (or so is the claim) by *not* being the acts of an embedded professional. In 1979 (and in the years before) I was arguing for politics and against transcendence; now I am arguing for politics and against Politics (the new transcendence). As Donne might have said, small change when we are to (materialist) bodies gone.

It would seem then that there is some point to publishing this essay even nine years later (I have heeded, involuntarily, Horace's advice), since its argument is still being resisted, although from another direction. That argument, to rehearse it one last time, is that professional concerns and urgencies, rather than being impediments to responsible (meritorious) action, are determinative of the shape responsible action can take. One does not perform acts of criticism by breaking free of the profession's norms and constraints whether in the service of timeless masterpieces or in the name of political liberation, and whenever the claim to have broken free is made you can be sure that it is underwritten, authorized, and rendered intelligible by the very disciplinary boundaries it purports to have left behind.

9. Short People Got No
Reason to Live: Reading Irony

Not too many years ago Randy Newman wrote and recorded a popular song that quickly became notorious. It was called "Short People" and began by declaring that "short people got no reason, short people got no reason, short people got no reason to live." The song went on to rehearse in detail the shortcomings of short people, which included small voices, beady little eyes, and the inconvenience of having to pick them up in order to say "hello." It wasn't long before groups of short people were organizing to lobby against the song; it was banned in Boston, and there was a bill to the same effect introduced into the Maryland legislature. In the midst of the hullabaloo occasioned by the song, its author rose (metaphorically, of course) to say that he had been misunderstood: it was not part of his intention to ridicule short people; rather, he explained, it was his hope that by choosing an object of prejudice so absurd, he might expose the absurdity of all prejudice, whether its objects were Jews or women or blacks or Catholics, or whatever. He was, in short, or so he claimed, being ironic.

Not surprisingly, Newman's statement did not settle the matter. His critics, it seems, were unimpressed by what he said, and they had various ways of discounting it. Some simply declared that he had lied. Others invoked the familiar distinction between intention and utterance: he may have intended no slur on short people, but his words say otherwise. Still others turned to psychology and explained that while Newman perhaps *thought* that he was free of prejudice, his song displayed his true feelings, feelings he had hidden even from himself. In short (a phrase that should, I suppose, be used sparingly in this chapter), rather than providing a point of clarity and stability, Newman's explanations (not heard as explanations at all, but as rationalizations or lies) merely extended the area of interpretive dispute.

I find this incident fraught with implications for the practice of literary studies, and especially for the practice and perception of irony, for what Newman perhaps has learned (I say perhaps because I am in no better position than anyone else to rule absolutely) is what Defoe and others had already learned to their respective costs: irony is a risky business because one cannot at all be certain that readers will be directed to the ironic meanings one intends. According to our most recent theorist of irony, such problems are special or marginal rather than general, for, in general—that is, for the most part—ironies are stable. I am referring, of course, to Wayne Booth, who roundly declares, "I can without blushing say: I *know* that Jane Austen intended Mr. Bennet's statement as meaning something radically different from what he *seems* to say."[1] Indeed, Professor Booth knows a great deal more than that about a great many stably ironic works, and the principles underlying his knowledge are the subject of his book, *A Rhetoric of Irony,* a book that instructs us both in the ways of detecting irony and in the ways of processing it. Stable ironies, Booth explains, have four identifying marks:

1. They are intended, . . . deliberately created by human beings to be heard or read or understood with some precision by other human beings. . . .

2. They are all *covert,* intended to be reconstructed with meanings different from those on the surface. . . .

3. They are all nevertheless *stable* or fixed, in the sense that once a reconstruction of meaning has been made, the reader is not then invited to undermine it with further demolitions and reconstructions. . . .

4. They are all *finite* in application; . . . the reconstructed meanings are in some sense local, limited. . . . We can say with great security certain things that are violated by the overt words of the discourse.[2]

These "marks" are aggressively noted, and it is obvious that they represent an attempt by Booth to set limits on the operation of irony, so that its undermining of overt or literal meanings will have a fixed and specifiable shape; but, unfortunately, they will not do as marks that *signal* the presence of irony (stable or otherwise), because it is precisely *their* presence that is in dispute when there is a debate as to whether or not a particular work is ironic. That is, one cannot argue for an ironic interpretation by pointing to these marks, because one will be able to point to them only as a consequence of an interpretation that has already been hazarded. Thus, for example, no one of the parties to the "Short People" dispute believes that the meanings he perceives were not intended; it is just that whatever intention is specified, it will be as much a product of interpretation as the reading it directs. Nor is it any help to say that an ironic meaning is always "covert," because the question of whether or not there *is* a covert meaning is precisely what is at issue, and therefore the covertness of a proposed meaning is not an argument for it; it is an argument. Things are no better with the third of Booth's marks, stability or fixity; the meanings proposed for "Short People" are *all* stable in that they do not involve further demolitions or reconstructions, but they are stable in different directions; that is, in as many directions as there are determinations of Newman's intention; and, moreover, in their various stabilities these same meanings are all finite and limited, offered, as Booth stipulates, with "great security" and certainty; it is just that not everyone is certain in the same way.

The certainty Booth desires is of quite a different order, for it would have to rest on something that was not itself a matter of opinion, and therefore subject to challenge; but what the Randy Newman example shows is that whatever one rests on in the course of identifying an irony will have exactly the same status as the reading that follows (with certainty) from it; that is, it will be the product of an interpretation. This holds equally for the steps, also four in number, by which an ironic meaning is supposedly processed or reconstructed. Step one, Booth tells us, is that "the reader is required to reject the literal meaning," because he will be "unable to escape recognizing either some incongruity among the words or between the words and something else that he knows." As an example, Booth cites this fragment from Voltaire's *Candide,* "When all was over and the rival kings were celebrating their victory with Te Deums in their respective camps," and declares that "the statement simply cannot be accepted at face value" (*B*-10). (The fact that I am always forced to explain the incongruity to an audience or a class in itself renders the declaration suspect.) But the incongruity will be inescapable only if it is assumed that the victory being celebrated by the two kings is the same one; if it has been established that the two kings entered the battle with different, but mutually compatible, objectives, then it would involve no contradiction at all to say that each had an occasion to celebrate a victory. The point is that incongruities do not announce themselves, as Booth assumes they do; rather, they emerge in the context of interpretive assumptions, and therefore the registering of an incongruity cannot be the basis of an interpretation, since it is the product of one.

This means that Booth's second step—the trying out of "alternative interpretations or explanations" (*B*-11), will be performed in relation to an incongruity that is itself an "alternative interpretation." And when the third step is taken, and the alternative readings are sorted out by referring them to "the author's knowledge or beliefs," still another interpretive construct will have been introduced, for the characterization of that knowledge and those beliefs will be, as Booth says, a "decision" (*B*-11), a decision based not on direct inspection, but on a conjectural reconstruction of what the author might have known or believed. It is on the basis of that decision, made with reference to alternatives that are only alternatives in relation to an incongruity that is itself interpretively produced, that we finally take step four and "choose a new meaning or cluster of meanings with which we can rest secure" (*B*-12). That security, however, is as precarious as any of the interpretive links with which it has been fashioned. So long as they are in place, everything seems stable and incontestable; but as soon as any one of them is put into question—by disputing the presence of an incongruity, by adding one more to our list of alternative readings, by revising our sense of an author's beliefs—the entire edifice trembles, and the debate over whether an utterance is ironic or over which of several ironic meanings is the right one will begin again.

This is precisely the conclusion that Booth wishes to avoid, because he believes that to reach it is to abandon all hope of ever resting confidently in a reading or of being able to say to another, "My reading is better than yours." The stakes in this enterprise are very high, for, as Booth explains, "if irony is, as Kierkegaard and the German romantics taught the world, 'absolute infinite negativity,' and if, as many believe, the world or universe or creation provides at no point a hard and fast resistance to further ironic corrosion, then all meanings dissolve into one supreme meaning: No meaning" (*B*-93). What Booth sees (although not always as clearly as one might wish) is that the shoring up of stable irony is the shoring up of meaning itself: "If the universe is ultimately an absurd multiverse, then all propositions about or portraits of any part of it are ultimately absurd . . . [and] there is no such thing as a 'fundamental violation' of the text" (*B*-267). This is a dark vision, indeed, and one can only agree with Booth's desire to resist it and with his assertion that it is counterintuitive, given the wide range of communicative certainties that characterize our daily experience. What is required, of course, is an explanation of those certainties, and my quarrel with Booth is not that he seeks it, but that he finds it in the wrong places.

He finds it first of all in the Hirschian distinction between meaning and significance, a distinction between what the words say and what any number of interpreters, proceeding from any number of viewpoints with any number of purposes, might be able to make of them. Debates about significance are inevitable, but they can also be principled and grounded, because "running constant throughout any such debate would be agreement about meaning" (*B*-21); or, again, "the central meaning of the words is fixed and univocal regardless of how many peripheral and contradictory significances different readers may add" (*B*-91). It follows, then, that "we have grossly exaggerated the actual disagreement even about the hard cases," for "in thousands of undisputed matters" we "read precisely the same work, but have chosen . . . to debate about what is debatable" (*B*-133). From this argument, it is a short step (really no step at all) to the notion of the "work itself"—identified with meaning—as the point of resistance to "ironic corrosion." That is, the work is "a structure of meanings, an order which rules out some readings as entirely fallacious, shows other readings to be partially so, and confirms others as more or less adequate" (*B*-242). It is the availability of that structure *before* significances are added to it that authorizes Booth to reject a reading in which "Claudius is the moral center of *Hamlet*," in the full confidence that "nothing in the work requires" him to accept it (*B*-19).

If these arguments seem circular, it is because they all rest on a single point, the perspicuity and independence of literal meaning. Indeed, each of Booth's key distinctions—between meaning and significance, between a "central meaning" and that which is debatable, between the "work itself" and what different readers and different circumstances might add to it—is no more than a distinction between a literal meaning, that which is indisputably and irreducibly "there," and interpretation, that which issues from some special perspective or set of interests. It is literal meaning, then, that grounds the interpretive process and provides a core of agreement, on the basis of which *principled* debate can then go on; for each of the readings generated in the course of debate will have to pass the minimal test of being compatible under the structure of meanings that remains fixed and univocal. In the case of "Short People," for example, any reading of Newman's intentions will at the very least have to take into account the fact that he uttered the words, "Short people got no reason to live," and meant them literally, even if it is then argued that he intends us to set aside that literal meaning for one that is ironic.

This argument will hold, however, only if the specification of literal meaning occurs independently of the interpretive activity of which it is to be the ground; that is, only if everyone who hears the utterance "short people got no reason to live," will hear it, at some basic level, in the same way. But, in fact, the dispute over the song is a dispute *about* its literal meaning, a dispute that arises because the words are heard, from the first, within different assumptions as to the circumstance of their production. If one assumes, as many of Newman's critics do, that the speaker, in saying that short people got no reason to live, is rendering a *judgment,* then the words will literally and immediately mean that short people do not deserve to live (and the way would then be open to arguing whether *that* literal meaning is offered seriously); but if one reconceives the speaker and imagines that he himself is a short person, then it is likely that the utterance will be heard as a *complaint,* and the words will literally mean that short people, because of the indignities and inconveniences they suffer, have nothing to live *for* (i.e., short people got no reason to live). In both cases there is a literal meaning and it is at once obvious and inescapable, but it is not the same one. The conclusion, a distressing one for Booth, is that literal meaning is no more stable (in the sense of being unchanging) than the interpretations it supposedly authorizes. Literal meaning, rather than being independent of perspective, is a product of perspective (it is the meaning that, given a perspective, will immediately emerge); it is itself an interpretation and cannot therefore be the indisputable ground on which subsequent interpretations securely rest.

This is not an argument that Booth confronts because he never feels obliged to prove the case for literal meaning; he simply assumes it as something so necessary to his own position that any challenge to it would be unthinkable. There simply *must* be a level of fixed and unvarying meaning, for if there were not, rational inquiry would be impossible. To the extent that he provides evidence for his conviction, it is evidence drawn from the history of literary criticism and, more specifically, from events in that history that have *not* occurred. That is, whenever Booth feels himself in danger of giving interpretation more than its due, he pulls himself (and us) back into line by rehearsing a list of interpretations that have not been put forward:

> We disagree about many "larger" issues: whether the Houyhnnms are to be seen as totally admirable, whether the Duke in *Measure for Measure* behaves badly, whether Mary Crawford in *Mansfield Park* is not unfairly treated by Jane Austen's moralizing voice. But nobody has suggested, even in this age of critical fecundity, that "A Modest Proposal" is a tragedy, or a paean to the British landlords or to Irish collaborators, or even a modest proposal for preventing the children of Ireland from being a burden to their parents or country. And nobody has suggested that "My Mistress' Eyes" or *Northanger Abbey* should be read either as non-ironic or as totally ironic, with no clear stop signs. Swift and Shakespeare and Jane Austen will not, after all, allow such freedoms; whether we like it or not, they determine, through the literary forms they created, both where we begin and where we stop (*B*-133–34).

The line of reasoning that follows from these examples is clear: in the long history of literary studies, there are certain interpretations that have never been offered seriously, interpretations that all of us would regard as obviously absurd. The explanation can only be that something is excluding these interpretations, while authorizing, at least as possibilities, a number of others; and that something could only be the intentions of the author as they are embodied in the verbal forms he has created, that is, in the literal meaning of the text.

This argument has a certain prima facie force, but it depends on an assumption that is never examined, the assumption that what *has* not happened is what *could* not happen. That is, for Booth the fact that no one has ever suggested this or that reading is tantamount to a proof that no one ever will, or at the least to a proof that if any one ever did, he would not be given a hearing. Unfortunately (or fortunately, depending on where you stand on these issues), Booth himself provides a counterexample to his argument when he turns, at one point, to Swift's "Verses on the Death of Dr. Swift," and specifically to the controversy over whether the lines spoken in praise of Swift by "one quite indifferent" are to be read ironically. Only in a footnote—it is almost as if Booth were trying to hide from himself the implications of what he is about to report—do we learn that the controversy is of recent date, and that, until 1963, "nobody had suggested irony in Swift's self-praise" (*B*-121). In that year Barry Slepian published an article suggesting just that,[3] and, as Booth reports, "most of the discussions since 1963 have accepted his arguments." That is, the ironic reading did not exist until a single critic proposed it.

What is remarkable is that Booth, having taken note of this fact of literary history, does not see its relationship to his own position; in particular, he does not see that it undermines the case not only for stable irony, but for stability in general. It is crucial to Booth's argument that there be at least some works of which it can be said that they are indisputably either straightforward or ironic, and he takes great comfort from the existence of works that have always been read one way or the other. Here, however, is a work or a part of a work that until 1963 was considered ironic by nobody, and since 1963 has been considered ironic by nearly everybody; and if *A Rhetoric of Irony* had been published in 1962, the ironic reading of the last section of "Verses on the Death of Dr. Swift" might have been one of those of which Booth could have said, "No one has ever proposed it."

What are we to make of this? How can we take it into account without totally undermining our faith in rational inquiry and principled debate? The answer to this question will be found in a better understanding of how Slepian was able to do what he did. What is the explanation for his success? In Booth's model the explanation could take one of only two forms: either Slepian is the first person in 230 years (with the exception of Swift) to have recognized the irony that was always there, or the lines are in fact not ironic, and for some reason he has succeeded in exercising almost mesmeric powers over his fellow Swiftians; that is, he either saw the text clearly (where no one else had) or persuaded others to see a text that wasn't there. Of course, he did neither; what he did was argue, and he argued in such a way as to persuade a significant number of his colleagues to see what he saw. He did not do this by simply *pointing* to the facts of the text (although that is the claim made by everyone who enters these waters); rather, he labored to *establish* the facts of the text, that is, to establish a perspective or a way of seeing from the vantage point of which the text would have for others the shape it had for him.

This is not to say that his was an act of unconstrained creation. The establishing of a perspective proceeds according to quite regular rules, rules that Slepian followed, even though he may have been unaware of them. The first rule is that one must remove the perspective that is already there, the perspective that is responsible for the text that everyone has hitherto seen. In this case that perspective was established by two of the poem's first readers, Dr. William King, to whom Swift sent the manuscript for publication, and Alexander Pope, who apparently agreed with King's judgment that "the latter part of the poem might be thought by the public a little vain, if so much were said by himself of himself" (S-250). It was on the basis of this judgment that the two men, in consultation with others of Swift's friends, altered the poem and published a version that was immediately repudiated by the author. The text of the poem was therefore corrupt from its first appearance, and the "true" text was not available until 1937, when Harold Williams published his authoritative edition.

There is a lesson here for those who speak confidently of *the* text, but I will not belabor it, since I am more interested in the fact that the poem's textual history begins with the conviction that in lines 307–484, Swift is engaged in an indecorous act of self-praise. That conviction was not repudiated after 1937, but took a new and diagnostic form in the speculation by John Middleton Murry that at the time the poem was written, Swift's mind was already failing: "The sardonic objectivity gives place to an extravagance of self-laudation. So striking a lapse from decorum must be ascribed to a radical weakening of Swift's vigour of mind."[4] The Swift that Slepian inherits is the product of this interpretive tradition, and he makes his first and decisive move when he challenges that tradition in the name of the "real" Swift. "I think that a close look at 'Verses on the Death of Dr. Swift' will disclose that Jonathan Swift had a better understanding of the poem than Alexander Pope and John Middleton Murry" (S-251). This is a powerful move because it trades on the privileged status accorded to authorial intention in the Anglo-American literary institution; it is also something of a polemical sleight of hand, since Pope and Murry do not oppose their understandings to Swift's; they merely have a different view of Swift's understanding than Slepian does, or to put it more precisely they see a different Swift in relation to whom the words they read have an obvious and immediate meaning. What Slepian must do is replace their Swift with another, and when he does, the words of the poem will have the meaning that this new Swift *must* have intended. That is, while Slepian proposes simply to take a "close look" at the poem, what he really does is defer that look until he has positioned his readers in such a way that the look *they* take will produce the poem he wants them to see.

Slepian does this in workmanlike fashion, announcing that he will "first . . . dispose of Murry's biographical explanations" (S-251). By that he does not mean that he will challenge the relevance of biographical explanations in the manner of a doctrinaire New Critic; rather, he will propose an alternative set of explanations and thus dispose of Murry's Swift. In place of a Swift who is senile and wandering, Slepian puts the Swift of Thomas Sheridan, an early biographer, who declares that during this period, Swift's "faculties do not seem to have been at all impaired by the near approaches of old age and his poetical fountain . . . still flowed in as clear and pure a stream." Slepian then cites the evidence of "well-sustained" poems that were written after this one, and concludes by asserting that "in 1732 Swift's mind was not 'weakening'" (S-253). (Of course, it could have weakened intermittently, but I am not so much interested in assessing Slepian's arguments as in analyzing the way in which he makes them.)

Slepian next disposes of the Swift of Pope and King, the man blind to his own vanity even in a poem whose very subject is vanity. He first argues from probability; it is much more likely "that Swift was up to his usual ironical tricks" (S-252). A second argument is stronger and more complicated: in the readings of Pope and Murry, the offending lines constitute an "incongruous addendum" (S-252); but Slepian promises to demonstrate that they are "the necessary completion of a complex pattern." That is, he promises to make the poem better. In the literary courtroom there is no more powerful argument; for while critics, like other researchers, claim to be interested only in the truth, they are committed to finding a specifically *literary* truth, one that will validate the credentials of the work they have undertaken to examine. So that if Slepian can come up with a reading that improves the poem's reputation, the probability of its being accepted as a true reading will be very high.

Slepian begins by invoking another powerful institutional formula: the poem can be easily divided into three parts. An entire essay could be written on the effectiveness of declaring that a poem has three parts, an effectiveness that may have an explanation in the tendency of literary criticism, at least since Matthew Arnold, to appropriate the discourse of religion. At any rate, once you are told that a poem has three parts, and you know too that one of those parts has always been considered an excrescence, you know, with all the certainty that attends membership in the literary community, that the third part is about to be brought into a harmonious relationship with the other two and so contribute to the making of an "organic whole." Moreover, you know that that is what a critic is supposed to do, and when he does it, you are willing to give the reading that results more than the benefit of the doubt. In this case it is done in less than four pages and in two swift (no irony intended) stages. First, Slepian points out that "no critic" in commenting on the first two parts of the poem has mistaken Swift's ironies and exaggerations for statements intended literally" (S-254). It follows then, from the unannounced principle that the mode of a poem should be the same throughout, that the third part is also ironic, and ironic in a way that makes it compatible with parts one and two. That way is found when Slepian declares that in this last section Swift makes himself the object of his own irony; by characterizing himself as "humble, fearless, altruistic, diligent, innocent, and resolute, he is not presenting an apologia, but making an assertion of his own vanity necessary to complete his thesis that all mankind is egotistical, selfish, and proud" (S-256). The poem is thus given a perfect New Critical shape: "The first part . . . says that people are vain; the second part that other men are vain; the third part that Swift is vain" (S-256). Quod erat demonstrandum.

Slepian, however, is unwilling to take credit for his accomplishment and insists on yielding it to Swift, who, he says, "has left clues . . . to show that he was not really taking himself seriously"; he himself has merely picked up on these clues, where others, for over 200 years, have missed them. Slepian's modesty is no doubt sincere, but it is also (even if unself-consciously) strategic, since it displays his conformity with another unwritten, but powerful, rule, the rule that a critic does not create, but only discovers meanings. Nevertheless, it is obvious that the clues Slepian has persuaded so many other readers to see become available only as a consequence of the change in perspective he brings about in this brief article. "Brings about" is perhaps too strong, because it suggests a wholly free act, whereas what Slepian has wrought is a consequence of his having made arguments that are recognized as telling by his peers, according to standards—of truth, evidence, adequacy—that are inseparable from the institution's notions of what its members are supposed to do. These notions, or conventions, are enabling as well as constraining, and they are in large part responsible for Slepian's success. In other words, he succeeds neither because he alone is uniquely in touch with the work itself nor because he has created the work out of whole cloth, but because, in accordance with procedures authorized by the institution, he has altered the conditions of seeing—the conditions under which one might take a "close look"— in such a way as to cause many to see a work other than the work they would have seen before he wrote.

Of course, the poem as it was previously seen was no less the product of some successful attempt (by a Pope or a Murry) to establish the conditions of seeing. To put it another way, while Slepian argues, as Booth insists that we must, from givens, he argues from givens that are only in place as a result of the kind of act he is himself performing. One of the givens that is in place when Slepian begins to write is the obvious irony of the poem's first two sections; and it is then open to him to presume on that irony when he moves to extend it to the third section, in a version of the "no one has suggested" argument ("no critic has mistaken Swift's ironies . . . for statements intended literally"); but it would be equally possible for someone to argue from the opposite direction, that is, from the fact that no one (before Slepian) had read irony into section three, to the demonstration that sections one and two are not really ironic either. And that is just what has happened since 1963. Writing in response to Slepian, Marshall Waingrow rejects the ironic reading of the encomium, but agrees that it does display Swift's vanity.[5] However, Waingrow contends, because the vanity is acknowledged, it can serve as a proper foundation for virtuous action (*W*-513). In effect, Waingrow is urging a change in the genre of the poem; in his reading it is less a satiric performance than a moral or homiletic one in which Swift offers himself as a model, necessarily flawed, of "moral perception." Once the third section of the poem has been read in this way, it is inevitable that the first and second sections will be brought into line. This step is taken by John Irwin Fischer, who sees in couplets like "I can not read a Line / But with a Sigh, I wish it mine" a "serious confession of Swift's envy" and "an act of true magnanimity." In Fischer's reading, every line "points" a moral, and the distinction between straightforward and ironic passages loses its force as what was once a poem becomes something very much like a sermon. (Swift's sermons are an important source for his argument.)

Of course, the poem can be read as a sermon only if the speaker is identified not with a persona, but with Swift himself, and indeed the critical history of the poem coincides with the rise and fall of the persona as a central tool of literary analysis. As a notion, the persona operates to further the New Critical goal of enforcing a distinction between literary or aesthetic facts and the facts of an author's life. One sees this clearly, for example, in Maynard Mack's famous essay, "The Muse of Satire," which is essentially a set of directions for turning "apparently very personal poems" into satiric fictions.[6] By the time Slepian writes, this is a standard strategy, and he is able to rely on it (even though he does not invoke it) when he argues that Swift is not speaking seriously—that is, in his own person. But when Waingrow and Fischer elaborate a reading that is unashamedly autobiographical, it is a sign that it is once again becoming permissible to regard a literary work as the expression of deeply held personal views. In 1973 Robert Uphaus explicitly dismisses the persona theory—"Swift . . . is not exploiting a literary convention which we may conveniently dub the *vir bonus*"—and declares that "the man, Jonathan Swift, is the poem's matter, and his mind, rather than poetic convention, is the poem's governing form."[7] As more and more of the poem is returned to Swift, less and less is reserved for irony. Uphaus is willing to admit to the presence of some irony in the poem—it does not drop "completely out of sight"—but, he concludes, "the *over-all* effect . . . is hardly ironic" (*U*-415). In ten years we have gone from Slepian's all-ironic poem (itself put in place of a poem that was only two-thirds ironic) to a poem that is only fitfully ironic, if it is ironic at all.

This does not mean, however, that Slepian's reading has simply been set aside and no longer exerts any influence. Indeed, its continuing influence is seen precisely in the readings that are opposed to it, for they are constrained even in their opposition by what Slepian has established. In particular, he has established as central the issue of Swift's artistry. Having made the poem better by rescuing it from the charges of Pope and Murry, he has brought about a situation in which it would be professionally unwise for anyone to make it worse. As a result, a critic who wants to argue with Slepian has to argue in such a way as to validate Swift's artistry even more strongly than Slepian does. That is, while one can certainly argue for a different "Verses on the Death of Dr. Swift," one would have great difficulty in arguing for a bad, or even an imperfect, "Verses on the Death of Dr. Swift." (Neither Murry's mad and senile Swift nor Pope's embarrassingly vain Swift is any longer with us, although one could certainly imagine circumstances under which they could be revived.) Just as Slepian could not have been successful had he not pointed to the givens and taken-for-granteds that were in place when he wrote, so no one who writes today will be successful if he fails to take into account the givens Slepian established.

This account of the critical process at once confirms and problematizes Booth's argument in *A Rhetoric of Irony.* In Booth's view rational debate rests on a set of independent facts to which all parties subscribe; but what the recent history of Swift's poem shows is that, while debate is certainly grounded on facts, they are facts that have themselves been established as the result of debate. Membership in the category of the indisputable is determined in the course of disputes; givens are not given but made, and once made, they can serve as the basis for unchallengeable observations, until they are themselves challenged in the name of givens that have been made by someone else. The constraints and certainties that Booth seeks in all the wrong places—in a system of literal meaning, in the distinction between meaning and significance, in the fact that there are readings that no one has ever suggested—are to be found in the very process he would have them control. The result is that two of Booth's worst fears are confirmed, but in a way that removes their sting. The first fear is that what is ironic will be for the reader to decide, for in the absence of independent criteria, he may see ironies or not as he pleases. This, however, is an empty fear, for the decision a reader makes will have been possible only in relation to decision procedures that have been authorized by the institution. Someone who decides for reasons the institution doesn't recognize, that is, someone who decides the poem is ironic because its author's name is Jonathan, will not succeed in persuading anyone else to his view (at least not now).

This is precisely Booth's second fear: that the question of whether or not a work is ironic will be settled by whoever happens to be the most persuasive: "The critic with the most persuasive style wins because there are after all no rules imposed by 'the work itself' and there is no referee" (B-133). This is a fear Booth can feel because he conceives of persuasion as something that operates without constraints—as a form of sheer brute power—unless there is an independent object such "as the work itself" to control it; but power, like anything else, is a context-specific entity, and what will be persuasive in a situation is not a matter of "style" (a word that is particularly empty), but a function of the understood goals and practices, notions of what counts as evidence, and of what will be heard as a relevant argument, that define the shape of an activity in a particular historical moment. So that while there are no rules imposed by the work itself (an entity that is produced by persuasion and does not precede it), there are always rules, or rules of thumb, that are constitutive both of the possibilities and of the limits of what can be said and what can be demonstrated. One persuades neither on the basis of independent entities nor on the basis of pure will (another chimera), but on the basis of grounds that have themselves been established by prior acts of persuasion; and what one persuades *to* are new grounds. The whole of Booth's theory rests on the possibility and the undoubted fact of agreement; but he seems to think that there are two kinds of agreement, a good kind, to which persons are compelled by facts that are unassailable; and a bad kind, to which persons are forced by the illegitimate power of a discourse that rests on nothing. But unassailable facts are unassailable only because an act of persuasion has been so successful that it is no longer regarded as one, and instead has the status of a simple assertion about the world. In short, there are no facts that are not the product of persuasion, and therefore no facts that stand to the side of its operations; all agreements are the result of the process for which Booth seeks an independent ground, and therefore no agreement, however securely based it may seem for the moment, is invulnerable to challenge.

Thus when a community of readers agrees that a work, or a part of a work, is ironic, that agreement will have come about because the community has been persuaded to a set of assumptions, to a *way* of reading, that produces the ironic meanings that all of its members "see"; and when and if that community is persuaded to another way, those meanings will disappear and be replaced by others that will seem equally obvious and inescapable. Irony, then, is neither the property of works nor the creation of an unfettered imagination, but a way of reading, an interpretive strategy that produces the object of its attention, an object that will be perspicuous to those who share or have been persuaded to share the same strategy. In general, that strategy has just the shape Booth says it does. One assumes for the speaker an intention other than the intention that would have produced the meaning the words seem immediately to have, the literal meaning; but the meaning the words seem immediately to have is itself the product of an assumed intention within imagined circumstances; and therefore, when that literal meaning has been set aside for an ironic one, what has happened is that one interpretive construct has been replaced by another. That is to say, *if irony is a way of reading, so is literalness;* neither way is prior to the other, in the sense of being a mode of calculation rather than interpretation; both are interpretive ways, which are set in motion by cues and considerations that are themselves in place as a consequence of an interpretive act.[8]

The point is a difficult one, but it may be clearer if we turn, for the last time, to Swift's poem. I can decide, as some readers have, that "Verses on the Death of Dr. Swift" is ironic, because there is a contradiction between Swift's claim that he lashes vices and not names (1.460), and his performance in this very poem. Or I can decide, as others have, that this claim is made seriously, and that for any number of reasons, Swift was simply blind to the contradiction. But I can also decide that the line is perfectly serious, because Swift conceives of the men he has named as the very incarnations of the vices he would lash, and therefore not as persons at all. In so deciding, I would be reading the line in such a way as to remove the contradiction it supposedly entails. But the presence or absence of a contradiction is one of those literal facts that are supposedly specifiable apart from interpretation. If contradictions can be made to appear and disappear by varying the assumptions within which reading occurs, then the literal level of meaning is as much an interpretive construct—the product of a way of reading—as the level of meaning we call ironic.

It is Booth's strategy in *A Rhetoric of Irony* to stabilize irony by linking it firmly to literal meaning. In my argument that link has been made even firmer (indeed, too firm for comfort) by undoing the distinction between them, at least insofar as it is a distinction between something that is interpreted and something that is not. That is, by making literal and ironic readings equally the products of interpretation, I may have seemed to undermine stability altogether, because if interpretation covers the field, there is nothing on which a particular interpretation can rest. But what I have been trying to show is that interpretations rest on other interpretations, or, more precisely, on assumptions—about what is possible, necessary, telling, essential, and so on—so deeply held that they are not thought of as assumptions at all; and because they are not thought of as assumptions, the activities they make possible and the facts they entail seem not to be matters of opinion or debate, but a part of the world. Of course, it is not inconceivable that these assumptions could themselves be put into question, but that could only happen because other assumptions will have acquired the force once theirs, and are, at least for the time being, unquestioned in their turn. Rational debate—about whether or not a work is ironic or about anything else—is always possible; not, however, because it is anchored in a reality outside it, but because it occurs in a history, a history in the course of which realities and anchors have been established, although it is always possible, and indeed inevitable, that they will have to be established again. For Booth the great question is, How can you know without doubt whether or not a work is ironic? My answer is that you always know, but that what you know, because it rests on a structure of assumptions and beliefs (which produce both literal and ironic meanings), is subject to challenge or revision, as a result of which you will still always know, even though what you know will be different. For someone like Booth such a state of affairs is distressing because it seems to doom us to an infinite regress of unstable interpretations; but one can just as easily say that it graces us with an endless succession of interpretive certainties, a reassuring sequence in which one set of obvious and indisputable facts gives way to another.

10. Profession Despise Thyself:
Fear and Self-Loathing in Literary Studies

In September 1982 columnist Peter A. Jay of the *Baltimore Sun* turned from his usual concern with the intricacies of city politics to the absurdities, or so he perceived them, of the academy.[1] His specific target was the world of English Studies, and he began by observing that "Professors, especially professors of literature, have always been fair game." My purpose here is to inquire into the reason why this should be so, why professors of literature should so often be the objects of criticism and ridicule, and why the source of the criticism is so often the literary community itself. Jay is not a member of that community, but the charges he levels are familiar; we have all heard them, and some of us may even have made them. The bill of indictment contains several particulars, but the basic complaint is that teachers of literature, and especially of English, have abandoned their proper study, "the study of life itself, as seen by writers of skill and vision," and given themselves over to the trivialities that accompany "specialization run amok," to topics (the examples are Jay's) like "Lesbian Feminist Poetry in Texas" and "The Trickster Figure in Chicano and Black Literature" or "other ephemera." Rather than committing themselves to "the broad stream of intellectual history," these men and women have become "academic timeservers trying to make their field so obscure, and its language so arcane, that no one can possibly understand it but themselves and a handful of other insiders." As a result, departments of English find themselves without clients and "now pander to the whim of the moment in a desperate attempt to attract . . . paying bodies."

One might pause here to note an apparent contradiction. On the one hand, teachers of literature are faulted for having become so specialized as to exclude all but a few from their circle; on the other, they are frantically reaching out to a mass audience. But I am less interested in analyzing the internal logic (such as it is) of Jay's argument than in identifying the set of assumptions that generate it, for they are the assumptions that underlie the fact that professors of literature are always fair game. First of all, there is the assumption that the category of literature is made up of works that transcend the circumstances of particular times and places; such works are, by definition, opposed to "ephemera" and the "whim[s] of the moment" and penetrate instead into the study of life itself. It follows, then, and this is a corollary assumption, that works which advocate or have their origin in particular attitudes, strategies, sectarian projects, or political programs do not qualify as literature and should not be treated as such by literary scholars.

Two other assumptions do not at first sight seem to follow, but in fact they do. The first is the assumption that it is wrong for teachers and students of literature to hearken to the marketplace, that is, to the needs and desires of potential paying customers, and the second is the assumption that those aspects of the academy which smack of the marketplace—matters of publication, tenure, and professional power—should be avoided and deplored. Whatever a professor of literature does, he or she shouldn't do it merely in order to get promoted, to become an expert in some small subject that no one has ever thought important, or to establish credentials at the expense of some fellow worker in the institutional vineyard. The relationship between these strictures and the definition of literature as something transcendent may seem obscure, but it will become clear as soon as one realizes that what is being demanded is a procedural purity that matches, in the sense of being answerable to, the presumed purity of the enterprise. That is, if literary works are produced in a realm far removed from the pressures and temptations of the everyday world—the world of commerce, competition, and politics—the business (not really a business at all) of honoring and explicating those works should be similarly removed, at least insofar as is possible.

Once one has these interrelated assumptions in view, it is easy to see why professors of literature are fair game: almost anything they do as professionals is likely to be held against them because it will always be possible to attribute to them some base or impure motive. In fact, insofar as they conduct themselves as professionals, their motives can only be base and impure, a conclusion Jay does not explicitly reach but surely implies when he deplores the "prevailing view" that it is far better to be "the world's greatest expert on Texas lesbian-feminist poets than to be a serious scholar who understands the broad stream of intellectual history." The crucial point about this comparison is the vagueness of Jay's preferred alternative in relation to the specificity of the alternative he scorns. What does it mean to understand the broad stream of intellectual history? The answer is that it doesn't mean anything in particular—it is as empty as Jay's other large phrase, "the study of life itself"—but it also means that a commitment to anything in particular is likely to be seen as a violation of it, whatever it is. That is to say, Texas lesbian-feminist poetry only looks like a particularly obvious instance of "specialization run amok"; but in fact it is specialization itself that is the object of Jay's criticism, and when push came to shove his position would commit him to opposing any focus narrower than the very broad—indeed, totally unbounded—focus he celebrates. To be an expert on anything at all—on seventeenth-century Protestant poetics or eighteenth-century political satire or nineteenth-century philology—is to be guilty of the main charge; and if specialization, rather than any particular instance of it, is Jay's true target, then his real objection is to the profession of letters itself, with all its attendant machinery, periods, journals, newsletters, articles, monographs, panels, symposia, conventions, textbooks, bibliographies, departments, committees, recruiting, placement, promotion, prizes, and the like.

Now it may seem to be stretching a point to conclude that anyone who attacks academic specialization is attacking the academy, but the conclusion is inevitable because specialization is the business of the academy, and if an argument against specialization is pursued far enough, it will shrink the area in which the academy can do business to almost nothing. As an example, consider another anti-professionalist piece, written by Pulitzer Prize-winning journalist Jonathan Yardley for a November 1982 edition of the *Washington Post*.[2] Yardley was disturbed by the publication of a manuscript version of Virginia Woolf's first novel, *The Voyage Out*. In his view the publication is an unfortunate "byproduct of academic specialization" and is an example of an "excess of scholarly enterprise," of interest only to the "Woolf specialist" for whom "each new shred of information is grist for the mill that produces dissertations and offprints, and papers and seminars—the effluvia of English departments." But if you take away dissertations, offprints, papers, and seminars, it is English departments themselves that become effluvia ("fumes emanating from decaying matter") because you are taking away most of what they do.

Yardley's argument, like Jay's, has a larger target than its rhetoric suggests, for once you have identified the proper object of literary study with something so general as the study of life itself, it is hard to see why there would be any need for an army of specialists whose business it was to tell you about literature. Isn't everyone, after all, an expert in life itself, fully competent to read and understand the work of those who have taken life as their subject? In Yardley's vision of things, the transaction between an author and his general readership is only short-circuited and overcomplicated by the superfluous efforts of specialists who must invent problems in order to have something to do and thus justify their positions and their salaries. Specialization (that is to say, professional literary study) is an affront both to the reader, who finds a formidable machinery and an alien vocabulary barring his access to the text, and to the author, whose larger intentions are ignored or set aside so that scholars can go about their work of "systematically raking through the odds and ends of literature." As a result, Yardley complains, the focus shifts from the "creative powers of the author" to the merely "re-creative methods of the specialist." Rather than enlarging and enriching "our understanding of a writer's life and career," professional literary scholarship "enlarges and enriches . . . our appreciation of a particular scholar's zeal and ingenuity."

To a certain extent Jay and Yardley are testifying to the ambivalence with which our society regards professionalism. On the one hand, the word "professional" is an honorific that is displayed prominently in the various media where we are invited to put our trust in this or that product or service because it is offered to us by professionals, by people who know what they are doing, who practice "state-of-the-art" skills and are in every way "up to date." The professional is the expert who possesses a competence not available to the man or woman in the street, and in a highly industrialized and technical society that competence is a necessary and valuable public resource. In another context, however, professionalism wears a darker face, the face of manipulation and self-aggrandizement. In this context professionalism is almost always accompanied by the adjective "mere" and stands for an activity in which a small and self-selected group conspires against the laity by claiming a superiority that is based finally on nothing more than an obfuscating jargon and the seized control of the machinery of production and distribution. From this perspective the individual professional is no longer a highly motivated servant of the public but a self-serving careerist whose vision extends only to the next rung on the ladder of advancement. When there is no more room on the ladder, it is simply extended by adding the bureaucracy of a new specialization defended by the members of the profession as a necessary response to the growing complexity of the field, but seen by the profession's critics as a transparent rationalization for extending its sway and further securing its privileges. The apparent contradiction between these views of professionalism is usually negotiated by the positing of two kinds of professionalism, one good and one bad. Good professionalism elaborates its machinery only to the extent demanded by its central and founding values; bad professionalism allows those values to be entirely overwhelmed by its machinery, which then becomes an end in itself. As Richard Ohmann puts in a particularly concise formulation of the anti-professionalist credo: when the "ethos of professionalism" takes over, "procedures supplant values and people are absorbed in structures."[3]

Literary anti-professionalism, as represented by Jay and Yardley, is obviously a version of this general indictment. But it is also more, in part, as we have seen, because the value that is either to be nourished or overwhelmed is defined in such a way as to remove the possibility of any legitimate link between it and most forms of critical activity. Indeed, given the twin assumptions that literature embodies values independent of any quotidian practice and that the work (in the static sense) of literature is already complete, critical activity becomes at once superfluous and dangerous. It is superfluous because (with the possible exception of the production of "definitive" editions) there is nothing to be done, no practical task that will validate the profession's right to exist, no buildings to be designed and constructed, no social ills to be identified and remedied, no diseases to be diagnosed and cured. And it is dangerous because in the absence of essential tasks, critics will be tempted to invent tasks (and problems and programs and agendas) that will soon come to obscure and even obliterate a value or repository of value that would have been better off left alone. It is this situation that explains the virulence of literary anti-professionalism: while most professions are criticized for betraying their ideals, this profession betrays its ideals by being practiced at all, by being, as a professor of medicine once put it to me, "a parasite on the carcass of literature." This also explains the fact that while in most cases anti-professional indictments are leveled from the outside, literary anti-professionalism is a feature of the profession itself, and indeed is the founding gesture of the profession insofar as it begins by thinking of itself as secondary and as removed from the world. Literary critics can hardly defend themselves against the accusations of irrelevance and self-promotion when the source of those accusations is what they themselves think and write.

As an example, consider an essay, "The Crisis in English Studies," written by Walter Jackson Bate for *Harvard Magazine* (September–October 1982). That essay has been reprinted and widely circulated, and it is cited by both Jay and Yardley as the chief, if not only, begetter of their own efforts. It is therefore doing real work in the world, and in what follows I will argue, first, that the work it is doing is pernicious, and, second, that the work it is doing is political, even though, like most anti-professionalist polemics, it presents itself as a program for removing politics and political considerations from a realm that should be independent of them. Predictably, Bate advertises his essay as a brief against "the new ersatz specialism," the effect of which has been to bypass "integrity and generality of vision" in favor of the narrow perspective of "restricted" and "manageable" fields and subfields.[4] Bate finds the roots of this unhappy situation in the late nineteenth century and, more specifically, in the formation in the 1880s of English departments. But since he is himself a member of an English department, one can hardly expect him to argue, as Jay and Yardley at least implicitly do, that there shouldn't be any; rather, he argues, almost explicitly, that there should only be one. This is the explanation for what at first seems to be a peculiar feature of Bate's essay: the crisis of his title is not a crisis of the marketplace. Although Bate does refer (and Jay after him) to the fact that at a certain point "the bottom fell out of the academic job market," in his view the real crisis is not an economic but a spiritual one, and its chief signs are not lacks but surpluses—so much so that in the last analysis he welcomes the unhappy market situation as a means of curbing the excesses of expansion and specialization. Although it is not open to Bate, given his position, to call for the end of the profession, he can call for a profession so reduced in scope that its boundaries are more or less identical with the confines of Cambridge.

This call is issued in the form of three interrelated complaints. First of all, Bate complains that there are too many Ph.D.'s, not because there are too few jobs but because they are not Ph.D's of the right kind; that is, they come from inferior institutions and especially from state universities which, he points out, went from a modest production of five or so a year "to producing seventy or eighty" (p. 50). His second complaint is that as the community of literary academics expands, its members expand the scope of their investigations to include documents and topics hitherto not regarded as literary at all, so that as things stand now, there are just too many things to teach. Bate cites, as examples of undesirable new courses and specialities, women's studies, gay studies, ethnic studies, and business English (an apparent anomaly on this list, but one that fits perfectly, as I shall show in a minute). From these two complaints, the third follows inevitably: there are too many people giving too many papers at too many panels at the convention of the Modern Language Association. It is here that we find, singled out for opprobrious mention, "Lesbian Feminist Poetry in Texas" and "The Trickster Figure in Chicano and Black Literature," as well as two others that Jay did not repeat, perhaps because he did not know enough to recognize what is for Bate their obvious absurdity: "Deconstruction as Politics" and "The Absent Father in Fact, Metaphor, and Metaphysics in the Middle Generation of American Poets."

Now, putting aside the job situation, as Bate puts it aside, this is a strange crisis, since it bears all the marks of disciplinary health: an army of active researchers, exploring new territories, sharing their discoveries and projects with one another, meeting regularly to explain, debate, and proselytize. What could be wrong? What is wrong, paradoxically, is the very fact that the profession, at least in intellectual terms, is healthy; for that means that it is not standing still and that its shape and the shape of its projects are continually changing. Widespread professional activity is at once a sign of these changes and an indication that they will continue. One imagines that part of what troubles Bate about a panel on the absent father in the middle generation of American poets is the possibility, indeed the certainty, that someone will want to ask and answer the question, What about the absent father in the *early* generation of American poets? And if there is a trickster figure in Chicano literature and in black literature, there is sure to be one in Yiddish literature and in the literature of the South and of the Old West. In short, there is no end to all this, just an ever-expanding horizon of new projects, new distinctions, new specializations, and, in Edmund Spenser's words, "endlesse worke."

It is this prospect that distresses Bate, not only because it will further fragment an enterprise whose coherence he believes to be in danger but because it will disperse the power and authority that was once centralized in Harvard and its sister institutions. For not only is the horizon lengthening, it is also broadening. Not only are there too many practitioners finding too many things to do, but these practitioners seem unwilling to confine themselves to the great tradition of supposedly apolitical art ("the best that has been thought and said") and insist, instead, on bringing into the canon (no longer *the* canon) texts produced by hitherto excluded groups—gays, Chicanos, women (even women who are not named George or safely tucked away in a bedroom for life), and filmmakers. And the inevitable consequence is that literary culture is no longer easily distinguishable from the social and political contexts that literature, at least in its high humanist definition, is supposed to transcend. It is even worse in the case of business English, at first a strange item to bring up the rear of this list, until one realizes that it represents the greatest outrage of all, the pollution of literature by the despised world of commerce. As Bate scathingly observes, if you study business English, you can perhaps get a job in a business school where, he notes with scorn, they "have money." And if you study film, you may get a job as a film reviewer and then settle down to a career that demands "little more than passive receptivity, the memory of miscellaneous titles, and facility with journalistic jargon" (p. 51).

One begins to see how draconian are the measures that must be taken if the enterprise is to be returned to the state Bate associates with earlier and happier days; any number of worlds and activities will have to be excluded. There shall be no blacks, no gays, no Chicanos, no filmmakers, no journalists, no women, no businessmen, and even, in some strange sense, no jobs. Bate, however, cannot mean this literally. He knows as well as anyone else (although it is part of what he laments) that, since the end of World War II, men and women of every religious, ethnic, national, and sexual persuasion from every possible social class have found their way into the world of letters. What he objects to (and in these circumstances, it is all that he *can* object to) is the tendency of these men and women to comport themselves *as* gays, blacks, Chicanos, and so forth, rather than as literary persons who just happen to be of a certain race, sex, or color. That is, the social diversity of the members of the literary community would be tolerable if their differences were subordinated to some general project, to some ideal that was not particularized in any way that corresponded to the interests and concerns of this or that group. Like Jay, Bate's real complaint is against specificity (for which, read specialization), and, again like Jay, he never quite names (except in the vaguest of terms) the positive value to which specificity stands opposed because to name it would be to render it too specific. In order to function as a value at once all-inclusive and yet nonbounded, it must remain undefined, ineffable, operating more or less in the manner of a religious mystery.

Bate is himself not explicit on this point, but we can piece out the gaps in his argument by turning to the essay "Poet: Patriot: Interpreter" written by Donald Davie for the September 1982 issue of *Critical Inquiry*. In the postscript to that essay Davie addresses himself to the question of professionalism and takes me to task for not realizing that literary study is not a profession at all but a "vocation" or a "calling." These, he says, are "less easily institutionalized" concepts and point to the responsibility of the true man or woman of letters to "bypass" the network formed by the "micro-politics of the MLA" and the "macro-politics" of the state, "as the truly independent and illuminating interpreters always have."[5] This obviously theological vocabulary makes explicit something that is only hinted at by Bate: anti-professionalism is basically a manifestation of the traditional Protestant distrust of forms in favor of a spirit that the letter of forms is always threatening to kill. The illuminating and independent interpreters of whom Davie speaks are illuminated from within and are independent of any of the horizontal constraints that would attach them to the interests and concerns of partisan and particular communities. Insofar as they themselves form a community, it is a community of *illuminati,* held together by an ability to commune directly, as it were, with "an illustrious shade like Spenser."[6]

Essentially, then, literary antiprofessionalism derives from a militantly ahistorical view of literary study, a view in which the objects of study—poems, plays, novels, a canon—stand always ready to be interrogated, and the machinery of professional life—departments, journals, promotions, and so forth—only get in the way. It is this view that underwrites Bate's firm distinction between what he calls the " 'accumulative' sciences," where knowledge is progressive and where "one can often build directly and logically on the bricks laid by predecessors," and the humanities, where "you are dealing with human nature," something that is varied in its manifestations but always the same in its essence (pp. 48, 53). In the accumulative sciences a specialized framework makes sense because there is a premium on the discovery of new facts and principles; but the facts of human nature are always before us and are available to what Bate calls "that wonderful quality, commonsense" (p. 53). Therefore, a disciplinary apparatus or network that merely reflects the narrowness of current professional concerns is at once unnecessary and dangerous, since it will tend to produce persons who are intent only on "having something new or . . . *different* to say—or simply finding something with which to take issue" (p. 49). These activities, the implication is, may have something to do with "rampant careerism" (a direct reflection of the oft excoriated "rampant specialization"), but they have nothing to do with the task of producing an accurate account of literature.

The counterview is presented in the essay to which Davie is responding. In that essay, "No Bias, No Merit: The Case Against Blind Submission," I argue that whatever account we have of a work or a period or of the entire canon is an account that is possible and intelligible only within the assumptions embodied in current professional practice. Rather than standing independently of our efforts, works, periods, and canons have the shape they do precisely because of our efforts, and therefore no act of literary criticism, no matter how minimally "descriptive," can be said to "bypass" the network that enables it. Changes in our critical vocabularies cannot be dismissed as mere shifts in fashion, because someone who has something "new or different to say" and says it persuasively will have changed the very objects of our attention. Obviously, if this argument is pursued (and I shall not pursue it here), it will go a long way toward challenging the supposed secondariness of literary criticism, and it also constitutes a challenge to the distinction, implicit in Bate's strictures, between responsible behavior and behavior that is "merely" professional; a behavior that seems reasonable or appropriate will seem so only in the context of the needs and goals currently recognized by the profession. What this means is that although anti-professionalism is (as Bate demonstrates) an attitude one can profess, it is not an activity one can practice. While one can certainly say anti-professional things, one cannot be an anti-professional in the strong sense of operating independently of the profession. The things one might say become available only within the profession's present shape and would have the effect, if they were hearkened to,

not of eliminating the profession but of giving it and its objects another, no less professional, shape. To put it another way, insofar as it
can have any consequences (apart from the impossible consequence of
bypassing the profession), anti-professionalism is a form of professional
behavior engaged in for the purpose of furthering some professional
project.

Again, we have a ready example in the essay by Bate, which, while
it is strongly anti-professional in its rhetoric, is in fact thoroughly professional in its strategy and goal. Indeed, the only thing about it that is
less than professional is its scholarship. In an attempt to account for
the deplorable present state of affairs Bate writes a history of the decline
and fixes 1980 as the date at which many teachers of English became
"strongly impressed" by structuralism (p. 51). Now Bate and I travel
in different circles, but I seem to recall that even in the remote landscapes of the Far West, as well as at Middle West outposts in Illinois,
Iowa, Michigan, and Chicago, not to mention the Eastern strongholds
of Yale, Columbia, Cornell, Johns Hopkins, and Brown, teachers of
English were already "impressed" by structuralism in the early and
mid-sixties, so much so that innumerable conferences and panels were
convened, the proceedings of which were then published, reviewed,
and debated. At about the same time, or a little later, a number of
authors on both sides of the Atlantic began to offer themselves as
guides: Jean Piaget, Edmund Leach, Robert Scholes, Edward Said, Leo
Bersani, Jonathan Culler, Geoffrey Hartman, Eugenio Donato, Sey-
mour Chatman, Roman Jakobson, Roland Barthes, Edward Wasiolek,
Serge Dubrovsky, Stephen Heath, Frank Kermode, J. Hillis Miller,
Fredric Jameson, and so forth. By the late sixties and early seventies the
death of structuralism had been announced several times, and for most
teachers of English the word now has something of a period flavor.

Bate turns next in his history to what he calls "the strange step-
child of structuralism known as 'deconstructionism'" (p. 52). One is
hardly surprised that he attaches himself to the tired and discredited
characterization of deconstruction as a "nihilistic view of literature, of
human communication, and of life itself." But one *is* surprised to find
him declaring roundly that "Derrida . . . never turns to the really
major philosophers" (p. 52). What could this mean? Either Bate is
denying the title of major philosopher to Plato, Aristotle, Leibniz,
Rousseau, Kant, Spinoza, Hegel, Freud, Husserl, Nietzsche, Heidegger,
and Austin, which would certainly be a revisionist view of the philo-

sophical tradition, but one that would require him to produce some arguments—or he has never read any Derrida and is gathering his information from hearsay or from the pages of *Newsweek*.

One could go on in this vein, documenting Bate's plain errors of fact, but the exercise would be beside the point, because his aim in this essay is not scholarly (although some of the trappings of scholarship are in evidence) but political. That is, he is not even attempting to give an accurate account of structuralism or of Derrida; rather, he is doing everything he can to discredit them, and he is doing this because by the evidence he himself marshals, literary students of the present generation are more and more influenced by the theoretical perspectives they represent and are therefore less and less under the sway of the high humanism of which the Harvard English department remains the institutional embodiment. A full account of the context from which Bate's essay emerges would require a history of that department, and I certainly cannot claim the detailed knowledge that would be necessary for the writing of such a history. But even from the viewpoint of an outsider, certain facts about the relationship between the Harvard English department and the rest of the profession seem obvious and unmistakable. At one time, not too long ago (certainly within my living memory), Harvard's was the most influential department in the country, not only because it nurtured values to which many in the profession would have pledged allegiance but because so many products of that department were influentially placed in other departments where they carried on Harvard traditions and continued to think of themselves as Harvard men. Moreover, those same men, as well as those who remained in Cambridge as keepers of the flame, were actively involved in the various associations by means of which knowledge was disseminated and professional projects were staffed. In short, the power and influence of Harvard was realized in a professional network, which rather than being bypassed was very much cultivated and even controlled.

That situation has now changed, partly as the result of two developments. First, there have grown up a number of competing versions of literary culture (Bate's essay is at once a documentation of and a complaint against this fact), and, second, the response of the Harvard English department to these rival ideologies has been to withdraw and leave them the field. That is, rather than assimilating or actively combating the "new doctrines," the department has more or less ignored them, even as their adherents have more and more seized the professional opportunities—to appear in journals, to speak at symposia, to proselytize at the MLA—that have been left open. As a result, the department has become something of a historical curiosity, a preserved relic of a time gone by, and has ceased to be an active force in the profession at large.

This melancholy decline weighs heavily on Bate's essay, which makes questionable sense as a piece of intellectual history but makes perfect sense as the attempt of a dispossessed monopolist to regain the professional power and control that he and his colleagues have long since lost. It is in this sense that Bate's anti-professionalist argument is a piece of professional behavior designed to secure specific professional goals; and indeed so thoroughly professional is Bate's performance that it might serve as an illustration of the principles of professional activity as they have been set down by Magali Sarfatti Larson in her excellent study of *The Rise of Professionalism.* The first thing a profession must do, Larson explains, is lay claim to a "superior expertise," a kind of knowledge that is "distinctively its own."[7] That knowledge must at once be universal in the sense that its beneficiaries are all of mankind and special in the sense that only a select few are empowered to dispense it. The danger, then, is that the knowledge base will be too wide, a danger Bate moves against in two ways: (1) by resisting the claims of a number of groups—gays, women, Chicanos, blacks—to any professional expertise and (2) by equating that expertise with a quality of mind or spirit—in fact, a sensibility—that has no visible marks and indeed by definition can have none. This means that there will have to be some mechanism for identifying that quality or spirit, and it is at this point that Bate displays his understanding of the second requirement for professional or market control: one must restrict access to the machinery for producing competent members. A profession is a profession because it has no "real" commodity but offers only a service; therefore, its most important activity is the credentialing of those who will be authorized to provide that service—thus Bate's dismay at the proliferation of degree-granting institutions and his evident pleasure at the fact that "the very grimness of the job situation has for some years been gradually shaking out of graduate study many who had formerly drifted into it" (p. 53). Presumably, when all the shaking out is done, the center of credentialing will once again be Harvard, and once again there will be Harvard-dominated departments, chaired by men of crimson blood, all over the country.

But of course, it will not be that easy. As Bate's lament for times past demonstrates, too much has happened in recent years; the profession has become more and more varied, and it will take more than attrition, natural and unnatural, to rehomogenize it and return Harvard to the central role it once enjoyed. But Bate is not without resources, and as he plays his final card, he reveals how thoroughly he has mastered the techniques by which one achieves professional control: he calls in the state, or in this case, the administration. As Larson explains, in order to enforce the claim of a group to the "sole control of superior expertise" and thus eliminate competition, it is necessary to seek an alliance with state authority. This is justified as a way of protecting the public from incompetent professionals, but the goal is in fact to create a bottleneck such that the public can turn only in one direction when it desires a certain service, and this is what happens when the force of law or legislation declares that only one version of that service is legitimate.

In the closing paragraphs of his essay, when he turns from criticism and lament to recommendation, Bate does not turn to his fellow English teachers, who are apparently too far gone to heed the call of reason, but to "the administrations of universities and colleges," urging them to intervene strongly in the process of hiring and promotion (p. 52). Specifically, he urges them to "seek pluralism." By that he doesn't mean, as he hastens to add, that a department should appoint persons of varying but strong views, but that pluralism should be sought in "individual appointments." This counsel seems curious until one realizes that what Bate is asking for is appointments of those who are not committed to anything in particular and who will therefore already be committed to the bodiless generality at whose shrine he would have us worship. That is, he is asking the administrators *not* to send him (or anyone else) any blacks, women, Chicanos, gays, film critics, and so forth. After all, he says, in an analogy that is revealing, "war is too important to leave to the generals" (p. 53). The ironies could not be greater: an essay that mounts an extended attack on the "chopping up" of the humanities into specialized bureaucracies ends by appealing to the most specialized bureaucracy of all: a diatribe against the excesses of professionalism is only a preliminary to a plan for regaining professional control: a decline that supposedly began with the formation of English departments will be reversed not by doing away with departments but by forcibly staffing them with members who subscribe to Bate's peculiar version of mystical pluralism. Of course, Bate in no way acknowledges the political and professional thrust of his recommendations and attributes to himself only the most pious of motives. Literature, he says, is a cultural heritage and must be protected; "it belongs to all of us" (p. 53). But it is the very fact that the base of literary authority has been broadened in recent years that has galvanized him into action, and what he really means is that literature should once again belong to him.

It might seem at this point that I am courting a contradiction: If anti-professionalism is a form of professional behavior, and if professional behavior covers the field (in the sense that anything one might urge will be a manifestation of it), then how can I fault Bate for using anti-professionalism to further a professional project? By collapsing the distinction (on which anti-professionalism runs) between activity that is professionally motivated and activity motivated by a commitment to abstract and general values, have I not deprived myself of a basis for making judgments, since one form of activity would seem to be no different from or better than any other? The answer is no, because the consequence of turning everything into professionalism is not to deny value but to redistribute it. One deconstructs an opposition not by reversing the hierarchy of its poles but by denying to either pole the independence that makes the opposition possible in the first place. If my argument is that there can be no literary criticism or pedagogy that is not a form of professionalism, it is also that there can be no form of professionalism that is not an extension of some value or set of values. Whereas before one was asked to choose between professionalism and some category of pure value (which, significantly, could only be named in the vaguest terms), the choice can now be seen as a choice between different versions of professionalism, each with its attendant values. To say that anti-professionalism is a form of professional behavior (and is therefore in a philosophical sense incoherent) is not to have closed the discussion but to have identified the basis on which it can continue by identifying the questions that should now be asked: What kind of professional behavior is anti-professionalism? and What are its consequences? The answer is that, at least in its literary form, it urges impossible goals (the breaking free or bypassing of the professional network) and therefore has the consequence of making people ashamed of what they are doing. The psychological distress that marks this profession, the fact that so many of its members exist in a shamefaced relationship with the machinery that enables their labors, is in part attributable, I think, to literary anti-professionalism, which is, as a form of professional behavior, almost always damaging.

It is damaging even when it informs a discourse diametrically opposed to Bate's and infinitely more attractive. Edward Said's recent essay, "Opponents, Audiences, Constituencies, and Community," which also appeared in the September 1982 issue of *Critical Inquiry,* is everything that Bate's is not: generous, learned, humane, compassionate, responsible. Indeed, Said could even be responding to Bate (although chronologically this is not possible) when he deplores literature departments whose curricula "are constructed almost entirely out of monuments, canonized into rigid dynastic formation, serviced and reserviced monotonously by a shrinking guild of humble servitors."[8] Where Bate counsels withdrawal into an ever smaller and narrowly elite professional priesthood, Said urges literary intellectuals to break out of their disciplinary ghettos and insert themselves into the social and political processes of the larger world (see p. 25). Yet despite everything that separates them, Bate and Said share one conviction: for each the villain in the piece is, in Said's words, "the cult of expertise and professionalism" (p. 2). Where Bate believes that professionalism and specialization have resulted in a loss of focus and in the dispersion of a shared cultural heritage, Said believes that these same phenomena have operated to turn that heritage into something like a museum piece, lovingly attended to by an ever more exclusive guild and thereby rendered "marginal," "harmless," and "non-political in the extreme" (p. 19).

Obviously, these arguments could not both be right, and I think they are both wrong, and wrong in the same way. Bate and Said think that the choice is between professionalism and some extra-institutional form of behavior (of which, of course, they would give very different descriptions), whereas it seems to me (1) that the choice is between the various forms professional life can take and (2) that the notion of extra-institutional activity is incoherent. To put it another way, one can agree (as I do) with Said's distress at the marginality of the humanities without agreeing that the way to escape marginality is to break out of "confining institutions." Marginality is not a function of professionalism but of a particular turn that professional life, at least professional *literary* life, has taken in this century. And if one wishes (as Said and I do) to change the conditions of marginality, then one must work not to eliminate professionalism but to see that it takes another turn. This is no simple matter. Presumably the fact (if it is a fact) that the humanities are now marginal has its source in historical developments, in the relationship of the humanities to other departments in the university structure, in the relationship of the university to business and government, and in the internal dynamics of literary studies with its definitions, assumed purposes and goals, authorized and orthodox practices, and so forth. In short, the present situation is the result of massive and massively deployed forces; but the way to counteract them is not to wave some magical moral wand (whether it bears the slogan "back to the great tradition" or "forward to the political awakening") but to set in motion other forces, equally institutional and professional, which eventually, one hopes, will have the effect of restructuring the shape of professional life.

The point may seem a small one. After all, if I agree with Said that the condition of marginality is harmful and should be changed, why does it matter all that much that he has misidentified that condition's cause? Especially since, if I am right, any course of action he proposes will perforce be a course of action that is institutional and professional. The answer lies in what I have already cited as the chief consequence of literary anti-professionalism: it makes people ashamed of what they are doing; and in that context Bate's and Said's arguments are mirror versions of one another. Bate's anti-professionalism encourages us to chide ourselves because the world is too much with us, because we have abandoned general and abiding truths for the particular and ephemeral concerns of everyday political life as represented by blacks, Chicanos, gays, and so forth. And Said's anti-professionalism encourages us to chide ourselves because we are not sufficiently of the world, because we have decided to "explicate Wordsworth and Schlegel" while others "run the country" (p. 23). If we listen to Said, we shall despise ourselves for being too marginal, and if we listen to Bate, we shall despise ourselves for not being marginal enough. It is my contention that we should listen to neither (at least on this point) and address ourselves instead to the question raised by the juxtaposition of their two essays. In the service of what values and with the hope of what consequences do we want to see our professional life arranged? This is not a simple question, nor will the answers one gives it be easily transformed into the implementation of this or that goal. But it is at least a question that does not have as a presupposition the unachievable desire of eliminating our professional life altogether in favor of some otherworldly, or more totally worldly, ideal.

These are the choices offered us by anti-professionalists of the right and left, and insofar as these choices correspond to beliefs held by many literary academics—the belief, on the one hand, that to study literature professionally is to spoil it, and, on the other hand, that to study literature professionally is to evade one's responsibility—they go a long way toward explaining why professors of literature are always fair game. We are fair game because we have arranged it that way by subscribing to views of our enterprise in relation to which our activities can only be either superfluous or immoral ("How can you study Milton while the Third World starves?"). We have at once loaded the gun and presented ourselves as willing and perspicuous targets; and if we are, as Bate claims, a "laughing stock in the national press" (p. 52), it is not because of the reasons he gives but because of the behavior he himself exemplifies when he provides, to those in the press who would pillory us, more ammunition than they need. If there is anything like a "crisis in English studies," it is a crisis in confidence, and it is one that we have in part created by taking ourselves too seriously as a priesthood of a culture already made, and not seriously enough as professionals whose business it is to make and remake that culture, even as we celebrate it.

11. Anti-Professionalism

I Every so often one hears the story of the editor who is sent a relatively minor Shakespeare sonnet or an early poem by Keats and rejects it as mannered and artificial. The story is usually tagged by one of two morals. Either it indicates that we have been deceived by custom and critical orthodoxy into venerating something without value, or, alternatively, it indicates how easy it is for something of value to go unrecognized by those whose judgments are in bondage to this or that critical fashion. It would seem that these morals are contradictory and are drawn from opposing positions; but, in fact, the positions are finally the same in one important respect: they both affirm, although in different ways and with different emphases, the independence of value from the judgments delivered by the agencies of professional authority, whether that authority is seen as supported only by unexamined tradition or as representing nothing more than the partisan opinion of the most recent victor in the struggle for institutional power. Both the moralist who thinks that a poem of little intrinsic worth has been kept afloat by the vested interests of an entrenched elite and the moralist who thinks that a great work of art is in danger of being sacrificed to the ever-changing interests of academic opportunists make the very same assumption about the relationship between a socially organized activity and the objects of its attention—the assumption that questions of merit have nothing essentially to do with the acts of description and judgment that have their source in the largely political machinery of professional bureaucracies.

I want to call that the anti-professional assumption, and I define anti-professionalism as any attitude or argument that enforces a distinction between professional labors on the one hand and the identification and promotion of what is true or valuable on the other. In some formulations that distinction is very firm and amounts to an equation of professionalism with everything that is evil and corrupting. It is in this spirit that Burton Bledstein ends his study of *The Culture of Professionalism*,[1] calling his readers to an awareness of the "arrogance, shallowness, and potential abuses . . . by venal individuals who justify their special treatment and betray society's trust by invoking professional privilege, confidence, and secrecy."[2] In many of Bledstein's examples this betrayal takes the form of allowing professional considerations to overwhelm considerations of public and client welfare. Thus he cites late nineteenth-century "[g]ynecologists and psychiatrists" who "diagnosed female hysteria as a pathological problem with a scientific etiology related to an individual's physical history rather than anger the public by suggesting that it was a cultural problem related to dissatisfied females in the middle-class home."[3] Underlying this criticism is something like the following scenario: faced with a situation in which they could choose from a number of explanations, these doctors chose that explanation that would strengthen their already entrenched interest by solidifying rather than alienating the support of middle-class America. It is a perfectly reasonable scenario, especially given the antiprofessionalist perspective, but it depends on assumptions about the nature of choice and the freedom of choosing agents that I will later challenge. For the meantime, however, we may note that in this particular example the professional's betrayal of his clients is simultaneously a betrayal of the truth. This is a particularly damning charge because, as M. S. Larson points out in *The Rise of Professionalism*,[4] professions characteristically justify their special status by claiming "cognitive exclusiveness,"[5] a unique access to some area of knowledge that is deemed crucial to the well-being of society; but that claim is more than compromised if knowledge is withheld from the public so that the profession's privileged position can remain secure. In the popular mind this particular form of professional abuse is typified by the behavior of lawyers who are entrusted with the determination and protection of truth, but who in practice deliberately obfuscate it by deploying procedural stratagems that constitute the real center of their craft and, finally, of their commitment. In the process, or so the story goes, the very values for which the enterprise supposedly exists—justice and the promotion of the general welfare—are sacrificed to the special interests that the legal profession at once represents and embodies.

The list of casualties left in the wake of professionalism grows—

the client, society, truth, value; but perhaps the casualty most often lamented in anti-professionalist polemics is the self or soul of the professional himself. For it follows that if a profession has given itself over to hypocrisy, secrecy, expansion for expansion's sake, mindless specialization, and the like, its members have necessarily surrendered their values and ideals to these same false priorities. Indeed, in this view, it is not too much to say (and many have said it) that in the act of becoming a professional one is in danger of losing his very humanity. This is the burden, for example, of a recent book-length complaint by a number of lawyers and law professors against the narrowing effects of their own education and professional experience. "We become accultured," they write,

> to an unnecessarily limiting way of seeing and experiencing law and lawyering, a way which can separate lawyers (as well as the other actors in the legal system) from their sense of humanity and their own values. When that separation occurs, the profession easily becomes experienced as only a job or role, and human problems as only legal issues. Care and responsibility yield to exigencies and stratagems; and legal education, instead of reflecting the aspiration and searching that embody law and lawyering, can all too easily become an exercise in attempted mastery and growing cynicism.[6]

In these sentences the authors produce a virtual compendium of anti-professionalist attitudes and arguments. Professionalism is indicted as a threat to humanity and to values; the openness of disinterested inquiry is replaced by the unworthy goal of "mastery" or manipulation, and, in the course of achieving mastery the professional is himself mastered (that is, taken over) by the constricted "roles and patterns" that are at once his weapons and his prison.[7] The professional, in short, becomes his own victim as the cynicism he practices transforms him into its image, leaving him with the base motives of an empty and self-serving careerism.

In addition to illustrating with force and concision what anti-professionalists are against, this paragraph allows us to infer what anti-professionalists are *for:* along with care, responsibility, humanity, and value, they are for openness, freedom, and sincerity—that is, for the real self as opposed to the self that has been lost or submerged in a "role." When the authors speak here of "actors in the legal system" their vocabulary is not neutrally employed; it is clear that acting or playing a "part" is an inferior form of behavior, not least because it binds the acting agent to the motivations of the "legal system"[8] and deprives him of the motivations he would have otherwise (and freely) chosen. In short, the actor enmeshed in a system is doing things for the wrong reasons, not for the reasons that would recommend themselves to him if he were not thus "constricted," but for reasons that attach to the limited and suspect goals of the professional enterprise. This complaint is often heard in anti-professional literature and is perhaps most familiar to us in the context of academic professionalism where it is regularly lamented that scholars are constrained in what they do by the desire to be promoted or by the fear that they won't be, and that therefore they write and publish only in order to augment their bibliographies and not out of true conviction or in response to an independently perceived need. As a result (the complaint continues), our journals are filled with publications that offer novelty rather than truth, since, as Richard Levin scathingly observes, university teachers "know that their interpretations are not likely to be published unless they say something . . . that has never been said before, which all too often means . . . that they must say something very strange."[9] Levin has in mind teachers of literature (and his indictment has been echoed recently by W. J. Bate, and was anticipated by Richard Ohmann, Mel Topf, and many others),[10] but the point is a general one: the pressure of professional life leads to the proliferation of work (research projects, publications, etc.) that has no justification in anything but the artificial demands of an empty and self-serving careerism.

Typically, careerism is seen not only as the corrupter of motives, but as the perverter of judgment. Not only does it tempt professionals to do things for the wrong—that is, "merely professional"—reasons, it tempts them to find authority in the accidental fact of professional status rather than in the true authority of carefully marshaled evidence and perspicuously powerful arguments. In the words of Frederick Crews, the authority inherent in some official or quasi-official professional position is "seized" rather than "earned"; it is false authority which proceeds not from "independent criteria of judgment," but from the anticipation of reward or punishment at the hands of "entrenched leaders."[11] Consequently, we have the spectacle of younger professionals who obsequiously adopt the opinions of their bureaucratic superiors, "imitating their mannerisms, praising their cleverness, using their favorite code words."[12]

Observers like E. D. Hirsch fear that if such behavior were to become normative, the communal enterprise itself would be in danger of collapsing as the march of intellectual progress was interrupted (if not stopped altogether) by every "drift in the currents of intellectual fashion."[13]

In Hirsch's apocalyptic scenario "fashion" is an enemy named by an even larger word, "rhetoric," which he sees as the most serious threat to the "logical integrity of inquiry."[14] "Obviously," he declares, "the consolidated knowledge within a discipline has nothing directly to do with rhetoric."[15] Obviously, this is not only an observation; it is an exhortation. Rhetoric *should* have nothing to do with the consolidated knowledge of a discipline, and the fear that it may have all too much to do with it is what animates Hirsch's enterprise. Hirsch thus stands in a long line that begins with Aristotle when, in the opening paragraphs of the third book of *The Rhetoric*,[16] he confesses himself uneasy and even ashamed that he must now descend to a discussion of so meretricious a topic as style. "Nobody," he declares wistfully, "uses fine language when teaching geometry."[17] Aristotle's point is that geometrical proofs strike the reason with an immediate and self-sufficient force, and therefore there is no need to wrap them up in some attractive verbal package. In this opposition of the central or essential to the superficial or ephemeral, we have the essence of the long quarrel between rhetoric and philosophy, a quarrel that philosophy has by and large won since more often than not rhetoric is identified as the art of illegitimate appeal, as a repertoire of tricks or manipulative techniques by means of which some special interest, or point of view, or temporary fashion, passes itself off as the truth. The rhetorical, then, is that which stands between us and the truth, obscuring it, preventing us from allying ourselves with it, and tying us instead to some false or partial god. These are exactly the charges that are leveled against professionalism, and it seems clear that anti-professionalism is basically an up-to-date, twentieth-century form of the traditional hostility to rhetoric.

In identifying anti-professionalism with anti-rhetoricity, I am not doing anything simple or simply dismissive. The anti-rhetorical stance, which is also the anti-professional stance, is complex and comprehensive, and in the preceding paragraphs I have been trying to build up a sense of its complexity by demonstrating that underlying its polemics are an epistemology, a theory of values, and a conception of the self. In the context of that effort Hirsch is particularly helpful. His arguments are more reasoned than any we have yet examined, and he allows us to be more precise both about the components of anti-professionalism and about the positive program in relation to which professionalism is the negative example. In the space of just two pages rhetoric and professional irresponsibility are identified with "advocacy," "vanity," "ideology," and a "decline in commitment,"[18] and each word or phrase directs us to an important feature of the anti-professional stance. The linking of advocacy and vanity is especially illuminating because it specifies for us the nature of the "real self," in whose name anti-professionalism levels its indictment. By "advocacy" Hirsch means the urging of a particular or partisan point of view, of a special interest, and it follows, at least in his arguments, that one who advocates does so in the "spirit of vanity"[19] because he prefers an interest to which he is personally attached to the *dis*interested pursuit of truth. This is made clear when Hirsch contrasts both advocacy and vanity (components, as he sees them, or runaway professionalism) with "selfless devotion to the communal enterprise."[20] As it is used here, "selfless" should be read quite literally. What is required is a self that has no interests "of its own" or has set them aside in favor of something larger; for only that selfless self will be able to espy and embrace a piece of rationality or truth that is itself independent of any interest. In order to be such a self, however, one must resist or turn away from the lure of one's "self-interest" or of other partial and partisan appeals and commit oneself to the communal enterprise (also identified as an enterprise without or above interest); one must, that is, perform an act of the will in which a choice is made against ideology and for the truth. If this choice is not made, there will be a "decline in commitment to the critical testing of hypotheses against all the known relevant evidence";[21] skepticism will become "widespread" as "the process of knowledge ceases,"[22] and rhetoric—in the form of activities grounded in nothing but "[m]ere individual preference,"[23] and the selfish exploitation of the institutions of scholarship[24]—will triumph. In short, professionalism will triumph as the "logic of inquiry"[25] is supplanted by "anti-rationalism, faddism, and extreme relativism."[26]

These are strong words, and they show us what is at stake in anti-professionalist polemics—the protection and nourishing of a set of related and finally equivalent acontextual entities. First, there is a truth that exists independently of any temporal or local concern; and then there is knowledge about this truth, a knowledge that is itself dependent on no particular perspective but has as its object this same trans-perspectival truth; and finally, and most importantly, there is a self or knowing consciousness that is under the sway of no partial vision, and is therefore free (in a very strong sense) first to identify and then to embrace the truth to which a disinterested knowledge inescapably points. On the other side, this happy eventuality is continually threat-ened by the contingent, the accidental, the merely fashionable, the narrowly political, the superficial, the blindly interested, the inessen-tial, the merely historical, the rhetorical, by everything that seems to so many to be the content of professionalism once it has been divorced from or has forgotten the higher purposes and values it is supposed to serve.

Now one can quarrel with this picture of things, as I shall before this essay concludes, but within its own terms it is powerful and per-fectly coherent. That is, if one is operating from within what we might call an ideology of essences—a commitment to the centrality and ulti-mate availability of transcendent truths and values—one will neces-sarily view with suspicion and fear activities and structures that are informed by partisan purposes (the spirits of advocacy and vanity) and directed toward local and limited (i.e., historical) goals. Anti-profes-sionalism, in short, follows inevitably from essentialism, so much so that an essentialist who wishes in some sense to give professionalism its due cannot avoid falling into the anti-professionalist stance. A case in point is Stephen Toulmin who has devoted a large volume (and two successors are promised) to a project that at first glance looks like the opposite of anti-professionalism. Toulmin's thesis in *Human Under-standing*[27] is that it is "a mistake to identify rationality and logicality—to suppose, that is, that the rational ambitions of any historically devel-oping intellectual activity can be understood entirely in terms of the propositional or conceptual systems in which its intellectual content may be expressed at one or another time."[28] A rational activity, he continues, is not to be explained by reference to " 'fixed and universal' principles of understanding" or to some " 'invariant forms of reason' ";[29] rather, "it is an *intellectual enterprise* whose 'rationality' lies in the procedures governing its historical development and evolution."[30] His conclusion is worth quoting in full:

[N]o system of concepts and/or propositions can be "intrinsi-cally" rational, or claim a sovereign and necessary authority over

our intellectual allegiance. From now on, we must attempt instead
to understand the historical processes by which new families of
concepts and beliefs are generated, applied, and modified in the
evolution of our intellectual enterprises. . . .[31]

It would seem that anyone who wrote these sentences must be
insulated against making the mistake (which he himself names) of
devaluing history and historical process; but even as he elaborates this
argument, Toulmin is invoking and developing a set of related distinctions that will finally subvert it. The first distinction is between "reasons" and "causes." By "reasons" he means an analysis of intellectual
activity that is made "in terms of reasons, . . . arguments, and justifications—that is in terms of 'rational' categories"; while by "causes" he
means an analysis that is made "in terms of forces, causes, compulsions, and explanations—that is, in terms of 'causal' categories."[32]
Causal categories turn out to include such things as the centers of professional influence (what Toulmin calls "current reference-group[s]"),
learned societies, the "invisible colleges," journals that "define the
forum of competition within which the effective disciplinary contest . . . is conducted,"[33] the "roles, offices, and positions"[34] held by
prominent workers in the field, and the institutional authority of essays
and books produced by such workers—in short, all of the factors and
considerations that make up what one understands by the notion of
"professionalism."

As one comes upon it, the distinction between reasons and causes
seems innocent and even promising because, after all, it is Toulmin's
argument that "causal categories," and therefore the activities of intellectuals as *professionals,* have been too long ignored and dismissed
to the detriment of our understanding of intellectual change. But simply by making the distinction—by assuming that rational categories
are one thing and causal categories another—Toulmin has assured that
sooner or later the latter will be dismissed in the context of a reasser-
tion, in some form, of the opposition of the essential to the contingent.
That is to say, unless one argues (as I shall finally argue) that the rational is itself an historical category—fashioned and refashioned by the
very causal forces to which Toulmin draws our attention—the rational
will inevitably be seen as a category that is transhistorical and therefore as a category that is finally independent of the "causal" forces that
either nourish or threaten it.

This is exactly what happens when the distinction between reasons and causes is folded into yet another distinction between the "disciplinary" and the "professional," where the "disciplinary" refers to the "rational [and] justificatory"[35] aspect of an enterprise, and the "professional" to the "organizations, institutions, and procedures"[36] by means of which the rational *happened* to have come to light. The overt assertion is that these aspects are "complementary"[37] and "interact,"[38] but the real assertion emerges in the questions that more and more rule Toulmin's inquiry and reveal its bias:

> How far do the structure, performance, and distribution of power within the professional institutions . . . enable them to meet the proper needs of the discipline for which they are acting?
>
> . . . .
>
> . . . How . . . do we recognize one set of factors or considerations as relevant to the intellectual content of a science, another to its human activities and institutional organizations?[39]

In these questions one clearly hears the silent "mere" before "human activities and institutional organizations," and one can easily infer the list of "improper needs" that stand in a relation of opposition and thwarting to the needs that are proper. Improper needs are the needs created by professional institutions, needs fueled by the spirits of advocacy and vanity, needs that threaten to blur the crucial distinction "between the intrinsic authority of ideas" (Toulmin apparently forgets that the notion of the intrinsic is one he has just challenged) and the "magisterial authority of books, men and institutions."[40] With this third distinction joining that between reasons and causes and between the disciplinary and the professional, the independence and (ideal) self-sufficiency of the rational is firmly established, notwithstanding Toulmin's claims to be establishing the contrary, and his pages begin to ring with the familiar anti-professionalist indictments. The observation that "even the best argument in the world could win the institutional authority merited by its intrinsic intellectual authority only if the professional circumstances were favourable,"[41] soon turns into a complaint against the "tyranny" of professional power, as a result of which "[p]apers are refused publication, academic posts are denied, professional honours are withheld . . . not for lack of worthwhile disciplinary arguments, but through professional disagreement with the editor, the research director, or the influential professor."[42] Presumably, the "best argument" should be recognizable independently of the criteria for judgment employed by any particular professional group, criteria that must be *seen through* if the best is not to be bested by the "merely" influential or institutionally authoritative; and presumably too, "professional disagreements" have only to do with base matters of patronage, preferment, and political infighting, and could only accidentally hook up with the rational considerations that are truly central to a discipline. In statements like these the deliberate and calm surface of Toulmin's prose (in its way a model of discursive decorum) gives way to the shrillness characteristic of Bate, Levin, Crews, and Bledstein and the full voice of anti-professionalism has emerged.[43]

That voice is underwritten by exactly the essentialist epistemology of which anti-professionalism is a manifestation, and the very center of that epistemology is revealed in what Paul de Man would call a moment of blindness and insight. The insight is that throughout Western history, words like " 'force,' 'weight,' and 'power' "[44] have been used to characterize and evaluate both rational arguments and arguments that proceed from institutional and professional authority; that is, the same vocabulary has been used to assess arguments "which are intellectually 'weighty' on their own account" and arguments which " 'carry weight with' the actual participants in a scientific debate."[45] One would think that this observation might lead to the conclusion—supported by the evidence of long practice—that the two kinds of argument are not finally to be distinguished, that what seems "weighty" on its own account and without any further (rhetorical) justification seems so because the justification has already been made and made so persuasively that what follows from it seems to follow as a matter of course. One would think, in other words, that Toulmin would be led by his own project to see that an intrinsically rational argument is nothing more (or less) than a rhetorical or interested argument that has become so deeply established that its truth seems (for anyone operating in the relevant community) to be self-evident. Toulmin, however, sees something else; he sees confusion, a blurring of differences and of a distinction that he cannot let go of because at a basic level it is within its confines that he does his thinking. Those confines are securely and historically identified when he sighs, "No doubt a 'weighty' argument deserves to 'carry weight with' all informed reasoners, but it may not succeed in doing so."[46] Or, in other words, no one uses fine language when teaching geometry.

II

The foregoing remarks should be read less as a criticism of Toulmin than as a demonstration of the way in which his deepest convictions take over his argument and turn it in a direction different from the one he announces. One might even say that I am praising Toulmin for finally being consistent with his first principles; his blindness to the constitutive power of history, to its ability even to shape and reshape the category of the rational, follows "naturally" from his insight (a mistaken one in my opinion) that "[r]ationality . . . has its own 'courts' in which all clear-headed men . . . are qualified to act" even when they represent different " 'jurisdictions' of rationality."[47] In short, as a member of the intellectual "right"—defined here by its commitment to essence and foundations—Toulmin comes by his antihistoricism and his anti-professionalism honestly.

Not so the anti-professionalists of the intellectual left. By "intellectual left" I mean all those who have contributed to the assault on foundationalism and who have argued, from a variety of directions and with differing purposes, that the present arrangement of things—including, in addition to the lines of power and influence, the categories of knowledge with their attendant specification or factuality or truth—is not natural or given, but is conventional and has been instituted by the operation of historical and political (in the sense of interested) forces, even though it now wears the face of "common sense." Members of the intellectual left would include, among others, followers and readers of Marx, Vico, Foucault, Derrida, Barthes, Althusser, Gramsci, Jameson, Weber, Durkheim, Schutz, Kuhn, Hanson, Goffman, Rorty, Putnam, and Wittgenstein, and their common rallying cry would be "back (or forward) to history."

It would follow or seem to follow that the left would be an infertile ground for anti-professionalism, since anti-professionalism is grounded so firmly in a way of thinking that identifies the historical with the merely contingent. But the reverse is true. Anti-professionalist indictments are found as readily on the left as on the right, and, if anything, the left-wing version tends to be the more shrill. Moreover,

what is consistency (of a challengeable kind) on the right is obvious—
and hence almost mysterious—self-contradiction on the left. When an
intellectual on the left makes a turn to anti-professionalism, the move
is quite literally breathtaking and involves a forgetting of one's own
declared principles that provokes admiration (in the old-fashioned
sense of "wonder").

As a spectacular example, consider Robert W. Gordon's essay
"New Developments in Legal Theory."[48] Gordon is writing as a member of the Critical Legal Studies movement, a group of left-leaning
lawyers and law professors who have discovered that legal reasoning is
not "a set of neutral techniques available to everyone"[49] but is everywhere informed by policy, and that judicial decisionmaking, despite
claims to objectivity and neutrality, rests on "[s]ocial and political judgments about the substance, parties, and context of a case . . . even
when they are not the explicit or conscious basis of decision."[50] They
have discovered, in short, that rather than being grounded in natural
and logical necessity, the legal process always reflects the interests and
concerns of some political or economic agenda, and they move from
this discovery to a "critical exercise, whose point is to unfreeze the
world as it appears to common sense as a bunch of more or less objectively determined social relations and to make it appear as (we believe)
it really is: people acting, imagining, rationalizing, justifying."[51]

Now this is a traditional enough project—it is the whole of the
sociology of knowledge; it is what the Russian Formalists meant by
defamiliarization, and what the ethnomethodologists intend by the term
"overbuilding"; and it is the program, if anything is, of deconstruction—but in Gordon's pages and in the pages of his cohorts, it takes a
turn that finally violates the insight on which it is based. That turn
turns itself, in part, on an equivocation in the use of the word "constructed." Used in one sense, it is part of the assertion that "[t]he way
human beings experience the world is by collectively building and
maintaining systems of shared meanings that make it possible for us to
interpret one another's words and actions."[52] That is to say, "systems
of shared meaning" do not have their source in distinctions and possibilities (for action) that precede and constrain human activity; rather
human activity is itself always engaged in constructing the systems in
relation to which its own actions and their meanings become at once
possible and intelligible; and " '[l]aw' is just one among many such
systems of meaning that people construct."[53] In sentences like this the

notion of "construction" functions primarily as a counterassertion to the notion of the natural or inevitable, to the *un*constructed; it does not suggest anything so specific or discreetly agential as implementing a "construction *plan*." That however, is precisely what is suggested in a sequence that turns the philosophical force of "construction" into a political accusation:

> In the West, legal belief-structures, together with economic and political ones, have been constructed to accomplish this sorting out. The systems, of course, have been built by elites who have thought they had some stake in rationalizing their dominant power positions, so they have tended to define rights in such a way as to reinforce existing hierarchies of wealth and privilege.[54]

All of a sudden "constructed" means "fabricated" or "made up," and the scenario is one in which the act of construction is performed by persons who build "belief-structures" in order to impose them on those they would dominate. The trouble with this scenario is that it makes sense only within the assumptions—of neutrality and pure rationality—that Gordon is at pains to deny. For as soon as beliefs have been identified, as they are here, with the materials of fabrication, they have been implicitly (and negatively) contrasted to something that is *not* fabricated, something that is natural and objective. But it is the natural and the objective—or at least their presumption—that Gordon proposes to dislodge in favor of these historical realities created by "people acting, imagining, rationalizing, justifying"; that is to say, by people who are implementing their beliefs. By making beliefs into the material of conspiracy and deception, he covertly reintroduces as a standard the very vantage point—independent at once of both belief and history—he is supposedly rejecting; and that reintroduction becomes overt and explicit when we are urged "to struggle against being demobilized by our own conventional beliefs . . . to try to use the ordinary rational tools of intellectual inquiry to expose belief-structures that claim that things as they are must necessarily be the way they are."[55] In other words, let us free ourselves from the confining perspective of particular beliefs (even when they are our own) and with the help of an *acontextual* and transcultural algorithm ("the ordinary rational tools of intellectual inquiry")[56] come to see things as they really are. This counsel would make perfect (if problematical) sense were it given by a Hirsch or a Toulmin, but given by Gordon it amounts to saying,

"Now that we understand that history and convention rather than nature deliver to us our world and all its facts and all our ways of conceiving and constructing it, let us remove the weight of history from our backs and start again."

The full force of this contradiction becomes clear in the next paragraph when Gordon declares that the "discovery" that the "belief-structures that rule our lives are not found in nature but are historically contingent" is "liberating"; but the discovery can only be liberating (in a strong sense) if by some act of magic the insight that one is historically conditioned is itself not historically achieved and enables one (presumably for the first time) to operate outside of history. Gordon's capitulation to the essentialist ideology he opposes is complete when he fully specifies what he means by liberating: "This discovery is . . . liberating . . . because uncovering those [belief-] structures makes us see how arbitrary our categories for dividing up experience are."[57] By "arbitrary" Gordon can only mean not grounded in nature, for by his own account they are not arbitrary, in the sense of being whimsical or without motivation; rather, they are part and parcel of very motivated (that is, interested) ways of building and living within social structures, ways that have themselves been instituted against a background of other ways, no less interested and no less historical. What Gordon wants (although by his own principle he should want no such thing) are categories uninvolved in interest; and it is in the context of that absolutist and essentialist desire that the ways and categories we have can be termed arbitrary.

Exactly the same line of reasoning is displayed by Gordon's colleague Duncan Kennedy when he moves from the observation that legal reasoning is everywhere informed by policy to the conclusion that those who teach legal reasoning teach "nonsense," "*only* argumentative techniques," "policy and nothing more."[58] But arguments based on policy can be devalued and declared nonsensical only if one assumes the existence and availability of arguments (not really arguments at all) based on a sense beyond policy, a sense which, because it is apolitical or extrapolitical, can serve as a reference point from which the merely political can be identified and judged. Kennedy is right to say that teachers who persuade students that "legal reasoning is distinct, *as a method* . . . from ethical and political discourse in general"[59] have persuaded them to something false; but that is not the same as saying that they teach nonsense; they teach a very interested sense and teach it as if there were no other. The way to counter this is to teach or urge some other interested sense, some other ethical or political vision, by means of alternative arguments which, if successful, will be the new content of legal reasoning. This is in fact what Kennedy is doing in his essay, but it isn't what he thinks he's doing—he thinks he's clearing away the "mystification" (the word is his)[60] of mere argument and therefore replacing nonsense with sense; but he can only think that in relation to a sense that is compelling apart from argument, a sense informed not by policy, but by something more real; and once he begins to think that way he has already bought into the ahistorical vision of his opponents, a vision in which essential truths are always in danger of being obscured by the special (i.e., rhetorical) pleading of partisan interest.

He buys into that vision again when he declares that "the classroom distinction between the unproblematic, legal case and the policy-oriented case is a *mere artifact*."[61] "Artifact" functions in Kennedy's discourse as "construction" does in Gordon's: it is a "hinge" word, poised between the insight that reality as we know and inhabit it is institutional and therefore "man-made" and the desire (which contradicts the insight) for a reality that has been made by nature. That desire is the content of "mere," a word that marks the passage (already negotiated) from an observation—that the distinction between the unproblematic and the policy-oriented case is conventional—to a judgment—that because it is conventional, it is unreal. By delivering that judgment, Kennedy not only invokes a standard of reality—as extraconventional and ahistorical—that more properly belongs to his opponents, but he also mistakes the nature of his own project. He thinks that what he must do is expose as "merely" interested or artifactual the distinctions presently encoded in legal reasoning; and he thinks too that once this is done distinctions of a more substantial kind will emerge and exert their self-sufficient (disinterested) force. But what will really happen is that one set of interested distinctions will be replaced by another. That is to say, the distinction between unproblematic and policy-oriented cases is not the product of some ideological conspiracy practiced upon an unwitting and deceived laity; rather, it reflects a set of historically instituted circumstances in which some issues are regarded as settled and others are regarded as "up for grabs"; and if Kennedy succeeds in unsettling what now seems settled so that the lines between the unproblematic and the policy-oriented are redrawn, he will not have exchanged a mere artifact for the real thing, but he will have dislodged one artifact—understood nonpejoratively as a man-made structure of understanding—in favor of another.

Kennedy's inability to see this is of a piece with Gordon's inability to see that the alternative to "conventional beliefs" is not "liberation," but other conventional beliefs, urged not in a recently cleared space by a recently cleared vision, but in the institutional space that defines both the present shape of things and the possible courses of action by which that shape might be altered. Both men proceed, in an almost unintelligible sequence, from the insight that the received picture of things is not given but historically contingent to the conclusion that history should be repudiated in favor of a truth that transcends it.

It is only a short step (really no step at all) from this sequence to the reinvocation of the acontextualities that underwrite anti-professionalism: a self that is able to see through the mystification of "rhetoric" and achieve an independent clarity of vision; a truth that is perspicuous independently of argument, and which argument tends only to obscure; and a society where pure merit is recognized and the invidious rankings imposed by institutional hierarchies are no more. If Kennedy's specific targets are institutional practices like grading and tenure, his real target is the institution itself in all of its manifestations, from law school to clerkships to apprenticeships to full partnerships to judgeships and beyond; and his essay, like Gordon's, takes its place in the general project of the Critical Legal Studies movement, a militantly anti-professional project whose goal is "to abolish . . . hierarchies, to take control over the whole of our lives, and to shape them toward the satisfaction of our real human needs."[62] The key word in this last sentence—taken from Peter Gabel and Jay Feinman's essay "Contract Law as Ideology"—is "real," for it identifies both the complaint and the program of anti-professionalism wherever it appears, and one of my contentions is that it appears everywhere. The complaint is that a set of related and finally equivalent realities—real truth, real values, real knowledge, real authority, real motives, real need, real merit, the real self—is in continual danger of being overwhelmed or obscured or usurped by artifacts (fictions, fabrications, constructions) that have been created (imposed, manufactured) by forces and agencies that are merely professional or merely institutional or merely conventional or merely rhetorical or merely historical; and the program is simply to sweep away these artifacts—and with them professions, institutions, conventions, rhetorics, and history—so that uncorrupted and incorruptible essences can once again be espied and embraced. What is surprising, as I have already noted, is to find this the declared program of intellectuals who think of themselves as being on the left, and who therefore begin their considerations with a strong sense of the constitutive power of history and convention, and this leads me to the declaration of a rule that is already implicit in my analysis: at the moment that a left-wing intellectual turns anti-professional, he has become a right-wing intellectual in disguise.

Consider, as a case in point, Richard Ohmann, whose *English in America*[63] is a story of conversion. As Ohmann tells it, he was once a more or less typical liberal humanist who believed in "the redemptive power of literature," which, because it transcends politics, helps us to build "a world apart from the utilitarian one where words and forms advance pragmatic interests."[64] Not surprisingly, he saw professions and professional structures (departments, committees, organized research, institutional hierarchies, etc.) as obviously utilitarian and pragmatic and therefore as "destructive of community."[65] More precisely, they are destructive of the value of literary experience, an experience that puts us in touch with "an infinitely complicated and irreducible reality"[66] by immersing us in language that is "ordered in special ways": "[I]t is divorced from present circumstances and from utilitarian concerns. It neither conveys information nor furthers an argument nor embodies a command nor passes a judgment."[67] But, of course, in active professional life judgments are passed all the time, argument and counter-argument form the primary mode of transaction, and information (about contexts, lives, and even institutional happenings) is the chief currency. Obviously, then, the profession exists in a negative and corrupting relationship to the value it supposedly serves and as mere "machinery" constitutes a "barrier to free development."[68] That development will be encouraged only if we "relinquish the mind-forged manacles of our . . . categories"[69] and repudiate the merely professional practices of "more research, more . . . articles . . . more seeking out of neglected works, more coverage . . . more minute specialization"—all of which are equated with "time serving and ambition."[70]

It hardly need be said that this is the classical anti-professionalist indictment, and it has the additional (expository) virtue of being absolutely explicit about its assumptions and imperatives: an atemporal value capable of lifting those who embrace it to an answerable level of transcendence is threatened by the all too temporal pressures of bureau-cracies, committees, hierarchies, promotion, etc. The case is particularly pure because it is a literary one; for while in other disciplines anti-professionalism requires a conscious effort to detach the service or commodity from the social and cultural contexts in which it seems inextricably embedded, in literary studies, at least as they have been practiced for much of this century, the commodity is *defined* by its inde-pendence of those same contexts, and anti-professionalism is the very content of the profession itself. It is Ohmann's claim, however, to have seen through all of this and to have realized that in taking this line he was falling in with "assumptions . . . so familiar among literate peo-ple of the last 175 years that I was unaware of them as challengeable premises and thought of them as plain facts."[71] Ohmann, in short, has discovered history and with it the fact that "institutions don't exist in vacuums or in the pure atmosphere of their ideals," but "are part of the social order."[72] Armed with this insight, he proceeds to a reexamination of the profession of English, an examination in which, presumably, both the questions to be asked and the answers one hopes to find will be very different.

Everything, however, turns out to be the same. The goal is still the "free development" of human potential and the barrier to that goal is still professional and institutional procedures which are declared to be in a relation of subversion and corruption to genuine values.[73] To be sure, the freedom to be sought is not, as it was earlier, the freedom to enter into a contemplative relationship with the great works of litera-ture, but the freedom to build a just and equitable society; that society, however, is imagined just as it was before the conversion, a "world apart from the utilitarian one where words and forms advance prag-matic interests,"[74] and the great works of literature are once again the vehicle by which captive selves will be liberated from the false visions of partial perspectives and turned toward abiding truths. Rather than serving to lift us above the ordinary and everyday, literature (especially poetry) now enables us to see through the ordinary and the everyday ("small change when we are to bodies gone")[75] and thereby puts us in a position to change what we have seen through. "[E]very good poem, play, or novel," Ohmann declares, "is revolutionary, in that it strikes through well-grooved habits of seeing and understanding";[76] and again, "[t]he poem disrupts the routine perceptions of everyday, and makes us see the world with new vision."[77]

It is tempting to linger over the obviously Neoplatonic sources of this supposedly revolutionary doctrine and to point out how traditional and how romantic a conception of literature this is; but for our purposes it is enough to observe that the entire program rests on the hope (and the possibility) of a self that can rise above its historical situation to a state where the false imperatives of merely institutional forms will be exchanged for the true imperatives that can now be espied by a newly cleaned vision, that is, by a newly free self. Much of Ohmann's analysis is devoted to demonstrating how and why the self is not yet free, imprisoned as it is in the perspectives imposed by professional structures; and the main indictment of those structures is that they impose choices on persons who would choose otherwise if they were truly liberated. Here a chief exhibit is a listing placed by the English department of Missouri Southern College in a publication entitled *Vacancies in College and University Departments of English for Fall 1971*.[78] Missouri Southern is described in the listing as a "new and growing four year institution," and the announced vacancy is for a specialist in Renaissance literature.[79] Ohmann interrogates the announcement by asking whose needs will be served by the presence of a Renaissance specialist in a small college in Joplin, Missouri. He observes that the prospective candidates for the position probably did not enter the profession with the expectation or hope of being anything "as specific as a Renaissance scholar"; instead, they probably "chose graduate work because they like[d] literature";[80] but that choice did not survive the coercing pressures of graduate education and, by the end of five or six years, lovers of literature have been made into technicians capable of filling one of the slots mandated by the professional bureaucracy. An even greater coercion has been practiced on the people of Missouri and the students of Missouri Southern who certainly did not themselves "feel a need to have this field covered at Joplin."[81] But if the choice either to be or to hire a Renaissance scholar does not originate with the state or with the students or even with the scholar himself, what is its source? Ohmann's answer is that its source is the internal requirements of the profession itself, conceived of as a grid of institutional or bureaucratic spaces that create needs and the actions that fill them independently of what anyone or any group "really" wants. In short, professional activity is not authorized by anything more substantive than the procedural exigencies built into the profession: "The profession exists so that there may be a means of accreditation and advancement for people in the profession, not out of any inner necessity and certainly not out of cultural need or the need of individual teachers."[82]

This answer seems to me to be the right one, but it does not seem to me, as it does to Ohmann, to be the matter of scandal; it is merely a recognition of the fact that needs and values do not exist independently of socially organized activities but emerge simultaneously with the institutional and conventional structures within which they are intelligible. When Ohmann says of the decisions to be or to hire a Renaissance specialist that "each choice is embedded in a network of decisions that were *not* choices,"[83] he is right; these decisions are only thinkable in relation to the already-in-place forms of socially organized activity that mark them as options; but when he turns this observation into an indictment and complains that such choices—enabled by structural possibilities that were not themselves consciously chosen—are not real choices, he falls into the trap of reserving "real" for choices that depend on no previously instituted circumstances whatsoever—choices that would be, in some strong sense, original. The problem is that it is hard even to imagine what those choices would be like; by what noninstitutional standards would they be made? What kinds of persons, at once abstracted from the concerns and alternatives built into conventional forms of behavior and yet *still acting,* would make them? The answers to these questions are distressingly familiar: What Ohmann desires are wholly free choices, made according to standards more objective than any attached to a particular perspective or partisan vision and by persons who are themselves above faction and entirely disinterested. The fact that this desire flatly contradicts his call for behavior that is *"more political"*[84] indicates the extent to which his "conversion" from mainstream liberalism to radical socialism is undone by his continuing anti-professionalism and constitutes dramatic proof of my general rule that a left-wing anti-professional is always a right-wing intellectual in disguise.

To put it another way, Ohmann's new historicism turns out to be barely skin-deep and amounts finally to a distrust of the historical more thoroughgoing than any he had evidenced before. In effect, he makes the same breathtaking move we have already seen in Gordon and Kennedy. Once, he tells us, I was blind to history's force, believing innocently in the availability and power of essences; now I see that the deposits of history everywhere surround us and even inform our ways of thinking; therefore let us resolve to think our way past or through history so that we may once again be free. Even when he is trying to be militantly historicist, Ohmann's essential essentialism shows through. "There is just no sense," he says, "in pondering the function of literature without relating it to the actual society that uses it, to the centers of power within that society, and to the institutions that mediate between literature and the people."[85] This all seems fine until one notices that the "it" in the sentence remains constant and is simply put to different uses by different interests. Literature, in short, stays the same; only its historical fortunes change; moreover, although its function may vary with varying political conditions, it does have a *true* function, the function of being iconoclastic and revolutionary. It never seems to occur to Ohmann that not only the uses of literature, but the items and qualities subsumed under the category, can change; it never occurs to him that literature is not an essential, but a conventional category, the content and scope of which is continually a matter of debate and adjudication between historically conditioned agents.

No such failure of insight can be attributed to Terry Eagleton who begins his recent *Literary Theory: An Introduction*[86] by historicizing what Ohmann leaves essential. Literature, Eagleton argues, is not a "definite signified,"[87] that is, a "distinct bounded object of knowledge"[88] with unique and stable properties; rather, he asserts (following Barthes), literature is what gets taught;[89] and what gets taught is at once incredibly diverse and continually changing. The line between the literary and nonliterary is continually being renegotiated; the content of key terms like "poetic diction" is continually in dispute; and the items in what is called "the canon" don't survive from one anthology to the next. In fact, "you cannot engage in an historical analysis of literature without recognizing that literature itself is a recent historical invention."[90] And if that is true of literature, it is even more true of literary theory, an activity that has no stable object to be theoretical about and is therefore indistinguishable "from philosophy, linguistics, psychology, cultural and sociological thought."[91] It follows, then, that literary theorists, critics, and teachers are custodians not of an essence, but "of a discourse," and their task is "to preserve this discourse, extend and elaborate it as necessary, defend it from other forms of discourse, initiate newcomers into it and determine whether or not they have successfully mastered it."[92]

From the point of view I will finally urge, this is exemplary, for it draws a straight (and to my mind correct) line from a thoroughgoing historicism to the insight that the features of the literary landscape are the products of institutional and professional forces. But then, inexplicably, Eagleton comes to a conclusion that puts him in the same camp with Ohmann, Gordon, Kennedy, and all the rest. "Literature," he declares, "is an illusion," and, moreover, "literary theory is an illusion too."[93] "Illusion" is a word like "construction" as Gordon uses it or "artifact" as Kennedy uses it; it marks the passage (apparently unnoticed by the author) from observation to judgment, from the description of something as conventional and historical to the declaration that therefore it is unreal. But one cannot say that because literature and literary theory are conventional—that is, effects of discourse—they are illusory without invoking as a standard of illusion a reality that is independent of convention, an essential reality; and once one has done that (however knowingly or unknowingly), the familiar antiprofessionalist complaint against structures and practices that stand between us and what is true and valuable and sincere cannot be far behind.

In Eagleton's case, it arrives immediately. After having pointed out (quite correctly) that "[b]ecoming certified . . . as proficient in literary studies is a matter of being able to talk and write in certain ways," he comments indignantly, "[i]t is this which is being taught, examined and certificated, not what you personally think or believe."[94] This is just like Ohmann's complaint that in composition courses a student's sense of purpose "emerges from the matrix of the theme assignment" rather than from anything "he brings from life."[95] Behind both statements is the assumption that true purposes and genuine beliefs exist apart from social and institutional forms which provide artificial or manufactured motives that are subversive of the real self. It is hardly surprising that in a few pages Eagleton's fulminations are indistinguishable from those of Bate, Toulmin, Hirsch, et al., as reasoned analysis gives way to formulaic and shrill diatribes against "the largely wasted energy which postgraduate students are required to pour into obscure, often spurious research topics in order to produce dissertations which are frequently no more than sterile academic exercises, and which few others will ever read."[96] After something like this, the conclusion that "professionalism . . . is . . . bereft of any social validation of its activities"[97] is at once expected and incomprehensible; expected because it has long since become the content of every description/accusation;

incomprehensible because "social validation" is precisely the kind of validation that professional activities have. Indeed, Eagleton's real complaint (although he would hardly acknowledge it) is that the validation of professional activities is "merely" social.

How do we account for this? How do we explain an argument that begins so promisingly, but then degenerates into the automatic and confused thinking displayed in these last quotations? The answer is to be found in a moment when it is possible to register one of two responses to the crucial insight impelling the work of left-wing intellectuals—the insight that our sense of what is obligatory, routine, ordinary, reasonable, authoritative, matter-of-fact, and even possible is grounded neither in nature nor in inevitability but in background conditions and assumptions that have been put into place by interested agents. One response, and the one almost always given, is outrage and horror, more or less equivalent to the discovery of the worm in the apple; and the reaction to that response is, as we have seen, first, indictment and then a call for action designed to free us from the impositions and deceptions to which we have become captive. The other response is less dramatic and takes the form of a project, of new research, in which the goal is to provide a full and analytical map of what have been called the "conditions of possibility," the conditions that underlie what at any point in the history of a society or an institution are taken to be the components of common sense.

Now, of course, these two responses are not mutually exclusive. One can engage in research of this kind and find oneself opposed to what it uncovers, but that is quite different from assuming at the outset that what is to be opposed is institutionalization or professionalization per se rather than this or that form of it, for that assumption (indistinguishable from essentialism) will work to preclude the sustained and serious investigation of institutional arrangements, since the investigator will be in a rush to deplore the fact that such arrangements exist. Just such a rush marks and mars the writings of those engaged in the GRIP project. One can hardly quarrel with the announced agenda of that project:

We would study the entire process of training and professional life that form a professional literary critic. We would examine how the professional comes to recognize only certain objects as worthy of study, for instance, how he or she regards only specifi-

cally defined work as important to perform; how he or she learns
the rules for social behavior in the profession.[98]

The statement is by James Fanto, but the title of his piece—"Contesting Authority: The Marginal"—indicates in advance why its promise
will never be fulfilled. He wishes to examine the lines of authority and
influence not in order to understand them or even to propose that they
be altered, but to express outrage that these or any other lines should
be in place. Consequently, when he comes to describe the hierarchical
form of the profession, he can only view it as a grand deception practiced on the public and on victimized initiates: "The profession . . .
establishes a hierarchy and sets some individuals . . . at its summit
together with the symbols associated with their names. . . . [T]hose
new to the profession receive these symbols—they are formed by them;
they submit to their authority."[99] What is missing here is any notice of
the *content* of what Fanto calls "symbols," the research accomplishments, methodological techniques, powerful interpretations, pedagogical innovations, etc., that bring some men and women to the "summit"
and form the basis of the authority that in Fanto's account is magically
and arbitrarily conferred (seized rather than earned). He is so convinced beforehand that the deference accorded to institutional superiors
is without foundation that he never bothers to catalog the tasks, long-
standing puzzles, crucial problems, the negotiation and completion of
which leads to professional recognition and promotion. To be sure,
these tasks, problems, and puzzles can be challenged as not worth
doing, and there are some who "rise" independently of any such accomplishments; but, nevertheless, there is a great deal more to the acquiring
of professional power than "the frequent celebration of the master in
reviews"[100] and other such gestures of servility that seem to make up
Fanto's entire understanding of the matter.

Fanto writes his essay as a tribute to the "marginal" figure, the
man or woman who struggles against the profession's hegemony in the
name, supposedly, of values that exist independently of the profession
and of any institution whatsoever. At one point, however, he acknowledges that the stance of opposition is not really "outside" but "remains
within the perspective of the profession and perhaps even falls into a
position already inscribed in the profession."[101] Indeed, he adds, "an
appeal to one's own professional purity . . . can often serve as a
strategy for displacing individuals and groups above one on the profes-

sional hierarchy."[102] But this moment of insight is brief and soon gives way to the familiar anti-professional blindness, as Fanto, in the very next paragraph, urges "resistance" to "institutions and social networks" and a continual scrutiny of "one's own position to guard against the reappearance of . . . professional power in one's own discourse and actions."[103] We could pause here to ask on the basis of what non-institutional standards and from what asocial position this resistance will be mounted, but by now, I trust, the questions are superfluous and the answer obvious.

What Fanto and his fellows in the GRIP project seem never to realize (despite the fact that they are all readers of Foucault) is that power not only constrains and excludes, but also enables, and that without some institutionally articulated spaces in which actions become possible and judgments become inevitable (because they are obligatory), there would be nothing to do and no values to support. David Shumway, for example, is only able to see tyranny and the mechanism of exclusion in the "disciplinary regime" of the modern academy, and he lists among the chief mechanisms the examination and the hiring process:

> Beginning with the tests that one takes as an undergraduate, continuing through qualifying examinations, to the dissertation itself and the examination on it, disciplines exclude and categorize their adherents by means of examination. The hiring process with its *vitae,* dossiers, and interviews—all disciplinary instruments—is today perhaps the most powerful means of disciplinary exclusion.[104]

It is hard to see what this can mean except that some people get hired and others don't, and it is even harder to imagine an alternative arrangement, one that would result (presumably) in some form of universal academic employment with each of us conferring on ourselves the appropriate degrees and titles. (Although perhaps there would be none, since titles are evidence of invidious distinctions.) Of course, it could certainly be the case that the procedures and criteria by which the academy makes its judgments are in need of revision or even of a total overhauling, but one cannot completely jettison those procedures and criteria or refrain from those judgments without eliminating the achievements that are at once thinkable and recognizable only because they are in place. What Shumway doesn't see is that the very values he would protect—true judgment, true merit, true authority—are functions of the forms and structures he sees as dangers; and he doesn't see that because, like all anti-professionals, he is finally committed to an essentialism that renders *all* forms and structures automatically suspect, even when they are the very heart of one's project. It is this that explains why Shumway can at once observe that a paradigm is displaced when those at the institutional center of "intellectual authority" believe it to be "inadequate" and yet complain that it has not been "proven to be inadequate."[105] Again, what could this possibly mean except that Shumway is holding out for a standard of proof that is altogether independent of the standards in force in an institution? What could it mean except that at the very moment of embarking on a study of the constitutive power of disciplines and professions, he displays an inability to see that power as anything but the vehicle of conspiracy, even though he himself has declared that the "issue of conspiracy is almost always a red herring."[106]

It may be a red herring, but it is one that leads the entire GRIP project astray in a way that is concisely illustrated by three successive sentences in James Sosnoski's "The *Magister Implicatus* as an Institutionalized Authority Figure."[107] Sosnoski begins by announcing that "[t]he 'official' set of beliefs linking individuals to institutions are the subject of my investigation."[108] He then declares that "[t]hese beliefs are quite powerful." And he adds immediately, "They make us behave in ways that we would choose not to."[109] What this third sentence does is assure that the investigation of his "subject" will be impoverished even before it begins; for having decided in advance that the effect of institutions on individuals is disabling—depriving them of choices and of meaningful forms of behavior—Sosnoski is himself disabled from considering the many ways in which institutions *enrich* individual possibilities by making available alternative courses of action, including action designed to supply perceived deficiencies and remedy existing ills. The result is a performance in which observations that could be the basis of a rich and textured analysis are too soon transformed into indictments. Sosnoski points out, for example, that critical discourse is informed by questions, and that both the questions and their acceptable answers make "sense only within the context of the conceptual framework that identified the problem"[110] in the first place. Moreover, he adds, institutional questions—such as those found in textbooks and on examinations—are in fact instructions "to perform a particular task in a particular manner,"[111] and thus "are the principal instruments of literary training."[112] It looks for a moment as if this insight will generate an inquiry into the history of these questions, a history that might then lead to an exploration of the relationship between the shape of literary studies and the larger intellectual shape of the culture; but while Sosnoski makes some gestures in that direction, he quickly returns to his limited (and limiting) focus and falls to deploring the deadening effects of discipleship ("Critical schooling produces critical schools")[113] and complaining that the net result of literary training is to substitute mere professional authority for the authority that should be reserved for true "competence."[114] By invoking this distinction, Sosnoski reveals himself as one more card-carrying anti-professional, interested in studying institutions only so that he can expose their tendency to replace "real" values and "genuine" motives with values and motives that have their source only in a desire to manipulate and control; and he reveals too (and inevitably) that his goal is not the reform of institutions and professions, but a world in which their "warranting frameworks" and practices of initiation and directing questions are no longer operative.

A sense of what that world would be like emerges in the final pages of the essay when Sosnoski presents his positive recommendations. We should, he counsels, "introduce a protocol to AGREE TO AGREE to replace our present polemical protocol to AGREE TO DISAGREE."[115] This statement is remarkable in several respects, but chiefly for its suggestion that agreeing and disagreeing are *styles* of intellectual behavior rather than evidence of deeply held beliefs that may or may not be in conflict. But if one sees that disagreement reflects differences in commitment rather than a mere fashion in intellectual inquiry, the recommendation to leave off disagreeing will sound rather strange; it will sound like a recommendation to put off one's beliefs, and that recommendation will make sense only if beliefs are thought to be acquired and discarded much as one acquires and discards pieces of clothing. Like Gordon, Sosnoski has a picture of the way we come to hold our beliefs and of the ease of changing them (simply by changing a rule of operating procedure) that allows him to see them as obstacles to genuine action by persons who agree to "share ideas." But simply to identify that picture is to raise some familiar questions: what would persons who had divested themselves of belief be like, and where would the ideas they share come from if they didn't come from interested (and therefore polemical) perspectives, and if they came from those perspectives how could they be meaningfully shared unless there were a way to discriminate between them, and if there were such a way, what could it be except some calculus that transcended polemic because it transcended politics? Either these questions are unanswerable because there could be no such persons or such ideas and because there is no such calculus, or they can be answered only by invoking and affirming the acontextual fictions—unsituated selves, presuppositionless ideas, disinterested action, independent criteria—that Sosnoski, himself so polemical and political, should be loath to embrace. Once again we see that for an intellectual of the left, anti-professionalism is at once debilitating because it precludes action on any level except the Utopian, and contradictory because it leads inevitably to an essentialism that has its proper home on the right.

III

It is time to take stock of our argument and see where it has taken us. What I have tried to demonstrate is that anti-professionalism, as a set of attitudes and arguments, is indefensible no matter what forms it takes: it is indefensible on the right because it begins with incorrect assumptions (about the possibility of free selves choosing extrainstitutional values by means of independent criteria), and it is indefensible on the left because it contradicts the correct (historicist and conventional) assumptions with which left-wing intellectuals, as I have defined them, begin. Having said as much and said it at such length, I still have left unanswered the questions most readers would probably want to raise: First of all, if anti-professionalism is as vulnerable (not to say silly) as I have made it out to be, why is there so much of it? And, second, if one gives up anti-professionalism as a way of responding to institutional life, what then remains? What is the alternative?

To take the second question first, it might seem that the only alternative to anti-professionalism is quietism or acquiescence in the status quo because by discrediting it I have taken away the basis on which this or that professional practice might be criticized. But, in fact, the only thing that follows from my argument is that a practice cannot (or should not) be criticized *because* it is professional, because it is underwritten by institutionally defined goals and engaged in for institution-specific reasons; since here are no goals and reasons that are not institutional, that do not follow from the already-in-place assumptions, stipulated definitions, and categories of understanding of a socially organized activity, it makes no sense to fault someone for acting in the only way one can possibly act. This does not, however, rule out opposition, for someone can always be faulted for acting in institutional ways that have consequences you deplore; and you can always argue that certain institutional ways (and their consequences) should be altered or even abolished, although such arguments will themselves be made on behalf of other institutional ways (and *their* consequences). In short, the alternative to anti-professionalist behavior (which on my account is impossible) is behavior of the kind we are already engaged in. One could call it business as usual so long as "business as usual" is understood to include looking around (with institution-informed eyes) to see conditions (institutionally established) that are unjust or merely inefficient (with justice and efficiency institutionally defined) and proposing remedies and changes that will improve the situation. Of course, what is a change and what is a remedy and what is an improvement will be matters of dispute between agents embedded in different organizational settings with different priorities and interests, but none of the parties to the dispute will be acting purely, that is, with no ax to grind; and no one will be grinding an ax that is not an extension of some rationally defensible sense of the enterprise.

Doing away with anti-professionalism, then, will have as little effect as anti-professionalism itself; if action independent of institutions is impossible, it hardly seems to matter whether it is advocated or derided; it will still be impossible. And yet anti-professionalism thrives, and I return to my first question. Why is there so much of it? The answer is to be found in the history of professionalism and in the way it has defined itself as a project. As M. S. Larson recounts it, professionalism is a "typical product of the 'great transformation,' "[116] the passage from a decentralized and rural society where status is a function of birth and of geography to the modern urbanized state in which status is acquired by climbing the ladder provided by corporate and professional organizations. In this new world, power, influence, and authority are achieved not by the "accidents" of class but by the demonstration of merit on the part of individuals who rise to prominence by virtue of their native ability. This, at any rate, is the story the rising or bourgeois class tells itself and also tells those others who do not rise and who for the most part are excluded from even approaching the ladder by the new mechanisms of selection and discrimination (religion, ethnic background, examinations, degrees, etc.). Professionalism, then, at least as it presents itself, promotes and enhances individual effort; it gives people the opportunity to "make it on their own," and it allows those who do make it to believe they deserve everything they receive; and it allows them to believe too that those who fail simply didn't work hard enough or didn't have "what it takes" in the first place.

Larson calls this story the "ideology of professionalism," and she identifies it with democratic liberalism: "The notion that 'the individual is essentially the proprietor of his own person and capacities, for which he owes nothing to society,' is a cornerstone of the bourgeois theory of democratic liberalism."[117] It is an ideology both because it serves certain well-defined interests (despite its claims to neutrality and to equal access) and because it is at variance with the facts as Larson understands them. She points out that rather than owing nothing to society, the professional owes everything to society, including the self whose independence is his strongest claim and justification. That is, it is only with reference to the articulation and hierarchies of a professional bureaucracy that a sense of the self and its worth—its merit—emerges and becomes measurable. The ladder of advancement is not only a structural fact, it is a fact that tells the person who occupies a place on it who he is and what he has accomplished; by providing goals, aspirations, and alternative courses of action, the ladder also provides the "means of self-assertion."[118] "[C]areer," she concludes in a powerful aphorism, "is a pattern of organization of the self,"[119] which is another way of saying that the self of the professional is constituted and legitimized by the very structures—social and institutional—from which it is supposedly aloof.

Given this analysis (which seems to me entirely persuasive), it is obvious that professional life is a continual attempt to mediate and ameliorate this tension. A professional must find a way to operate in the context of purposes, motivations, and possibilities that precede and even define him and yet maintain the conviction that he is "essentially the proprietor of his own person and capacities." *The way he finds is anti-professionalism.* As we have seen again and again, anti-professionalism is by and large a protest against those aspects of professionalism that constitute a threat to individual freedom, true merit, genuine authority. It is therefore the strongest representation within the professional community of the ideals which give that community its (ideological) form. Far from being a stance taken at the margins or the periphery (as someone like Fanto would have it), anti-professionalism is the very center of the professional ethos, constituting by the very vigor of its opposition the true form of that which it opposes. Professionalism cannot do without anti-professionalism: it is the chief support and maintenance of the professional ideology; its presence is a continual assertion and sign of the purity of the profession's intentions. In short, the ideology of anti-professionalism—of essential and independent values chosen freely by an independent self—is nothing more or less than the ideology of professionalism taking itself seriously. (The more seriously it is taken, the more virulent will be the anti-professionalism; thus the peculiar form of literary anti-professionalism, which is more often than not the overt form of literary practice.)

This, then, is the answer to the question, why, if anti-professionalism is incoherent, is there so much of it? Anti-professionalism is professionalism itself in its purest form. Does this mean that at the heart of professional life is a blatant contradiction that should be recognized and extirpated? Not at all, for if it is, in some sense, a contradiction, it is also emblematic of a necessary condition of human life. Let me explain. Throughout this essay I have been urging what might be called a strong interpretivist or conventionalist view, a view in which facts, values, reasons, criteria, etc., rather than being independent of interpretive history, are the products of that history. But, at the same time, I have resisted any suggestion that those who stipulate to those facts or hold those values or advance those reasons are operating under a delusion that would be removed if they came to realize that their ways of thinking and evaluating were conventional rather than natural. Such a realization could only have that effect if it enabled the individual who was constituted by historical and cultural forces to "see through" those forces and thus stand to the side of his own convictions and beliefs. But that is the one thing a historically conditioned consciousness cannot do—scrutinize its own beliefs, conduct a rational examination of its own convictions; for in order to begin such a scrutiny, it would first have to escape the grounds of its own possibility and it could only do that if it were not historically conditioned and were instead an acontextual or unsituated entity of the kind that is rendered unavailable by the first principle of the interpretivist or conventionalist view.

What this means, finally, is that even if one is convinced (as I am) that the world he sees and the values he espouses are constructions, or, as some say, "effects of discourse," that conviction will in no way render that world any less perspicuous or those values any less compelling. It is thus a condition of human life always to be operating as an extension of beliefs and assumptions that are historically contingent, and yet to be holding those beliefs and assumptions with an absoluteness that is the necessary consequence of the absoluteness with which they hold—inform, shape, constitute—us. Professionalism is, as I have said, a very emblem of that condition. The professional who is "spoken" in his every thought and action by the institution and yet "speaks" in the name of essences that transcend the institution and provide a vantage point for its critique is not acting out a contradiction, but simply acting in the only way human beings can. From the beginning, my argument has been that anti-professionalism is indefensible because it imagines a form of life—free, independent, acontextual—that cannot be lived; that argument now takes its final and curious turn by concluding that professionalism itself cannot be lived apart from such an imagining. In my efforts to rehabilitate professionalism, I have come full circle and have ended up by rehabilitating anti-professionalism too.

12. Transmuting the Lump:
Paradise Lost, 1942-1979

I In 1972 Raymond Waddington began an article on books XI and XII of *Paradise Lost* in a way that is remarkable both for what it reveals and for what it conceals. What it reveals is that something has changed: "Few of us today could risk echoing C. S. Lewis's condemnation of the concluding books of *Paradise Lost* as an 'untransmuted lump of futurity.' "[1] Waddington is taking note of the fact that Lewis's judgment has apparently been reversed and the concluding books of the poem are now held in more esteem than they once were. His view of that reversal (insofar as he could be said to have one) is not directly stated, but emerges inadvertently, as it were, in a footnote where the bibliographical reference to Lewis's book gives the date of publication as 1969. In fact, *A Preface to "Paradise Lost"* was published in 1942. It is not that Waddington is inaccurate in any narrow technical sense; the edition he was consulting is a reprint or reissue, and he commits no scholarly error by citing its date. One can say, then, that it really doesn't matter, and obviously for Waddington it doesn't; but that is just the fact that calls out for explanation (the French would term it a "scandal"), because in this and other sentences Waddington is reporting on the *history* of recent criticism, and it is, at the very least, a curious history that displays an unconcern with the dates of its events. The explanation, even more curious perhaps than the fact, is that Waddington doesn't really regard it as a history at all, that is, as a succession of developing norms, perspectives, possibilities, alternatives; rather, he regards it simply as a change of states—from wrong to right—a change that might as well have occurred in an instant as in thirty years, and one that need not have occurred at all if only Lewis had been more discerning. "Lewis's phrasing," says Waddington in the very next sentence, "emphasizes a failure to comprehend structure." It is not a failure that is time-bound because it exists in relation to a structure that was always there to be seen. Lewis simply didn't see it (the reason he didn't see it is never inquired into; both failures and successes are always mysterious or miraculous in this view of things). The fact that others have seen it since is important, but the precise date at which they saw it is not. Thus Lawrence Sasek's 1962 article "The Drama of *Paradise Lost*, Books XI and XII" is cited in the anthologized version of 1965, and Northrop Frye's remarks in *The Return of Eden* are dated 1966, no mention being made of the fact that the substance of the book was first presented as the Huron College Centennial Lectures in 1963. The result is to obscure the extraordinary and apparently spontaneous proliferation of articles defending the concluding books in the short period between 1958 and 1963. In his only gesture toward historical understanding, Waddington observes that "a generation of readers has shared the conviction" that Lewis was mistaken in his condemnation, but he leaves unasked and unanswered the question of what conviction the previous generation (1942–58) was sharing and why it was so slow to perceive what is now so clear to so many.

Waddington's lack of interest in the historical conditions that enabled the work of his predecessors goes hand in hand with a lack of interest in the conditions that enable his own work. He is obviously doing something in these opening sentences, but he does not pause to reflect on what he does because it never occurs to him that one could do anything else; that is, the values, standards, goals, and understood practices on which he relies are not regarded by him as requiring explanation or defense; they are simply attendant upon clear seeing. Thus, for example, he seems unaware that his vocabulary is at once charged and ideological: "Lewis's phrasing emphasizes a failure to comprehend structure; and while an occasional Broadbent or Martz will inveigh against the execution of Books XI and XII, a generation of readers has shared the conviction that, as in *Paradise Regained*, where the design also is subtle and complex, structure and function are very firmly controlled by the poet." Words like "design," "subtle," "complex," "structure," "function," and "control" are meaningful and meaningfully honorific only within the assumption of a set of notions about what constitutes poetry and poetic qualities. In general, these are formalist notions, and for one who holds them, or is held by them, "design" immediately means "pattern" and not purpose or intended goal, while "function" refers to the relationship between the parts of an artifact and not to the role played by that artifact in a society, and "control" is something that is exerted over the various elements of a structure (itself defined formally) rather than over the responses of a reader (although that is presumed to follow as a matter of course). A reader who understands these words as Waddington intends him to (an intention of which he is not consciously aware) will not reflect on them as he reads because they are not received as discrete bits of vocabulary, but form part of a system of understanding in which what could possibly be meant by this or that term is stipulated in advance. That system is not something that is brought to bear on a literary landscape; it *speaks* that landscape and declares the shape of everything in it, including the entities that populate it and the questions that can properly be put to them. No term is ever innocently employed, not even the term "poet," which is here as system-specific as any other and is understood (implicitly) as "poet-rather-than-moralist-or-philosopher." That is, a formalist perspective on literary matters will deny the title "poet" (and the category "poem") to anyone else whose intentions are overtly didactic or political, a fact (also system-specific) that explains a great deal about the critical history of *Paradise Lost,* books XI and XII.

Now Waddington knows all of this, but he knows it in an uncritical way; that is, he doesn't know it as something that could be otherwise, as knowledge that has been made possible by the institution of certain historical conditions. Rather, he knows it as the simple truth, a truth that might have emerged at any time, but just happened to have emerged in the last generation. A case in point is the appearance in his very first sentence of the word "risk": "Few of us today could risk echoing C. S. Lewis's condemnation. . . ." From the point of view I will urge in this essay the word is a crucial one, because it indicates the extent to which what one can reasonably and prudently say is a function of assumptions currently in force in the profession. But to Waddington it indicates no such thing: it indicates simply that C. S. Lewis has been proved wrong and few of us (and they a very curious few) would want to risk being associated with error. Waddington has no real interest in the risk he points out (he doesn't think it interesting) even as he so carefully avoids it by aligning himself with "the most influential readings." He exercises professional prudence, but he doesn't seem to realize that by doing so he is choosing a strategy, a course of action with consequences that can be contrasted with the consequences of alternative courses; instead, he regards himself as simply saying the obvious as it is dictated by facts that have been established for all time.

In a sense, then, Waddington writes against himself: he reports on a process—the process by which the details, large and small, of a literary topic are first established and then altered—but at the same time he discounts that process as something that has any real relationship either to his task or to its object. He quite self-consciously locates himself in a community, but presents himself as a single agent who just happens to be in agreement with other single agents who have come to see what he sees. His predecessors are presented as discrete workers, each of whose conclusions provide *"independent* corroboration" of the assertions put forward by the others. In his sentences Miltonists are always "recognizing" this or "becoming aware" of that; the dominant image is one of seeing, either clearly or through a glass darkly, and seeing is itself never seen as contextually determined, as an activity that is performed in accordance with the possibilities and options that are inherent in a particular historical moment. The result is literary history in a mode with which we are all familiar: a finite number of unchanging questions is addressed to a finite set of unchanging objects by persons whose perspicuity (or lack thereof) is the consequence of individual education and experience. I would like here to suggest the possibility of another kind of history, one that begins with the assumption that literary works are the products as well as the objects of our activity, that they are constituted by questions which are themselves meaningful only in relation to prevailing institutional conditions, and that what makes convincing sense (of a kind that can be shared by a "generation") is a function of the ideological and political situation of avowedly professional readers and writers who know very well (as Waddington himself knows) that what they can reasonably and profitably do depends very much on what has been done before them. Waddington's essay seems to me to be at once a document in, and an example of, this kind of history—we can call it history as persuasion—and in what follows I will take it (along with its predecessors and successors) more seriously than he does.

We can begin by simply stating the problem, although to do so is itself a contentious and polemical act. How is it that in 1942 it was possible to regard books XI and XII of *Paradise Lost* as barely belonging to the poem, whereas by 1979—and here I would instance Edward Tayler's fine book *Milton's Poetry: Its Development in Time*[2]—books XI and XII are regarded as the poem's very center? We will put aside, for the moment, the standard answer to that question—in 1979 we are now in a position to see the truth—and look for an answer in the poem's critical history, regarded not as a record of discrete insights but as a linked and dynamic sequence of constitutive acts enabled by a set of specifiable conditions. The first thing to note is that the "risk" of which Waddington speaks is attendant on every critical gesture and is therefore not irrelevant to the case of C. S. Lewis himself. Did Lewis take a risk when he said what he said? If so, what was it? If not, why not? Those questions should in turn be considered in terms of the more general question of the nature of risk in literary studies. How is it calculated? What is at stake? Of course, it is not calculated at all if by that word one means a self-conscious choice of this or that approach in relation to the probability of professional rewards; rather, the choices that occur to one "naturally" are already understood in terms of the needs of the profession and therefore come already calculated; one could not think of a course of action that was unrelated to conditions prevailing in the profession because those very conditions form the background— the all-pervasive but unarticulated context—within which thinking about possible courses of action goes on. Thus any reading one proposes will have a relationship—of confirmation, challenge, modification, reversal—to previous readings, and this means that any reading one proposes will be political, since it will advance or retard someone's interest and declare itself on issues in relation to which sides have already been chosen.

This is not to say that the relationship between a critical act and its predecessors is ever simple, or describable by a direct line of cause and effect. Untangling the filiations and antecedents of even a single assertion will lead not to an explanation (in the sense borrowed from the physical sciences) but to an awareness of the complexity that underlies the intelligibility and value of any critical gesture. Thus, for example, when Lewis condemns the concluding books of *Paradise Lost,* he is doing not a single thing, but several things, with varying degrees of self-consciousness. First of all, he is allying himself with a long tradition that is already in place by 1712 when Addison observes that books XI and XII are "not generally reckoned among the most shining Books of the poem" (*Spectator,* no. 363).[3] Addison comes to praise, and he defends the books by pointing out that without them the story of the fall of man "would not have been complete, and consequently his Action would have been imperfect" (p. 216), but at the same time he establishes the basic line of complaint when he declares (p. 217) that "if Milton's poem flags anywhere, it is in this Narration, where in some Places the Author has been so attentive to his Divinity, that he has neglected his Poetry."

The terms of Addison's qualified praise are exactly the terms of Lewis's qualified censure: the example of Virgil is cited by both men; both point to particularly "fine moments," and both are uneasy about the proportions of doctrine to poetry. But if on one level Lewis is merely reconfirming an old orthodoxy, on another level he is challenging a new one, the orthodoxy of anti-Miltonism, as it was represented in the writings of T. S. Eliot and F. R. Leavis. It was Leavis who had announced in 1933 that "Milton's dislodgement, in the past decade, after his two centuries of predominance, was effected with remarkably little fuss."[4] To our ears this sounds like either a premature or partial judgment or an effort to get away with an outrageous assertion by presenting it as a commonplace; but in fact what Douglas Bush was later to call "these smug words"[5] (the question of who is smugger than whom in these controversies is a nice one) were more than a little justified when Leavis wrote, and as late as 1945 Bush feels compelled to devote the entire first chapter of *"Paradise Lost" in Our Time* to "The Modern Reaction Against Milton." The strength of that reaction is to be measured not by the numbers it embraced but by the names associated with it: in addition to Leavis, Ezra Pound, John Middleton Murry, Herbert Read, F. L. Lucas, Bonamy Dobrée, G. Wilson Knight, and, of course, Eliot. It is hard for us in a time when the absence of critical authority is lamented to imagine the influence attributed to Eliot in these discussions; but the attribution is made by all parties. Leavis, in the second sentence of his essay, declares that "the irresistible argument was, of course, Mr. Eliot's creative achievement" (the "of course" tells its own story); twenty-five years later B. A. Wright is still complaining that "young men and women go up to the universities to read Honours English without having read a line of Milton, for their teachers have told them that they need not bother about a poet of exploded reputation."[6] "Mr. Eliot," writes a historian of the period, "was able to turn a generation of practitioners and readers of verse away from Milton toward Donne and the metaphysicals."[7]

What is clear from these reports is that the weight of Eliot's judgment is a *political* fact rather than a fact that reflects the "truth" (independently determined) of his opinions. Anyone who would advance another judgment, therefore, must make his case in the context of Eliot's authority. He must argue not *about* Milton (as if Milton were an entity whose characteristics were a matter of public and obvious record), but against Eliot, and, ultimately, with the whole set of assumptions and presuppositions within which Milton emerges as a morally bad man whose poetry was insufficiently faithful to the felt complexities of human experience. Here, then, in 1942 is a risk that Lewis must take, and the inescapably political (read "historical") nature of critical debate is reflected in the care with which he orders his response to Eliot and the other anti-Miltonists. First, he disposes of those (unnamed) who are of too gross a sensibility even to be answered (this is a strategy he borrows from the poet), critics "who hate Milton through fear and envy."[8] Next he considers "a much more respectable class of readers" (p. 131), those who find Milton's verse insufficiently in touch with the texture of felt human life. In this group Leavis is the chief figure, and he receives the respect due an equal: "Dr. Leavis does not differ from me about the properties of Milton's epic verse. . . . It is not that he and I see different things when we look at *Paradise Lost.* He sees and hates the very same that I see and love" (p. 130). When he comes to Eliot, however, Lewis's strategy changes. Rather than dismissing him, or simply agreeing to disagree, as equals always can, he first acknowledges his superiority and then makes it the grounds for discounting him. If some readers are not good enough for the poem, Eliot is *too* good for it; he has removed himself from its precincts "in order to fast and pray in the wilderness" (p. 132). The act is a noble one, and Lewis says of Eliot "I honour him," but it is finally an act too difficult for most men who "live in merry middle earth" and find it "necessary to have middle things" (p. 133).

Thus Lewis himself takes a middle position, between Leavis's demand for "a particular kind of realism" (p. 131) and Eliot's desire for an otherworldly purity, and in the context of that position his condemnation of books XI and XII makes a different kind of sense than the sense made of it by Waddington and others. First of all, it is part of a *defense* of Milton in the face of the two-pronged attack on the abstractness of his verse and on the unacceptability of his religious ideas. Lewis handles the first or artistic objection by celebrating the ritual and formulaic qualities that Eliot and others deplore. The objection to Milton's theology is met, curiously enough, by denying the centrality of religion to his poem: "I am not sure that *Paradise Lost* was intended to be a religious poem . . . and I am sure it need not be" (p. 128). Once again, Lewis has recourse to a traditional line of argument. Nineteenth-century Miltonists tended more and more to displace the burden of critical attention from Milton's ideas to his art—the negative form of this is well represented by Raleigh's famous pronouncement that *"Paradise Lost* is a monument to dead ideas"[9]—and for Lewis the art of *Paradise Lost,* as apart from its theological content, resides in its plot. Of course, the contents of the plot are in some sense religious—Lewis is not making a case for ignorance of the theology—but our relationship to those contents does not and should not result in "a religious exercise." If it begins to feel like one, if "we remember that we also have our places in this plot, that we also . . . are moving either towards the Messianic or towards the Satanic position, then we are entering the world of religion." And when we do that, Lewis continues, "our epic holiday is over; we rightly shut up our Milton." Whereas in the religious life "man faces God" directly, in our literary experience we are the observers of feigned encounters: "We are not invited . . . to *enjoy* the spiritual life, but to *contemplate* the whole pattern within which the spiritual life arises."

The assumptions that inform these statements are crucial for the entire history I hope to explore in this essay—indeed, it is when they have been dislodged that books XI and XII will have been fully rehabilitated—but for the present it is enough to point out the justification they provide for Lewis's dismissal of those books. If the criterion of evaluation is structural—a matter of a functional relationship to the unfolding of a plot—then it follows that a lengthy rehearsal of theological doctrine, punctuated only now and then by any interaction between characters, is by definition "inartistic" (p. 125). In making this judgment Lewis is able at once to affirm a basic principle of both Eliot's and Leavis's criticism—that literature must be evaluated as *literature* and not as something else (morality, religion, politics)—and to indicate that their application of that principle in the case of Milton is excessively draconian. One need not reject all of *Paradise Lost* because in some parts of it the poet has been so attentive to his divinity that he has neglected his poetry. In effect, then, books XI and XII of *Paradise Lost* are sacrificed by Lewis so that he can defend the rest of the poem in the face of its influential detractors. The gesture that Waddington sees as a failure to comprehend structure (that is, he sees it only in relationship to his own view of the matter) is, if understood historically, an attempt to *assert* structure, both as a principle of literary judgment and as a property of Milton's poem. Lewis is fighting a battle that has been won by the time that Waddington writes, and, in fact, Waddington is able to proceed within the assumption of the poem's greatness only because of what is begun in the very pages he deplores. (In 1972 there is still a "Milton controversy," but it isn't the controversy that determines the significance of what Lewis does in 1942, although what Lewis does in 1942 finally makes it possible for Waddington to do what he does in 1972.)

In short, what looks from the vantage point of 1972 like an aberrant judgment, now happily corrected, is, in the context of its production, a perfectly understandable act that is politically astute and marvelously economical. By regarding the concluding books of Milton's poem as "a grave structural flaw," Lewis manages at one and the same time (1) to identify himself with a long and honorable tradition in which these books are said to represent a "falling off"; (2) to defend strongly the rest of the poem and to defend it in precisely the terms—aesthetic terms—that undergird the anti-Miltonist position; (3) to display his credentials as a literary critic and thereby blunt somewhat the force of his earlier assertion that his chief qualification as commentator is the fact that he himself is a Christian (p. 64); and (4) to reaffirm (and therefore buy into) the central tenet of twentieth-century criticism, the autonomy of poetry as distinct from the materials that inform it whether they be religious, political, or economic.

By so praising the astuteness and economy of what Lewis does, I do not mean to suggest that he was wholly successful. In fact, contemporary reviews indicate that at least one part of his strategy failed. Despite his assertions to the contrary, the argument of his book was not seen as primarily literary, but as religious. For an appreciative reviewer like Edward Wagenknecht the appearance of *A Preface to Paradise Lost* means that "there is no longer any reason for failing to recognize that the defense of Christian culture did not end when Chesterton fell to the earth" (*New York Times Book Review,* May 23, 1943, p. 10), while for an anonymous reviewer in the *Durham University Journal,* Lewis's religious opinions are irrelevant: "Such Buchamite confession is out of place in a work of literary criticism. . . . We are not interested in Lewis's Christianity but in the quality of his literary perception" (vol. 35, no. 3, June 1943, p. 72). The fact is that Lewis is committed to a difficult argument whose internal contradiction reflects a contradiction writ large in the literary community of the period: on the one hand he wants to make the case for *Paradise Lost* on largely literary grounds; but on the other he is concerned most of the time to correct what seem to him mistaken characterizations of Milton's religious and political views. One must be very agile, indeed, to be able to say at one point that "Milton's thought, when purged of its theology, does not exist" (p. 64), and yet to insist at another that "in some very important senses *Paradise Lost* is not a religious poem" (p. 127). Of course, what Lewis means, as I have already indicated, is that it is not a religious poem because its aim is not to evoke a religious response, but this formulation does little more than invoke, without explaining, a distinction between the ideas informing a work and the manner of that work's reception. The fact that such a distinction is basic to mid-twentieth-century aesthetic principles does not render it unproblematic; and the problems it involves are particularly difficult to avoid when the work in question is *Paradise Lost.* One sees this clearly when Lewis argues that "the adverse criticism of Milton is not so much a literary phenomenon as the shadow cast upon literature by revolutionary politics, antinomian ethics, and the worship of Man by Man" (p. 129). Now, there are two ways to read this, either as a warning against confusing literary issues with issues of religion and politics (that confusion would then be the shadow), or a statement that false, as opposed to true, conceptions of religion and politics have obscured (cast a shadow over) the poem's true literary quality. It is the difference between saying that literary judgments must be made independently of ideas and saying that you have to have the right ideas in order to make correct literary judgments. It is a difference that Lewis continually fudges, and, as a result, he is often in the position of affirming a principle even as it is being undermined by his practice.

Consider, for example, his final (and famous) view of the argument with Leavis: "The disagreement between us tends to escape from the realm of literary criticism. We differ not about the nature of Milton's poetry, but about the nature of man, or even the nature of joy itself" (p. 130). The Milton controversy, in all of its successive phases, shows how Lewis is at once right and wrong; critical debates at a certain level are always about the nature of man, and differences on that level lead directly to different characterizations of the poetry. Lewis's account of Satan's function as a character in the epic is inseparable from his notion of what heroism is, and a critic for whom heroism is defined differently will produce a different description of Satan's action, language, and rhetoric. It is not simply that the same poetic "facts" will receive opposing interpretations from opposing points of view, but that opposing points of view will lead to opposing specifications of what the poetic facts are. One can understand why Lewis would wish to separate literary from extraliterary judgments—the aesthetic of his time demands it—but the regularity with which his arguments and the arguments of others begin and end with religious, moral, and philosophical pronouncements makes it obvious that such a separation is impossible.

II

That impossibility is particularly evident in the case of *Paradise Lost,* where discussions are from the very first involved with God and man, and it is even more evident in 1942 when literary critics, like everyone else, were concerned with issues of war. It may seem strange to bracket together a controversy about a seventeenth-century poem and a global conflict; but the strangeness only testifies to the way in which literary history has managed to erase a portion of itself. In the two full-length studies of Milton criticism published since 1960 there is no discussion of World War II at all. K. L. Sharma remarks in one place that by the mid-forties "political events had somewhat turned the tide in favour of Milton" (p. 5), and in another observes that while the Romantic revolutionaries could be "reminded by Satan of Prometheus," in the Second World War "Satan came to remind readers of Hitler" (p. 26); but these are occasional observations and do not add up to any serious consideration of the relationship of political to literary events. Patrick Murray's *Milton: The Modern Phase* (1967) is written as if World War II had never occurred and as if G. Wilson Knight's *The Chariot of Wrath* had never been written. (Sharma also ignores it.) Knight's book, published in 1942, is subtitled *The Message of John Milton to Democracy at War* and bears on its title page a passage from an address delivered by Winston Churchill. Knight begins with the assumption of a "recurring pattern in human affairs" (p. 39). He then draws an obvious parallel between the crisis of the 1640s and the turmoil of the 1940s, and declares that "the ideas and energies thrown up in the civil disruption of which Milton is the living voice are valuable pointers towards understanding of the inward mechanisms of the British Constitution" (p. 17).

Milton's concern, especially in his prose writings, to define the relationship between the individual and the state, between virtue and civil authority, between legitimate and illegitimate force, makes him an inevitable point of reference for the issues facing wartime Britain, especially since one of his chief claims is to be a national poet, speaking to and for a particularly British form of heroism. It is thus "scarcely strange," Knight avers, "that within his greater poetry the action should be variously prophetic, and even shape itself into one remarkable prefiguration of our own gigantic, and itself archetypal, world-conflict" (p. 83). The continuity that allows Knight to make this statement is a religious one, and he is able to cite a number of contemporary voices who believe with him that the struggle against Hitler is the latest battle in the age-old war against the Antichrist. "It is undeniable," asserts one of his sources, a psychologist, "that the present division in Europe has to do with the pagan-Christian conflict within the soul of Christendom" (p. 146). Within this perspective Knight feels justified in finding innumerable points of contact between Milton's characters and the heroes and villains of World War II, and there is even a suggestion that he himself is a Miltonic figure, taking up verbal arms "against aspiring will-to-power and cunning use of mechanized resource" (p. 149). His vision, like Milton's, is global and even cosmic, and he joins the poet in rousing the nation and the world to a great action: "The challenge is here; my reasons have been presented; and the great passage on Britain roused in *Areopagitica* may, with profit, be remembered" (p. 158). It would seem that Milton's hope expressed in 1642 in *The Reason of Church Government* that he might "inbreed and cherish in a great people the seeds of virtue and public civility" is finally being realized three hundred years later.

I am not endorsing this reading of Milton (which is, in the 1980s, once again in fashion, although in a somewhat different form), merely pointing out that it cannot be dismissed as an eccentric one. Knight's book was reviewed seriously, and its literary/political thesis was noted as one of its strengths. "Professor Knight," Geoffrey Tillotson enthuses, "is able to give us not only a book of literary criticism but also a war book about Britain and Hitler (power allied to badness)," and he concludes that readers "will find few critics of Milton capable of helping them in more ways" (*English* 4, 1942–43, pp. 130–31). Douglas Bush is less happy with Knight's "whirlwind apotheosis" (p. 6) and would prefer a more "intelligible criticism," but he too finds the linking of Milton and the war a natural one: "If there be any people who think that the rise or fall of Milton's fame is not of much moment in a war-torn world, we may remember . . . that Milton is one of the great portions of that heritage for which the war has been fought" (p. 3). It follows, then, that "indifference or hostility to him is not a mere matter of liking or disliking a particular poet; it belongs to the much larger question of whether the tastes and standards of our generation reflect spiritual health or disease" (p. 3). Statements like these (and there are countless others that could be cited in the years 1940–45) represent more than an attitude toward Milton; they constitute a way of reading him, a way that ultimately produces a Milton significantly changed from the beleaguered figure attacked by Leavis and Eliot in the thirties. In Knight's reading, for example, the sixth book of *Paradise Lost,* as much maligned in its way as books XI and XII, is given a new prominence and value as a prototype of the Allied-Axis conflict and as an exploration of the relationship between godliness and power. Knight reserves his highest praise for the War in Heaven, declaring at one point that the onrushing chariot of God, "at once a super-tank" and a "super bomber," is "the most spectacular incident in *Paradise Lost,* perhaps in England's, perhaps even—outside the Bible—in the world's literature" (p. 162).

This brief look into a forgotten chapter in Milton criticism beckons us to investigations we cannot here undertake. There is at least an essay and perhaps a book to be written about the political/military uses to which Milton has been put (some work has already been done with reference to American conflicts), and another, perhaps, that would study the way in which critical estimates of the poetry have led to its appropriation for purposes of propaganda which in turn has fed back into the critical estimates. One would want to inquire also into the conditions that bring literary criticism into such a close proximity with great political events that the line between them is thoroughly blurred. On Sunday, May 30, 1942, the editorial writer of *The Times Literary Supplement* credits Knight with bringing forward a Milton who is "a living champion, a national oracle, whose voice his countrymen of today will do well to remember" (p. 271). Is it only during world conflicts that our activities can acquire such immediate relevance, or is it the case (as many have recently argued) that literary studies are always implicated in political agendas and especially so when the academy thinks of itself as isolated and innocent? To become aware of Milton's wartime fortunes is to have these and other questions arise naturally, but, for the time, they must be put aside so that I can continue to pursue the question with which we began. How is it that *Paradise Lost,* books XI and XII, were so thoroughly reevaluated in the period between Mr. Lewis's strictures and Waddington's first sentence? In relation to that question Knight's book is important because it contributes to the effort (of which Lewis was also a part) to defend Milton against the charges of his detractors. Thus in addition to praising Knight's contribution to the Allied cause, Tillotson also finds him redressing "some of the recent literary slandering of Milton in the same way as R. W. Chambers's recent Wharton lecture redresses some of the personal slandering of him." One could say, then, that in these years the poet and the Allied cause are in one another's service. Milton is doing his part in the great effort to save democracy, and democracy is repaying the favor by elevating Milton to a position so lofty that his enemies will be unable to bring him down.

Of course, even if *Paradise Lost* has its dramatic moments on the world stage (along with *Areopagitica,* it was thought by many to be the quintessential expression of what everyone was fighting for), the sustained battles over its meaning and shape were still being fought in the academic trenches. In that battle, as I have already indicated, Lewis plays an ambiguous role. On the one hand, he is certainly among Milton's strongest champions; but in making his case he finds it necessary to "sacrifice" books XI and XII to the cause, and therefore he produces the phrase that seems so authoritatively to condemn them. Paradoxically, however, the very authority of Lewis's judgment is productive of its own eventual reversal: that is, it defines in a negative way the nature of the project that will end in the elevation of books XI and XII to their present place of honor. That project will be guided by the terms of Lewis's dismissal. Those terms, as we have seen, are at once ideational and literary: the materials of these books are inappropriate to a literary work because they are doctrinal and didactic; and, moreover, "the actual writing . . . is curiously bad" (p. 125), and it is bad because the books are insufficiently dramatic. Lewis delivers these strictures as if they represented discrete and independent judgments, but in fact, each judgment is a reflection of the others. If the content is didactic rather than "poetic," the style will necessarily be bad because it will not reflect the subtle particulars of "lived experience," and because it does not reflect those particulars, but has reference instead to static abstractions, the result will of course lack drama. The opposition of poetry and doctrine entails a bias for some styles and against others, and entails too a bias in favor of the vivid representation of action in the world. So long as this set of mutual entailments is firmly in place, there will be little that a would-be defender of books XI and XII will be able to say.

I observed earlier that Waddington leaves unexplained the fact that fifteen years passed before there was any substantial challenge to Lewis's condemnation. Part of the explanation is to be found in the extent to which large features of the literary landscape would have to change before there could be any corresponding change in the arguments that could even be conceived (never mind heard) in the service of a possible defense. One sees this clearly in the early but ineffective effort of E. N. S. Thompson to redress the critical balance. The date is 1943 and Thompson himself knows how unpromising is the task he has undertaken: his very first sentence declares, "A plea for the last two books of *Paradise Lost* will seem at the present time decidedly quixotic."[10] He cites the "incorrigibles" who object to "all that Milton wrote," but he is even more dismayed "to find a staunch supporter like Mr. C. S. Lewis rendering an unfavorable judgment." Nevertheless, Thompson is determined "to put on record my impression that the details of this historical survey are poetically chosen and ordered effectively to the poet's chief end." Notice what this statement of intention does *not* promise: it does not promise to defend the survey as history or as doctrine, but to demonstrate that nevertheless it is employed poetically and contributes to a poetic end. Lewis's assumptions are left unchallenged, and Thompson is content to argue that this part of the poem exhibits many of the qualities generally admired in the earlier books ("the sentences are . . . no more cumbrous than Satan's first speech in book II"). His strategy is two-pronged. He answers the stylistic objection by presenting isolated passages and praising them as "finely etched pictures," and he answers the objection that these last books are structurally unrelated to the poem's plot by claiming that they are necessary to a psychological plot, the plot of Adam's education. Since Adam has had "precious little personal experience" (p. 376), he needs the knowledge and wisdom conveyed to him by the succession of tableaus and commentary: "Each scene adds something to Adam's fund of experience, just as the pictured scenes in the Purgatorio enlighten Dante toiling up the steep mountain path" (p. 378).

The emphasis on the psychology of education is hardly new. In 1734 Jonathan Richardson observes admiringly, "tis Delightful to see how Finely Milton *observes* all the Growth of the New Man. Creation was all at Once, Regeneration is like the Natural Progression: we are Babes, and come by Degrees to be Strong Men in *Christ.*"[11] The difference is that Richardson's admiration is for a theological pattern whereas Thompson offers his reading in order to counter the charge that in these books the theology has crowded out the poetry. In Thompson's account the lessons Adam learns are not doctrinal but political and ethical, and the progress of his education is from the relatively simple lessons of book XI to "the more complex social and political problems" of book XII. For Richardson the claims of the aesthetic and the theological do not pull against one another because the two categories are not mutually exclusive; but for Thompson, to defend the one is to devalue the other, and therefore he is forced to leave large sections of the text out of his account, an account that will have little chance of reversing the judgment so authoritatively made by Lewis.

Thompson's difficulty is seen in another form in the work of B. A. Rajan, who in 1947 also attempts something like a defense of books XI and XII. Like Thompson, Rajan begins by conceding so much that there is very little left for him to defend. "I myself," he says, "am not in love with the last books."[12] "They are bleak and barren and pessimistic." "The achievement falters" (p. 85). "Entire scenes do nothing" (p. 84). Milton is "tired in spirit" (p. 92). "There is no progression of poetic fervour to support the mechanical development of the epic." Rajan has an explanation for these weaknesses, but it turns out to be a curious and finally damaging one. The pessimism and dispiritedness, and the resulting flatness of the writing, are "unmistakable" (p. 83), but "they are not part and parcel of Milton's poetic design" (p. 84); rather, they are "intrusions in that design . . . the clenched, spasmodic despair of the man who will one day write *Samson Agonistes,* but intrusions nevertheless which are in no way evidence of Milton's epic intention." Milton, in short, was out of control. "The unevenness of the last two books reflects a desperate attempt to find peace of mind" (p. 84), and by dramatizing his own anxieties the poet violates the decorum of the epic mode, forgetting that if self-exploration is your concern, "there are other forms of writing you can employ" (p. 85).

One might pause over this remarkable argument and examine its sources in contemporary theories of epic and lyric; but for our purpose it is enough to point it out as an instance of the problem facing anyone who would challenge the conventional wisdom about books XI and XII without first challenging the assumptions (about what is and is not poetic) in the context of which that wisdom seems inescapable. It will not be enough to produce instances of "finely etched pictures" (thus countering Eliot's charge of visual deficiency) or explain away large portions of the verse as irrelevant to Milton's poetic intention; rather what is required is a redefinition of the poetic that does not exclude the theological and a redefinition of the theological that makes points of doctrine available for dramatization. This is exactly what happens in the period of 1958–72, and it happens in part because the argument from psychology—in which the sweep of books XI and XII is justified as a backdrop for Adam's education—will also become the argument from theology, as that education is seen to be specifically religious, tied to the states of regeneration as Milton describes them in his *On Christian Doctrine*. At the same time this double argument will be extended to the reader, whose experience will be seen in a relationship of symmetry and asymmetry to Adam's, and who will, in effect, be incorporated into the poem as one of its characters. (This strategy is already implicit in Richardson's observation, on p. 535, that at the end of book XII Adam is brought "into the Condition in Which We Are, on *Even Ground* with Us.")

Looking back, it is tempting to say that the components of this unified reading are all present, and that Thompson and Rajan fail, for a variety of reasons, to put them together; but, in fact, it would have been impossible for them or for anyone else to put them together because the intellectual framework, in which they are, in a sense, already together, did not yet exist. The framework that did exist rigorously separated poetry and theology, and refused to extend the drama and tension of art to the lived experience of a reader who might then be moved to this or that decision about his obligations or responsibilities or proper course of action. That kind of reader response was, as Lewis so forcefully insisted, not appropriate to the aesthetic experience in which issues of choice and decision (in the sense of conversion) are encountered not directly but "in profile." Indeed, if someone were to have argued, in 1942 or 1947, that the excellence of books XI and XII inhered in their capacity to provoke a self-examination of a specifically religious kind, he would in effect have been arguing that they weren't poetry.

The doctrine of poetic autonomy is so strong in the period that it rules quite different critical practices with the result that none of the competing schools is in a position to make an effective case for books XI and XII. Rajan, like Thompson, is an historical critic, a follower of Lewis, although he would like to dissent from Lewis's verdict on the last two books. But even though he is committed to the recovery of a historical perspective (the title of his book is, after all, *"Paradise Lost" and the Seventeenth Century Reader*), his ruling principle is that "there is nothing we can rely on except the poetry" (p 36); and that principle prevents him from taking his historical materials seriously, that is, as having any bearing on the question of poetic quality. "A preoccupation with doctrine," he declares, "will not help us." The relationship between Milton's religious beliefs and his poetry is interesting, but "I cannot see that it is aesthetically relevant." It is hardly a surprise, then, when he cannot see that large parts of books XI and XII are aesthetically relevant and falls to making excuses for them that are more damning than Lewis's censure.

The aesthetic irrelevance of books XI and XII is even more assured in relation to the other dominant critical practice of the period, the close readings of New Criticism. For the New Critics the autonomy of poetry is at once an article of faith and the basis of a program. That program is one of exclusion: it is not simply that historical materials are to be considered only insofar as they further a poetic end; the New Critic (at least in his more doctrinaire moments) is afraid that the poetic end will be obscured if the historical materials receive any sustained consideration whatsoever. This is so because New Criticism defines the poetic end and poetry itself at once universally and narrowly: universally because the qualities that identify poetry are understood not to change over time; narrowly because those qualities are small in number and identical with those recently discovered to reside in the metaphysicals. Listen, for example, to this representative and authoritative statement by Cleanth Brooks: "Our age rejoices in having recovered Donne; but in doing so we have recovered not just Donne's poetry, but poetry. This is so generally true that for many of us the quality of poetry—as distinguished from that of the more empty rhetorics—is bound up with functional metaphor, with dramatic tension, and with the fusion of thought and emotion—qualities which we associate with the poetry of Donne."[13]

The date is 1951 and the essay's title is "Milton and the New

Criticism." As an admirer of Milton, Brooks's task is clear. He must rescue the poet from Eliot's praise of him as the builder of "mazes of sounds" (for in such an account Milton becomes one "of the more empty rhetorics"), and he must do so by demonstrating that his verse is characterized by functional metaphor, dramatic tension, and the fusion of thought and emotion. For as Brooks himself forthrightly declares in the very next sentence, "We try to find these qualities . . . in the work of anyone to whom we give the name poet" (p. 3). What is at stake, then, is Milton's very right to be called a poet, and what follows, predictably, is a series of analyses, largely of similes from the early books of *Paradise Lost*, in which the requisite Donnean characteristics are duly discovered. Before the essay concludes, the poet of large and overarching designs (which may or may not falter in the execution) has been replaced by the poet of innumerable local effects, of complex and multiple resonant images, of a richness of texture that is inseparable from a richness of thought.

Brooks's performance is an impressive demonstration of the way in which a strongly held definition of poetry can become a strategy for turning particular poems into verse that has been rendered answerable to the definition. Significantly for our purposes, the execution of that strategy does not involve any references to books XI and XII. Nor is this surprising: if one is engaged in a defense of Milton which requires that his verse, at least in certain respects, be indistinguishable from Donne's, the last place one is going to look for support is a portion of the poem that has always been characterized as a stylistic "falling off." Not only does it make good sense for Brooks to ignore books XI and XII when making his case; given the assumptions within which he works, he can ignore them with impunity. It is a tenet of New Critical theory that the essence of poetry involves a moment of lyric intensity; a long poem, then, is almost a contradiction in terms (and here the remarks of Poe are relevant), and one does not expect something the size of *Paradise Lost* to display at all points the qualities that mark it as poetic. Brooks is therefore under no obligation to take account of every moment in the poem because it is no part of his aesthetic to require a uniformity of texture or achievement. The situation is quite different in the case of the literary historian who is committed to finding in *Paradise Lost* the working out of a coherent and sustained design (whether that design be epic, or cosmological, or moral); he has the obligation to account for everything, and if something in the poem does not seem to contribute to the design or appears to be a fault in its execution, it must be explained or explained away. The result is the succession of excuses, rationalizations, and weak justifications that we have seen in the work of Lewis, Thompson, and Rajan, and the larger result is that, however opposed in aims and principles the New and the historical critics may be, they are united in their inability to make anything admirable out of books XI and XII of *Paradise Lost.* The only difference between them is that for the literary historian that inability is a cause for regret; he would like to be able to validate the merit of these books because to do so would be to strengthen his *general* account of Milton. Brooks has no such regrets since his defense of Milton requires only that he adduce a sufficient number of examples of the right kind of verse; and if books XI and XII do not yield such examples, he will simply pass over them in silence.

Silence seems to be the general strategy of New Criticism with respect to books XI and XII, even when the critic is committed to a comprehensive reading. Something of the state of the art can be inferred from Arnold Stein's *Answerable Style* (1953). Stein's book is the first extended effort to apply New Critical principles to the whole of *Paradise Lost,* and his achievement stands behind much of what has been written since. Stein offers a powerful alternative to the Leavis-Eliot characterization of Milton's style as abstract and remote. Like Brooks, he adduces several passages in which Milton could be reasonably compared to Donne, but his main strategy is to agree with Leavis and Eliot when they observe that Milton does not try to get beyond poetry and then to demonstrate how, within the confines he has chosen, the poet achieves a complexity and precision that are perfectly answerable both to his vision and his purpose. In Stein's reading, Milton's monolithic certainty, so offensive to readers in love with a more tentative style, does not produce a sameness of texture, but frees him to present a variety of textures without ever losing hold of that which finally grounds and controls them. Milton, Stein says, "has a sure metaphysical grasp of the principle, the center, which can admit all kinds of surface complexity, and indeed must, to prove his grasp; he justifies the great theme in the process of mastering idea and texture in the perspectives of the whole cumulative weight of the epic structure. . . . He presents the immediacy of the moment in the conscious perspective of time" (p. 155). This is an impressive statement which promises a way of bringing together the New Critical emphasis on local texture with the traditional concern for Milton's epic structures, and in the earlier chapters of *Answerable Style* the promise is more than redeemed by a succession of influential analyses. (The reading of book VI is still powerful after thirty-five years.) The promise, however, is *not* extended to books XI and XII of which nothing is said until the penultimate paragraph:

> These books fulfill the rhythm of the poem and they satisfy two kinds of time; they allow Adam a necessary interval to convalesce as man and hero under the aspects of human history and eternity. During this time he becomes a conscious tragic hero . . . accepting, with all passion spent, fully man's condition, and he himself now a fully experienced man; and becomes a mythic hero reborn; and finally becomes man, with all his history behind and before him. (p. 161)

This is finely said, but in essence it is no more than what was said eight years before by Thompson; books XI and XII provide space and time for Adam's education into mortality. Although Stein's book was instrumental in changing the ways in which we thought and talked about *Paradise Lost,* it left unchanged the traditional negative view of its closing books.

III

It is now 1953 in our story, and if I were given to melodrama, I might say that "things are looking bad for books XI and XII of *Paradise Lost."* The two dominant critical schools are either disinclined or unable to effect their rehabilitation; and if one were to measure the state of the art by James Thorpe's anthology of Milton criticism from four centuries (published in 1950), there would seem to be no reason to believe that there would soon be any change for the better. But, in fact, the forces of change are already evident in the very documents that seem to argue against it. First of all, the recharacterization of books XI and XII has become a *project:* that is, it is on the list (invisible, of course) of those things that need to be done. This was in part the result of Lewis's fortunately unfortunate phrasing—"untransmuted lump of futurity" is a judgment in search of an argument—and in part the result of a general change in the basic mode of critical practice. The old mode called for two actions: one either first praised the beauties and then pointed out the deficiencies, or first pointed out the deficiencies and then praised the beauties. The assumption underlying the new mode, however, is that everything written by a poet is or should be equally poetic, and a corollary assumption that poets should be given the benefit of the doubt leads to a practice in which the understood task for criticism is to demonstrate that every rift is loaded with ore.

This new practice is nowhere announced as now beginning, but it grows up alongside the ever more institutionalized practice of close reading of which it is a logical extension. If we think of close reading as a technique for bringing out the complexity of individual poetic moments, then the question of what to do with long poems can have two possible answers. Following the lead of Poe (whose pronouncements underlie much of New Critical theory), one can decide "that a long poem does not exist . . . [it] is simply a flat contradiction in terms";[14] it would then be permissible to ignore those portions of a long work that did not seem truly poetic, just as so many critics took to ignoring the last two books of *Paradise Lost*. Or, alternatively, one can "save" the long poem by regarding it as an extended short poem (a strategy Poe considers, but ironically), by de-emphasizing the narrative or sequential dimension and concentrating instead on the analysis of innumerable local effects. This is the course taken by New Criticism, which thus commits itself to finding poetic qualities (of tension, paradox, irony) in every corner of a work, however long. It might seem that such a program runs the danger of turning poems into discontinuous fragments, held together only by the physical ligatures of paper and pages; but fragmentation is avoided by invoking another New Critical principle, the doctrine of organic unity: all the parts of a long poem are unified in their relation to a single theme or vision which informs them and of which they are the (repeated) expression. Consequently, sequence is once again legitimated, not, however, as the generator of meaning (as it is in the logic of narrative) but as a succession of spaces in which the same meaning is endlessly and variously displayed. This is the triumph of the New Critical privileging of the image: the long poem becomes an extended metaphor, a symbolic object whose structure does not so much develop as it exfoliates.

One could put this another way by observing that in extending its particular kind of attention to longer poems, New Critical practice spatializes time. It is thus itself an extension of modernism, of the tendency in modernist aesthetics to conceive of the work of art not as a series of propositions about an exterior reality but as a system of significations regulated by internal laws. The art object so conceived becomes a spatial field or gestalt in which every point is related to every other point, and while it is true that the relations between points can only be apprehended in time, the final and desired apprehension is one in which the temporal medium has been transcended and the network of internal references and cross-references can be grasped in a single moment of unified vision. When that happens, as Joseph Frank points out in "Spatial Form in Modern Literature," "past and present are seen spatially, locked in a timeless unity." In place of the "objective historical imagination" modern writers put the "mythical imagination . . . the imagination that sees the actions and events of a particular time merely as the bodying forth of eternal prototypes," and these prototypes, Frank continues, "are created by transmuting the time-world of history into the timeless world of myth."[15]

It is finally no accident, I think, that Frank's formulation here is an uncanny prediction of the way in which the lump of *Paradise Lost,* books XI and XII, will finally be redeemed: that apparently awkward history will, quite literally, be transmuted into the timeless world of myth. I am not suggesting any simple cause-and-effect relationship between Frank's essay, seminal and influential though it was, and the eventually happy fate of Milton's orphaned books. The relationship, while real, is a much more overdetermined one in that Frank is only one of many who are announcing, from variety of perspectives, a shift from temporal to spatial ways of thinking: his use of the word "myth" calls to mind another great spatializer of the period, Northrop Frye, whose labors in *The Anatomy of Criticism* (1957) could also be well (and prophetically) described as a transmutation of the actions and events of a particular time into the timeless world of "eternal prototypes." Frye's prototypes are, of course, his archetypes, those large recurring patterns and images that together form an overarching and abiding grid in relation to which particular works (and if someone, not Frye, were so minded, particular lines) can be placed and understood: not understood, however, in their details—that is the work of a criticism devoted to explication—but understood as instances of a structure that makes them possible and intelligible. Frye, like the New Critics, is a formalist and a believer in the autonomy of literature, but for him literature means the general and generating literary structures, and the task of formal description is to get a proper account of them. In order to accomplish that task, as Frye points out, one does not take the "close look" that defines New Critical practice; rather, one "stands back" so that the outlines of the "archetypal organization" can come into view.[16] This standing back is obviously ahistorical and leads to the de-emphasis on the succession of forms in favor of the enumeration of those forms that repeatedly appear. Nor are those forms exclusively literary in any narrow sense. Frye is as committed as any New Critic to the study of literature *as* literature, but for him literature is not simply a collection of techniques, but an imaginative ordering, in words, of all the modes of being characteristic of human life. "Literature neither reflects nor escapes from ordinary life: what it does is reflect the world as human imagination conceives it, in mythical, romantic, heroic and ironic as well as realistic and fantastic terms."[17]

One effect of Frye's archetypal or mythic vision is to break down the barriers between the literary and other realism, not, however, by diluting or subordinating the literary (the great fear of twentieth-century aesthetics), but by appropriating for it everything that is centrally and essentially human. The same inclusiveness also characterizes other "mythologizing" systems that were to become increasingly influential in the 1940s and 1950s: Cassirer's theory of symbolic forms, Jung's theory of archetypes, Freud's theory of the unconscious. These systems are very different from one another, but they are alike in their privileging of a primitive or original state in which subject/object and all the other distinctions that rationality brings are not in force, and the entities we think of as already distributed in time and space exist together in a moment of simultaneity and primal fluidity, a moment in which the logic of metamorphosis has not yet given way to the logic of discreteness, and, as Cassirer puts it, "everything may be turned into everything."[18]

It follows that in each of these systems (although in varying degrees), the fall occurs with differentiation, with the dispersal into objectified space and irreversible time of what was once whole and unified; and it further follows that the tendency in these systems to value the "edenic" or "prerational" leads to the devaluing of the discursive and the sequential, that is, of narrative. In a passage that refers with approval to Jung and Cassirer, Frye contrasts the "epiphanic moment, the flash of instantaneous apprehension with no direct reference to times" to the dilution of that moment in the "forms of proverbs, riddles . . . and folk tales" where "there already is a considerable element of narrative."[19] The rhetoric here, as in the writings of the other great spatializers, is the rhetoric of loss, and what is lost is an immediate and instantaneous apprehension of essence (be it mythic, archetypal, psychic, etc.), an apprehension that has been dulled or obscured by too close an immersion in the effects for which essence is ultimately responsible. For different reasons the recovery of the instantaneous or epiphanic is associated by many of these same thinkers with the production and experience of poetry, and, more particularly, with poetic or metaphoric language, in which, it is asserted, the constraints and distortions of discursive temporalizing language are loosened and, in moments of true vision, undone (one thinks here, for example, of Philip Wheelwright). This is thought to be more true of certain kinds of poetry than of other kinds. Lyric poetry, romance, and epic in the mode of the *Odyssey* or the *Orlando Furioso* are more likely to embody and induce the vision of wholeness than are the realistic novel, the political satire, or the more plot-centered epic mode of the *Aeneid* or *Jerusalem Delivered;* but it is always possible to reverse this judgment (sometimes made only implicitly or by acts of omission) by arguing that works that appear to be structured along lines of sequence and plot are in fact works in which those lines are repeatedly broken and blurred, so that attention is continually called to a timeless realm of underlying and constitutive truths (or archetypes, or myths).

Just such an argument was being made, in small and large ways, for *Paradise Lost* in the late 1950s. In 1958 both Geoffrey Hartman and Kingsley Widmer published essays in *English Literary History* that illustrate the way in which the technique of close reading was contributing to the spatialization of Milton's epic. Hartman's "Milton's Counterplot," a classic piece that has often been anthologized, anticipates in its brief compass much of the work that will be done in the next decade. In his argument the counterplot of *Paradise Lost* is found in those places where the apparent urgency of superficially dramatic moments (usually with Satan at their center) is undercut by references to God's "divine imperturbability" and his "omnipotent knowledge that the creation will outlive death and sin."[20] This counterplot, while expressed only in an "indirect manner," is everywhere present: "The root-feeling . . . for imperturbable Providence radiates from many levels of the text." Hartman chooses in this essay to operate at the level of the simile, and he demonstrates, in a series of brilliant analyses, how at the center of a Miltonic simile the restless activity of the diabolic host is often viewed from a vantage point of "aesthetic distance" (p. 391), of "a calm and cold radiance" (p. 390). The result is that "a simile intended to sharpen our view of the innumerable stunned host of hell, just as it is about to be roused by Satan, at the same time sharpens our sense of the imperturbable order of the creation . . . and of the survival of man through Providence and his safe-shored will" (p. 391).

The counterplot, then, is a device or machine for arresting the forward action of narrative and directing us (insofar as it is possible) to God's "Prospect high / Wherein past, present, future he beholds" (III, 77–78). The imperturbability of God's heavenly Prospect (like many of Milton's heroes, he sits) is contrasted to the busy restlessness of Satanic activity, and if one takes this contrast seriously, as criticism now begins to do, the very concept of action is redefined away from gestures of visible movement and toward the maintenance of a still, calm center. Obviously, such a redefinition is an important part of the general effort to devalue plot and sequence in what had always been thought of as a heroic poem, that is, a poem that celebrates heroics. It is a redefinition to which Widmer contributes in his essay "The Iconography of Renunciation: The Miltonic Simile."[21] What is being renounced in the similes and elsewhere, according to Widmer, is "the flux . . . of worldly activity," which is, he asserts, essentially evil, and in its place Milton elevates the "unchanging and absolute good" of the divine. In the poems this new heroism is represented not by movement and energy but by "the immutable Lord, the untemptable Christ, the renunciatory Samson, the poetic mind fixed only on a single revelation" (p. 84). Widmer's discussion traverses much of the same territory as Hartman's and yields a similar account of ironic reversals, double perspectives, and subversions of narrative progress. In the end the entire poem, apparently so full of detail and dramatic gesture, has been transformed by Widmer into a "fascinating and shocking master simile: the world as evil and virtue as renunciation" (p. 86).

This master simile is "shocking" because it would seem to run counter to the then orthodox view of Milton as a Christian humanist, with the emphasis on the "humanist," that is, "upon the positive values of classical learning, religious and ethical moderation, and general reasonableness." Widmer's Milton, on the other hand, is "absolutist" (p. 75), unyielding, and dismissive of "the texture of reality and plenitudinous human actuality" (p. 86). This is a noteworthy point because it is an early indication of another of the changes that will eventually lead to the rehabilitation of books XI and XII. To the extent that Milton is thought of as holding *moderate* religious views— views that coexist harmoniously with the claims of humanism—it will be easy to regard books XI and XII as a regrettable and uncharacteristic instance of immoderation in which human values are insufficiently acknowledged. ("The Author has been so attentive to his Divinity, that he has neglected his Poetry.") But once Milton's religious temper is recharacterized in the direction suggested by Widmer, the doctrinal emphasis of books XI and XII will seem legitimate and central. This is precisely what will happen in the 1960s and 1970s, but hasn't happened yet in 1959, although the way is being prepared by the spatialization of the poem, which involves, as we have seen, a change from the celebration of infinite variety (regarded by earlier critics as one of Milton's glories) to a celebration of a single monolithic vision.

An important document in this change is Isabel MacCaffrey's *"Paradise Lost" as Myth*.[22] Published in 1959, MacCaffrey's book is the first self-conscious attempt to turn *Paradise Lost* into the kind of spatial object increasingly admired by modernist critics and readers. As myth, *Paradise Lost* records a prehistoric event from which all later realities are descended, "and, therefore, the reality of occurrences in time . . . no longer *depends* on their recurrent manifestations; rather, their existence is made to depend on the prior reality of a metaphysical condition that is their cause" (pp. 15–16). It is Milton's achievement, MacCaffrey declares, "to allow us temporarily to share a manner of seeing that will capture accurately the outlines of a peculiar kind of reality," and he does this by inventing "a series of techniques profoundly original . . . and among them a style reverberatory . . . and a 'spatial' structural pattern of interlocking, mutually dependent parts" (pp. 42–43). Consequently, MacCaffrey continues:

> The "normal" straightforward narrative patterns traditional to story-tellers will be inappropriate; suspense will be replaced by the tacit comment of interconnecting . . . threads. The mythical narrative slights chronology in favor of a folded structure which continually returns upon itself, or a spiral that circles about a single center; in this it reproduces the very shape of the myth itself which is circularly designed for resonance and cross-reference.

It follows that a poem constructed along these principles will not display a developing meaning—a meaning that is being processed by the events of a narrative—but will rather represent, again and again, a meaning that is as present in the first line as it is in the last. In *Paradise Lost* "meanings are deepened or heightened, but their direction and configuration [are] not essentially changed" (p. 51).

One can draw a direct line from this view of the poem to the eventual "upgrading" of books XI and XII, if only because the various rationales for leaving those books in the interpretive limbo they had come to occupy now become unavailable: one can no longer say, for example, that the poem is for all intents and purposes over at the end of book X, and that, except for the last hundred lines or so, books XI and XII are superfluous. One can no longer say that because as a judgment it is intelligible only within a strongly temporal reading, a reading in relation to which one asks of a line or a passage or a book, "In what ways does it contribute to the plot?" or "What is its relevance to the poem's developing meaning?" or (in a somewhat older tradition) "How well does it conform to a conventional epic practice?" (the visit to the underworld, the catalog of ships, the revelation to a hero of his future history). These questions assume the independence from one another of poetic "components" as they are arranged along a sequence, and within that assumption it makes sense to interrogate those components separately and to pronounce one of them successful or unsuccessful. (And in some cases this pronouncement will be made with reference to models *external* to the poem, to stylistic models or to the model of "the epic.") But within the assumption of a spatial or mythic poem of the sort MacCaffrey believes *Paradise Lost* to be, there are no separable components, since every coordinate of the spatial object displays the same significances and resonances. One must therefore ask a new question: In what ways does the line or passage or book realize the poem's single and all-pervasive vision? And that question will also be a program: that is, to ask it is to have assumed the shape of its answer, a shape in which one portion of the text will be shown to have exactly the same properties as every other portion. It is therefore not at all surprising to find MacCaffrey asserting that the major and archetypal images of books I and II "are continued into history in the final books of *Paradise Lost*" (p. 175). Her reading of these books consists of finding in every instance that a detail or an action is a version of something we have seen innumerable times before: "Each of the elements has its mythical prototype in the books that have gone before, and the evil fortune of the Egyptians is shown manifestly to be a product of the same self-destructive power that brought the fallen angels to their ill mansion" (pp. 176–77). The argument, in short, is that books XI and XII are just like books I and II, and the significance of the argument for the story I am telling can be seen in the fact that, traditionally, one of the reasons for dismissing books XI and XII is that they weren't like books I and II at all. (Later the argument will go in the other direction, i.e., of making I and II, and all the rest, just like the newly characterized XI and XII.)

By 1959, then, not only is the rehabilitation of books XI and XII a recognized and official project, it is a project of a very specific kind; and the fact that it is now that kind of project means that many of the obstacles to its success have already been removed, although no one in particular has set out to remove them. Those obstacles were contained, you will recall, in the charges usually made against the books: they are insufficiently poetic; they do not contribute to the unfolding of the plot; they are inert and undramatic. The charge of poetic insufficiency has been answered by a shift in the mode of characterizing the poetic texture: no longer does one look at isolated lines and passages and test them for the requisite qualities; rather, one notes the relationship between any local detail and a host of other details, all of which combine to form a single resonance. As MacCaffrey puts it, "Not the thickness of individual denotation, but the density of endless implication, weights Milton's images" (p. 177). The charge of structural irrelevance has been answered by a reconceiving of the structure, which is no longer a succession of actions that follow one another in time, but a sustained projection of a single overriding and omnipresent master-meaning; and the charge that these books are undramatic is in the process of being answered by a redefinition of action, away from the theatrical and visible response to the pressure of occasions and toward the interior maintenance of a single unswerving position.

These shifts in literary practice are also parts of a larger shift by which the chief obstacle to the transmutation of Lewis's lump—the rigid separation of poetry from doctrine—will finally be removed. The identification of large mythic or archetypal patterns as constitutive of human experience leads to the habit of seeing different realms of that experience as transformations of one another rather than as areas of opposing or mutually exclusive concerns. If the myth of the birth of the hero or of the hero's fall or of the entry into Paradise are basic constituents of human forms of thought, their appearance in epic or romance on one hand and in a variety of religions on the other is neither surprising nor the occasion for debates as to whether in focusing on them one is subordinating the aesthetic to the theological (or vice versa); and by the same reasoning the presence in a literary work of doctrinal patterns need not be the cause for a special anxiety, since those patterns do not enforce a narrowly religious reading but ask to be tracked to their source in an underlying and pervasive myth. As Frye says in the *Anatomy,* "the literary critic, like the historian, is compelled to treat every religion in the same way religions treat each other, as though it were a human hypothesis" (p. 126). As a human hypothesis a religion is just as available for aesthetic "appropriation" as any other body of assertions, and mutatis mutandis a literary work will not be in danger of losing its credentials as literary because it contains small or large amounts of religious materials. The effect of mythologizing thought is to relativize its various instantiations, to blunt the claim of any one to have precedence over the others, and to encourage exercises in which the uncovering of analogies is central and the banishing of one analogous system from the precincts of another is beside the point.

Given such liberalization of the "aesthetic" (which is inseparable from an aestheticization of the religious), the way is open to reexamining the untransmuted lump of books XI and XII with an eye toward discovering in them patterns and reoccurrences of the kind criticism is increasingly committed to find. It is at this moment that typology appears as a tool of *literary* analysis. In Waddington's survey typology is cited as the basis for some of "the most influential readings" of books XI and XII, but as far as one can tell the sudden emergence of typological interpretations is a phenomenon without an explanation, something on the order of an eruption. But from the vantage point of the history we have been tracing here, the phenomenon makes perfect and inevitable sense. First of all, typology is, like Frye's archetypes and Frank's modernism and Cassirer's symbolic structures, a machine for the spatialization of time. Typology is a way of reading the Old Testament so that its events are seen as prefigurations or "shadows" of events in the New, and especially of events in the life of Christ. In typological interpretations the actions of men and nations derive their significance not from the conditions of their historical production, but from a master significance—Christ's work of incarnation and redemption—which is "before" history in the sense of having already occurred in eternity and is nevertheless the content of history in that every event at once reflects and anticipates it. Obviously, to read history in this way is to be always referring its events upward to the everpresent source of their meaning rather than forward to the meaning that may seem to be generated by sequence, and, just as obviously, this way of reading shares a great deal with the mythologizing systems that have become so central to literary analysis. It assumes a structure in which all points radiate out from a stabilizing and generating center; it invites us to apprehend that structure by turning away from the movement of a temporal succession to the stasis of an inclusive and eternal vision; and by characterizing that vision it provides us with a program for discovering it in everything we see. No matter what significance may seem to be conferred on an action or event by empirical circumstances, its true significance can only inhere in some relationship (of anticipation, opposition, promise) to the truth proclaimed and borne by Jesus Christ. As Augustine puts it, in a classic formulation of figurative or typological reading, "to the healthy and pure internal eye He is everywhere" and therefore "what is read should be subjected to diligent scrutiny until an interpretation contributing to the reign of charity is produced."[23]

As a system, then, typology is characterized by just those emphases and strategies that were contributing in the late fifties to the making of *Paradise Lost* into a modernist poem. Moreover, it has the incalculable and, one is tempted to say, decisive advantage of being itself a topic in the poem, and in just that part of the poem whose reputation needed to be refurbished. Midway through book XII, the archangel Michael, in response to a question from Adam, delivers himself of an answer that is as concise and elegant an explanation of typology as one could wish:

> Law can discover sin, but not remove,
> Save by those shadowy expiations weak,
> The blood of bulls and goats, they may conclude
> Some blood more precious must be paid for man,
> Just for unjust, that in such righteousness
> To them by faith imputed, they may find
> Justification toward God, and peace
> Of conscience, which the law by ceremonies

Cannot appease, nor man the moral part
Perform, and not performing cannot live,
So law appears imperfect, and but given
With purpose to resign them in full time
Up to a better covenant, disciplined
From shadowy types to truth, from flesh to spirit,
From imposition of strict laws, to free
Acceptance of large grace, from servile fear
To filial, works of law to works of faith. (290–306)

From the hindsight perspective of 1982 or 1972 one might wonder why this and related passages did not alert readers to the typological
structure of books XI and XII earlier than they in fact did. The explanation is that first of all the typological tradition had only recently
been recovered and become an object of study by historians of religion.
So that when literary critics begin to work with typological materials
the sources and accounts they cite—in the writings of Danielou, de
Lubac, Auerbach, Lampe, Wolcombe, Hanson—have themselves only
become available in the period of 1957–64. But even if these materials
had been available earlier, readers of Milton would not have been
drawn to them for the same reason they were not drawn to the study
of books XI and XII: they would have been regarded as nonliterary,
and any demonstration that by referring to them one could make sense
out of books XI and XII would have been a demonstration or redem-
onstration of the fact that in those books the poet was more attentive
to his divinity than his poetry. The point is one I have made before: the
network of relevancies, connections, and analogies that make for literary illumination cannot be fashioned from materials that are just lying
around waiting for someone clever enough to put them together;
rather, they must, in some sense, already *be* together, or already embedded within some general way of thinking in the light of which their
relationship just "cries out" for observation and elaboration.

This is what has happened to typology and literature by 1958,
and it had been happening for quite a while in ways indirectly, but
powerfully, related to books XI and XII. Frye complains, in 1957, that
"biblical typology is so dead a language now that most readers, including scholars, cannot construe the superficial meaning of any poem
which employs it" (*Anatomy,* p. 14), but his complaint is surely an exaggeration which can be challenged in part by his own practice. In

1956 he had published "The Typology of *Paradise Regained*," an influential essay that concisely summarizes the principles of typology and offers an important early account of the heroism that is proper to the typological vision, a heroism characterized not by movement and action, but by patience and waiting. Frye is able to cite in support of his argument Elizabeth Pope's *Paradise Regained: The Tradition and the Poem* (1947), and he might also have cited Michael Krouse's *Milton's Samson and the Christian Tradition* (1949), a comprehensive survey of the typological uses to which the legend of the Hebrew strongman had been put. Both studies grew out of dissertations directed by Don Cameron Allen, who was already working this vein by 1937 and had recently (1953) been arguing for the theological basis of Milton's closet drama, an argument that was also being pursued in slightly different ways by A. S. P. Woodhouse and John Steadman. Obviously, the invoking of theological contexts in the course of literary discussions is becoming more and more respectable, and that respectability is to some extent a spillover from the growing vogue in Medieval studies of typological criticism in the work of D. W. Robertson and others. It is always easier for an interpretive strategy to make its way *up* the chronological ladder rather than down, because it is always easier to argue for the continuing influence of an older way of thinking than for the retroactive relevance of a method only newly discovered. Once typology had become accepted as an interpretive strategy by Chaucerians, it was only a matter of time before it was taken up by Spenserians and Miltonists. In 1959 William Madsen read a paper entitled "Earth the Shadow of Heaven: Typological Symbolism in *Paradise Lost*" at the convention of the Modern Language Association, and the era of typological criticism in Milton studies could be said to have officially arrived.

IV

It is at this point that the generation of which Waddington speaks—the generation of readers who share a conviction of the excellence of books XI and XII—also arrives, although I should hasten to say that it does not arrive all at once or with its arguments fully articulated. That is, while the preceding pages have traced the emergence of the conditions—small and large—within which the rehabilitation of books XI and XII becomes possible and even inevitable, the fact of those conditions does not mean that the work will immediately be done, and, indeed, many critics are still able to operate as if none of the shifts in definition and emphasis described here had ever occurred. What is important is a change in atmosphere, a change in which the presumption of innocence has replaced the presumption of guilt, a change that leads in only five years to the reversal of a judgment that had stood, more or less, for over two hundred and fifty. That reversal occurs not only because new arguments (reflecting new understandings of what is and is not poetic) become available, but because old arguments are now heard with more force than was possible when there was not an audience *eager* to hear them. Thus one of the interesting things about F. T. Prince's essay "On the Last Two Books of *Paradise Lost*," always cited as the first strongly effective defense, is its continuity with the unsuccessful defense offered fifteen years earlier by Thompson. Like Thompson, Prince assumes that "our function as critics should be to assess [*Paradise Lost*'s] qualities as a poem, to explore the poetic results which Milton has obtained from his materials." If those materials are religious, as they are here, we must certainly be ready to respond to them "in imagination," but "we need not commit ourselves to any decision upon their truth or untruth."[24] Prince then proceeds to find, as Thompson did before him, a *dramatic* coherence in the sequence of Adam's responses, "in the vibration of the story in [his] reacting consciousness." For Prince, however, the pattern of reaction is not confined to the special circumstances of the last two books, but is another instance of a dramatic method employed by Milton throughout, the use of characters as "registers of consciousness" (p. 237); "so we have Adam's description of his first impressions of Paradise and of his feelings for Eve, and Eve's corresponding account of her first sensations." Prince thus demonstrates, without any particular self-consciousness, his conformity to the new mode of critical practice in which the sameness of the poem from beginning to end is assumed, and indeed he opens his essay by declaring that "in *Paradise Lost,* every part contributes to the whole; there is no waste or loose matter: unity of design and execution is sustained from beginning to end." The burden of proof is no longer on the poem or on any part of it, but on the critic who would argue *against* the success and coherence of its design. It is this presumption in the poem's favor that leads Prince to seek unifying structures and to find ways for turning old deficiencies into new beauties. Thus he argues that the lowering of the level of intensity in the last two books is a wonderful accommodation by Milton to the experience of reading a long poem where necessarily "the nature of our interest changes" and "our interest itself must in some degree flag" (p. 244). It is Milton's achievement to make this fact about the reader's psychology coincide with a fact about his narrative, the somewhat anticlimactic turn from high drama (will they or won't they) to the serious and somber business of settling into human life as we know it. It is a sign of Milton's artistry and control that he shows "an instinctive grasp of the ebb and flow of interest in a long poem, and that . . . he has utilized the inevitable shift in our attention to coincide with the mood of the last phase" (p. 247).

Persuasive or not as it may be, this argument is a perfect illustration of the changed assumptions within which Prince and everyone else now work: no longer is a work scrutinized for its conformity or failure to conform to principles of poetic excellence; rather, poetic excellence is a given and any "fact" about a poem that seems to deny it must be "reseen" as its strongest confirmation. Prince's "move" here looks forward to the later and more ambitious argument by which every puzzling or apparently discordant feature of *Paradise Lost* will be found significant in relation to the reader's experience, but at this stage of our history it simply bespeaks the now standard willingness to give the poet the benefit of every doubt. That same willingness is, as we have seen, inseparable from the conception of the work as a spatial object everywhere infused with the same meaning, and the critic who holds this conception will be inclined to make connections between observations that might otherwise seem discrete. Thus for Prince, seeing Adam as a figure for "the human consciousness itself" in all of its triumphs and falls means seeing the figures of XI and XII as instances of the same "repeated lapses and renewals of effort," and this means that the theological personages of Michael's narrative are given a dramatic and structural significance. Again, Prince is at once saying something new and saying something that the expanded notion of what can be treated as literary allows if not directs him to say. He and Thompson share the same assumptions, but in another sense they are not the same, since the key terms—poet, drama, religion—are understood to have different boundaries and to call into being different interpretive activities. Although Thompson wanted to say the things that are now said by Prince, he was unable in 1943 to extend his observations in ways that are inevitable in 1958, given the changed landscape in which all critics now labor.

This includes even those critics who continue to be hostile to books XI and XII despite the new respectability, indeed urgency, of showering them with praise. J. B. Broadbent, to cite a single example, is one of a long line of Cambridge critics for whom Milton is always suspect because he is not more like D. H. Lawrence. In the course of his chapter on the concluding books, Broadbent rehearses many of the old complaints: they are undramatic; the verse is "arthritic"; the ethic is disappointingly stoic, "a stubborn Petrine determination to be unpolluted by evil."[25] But for all of that Broadbent cannot help but participate in the project that is now central to Milton studies. He finds innumerable linkages backward to books I and II and comments that "these linkages do much to focus ethic in aesthetic" (p. 274). Even as he labels it "megalomaniac" (p. 281), he recognizes "the claim of Christianity . . . to continuing apprehension of the point of intersection of the timeless with time," and he is aware of the relationship between that claim and what Milton is attempting, however misguidedly, in these books. In short, despite his sympathies or his lack of sympathy, Broadbent, like everyone else, leaves books XI and XII better than he found them.

In Waddington's account of these matters there are only two events, a fall in 1942 from true perception in the form of Lewis's unfortunate pronouncement and a recovery begun in 1958 when Prince and a host of others suddenly have their visions cleared; but from the perspective that has been presented here Lewis saw what it was possible for him to see and saw it not in an aberrant but in a thoroughly traditional way, and Prince's clear-sightedness is similarly an extension of the conditions of seeing—established gradually in the years since 1942—that make what he now says seem so obvious.

One is not surprised, then, to find any number of critics contributing to a project now firmly under way, even though many of them are not self-consciously aware of it as a project. There is no evidence that John M. Steadman and John E. Parish had their eyes on the story I have been telling when, in 1959, they present accounts of the theological traditions that find their way into the last books of Milton's poem; nevertheless, the *reason* they give for offering these accounts (of the prophesized redeemer and the curse on the serpent) is that they help us understand how Milton "maintains suspense throughout the last three books of *Paradise Lost* and gives them dramatic unity."[26] What is remarkable is that neither Steadman nor Parish feels obliged to argue for the assumption that underlies their assertions, the assumption that these books do in fact display "dramatic unity" (whereas not much earlier they would have been denied both unity and drama) and the corollary assumption that the possession of these *aesthetic* qualities can be validated by the introduction of materials from theology. One year later, Dick Taylor, Jr., explicating another theological tradition, the expulsion from Paradise, is even more emphatic in his linking of the (now undoubted) dramatic effectiveness of the books with Milton's theological concerns. In Taylor's reading, Milton "weaves" those concerns "into the structural and thematic fabric of his poem, achieving a more effective dramatic significance" than did his predecessors,[27] a pattern that finds its fulfillment in the actual story of Christ's coming (p. 79), a moment toward which "Milton has carefully built" (p. 77). Taylor himself is already building on Parish and Steadman whom he acknowledges in his first footnote along with Prince as among those now arguing for a more "favorable" view of the formerly untransmuted lump.

That more favorable view is forthrightly announced (and assumed) in the title of Lawrence Sasek's 1962 essay "The Drama of *Paradise Lost,* Books XI and XII."[28] Sasek is also noteworthy in that he self-consciously locates himself in the history I have been recounting, and sees himself raising the banner originally unfurled by Thompson, who, he laments (no doubt with satisfaction), "apparently failed to convince critics that the last two books were more than a necessary but uninspired conclusion, attaining the poetic intensity of the preceding books only in isolated passages" (p. 182). Nineteen years later, Sasek will do what Thompson failed to do, and he proceeds to do it in terms that are increasingly familiar. The historical materials are not haphazardly ("lumpily") marshaled, but "are selected for their effect on Adam." The conclusion is ringing and confident:

> The last two books of *Paradise Lost* therefore present a drama in which the character of Adam is molded into an example of Christian fortitude. They dramatize the final stage in Adam's development from innocence through sin, through reconciliation with God, to a full knowledge and acceptance of God's judgment.

Sasek ends by expressing the hope that in the future books XI and XII will "receive more respect than they are generally given" (p. 196), but the future he looks forward to has already arrived. It is only the fourth year in the revolution A.P. (after Prince), and yet Sasek's essay is more than a little out-of-date. He seems unaware of the work of Prince, Parish, and Steadman and presents himself as more of a pioneer than he could possibly be. The reverse is true of Jackson Cope who in the same crucial year begins his *The Metaphoric Structure of Paradise Lost* by rehearsing the developments in intellectual history to which he is the self-conscious heir. The entire first chapter of the book analyzes the shifts and attitudes and perspectives that make its writing possible. "No observer of the Renaissance need be told," Cope declares in his very first sentence, "that literary criticism in recent years has removed its focal interest from John Donne and the metaphysical poets to John Milton" (p. 1). Cope finds the shift in focus from Donne to Milton "closely paralleled by another," by the fact "that almost without our noticing, the once flourishing *explication de textes* has become largely a classroom exercise" (p. 1); that technique, which attends so closely to the moment-by-moment experience of verse, has been succeeded, says Cope, by a method of analysis more spatial in conception, one in which the "flow of time . . . is . . . frozen into the labyrinthine planes of a spatial block . . . whose form has neither beginning, middle, end, nor center, and must be effectively conceived as a simultaneity of multiple views" (pp. 14–15). In the course of articulating the forthright modernism that will generate his analysis, Cope pays tribute to the influences I have noted above: Joseph Frank, Northrop Frye, Ernst Cassirer, and, of course, Isabel MacCaffrey, who is praised as "the most truly 'metaphorical' [i.e., spatializing] reader among Milton's admirers" (p. 24).

Although Cope announces the passing of the Donne tradition and everything it represents, he is enough under its influence that he finds almost nothing to say about books XI and XII; but his place in our story is secure because he so explicitly articulates the assumptions within which work on those books can now confidently go forward. The same banner year of 1962 sees the publication of a state-of-the-art analysis in the final chapter of Joseph Summers's *The Muse's Method*. Summers begins by recalling, as it is now obligatory to do, the harshly critical tradition that stretches from Addison to Lewis and admits that until the "fairly recent past . . . I have found myself in agreement . . . with each of the opinions I have quoted concerning the sunset of genius or the actual failure of the last two books of *Paradise Lost*" (pp. 187–88). Nevertheless, by a process he does not explicate, but is, I would maintain, the process whose arc I am even now describing, he has come to the point where he believes "that Milton knew what he intended in the last two books, and that he accomplished his intent" (p. 188). What follows differs from his predecessors largely in the detail and scope of the reading (the chapter is nearly forty pages), but essentially the burden of his argument is familiar:

> The final books complete the education of Adam and the reader. . . . In the visions . . . Adam is granted the opportunity to make the usual human mistakes. In his responses . . . he embraces the false consolations (and despairs) of philosophy, and the false or mistaken conclusions of religion; and then, through angelic guidance, he is led to recognize their falseness. . . . The final books provide for both Adam and the reader the final temptations. If each sustains the vision of Providence, he will have earned it. (pp. 190–91)

What is new or at least newly emphasized here (recall Jonathan Richardson in 1734) is the role of the reader in the poem's educational scheme, and that emphasis will in the next few years be picked up and elaborated by several critics, including the author of this account.

It is not too much to say that by 1962 everything is done; the lump has been transmuted, and the terms of that transmutation are conveniently on display in a single sentence of a much praised essay by Barbara Lewalski published in the following year. Responding yet once more to the oft rehearsed criticism of books XI and XII "as an unwieldy mass of doctrine, didacticism, and dullness," Lewalski declares: "The evidence rather suggests that the prophecy is a highly complex aesthetic structure organized so as to project the great themes of the poem on the epic screen of all human history, and at the same time, by means of this projection, to promote Adam's own development as a dramatic character."[29] All the key words are there, ready to be affirmed and assumed by Waddington and countless others: "complex," "aesthetic," "structure," "organized," "great," "development," "dramatic." What is significant is that each of these words would earlier have represented a *claim* greatly in need of support; now they are offered as descriptive of what anyone should be able to see. There will henceforth be few or any who will "risk echoing C. S. Lewis's condemnation of the concluding books of *Paradise Lost* as an 'untransmuted lump of futurity.'"

This does not mean that work stops. There are finishing touches to be put on, many of them supplied by H. R. MacCallum's masterful essay, "Milton and Sacred History: Books XI and XII of *Paradise Lost.*"[30] And, of course, the grumbling is not completely silenced. Louis Martz in *The Paradise Within* (New Haven, 1964) repeats the old charges and while acknowledging the soundness of Milton's theological design concludes that "poetically it is a disaster" (p. 150). In the same year Christopher Ricks (*Milton's Grand Style*) does not comment directly, but in his extended (Empsonian) defense of Milton's style (a defense that is brilliant but directed at charges no longer being made) passages from the last books are few and far between. For the most part, however, the new orthodoxy is established, and in 1966 (well ahead of Waddington's first sentence) Larry Champion can say that "most critics . . . see the final books as essential to the epic."[31] As the decade wears on, more voices join the chorus in essays and books (by Dennis Burden, Stanley Fish, John Lawry, John Reesing, William Madsen), all proclaiming in different tones what everyone now knows.

In 1968 B. A. Rajan reappears, in the manner of a character last seen in the first act of a play now concluding, to pronounce on what has passed since he last pronounced in 1947:

> Twenty-five years ago the high hill from which Adam looked down upon history commanded a territory which was largely unexplored. E. N. S. Thompson's defense of the last two books had yet to be written, and C. S. Lewis' dismissal of them as an "untransmuted lump of futurity" was the reigning judgment, challenged only by the imperceptive or by those who had no choice, but to be original. Scholarship abhors a vacuum even more than nature, and there has been no lack of articles moving into these enticing open spaces. . . . The structural relevance of the last two books had been firmly defended; their place in the great pattern had been shown; and all is as it ought to be in the celestial cycle. Lewis' judgment is now a chastening warning that the race is not really to the swift or superficial but rather to the blear-eyed scholar with the true patience needed to struggle with sacred history.[32]

Rajan's sentences are so elegant, urbane, and witty that I am tempted to appropriate them for a final word. But in criticism, as in nature, there is no final word, only the words provoked by those intended as final. In this case the words that continue to come are directed not at books XI and XII, now securely arrayed in their new glory, but at books I–X, which must be redescribed so as to be integrated with the lump they once so obviously excelled. Even when some things change within the profession, other things remain very much the same. In the late sixties the premium on unity is as strong as ever (it will be some time before the age of fragmentation, dispersal, and discontinuity is ushered in), and if one part of a "great" poem has been recharacterized, it is incumbent upon the community to recharacterize the rest, lest the whole seem disunified and less great. One sees the future clearly when Mary Ann Radzinowicz declares that "the final books which seem purely didactic to some are not didactic in any way the whole poem isn't."[33] Her project will be the reverse of that undertaken a generation earlier: rather than demonstrating that books XI and XII are just like books I–X, she will demonstrate that books I–X are just like books XI and XII. No longer the undoubted benchmark of judgment, aesthetic or poetic quality is now something to be pushed away or at least subordinated to the theology once scorned in its name. In her final paragraph Radzinowicz proclaims the poem reunified, but from the end backward: "when the poem ends with the father and mother of mankind leaving Eden on their long journey, the last words give us no image of them which the whole poem was not preparing from the beginning" (p. 50).

Given this conclusion, one could even argue that the earlier books are not necessary and thereby turn upside down the view of those many who wished Milton had stopped at ten. Edward Tayler does not make that argument, but he does focus exclusively on the final books in his *Milton's Poetry: Its Development in Time* (Pittsburgh, 1979), employing the rest of the poem as a gloss upon its conclusion. Tayler does not defend his procedure; it seems obvious to him. After all, the subject of the epic is the "cycle of loss and restoration, the *circular* movement from Eden to Eden" (p. 63), the dominant pattern "is that of anticipation and fulfillment, which is in turn the pattern of providential time from shadowy types to truth," and "these patterns emerge most explicitly in the last two books" (p. 71). Tayler adds, in a way that is unnecessary but convenient for my purposes, that these "books may be denominated an 'untransmuted lump of futurity' (in C. S. Lewis's notorious phrasing) only if we remain ignorant of the proper way to 'measure' the 'Race of time.'" It is an ignorance that the profession's race of time, as I have reported it, has taken from us forever.

V

Now that the story, or at least that part of it I command, has been told, certain questions beg to be asked, the chief of which may be, "what's the point?" The point is surely not (despite early appearances) to fault Raymond Waddington for failing to be aware of the conditions that enable his perceptions. Indeed, to demand that he be aware of those conditions would be to demand that he be outside them, and it has been my thesis that these conditions cannot be escaped. Waddington cannot be asked to have a perspective on his professional situation because that situation *is* his perspective. Nor can the point be to say something about *Paradise Lost*. That would be the point of another enterprise, the enterprise of literary or practical criticism. In that enterprise one answers questions like, "what is the function of this episode?" or "to what extent is Milton's attempt to represent innocence successful?" or "what is the relationship between *Paradise Lost* as a domestic epic and the emergence in the next century of the bourgeois novel?" or "in what figures and actions do we find the assertion of feminine as opposed to patriarchal values?" Like any other Miltonist, I have answers to these questions, but the answers are unrelated to the evidence marshaled here even though my ability to give them (like Waddington's) follows from some set of institutional conditions in which I am embedded. It is just that knowing I am embedded in those conditions does not relax their hold; the knowledge that a history has produced me and enabled my perceptions does not alter those perceptions or cause me to see something other than what I see when I turn the pages of the poem. Paradoxical though it might seem, the shape of my performance as a literary critic is logically independent of any analysis (including this one) I might offer of the assumptions within which that performance unfolds. Moreover, if this is so, then the point cannot be to give recommendations for reading Milton. I have not passed judgment on what the critics in my story have had to say about the poem, and therefore one cannot conclude from my account of its critical history that this or that direction is the right one. It would be entirely proper for someone who had read this essay to decide that it was all very interesting, but that C. S. Lewis was right after all.

What, then, is the point? Simply to read the history, to give an account of how certain descriptions of the poem have come to the fore without anointing or rejecting any of them. Of course, by limiting the essay to that ambition I do not escape criticism but invite it precisely on the question of what kind of history it is. In reaction to an earlier version some have labeled it "internalist." Thus Gary Saul Morson writes that "Fish's history is based on the 'internalist' premise that the dynamics of the profession are the sole determinants of its development; external forces need not be considered because they can be effective only insofar as the profession's own requirements lead to their incorporation."[34] It would seem more reasonable, Morson goes on, "to assume that all cultural institutions or systems continuously interact with a variety of external and internal forces, some of which may be welcome (to someone), and some unwelcome." I have spoken to these issues in an earlier chapter (see "Change," chapter 7), but a few more words at the end of this long chronicle would not be out of place.

First of all, it is certainly true that my history is "internalist" as Morson uses the term, and it is also true that one could relate the changes I note in the conditions of professional production to changes in the external world. Indeed, I attempt something in that direction in the brief discussion of the effect on *Paradise Lost* of World War II, but the focus remains narrowly literary, and even within those confines many questions are left unaddressed: To what extent does the fact that many academic careers were interrupted (some permanently) explain the lag between Lewis's (in)famous pronouncement and its eventual reversal? How can we assess the effect on scholarly production (or on scholarly thinking) of shortages in paper, restrictions on publications, etc.? How do postwar changes in the size and constitution of student populations put pressure on literary studies in general and Milton studies in particular? Here one might profitably focus on the extraordinarily large number of Jewish scholars who begin to populate Renaissance studies. For many Miltonists writing before 1945 the problem was to reconcile one's assumed Christianity with the thesis of poetic autonomy; but for many Jewish academics Christianity was an object of study like any other, and consequently they were not about to be made uneasy, as Samuel Johnson was, by the mingling of poetic fictions with "the most awful and sacred truths." What influence did the influx of this group and of others hitherto excluded from the academy, either by finances or by visible and invisible quotas, have on the study of *Paradise Lost?* The question is an interesting one, but it is not answered or even considered here.

Nor do I consider the questions that might be put to the answers I do provide. If one important factor in the rehabilitation of books XI and XII was the shift from temporal to spatial modes of thinking, to what other and larger shifts is this one connected? Does it have something to do with the increasing internationalization of economic and social structures, or with the development of communications systems that result in McLuhan's "global village"? Or should we look to the rise of the Third World and the increasing awareness that one can no longer think in terms of centers of political authority in relation to which lesser places are clearly and acceptingly subordinate? And if these questions seem too large, there are smaller questions that are nevertheless larger than the ones I choose to ask. To what extent is the emergence of spatial models part of an effort to remove literary studies from the isolation they occupy in New Critical practice? And is this effort part of a more general effort to reinvent American education in the wake of the perceived failure of the progressive movement? And is that effort part of an even more general effort to reassert the homogenous nature of American life? If one answers this last question in the affirmative, then perhaps the story I have been telling—of unity triumphant—is part of a larger story of containment, of the effort of a mid-twentieth-century hegemonic culture to domesticate the differences that give the lie to its claims of unity. The rise of books XI and XII would then be a somewhat more sinister phenomenon than I have made it out to be.

One could go on in this mode forever and produce a catalog of paths this chapter does not pursue that would be longer (God forbid) than the chapter itself. All that would mean, however, is that it would have been possible to tell stories other than the one I have told, and obviously Morson thinks that another story is what I should be telling. However, he also thinks that this other story, in which "events outside the profession" would receive more focused attention, would not only be different, but more "complex" and because more complex, more truly historical, and because more truly historical, better; and on this point I cannot agree. Morson contrasts my piece with another that "emphasizes the interaction of complex forces affecting authorship, conventions, social milieus, forms of publication, habits of reading or listening" (p. 27), and that is a just description of an essay whose burden is precisely the complexity of such matters. The author (William Mills Todd) does not get down to particular cases because that's not what he's interested in doing; he's interested in elaborating a general framework (with the help of some Jakobsonian categories) within which particular cases might be considered; since the instances he cites are exemplary of his general thesis and not of interest in their own right, he does not elaborate them. This is not to criticize Todd, but to point out that the story you tell (or don't tell) depends on the angle of interest from which you proceed and that in a universe where all projects are angled—mounted from a perspective, pursued within a purpose—no story is more complete or truly historical than any other, except on a scale that is itself angled and perspectival. Morson says of my tale that it "excludes much historical complexity," as if historical complexity was an inert and preinterpretive entity to which one could be more or less responsible; but complexity is itself a standard that operates only within particular angles and purposes, and in relation to a particular purpose (such as trying to figure out how books XI and XII got to be so much better than they once were), the bringing in of additional perspectives would result not in complexity but in irrelevance and (perhaps) in narrative paralysis (you'd never get from one point to the next).

Consider, for example, another of Morson's criticisms, that my account proceeds "as if the principal consumers of literary classics were college professors and the students they have trained" (pp. 17–18); and he adds, "in many cultures readers are not necessarily university products and do not share the assumptions, values, interests, that such accounts presuppose." Indeed, this is true even of our culture; the classics are read not only by specialists in literary criticism, but by those with no formal education or those whose formal education ended many years ago, and who would therefore not have been exposed at all to the events that make up my story. It would be possible and valuable to study the differences between what such readers think of *Paradise Lost* and what is thought by up-to-date Miltonists, and to study also the routes by which interpretations produced in the High Academy make their way into the larger culture and begin to affect the practice of readers who know nothing about them. But that would be a study *different*—not more complete or more historical—than the one I attempt. For my purposes (which are neither larger nor smaller than anyone else's) the only actors *are* college professors and the students they train because it is they who undertake the tasks, write the essays, and respond to one another within a general response to the conditions of the profession. The readers who are not professional are simply not actors in this story, and it would be beside any possible point to bring them in.

Of course, the "conditions of the profession" are not monolithic:

there are many who are "in the profession" but in places and in circumstances that scarcely allow them either the leisure or the resources to
participate in something so rarified as the rehabilitation of books XI and
XII of *Paradise Lost*. They do not get into this story, and there is, of
course, a story to be told about why they do not and what their exclusion means in relation to the structures of power prevailing both in the
university culture and the culture at large. But I'm not telling *that*
story; I'm telling this one, and if I can be criticized it is for choosing
to tell it, since by doing so I may be thought to have reinforced (by not
questioning) the lines of authority it traces out. In response to *that* criticism—you should be doing some other kind of work—I could only say
that it is "internal" history that interests me. I want to know about the
dynamics of the profession and how the conditions of its practice change.
Moreover, I would add, were I to "expand" my focus, I would lose it;
that is, if I were to inquire seriously into the dynamics behind the dynamic, my chosen subject would disappear, and I don't want it to. Of
course, my choices will only be viable professionally (the perspective is
determinedly retained) if they are of interest to others. If no one cares
to read about how parts of *Paradise Lost* were decisively recharacterized
with what implications for the relationship between texts and the labors
of critics and scholars, then a judgment much severer than Morson's—
the judgment of the marketplace—will have been rendered.

Of course (and this really is my final point), "internal" is itself on
historical notion. What is internal to the profession (this or any other)
will vary, both within the profession (the "world" of Milton studies
and the "world" of composition theory would require quite different descriptions) and at various times. There is very little reference in this essay to the relationship between Milton studies and political/social movements in the United States and Britain, but if the account were to
continue into the 1980s (it now stops at 1979), political and social
movements would figure prominently. Not, however, because the focus
would have become less internal, but because the configuration of the
internal will have changed. Whereas for Arthur Barker, writing in
1942 (*Milton and the Puritan Dilemma*), Milton's radicalism is a
fact to be documented and historically placed, for more recent writers
the same fact is intimately related to the commitments they have made
or want to make across a range of national and international problems.
When Fredric Jameson begins an essay by announcing that "nothing is
more appropriate, in the second year of the Iranian Revolution and the

first of the Islamic Republic, than a return to 1642 and a meditation on the work of the greatest English political poet,"[35] it is clear that politics is in Milton studies in a new way (although it is much the same way that politics was in Milton studies in those few years when the poem was read as an allegory of the Second World War). Many Miltonists now feel obliged to show that the stand they take on a question raised by the poem is continuous with and a furtherance of a stand they wish to take in the "larger" arena of politics. Much the same thing can be said about the relation of Milton criticism to feminism. There was, of course, a feminist movement in the 1960s and 1970s and alongside it the perennial question of Milton's attitude toward women; but it is only in the 1980s that these merge in a way that makes "Milton and women" more than a topic for classroom discussion. The reason is that where feminism was once a phenomenon with which Milton studies might or might not connect, it is now an assumed and obligatory context of concern. In short, feminism is now *internal* to Milton studies, a frame of reference constitutive of its gestures, and one a critic ignores at the risk of calling into question his or her credentials as a competent professional. "Few of us today could risk. . . ." (The arrival of this state of affairs was anticipated and resisted in the 1970s, and the battle takes place, appropriately enough, in the pages of *Milton Studies*.) Of course, there are those who would say that feminism's relation to Milton studies was most crucial and revealing when it was unacknowledged, when the true story was the story of how the ideology of patriarchy was reproduced in a criticism that refused to recognize it, when the feminist perspective was suppressed so that the illusion of male sufficiency could be preserved. Again, I can only say that while that story would be a powerful and salutary one, it is not mine. In the age of the political unconscious I am still drawn to the workings of the political conscious, to the *surfaces* of things and, I suppose, to superficiality in general; and for that, as for so much else, I remain unrepentant.

13. Don't Know Much About the Middle Ages: Posner on Law and Literature

The thesis of Richard Posner's *Law and Literature: A Relation Rear-gued*[1] is that the study of literature and the interpretation of statutes are very different activities and that one "has little to contribute"[2] to the other. Let me say at the outset that Judge Posner is right. Literary and legal interpretation are distinct, and the skills they separately require are not readily convertible. But while Posner's large point is well taken, the reasons with which he supports it are not, for they take the form of a series of distinctions no one of which can be maintained.

The basic distinction concerns the vexed matter of intention and is framed in terms made familiar to us by recent debates about constitu-tional interpretation. There are, according to Posner, two ways of read-ing: one that "requires [the interpreter] to discern" the intention of the author or authors of a text and another that requires the interpreter "merely to assign some coherent and satisfying meaning" to a text, in-dependently of what any author might or might not have intended.[3] The first kind of reading is appropriate for legal texts, while the second, identified by Posner as "New Critical," is appropriate for literary texts.[4] While it would be possible in Posner's view to read either kind of text in either way—to interpret a poem as the realization of a specific inten-tion or to interpret a statute as if it were an "interesting verbal arti-fact"[5]—the results would be "otiose"[6] and distorting, reducing the rich-ness of a beautiful artifact to the statement of an author's "banal" intention,[7] on the one hand, depriving the words of a statute "of their historical context,"[8] and thus of their power to constrain, on the other. It is clear that for Posner, as for many others, the issue of intention is one with the issue of constraint. Those who ignore intention, either be-cause they are bad jurists or good literary critics, cut themselves loose from contextual constraints; while those who defer to intention allow contextual constraints to limit the scope of their interpretive activity.

Every part of this picture is wrong. There is only one way to read or interpret, and that is the way of intention. But to read intentionally is not to be constrained relative to some other (nonexistent) way of reading. The reason for both truths is the same: *Words are intelligible only within the assumption of some context of intentional production, some already-in-place predecision as to what kind of person, with what kind of purposes, in relation to what specific goals in a particular situation, is speaking or writing.* To approach the matter from the other direction: Meanings are not embedded in words but emerge and are perspicuous in the light of background conditions of intelligibility. One could not "merely . . . assign some coherent . . . meaning"[9] to a text independent of a consideration of intention because any meaning one might assign would be thinkable only in the light of an intentional structure already assumed. In those cases in which meanings seem immediately available without recourse to anything but the words themselves, it is because the intentional structure—the conditions of intelligibility that limit the meanings words can have before they are produced—is so deeply in place that we are not aware of it and seem to experience its effects directly, without mediation. Consider the small example of the utterance, "Can you pass the salt?" immediately construed by the vast majority of native speakers as a request for performance of a specific action rather than as a question about the hearer's physical abilities; but this is so only because in the very hearing of the utterance we assume the mealtime setting populated by agents concerned with eating and drinking in the context of communal resources. If one varies the setting and reconceives it as a conversation between a doctor and a patient recovering from surgery, the utterance "Can you pass the salt?" could indeed be heard as a question about the hearer's physical ability and could be so heard immediately and *literally*. I say "literally" to anticipate and prevent the mistake of thinking that what the example displays is a distinction between the literal meaning of an utterance and the meaning it acquires when placed in a particular context. Both meanings—the meaning of "request for performance" and the meaning "inquiry into one's capacities"—are literal given the in-place force of some intentional context of production. Independently of some such already assumed context (and there could be many more than two), the utterance wouldn't have any meaning at all and wouldn't *be* an utterance, but merely a succession of noises or marks.

To put the point proverbially, intentions (or their assumption) come first; meanings second. Therefore, there can be no distinction between intentional construing and some other, more freewheeling kind. But this does not mean that interpretation is as safely constrained as some proponents of intentionalism claim it is, because while it is true that interpretation cannot proceed independent of intention, it is also true that intentions are themselves interpretively produced and therefore cannot serve (except in the most general and nonvoluntarist sense) as a check on interpretive activity. In the example of "Can you pass the salt?" it is always possible that someone at a dinner table may hear the question as one about his abilities, or that a patient may hear his doctor asking him to pass the salt (perhaps as a preliminary to an experiment). The fact that interpretation is irremediably intentional means only that one cannot choose between intentional reading and something else; but that still leaves the problem of determining exactly what the intention of which an utterance is the expression *is*. Since one cannot read back from the utterance to the intention (for that would be possible only if utterances were meaningful apart from intention, or, to put it more precisely, had as part of their meaning a specification of the intention behind them), the intention must be supplied or constructed by the very interpreter who will then cite it in support of the meanings he "finds."

This conclusion may seem paradoxical, but it is not: All interpretation is intentional—assuming as the ground of its possibility a purposeful agent who has produced its object—but intentions do not constrain interpretation because the shape of the agent's purpose can itself be the matter of interpretive dispute. Undoing the distinction between reading with and without the anchor of intention also undoes the possibility of distinguishing between reading that is constrained and reading that is not, and this in turn undoes *every* distinction invoked by Posner in the course of his essay. I have counted fifteen distinctions, and they are all the same. Each posits an opposition between an interpretive activity that is answerable to public (factual, historical) and formal (verbal, logical) requirements, and an interpretive activity that is (at least relatively) free to go its own untrammeled way. In addition to the one already noted (between intentional and nonintentional interpretation), there are (1) the distinction between "interpretation" and "construction";[10] (2) the distinction between words moored by history and context and words "wrenched free of their historical context";[11] (3) the distinction between defined and "undefined lawmaking power";[12] (4) the distinction between "highly specific language"[13] and vague, nonspecific language; (5) the distinction between legislation that limits the judiciary and legislation that gives the judiciary a "blank check";[14] (6) the distinction between language (poetry, for example) that is simply "beautiful and moving" and language that has legal or political "significance";[15] (7) the distinction between verbal production that is purposeful and occasional and verbal production that is "unconscious" or the effusion of genius; (8) the distinction between language bounded by "period and culture" and language that is able to "transcend boundaries" because it has a "certain generality and even universality," that is, means nothing *in particular;*[16] (9) the distinction between bound and free ("irresponsible") reading;[17] (10) the distinction between judging as an activity constrained by "authoritative texts" and literary criticism as an activity that deals with texts that are themselves detached from issues of authority and power;[18] (11) the distinction between nonambiguous and ambiguous texts;[19] (12) the distinction between nonrhetorical and rhetorical modes of discourse; (13) the distinction between scientific discourse and discourse less responsible to canons of logic and proof;[20] (14) the distinction between neutral, colorless language and language colored by style;[21] and (15) the distinction between scientific language and persuasive language.[22]

Since everything that Posner says flows from these distinctions, they are, in the end, what he is asserting, and I content that none of them can be maintained, at least not in the way required by his argument. Consider for example the cluster formed by numbers 12 through 15. Scientific language, according to Posner, is distinguished by logic rather than style; that is to say (and these claims are of course interchangeable), scientific discourse relies not on rhetoric, but on something akin to mathematical demonstration,[23] and it is the nature of mathematical demonstration or experimental proof to dispense with the techniques of persuasion, techniques more appropriate to "areas of uncertainty" where "direct confirmation" of a hypothesis is unavailable.[24] Within its own circle this is a tight argument, but the argument falls with the fall of its basic premise: "Not all modes of discourse are rhetorical."[25] All modes of discourse *are* rhetorical, where "rhetorical" means proceeding on the basis of assumptions and distinctions that are open to challenge, even though there may be times when no one is challenging them. The derivations that make up a scientific proof or a deductive argument in law rely for their force—that is, for their persuasiveness—on distinctions (such as that between rest and motion or public and private) that have themselves been put in place by debates just like those in relation to which they are now regarded as uncontroversial and directly confirming. It is because they are now (that is, for a time) uncontroversial that the assertion of such distinctions will be thought of as devoid of "style"; but in fact their assertion will be assertion in a style that by virtue of an institutional success has won the right to offer itself as impersonal, as proceeding from no particular point of view. The difference then between science or law, on the one hand, and literary criticism, on the other, is not the difference between rhetoric (or style) and something else, but between the different rhetorics that are powerful in the precincts of different disciplines; and the difference between the rhetoric of science—the rhetoric of proof, deduction, and mathematical certainty—and other rhetorics in modern society is a difference between a prestige discourse, a discourse that has for historical reasons become associated with the presentation of truth, and the discourses that will for a time measure themselves against it. I am not saying that these differences are illusory or that they don't have real consequences, only that their reality and their consequentiality are historical achievements—achievements fashioned on the anvil of argument and debate— and that as historical achievements they can be undone in much the same way as they were achieved.

I have stressed the word "historical" in the previous paragraph because it names the sense Posner most egregiously lacks. He seems not to understand that the distinctions he so confidently invokes belong not to the nature of things but to conditions that have been put in place by exactly the labors—interpretive labors—that are supposedly constrained by those distinctions. He thus falls repeatedly into the error of regarding as universal the imperatives (both moral and methodological) that are perspicuous only within local (and therefore revisable) structures of conviction and belief. Consider, for example, the many-layered argument he makes regarding the constraints on interpretation inherent in the Eighth Amendment (forbidding "cruel and unusual punishment"). Because it has its origin in an historical context, Posner explains, a reader is not "free to imprint his own reading on the amendment"; and if a court were to go so far as to find in the provision "a prohibition against sexually segregated prisons," its performance "would be as irresponsible as a literary critic's reading of Virgil's *Fourth Eclogue,* written before the birth of Christ, as a Christian allegory—which, as a matter of fact, is how it was read during the Middle Ages."[26] Here Posner avails himself of what we might call the strategy of the double absurdity. He thinks it absurd that anyone would so interpret the amendment and he underlines his point by linking that interpretation with one even more obviously absurd, the impossibly anachronistic reading by a Christian exegete of a pagan poem. The point seems indisputable until one realizes that anachronism itself is a cultural concept, tied to a view of time as linear and irreversible and to a notion of agency as the property of discrete individuals. The possibility of regarding something as anachronistic emerges only within the assumptions we have inherited from the Enlightenment, assumptions that have conferred on science and its procedures the prestige they enjoy in Posner's essay; but within an older set of assumptions that are, in the end, inseparable from the hegemony of religion—the prestige discourse that science replaced—the reading of a poem in terms its (so-called) author could not possibly have known would be regarded not as anachronistic, but as obvious and obligatory. That is to say, readers in the Middle Ages proceeded within the undoubted conviction of God's authorship of all human actions, physical and verbal, and given that conviction (which could not have been judged unreasonable, since it formed the field of relevance within which reasons emerged), a Christian reading of Virgil's poem, a reading that implied an author not bound by the constraints of chronology, would not be irresponsible, but compelled. Indeed, it would be incumbent upon anyone who wanted to take Virgil seriously—as opposed to dismissing him as an epiphenomenon of carnal history—to produce such a reading, and so bring him into line with the truths proclaimed by the Holy Scriptures. That is why, as Posner obligingly reports, the poem was read that way in the Middle Ages, not because (as his tone implies) medieval men and women didn't know any better, but because given what they knew with a certainty no less firm than that provided by the rhetoric of science, to read that way was nothing more (or less) than the exercise of common sense.

The point is a general one and will hold for Posner's "reading" of the way in which the Eighth Amendment could not be read responsibly. Here, rather than looking backward to conditions of intelligibility that are no longer as generally in force as they once were, one need only look forward to new conditions of intelligibility that have not yet fully emerged: All that is necessary for the practice of sexually segregating prisoners to be considered "cruel and unusual" would be a conviction strongly held in a society that sexuality and its exercise were at the very center of man's being; so that if people were asked, "What is the worst, most unbearable, organization of social life you can think of?," one often-given answer would be "sexually segregated." At that point (and it is a point some in *our* society have already reached), the classification of the practice as one enjoined by the Eighth Amendment would be obvious, would "go without saying," and to assert otherwise would amount to being irresponsible.

Let me be clear. I am not saying that "anything goes," that interpreters of the Eighth Amendment (or Virgil's *Eclogues*) are presented with a "blank check" to be filled in as they like; only that insofar as the filling in of the check is constrained (and it always will be; Posner's positing of a wholly free interpretive activity is as mistaken—it is the same mistake—as his positing of an interpretive act that is wholly prescribed), the constraints will inhere not in the language of the text (statute or poem) or in the context (unproblematically conceived by Posner as a "higher" and self-declaring text) in which it is embedded, but in the cultural assumptions within which both texts and contexts take shape for situated agents. And it will do no good to ask for a specification of those cultural assumptions (so that they could then serve as the constraint neither text nor context provides) because specifying is itself an act that occurs with assumptions that it cannot, at the moment of occurrence, specify. The moral is not that there are no such things as texts or acts, but that our ability to point to them or perform them depends on prearticulations and demarcations they cannot contain; and it is only so long as such prearticulations and demarcations are in place—and in a place we cannot locate because it locates and defines us—that texts and acts will have the immediate palpability they seem always to have.

The mistake is to confuse that palpability—the immediacy with which shapes make themselves available *within* local and historical conditions of intelligibility—with something inherent in those shapes, for that is the mistake of claiming for interpretively produced entities the status of being constraints on interpretation. It is a mistake Posner repeatedly makes when he distinguishes straightforward and specific language from vague and literary language, and argues (in, to be sure, a commonsense fashion) that the first is more constraining than the second. (This is the burden of numbers 2 through 11 on my list.) Here, for example, is his discussion of a supposedly unambiguous contract in relation to the operation of the parol evidence rule:

> If a document states that it is the complete integration of the parties' contract, and the price stated in the document is $100 per pound, the parol evidence rule will prevent the seller from later offering testimony that in the negotiations leading up to the contract the parties had agreed that the price would be $100 per pound only for the first ten pounds after which it would be $120 a pound. The document is not ambiguous.[27]

But Posner misses the point. The document is neither ambiguous nor unambiguous in and of itself. The document isn't *anything* in and of itself, but acquires a shape and a significance only within the assumed background circumstances of its possible use, and it is those circumstances—which cannot be *in* the document, but are the light in which "it" appears and becomes what "it," for a time at least, is—that determine whether or not it is ambiguous and determine too the kind of straightforwardness it is (again for a time) taken to possess.

It could well be that in the industry related to the contract of Posner's example it is understood by everyone experienced in the trade that when a price per pound has been negotiated, it goes without saying that there is an escalation of 20 percent after the first ten pounds. Within that understanding, the document would have, and have obviously and without dispute, the meaning Posner scoffs at. Of course, within a *different* understanding, a different sense of the way business is typically done, the document will have just the obvious meaning Posner claims for it, but that obvious meaning will be no less circumstantial—no less the product of interpretive assumptions that are not in the text because it is within *them* that the text acquires intelligibility—than the meaning he rejects.[28] This does not mean that the document is ambiguous, but that the shape of its straightforwardness (or of its ambiguity should that be the face it presents) will always be a function of something prior to it. Of course, one could always attempt to make that something (I have been calling it the background conditions of intelligibility) explicit and thereby (and this is Posner's word) "control" the document's interpretation; but the intelligibility of the language in which the background conditions were supposedly made explicit would itself be a function of still other background conditions that would not be "in" the text but would nevertheless determine what everyone (or nearly everyone; there is always room for dispute) took to be its meaning.[29] As a frequent flyer, I have been amused by the efforts of airlines to police their lavatories. In particular, I've noticed the now almost desperate search for a sign whose wording will make absolutely and explicitly clear what should and should not be flushed down the toilet. The latest (and doomed) effort goes something like this: "Only toilet paper and tissue should be deposited in the toilet." How long will it be, I wonder, before flight attendants and maintenance men begin to find bodily waste, liquid and solid, deposited in the most inconvenient places, if only by wags who recognize and testify to the folly of thinking that language can be made so explicit as to preclude interpretation. Of course, one could add feces and urine to the list of proper things to deposit, but that would only fuel the game, not stop it. What stops the game when it is stopped (as it almost always is) is not the explicitness of words, but the tacit assumptions (concerning what toilets are for, and, on an even more basic level, what is and is not waste in a post-agricultural society) within which the words immediately take on an unproblematic (though interpretively produced) shape.

The point is a simple one: All shapes are interpretively produced, and since the conditions of interpretation are themselves unstable—the possibility of seeing something in a "new light," and therefore of seeing a *new* something, is ever and unpredictably present—the shapes that seem perspicuous to us now may not seem so or may seem differently so tomorrow. This applies not only to the shape of statutes, poems, and signs in airplane lavatories, but to the disciplines and forms of life within which statutes, poems, and signs become available to us. There is a temptation when considering these issues to concede the interpretive status of the objects and texts within an enterprise while claiming for the enterprise itself a reality less mutable and permutable, to argue, for example, that while legal and literary texts may change with changes in the conditions of interpretation, the disciplines themselves remain stable—continue always to be what they essentially are—as do the differences between them. Something like this seems to lie behind Posner's insistence that when all is said and done "the study of literature has little to contribute to the interpretation of statutes and constitutions."[30] As I have already indicated, this seems to me a correct judgment; but while for Posner the judgment follows from the essential

nature of the two disciplines, I see it as an accurate account of interpretive conditions presently—but not inevitably—in force. That is,
while I agree with his assertion of difference, I disagree with his specification of its source and with his assumption of its durability.

The source for many of the differences Posner invokes is the supposedly master difference between legal and literary language. While
the first is specific and historically tethered, the second is inherently
ambiguous and unconstrained: "[E]very great work of literature may
well be unclear."[31] This is simply the distinction between clear and
unclear contracts writ large, as a distinction *between* disciplines rather
than a distinction within a discipline, and it falls by the same argument:
To the extent that literary texts are "unclear"—do not yield straightforward messages as do statutes or signs in lavatories—it is not because
something called "literary language" has certain properties, but because
literary critics (or at least some of them) approach their task already
in possession of, or possessed by, a sense of what the object of their
professional attention is like, and that sense, put into operation as a
reading strategy, produces both the literary text and its (supposedly
antecedent) properties. As I put the point some time ago:

> If your definition of poetry tells you that the language of poetry
> is complex, you will scrutinize the language of something identi-
> fied as a poem in such a way as to bring out the complexity you
> know to be "there." You will, for example, be on the lookout for
> latent ambiguities . . . you will search for meanings that subvert
> or exist in a tension with the meanings that first present them-
> selves. . . . Nor, as you do these things, will you have any sense
> of performing in a willful manner, for you will only be doing
> what you learned to do in the course of becoming a skilled reader
> of poetry.[32]

All of which is to say that as a fully situated member of an interpretive
community, be it literary or legal, you "naturally" look at the objects
of the community's concerns with eyes already informed by community
imperatives, urgencies, and goals. Therefore if it is the goal of your
community to derive single lines of direction from particular texts
(identified as the Constitution, statutes, precedents), your *first* glance
at such a text will be informed by that interpretive disposition (indistinguishable from what you think, in advance, the text is *for* and also
from what you take to be your relation to it), and you will see, and by

seeing produce, that kind of text. Conversely, if it is the goal of your community to derive as many lines of direction as possible from a text, your first glance at it will be informed by *that* interpretive disposition (and, remember, reading independently of an interpretive disposition, of some already-in-place sense of the enterprise in relation to which this *is* a text, is impossible) and multiple meanings will force themselves upon your attention. Obviously, with respect to the two communities and their enterprises, interpretive activity will be different, but rather than being a difference that follows from the essential nature of law and literature or from the essential properties of legal and literary language, the difference will be *originary,* assumed in advance and then put into operation so as to produce the formal "evidence" of its rightness, the evidence of straightforward or ambiguous language, or of legal as opposed to literary significances.

One cannot then ground the difference between literary and legal interpretation in the different kinds of texts they address, because the textual differences are themselves constituted by already differing interpretive strategies, and not the other way round. Nor can one turn this insight into a new reification of difference by assuming that the strategies specific to law and literature are themselves basic and unchanging, for they are no less historically achieved (and therefore contingent) than the texts they enable us to produce. While it is true that an agent embedded in an enterprise proceeds with a firm, if tacit, sense of what the enterprise is (of what and who it is for and by what routines it accomplishes its ends) and therefore with a sense of the differences between it and the other enterprises that it is not, that sense is itself revisable, and if it is revised (it needn't be—there is nothing inevitable about any of this), the difference between the enterprise conceived of as a set of interpretive dispositions and some others may become less sharp. As things stand now in our culture, a person embedded in the legal world reads in a way designed to *resolve* interpretive crises (although as Walter Michaels reminds me, after he was reminded of it by a practicing lawyer, at some stages in the preparation and even the arguing of cases, the proliferating of interpretive crises is just the skill called for), while someone embedded in the literary world reads in a way designed to *multiply* interpretive crises.[33] It could, however, be otherwise, and is otherwise even today in some Latin American cultures where literary productions are understood to issue from specific political agendas in whose direction they unambiguously point. (We all, of course, remember the Cultural Revolution in China, with its stipulation as to the content and message of works that purported to be literature.) To the objection that in such cultures the essence of the literary has been violated, one must reply that what the examples show (and countless others could be educed; the story Posner tells in which the literary is equated with the effusions of genius as it rises above the constraints of any local sociopolitical context has been told only since the beginning of the nineteenth century, and one might reasonably argue that in the long sweep of history it is an anomaly) is that literature has no essence, only the succession of forms it takes in different social settings where the *space* of the literary—its differential relationship to the activities that limit and enable its possible actions—is differently opened up.[34]

At times Posner seems to see this, at least on the legal side of the question, as when, after declaring, "If I want to learn about fee entails I do not go to *Felix Holt*," he adds, "Obviously this is not true in cultures where the only information about law is found in what we call literature, though contemporaries thought of it as history. . . ."[35] Again, I want to agree with Posner that in our culture a legal agent does not go to novelists for legal instruction when more authorized sources of instruction are readily available; but I would insist that these other cultures (which would include the medieval culture whose infrastructure he dismisses or ignores) are fully as realized as ours and that the institutional arrangements they display—arrangements that in some cultures result in law being indistinguishable from religion or prophecy—do not *necessarily* (although it may turn out to be so empirically) represent primitive stages of realization that the race has long since gone beyond. I am not here retailing some cheap relativism which would disable us from preferring our arrangements to theirs; rather, I am saying that whatever preferences we have are themselves historically constituted in relation to various contending political and social agendas, and that when we defend them or reiterate them (as Posner does here) we are doing so not in the name of some transparent truth, but in the name of interests whose universality is always contestable.

What are Posner's interests? The question may seem abrupt and unrelated to the linguistic and philosophical arguments of the preceding pages, but it is a question Posner himself invites in those places where he invokes the notion of "power" as still another way of distinguishing between legal and literary interpretation. The argument is that since literary critics operate in a realm where consequences are minimal—what harm, after all, will be done if a critic substitutes "his will for that of Wordsworth or Yeats"[36]—it does not matter that much if their actions are (relatively) unconstrained. Lawyers and judges, on the other hand, operate in the public world of government and regulation and "[i]n our society the exercise of power by appointed officials . . . is tolerated only in the belief that the power is somehow constrained."[37] While "[t]he critic who interprets an ambiguous work of literature is not imposing his view on anyone else . . . the court that interprets an ambiguous provision . . . is imposing its view on the rest of society, often with far-reaching practical consequences."[38] One could question this distinction from several directions, by arguing, for example, that the actions of literary critics can have consequences as far-reaching and practical as the decision of any court. The judgment of an authoritively placed literary critic (Matthew Arnold, Lionel Trilling, T. S. Eliot) can have a profound and *direct* effect on what gets taught in the schools, what appears in the curriculum, what gains entrance into the canon, what gets published, reviewed, anthologized, disseminated, and in all of these ways can finally have an effect on the very structure of a culture, its favored myths, storehouse of moral values, modes of intellectual inquiry, etc. I am not saying that these effects are the same as the effects of a judicial pronouncement (although the edicts of some literary critics have precisely that force), but that they are no less "far-reaching," and that the difference between them is the difference between differing spheres of and routes to consequentiality, not the difference between consequentiality and its opposite.

This is a version of the argument I have been making all along in which I challenge Posner's laying down of essentialist distinctions by the double strategy of first denying the distinctions and then historicizing them. But for the moment I am less interested in challenging the distinction between legal and literary consequentiality than in asking for what reason—in the service of what agenda—Posner makes it, and the answer to this question puts a new twist on his discussion of power. For it turns out that Posner's attribution of powerlessness to literary interpretation, at least in comparison to legal interpretation, is itself a (disguised) move in a power game. The stakes in the game are named in the very first sentence of the essay: "After a century as an autonomous discipline, academic law in America is busily ransacking the social sciences and the humanities for insights and approaches with which to enrich our understanding of the legal system."[39] The issue then is the autonomy of academic law, and it has been the issue in every one of the distinctions so far discussed. The implication is that Posner will reassert that autonomy in the face of recent challenges to it. But that is a less than candid view of the matter since he says nothing at all about the social sciences (and it is hard to see how he could, given his determination to hand over academic law to one of them on a silver platter); rather, he turns his critical attention to literary studies and argues, as we have seen, for their irrelevance to the legal system, an irrelevance attributed at least in part to the extent to which they are removed from the operations of real power. But what is presented as a dismissal rendered from a position of strength—the sitting judge hears the case of the petitioning literary critics and finds it weak—is an action far more defensive, for what Posner fails to report are the incursions *already* made into academic law, and particularly into the domain of legal interpretation, by literary studies. His admonition—don't look for very much help from literary studies—comes too late; for, as he surely knows, recent years have seen an unprecedented traffic between legal and literary studies, with the former borrowing and appropriating far more than the latter, and to considerable effect. Not only is it now difficult to tell some numbers of the *Stanford Law Review* or *The Yale Law Journal* from *Diacritics* and *Critical Inquiry,* but the issues debated in their pages have spilled out into tenure battles, the restructuring of curricula and even of whole law schools, and produced a general sense in the legal profession of a new crisis in which its authority—internal and external—is being put into question as never before. This, of course, is what the Critical Legal Studies Movement is all about, and it is from the literary analysis of interpretation that this movement takes many of its arguments and techniques. The fact that Posner does not even refer to the movement is of a piece with the strategy I have already noted: Committed to a weak position—weak because the developments he warns against have already occurred—he hides its weakness by neglecting to mention those developments.

Of course, he does more than that: He puts forward an argument against the significance of the developments he neglects to mention. It is, he declares, a "great false hope" that literary theory "will change the way in which lawyers think about the interpretation of statutes and the Constitution."[40] That, it seems to me, is an empirical question, and the evidence is not yet in. I agree with Posner that, given the present construction of the legal world, a deconstructive interpretive theory will not be readily translatable into a viable legal practice (this is, of course, the problematic that continually engages the Critical Legal Studies Movement); but it could be the case that the dissemination of such a theory might play a role in altering the way in which the legal world is constructed by altering the ways in which legal actors conceive of their activities. Indeed, there is already evidence that literary theory *has* changed the way in which some lawyers think about the interpretation of statutes and the Constitution, and it is at least possible (but not inevitable) that this change in the characterization of interpretive labors (of what they are "really" like) could play a role in changing those labors themselves. The evidence I am thinking of includes citations by courts of pieces in the pioneering *Texas Law Review* special issue on interpretation[41] and the introduction into the Bork hearings of arguments about intention and literal meaning that are obviously derived from the writing of prominent literary critics. To be sure, the evidence is inconclusive and the vast majority of legal business is still done within the traditional notions of literal meanings, transparent intentions, determinate texts, and stable precedents; but if certain forces in the legal academy grow more numerous and outlive their detractors (the second is a certain occurrence), then who knows?

I referred earlier to some significant omissions in Posner's argument: His silence on the subject of economics after mentioning the social sciences in his first sentence; his failure to acknowledge the Critical Legal Studies Movement even by name, although one member of that movement (Gary Peller) is scorned in a footnote.[42] I call these omissions significant because they alert us, as omissions often do, to the real and not-so-hidden agenda that lurks behind the agenda forthrightly proclaimed. Although Posner says nothing about economics, the effort he mounts here to deauthorize literary studies is intended to clear the field so that the authority of economics in the legal academy can be secured; and since members of the Critical Legal Studies Movement are among the most prominent and forceful opponents of Law and Economics, Posner is obliged to disarm them, which is precisely what he will succeed in doing if he manages to discredit the discipline from which they take so much of their arsenal. The entire essay, then, is something of a feint; it directs our attention to the supposed limitations of literary interpretation, but its primary, if unstated, purpose is to legitimize the interpretive strategies authorized by economics.

By and large, the feint is successful, but there are several ostensibly literary moments where the economic agenda peeps through. One occurs in the context of Posner's repeated assertion that literary works are not to be read with the intentions of the author in mind since when they are deciphered or reported the intentions of authors—statements as to what they meant—are often banal. His example is the poetry of Ezra Pound, which, he says, is "quite beautiful"; but its beauty, he continues, has nothing to do with the messages Pound apparently intends, which are at times "false and even absurd," as in those passages "that denounce usury."[43] Now Pound has been faulted for many things, but one wonders what kind of reader would single out the critique of usury as a particularly objectionable feature of his poetry. The answer, of course, is a proponent of the doctrines of Law and Economics, and it would seem that at some level Posner detects in the perspectives offered by literary and deconstructive theory a danger to the program with which he is so closely associated. It is, after all, a thesis of deconstructive theory that forms of representation, of which any system of currency is an instance, are always agencies of power and manipulation and never simply stand in for natural forces like the market. Perhaps the trouble with literary studies is not that they are irrelevant but that, at least potentially, they are too relevant.

A second moment at which Posner's possibly wider agenda can be spied occurs in a footnote. The note is to a discussion of Shakespeare's *The Merchant of Venice* in which Posner argues that although "[a]t one level the play is about the enforcement of a contract that contains a penalty clause,"[44] that is not its real point. The real point, he tells us, is, metaphorical and general rather than political and therefore it is nothing one need worry about. The footnote to the argument cites a 1964 book entitled *Shakespeare's Politics* by one A. Bloom, whom we have come to know as Allan Bloom, the author of *The Closing of the American Mind*,[45] a sustained diatribe against exactly the theory and theorizing that Posner is declaring to be beside the legal point. One could pursue many paths here, beginning perhaps with a counter-reading of *The Merchant of Venice* in which the center of the play is precisely the contract, and its lesson is the rejection of both literalism and usury as complementary realizations of a spiritual poverty, a lesson Posner would surely find uncomfortable. Or one could explore the "Chicago connection," which finds a neoconservative disciple of Leo Strauss cited by a neoconservative legal economist who in the company of (among others) a prominent former dean of the University of Chicago Law School supported the nomination to the Supreme Court of a neoconservative literalist and formalist who publicly attributed his theoretical awakening to a period spent in that same university. Or one could go in still another direction and note the repeated appearance in Posner's notes of E. D. Hirsch, another intellectual with connections to Chicago who, along with the aforementioned Bloom, is providing former Secretary of Education William Bennett and others with ammunition for their attack on the humanities in general and on literary interpretivism in particular; an attack that has been recently stepped up in the press, and will soon, I am told, be receiving congressional attention. But whichever path one followed (and there are others) the result would be to highlight the extent to which Posner's essay, as innocently occasional as it might seem, is part and parcel of a wholesale effort to restructure several key American institutions in accordance with a very definite, and some would say extreme, political and moral vision.

It might seem that I am inflating the significance of what is after all a slight and flawed piece, full of misinformation and blunders (including the howler of criticizing Shakespeare for his "failure" to publish his plays[46]), uncomprehending of the positions to which it is opposed, finally less an argument than a collection of outdated pieties. Indeed, it might seem sufficient to leave the judgment of it to the full verse from which my title is taken:

> Don't know much about the Middle Ages,
> Look at the pictures and turn the pages;
> Don't know much about no rise and fall;
> Don't know much about nothing at all.[47]

But while there would be a certain satisfaction in this gesture, it would be too easy and it would reproduce the mistake for which I have criticized Posner, the mistake of accepting at face value the boundaries that separate disciplines and render their respective activities discrete from one another. In fact, neither disciplines nor the activities they enable are discrete; they exist in networks of affiliation and reciprocity that can sometimes be glimpsed (as they are here) in footnotes that reveal how a position taken in one corner of the institutional world is authorized by and authorizes in its turn positions of a similar kind taken elsewhere. Given the *structural* interdependence between disciplines, the effects of a piece of writing will always extend to contexts apparently far removed from the ones explicitly addressed; and this will be especially true in the case of someone like Posner, who is, after all, an appellate judge of national reputation and a scholar of enormous influence. This means that when he pronounces on something—even when, as in this case, the pronouncement is uninformed and slipshod—he will receive a respectful hearing, and therefore it is incumbent upon those who find his views not only wrong, but supportive of wrong views now being put forward in other (sometimes high) places, to challenge them in the strongest terms possible.

Consequences

14. Consequences

Nothing I wrote in *Is There a Text in This Class?* has provoked more opposition or consternation than my (negative) claim that the argument of the book has no consequences for the practice of literary criticism.[1] To many it seemed counterintuitive to maintain (as I did) that an argument in theory could leave untouched the practice it considers: After all, isn't the very point of theory to throw light on or reform or guide practice? In answer to this question I want to say, first, that this is certainly theory's claim—so much so that independently of the claim there is no reason to think of it as a separate activity—and, second, that the claim is unsupportable. Here, I am in agreement with Steven Knapp and Walter Benn Michaels, who are almost alone in agreeing with me and who fault me not for making the "no consequences" argument but for occasionally falling away from it. Those who dislike *Is There a Text in This Class?* tend to dislike "Against Theory" even more, and it is part of my purpose here to account for the hostility to both pieces. But since the issues at stake are fundamental, it is incumbent to begin at the beginning with a discussion of what theory is and is not.

"Against Theory" opens with a straightforward (if compressed) definition: "By 'theory' we mean a special project in literary criticism: the attempt to govern interpretations of particular texts by appealing to an account of interpretation in general" (p. 723). In the second sentence the authors declare that this definition of theory excludes much that has been thought to fall under its rubric and especially excludes projects of a general nature "such as narratology, stylistics, and prosody" (p. 723). On first blush this exclusion seems arbitrary and appears to be vulnerable to the charge (made by several respondents) that by defining theory so narrowly Knapp and Michaels at once assure the impregnability of their thesis and render it trivial. I believe, on the contrary, that the definition is correct and that, moreover, it is a reformulation of a familiar and even uncontroversial distinction. In E. D. Hirsch's work, for example, we meet it as a distinction between general and local hermeneutics. "Local hermeneutics," Hirsch explains,

> consists of rules of thumb rather than rules. . . . Local hermeneutics can . . . provide models and methods that are reliable most of the time. General hermeneutics lays claim to principles that hold true all of the time. . . . That is why general hermeneutics is, so far, the only aspect of interpretation that has earned the right to be named a "theory."[2]

By "general hermeneutics," Hirsch means a procedure whose steps, if they are faithfully and strictly followed, will "always yield correct results";[3] "local hermeneutics," on the other hand, are calculations of probability based on an insider's knowledge of what is likely to be successful in a particular field of practice. When Cicero advises that in cases where a client's character is an issue a lawyer should attribute a bad reputation to "the envy of a few people, or back biting, or false opinion" or, failing that, argue that "the defendant's life and character are not under investigation, but only the crime of which he is accused," he is presenting and urging a local hermeneutics. But when Raoul Berger insists that the meaning of the Constitution can be determined only by determining the intentions of the framers, he is presenting and urging a general hermeneutics.[4] In one case the practitioner is being told "[i]n a situation like this, here are some of the things you can do," where it is left to the agent to determine whether or not he has encountered a situation "like this" and which of the possible courses of action is relevant. In the other case the practitioner is being told "[w]hen you want to know the truth or discover the meaning, do this," where "this" is a set of wholly explicit instructions that leaves no room for interpretive decisions by the agent. In one case the practitioner is being given a "rule of thumb," something that would in certain circumstances be a good thing to try if you want to succeed in the game; in the other he is being given a rule, something that is necessary to do if you want to be right, where "being right" is not a matter of being in tune with the temporary and shifting norms of a context but of having adhered to the dictates of an abiding and general rationality. A rule is formalizable: it can be programmed on a computer and, therefore, can be followed by anyone who has been equipped with explicit (noncircular) definitions and equally explicit directions for carrying out a procedure. A rule of thumb, on the other hand, cannot be formalized, because the conditions of its application vary with the contextual circumstances of an ongoing practice; as those circumstances change, the very meaning of the rule (the instructions it is understood to give) changes too, at least for someone sufficiently inside the practice to be sensitive to its shifting demands. To put it another way, the rule-of-thumb reader begins with a knowledge of the outcome he desires, and it is within such knowledge that the rule assumes a shape, becomes readable; the rule follower, in contrast, defers to the self-declaring shape of the rule, which then generates the correct outcome independently of his judgment. The model for the "true" rule and, therefore, for theory is mathematics, for as John Lyons points out, if two people apply the rules of mathematics and come up with different results, we can be sure that one of them is mistaken, that is, has misapplied the rules.[5]

Lyons turns to the analogy from mathematics in the course of an explication of Chomskian linguistics, and the Chomsky project provides an excellent example of what a model of the formal, or rule-governed, type would be like. The Chomskian revolution, as Jerrold Katz and Thomas Bever have written, involved "the shift from a conception of grammar as cataloging the data of a corpus to a conception of grammar as explicating the internalized rules underlying the speaker's ability to produce and understand sentences."[6] Basically this is a turn from an empirical activity—the deriving of grammatical rules from a finite body of observed sentences—to a rational activity—the discovery of a set of constraints which, rather than being generalizations from observed behavior, are explanatory of that behavior in the sense that they are what make it possible. These constraints are not acquired through experience (education, historical conditioning, local habits) but are innate; experience serves only to actualize or "trigger" them. They have their source not in culture but in nature, and therefore they are *abstract* (without empirical content), *general* (not to be identified with any particular race, location, or historical period but with the species), and *invariant* (do not differ from language to language). As a system of rules, they are "independent of the features of the actual world and thus hold in any possible one" ("FRE," p. 40).

It follows that any attempt to model these constraints—to construct a device that will replicate their operations—must be equally independent in all these ways, that is, it must be formal, abstract, general, and invariant. It is Chomsky's project to construct such a device, a model of an innate human ability, a "competence model" which reflects the timeless and contextless workings of an abiding formalism, as opposed to a "performance model" which would reflect the empirical and contingent regularities of the behavior of some particular linguistic community. Once constructed, a competence model would function in the manner of a "mechanical computation" ("FRE," p. 38); that is, to "apply" it would be to set in motion a self-executing machine or calculus that would assign, without any interpretive activity on the part of the applier, the same description to a sentence that would be assigned by "an ideal speaker-listener, in a completely homogeneous speech-community, who knows its language perfectly."[7] If such a speaker were presented with the sentence "He danced his did," he would reject it as ungrammatical or irregular or deviant. Accordingly, a grammar modeled on his ability (or intuition) would refuse to assign the sentence a description—the generative device would find itself blocked by an item that violated its rules. If such a speaker were presented with the sentence "Flying planes can be dangerous," he would recognize it as ambiguous; accordingly, a generative grammar would assign the sentence not one but two structural (or "deep") descriptions. And if such a speaker were presented with the pair of sentences "John hit the ball" and "The ball was hit by John," he would recognize them as being synonymous, and, accordingly, the generative grammar would assign them a single structural description.

It is important to realize that this ideal speaker and the grammar modeled on his competence would perform their tasks without taking into account the circumstances of a sentence's production, or the beliefs of the speaker and hearer, or the idiomatic patterns of a particular community.[8] The speaker who knows the language of his community "perfectly" in Chomsky's idealization knows that system independently of its actualization in real-life situations: that knowledge is his competence, and the grammar that captures it divides strings in a language "into the well-formed and the ill-formed just on the basis of their syntactic structure, without reference to the way things are in the world, what speakers, hearers, or anyone else believe, etc." ("FRE," p. 31). That is why, as Judith Greene puts it, "the only real test . . . of a grammar is to devise a set of formal rules which, if fed to a computer operating with no prior knowledge of the language, would still be capable of generating only correct grammatical sentences."[9]

This is precisely the goal of Chomskian theory—the construction of "a system of rules that in some explicit and well-defined way assigns structural descriptions to sentences," where "explicit" means mechanical or algorithmic and the assigning is done not by the agent but by the system (*ATS*, p. 8). Needless to say, there has been much dispute concerning the possibility (and even desirability) of achieving that goal, and there have been many challenges to the basic distinctions (between competence and performance, between grammaticality and acceptability, between syntax and semantics, between grammatical knowledge and the knowledge of the world) that permit the goal, first, to be formulated and, then, to guide a program of research. But putting aside the merits of the Chomsky program and the question of whether it could ever succeed, the point I want to make here is that as a program it is theoretical and can stand as a fully developed example of what Knapp and Michaels mean when they say that theory is a *special* project and what Hirsch means when he insists that only such a project—a general hermeneutics—"has earned the right to be named a 'theory.'" The Chomsky project is theoretical because what it seeks is a method, a recipe with premeasured ingredients which when ordered and combined according to absolutely explicit instructions—instructions that "[do] not rely on the intelligence of the understanding reader" (*ATS*, p. 4)—will produce the desired result. In linguistics that result would be the assigning of correct descriptions to sentences; in literary studies the result would be the assigning of valid interpretations to works of literature. In both cases (and in any other that could be imagined) the practitioner gives himself over to the theoretical machine, surrenders his judgment to it, in order to reach conclusions that in no way depend on his education, or point of view, or cultural situation, conclusions that can then be checked by anyone who similarly binds himself to those rules and carries out their instructions.

Thus understood, theory can be seen as an effort to govern practice in two senses: (1) it is an attempt to *guide* practice from a position above or outside it (see pp. 723 and 742), and (2) it is an attempt to *reform* practice by neutralizing interest, by substituting for the parochial perspective of some local or partisan point of view the perspective of a general rationality to which the individual subordinates his contextually conditioned opinions and beliefs. (Not incidentally, this is the claim and the dream of Baconian method, of which so many modern theoretical projects are heirs.) Only if this substitution is accomplished will interpretation be principled, that is, impelled by formal and universal rules that apply always and everywhere rather than by rules of thumb that reflect the contingent practices of particular communities.

The argument *against* theory is simply that this substitution of the general for the local has never been and will never be achieved. Theory is an impossible project which will never succeed. It will never succeed simply because the primary data and formal laws necessary to its success will always be spied or picked out from within the contextual circumstances of which they are supposedly independent. The objective facts and rules of calculation that are to ground interpretation and render it principled are themselves interpretive products: they are, therefore, always and already contaminated by the interested judgments they claim to transcend. The contingencies that are to be excluded in favor of the invariant constitute the field within which what will (for a time) be termed the invariant emerges.

Once again, a ready example offers itself in the history of Chomskian linguistics. In order to get started, Chomsky must exclude from his "absolute formulations . . . any factor that should be considered as a matter of performance rather than competence." He does this, as Katz and Bever observe, "by simply considering the former [performance] as something to be abstracted away from, the way the physicist excludes friction, air resistance, and so on from the formulation of mechanical laws" ("FRE," p. 21). This act of abstracting-away-from must of course begin with data, and in this case the data are (or are supposed to be) sentences that depend for their interpretation not on performance factors—on the knowledge of a speaker's beliefs or of particular customs or conventions—but on the rules of grammar.[10] The trick then is to think of sentences that would be heard in the same way by all competent speakers no matter what their educational experience, or class membership, or partisan affiliation, or special knowledge, sentences which, invariant across contexts, could form the basis of an acontextual and formal description of the language and its rules.

The trouble is that there are no such sentences. As I have argued elsewhere, even to think of a sentence is to have already assumed the conditions both of its production and its intelligibility—conditions that include a speaker, with an intention and a purpose, in a situation.[11] To be sure, there are sentences which, when presented, seem to be intelligible in isolation, independently of any contextual setting. This simply means, however, that the context is so established, so deeply assumed, that it is invisible to the observer—he does not realize that what appears to him to be immediately obvious and readable is a function of its being in place. It follows, then, that any rules arrived at by abstracting away from such sentences will be rules only within the silent or deep context that allowed them to emerge and become describable. Rather than being distinct from circumstantial (and therefore variable) conditions, linguistic knowledge is unthinkable apart from these circumstances. Linguistic knowledge is contextual rather than abstract, local rather than general, dynamic rather than invariant; every rule is a rule of thumb; every competence grammar is a performance grammar in disguise.[12]

This, then, is why theory will never succeed: it cannot help but borrow its terms and its contents from that which it claims to transcend, the mutable world of practice, belief, assumptions, point of view, and so forth. And, by definition, something that cannot succeed cannot have consequences, cannot achieve the goals it has set for itself by being or claiming to be theory, the goals of guiding and/or reforming practice. Theory cannot guide practice because its rules and procedures are no more than generalizations from practice's history (and from only a small piece of that history), and theory cannot reform practice because, rather than neutralizing interest, it begins and ends in interest and raises the imperatives of interest—of some local, particular, partisan project—to the status of universals.

Thus far I have been talking about "foundationalist" theory (what Knapp and Michaels call "positive theory"), theory that promises to put our calculations and determinations on a firmer footing than can be provided by mere belief or unjustified practice. In recent years, however, the focus of attention has been more on "anti-foundationalist" theory (what Knapp and Michaels call "negative theory"), on arguments whose force it is precisely to deny the possibility (and even the intelligibility) of what foundationalist theory promises. Anti-foundationalist theory is sometimes Kuhnian, sometimes Derridean, sometimes pragmatist, sometimes Marxist, sometimes anarchist, but it is always historicist; that is, its strategy is always the one I have pursued in the previous paragraphs, namely, to demonstrate that the norms and standards and rules that foundationalist theory would oppose to history, convention, and local practice are in every instance a function or extension of history, convention, and local practice. As Richard Rorty puts it: "There are no essences anywhere in the area. There is no wholesale, epistemo-

logical way to direct, or criticize or underwrite the course of inquiry. . . . It is the vocabulary of practice rather than of theory . . .
in which one can say something useful about truth."[13] (Notice that
this does not mean that a notion like "truth" ceases to be operative,
only that it will always have reference to a moment in the history of
inquiry rather than to some God or material objectivity or invariant
calculus that underwrites all our inquiries.)

The fact that there are two kinds of theory (or, rather, theoretical
discourse—anti-foundationalism really isn't a theory at all; it is an
argument against the possibility of theory) complicates the question of
consequences, although in the end the relationship of both kinds of
theory to the question turns out to be the same. As we have seen, those
who believe in the consequences of foundationalist theory are possessed
by a hope—let us call it "theory hope"—the hope that our claims to
knowledge can be "justified on the basis of some objective method of
assessing such claims" rather than on the basis of the individual beliefs
that have been derived from the accidents of education and experience.[14] Anti-foundationalist theory tells us that no such justification
will ever be available and that therefore there is no way of testing our
beliefs against something whose source is not also a belief. As we shall
see, anti-foundationalism comes with its own version of "theory hope,"
but the emotion its arguments more often provoke is "theory fear," the
fear that those who have been persuaded by such arguments will abandon principled inquiry and go their unconstrained way in response to
the dictates of fashion, opinion, or whim. Expressions of theory fear
abound (one can find them now even in daily newspapers and popular
magazines), and in their more dramatic forms they approach the status
of prophecies of doom. Here, for example, is Israel Scheffler's view of
what will happen if we are persuaded by the writings of Thomas Kuhn:

> Independent and public controls are no more, communication has
> failed, the common universe of things is a delusion, reality itself is
> made . . . rather than discovered. . . . In place of a community
> of rational men following objective procedures in the pursuit of
> truth, we have a set of isolated monads, within each of which
> belief forms without systematic constraints.[15]

For Scheffler (and many others) the consequences of anti-foundationalist theory are disastrous and amount to the loss of everything we
associate with rational inquiry: public and shared standards, criteria for

preferring one reading of a text or of the world to another, checks against irresponsibility, etc. But this follows only if anti-foundational-ism is an argument for unbridled subjectivity, for the absence of con-straints on the individual; whereas, in fact, it is an argument for the situated subject, for the individual who is always constrained by the local or community standards and criteria of which his judgment is an extension. Thus the lesson of anti-foundationalism is not only that external and independent guides will never be found but that it is unnecessary to seek them, because you will always be guided by the rules or rules of thumb that are the content of any settled practice, by the assumed definitions, distinctions, criteria of evidence, measures of ade-quacy, and such, which not only define the practice but structure the understanding of the agent who thinks of himself as a "competent member." That agent cannot distance himself from these rules, because it is only within them that he can think about alternative courses of action or, indeed, think at all. Thus anti-foundationalism cannot pos-sibly have the consequences Scheffler fears; for, rather than unmooring the subject, it reveals the subject to be always and already tethered to the contextual setting that constitutes him and enables his "rational" acts.

Neither can anti-foundationalism have the consequences for which some of its proponents *hope,* the consequences of freeing us from the hold of unwarranted absolutes so that we may more flexibly pursue the goals of human flourishing or liberal conversation. The reasoning be-hind this hope is that since we now know that our convictions about truth and factuality have not been imposed on us by the world, or im-printed in our brains, but are derived from the practices of ideologically motivated communities, we can set them aside in favor of convictions that we choose freely. But this is simply to imagine the moment of unconstrained choice from the other direction, as a goal rather than as an abyss. Anti-foundationalist fear and anti-foundationalist hope turn out to differ only in emphasis. Those who express the one are concerned lest we kick ourselves loose from constraints; those who profess the other look forward to finally being able to do so. Both make the mis-take of thinking than anti-foundationalism, by demonstrating the con-textual source of conviction, cuts the ground out from under convic-tion—it is just that, for one party, this is the good news and, for the other, it is the news that chaos has come again. But, in fact, anti-founda-tionalism says nothing about what we can now do or not do; it is an account of what we have always been doing and cannot help but do (no matter what our views on epistemology)—act in accordance with the standards and norms that are the content of our beliefs and, therefore, the very structure of our consciousnesses. The fact that we now have a new explanation of how we got our beliefs—the fact, in short, that we now have a new belief—does not free us from our other beliefs or cause us to doubt them. I may now be convinced that what I think about *Paradise Lost* is a function of my education, professional training, the history of Milton studies, and so on, but that conviction does not lead me to think something else about *Paradise Lost* or to lose confidence in what I think. These consequences would follow only if I also believed in the possibility of a method independent of belief by which the truth about *Paradise Lost* could be determined; but if I believed that, I wouldn't be an anti-foundationalist at all. In short, the theory hope expressed by some anti-foundationalists is incoherent within the anti-foundationalist perspective, since it assumes, in its dream of beginning anew, everything that anti-foundationalism rejects.

Of course, it could be the case that if I were shown that some of my convictions (about Milton or anything else) could be traced to sources in sets of assumptions or points of view I found distressing, I might be moved either to alter those convictions or reexamine my sense of what is and is not distressing. This, however, would be a quite specific reconsideration provoked by a perceived inconsistency in my beliefs (and it would have to be an inconsistency that struck me as intolerable), not a general reconsideration of my beliefs in the face of a belief about their source. To be sure, such a general reconsideration would be possible if the source to which I had come to attribute them was deemed by me to be discreditable (hallucinatory drugs, political indoctrination)—although even then I could still decide that I was sticking with what I now knew no matter where it came from—but human history could not be that kind of discreditable source for me as an anti-foundationalist, since anti-foundationalism teaches (and teaches without regret or nostalgia) that human history is the context within which we know. To put it another way, an anti-foundationalist (like anyone else) can always reject something because its source has been shown to be some piece of human history he finds reprehensible, but an anti-foundationalist cannot (without at that moment becoming a foundationalist) reject something simply because its source has been shown to be human history as opposed to something independent of it.

All of which is to say again what I have been saying all along: theory has no consequences. Foundationalist theory has no consequences because its project cannot succeed, and anti-foundationalist theory has no consequences because, as a belief about how we got our beliefs, it leaves untouched (at least in principle) the beliefs of whose history it is an explanation. The case seems open-and-shut, but I am aware that many will maintain that theory *must* have consequences. It is to their objections and arguments that I now turn.

The first objection has already been disposed of, at least implicitly. It is Adena Rosmarin's objection and amounts to asking, Why restrict theory either to foundationalist attempts to ground practice by some Archimedean principle or to anti-foundationalist demonstrations that all such attempts will necessarily fail? Why exclude from the category "theory" much that has always been regarded as theory—works like W. J. Harvey's *Character in the Novel,* or Barbara Herrnstein Smith's *Poetic Closure,* or William Empson's *Seven Types of Ambiguity*— works whose claims are general and extend beyond the interpretation of specific texts to the uncovering of regularities that are common to a great many texts? The answer is that the regularities thus uncovered, rather than standing apart from practice and constituting an abstract picture of its possibilities, would be derived from practice and constitute a report on its current shape or on the shape it once had in an earlier period. It is possible to think of these regularities as rules, but they would be neither invariant nor predictive since they would be drawn from a finite corpus of data and would hold (if they did hold) only for that corpus; each time history brought forward new instances, it would be necessary to rewrite the "rules," that is, recharacterize the regularities. In Chomsky's terms, the result would be a succession of performance grammars, grammars that reflect the shifting and contingent conditions of a community's practice rather than capture the laws that constrain what the members of a community can possibly do. The result, in short, would be *empirical generalizations* rather than a general hermeneutics.

Still, one might ask, Why not call such generalizations "theory"? Of course, there is nothing to prevent us from doing so, but the effect of such a liberal definition would be to blur the distinction between theory and everything that is not theory, so that, for example, essays on the functions of prefaces in Renaissance drama would be theory, and books on the pastoral would be theory, and studies of Renaissance self-fashioning or self-consuming artifacts would be theory. One is tempted to call such efforts theory in part because they often serve as models for subsequent work: one could study self-fashioning in the eighteenth century or self-consuming artifacts as a feature of modernism. Such activities, though, would be instances not of following a theory but of extending a practice, of employing a set of heuristic questions, or a thematics, or a trenchant distinction in such a way as to produce a new or at least novel description of familiar material. Much of what is done in literary studies and elsewhere conforms to this pattern. If we like, we can always call such imitations of a powerful practice "theory," but nothing whatsoever will have been gained, and we will have lost any sense that theory is special. After all, it is only if theory is special that the question of its consequences is in any way urgent. In other words, the consequentiality of theory goes without saying and is, therefore, totally uninteresting if *everything* is theory.

And yet the argument that everything is theory is sometimes put forward in *support* of theory's special status. Those who make this argument think it follows from the chief lesson of anti-foundational-ism, the lesson that there are no unmediated facts nor any neutral per-ception and that everything we know and see is known and seen under a description or as a function of some paradigm. The conclusion drawn from this lesson is that every practice presupposes a structure of assump-tions within which it is intelligible—there is no such thing as *simply* acting—and the conclusion drawn from that conclusion is that every practice is underwritten by a theory. The first conclusion seems to me to be correct—any practice one engages in is conceivable only in rela-tion to some belief or set of beliefs—but the second conclusion is, I think, false, because beliefs are not theories. A theory is a special achievement of consciousness; a belief is a prerequisite for being con-scious at all. Beliefs are not what you think *about* but what you think *with,* and it is within the space provided by their articulations that men-tal activity—including the activity of theorizing—goes on. Theories are something you can have—you can wield them and hold them at a dis-tance; beliefs have *you,* in the sense that there can be no distance between them and the acts they enable. In order to make even the sim-plest of assertions or perform the most elementary action, I must already be proceeding in the context of innumerable beliefs which can-not be the object of my attention because they are the content of my attention: beliefs on the order of the identity of persons, the existence

of animate and inanimate entities, the stability of objects, in addition
to the countless beliefs that underwrite the possibility and intelligibility
of events in my local culture—beliefs that give me, without reflection,
a world populated by streets, sidewalks, telephone poles, restaurants,
figures of authority and figures of fun, worthy and unworthy tasks,
achievable and unachievable goals, and so on. The description of what
assumptions must already be in place for me to enter an elevator, or
stand in line in a supermarket, or ask for the check in a restaurant
would fill volumes, volumes that would themselves be intelligible only
within a set of assumptions they in turn did not contain. Do these volumes—and the volumes that would be necessary to *their* description—
constitute a theory? Am I following or enacting a theory when I stop
for a red light, or use my American Express card, or rise to speak at a
conference? Are you now furiously theorizing as you sit reading what
I have to say? And if you are persuaded by me to alter your understanding of what is and is not a theory, is your new definition of theory a
new theory of theory? Clearly it is possible to answer yes to all these
questions, but just as clearly that answer will render the notion "theory" *and* the issue of its consequences trivial by making "theory" the
name for ordinary, contingent, unpredictable, everyday behavior.

Now it may be easy enough to see the absurdity of giving the
label "theoretical" to everyday actions that follow from the first or
ground-level beliefs that give us our world. The difficulty arises with
actions that seem more momentous and are attached to large questions
of policy and morality; such actions, we tend to feel, must follow from
something more "considered" than a mere belief, must follow, rather,
from a theory. Thus, for example, consider the case of two legislators
who must vote on a fair housing bill: one is committed to the protection of individual freedom and insists that it trump all competing
considerations; the other is some kind of utilitarian and is committed
to the greatest good for the greatest number. Isn't it accurate to say
that these two hold different theories and that their respective theories
will lead them to cast different votes—the first, against, and the second,
in favor of, fair housing? Well, first, it is not at all certain that the
actions of the two are predictable on the basis of what we are for now
calling their "theories." A utilitarian may well think that, in the long
run, the greatest number will reap the greatest good if property rights
are given more weight than access rights; a libertarian could well decide that access rights are more crucial to the promotion of individual

freedom and choice than property rights. In short, nothing particular follows from the fact that the two agents in my example would, if asked, declare themselves adherents of different theories. But would they even be theories? I would say not. Someone who declares himself committed to the promotion of individual freedom does not have a theory; he has a belief. He believes that something is more important than something else—and if you were to inquire into the grounds of his belief, you would discover not a theory but other beliefs that at once support and are supported by the belief to which he is currently testifying. Now, to be sure, these clustered beliefs affect behavior—not because they are consulted when a problem presents itself, however, but because it is within the world they deliver that the problem and its possible solutions take shape. To put it another way, when one acts on the basis of a belief, one is just engaged in reasoning, not in theoretical reasoning, and it makes no difference whether the belief is so deep as to be invisible or is invoked within a highly dramatic, even spectacular, situation. The sequence "I believe in the promotion of individual freedom, and therefore I will vote in this rather than in that way" is not different in kind from the sequence "I believe in the solidity of matter and therefore I will open the door rather than attempt to walk through the walls." It seems curious to call the reasoning (if that is the word) in the second sequence "theoretical," and I am saying that it would be no less curious to give that name to the reasoning in the first. The fact that someone has a very general, even philosophical, belief—a belief concerning recognizably "big" issues—does not mean that he has a theory; it just means that he has a very general belief. If someone wants to say that his very general belief has a consequential (although not predictable) relationship to his action, I am certainly not going to argue, since to say that is to say what I said at the beginning of this section: it is belief and not theory that underwrites action.

It is simply a mistake, then, to think that someone who identifies himself as a believer in individual freedom or in the greatest good for the greatest number has declared his allegiance to a theory. But there are instances in which it is indeed proper to say that someone who takes this rather than that position is opting for this rather than that theory, and in those instances the question of the consequences of theory is once again alive. Here, a recent essay by Thomas Grey of the Stanford Law School provides a useful example. Grey is concerned with the consequences for the judicial process of two theories of constitutional interpretation. Those who hold the first theory he calls "textualists," and in their view "judges should get operative norms only from the text," that is, from the Constitution. Those who hold the other theory he calls "supplementers," and in their view "judges may find supplemental norms through [the] interpretation of text analogs" such as previous judicial decisions or background social phenomena.[16] I regard these two positions as theoretical because they amount to alternative sets of instructions for reaching correct or valid interpretive conclusions. Someone who says "I am committed to promoting individual freedom" still has the task, in every situation, of deciding which among the alternative courses of action will further his ends. But a judge who says "I get my operative norms only from the text" knows exactly what to do in every situation: he looks to the text and restricts himself to the norms he finds there. On the other side, his "supplementalist" opponent also knows what to do: he looks for norms not only in the text but in a number of other, authorized, places. Grey forthrightly identifies himself as a supplementer, arguing that if lawyers and judges come to think of themselves as supplementers rather than textualists, as one kind of theorist rather than as another, they "will thereby be marginally more free than they otherwise would be to infuse into constitutional law their current interpretations of our society's values."

For Grey, then, the consequences of theory are real and important. It seems obvious to him that (1) if two judges, one a textualist and the other a supplementer, were presented with the same case they would decide it differently, and (2) the differences in their decisions would be a function of the differences in their theories. This assumes, however, that the two theories give instructions that it is possible to follow and that someone *could* first identify the norms encoded in the text and then choose either to abide by them or to supplement them. But as Grey himself acknowledges, interpretation is not a two-stage process in which the interpreter first picks out a "context-independent semantic meaning" and then, if he chooses, consults this or that context; rather, it is within some or other context—of assumptions, concerns, priorities, expectations—that what an interpreter sees as the "semantic meaning" emerges, and therefore he is never in the position of being able to focus on that meaning independently of background or "supplemental" considerations. The semantic meaning of the text does not announce itself; it must be decided upon, that is, interpreted. Since this is also true of contexts—they too must be construed—the distinction between text and context is

impossible to maintain and cannot be the basis of demarcating alternative theories with their attendant consequences. In short, no text reads
itself, and anything you decide to take into account—any supplement—
is a text; therefore interpreters of the Constitution are always and *necessarily* both textualists and supplementers, and the only argument between them is an argument over which text it is that is going to be read
or, if you prefer, which set of background conditions will be specified as
the text. Those arguments have substance, and on many occasions their
outcomes will have consequences, but they will not be the consequences
of having followed one or the other of these two theories because,
while they truly are theories, they cannot be followed. If the two judges
in our example did in fact happen to reach different decisions about the
same case, it would not be because they have different theories of interpretation but because they interpret from within different sets of priorities or concerns, that is, from within different sets of beliefs. It is
entirely possible, moreover, that despite the declared differences in
theoretical allegiance, the two could reach exactly the same decision
whenever the text to which the one has confined himself is perspicuous
against the same set of supplemental concerns or perspectives that
forms the other's text.

And yet it would be too much to say that declarations of theoretical allegiances—even allegiances to theories that cannot be made operative—are inconsequential. As Grey notes, such declarations have a
political force. "Most lawyers," he points out, "share with the public a
'pre-realist' consensus that in doing judicial review, judges should generate their decisive norms by constitutional interpretation only." In
short, there is a consensus that they should be textualists; therefore,
Grey contends, "For me to call my views 'noninterpretive' [supplemen-
talist] will obviously not improve my chances of winning the argument." Now one could dismiss this as a piece of cynical advice ("Call
yourself a textualist no matter how you proceed"), but it seems to me
to point to a significant truth: rather than dictating or generating arguments, theoretical positions are parts of arguments and are often invoked because of a perceived connection between them and certain
political and ideological stands. That is, given a certain set of political
circumstances, one or another theory will be a component in this or
that agenda or program. So, for example, in a struggle for power between the judiciary and the legislature, one party may gravitate "naturally"—that is, in terms of its current goals—toward one theory while

the other party—just as naturally and just as politically—identifies itself with the opposite theory. Moreover, in the course of a generation or two, the identifications may be reversed, as new circumstances find the onetime textualists now calling themselves supplementers (or legal realists, or "noninterpretivists") and vice versa. In short, declaring a theoretical allegiance will often be consequential—not, however, because the declaration dictates a course of action but because a course of action already in full flower appropriates it and gives it significance.

Thus we see that even when something is a theory and is consequential—in the sense that espousing it counts for something—it is not consequential in the way theorists claim. Indeed, on the evidence of the examples we have so far considered, the possible relationships between theories and consequences reduce to three: either (1) it *is* a theory but has no consequences because, as a set of directions purged of interest and independent of presuppositions, it cannot be implemented, or (2) it has consequences but is not a theory—rather, it is a belief or a conviction, as in the case of the promotion of individual freedom, or (3) it is a theory and does have consequences, but they are political rather than theoretical, as when, for very good practical reasons, somebody calls himself a textualist or a supplementer.

Nevertheless there still is a position to which a "consequentialist" might retreat: perhaps theory, strictly speaking, is an impossible project that could never succeed, and perhaps beliefs and assumptions, while consequential, are not theories—but, Isn't the foregrounding of beliefs and assumptions "theory"?—and, Doesn't the foregrounding of beliefs and assumptions make us more aware of them?—and, Isn't that a consequence, and one which will itself have consequences? In short, theory may be just an activity within practice, but—as this position would have it—Isn't it a special *kind* of activity? This claim has two versions, one weak and one strong. The strong version is untenable because it reinvents foundationalism, and the weak version is so weak that to grant it is to have granted nothing at all. The strong claim reinvents foundationalism because it imagines a position from which our beliefs can be scrutinized; that is, it imagines a position outside belief, the transcendental position assumed and sought by theorists of the Chomsky type. The argument against the strong claim is the anti-foundationalist argument: we can never get to the side of our beliefs and, therefore, any perspective we have on one or more of them will be grounded in others of them in relation to which we can have no perspective because we have no distance. The weak claim begins by accepting this argument but still manages to find a space in which theory does its special work: although we can never get an absolute perspective on our beliefs, we can still get a perspective on *some* of our beliefs in relation to some others; and if this happens, it may be that from within the enclosure of our beliefs we will spy contradictions of which we had been unaware and, thereby, be provoked to ask and answer some fundamental questions. In short, and in familiar language, theory—or the foregrounding of assumptions—promotes critical self-consciousness.

Now it is certainly the case that people are on occasion moved to reconsider their assumptions and beliefs and then to change them, and it is also the case that—as a consequence—there may be a corresponding change in practice. The trouble is, such reconsiderations can be brought about by almost anything and have no unique relationship to something called "theory." Some years ago Lawrance Thompson published a biography of Robert Frost in which the poet was revealed to have been a most unpleasant, not to say evil, person. The book produced much consternation, especially among those who had assumed that there was (or should be) a correlation between the quality of a man's art and his character. Underlying this assumption was a traditional and powerful view of the nature and function of literature. In that view (still held by many today), literature is ennobling: it enlarges and refines the sensibility and operates to make its readers better persons. It follows, then, that those who are able to produce nobility in others should themselves be noble—but here was an undeniably great artist who was, by all the evidence Thompson had marshaled, perfectly vile. Presumably, Thompson's book induced some who held this view to reconsider it; that is, they had been made aware of their assumptions. What moved them, however, was not theory but a work of traditional scholarship that did not even pretend to be criticism.

The impulse to reexamine the principles underlying one's practice can be provoked, moreover, by something that is not even within the field of practice: by turning forty, or by a dramatic alteration in one's economic situation, by a marriage, or by a divorce. Of course, it can also be provoked by theory—but not necessarily. That is, you could engage in the exercise of foregrounding your assumptions and even come to see that some of them were incompatible with some piece of your practice and, nevertheless, respond with a shrug, and decide to let things be. The man who declares himself committed to the redistribution of authority and the diffusion of power may be an absolute autocrat in the classroom, and when this is pointed out to him or when he points it out to himself, he may mutter something about the limited attention span of today's youth and go on as before. Even when theory (so called) produces self-consciousness, it need not be "critical"; it need not be the prelude to change. Once again, we reach the conclusion that there is no sense in which theory is special: it cannot provide us with a perspective independent of our beliefs, and the perspective it can occasionally (but not necessarily) provide on some of our beliefs relative to others can be provided by much that is not theory.

If one has followed the argument thus far, it begins to be difficult to understand why anyone has ever thought that theory should have consequences. Yet, since many have thought so and will continue to think so even after I have done, it is time to inquire into the reasons for their conviction. One reason, and a very powerful one, is the institutional success of philosophy in persuading us that the answers to its questions are directly relevant to everything we do when we are not doing philosophy. As Richard Rorty has put it:

> Philosophers usually think of their discipline as one which discusses perennial, eternal problems—problems which arise as soon as one reflects. . . . Philosophy can be foundational in respect to the rest of culture because culture is the assemblage of claims to knowledge, and philosophy adjudicates such claims.[17]

The idea, then, is that whatever the surface configurations of our actions, *at bottom* we are being guided by principles of the kind that philosophy takes as its special province. Thus it is to philosophy that we should look to get a perspective on those principles and on the actions we perform in everyday life.

The relevance of philosophy to every aspect of human culture has been assumed for so long that it now seems less an assertion or an argument than a piece of plain common sense. But it is, in fact, an argument, and one whose content is the debatable proposition that almost everything we do is a disguised and probably confused version of philosophy. That proposition will begin to seem less plausible if we remember that philosophy is not the name of a natural kind but of an academic discipline and, moreover, of a discipline whose traditions are so special as to constitute a prima facie denial of its territorial ambitions. Philosophy is that area of inquiry in which one asks questions about the nature of knowledge, truth, fact, meaning, mind, action, and so forth, and gives answers that fall within a predictable range of positions called realism, idealism, relativism, pragmatism, materialism, mentalism, Platonism, Aristotelianism, Kantianism, etc. Of course, other areas of inquiry are similarly well developed and articulated and come complete with their own array of positions, problems, solutions, and decorums. One of these is literary criticism, where the task is the description and evaluation of verbal artifacts and the categories of interrogation are historical (is it Romantic or neoclassic?), generic (is it masque or drama?), formal (is it episodic or organic?), stylistic (is it Senecan or Ciceronian?).

Now, although the traditions of philosophy and literary criticism display certain points of intersection and occasionally refer to each other, they are for all intents and purposes distinct, so much so that it is perfectly possible for someone wholly ignorant of one to operate quite successfully in the other. It makes no sense, then, to think that one is radically dependent on the other, to think, for example, that since there is something called "the philosophy of action" and since literary criticism is an action, anyone who wants to know how to do literary criticism should consult the philosophy of action. A literary critic already knows what to do simply by virtue of his being embedded in a field of practice; it is hard to see why his performance would be improved or altered by bringing to bear the categories and urgencies of another field of practice. Of course, it is always possible to step back from a field and put to it the kinds of questions that belong properly (that is, by history and convention) to philosophy, to ask, for example, what literary critics must believe about the world, truth, meaning, fact, evidence, etc., in order to go about their work in a way that seems to them at once routine and natural. But the lessons learned from such an interrogation would be philosophical, not literary, and the fact that it was possible to learn them would not prove that those who do criticism are really doing philosophy any more than the fact that every activity is potentially the object of philosophical analysis means that every activity is at base philosophical and should be ruled by philosophy's norms.

The point is obvious and, one would have thought, inescapable: philosophy is one thing, and literary criticism is another. But the point has been obscured by the fact that in the past twenty-five years philosophy has become something that literary critics also do or attempt to do. That is, they attempt to do theory, which is another name for philosophy; and if the argument for the consequences of theory seems strong when theory is a separate discipline, it seems even stronger when theory is a component of the field it purports to govern. But if theory (or philosophy) is now a practice in literary studies, it differs more from its fellow practices than they do from each other. A formalist and a critic of myth may be at odds, but they are in the same line of work and contesting for the same privilege, the privilege of saying what this poem or novel or play means. Theory, on the other hand, disdains particular acts of interpretation and aspires to provide an account of interpretation in general—and just as a philosophical analysis of an activity is not an instance of that activity but of philosophy, so an account of interpretation is not an interpretation but an account. They are different games, and they remain different even when they are played by the same person.

That is to say, as things stand now, a worker in the field may hold this or that theoretical position—think of himself as a foundationalist or an anti-foundationalist—and *also* be a practicing critic—think of himself as a Wordsworthian or a Miltonist. But, when he is performing as a Wordsworthian or a Miltonist, he will be asking the questions and giving the answers that belong to that tradition of inquiry, and his theoretical position will quite literally be beside the point. I may be convinced, as in fact I am, that my sense of what is going on in a literary work is a function of my history, education, professional training, ideological affiliation, and so on, but that conviction will be of no effect when I set out to determine who is the hero of *Paradise Lost;* for at that moment all of the categories, distinctions, imperatives, and urgencies that might at some other time become the object of a metacritical investigation will be firmly in place and form the enabling conditions of my actions. In short, theory is not consequential even when the practitioner is himself a theorist. Indeed, the practitioner may cease to be a theorist or may awake one morning (as I predict we all will) to find that theory has passed from the scene and still continue in his life's work without ever missing a beat.

This conclusion may seem to fly in the face of the evidence provided by those critics who, apparently, changed their practice when they changed their theory, who now discover aporias and radical de-centerings where they used to discover irony and unity. Doesn't this evidence itself constitute a strong empirical case for the consequences of theory?[18] Not at all—what it indicates is that thematizing remains the primary mode of literary criticism and that, as an action, thematizing can find its materials in theory as well as in anything else. In thematic criticism a work is discovered to be the literary expression or consideration of such and such concerns, be they economic or psychological, political or military, sexual, culinary, or whatever. What the thematic critic then produces are economic or psychological or sociological or political or philosophical readings. He does *not* produce—that is, he does not do—economics, psychology, sociology, political science, or philosophy. He may *quarry* these and other disciplines for vocabulary, distinctions, concerns, etc.—indeed, it is hard to see what else he could do—but to quarry from a discipline is not to become a practitioner of it. If I propose a religious reading of George Herbert's lyrics, am I practicing religion? If I read Gustave Flaubert in the light of medical knowledge in the nineteenth century, am I practicing medicine? Obviously not—and neither, when I find that a work is "about" the limits of language, or the conditions of assertion, or the relativity of truth, am I doing theory. If I were practicing religion, I would be urging, chastising, and preaching; if I were practicing medicine, I would be setting bones and handing out prescriptions; and if I were practicing theory, I would either be arguing for a set of formal and explicit rules or arguing that rules of that kind are never available. I would not be analyzing the way in which such arguments are distributed over a range of characters in a novel or underlie the dramatic structure of the Romantic lyric. It is only because theory as a form of practice now shares an institutional or disciplinary home with literary criticism that its thematization is taken as evidence of its power to alter literary criticism. In fact, the power flows in the other direction: like any other discipline or body of materials that is made into thematic hay, theory is not so much the consequential agent of a change as it is the passive object of an appropriation.

We have now achieved what appears to be a dramatic reversal. At the outset, the strong thesis in the field was that theory has consequences and that they are far-reaching and fundamental, but now theory has been deprived of any consequentiality whatsoever and stands revealed as the helpless plaything of the practice it claimed to inform. But certainly we have gone too far, and it is time to admit what everyone knows: theory has consequences; not, however, because it stands apart from and can guide practice but because it is itself a form of practice and therefore is consequential for practice as a matter of definition.[19] That is, any account of what now makes up the practice of literary criticism must include theory, which means that there was a time when theory was not a part of criticism's practice, and the fact that it now is has made a difference, has been consequential.

Of course, as consequences go, this is pretty low-level, but there is more. As a practice, theory has all the political and institutional consequences of other practices. Those who do it can be published, promoted, fired, feted, celebrated, reviled; there can be symposia devoted to it, journals committed to it; there can be departments of theory, schools of theory; it can be a rallying cry ("Give me theory or give me death!"), a banner, a target, a program, an agenda. All of these (and more) are consequences, and they would not be possible if there were no theory. But although these are certainly the consequences of theory, they are not theoretical consequences; that is, they are not the consequences of a practice that stands in a relationship of precedence and mastery to other practices. There is a world of difference between saying that theory is a form of practice and saying that theory informs practice: to say the one is to claim for theory no more than can be claimed for anything else; to say the other is to claim everything. So, even though the thesis that theory has no consequences holds only when the consequences are of a certain kind, they are the only consequences that matter, since they are the consequences that would mark theory off as special.

We can test this by thinking about the consequences that would satisfy a theorist. Surely Chomsky's theory has had consequences: it has revolutionized a discipline and extended its sway; its terms and goals structure everything that happens in the field; but it has not had (and, by my argument, could not have) the consequences of its claims—it has not provided the formal and algorithmic model of language acquisition and use whose promise generated all the activity in the first place. The theory's success, in short, has been largely political; as such, it is a success that can hardly be comforting to Chomsky since the political is what he, like every other theorist, desires to rise above. Paradoxically, the triumph of Chomskian theory from an institutional point of view is an illustration of its failure from the point of view of its fondest hope, the hope to transcend point of view by producing a picture of the language that holds for any or all institutions and is beholden to none. Chomsky is in the position of every other theorist: the consequences he seeks are impossible, and the consequences to which he has clear right and title make him indistinguishable from any other political agent and render theory a category about which there is nothing particular— because there is nothing general—to say.

There is nothing either particular or general to say about theory's political consequences because, while they are palpable, they are not predictable; they do not follow *from* theory but are something that *befalls* theory—although, again, not necessarily and not always in the same way. As a practice, theory will cut a different figure in different disciplines; only in philosophy will changes in theory receive immediate and consequential attention. But that is because philosophy (at least in the analytic tradition) *is* theory, is the foundational project Rorty describes. Thus to say that in philosophy a change in theory will change practice is only to say that when practice changes, it changes. In literary criticism, on the other hand, theory is only one practice among many, and its impact has varied with different locations and universities. In some places in the United States the appearance of a theoretical manifesto in *New Literary History, Diacritics,* or *Critical Inquiry* will be Monday-morning news to which one must respond; in other places it will be heard, if it is heard at all, as the report of a minor skirmish on a foreign field of battle. In a discipline of such diversity with respect to theory, the question of its consequences cannot even be meaningfully put.

In the world of legal studies the case is different again. There theory has recently become the center of debate, in large part because of a single issue, the legitimacy of judicial review, or, as it is sometimes called, the "countermajoritarian difficulty."[20] The difficulty takes the form of a question: How, in a democratic system, can one justify the fact that a group of men and women, who are appointed for life, pass judgment on the validity of legislation enacted by the elected representatives of the people? This question is quite literally a demand for theory, for a justifying argument that does not presuppose the interests of any party or the supremacy of any political goal or borrow its terms from the practice it would regulate. For the foundationalists, only such an argument will guarantee the coherence of the legal process—it simply *must* be found; the failure so far of the efforts to find it leads the anti-foundationalists, on the other hand, to conclude that the legal process is political through and through and is therefore a sham. Both parties agree that the issue of judicial review is "the most fundamental in the extensive domain of constitutional law" and that the stakes are very high.[21] As long as that agreement continues, theory is likely to flourish as a consequential form of legal practice.

Here, then, are three disciplines, in each of which theory is differently consequential, and those differences themselves are not stable but contingent and changeable. Philosophy and theory have not always been one, and still are not in some parts of the world—and may not even be so in our part of the world if Rorty and some others have anything to say about it. Theory has not always been a glamour stock in literary studies and has already ceased to be a growth industry; if the urgency attached in the legal world to the issue of judicial review should ever fade, theory could fade with it (although if it has become well enough established, it might migrate to another issue). Will it fade? Will it rise in other disciplines hitherto innocent of it? Will the consequences of its appearance or demise be large or small? These and other questions could be answered only if there were a general account of theory's career, but since the determining factors will always be local and contingent—who could have predicted that the emigration of European scholars in the late 1930s would bring literary theory to the United States or that marketplace conditions in the humanities would bring it (by way of disgruntled Ph.D.'s) to the law—no such account is available and we must wait upon the event. If the question of theory's consequences is itself not theoretical but empirical, it can only receive an empirical answer in the form of specific and historical investigations into the consequences that this or that theory did or did not have. The result of such investigations will vary—in some cases, there will be virtually nothing to report and, in others, the report will fill volumes—but in no case will the chronicling of theory's consequences demonstrate that theory has—by right, as an inherent property—consequences.

   Will there be consequences to an argument against theory's conse-quences? Since that too is an empirical question, the answer is "time will tell," but there are some consequences that would seem to be either likely or unlikely. A likely consequence attaches to the issue of justification. Should it happen that everyone were persuaded by the "no consequences" argument (an outcome that is itself extremely unlikely), the search for certain kinds of justification might very well cease or, at least, be carried on with altered hopes, and that would be a consequence. To return for a moment to the context of legal studies and the "countermajoritarian difficulty," the issue would lose its urgency and the debate would continue, if it continued, on different terms, if all parties were brought to see (1) that the demand for a justification of judicial review which did not presuppose but bracketed the interests, goals, agendas, lines of authority, and so on, already in place was a demand for something at once unobtainable and empty, and (2) that the unavailability of such a justification proved not that everything was a sham but that justifications are always interested and acquire their intelligibility and force from the very practices of which they are a public defense. That is, if both parties could be brought to see that political justifications are the only kind there are and that this fact does not render argument nugatory but necessary, they might fall to recommending their contrasting agendas for the frankly political consequences they would be likely to have and not for a theoretical purity they could never achieve. Such a turn of events would not change very much, since, if I am right, every argument is already interested and political no matter what its theoretical trappings—but at least certain kinds of objections would no longer have very much force and certain kinds of appeals would no longer seem tainted.

On the other side, there is at least one consequence of the success of the "no consequences" argument that is not only unlikely, but impossible, and can be ruled out in advance. The case for theory's inconsequentiality, even if it is persuasive, will not return us to some precritical state, whether it be thought of as a state of innocence or of knownothing ignorance. The consequences of theory as a form of practice are real even if the consequences of theory as a foundational or antifoundational project could not possibly exist—indeed, theory's "practical" consequences are real *because* its "theoretical" consequences could not exist. The discrediting of theory could have the consequence of returning us to some uncontaminated or unredeemed practice only if theory were the independent and abstract calculus of its strongest claims. The fact that theory is not and could not be that calculus and therefore could not have the consequences of its claims assures that it will always have the political consequences I have been describing. Although theory cannot be a lever for change from the outside, its existence on the inside—within the field of practice—is evidence that a change has already occurred, a change in which its mode of interrogation has now joined or displaced others. That change cannot be reversed, and its effects will continue long after the formal program of theory has been abandoned.

Will it be abandoned? Will theory stop? Certainly not as a result of arguments against it, mine, or anyone else's. Arguments against theory only keep it alive, by marking it as a site of general concern. Theory will stop only when it has played out its string, run its course, when the urgencies and fears of which it is the expression either fade or come to be expressed by something else. This is already happening in literary studies, and there could be no surer sign of it than the appearance in recent years of several major anthologies—by Josué Harari, Jane Tompkins, Robert Young—and of series that bear titles like New Accents but report only on what is old and well digested. The fading away of theory is signaled not by silence but by more and more talk, more journals, more symposia, and more entries in the contest for the right to sum up theory's story. There will come a time when it is a contest no one will want to win, when the announcement of still another survey of critical method is received not as a promise but as a threat, and when the calling of still another conference on the function of theory in our time will elicit only a groan. That time may have come: theory's day is dying; the hour is late; and the only thing left for a theorist to do is to say so, which is what I have been saying here, and, I think, not a moment too soon.

15. Anti-Foundationalism, Theory Hope, and the Teaching of Composition

In the past twenty years the literary landscape has been transformed by the emergence of theory. Although it remains true that theory is not seriously taught in the majority of our departments of literature and is a regular part of the curriculum in only a few avant-garde outposts, it is nevertheless the case that much of the energy—and especially the polemical energy—in the literary academy is centered on theory; so much so that even those whose acquaintance with theory is secondhand regularly debate its value and its consequences. Not surprisingly, the question of theory has found its way into discussions of the teaching and practice of writing, and, also not surprisingly, the appearance of theory in the world of composition has provoked the same expressions of hope and fear that attend its appearance in every other discipline.

It is theory hope—the promise that theory seems to offer—that is my subject, but it is a subject that cannot be approached without first posing the basic question of what, exactly, theory is. It is a large question and one that could be pursued on any number of levels, but I would like to begin at the most general level by saying that, in general, theory comes in two forms: although even as I say that I want to qualify it by saying that by some arguments the second form of theory is not properly theory at all. Be that as it may, the two forms of discourse that at least announce themselves as theory are foundationalism and anti-foundationalism. By foundationalism I mean any attempt to ground inquiry and communication in something more firm and stable than mere belief or unexamined practice. The foundationalist strategy is first to identify that ground and then so to order our activities that they become anchored to it and are thereby rendered objective and principled. The ground so identified must have certain (related) characteristics: it must be invariant across contexts and even cultures; it must stand apart from political, partisan, and "subjective" concerns in relation to which it must act as a constraint; and it must provide a reference point or checkpoint against which claims to knowledge and success can be measured and adjudicated. In the long history of what Derrida has called the logocentric tradition of Western metaphysics, candidates for the status or position of "ground" have included God, the material or "brute act" world, rationality in general and logic in particular, a neutral-observation language, the set of eternal values, and the free and independent self. Every foundationalist project assumes the existence and availability of one or more of these grounds, and it is from this assumption that its program of research proceeds in the direction of building and elaborating a model.

As an example of such a model, it is convenient to recall the linguistics of Noam Chomsky, at least in its early or pure form. As Chomsky himself describes it, the goal of his theory is the construction of a "system of rules that in some explicit and well-defined way assigns structural descriptions to sentences" and does so in a way that "does not rely on the intelligence" of the assigning agent, of whose beliefs, cultural situation, educational experience, etc., the system remains independent. What it does rely on is a set of formal constraints which have the characteristics I have already cited: abstractness, generality, invariance across contexts. Once these constraints have been discovered and put in place, the resulting machine—Chomsky calls it a "competence grammar"—would be able to divide sentences "into the well-formed and the ill-formed just on the basis of their syntactical structure, without reference to the way things are in the world, or to what speakers, hearers, or anyone else believes."[1]

In short, the successful foundational project will have provided us with a "method," a recipe with premeasured ingredients which when ordered and combined according to absolutely explicit instructions—and the possibility of explicitness is another foundationalist assumption—will *produce,* all by itself, the correct result. In linguistics that result would be the assigning of correct descriptions to sentences; in literary studies the result would be the assigning of valid interpretation to poems and novels; and in the teaching of composition the result would be the "discovery of rules that are so fundamental as to be universal," rules that if followed would lead directly to coherence, intelligibility, readability, persuasiveness, etc.

In this last sentence I have quoted from an excellent essay by Patricia Bizzel, who goes on to rehearse some of the assumptions informing the work of foundationalist theorists of composition. They tend, she says, to see in all stages of the composing process "the same basic logical structures"; they tend also "to see differences in language use as superficial matters" because they believe that "the basic structure of language cannot change" and is "isomorphic with the innate mental structures" that enabled one to learn a language in the first place.[2] Students who have difficulty writing are somehow out of sync with their own innate structures, and it is a matter simply of getting them back in touch with the right internalized standards which they can then proceed to apply and actualize in different situations. One need only add to Bizzel's account the assumptions of a fixed and stable world with which both the innate mental structures and the universal forms of language are isomorphic, and a fixed and stable self whose operations are or should be as regular as the formalisms to which it is allied. As Richard Lanham puts it, in a capsule characterization, the foundationalist world picture includes "a positivistic social reality just 'out there' and a self just 'in here,' half way between the ears."[3] Robert Scholes offers another characterization in a chapter entitled "Is There a Fish in This Text?": "a complete self confronts a solid world, perceiving it directly and accurately, always capable of capturing it perfectly in a transparent language. Bring 'em back alive; just give us the facts ma'am; the way it was; tell it like it is; and that's the way it is."[4] Scholes rehearses this scenario only to ridicule it, to give it the label of a "naive epistemology," and to declare forthrightly what the essays by Bizzel and Lanham certainly imply, that "this . . . epistemology . . . is lying in ruins around us."[5]

What has ruined it, at least in these reports, is anti-foundationalism, a set of notions or way of thinking to which Scholes, Bizzel, and Lanham obviously subscribe. Anti-foundationalism teaches that questions of fact, truth, correctness, validity, and clarity can neither be posed nor answered in reference to some extracontextual, ahistorical, nonsituational reality, or rule, or law, or value; rather, anti-foundationalism asserts, all of these matters are intelligible and debatable only within the precincts of the contexts or situations or paradigms or communities that give them their local and changeable shape. It is not just that anti-foundationalism replaces the components of the foundationalist world-picture with other components; instead, it denies to those components the stability and independence and even the identity that is so necessary if they are to be thought of as grounds or anchors. Entities like the world, language, and the self can still be named; and value judgments having to do with validity, factuality, accuracy, and propriety can still be made; but in every case these entities and values, along with the procedures by which they are identified and marshaled, will be inextricable from the social and historical circumstances in which they do their work. In short, the very essentials that are in foundationalist discourse opposed to the local, the historical, the contingent, the variable, and the rhetorical, turn out to be irreducibly dependent on, and indeed to be functions of, the local, the historical, the contingent, the variable, and the rhetorical. Foundationalist theory fails, lies in ruins, because it is from the very first implicated in everything it claims to transcend.

Such, at any rate, is the anti-foundationalist argument, which has been made in a variety of ways and in a variety of disciplines: in philosophy by Richard Rorty, Hilary Putnam, W. V. Quine; in anthropology by Clifford Geertz and Victor Turner; in history by Hayden White; in sociology by the entire tradition of the sociology of knowledge and more recently by the ethnomethodologists; in hermeneutics by Heidegger, Gadamer, and Derrida; in the general sciences of man by Foucault; in the history of science by Thomas Kuhn; in the history of art by Michael Fried; in legal theory by Philip Bobbit and Sanford Levinson; in literary theory by Barbara Herrnstein Smith, Walter Michaels, Steven Knapp, John Fekete, Jonathan Culler, Terry Eagleton, Frank Lentricchia, Jane Tompkins, Stanley Fish, and on and on. Obviously it is not an isolated argument; in fact, today one could say that it is the *going* argument. And yet, it would be *too much* to say that the foundationalist argument lies in ruins. It is in fact remarkably resilient and resourceful in the face of attacks against it. The resistance or persistence of foundationalism usually takes the form of a counterattack in which the supposedly disastrous consequences of anti-foundationalism are paraded as a reason for rejecting it. Those consequences are usually said to extend to the loss of everything necessary to rational inquiry and successful communication. As one anti-anti-foundationalist, Israel Scheffler, puts it, without the anchor of determinate facts and an independent rationality, "controls are no more, communication has failed, the common universe of things is a delusion . . . in place of a community of rational men following objective procedures in the pursuit of truth, we have a set of isolated monads, within each of which belief forms without systematic constraints."[6]

This is a dark prophecy, a foundationalist nightmare vision in which a liberated self goes its unconstrained way believing and doing whatever it likes; but it is also a misreading of anti-foundationalism at one of its most crucial points, the insistence on situatedness. A situated self is a self whose every operation is a function of the conventional possibilities built into this or that context. Rather than unmooring the subject, as Scheffler charges, anti-foundationalism reveals the subject to be always and already tethered by the local or community norms and standards that constitute it and enable its rational acts. Such a subject can be many things: certain, confused, in turmoil, at rest, perplexed, sure. But the one thing it cannot be is free to originate its own set of isolated beliefs without systematic constraints. Whatever anti-foundationalism is or isn't, it cannot have the negative consequences feared by those who oppose it.

This brings us finally to the specific subject of this paper, the consequences of anti-foundationalism for those who do not oppose but welcome it and find in it the basis not of a fear but of a hope. As it is usually expressed, that hope follows directly from the demonstration that foundationalist methodology is based on a false picture of the human situation. Since it is not the case, as foundationalists assume, that the "scene" of communication includes a free and independent self facing a similarly independent world to which it can be linked by the rules of a universal language, a methodology based on these assumptions will necessarily fail of its goal. And conversely, if the true picture of the human situation is as anti-foundationalism gives it—a picture of men and women whose acts are socially constituted and who are embedded in a world no more stable than the historical and conventional forms of thought that bring it into being—if this is the correct picture of the human situation, then surely we can extrapolate from this picture a better set of methods for operating in the world we are constantly making and remaking, a better set of rationales and procedures for making judgments, and a better set of solutions to the problems that face us as teachers of writing.

Now, it is not hard to understand why so many have sought a methodological payoff for composition in the arguments of anti-foundationalism. Those arguments, with their talk of change, transformation, contextual variability, selves dissolved in institutional roles, etc., seem perfectly suited to the new emphasis on process over product, the replacement of a standard of correctness by the fluid and dynamic standard of effectiveness, the teaching of strategies rather than of rules and maxims, the ascendancy, in a word, of rhetoric. Indeed it is no longer accurate to call this shift in orientation "new" since, as Maxine Hairston has observed, at least in some quarters "the admonition to 'teach process, not product' is now conventional wisdom."[7] In anti-foundationalism it seems that the new conventional wisdom has found a new paradigm, one that we can presumably tap in order to put our wisdom into operation. This heady prospect is all the more attractive because it gives us a way of explaining what is at least perceived to be the failure of our efforts to date. We can now tell ourselves and others that if we have not succeeded it is because we have been laboring under the wrong epistemological assumptions, and now that we have found the right ones, success or at least dramatic improvement should follow.

As a card-carrying anti-foundationalist, I would certainly like to believe that the arguments to which I am committed will have a beneficial effect on the teaching of writing. But I am not convinced, and I would like to rehearse with you the reasons for my skepticism. On one point I am not a skeptic: there is at some level a natural "match" between anti-foundationalism and a process-oriented or rhetorical approach to composition. Indeed, another word for anti-foundationalism *is* rhetoric, and one could say without too much exaggeration that modern anti-foundationalism is old sophism writ analytic. The rehabilitation by anti-foundationalism of the claims of situation, history, politics, and convention in opposition to the more commonly successful claims of logic, brute fact empiricism, the natural, and the necessary marks one more chapter in the long history of the quarrel between philosophy and rhetoric, between the external and the temporal, between God's view and point of view. But does the fact that anti-foundationalist arguments and the slogan of writing as process in some sense "go together" mean that the first can serve as a methodological resource for the second or that, conversely, the elaboration of the second depends on a prior understanding of and commitment to the first? Let me break that question down into three smaller questions: first, does anti-foundationalism as a model of epistemology provide us with directions for achieving the epistemological state it describes? Second, is it the case that if we learn the lesson of anti-foundationalism, the lesson that we are always and already situated, we will thereby become more self-consciously situated and inhabit our situatedness in a more effective way? And third (and most practically) will the teaching of anti-foundationalism, to ourselves, and to our students, facilitate the teaching of writing? My answer to all three of these questions is no; moreover, it seems to me that it is an answer dictated by anti-foundationalism itself. It is also an answer implicit in one of Derrida's characteristically enigmatic pronouncements: "This situation has always already been announced."[8] By "this situation" Derrida means the situation in which knowledge is always and already mediated, the situation in which language rather than being the mere medium or instrument with which we interrogate the world is itself the origin of the world, of our modes of interrogation, and of ourselves. It is the situation that Derrida comes to announce in *Of Grammatology* and elsewhere; yet he says it "has always already been announced." Derrida's point is that since it has always been announced, it cannot be discovered, at least not in the sense that would give us a purchase on it that we did not have before. That is, the realization that something has always been the case does not make it more the case than it was before you realized that it was; you are still, epistemologically speaking, in the same position you were always in. The fact that we are now able to announce that we are situated does not make us more situated, and even when we could not announce it, being situated was our situation.

Ah, you say, but now we really *know* it because we know it self-consciously. But to say that is to make self-consciousness something one achieves in a space apart from situations and to make self-conscious knowledge a knowledge more firm and more "true" than the knowledge we have without reflection. This is, of course, a general assumption of liberal thought—that the only knowledge worth having is knowledge achieved disinterestedly, at a remove from one's implication in a particular situation—but it is an assumption wholly at odds with anti-foundationalism, and it is certainly curious to find it at the heart of an anti-foundationalist argument. That is, it is curious to have an argument that begins by denying the possibility of a knowledge that is independent of our beliefs and practices and ends by claiming as one of its consequences the achieving of just such an independence. But this is precisely what is claimed when the anti-foundationalist insight is said to provide us with a perspective on what we have been doing such that we are now in a position either to do it better or to do something we have not been able to do before. Indeed, any claim in which the notion of situatedness is said to be a lever that allows us to get a purchase on situations is finally a claim to have escaped situatedness, and is therefore nothing more or less than a reinvention of foundationalism by the very form of thought that has supposedly reduced it to ruins.

This is what happens in many of the essays in which anti-foundationalist theory is linked in a causal way to a revolution in the teaching of composition. As an example, consider Kenneth Bruffee's influential piece, "Liberal Education and the Social Justification of Belief." Drawing on the arguments of Kuhn, Rorty, and myself, Bruffee avails himself of the vocabulary of paradigms, interpretive communities, and the social justification of belief, and finds in it a program for the reform of teaching. We should, he says, introduce our students to "the notion of knowledge communities" and to the idea that knowledge is a function of belief rather than of an unmediated communication with the world or with a self-declaring truth. Once we help students "recognize that they are already members of communities of knowledgeable peers," then we can proceed to build from that knowledge to wider and wider communities.[9] The initial step, then, is one of "self-awareness," and in order to bring it about we should, according to Bruffee, ask students "to identify" in nonevaluative terms their own beliefs and the beliefs of the local, religious, ethnic, national, supranational, and special-interest communities they are already members of:

> Protestant students from Kansas City, Jewish students from Atlanta, Catholic students from Boston, Vietnamese from Michigan, Polish-Americans from Toledo, Chicanos, . . . blacks and whites, . . . middle class and poor, rock fans, bridge players, hockey addicts . . . people from potentially every conceivable community would become aware of what the beliefs of their own communities are, what the beliefs of other communities are, what distinguishes the beliefs of their own communities from the beliefs of other communities, and in what respects the beliefs of most communities are identical. . . . And it would help students learn how beliefs affect the way people within a community, and people of different communities, interact with each other. The curriculum would help students make these discoveries in part through self-conscious analysis, and in part through self-conscious efforts to join the several disciplinary communities that constitute the faculty of an institution of liberal education.[10]

The appearance of the word *liberal* in this last sentence is no accident, for what Bruffee has done in this paragraph is redescribe anti-foundationalism so that it becomes a new and fashionable version of democratic liberalism, a political vision that has at its center the goal of disinterestedly viewing contending partisan perspectives which are then either reconciled or subsumed in some higher or more general synthesis, in a larger and larger *consensus*—a word Bruffee uses again and again. Now I have nothing to say against this goal—at least not here—except that it is incompatible with anti-foundationalism because it assumes the possibility of getting a perspective on one's beliefs, a perspective from which those beliefs can be evaluated and compared with the similarly evaluated beliefs of others. That is, what anti-foundationalism teaches (and I apologize for saying this yet again) is the inescapability of situatedness, and if situatedness is inescapable, students could not possibly identify in nonevaluative ways their own beliefs, because as situated beings some set of beliefs of which they could not be aware would be enabling any identification they might make; and, therefore, the act of identification would from the very first be "evaluative" through and through. One could escape this logic only by saying that while the operations of the mind are always a function of context, in one operation—the identification of its own context and that of others—it is independent. Such an exemption is obviously contradictory and marks a return in Bruffee's discourse of the foundationalism he has supposedly banished. The project of building a larger and larger consensus on the insight of anti-foundationalism can only get started if the first tenet of anti-foundationalism—the situatedness of all knowledge and of all acts of knowing—is forgotten.

It is forgotten, as I have said, in the name of liberalism, and this brings up a point that deserves a paper of its own: anti-foundationalism has always been thought of as a position on the left, and one whose consequences will be favorable to the left-wing goals of reform and revolution. The reasoning is understandable: since the lesson of anti-foundationalism is that the world and its facts are not given but made, does it not follow that those who have learned the lesson will feel free to make them again? But even to ask the question in this way is to fall into the error I have already identified, the error of thinking that a conviction as to the circumstantiality of everything we know can afford us a perspective on our circumstantial knowledge and enable us to change it. What one must remember is that circumstantiality—another name for situatedness—is not something one can escape by recognizing it, since the act of recognition will itself occur within circumstances that cannot be the object of our self-conscious attention. Thus revolution and reform can take no particular warrant from anti-foundationalism, and to think otherwise is once again to make the mistake of making anti-foundationalism into a foundation.

To put the matter in a nutshell, the knowledge that one is in a situation has no particular payoff for any situation you happen to be in, because the constraints of that situation will not be relaxed by that knowledge. It follows, then, that teaching our students the lesson of anti-foundationalism, while it will put them in possession of a new philosophical perspective, will not give them a tool for operating in the world they already inhabit. Being told that you are in a situation will help you neither to dwell in it more perfectly nor to *write* within it more successfully. When Bizzel urges that we "teach students that there are such things as discourse conventions," that is, teach anti-foundationalism, she is open to the same criticism that she levels at foundationalist theorists who, she says, "assume that the rules we can formulate to *describe* behavior are the same rules that produce the behavior."[11] But that is also her assumption insofar as she believes that a description of how we come to know what we know can be turned into a set of directions for knowing. As a searching critique of method, anti-foundationalism cannot itself be made the basis of a method without losing its anti-foundationalist character.

But perhaps the link between anti-foundationalism and composition can be preserved by making it weaker. One might argue that even if anti-foundationalism cannot serve as a lever with which to master situations, it can direct us to a new area of instruction. This is in effect what is urged by Scholes when he says that "what the student needs from the teacher is help in seeing discourse structures themselves in all of their power and fullness"[12] and by Bizzel when she predicts that "the staple activity of . . . writing instruction will be analysis of the conventions of particular discourse communities."[13] Here the advice is, if all knowledge is situational, then let's teach situations.

The trouble with this advice is that in its strongest sense it cannot be followed, and in its weaker sense it cannot help but be followed, even when it hasn't been given. It can't be followed in the strong sense because it would amount to teaching situations as if (1) they were a new kind of object to which we could now turn our attention, and (2) we could achieve a distance from them such that our accounts of them would be a form of "true" knowledge. But both these "as ifs" once again reinvent foundationalism by substituting for the discredited notion of determinate facts the finally indistinguishable notion of determinate situations and by rendering unproblematic our relationship to these newly determining entities. The truth is that a situation is not an entity, but a bundle of tacit or unspoken assumptions that is simultaneously organizing the world and changing in response to its own organizing work. A situation is always on the wing, and any attempt to capture it will only succeed in fixing it in a shape it no longer has. Moreover, any attempt to capture it must itself be mounted from within a situation, and therefore the knowledge afforded by such an exercise is not only out-of-date but disputable. In short, if the teaching of the theory of situations is inefficacious, the teaching of situations themselves is impossible and a contradiction in terms.

In another sense, however, the weak sense, teaching situations is not only possible but inevitable, irrespective of one's "doctrinal" position. For if anti-foundationalism is correct and everything we know is always a function of situations, then everything we teach is always situational knowledge, whether we label it so or not. That is to say, even if a student is being presented with a piece of knowledge—of grammar, of propriety, of whatever—as if it were independent, detached, and transferable (i.e., "cashable" in any and all situations), it is not thereby *rendered* independent, detached, and transferable. Therefore composition teachers are always teaching situations because they can do nothing else.

Thus, for example, all classical rhetoricians regard metaphor and other figures as departures from ordinary or normative speech, as forms of inappropriateness that are nonetheless useful and even necessary in this or that situation; but while the normative is supposedly the measure of figurative appropriateness and is constantly invoked as the unchanging ground against which departures can be measured and assessed, it in fact never appears in the long catalogs offered us by Quintilian and others. What does appear is example after example of speech that is effective in particular situations; and so many are the situations and so protean and shifting are the figurative possibilities, that one cannot escape the conclusion that situatedness and not correctness is the rhetorician's true subject. Consequently, while those who have been taught by and now teach Quintilian may think that they are adhering to a foundationalist model, and may defend such a model against relativistic incursions, they are in fact teaching what Bizzel and Scholes and others now urge them to teach.

Or, for another example, consider the case of E. D. Hirsch, until recently one of the most prominent champions of a pedagogy based on normative notions of correctness, readability, and quantifiable effects. As many of you will know, Hirsch has recently recanted and now says along with everyone else that the "formal elements of language cannot be successfully separated from vast domains of underlying cultural information" and that therefore "we cannot do a good job of teaching, reading, and writing if we neglect . . . particular cultural vocabularies."[14] Does this mean that Hirsch wasn't doing a good job earlier or that he was teaching something beside cultural vocabularies before he came to recognize the impossibility of avoiding them? I would venture to guess that he was as good a teacher of composition before he saw the contextual light as he is now. Not only does being converted to anti-foundationalism bring with it no pedagogical payoff; being opposed to anti-foundationalism entails no pedagogical penalty.

Everything I have said so far can be reformulated in terms that might seem paradoxical, but are not: if all knowledge is situational and we are always and already in a situation, then we can never be at any distance from the knowledge we need. Anti-foundationalism cannot give us the knowledge we seek because its lesson is that we already have it. This is explicitly the lesson taught by Polanyi in the name of "tacit knowledge." Tacit knowledge is knowledge already known or dwelt in; it cannot be handed over in the form of rules or maxims and theories; there is, as James Reither observes, "no transition from 'knowing that' to 'knowing how.' " And yet, Reither apparently forgets his own observation when he asserts that knowing that knowledge is tacit "provides a theoretical rationale" for certain ways of teaching as opposed to others, for ways of teaching that will help "bring about" a "tacit integration" of otherwise empty maxims. But this is to turn the knowledge that knowledge is tacit into a recipe for achieving it, when of course the lesson of tacit knowledge is that it cannot be achieved by recipe, by the handing over of an explicit maxim, even when the maxim is itself. As an argument that denies the possibility of learning by rule, the theory of tacit knowledge cannot legitimate some set of rules for learning. Neither can it rule out any. According to Reither, once we know that knowledge is tacit, we know that "students cannot learn to write only by being told . . . hundreds upon hundreds of explicit maxims."[15] But this is itself a maxim and one that is contradicted by history: insofar as there has been and continues to be such a pedagogy, many of the students subjected to it have learned how to write; and they have learned how to write in part because the maxims they are given are not explicit at all, in the sense of being detached from a tacitly known practice, but are the precipitations of a practice, whether they are presented as such or not. The notion of tacit or situational knowledge is simply too powerful to be endangered by a method that is ignorant of it; indeed, in the strongest sense a method cannot be ignorant of it, no matter how much it tries. The lesson of tacit knowledge—the lesson that it cannot be the object or the beneficiary of self-consciousness—must be extended to the theory of itself. Knowing that knowledge is tacit cannot put us in more possession of it or enable us to possess it in a heightened way; and *not* knowing that knowledge is tacit cannot deprive us of it. To make the notion of tacit knowledge either into a recipe for learning or into a set of requirements for a "good" pedagogy is to exempt it from its own insight.

The conclusion I am reaching is a conclusion approached by J. Hillis Miller, who then immediately shies away from it. Miller reports that "empirical studies of the relative effectiveness of different theories of teaching writing are not . . . reassuring. They suggest that students will get somewhat better whatever the teacher does, perhaps through sheer praxis. One learns to write by writing."[16] Miller, as I have said, shies away from this conclusion, and he does so in the name of a belief "in the reasonableness of things"—a belief that translates into a conviction that there simply must be a connection between theory and practice. Miller's "swerve" is a strong testimony to the need felt by many to believe that what they do can be justified or explained by a set of principles that stands apart from their practice, by a theory. One cannot argue against that need, nor can one dismiss the narrative of self-discovery it often produces, the narrative in which conversion to a theory leads directly to a revolution in practice. But this is a narrative that belongs properly to a foundationalist hero, to someone who has just discovered a truth above the situational and now returns to implement it; it cannot, without contradiction, be the narrative of an anti-foundationalist hero who can only enact his heroism by refusing to take either comfort or method from his creed.

It is a hard move to make or not to make because it brings so little immediate satisfaction and leaves the would-be theorist with so little to do. After having announced that foundationalist epistemology "lies in ruins" Scholes asks, "what do we do in response to this situation?" and rehearses two alternative courses of action: "either we can assume that our practice has nothing to do with theory, or we can make the opposite assumption and try to use the new developments in . . . poststructuralist theory as the basis of a *new practice* in the teaching of composition."[17] Since this is only page five of a twenty-page essay, we know in advance which alternative Scholes will choose, and by choosing it he gives himself the incalculable advantage of having something to say and something to sell. I have had a lot to say, but I have nothing to sell, except the not-very-helpful news, if it is news, that practice has nothing to do with theory, at least in the sense of being enabled and justified by theory. This leaves me and you only a few worn and familiar bromides: practice makes perfect, you learn to write by writing, you must build on what you already know; but anti-foundationalism tells us that these bromides are enough, tells us that as situated beings our practice *can* make perfect, and that we already know more than we think. Perhaps I should apologize for taking up so much of your time in return for so small a yield; but the smallness of the yield has been my point. It is also the point of anti-foundationalism, which offers you nothing but the assurance that what it is unable to give you—knowledge, goals, purposes, strategies—is what you already have. And come to think of it, that may be an offer you can't refuse.

16. Still Wrong After All These Years

Ronald Dworkin's new book, *Law's Empire,* is quite long, but its basic argument is easily grasped. Dworkin is looking for an account of law that both fits legal practice and can serve as a justification of it. He finds that account in what he calls "law as integrity" (the latest version of what earlier in his work was termed first "articulate consistency" and then "chain practice"), a notion he defines in opposition to conventionalist and pragmatist accounts of law. A conventionalist account, as Dworkin characterizes it, is one which "restricts the law of a community to the explicit extension of its legal conventions like legislation and precedent" (p. 124). The consequence (an unfortunate one in Dworkin's view) is that when the conventions run out—when situations arise in the law that conventions do not cover—judges are left on their own and "must find some wholly forward-looking ground of decision" (p. 95). Although conventionalism begins by insisting on severe—indeed positivistic—constraints, it ends in a vision of constraints entirely left behind. Pragmatism's route to inadequacy is even shorter in Dworkin's story, for a pragmatist's first principle is that there are no first principles, merely the judge's opinion as to what, at any moment, is the best thing to do. In a pragmatist account of law, "judges do and should make whatever decisions seem to them best for the community's future," irrespective of "any form of consistency with the past as valuable for its own sake" (p. 95).

For law as integrity, in contrast, consistency is the chief obligation. It "requires a judge to test his interpretation of any part of the great network of political structures and decisions of his community by asking whether it could form part of a coherent theory justifying the network as a whole" (p. 245). That is to say, "law as integrity asks judges to assume . . . that the law is structured by a coherent set of principles about justice and fairness and procedural due process, and it asks them to enforce these in the fresh cases that come before them, so that each person's situation is fair and just according to the same standards" (p. 243). The contrast is clear and (apparently) powerful: conventionalism offers rigid and mechanical principles that are inadequate to the unfolding complexity of legal life, while pragmatism forsakes even the possibility of linking up with a history that principle has informed. Only law as integrity affords both flexibility and continuity, for when a fresh case presents an apparently novel face, law as integrity neither throws up its hands in resignation (as a strong conventionalism would) nor decides on the basis of wholly contemporary pressures (as pragmatism must). Rather, it labors to bring the case in line with a chain of decisions, attending not to the particular details or outcomes of those decisions but to the underlying story ("coherent theory") their succession tells. In short, law as integrity at once respects history (as pragmatism does not), but refuses to be bound by its surface or literal shape (as conventionalism is), looking instead to the *abstract* shape to which history points and from which it is derived.

In what follows I shall put forward three related objections to Dworkin's thesis. I shall argue first that his critique of conventionalism and pragmatism, however persuasive or unpersuasive it might be, is irrelevant because neither is a program according to which a judge might generate his practice. I shall then turn directly to the concept of "law as integrity" and question the claim (made frequently) that it represents an additional or extra step in adjudication—a "distinct virtue" (p. 411)—which can be invoked as a constraint against the appeal of lesser virtues and as a check against the pressures of the political and the personal. And, finally, I shall contend that if "law as integrity" is anything, it is either the name of what we already do (without any special prompting) or a rhetorical/political strategy by means of which we give a certain necessary coloring to what we've already done.

My first point, then, is that conventionalism and pragmatism are not names of possible forms of self-conscious action. Conventionalism is not a possible form of action because for one to be able to "perform" it—to "do" conventionalism—it would have to be the case that language, at least in some of its instantiations, can set limits on its own interpretation. That is, after all, what conventionalism, as Dworkin defines it, asserts: certain words found in certain authoritative texts (the Constitution, statutes, precedents) contain explicit directions that serve to guide the activities of legal actors. "A right or responsibility flows from past decisions only if it is explicit within them or can be made explicit through methods . . . accepted by the legal profession as a whole" (p. 95). The attraction of conventionalism is the constraint it seems to place on the interpretive power of judges and administrators; an avowedly conventional jurist will feel himself bound by the explicit or literal meaning of the appropriately identified texts.

But, of course, this entire picture of things, and the possibility of *being* a conventionalist, depends on the assumption that explicit or literal meanings do in fact exist, and it is my contention that they do not. It is also Dworkin's contention, at least when he (correctly) observes that conventionally authoritative texts, rather than limiting interpretation, are the objects of interpretation: different legal actors may point to the "same" authoritative texts but assert for them entirely different meanings, and their opinions will, as Dworkin says, "express an interpretation rather than a direct or uncontroversial application of the institution of legislation" (p. 123). In fact, there is no possibility of a direct or uncontroversial application of the institution of legislation or of anything else. To be sure, you can always cite a statute or a piece of the Constitution and declare roundly that you stand on it and will not go beyond it; but, in fact, you will *already* have gone beyond it, if by "it" you understand a meaning that declares itself and repels interpretation. Meanings only become perspicuous against a background of interpretive assumptions in the absence of which reading and understanding would be impossible. A meaning that seems to leap off the page, propelled by its own self-sufficiency, is a meaning that flows from interpretive assumptions so deeply embedded that they have become invisible.

They can sometimes be made visible by someone who hears the "same" words within different assumptions in relation to which a quite other meaning "leaps off the page." Consider, for example, the stipulation in the Constitution that no one shall be eligible to be president "who shall not have attained to the age of thirty-five years"—a clause often cited wistfully by those who wish that the entire document had been written in the same absolutely explicit and precise language. But its explicitness and precision seem less certain the moment one pauses to ask an apparently nonsensical question: What did the writers mean by thirty-five years of age? The commonsensical answer is that by thirty-five years of age they meant thirty-five years of age; but thirty-five is a point on a scale, and the scale is a scale of something; in this case a scale of *maturity* as determined in relation to such matters as life expectancy, the course of education, the balance between vigor and wisdom, etc. When the framers chose to specify thirty-five as the minimal age of the president they did so against a background of concerns and cultural conditions within which "thirty-five" had a certain meaning; and one could argue (should there for some reason be an effort to "relax" the requirement in either direction) that since those conditions have changed—life expectancy is much higher, the period of vigor much longer, the course of education much extended—the meaning of thirty-five has changed too, and "thirty-five" now means "fifty." One might object that this argument (which has already been developed in different ways by Mark Tushnet, Gary Peller, and Giradeau Spann, among others) could be made only by instituting special circumstances within which "thirty-five" received a meaning other than its literal one; but the circumstances within which the framers wrote and understood thirty-five were no less special; and therefore the literal meaning thirty-five had for them was no less contextually produced than the literal meaning thirty-five might now have for those who hear it within the assumption of contemporary political and social conditions.

The moral is clear: someone who stands on a literal or explicit meaning in facts stands on an interpretation, albeit an interpretation so firmly in place that it is impossible (at least for the time being) not to take as literal and unassailable the meanings it subtends. What is also clear is that this truth about meaning (it is always and already interpretive) means that conventionalism is not a possible program for judicial action, for to *be* a conventionalist is to bind oneself to meanings that have not been sullied by one's interpretive assumptions, and since there are no such meanings that is not something one could possibly do. Dworkin himself seems almost to say as much in his discussion of "soft" as opposed to "strict" conventionalism. Strict conventionalism is the impossible program we have been discussing; it "restricts the law of a community to the explicit extension of its legal conventions like legislation and precedent" (p. 124). Soft conventionalism, on the other hand, "insists that the law of a community includes everything within the implicit extension of these conventions" (p. 124). Of course, since what is and is not an implicit extension will always be a matter of dispute and interpretation, Dworkin is correct to conclude that soft conventionalism "is not really a form of conventionalism at all" (p. 127), and that "if conventionalism is to provide a distinct and muscular conception of law . . . it must be strict, not soft, conventionalism" (p. 128). I would add only that since it is a practical impossibility, strict conventionalism cannot provide a distinct and muscular conception of law either and that, therefore, there is no point in arguing against it.

The same thing can be said of pragmatism, although for slightly different reasons. A pragmatist, as Dworkin defines him, would be one who does not take into account "any form of consistency with the past" (p. 95). Not bound by any sense of obligation to history, he would "stand ready to revise his practice" and "the scope of what he counts as legal rights" in the light of his judgment as to which course of action best serves the community's future (pp. 154, 95). His actions would comprise "a set of discrete decisions" which he would be "free to make or amend one by one, with nothing but a strategic interest in the rest" (p. 167), with "no underlying commitment to any . . . fundamental public conception of justice" (p. 189). My question simply is, could there be such a person performing such actions, and my answer is, no. What, for example, would a "discrete decision" be like? If we are to take Dworkin at his word, it would be a decision that turned on a judgment of what was best for the community's future irrespective of the history of decisions, statutes, and invoking of precedents that preceded it. But where would one's sense of what was "best" come from if not from that very history, which, because it formed the basis of the agent's education, would be the content of his judgment? The very ability to formulate a decision in terms that would be recognizably legal depends on one's having internalized the norms, categorical distinctions, and evidentiary criteria that make up one's understanding of what the law is. That understanding is developed in the course of an educational experience whose materials are the unfolding succession of cases, holdings, dissents, legislative actions, etc., that are the stuff of law school instruction and of the later instruction one receives in a clerkship or as a junior associate. These are not materials the legal actor thinks *about;* they are the material with which and within which he thinks, and therefore whether he "knows" it or not, whether he likes it or not, his very thinking is irremediably historical, consistent with the past in the sense that it flows from the past.

Dworkin's discussion of pragmatism repeatedly refers to the actions of "self-conscious" pragmatists (p. 154)—lawyers and judges who, if asked to render an account of their practice, would reply in pragmatist terms and say that when they decide something they never seriously consider the history of the enterprise, but make "discrete decisions." My point is that even if there are those who would thus characterize their actions, they would be mistaken, and the mistake they would be making is the mistake Dworkin makes when he hypothesizes about them: the mistake of assuming a direct and causal relationship between one's account of one's practice and the actual shape of that practice. The mere fact that a lawyer or a judge *says* that he is doing something impossible (acting freely and in disregard of the past) doesn't make him capable of doing it. One can be a "self-conscious" pragmatist only in the sense that one can sincerely believe oneself to be acting on pragmatist principles (or, from Dworkin's perspective, nonprinciples), but self-conscious pragmatist action, as opposed to the philosophical action of thinking of oneself as a pragmatist, is not an available option, and therefore there is no need to counsel against it.

That, of course, has been my argument all along, that Dworkin's strictures against conventionalism and pragmatism are "academic" (in the familiar pejorative sense) because they are not positions one could put into practice; and this argument, if understood, already includes the argument that "law as integrity" is a position that one could not fail to put into practice. The reasoning is simple: if pragmatism is not an option for practice because the history it supposedly ignores is an ingredient of any judge's understanding, then law as integrity, which enjoins us to maintain a continuity with history, enjoins us to something we are already doing. This is a conclusion that Dworkin would certainly resist since it is his basic thesis that law as integrity is a "distinct political virtue" (pp. 166, 411), a thesis that is first developed in the context of a distinction between conversational and constructive (or creative) interpretation. Conversational interpretation is the name of what a hearer does when processing the words of a speaker: "it assigns meaning in the light of the motives and purposes and concerns it supposes the speaker to have, and it reports its conclusions as statements about his intention in saying what he did" (p. 50). Constructive interpretation, on the other hand, turns on the purposes not of "some author, but of the interpreter": "Roughly, constructive interpretation is a matter of imposing purpose on an object or practice in order to make of it the best possible example of the form or genre to which it is taken to belong" (p. 52).

Now, much in this book depends on what Dworkin intends when he counsels us, as he does here, to make of something the "best" it can be. On the evidence of what he says here, the procedure seems to be a two-step one in which the interpreter first determines the shape (or meaning) an object apparently has, and then wrestles it into another shape according to some prior sense of what it would be *best* for it to mean. The trouble with this account of interpretation is that it commits Dworkin to both of the positions he wants to avoid: strict conventionalism and freewheeling pragmatism. The account is conventionalist, or formalist, in that it posits an identity for the object apart from any interpretation of it (step one); but it is pragmatist, and, in fact, subjectivist, when it assigns to the interpreter the power of *imposing* purpose (step two). Indeed, if we take the word "imposing" seriously, this is not an account of interpretation at all, but an instance of what Dworkin has elsewhere stigmatized as "changing" or "altering."

Dworkin is obviously uneasy about moving in that direction, for he immediately checks himself with this defensive qualification: "It does not follow . . . that an interpreter can make of a practice or a work of art anything he would have wanted it to be. . . . For the history or shape of a practice or object constrains the available interpretations of it" (p. 52). But to say this is to fall right back into the formalist trap, for while the caveat may absolve the interpreter of the charge of willful imposition, it does so at the expense of his creativity; if the object or practice constrains what can be said about its purposes, then there is very little (if anything) for the interpreter to construct, and therefore no difference at all between conversational and constructive interpretation. At this point Dworkin again reacts against his own formulation, and in the next sentence he veers back in the direction of constructive creativity—returning purpose to the interpreter. "Creative interpretation, in the constructive view, is a matter of interaction between purpose and object." This time, however, he attempts to arrest the pendulum and soften his dilemma by means of the word "interaction," which suggests that purpose (and power) are distributed *between* the object and the interpreter. But that suggestion has no intelligible translation since, even if the object only dictates the *range* of the purposes that can be predicated of it, it still holds all the power, whereas, on the other hand, if the choice of purpose belongs to the interpreter, then the power is wholly his. Either the object or practice is *already* the best it can be and doesn't need the interpreter's help (in which case Dworkin is a positivist) or by *making* it the best it can be, the interpreter rides roughshod over the object and refashions it (in which case Dworkin is a subjectivist).

But, Dworkin might object, you miss the point. True, the interpreter imposes a purpose (and therefore a meaning) on the object, but the purpose is not his own and neither does it belong to the object, at least not in any simple or superficial way. Rather, it belongs to that "coherent theory" (p. 245) or abiding "set of principles" (p. 243) which, while they may not be explicit in particular decisions or statutes, are what "the explicit decisions presuppose by way of justification" (p. 96). The idea is that the continuity of legal practice is not something one can spot on its surface, but is something one can grasp only by seeing through the practice to the underlying and abstract assumptions of which particular decisions and statutes are the intended instantiations. That is the interpreter's task: to construct or reconstruct that abstract shape and then to characterize and decide the present case in a way that makes of it a confirmation and extension of that same shape. Such an interpreter is creative without being willful since he is guided by something independent of him, and he is also constrained without being slavishly so since the something that guides him is something he must construct.

This more complex picture is at first glance both coherent and satisfying, but at second glance it exhibits the old familiar problems. First of all, it rests on a distinction between legal practice as a set of discrete acts and legal practice as a continually unfolding story about such principles as justice, fairness, and equality. But the distinction is a false one, for it is not possible (except in a positivist world of isolated brute phenomena) to conceive of a legal act apart from just that story and those principles. Indeed, as I pointed out in the first of my exchanges with Dworkin, "a case could not even be seen as a case if it were not *from the very first* regarded as an item in a judicial field and therefore as the embodiment of some or other principle."[1] If one were to construe a case without any such regard or strong sense of the judicial field as both a structure and an ongoing narrative, the result would not be a case at all, but a set of facts and meanings that would touch only accidentally and intermittently on legal emphases and concerns. The truth of this could be attested to by those many law students who spend most of their first year not being able to make the *right* sense of the materials before them, until that happy (and mysterious) day when everything, or at least most things, suddenly become clear, at least to the extent that they now feel they are in the game. It is not that the novice student sees the practice detached from the principles underlying it; he doesn't see "the practice" at all but something else (perhaps some other practice if its assumptions are strongly enough the content of his perception). Conversely, the initiated student who has thoroughly internalized the distinctions, categories, and notions of relevance and irrelevance that comprise "thinking like a lawyer," cannot see anything *but* the practice (nor can he remember what it was like to not see it) and along with it, because it is inseparable from the practice, he sees the set of principles of whose unfolding the practice is the story.

Dworkin is right, then, to insist that present cases must be construed as instances of a general and continuing narrative about justice and equality. But he is wrong to think of that narrative as something that must be first constructed and then *added* to a first-level perception of discrete events, for the competent lawyer or judge is always and already an actor in that narrative and is necessarily telling its story with his every gesture. Dworkin comes close to seeing this when he entertains the possibility of collapsing the two categories of conversational and constructive interpretation into one:

> The constructive account of creative interpretation, therefore, could perhaps provide a more general account of creative interpretation in all its forms. We would then say that all interpretation strives to make an object the best it can be, as an instance of some assumed enterprise, and that interpretation takes different forms in different contexts only because different enterprises engage different standards of value or success. Artistic interpretation differs from scientific interpretation, we should say, only because we judge success in works of art by standards different from those we use to judge explanations of physical phenomena. (p. 53)

This is almost right: all interpretation *does* strive to make an object the best it can be if we understand "best" to mean nothing more (or less) than the standard of value or relevance that is the defining characteristic of that object. So that, for example, the defining characteristic of a judicial opinion would be that it presented itself as flowing from the principles of justice, of a scientific explanation that it strove to be accurate, of a work of art that it set out to be beautiful or profound or unified. In each instance the interpretation of the object would begin from within the assumption that it was *that* kind of object one was interpreting and therefore, simply by virtue of his interpretive "style" or angle of interpretive entry, the interpreter would *already*—from the very first—be seeing the object as an instance of its defining aspiration (to be accurate, or just, or beautiful). That is, he would be seeing it as "the best it could be," a standard *built into* that aspiration. All interpretation would then fall under the same category, but it would be conversational, assigning "meaning in the light of the motives and purposes and concerns it supposes the speaker to have." Those motives would be understood to include the motive of producing the kind of meaning appropriate to the enterprise and its built-in sense of value, and no effort to add value by a special act of construction would be necessary.

But Dworkin is committed to these being such a special or extra act—a distinct level of interpretive striving which distinguishes the truly responsible interpreter—and it is time to inquire into the reasons for his commitment. One reason returns us to his earliest work and to a fear that his writings consistently display: the fear of individual or subjective preference. In *Law's Empire* the additional interpretive step enjoined by the doctrine of "law as integrity" has precisely the function of constraining or checking preference. The idea is that a judge may, by virtue of his own opinions and desires, prefer a particular outcome in a case, but if he practices "law as integrity" he will be in possession of a "coherent theory," or set of abstract principles, which he will then interpose between the case and his own opinions (pp. 341, 258). Thus, for example, a judge "deciding" *McLoughlin*—a well-known case that turns on the question of compensation for emotional injury—may personally believe (a nonsense phrase that I use here only for the sake of argument) that no one should be compensated for emotional injury, but "if he accepts integrity"—that is, if he considers himself to be respecting and continuing an institutional history—"and knows that some victims of emotional injury have already been given a right to compensation, he will have a reason for deciding in favor of Mrs. McLoughlin nevertheless" (p. 177).

The example suggests that there are two kinds of reasons—personal ones and institutional ones—and that if a judge "accepts integrity" as his working principle the institutional reason will exert a pressure that would not be felt by a judge who feels free to discount the history of past decisions. But are the two kinds of reasons really so different? How does a judge come to "think it unjust to require compensation for any emotional injury" (p. 177)? Indeed, what makes a judge *capable* of having such a thought? It will be available to him only because his very ways of thinking have been formed by that institutional history in which notions like compensation, categories like emotional vs. physical injury, and distinctions between just and unjust were assumed and in place. In short, the so-called personal reason is no less institutional and attentive to history than the reason that derives from a commitment to "integrity," and, indeed, the very notion of a "personal" reason that a judge might assert against his obligation to the history of past decisions is finally incoherent. Any reason that finds its way into a judge's calculations will be perforce a *legal* one, and therefore one whose very existence is a function of that history (that is, of some view of it)—a history he could not possibly discount even if he declared himself to be doing so. (This is simply to repeat, from a slightly different angle, my argument against the possibility of a pragmatist judicial practice.)

This is not to deny that judges might have personal reasons of another more alarming kind. A judge hearing *McLoughlin* might be inclined to decide against the plaintiff because she reminds him of a hated stepmother or because she belongs to an ethnic group he reviles. But think of what he would have to do in order to "work" such "reasons" into his decision. He could not, of course, simply declare them, because they are not, at least in our culture, legal reasons and would be immediately stigmatized as inappropriate. Instead, he would be obliged to find recognizably legal reasons that could lead to an outcome in harmony with his prejudices; but if he did that he would not be ruled by those prejudices, but by the institutional requirement that only certain kinds of arguments—arguments drawn from the history of concerns and decisions—be employed.

We begin to see that the fear of personal preferences is an empty one, and I would go so far as to say that there are no such things as "personal preferences" if by that phrase one means preferences formed apart from contexts of principle. A preference is something one cannot have independently of some institution or enterprise within which the preference could emerge as an option, and an institution or enterprise is itself inconceivable independent of some general purpose or value— some principle—its activities express. It follows, then, that it is a mistake to oppose preference to principle. Rather, what opposition there is will be between preferences that are appropriate to a given enterprise and preferences that are appropriate to some other enterprise; and, more often than not, there is no choice to be made between them since the choice has *already* been made the moment you see yourself as being engaged in one enterprise rather than another. I may be a judge deciding a case involving voter fraud who "personally" prefers one political party to another (it would be hard to imagine a judge of whom this would not be true), but if I am thinking of myself as a judge, I automatically conceive of my task as a judicial one and comport myself accordingly. Or, on a scale of pleasurable activities, I might prefer watching a baseball game on television to having tea with my mother-in-law, but as a husband who wishes to remain happily married, I might prefer to do the prudent thing. The conflict, then, is never between preference and principle, but between preferences that represent different principles, and if I am deeply enough embedded in some principled enterprise, the conflict will never be actualized because some preferences simply will not come into play.

Of course, there can be conflict between the preferences—or pulls—that represent different principles within the umbrella of an overarching (and principled) enterprise. This is the situation that Dworkin imagines when he posits a judge whose conviction regarding the justness of compensation for emotional injury is at odds with his reading of the chain of decisions in which the matter has been in dispute. That judge, as Dworkin says, will have a reason for deciding in Mrs. McLoughlin's favor. That reason needn't be decisive, however, for the judge may view it as a challenge to the exercising of his judicial skills, or as an invitation either to reread the chain of decisions in a way that excludes the present case from its scope or to characterize the present case in a way that leads it to be seen as turning on an issue other than the issue linking the chain of decisions. The judge who succeeds in doing either will not have chosen preference over principle, or personal conviction over the obligation to continue the judicial enterprise. Rather, he will have continued the enterprise by combining two of its legitimate elements— notions of what is and is not just and a deference to the "conversation" in which the nature of justice has been debated—into a story that links them together. *Whatever shape that story then has will be a principled shape; that is to say, it will be a shape that reflects a commitment to law as integrity.*

What this means is that "law as integrity" is not the name of a *special* practice engaged in only by gifted or Herculean judges, but the name of the practice engaged in "naturally"—without any additional prompting—by any judge whose ways of conceiving his field of action are judicial, that is, by any judge. The moment he sees a case *as* a case, a judge is already seeing it as an item in a judicial history, and at the same moment he is already in the act of fashioning (with a view toward later telling) a story in which his exposition of the case exists in a seamless continuity with his exposition (and understanding) of the enterprise as a whole. In one of the many places at which he recommends "law as integrity" as a *method*, Dworkin declares that it is "possible for any judge to confront fresh and challenging issues as a matter of principle, and this is what law as integrity demands of him" (p. 258). My point is that it is impossible for a judge to do anything else and still be acting and thinking like a judge, and that therefore the demands of integrity are always and already being met. Dworkin's conditional clause, "if he accepts integrity" (p. 177), is superfluous since acceptance is simultaneous with his acceptance of his role. (It is as if one distinguished between those baseball players who thought it their obligation to try and score runs and those who thought it something else.) As an account of what legal actors do, "law as integrity" is powerful and persuasive; lawyers and judges do, in fact, see the law as "structured by a set of coherent principles" which they feel obliged to take into account and extend. But, precisely because this is what they already do by virtue of their being judges and lawyers, it is pointless to enjoin them to do it.

But enjoining them to do it is Dworkin's whole point, and this is the second reason for his commitment to "law as integrity" (the first, you will recall, is to keep personal preference in check): it gives Dworkin something to do and something to be. That something to do is to urge integrity, and the something to be is a philosopher. Indeed, from its very beginning, the book is an argument for the necessity of philosophy and for the superiority of that judge who is the most philosophical which, in Dworkin's terms, means the judge most capable of abstracting away from the everyday world of practical pressures. The Herculean or philosophical judge, mired as we all are in the machinations and calculations of political agents, is nevertheless "aware of a different, more abstract calculation: *pure* integrity . . . invites him to consider what the law would be if judges were free simply to pursue coherence in the principles of justice that flow through and unite different departments of law" (pp. 405–6). These principles are the con-

tent of "pure integrity" for they "offer the best justification of the present law seen from the perspective of no institution in particular" (p.
407); and since even the best judge is confined within the perspective
of his institution, "it falls to philosophers . . . to work out law's ambitions, the purer form of law within and beyond the law we have"
(p. 407).

I pass over the egregious elitism of this picture (the ladder of insight with ordinary, unreflective people at the bottom rung, conventionalists and pragmatists slightly higher, practitioners of law as integrity nearing the top and looking upward to the one philosopher who
resides wholly in integrity's realm) to note that this is the latest version
of an impulse that Dworkin's work has displayed from the very beginning, the impulse to ascend "from the battleground of power politics
to the forum of principle."[2] Thus in the last of his characterizations of
"law as integrity" Dworkin declares that its aim is "to lay principle over
practice to show the best route to a better future, keeping the right faith
with the past" (p. 413). As a recommendation, however, this makes
sense only if practice is or could be unprincipled, if it is merely a collection or succession of actions unrelated by any overarching norms or
goals. But as I have argued again and again, insofar as practice is always practice of *something* (of law, literary criticism, baseball), its gestures are already informed by the sense of value and continuity that
make that something a distinct activity. In short, one is always in the
forum of principle; it is simply that the forum of principle one is in
may not be the one acknowledged by others. The distinction between
principle and policy—the distinction with which Dworkin began his
career and which sustains it today—is finally a *political* distinction, a
distinction with the political aim of claiming for some policy the label
of principle.

This is not to say that the distinction is invoked insincerely or for
base motives; the motives will be those that are inherent in asserting
a position or point of view in which you believe, for in relation to that
point of view the assertions of others flow not from principle but from
policy (or false principle). It is just that whenever the distinction between principle and policy is invoked, the line it draws will be bright
and visible only within the assumptions of some policy that is, for the
moment, so deeply in force as to be beyond challenge; but the challenge can always be made, and when it is, that line—interpretive, constructed, and political to the core—will be drawn again. Either the fo-

rum of principle—"the perspective of no institution in particular"—is empty and therefore incapable of guiding or constraining, or it is the name of a policy (of an institutional perspective) that has achieved a particular political and institutional success. Either we could never ascend it or we are always and already within it—always in the grip of some vision that is at once the content and the set of practices of the enterprise in which we are embedded. I believe the latter to be the case, and therefore any discourse striving to operate within a "pure" form of principle will always be thin and (to say the least) uncompelling. This is why Dworkin's lengthy accounts of Hercules making his way through hypothetical cases, although they are intended to be the centerpiece of the book, are flat and uninteresting. To be interesting they would have to be nonhypothetical arguments Dworkin was actually making in the service of a specific program he wished us to adopt, for only then could they speak to concerns that we might actually have, concerns relative to issues of policy and politics (the only kind of issues there are). One of the ironies of *Law's Empire* is that the closer it gets to its announced ideal, the less of a claim it has on our serious attention.

To summarize, *Law's Empire* has a negative and a positive argument. The negative argument warns us against the dangers of conventionalism and pragmatism, but since these are not forms of possible judicial practice, the warning is unnecessary. The positive argument urges us to adopt "law as integrity," but since that is the form our judicial practice already and necessarily takes, the urging is superfluous. Behind both arguments lies the ideal of inhabiting a forum where principle is pure and personal and political appeals have been eliminated, but since that ideal is either empty or already filled with everything it would exclude, a book commending it to us is finally a book with very little to say.

Of course, there are incidental pleasures along the way, chief among them an excellent ten pages in which Dworkin distinguishes sharply between internal and external skepticism. Internal skepticism is that doubt one might have about an assertion from within a position that allows (indeed, demands) judgments of rightness and wrongness. Thus one might reject a way of characterizing *Hamlet* in the conviction that some other characterization is the correct one. An external skeptic, on the other hand, would reject the whole notion of correctness, since it is his thesis that all claims to correctness about *Hamlet* or anything else are ungrounded; his doubt is not about a particular assertion, but about the status of assertion in general. Dworkin's point is that "external skepticism cannot threaten any interpretive project" (p. 82), because any interpretive project will only have shape from within a set of moral or evaluative assumptions of just the kind that external skepticism refuses to acknowledge. It follows, then, that with respect to the issues that *are* issues within those assumptions, external skepticism's challenge is irrelevant. As a stance or attitude, it is, as Dworkin says, determinedly "disengaged" (p. 80), and because it is disengaged it has nothing to say; it does not reflect on judgments pronounced or heard by already engaged agents. What those agents are engaged in are practices, and within those practices judgments of correctness and incorrectness have all the traction one might desire. If we assert *Hamlet* is about delay and that slavery is wrong, the practices within which we hazard those assertions give them "all the meaning they need or could have" (p. 83), and the reality of that meaning is in no way compromised by the "metaphysical" (wholly abstract) pronouncements of external skepticism (p. 79).

Dworkin's point is not new, but it is one that cannot be made too often. Unfortunately, it is also one that undercuts his own project in exactly the ways I have here outlined. The superfluousness of "external skepticism" is precisely the superfluousness of "law as integrity." Just as external skepticism does not touch assertions internal to a particular interpretive system, so is "law as integrity" an unnecessary (and empty) addition to a system of practice that already displays what it would provide. Both notions are stand-ins for the general claim of philosophy to be a model of reflection that exists on a level superior to, and revelatory of, mere practice. But, in fact, "external skepticism" and "law as integrity" are themselves practices—philosophical practices, practices of speculation that emerge from the special context of academic philosophy where the constructing of a "perspective of no institution in particular" is the first order of business—and the mistake is to assume that as philosophical practices they have anything to say about practices internal to disciplines other than philosophy. It is a mistake Dworkin himself identifies and scorns when he observes that the external skeptic tries to speak from the outside and inside at once and doesn't see that the radical detachment of the one perspective wholly undermines its relevance to the other (p. 83). It is the mistake that Dworkin himself makes throughout the book. Indeed, it is the mistake that *is* the book.[3]

17. Dennis Martinez and the Uses of Theory

I On June 24, 1985, Dennis Martinez, then a pitcher for the Balti-more Orioles, was caught by journalist Ira Berkow in the act of talking to his manager, Earl Weaver, shortly before the beginning of a game with the Yankees. Berkow, sensing a story, approached Martinez and asked him "what words of wisdom had been imparted by the astute Weaver."[1] Now Martinez is a pitcher who is unlikely ever to make it into the baseball Hall of Fame, if only because he seems to experience every pitch as a discrete event, unrelated to either its predecessor or its suc-cessor, but if his baseball skills are suspect, his philosophical skills would seem to be beyond dispute. In response to Berkow's question, Martinez offered a two-stage narrative. In the first stage he reports the event. "He [Weaver] said, 'Throw strikes and keep 'em off the bases,' . . . and I said, 'O.K.'" This is already brilliant enough, both as an account of what transpires between fully situated members of a community and as a wonderfully deadpan rebuke to the outsider who assumes the pos-ture of an analyst. But Martinez is not content to leave the rebuke im-plicit, and in the second stage he drives the lesson home with a pre-cision Wittgenstein might envy: "What else could I say? What else could he say?" Or, in other words, "What did you expect?" Clearly, what Berkow expected was some set of directions or an articulated method or formula or rule or piece of instruction, which Martinez could first grasp (in almost the physical sense of holding it in his hand or in some appropriate corner of his mind) and then consult whenever a situation seemed to call for its application. What Berkow gets is the report of something quite different, not a formula or a method or a principle—in fact, no guidance at all—simply a reminder of something that Martinez must surely already know, that it is his job to throw a baseball in such a way as to prevent opposing players from hitting it with a stick.

Of course, there is more to it than that, but Weaver made no effort to "impart" that more, and indeed it would have been totally inappropriate for him to have done so. Were he either to explain the principles of pitching or to enumerate the possible situations that might arise during the game and suggest strategies to deal with those situations, Martinez would be understandably incredulous and justifiably resentful. What Martinez is saying to Berkow is something like this: "Look, it may be your job to characterize the game of baseball in terms of overriding theories, but it's my job to play it; and playing it has nothing to do with following words of wisdom, whether they are Weaver's or Aristotle's, and everything to do with already being someone whose sense of himself and his possible actions is inseparable from the kind of knowledge that words of wisdom would presume to impart." In short, what Weaver says amounts to "Go out and do it," where "do it" means go and play the game. That is why both Weaver's counsel and Martinez's response must be without content. What they know is either inside of them or (at least on this day) beyond them; and if they know it, they did not come to know it by submitting to a formalization; neither can any formalization capture what they know in such a way as to make it available to those who haven't come to know it in the same way.

Let me extend the point by assuming that Martinez has walked the first batter (an all too possible occurrence) and the second baseman trots up to say to him, "There's a man on first base." What could he possibly mean? Certainly he does not think that Martinez has already forgotten what he did only a few seconds ago. Rather, he is prompting Martinez to remember what having a man on first base involves: the repositioning of both outfielders and infielders to deal with eventualities that have just become more likely, the narrowing of the options available to the batter who may now adjust his stance or choke up on the bat or steel himself to be more patient and discriminating than he might otherwise have been; the necessity of keeping in mind the next and then the next batter who, even though they have not appeared, are already factors in the situation. All of this and more is, in a sense, contained in "There's a man on first base," although those simple words will only convey that information to someone who literally carries it

in his bones.² One can imagine Berkow approaching the second baseman to ask him what counsel he gave to Martinez, and hearing in response, "I said, 'There's a man on first base,' and he said, 'O.K.' What
else could he say? What else could I say?"

This doesn't mean that there's never anything else to say, in a
formal or theoretical sense, about baseball; only that it is not always
appropriate to say it, although there are times when it would not be
appropriate to say anything else. Presumably, as the second baseman
says what he says, an announcer up in the radio or television booth—
more than likely a former player—is saying just the kind of things
that someone like Berkow expects. That is, in the announcer's account
of what has just happened, both the pitcher and the second baseman
are in the act of consulting and applying a set of underlying rules or
formal principles that underlie the skills of baseball in general and
the skillful exercise of judgment in this situation in particular; and it
is often the announcer's claim to know even more about these rules
than the players themselves know. And, in fact, that is, I think, a justifiable claim, but it is a justifiable claim because knowledge of the rules
is the game he is in (and, of course, it follows that he would be an expert in his own game), while the players are in quite another game
which has, I would contend, only an oblique relationship to the announcer's account of it. My claim, in short, is that in this imagined scenario there are two distinct activities—playing baseball and explaining
playing baseball—and that, in a strict sense (which I shall soon elaborate), there is no relationship between them whatsoever.³

The point may be clearer if we turn to another example, taken
this time from the world of industrial research as reported by Donald
Schön.⁴ It seems that a research and development team was experiment-
ing with a paintbrush made of synthetic bristles. The bristles were superior in many ways to the old natural kind, but in one respect they
were unsatisfactory: they did not deliver paint to a surface smoothly.
The team tinkered with the bristles in an attempt to improve them, but
to no avail until someone suddenly said, "You know, a paintbrush is
a kind of a pump."⁵ In fact, no one (including the speaker) did know
that until it was hazarded as an observation; but once hazarded it constituted a suggestion: "Let's think of a paintbrush as a pump and see
where it gets us." Where it got them was to a reconception of the
entire problem which now appeared to be one not of individual bristles, but of the channels formed by bristles, channels whose properties

were hydraulic and which could therefore be interrogated with the familiar vocabulary of mechanical engineering.[6] In the end, the result was just the kind of paint flow the researchers were looking for, and the new paintbrush was promptly dubbed a "pumpoid."[7]

After rehearsing the story, Schön turns to the problem of describing what had happened and remarks that it would be tempting to conclude "that the researchers mapped their descriptions of 'pump' and 'pumping' onto their initial descriptions of 'paintbrush' and 'painting' ";[8] but this would be incorrect, says Schön, because it would make a groping developmental process into a formal and explicit program. Rather than beginning with two lists of the formal properties of brushes and pumps and mapping one onto the other, the researchers began with what Schön calls "an unarticulated perception of similarity"[9] which then provoked them to questions and experiments that elaborated and deepened the similarity to the point where it could be the object of an analytic description. "It is important to note," says Schön, "that the researchers were able to see painting as similar to pumping before they were able to say 'similar with respect to what.' "[10] That is, the formalization that one might think served as their guide in doing what they did was available to them only after they had done it. The similarity that now could be reduced to a list of matched components was the product and not the cause of the process of discovery. Only later and after the fact, Schön insists, did the researchers "develop an explicit account of the similarity, an account which later still became part of a general theory of 'pumpoids,' according to which they could regard paintbrushes and pumps, along with washcloths and mops, as instances of a single technological category."[11] Moreover, he concludes "to read the later model back onto the beginning of the process would be to engage in a kind of historical revisionism."[12] It would be to confuse a retrospective account of what they had done—an account in which the characteristics and capabilities of pumps and paintbrushes are matched up so as to illustrate their membership in a single category—with an account of how they had done it. Insofar as there is now something in the world called the "theory of pumpoids," it would be a mistake to think of that theory as guiding the process by which pumpoids emerged as a solution to the problem the researchers originally faced. The solution—provoked by the intuitive nontheoretical suggestion that we try thinking of paintbrushes as pumps—came first and the theory followed in response to whatever pressures prompted them to present their achievement in terms more orderly and rule-governed than their actual experience of it.

One can imagine a situation in which the pressures flowed from the need for funds: they now have built a model of a pumpoid, but they need $4.5 million to develop and manufacture it. What do they say in the application to the National Science Foundation or the Exxon Corporation? Well, one thing they wouldn't say—at least if they really wanted the money—would be, "Hey, one day Marty and Ellen and I were sitting around trying to make those bristles deliver paint, and out of the blue Ellen said, 'You know, you can think of a paintbrush as a kind of a pump.'" Rather, they would eliminate from their presentation all traces of the fumbling, groping process by which they came to their triumph and offer only their conclusions, now dressed up in the vocabulary of hydraulic flow and presented in terms as formal and mathematical as possible.

At this point, there would be those who would fault the researchers for falsifying their experience. They would be accused, in a word, of being dishonest, of suppressing what they knew to be the truth about the matter in order to secure monetary gain. But that would be much too harsh a judgment, and, indeed, would be incorrect, for it would assume that the practice of applying for grants was or should be continuous with the practice of discovering or inventing. Think of the two practices as different answers to a single question: What do we have to do in order to reach our goal? When the goal is making the paint flow and flow smoothly, then what you have to do is eliminate the condition (the researchers called it "gloppiness") that now impedes flow, and your procedure is to look around for ways to do that. Presenting theories is not going to be one of those ways, any more than it would be a way of preventing the runner on first base from scoring. But when the goal is to get money from a foundation, then representing yourself as having followed or applied a theory is a very good way, and when you have recourse to it you are not being dishonest, you are being effective—just as you are being effective when you try out the suggestion that a paintbrush is similar to a pump in the absence of any theory of what the similarity is. I call this the "thesis of the plural honesties," and what it says is that in one case you are honestly attempting to get the brush to deliver paint and in the other you are honestly trying to get the foundation to deliver money.

You might reasonably be wondering what this has to do with the discourse of law. Before I tell you, let me consolidate what I take to be the gains of my two examples. First, what they together suggest is that performing an activity—engaging in a practice—is one thing and discoursing on that practice another. Second, the practice of discoursing on practice does not stand in a relationship of superiority or governance to the practice that is its object.[13] There are some baseball players who can talk about their craft in an analytic fashion, but that does not make them better baseball players than they would be if they couldn't; and there are some researchers who are good at thinking up ex post facto accounts of their accomplishment, but those accounts are not to be understood as recipes for that accomplishment. Even if the practitioners happen to be in possession of a theory of the activity in which they are engaged, the shape of that activity is not the result of the application of that theory. They do not use their account of what they are doing (assuming that they have one) in order to do it. They can, however, use their account of what they are doing to do something else, to perform as a play-by-play analyst or apply for a grant.

What is at stake here are two uses of the word "use": on the one hand, "use" in the sense of "making use of" as a component of a practice; on the other, "use" in the sense of using in order to generate a practice. It is in the first sense that baseball analysts and grant applicants use theory, and it is in the second sense that no one (this, at least, is my thesis) uses theory. That is, no one follows or consults his formal model of the skill he is exercising in order properly to exercise it. This should not be understood as a distinction between activities that are theoretical and activities that are not. No activity is theoretical in the strong sense of unfolding according to the dictates of a theory, and this includes the activities (for example) of analyzing baseball or applying for grants; for while they are to be distinguished from playing baseball and inventing pumpoids precisely by the self-conscious recourse to a theoretical mode of talk, that talk no more generates the shape of their own enactment than it generates the shape of what the talk is about (playing baseball and inventing pumpoids). As activities, analyzing baseball and applying for grants are just like playing baseball and inventing pumpoids in that those who are engaged in them make use of whatever comes to hand in the effort to achieve a practice-specific goal. Even if the skill one exercises in a practice is the skill of talking theory, this does not make the practice theoretical; it just means that in the judgment of the practitioner who wants to get something done, talking theory is one of the resources he employs in the course of doing it. Again, this does not mean that the skill depends on (in the sense of flowing from) theory talk; it means simply that one expression of the skill is knowing when theory-talk will or will not be useful. While it is certainly the case that the successful performance of a skill will sometimes require the invocation of theory—even of a theory of that particular skill—it is never the case that the theory thus invoked is acting as a blueprint or set of directions according to which the performance is unfolding.

I should acknowledge here that what I intend by "theory" may seem to some to be excessively narrow.[14] I reserve that word for an abstract or algorithmic formulation that guides or governs practice from a position outside any particular conception of practice. A theory, in short, is something a practitioner consults when he wishes to perform correctly, with the term "correctly" here understood as meaning independently of his preconceptions, biases, or personal preferences. To be sure, the word "theory" is often used in other, looser ways, to designate high-order generalizations,[15] or strong declarations of basic beliefs, or programmatic statements of political or economic agendas, or descriptions of underlying assumptions. Here my argument is that to include such activities under the rubric of theory is finally to make everything theory, and if one does that there is nothing of a *general* kind to be said about theory. When I assert the lack of a relationship between theory and practice I refer to the kind of relationship (of precedence and priority) implied by the strongest notion of theory; the relationships that *do* exist between theory and practice (and there are many) are no different from the relationships between any form of talk and the practice of which it is a component.

II

This brings us at last to the law and to the practice that is the almost exclusive focus of contemporary legal debate, judging. Now judging is both a practice much theorized about and a practice that is itself filled with theory or theory-talk. As you may have suspected, what I want to say is that judging or doing judging is one thing and giving accounts or theories of judging is another, and that as practices they are independent, even though the successful performance of the first will often involve engaging in the second. That is, as a practice judging is one of those that includes as a part of its repertoire self-conscious re-flection on itself, and therefore it seems counterintuitive to say that such self-reflection—such theorizing—is not to some extent at least constitutive of what it is reflecting on; but that is just what I will be asserting, and asserting in direct opposition to what is assumed by al-most everyone in the legal academy, irrespective of doctrinal or po-litical affiliation. What everyone assumes is that much in judging de-pends on what theory of judging a judge holds, and whether or not he holds it self-consciously. Here are some representative statements:

(1) First, a judge must have a theory of law proper . . . some rule of recognition that explains how to derive a text ("the law"). Second, the judge must have some theory about facts that deter-mines which of the indefinitely large numbers of descriptions of "what happened" should be used in deciding the case. Third, a judge needs [a] theory of interpretation. . . . And fourth, a judge needs a theory about logic and its place in legal reasoning.[16]

(2) [W]e hope to develop a positive theoretical account of the grounds of law, a program of adjudication we can recommend to judges and use to criticize what they do.[17]

(3) [E]very branch of doctrine must rely tacitly if not explicitly upon some picture of the forms of human association that are right and realistic in the areas of social life with which it deals. If, for example, you are a constitutional lawyer, you need a theory of the democratic republic that would describe the proper rela-tion between state and society or the essential features of social organization and individual entitlement. . . . Without such a guiding vision, legal reasoning seems condemned to a game of easy analogies.[18]

These three statements are essentially in agreement with one an-other in several important respects. They hold first that judges and law-yers need a theory in order properly to perform their tasks; second, that a theory self-consciously wielded would provide both a program for judging and a model in relation to which individual acts of judging can themselves be judged; and third, that, in the absence of such a pro-gram or model, judging and lawyering are random, ad hoc activities, at the mercy of whatever presentation of the facts seems at the moment to be the most persuasive. As our third theorist puts it in his very next sentence, in the absence of a theory, "[i]t will always be possible to find, retrospectively, more or less convincing ways to make a set of distinctions, or failures to distinguish, look credible."[19] Remarkably, our three authors occupy very distinct and opposing positions in the world of legal theory. The author of the first statement is Michael Moore, who bills himself as a natural law theorist, as someone who believes that we should comport ourselves in relation to general and abiding truths, irrespective of what is urged on us by presently enacted law or conventional systems of opinion. The second statement is taken from the recent work of Ronald Dworkin, who urges judges to look to the history of the judicial enterprise—a history Moore would finally have us set aside—for a "coherent theory"[20] that would guide particular decisions. And the final statement comes to us from Roberto Unger, the prophet, if not the messiah, of the Critical Legal Studies Movement, who sees in judicial history a dismal record of mystification and oppression that will only be removed when a world of contending interests is replaced by a world in which men and women of enlarged sympathies exist in a relationship of reciprocal support that renders the machinery of legal culture obsolete. In short, the right, center, and left[21] of the legal academy are at odds with one another on every other point except on the point that what is required if our situation is to be improved (and perhaps even perfected) is the right theory.[22]

In what follows I will contend (1) that in whatever form it appears the argument for theory fails, (2) that theory is not and could not be used to do what Moore, Dworkin, and the Critical Legal Studies Movement want it to do, generate and/or guide practice, (3) that when theory is in fact "used" it is in the way Unger so dislikes, in order "retrospectively" to justify a decision reached on other grounds, (4) that theory is essentially a rhetorical and political phenomenon whose effects are purely contingent, and (5) that these truths are the occasion neither of cynicism nor of despair.

I will begin with Moore, whose essay, "A Natural Law Theory of Interpretation,"[23] illustrates an assumption that is crucial to the argument for theory, the assumption that the practice of judging will vary according to the theory the judge uses.[24] The question Moore asks is whether judges should use a conventionalist or realist theory in order to do their jobs. A conventionalist theory is one that in response to the question, "Where do values, meanings, and facts come from?" answers, "From culture and history," that is, from man-made or conventional structures. In response to the same question a realist theory would answer, "Facts, meanings, and values come from God and nature, or from the divine Nous or the eternal structure of rationality." It is Moore's thesis that it is always better—in the sense that you will get better results—to use a realist theory in the course of reaching a decision. For example, when a judge must determine the meaning of a statute or a phrase from the Constitution, he should be guided "by the real nature of the things to which the words refer and not by the conventions governing the ordinary usage of those words."[25] The reasoning is that "ordinary usage" is a reflection of what people happen to think about a matter rather than a reflection of what is really true. Thus, for example (the example is Moore's), a case might well turn on the question of whether or not someone was in fact dead, and Moore's counsel is that if as judges we must rule on this question on our way to delivering an opinion, we should be guided "not by some set of conventions we have agreed upon as to when someone will be said to be dead; rather, we will seek to apply "dead" only to people who are really dead, which we determine by applying the best scientific theory we can muster about what death really is."[26]

Now, as you may have noticed, this is a sentence that cannibalizes itself. The first part of the sentence is unexceptionable. It says: When you are called upon to stipulate as to a matter of fact, go with what you take to be the truth and not with a specification or definition that has been handed down by some political or institutional body. However, it is to just such a body that the second part of the sentence counsels us to go in search of what is really—that is, non-conventionally—true. We must, Moore says, apply "the best scientific theory we can muster about what death really is." Moore really isn't urging us to be realists at all; he's urging us to be one kind of conventionalist rather than another, and telling us that if we have been offered two conceptions of what death is, one by the legislature of California and the other by the most recent issue of the *New England Journal of Medicine,* we should go with the *New England Journal of Medicine.* Moreover, although Moore doesn't say so, the basis of his advice is a faith in the division of labor implicit in our present institutional structures: judges determine what the law is; scientists and research physicians determine what it is to be "really" dead. It is an arguable point, but on whatever side of the argument you happen to be, you will not be upholding the banner of epistemological realism. No matter how intriguing the choice between conventionalist and realist theories may be on a meta-critical level, it has no role whatsoever to play on the level of practical action, since wherever you turn in the world the sources of your knowledge and convictions will be conventional.

In a way Moore knows this, since he acknowledges (on the very same page) that the "best scientific theories" may be inadequate since they only reflect our present state of knowledge; but, he says, a realist will have the advantage of knowing, as his conventionalist opposite will not, that there is in fact something beyond our present state of knowledge, something toward which we are striving. "A realist . . . believes that there is more to what death is (and thus what 'death' means) than is captured by our current conventions." Yes, but that knowledge (or, more properly, belief) doesn't do him any good, doesn't place him in any better position than the conventionalist when it comes to making actual decisions and determinations. He must still rely on whatever body of conventional knowledge he takes to be authoritative for whatever reasons.

Does this mean that the self-proclaimed realist theorist is in fact a conventionalist theorist without knowing it? Not at all. What it means is that he is not a theorist of any kind, at least when he is in the process of deciding whether or not someone is dead. At that moment he is listening to arguments with an ear already informed by a sense of what is and is not evidence, and of what, in the field of evidence, is weighty and conclusive. To be sure, any sense of the evidentiary will have its source in—be a function of—some conventional system of assumptions in which authority is located in particular institutions or procedures, but the decisionmaker is not using that system (or any other); rather, it is what he sees with, or more precisely, it is within it that he sees, and he will see what he sees independently of whether his theory of knowledge (should he have one) is realist or conventionalist.[27] That is, the realist theorist will know, by virtue of his theory, that there is something beyond or behind the conventions that are currently established, but that knowledge will not help him either to set those conventions aside or to determine which of them is a better approximation of what the facts "really" (independently of convention) are. On the other side (which in my argument will turn out to be the same side), the conventionalist theorist will be similarly disappointed by his theory should he turn to it in a moment of epistemological need. What the conventionalist theorist's theory tells him is that knowledge and certainty have their source in culture and history rather than in nature and

God. What the conventionalist theorist's theory won't tell him is where precisely in culture and history to look for the resolution of a current dilemma. That is, his theory won't give him a method for deciding whether or not someone is dead; all it will do is assure him that whatever he decides, the basis of decision—the facts that seem indisputable to him, the procedures that he regards as obligatory, the inferences that simply cannot be avoided—will be conventional through and through. Nor will this conviction of conventionality and its pervasiveness lead him to distrust either the conclusion he reaches or the means he employs to reach it. Such distrust could only follow if being a conventionalist theorist meant that you had a heightened (and confidence-eroding) sense that everything you saw was "merely" conventional, that is, unreal; but the conventionalist theorist, no less than his realist counterpart, is wholly informed by whatever conventions now structure his consciousness and perception, and his conviction that conventions cover the field and are the source of everything he knows will not shake or even be seen to have a bearing on whatever convictions and pieces of knowledge those conventions have now delivered. He may be a conventionalist when you ask him whether knowledge derives from nature or from culture, but when he knows something it will be with all the confidence any realist could ever desire. In the case of either theorist the answer to the question "How is it that we know what we know?" cannot be translated into a recipe for knowing; you don't use your account of knowing in order to "do" knowing.

Curiously enough, this is the same conclusion Moore reaches, although with a different emphasis. There may be those who espouse a subjectivist or conventionalist epistemology, "but when it comes to daily living they make judgments and decisions as we all do: presupposing the existence of tables, chairs, and right answers to hard moral dilemmas and legal cases. They are skeptics in their explicitly philosophical moments, and realists *when it counts* in daily living."[28] Moore takes this as evidence that such theorists, no matter what they say, are using a realist, not a conventionalist, epistemology. I take it as evidence that they are not using any epistemology (or theory) at all. They are merely registering what they see and proceeding in ways that seem to them to be obligatory and routine, and they do these things not because they have applied this or that epistemology, but because within the beliefs and assumptions that constitute their perception and their sense of possible courses of action, there is nothing else they could do. What this means is that, as Moore later says, we are all realists; but we are all realists only in the sense that we all believe what we believe, and that we take what we believe to be true. This, in fact, is what it means to believe something—to take it to be the case—and it requires no special effort of the will, no assumption of a particular epistemological style, to be guided by that which, according to our lights, is really true. (What else could we do? What else could anyone do?). But if it is in this sense that we are all realists, then by the same argument we are all conventionalists. If it is only "according to our lights" that the category of the "really true" acquires its members, then the "really true" is always and already a conventional category, and there is no possibility of identifying a "really true" that is independent of any convention whatsoever. The conclusion—and it is not a paradoxical one—is that we are *both* realists and conventionalists, realists in that we "naturally" proceed in accordance with what we take to be the truth of the matter, and conventionalists in that what we take to be the truth of the matter will always have its source in conventions.

To this conclusion we must add another and more important one: The condition of being both realist and conventionalist is not a condition we self-consciously choose. Realism and conventionalism are the names of philosophical positions on the question of how it is that we know what we know; they are not the names of epistemological programs that one could self-consciously put into action. One could not determine to "do" conventionalism or realism, and therefore the shape of what one does in fact do will have no causal relationship to the account one might give of doing it. Two judges might differ in their assessments of whether someone was really dead for all kinds of reasons, but one of those reasons would not be a difference in their epistemological theories.

III

Another way to make my point would be to say that when judges do what they do, they do not do it in accordance with or at the behest of some systematic and coherent account of law and its relation to morality and society. Judging, in short, cannot be understood as an activity in the course of which practitioners regularly repair for guidance to an underlying set of rules and principles. But, one might object, that is exactly the description of judging that judges themselves offer. As Ronald Dworkin observes, "when good judges try to explain in some general way how they work . . . [t]hey say, for example, . . . that they are enforcing an internal logic of the law through some method that belongs more to philosophy than to politics, or that they are the agents through which the law works itself pure. . . ."[29] That is, they picture themselves as striving to achieve what Dworkin calls "articulate consistency,"[30] a way of deciding cases that ties the most recent decision to "some comprehensive theory of general principles and policies that is consistent with other decisions also thought right."[31] Dworkin's example is a congressman who "votes to prohibit abortion, on the ground that human life in any form is sacred, but then votes to permit the parents of babies born deformed to withhold medical treatment that will keep such babies alive."[32] Such a person, Dworkin announces, cannot, by the "principle of responsibility," be allowed these two votes "unless he can incorporate the difference within some general political theory he sincerely holds."[33] It is Dworkin's thesis that this act of "incorporation," this fashioning of "articulate consistency," is or should be the form of judicial decisionmaking. It is his claim that what judges do when they are really doing their job is work out the present decision in relation to a general theory whose demands must be met if the decision is to be a responsible one, and whose articulations guide, almost in the sense of generating, that decision. He acknowledges that this remains an ideal and that most judges unfortunately are not so self-consciously reflective about their practice and therefore are likely to display judicial behavior that is inconsistent, ramshackle, and ad hoc. The better judge, then, is the better philosopher; indeed, in Dworkin's view, a judge is always a philosopher whether he is aware of it or not, for "[a]ny practical legal argument, no matter how detailed and limited, assumes the kind of abstract foundation jurisprudence offers."[34] Therefore, "any judge's opinion is itself a piece of legal philosophy, even when the philosophy is hidden."[35] Bad judges are judges whose philosophy is hidden from themselves; they follow instructions they have never properly considered and derive their arguments from distinctions they have never subjected to scrutiny. The good judge is supremely aware of his philosophy and is always in the process of both consulting and refining it whenever he takes up the task of making a decision about a fresh case. The choice is clear. One can either be an unreflective judge and be at the mercy of one's theory, or one can be in command of one's theory and use it as a mode of "calculation"[36] to produce coherent and consistent opinions.[37]

There is, however, in Dworkin's work a quite different picture of a judge's situation and activity, and while this different picture often sits side by side with the appeal to theory and the injunction to use theory, it finally reveals that appeal and injunction to be superfluous. I shall call that different picture an "enriched notion of practice,"[38] a notion in which practice, rather than being in need of the guidance theory might claim to provide, is itself sufficient, is, in fact, self-sufficient, and in need of nothing additional. This notion often surfaces in Dworkin's writings and is, in fact, already present in the early essay "The Model of Rules I,"[39] where Dworkin says that legal principles, of the kind he urges us to apply, have their origin "not in a particular decision of some legislature or court, but in a sense of appropriateness developed in the profession . . . over time."[40] In Dworkin's later work, this "sense of appropriateness" is developed into a description of law as a "chain enterprise," an enterprise in which agents see themselves as continuing the work of their predecessors.[41] "Each judge must regard himself, in deciding the new case before him, as a partner in a complex chain enterprise of which . . . innumerable decisions, structures, conventions, and practices are the history; it is his job to continue that history into the future through what he does on the day."[42]

What this suggests is that the agent embedded in a chain enterprise is the natural heir of the constraints that make up the chain's history. As a link in the chain he is a repository of the purposes, values, understood goals, forms of reasoning, modes of justification, etc., that the chain at once displays and enacts. It would follow, then, that an agent so embedded would not need anything external to what he already carried within him as a stimulus or guide to right—that is, responsible—action; in short, he would not need a theory. Dworkin, however, manages to arrive at just the opposite conclusion. He contrives to turn the insight that practice constrains into an argument for the necessity of constraints in excess of practice. And he does this because he sees the weight of practice—that is, of its history—not as something the agent thinks within, but as something the agent thinks with.

To think *within* a practice is to have one's very perception and sense of possible and appropriate action issue "naturally"—without further reflection—from one's position as a deeply situated agent. Someone who looks with practice-informed eyes sees a field already organized in terms of perspicuous obligations, self-evidently authorized procedures, and obviously relevant pieces of evidence. To think *with* a practice—by self-consciously wielding some extrapolated model of its working—is to be ever calculating just what one's obligations are, what procedures are "really" legitimate, what evidence is in fact evidence, and so on.[43] It is to be a theoretician. Often Dworkin will begin by talking as if he imagines the agent in the first position—embedded within a practice in the sense that his every action is an extension of it; but he soon slides into imagining the agent—at least when he is expert—as happily distanced from practice's flow and in possession of some abstract formulation that insulates him against its pressures. Sometimes the shift occurs in the same sentence, as when he asserts in the essay "Hard Cases" that "institutional history acts not as a constraint on the political judgment of judges but as an ingredient of that judgment."[44] Now what I take to mean—or, to be more precise, what I want that to mean—is that at the moment when a judge sees a case in a certain way—as falling into this category, or requiring that kind of investigation—there would be no point to his consulting institutional history, because it is that history—not consulted but thoroughly internalized—that already constrains what he sees. As it turns out, however, that is not what Dworkin means at all, for he goes on to explain that institutional history is such an ingredient because it is "part of the background that any plausible judgment must accommodate."[45] With the word "accommodate," what seemed to have been together and indeed to have been one and the same—the shape of one's institutional history and the shape of one's judgment—are once again apart, with the first—institutional history—acting as a benchmark or minimal constraint to which the second—the act of judgment—must self-consciously conform. Moreover, in this picture—the picture in which theory is necessary—the agent could choose not to accommodate the institutional history and so proceed to act in an irresponsible and wayward manner. Finally, it is basic to Dworkin's view of the matter that theory—in the form of a coherent set of principles—operates as a constraint not only on an insufficiently constrained practice, but on an insufficiently constrained practitioner. Dworkin's inability to grasp the implications of an enriched notion of practice—even when he gestures in the direction of that notion—is at one with his inability to understand what it would mean to be an agent embedded in that practice, an agent who need not look to something in order to determine where he is or where he now might go because that determination is built into, comes along with, his already-in-place sense of being a competent member of the enterprise.

The distinction between my position and Dworkin's may seem small. After all, he, too, insists that the historical experience of practice is crucial. But the distinction is not small, but subtle and all-important, and I feel it most strongly in those moments when I find myself re-writing one of Dworkin's sentences. In *Law's Empire,* for example, he makes the following, apparently congenial, asssertion: "Any judge will develop, in the course of his training and experience, a fairly individualized working conception of law on which he will rely, perhaps unthinkingly."[46] As I read this, I emend it (almost involuntarily) to "Any judge will develop into a working conception of law." The point of the emendation is to indicate the extent to which an experienced—that is practiced—judge is working simply by being what practice has enabled him to be; and, on that understanding, the clause "on which he will rely" should be changed to "which he will be." Thus, "any judge, in the course of his training and experience, will develop into a working conception of law, which he will be." One might object that in this new version of the sentence, the clause "which he will be" is redundant: If a judge develops into a working conception of law then, of course, that's what he is and nothing more need be said about the matter. Exactly right. There is nothing additional to say about it. The clause is superfluous for the same reason that theory is superfluous: The internalized "know-how" or knowledge of "the ropes" that practice brings is sufficient unto the day and no theoretical apparatus is needed to do what practice is already doing, that is, providing the embedded agent with a sense of relevancies, obligations, directions for action, criteria, etc.

But there may be other things to do, and theory might be needed to do one or more of them. It is time to acknowledge or reacknowledge the force of one of Dworkin's observations, that when judges themselves try to explain how it is that they work they present themselves as striving for just that articulate consistency that he sees as guiding the process of decision-making. And what is perhaps even more telling, judges engage in the same mode of self-presentation—a mode in which a present decision is explained or justified by an assertion of its fit with the principles underlying past decisions—when they hand down their decisions in the form of an opinion. How are we (that is, how am I) to account for this? Are judges concealing an unattractive truth? Or do they not know what they are doing? Not at all; they know perfectly well what they are doing. They are engaging in the practice of self-presentation, that is, the practice of offering a persuasive account of why they have done what they have done—decide the case this way rather than that—which is not the same thing (why on earth should it be?) as offering an account of how they actually did it. Dworkin is on to something really important in his elaborate discussion of the search for "articulate consistency" and the requirements it imposes; but what he is on to is not a mechanism by which decisions are generated, but the complex of rhetorical gestures to which one has recourse when a decision, already made, must be put into presentable form. Dworkin, in short, is a rhetorician.

The point can be made by returning to a sentence we have already considered and focusing this time on a single word: "Institutional history is part of the background that any plausible judgment . . . must accommodate." You will recall that my objection was to the word "accommodate," with its suggestion that institutional history was something the agent consults in the process of making a decision, whereas in my view the shape decisionmaking must take is immediately obvious to the agent for whom institutional history is the very ground of consciousness. But my objection disappears if the weight of Dworkin's assertion falls on the word "plausible"—"that any plausible judgment . . . must accommodate"—for that would indicate an obligation of a different kind from the obligation to consult or follow a theory. It would indicate an obligation to present one's decision in a form most likely to secure its acceptance; what Dworkin would be suggesting is that nowadays the form most likely to secure acceptance involves the fashioning of a story in which the present decision is the inevitable production of a principled and consistent history.[47] In short, "articulate consistency" is not the name of a theoretical perspective from which decisions issue, but of a pragmatic strategy by means of which decisions are successfully inserted into a field of practice that requires of its decisions that they be filled with certain forms of talk, in this case with theory-talk. Indeed, in this view, theory would be no more (or less) than a kind of talk; it would be precisely the kind of talk one was advised to engage in when presenting one's decisions to members of the present legal community. A judge would do theory-talk in the same way and for the same reason that the industrial researchers in our earlier example did it, not in order to provide an accurate description of the process by which they came upon their invention, but in order better to dress the product of that process in a garb appropriate to a situation in which their goal—and therefore the ground rules—had changed. Their goal is now persuasion, and they cast around for appropriate means with which to effect it (this is, of course, the traditional Aristotelian definition of rhetoric) and find them, or at least a portion of them, in the rhetorical practice of talking theory. Just as it would be inappropriate (indeed, disastrous) for the researchers to begin by saying that "we were all sitting around one day, etc.," so would it be similarly inappropriate for a judge to say that "when I first saw this case, I saw it as already categorized and exhibiting certain characteristics and therefore calling for a certain description, and then I gave my clerk the assignment of putting together a story in which what I immediately saw was the product of a conscious act of intellection and deduction; and here's the story he brought back."[48] You just don't say that. You say something else, and what you say must employ the vocabulary and tone of theory.

Once Dworkin has been recharacterized as a rhetorician rather than a theorist, much of what he says becomes quite acute and to the point, although not to the point he thinks himself to be making. Thus when he advises against historical, psychological, and sociological self-presentations, on the grounds that "justification must be plausible and not sham,"[49] he is saying something that is itself historical, psychological, and sociological: that given the way things are now in the law business, you had better not offer a justification that takes its terms from these disciplines, but takes them instead from moral or political philosophy because right now that's the going talk, and to slight it would be to risk losing the sympathy of your audience. What is and is not "sham" is entirely a matter of what in the discipline is currently thought to be the proper repository of evidence and argument. Sham is what won't work, or as Dworkin himself observes in the very next sentence, sham is what will be "unappealing"; if it is unappealing, then "it cannot count as a justification at all."[50] Quite right. And Dworkin is right, too, when he labels the suggestion that we stop talking about "the law" and other big concepts in legal theory as "mostly bluff" because these concepts are "too deeply cemented into the structure of our political practices" to be so easily "given up."[51] I would only add that what they are deeply cemented into is precisely a political practice, the practice of persuasively urging one's decision in the appropriate forum. In that forum, to stop talking in philosophically conceptual terms would be to make a big political (i.e., rhetorical) mistake. It would not be a mistake because it would falsify our picture of what judicial decisionmaking is like—it has no relation to that picture—but because philosophically conceptual terms are what the legal community now expects to hear when it listens to a self-presentation.

Of course, Dworkin would not accept my praise of him as a rhetorician, as someone who is telling us what kinds of stances and poses will best effect our polemical ends. He is not content with giving good rhetorical advice; he wants that advice to link up with a deep epistemological truth of which it is the reflection. He wants the observation that (at least in the current scene) you are more likely to be persuasive if you present yourself as having first built and then followed a theory to be heard as a description of and as a recipe for responsible decisionmaking. He wants to think of himself as telling us not simply how to dress, but how to be. The trouble is that by asking to be judged on the basis of that high aspiration—the aspiration to be a philosopher-king—Dworkin risks emptying his enterprise of any value or significance because as an epistemological recommendation it has nothing to offer us. What it purports to offer is a program for determining where a case fits, how it should be characterized, what its features are, and on what side of it one will find the right. But these are all judgments which come along with what Dworkin himself identifies as the "sense of appropriateness" with which and within which the fully initiated (i.e., practiced) member already sees. Such a member has no need of the help of an elaborated theory that has been designed to generate the sense of appropriateness he not only already has, but already is.[52]

That is why Dworkin's repeated injunction to arrive at the "best" judgments we possibly can and be the best judges we can possibly be sounds so strange. One wants to say, with Dennis Martinez, "what else could we be or do except what, according to our lights, was the best?" That is, someone whose sense of appropriateness includes a firm conviction of what is and is not obligatory and what is and is not responsible judicial behavior will not have to look elsewhere for his convictions or for an understanding of what would be the "best" thing to do. "Be the best you can be" finally means nothing more than "act in the way your understanding of your role in the institution tells you to act." Like "throw strikes" and "keep 'em off the bases," it is not an invitation to acquire new knowledge, but a reminder of what you already know. "Keep 'em off the bases" could only have a positive content if a pitcher who thought himself to be acting as a pitcher could possibly decide to put as many men on base as he could; similarly, "Make your decisions the best they can be" could only have a positive content if a judge who thought himself to be acting as a judge could possibly decide to reach decisions that he would himself reverse on appeal. The pitcher who deliberately put men on base and the judge who issued willfully bizarre opinions would not be described as not having done their best, but as not having played their respective games. Those who are playing the game learn nothing from someone who tells them to be the best they can be. They are the recipients of the verbal equivalent of a pat on the back, and if Dworkin's claim is to be giving direction to judicial decisionmaking, the claim fails, and the best that *he* can be is a cheerleader. (C'mon, fellows, do your best.)

All of this changes, however, if the injunction to search for the best justification of your decision is understood not as a method for producing that decision, but as a strategy for presenting it after it has already been made. Then the injunction has a positive content, and it tells you something. It tells you that only half your work is done and that, as things now stand, the way to do the second half—the way to be persuasive—is to construct a certain kind of story in which your decision is more or less dictated by the inexorable laws of the judicial process. Now Dworkin has a real project: to give you examples of how that story has been constructed in the past and to provide you with rules of thumb that might be of help when you are asked to construct such a story in the future. It is not the project he announces; it is not the building of a grand theory. It is just a rhetoric, a manual of practical know-how; but precisely because it is a rhetoric and not a theory it might even be something you could actually use.

IV

Yes, but use to what purpose, one might ask, and the answer a Critical Legal Studies adherent might give is, use to the purpose of extending and perpetuating the sham the law already is. That is to say, by redescribing Dworkin as the writer of a handbook for judicial self-presentation, I could be said to have put my finger on what is wrong with current judicial practice: Most of it consists of a massive effort to hide from itself and from the general public the rhetorical basis of its operations. This is what Unger means when he complains about the practice of retrospectively finding ways to make distinctions credible, and it is precisely the charge Mark Kelman makes in his essay, "Interpretive Construction in the Substantive Criminal Law."[53] Kelman's thesis is that those who employ legal argument make claims for its rationality that cannot finally be maintained; they cannot be maintained because the steps in legal argument follow from an unacknowledged first step in which all the important questions are decided without reflection and, as it were, behind the institution's back. What results is what he calls "rational rhetoricism,"[54] the practice of allowing an apparently rational discourse to unfold with no acknowledgment whatsoever of the "nonrational" determinations that reside at its heart. Kelman, in short, is pointing to the truth I have been urging in this essay—the truth that the practice of deciding is one thing and the presentation in persuasive form of that decision another—and declaring it a scandal. The agent only "seems" to "deduce a single result on principle";[55] in fact, the result proceeds from the hidden bias of a point of view already assumed and is then dressed up as a "legal-sounding argument."[56]

Correctly understood, this is a complaint that agents are embedded in practice and that as long as they remain so—and remain so unthinkingly—they will never be able to see or to get a purchase on that which really informs their supposedly rational deliberations. We must, he says, be in a position where our "interpretive constructs"—those angles or prisms that give us our world and its "facts"[57]—are no longer obscured and have been made to surface; at that point, presumably, we will be less blinded by these constructs and less vulnerable to their now insidious (because covert) appeal. It is Kelman's effort in his essay to move us in the direction of that happy state, and he proceeds by exposing or debunking those "interpretive constructs" which, in his view, are doing us the most damage.

Chief among these is the unthinking assumption of a "narrow time frame" within which the moment of criminal action is seen as coterminous with the physical act of pulling the trigger or snatching the purse; if the time frame were broadened and one understood an action as including many of its antecedents, including those social and economic pressures felt by the actor, then the assignment of responsibility would be rendered more problematical and a space would open up in which the question of determinism could be seriously raised. Kel-

man's complaint is that we never self-consciously debate the appropriateness of alternative time frames and thus enter upon our deliberations
with many of the conceptual possibilities already excluded: "As best
I can tell, we do these interpretive constructions utterly un-self-con-
sciously. I have never seen or heard anyone declare that they are framing
time broadly or narrowly, unifying or disjoining an incident, broadly or
narrowly categorizing a defendant's . . . intent . . . let alone explain
why they are doing it."[58]

Kelman is, of course, right. He has never seen anyone self-consciously select his interpretative constructs; indeed, I would go further
and say that no matter how long he lives it is a sight he will never see,
because there has never been or ever will be anyone who could survey
interpretive possibilities from a vantage point that was not itself already
interpretive. The demand for self-consciousness is a demand for a state
of consciousness in which nothing has yet been settled and choices can
therefore be truly rational. But if all concepts or constructs remained
to be chosen, there would be nothing—no criteria, no norms of measurement, no calibration of value—with which or within which the
choosing could be done; indeed, there would be no chooser, for if the
question of direction were totally open the mind (such as it is) would
be incapable of going in any direction at all if only because it would be
unable to recognize one.

To put the matter baldly, already-in-place interpretive constructs
are a condition of consciousness. It may be, as Kelman laments, that the
thinking that goes on within them is biased (which means no more
than that it has direction), but without them (a pun seriously intended) there would be no thinking at all. It follows, then, that the
one thing you can't do in relation to interpretive constructs is choose
them, and it follows too that you can't be faulted either for not having
chosen them or for having chosen the wrong ones; moreover, it follows
that it makes no sense to condemn as "nonrational" the reasoning that
proceeds within interpretive constructs because that's the only kind of
rationality there is.[59] Finally, by the same reasoning, if you can't choose
your interpretive constructs, then neither can you know them (in the
sense of holding them in your hand for inspection), and if you can't
know them, you can hardly be expected to take them into account when
you come to explain the process by which you reached your conclusions.
Kelman's essay begins as a complaint against the disparity between the
self-presentation of action in the legal community and the true facts of

the decisionmaking process; but if the true facts—the always prior operation of interpretive constructs—are not available to reflection, then the complaint is against something that could not be avoided. Rather than being an argument against my thesis of the two practices—deciding and presenting deciding—Kelman's examples flesh out the thesis by showing how impossible it would be to achieve the distance from our interpretive constructions that would be necessary if we were to be fully cognizant of the springs of our practice and could draw on that cognizance in our discourse about our discourse.

Nor is it the case that the hold our interpretive constructs have on us will be loosened simply because we have been alerted to it by Kelman and his friends. To think otherwise is to fall into the characteristically left error of assuming that an insight into the source of our convictions (they come from culture, not from God) will render them less compelling.[60] If you have been persuaded to that insight, you will be able, like Kelman, to tell a general story about where our convictions come from; but that story will not reflect one way or the other on any single one of them, which will or will not be in force depending on the extent to which this or that interpretive construction is doing its work. Remember what the general story says: Whatever you take to be the case about a matter will be a function of interpretive constructs you have not chosen; but the fact that you have now heard the story and believe it doesn't put you in any better position either to choose your interpretive constructs or to neutralize the effects of those you still will not have chosen.

"It is illuminating and disquieting," Kelman asserts, "to see that we are nonrationally constructing the legal world over and over again. . . ."[61] In fact, it is neither. It is not illuminating because it does not throw any light on any act of construction that is currently in force, for although your theory will tell you that there is always one (or more) under your feet, it cannot tell you which one it is or how to identify it. It is not disquieting because in the absence of any alternative to interpretive construction, the fact that we are always doing it is neither here nor there. It just tells us that our determinations of right and wrong will always occur within a set of assumptions that could not be subject to our scrutiny; but since everyone else is in the same boat, the point is without consequence and leaves us exactly where we always were, committed to whatever facts and certainties our interpretive constructions make available, and ready to do battle with those who, in the grip of other interpretive constructions, are certain of a different set of facts. Kelman's deconstructive theory finally has the same status as Moore's theory of epistemological realism and Dworkin's theory of articulate consistency: It is entirely irrelevant to the practice it purports to critique and reform. It can neither guide that practice nor disturb it. Indeed, the insight that interpretive constructs underlie our perceptions and deductions cannot do anything at all. It cannot act as a direction to seek something other than interpretive constructs, because there is no such other thing to be found; and it cannot act as a caution against the influence of interpretive constructions now in place because that influence will already be at work contaminating any effort to guard against it. In the end, Kelman's indignation that we do interpretive construction unself-consciously draws the now familiar Dennis Martinez response: What else could we do? It is a realization that goes nowhere, an epistemological or theoretical insight which is of no use at all.

It cannot even be useful as an ingredient in the practice of self-presentation.[62] Unlike Dworkin's notion of articulate consistency, the doctrine of rational rhetoricism cannot be recommended as a strategy to those who wish to make their arguments and opinions as persuasive as possible. Imagine the judge or lawyer who makes every point in the company of the demonstration that the point depends on assumptions that one could always challenge. Imagine, too, that same judge or lawyer on the alert for those moments when his own discourse is in danger of becoming convincing, and meeting that danger by analyzing and laying bare the wholly rhetorical conditions that give force to what he has been saying. It would be too little to say of such a performer that he was falling down on the job of lawyering or judging; he wouldn't be doing that job at all, but some other, the job of literary criticism or of continental philosophizing. What Kelman and those who agree with him fail to understand is that no activity or practice can take into consideration everything that could possibly be taken into consideration, because it is the very definition of an activity or practice that it is an attempt to do *this* rather than *that*.

In a recently published book Peter Goodrich has complained that in "constructing the abstract world" of law—the world in which actions are easily specifiable and responsibility can always be determined—members of the legal community "have tended to be forgetful both of the irrationality and chance embedded in social life as well as of the instability and change intrinsic to human purpose and human personality."[63] But what would it mean for actors in the legal community to be *not* forgetful of these things, indeed to have them uppermost in their minds, dictating the shape of their thoughts? It would mean that they would not be legal actors, but psychologists, or sociologists, or statisticians. "Forgetfulness," in the sense of not keeping everything in mind at once, is a condition of action, and the difference between activities—between doing judging and doing literary criticism or doing sociology—is a difference between differing species of forgetfulness. The absurdity of demanding that everything be remembered is illustrated by Kelman's accusation that in framing and administering criminal law "we simply rule out the determinist claim that 'crime is unavoidable.' "[64] But all this means is that in order for there to be a criminal law, the claim of determinism cannot seriously be entertained, except as a fringe or special case—insanity, mental incapacity—which bounds and protects a central area of personal responsibility. It can hardly be a complaint against the criminal law that it pays little and selective attention to a point of view that would undo it. What Kelman is really complaining about is that there is a criminal law at all.

Now that, of course, is a perfectly reasonable complaint. If the criminal law depends on notions of personal responsibility and autonomous action which seem retrograde and harmful, perhaps we should do something to get rid of it. Perhaps so, but we won't get rid of it by assaulting it with a philosophical argument, even one that shows it to be less firmly grounded than many had assumed. That might be a knock-down argument in philosophy, but, despite what Dworkin and others might believe, law is not philosophy, and it will not fade away because a few guys in Cambridge and Palo Alto are now able to deconstruct it.

I can imagine Kelman and Dworkin and Moore and a host of others objecting that I still have not dealt with the most obvious deficiency of a legal culture that is not somehow undergirded by reason, by a theory: It leaves us with a field of practice that is ramshackle and inconsistent. As Kelman puts it, "*the* solution to legal dilemmas is inevitably partial. The 'victory' of one framework or the other is a temporary one than can never be made with assurance."[65] Or in the words of Roberto Unger, law, in the absence of some cohesive and coherent view, is simply "an endless series of ad hoc adjustments," "a collection of makeshift apologies."[66] The question I would ask is "makeshift in relation to what?" Surely not in relation to the pressures and urgencies that make a solution satisfying or an adjustment helpful.

The answer, as we have already seen, is makeshift in relation to a description of our several and various actions which would show them to follow from a single set of abstract principles, from a theory. But what that means is that "makeshift" and "ad hoc" are accusations not of our practices as they pursue their several goals, but of our practices as if it were their single goal to be available to a philosophical description. But if our practices had that goal, they wouldn't be our practices. They would be philosophy;[67] indeed, that is finally what the demand for theory and consistency amount to, a demand that there be only one practice and that philosophy be its name. Now there is, of course, a practice named philosophy, and it is in the business of abstracting away from other practices in order to see what can be said about things in general. But it seems bizarre to think that this should also be the business of practices that are not philosophy, to think that it is the obligation of agents in other practices periodically to rouse themselves and say, "Hey, what we're really doing is philosophy even though we call it judging or literary criticism, so let's consult some philosophers so that we can see if we're doing it right or doing it in some ad hoc or ramshackle way." It is hard to imagine why agents genuinely committed to a practice would hand over responsibility for judging it to some other practice, especially to a practice that takes place almost exclusively in college classrooms. It is quite easy to imagine why philosophers would think that an abdication in their direction makes perfect sense. Philosophers, after all, are like anyone else; they want people who don't do what they do to believe that what they do is universally enabling. They want us to believe that the only good king is a philosopher-king, and that the only good judge is a philosopher-judge, and that the only good baseball player is a philosopher-baseball player. Well, I don't know about you, but I hope that my kings, if I should ever have any, are good at being kings, and that my judges are good at being judges, and that the players on my team throw strikes and keep 'em off the bases.

18. Unger and Milton

Introduction

I propose to take Roberto Unger as seriously as he takes the questions he raises. One mark of his seriousness is his insistence on beginning at the beginning, asking each question as if it had never been asked before. As he puts it, with the combination of modesty and ambition that makes his voice so distinctive, "My purpose will be to think as simply as I can about the problems I discuss. In our age, philosophy has won some triumphs because a few men have managed to think with unusual simplicity."[1] Thinking simply about Unger, or trying to, means going back to his early work in an effort to understand more fully those later writings that have recently brought him public attention. I shall begin with *Knowledge and Politics* (1975), with a view toward identifying a structure of concerns that continues to underlie his more recent publications. For a while I shall try, quite uncritically, to lay out "as simply as I can" the very complex argument of a difficult book. It is only when I turn to "The Critical Legal Studies Movement" (and I shall make no attempt to characterize that movement, an effort that now constitutes a genre of its own) that I shall introduce my reservations and criticisms.

My use of Milton is at once illustrative and polemical. In general, the legal academy, even that part of it that admires Unger, has been puzzled and discomforted by him. This discomfort reflects, I think, the uncongeniality of theological discourse to the legal mind, and in linking Unger's thought to Milton's (with no suggestion of influence, although influence is by no means impossible) I hope to provide a context in which the nature and direction of his project become clear. At the same time I am preparing the way for my most general conclusion about Unger, which is that insofar as he is a religious thinker, concerned always to inform the particular moments of everyday life with the imperatives of a universal and godly vision, he will never be able to fashion the politics for which so many of his readers wait. (Speak, Unger.)

I

At a crucial moment in *Areopagitica* John Milton declares that "they are not skillful considerers of human things, who imagine to remove sin by removing the matter of sin."[2] Milton's point is that sin is not a property of objects but of persons, and that therefore the elimination from the landscape of (supposedly) sinful objects will finally do nothing to eliminate or even reduce a sin that lives within, a sin that cannot be starved because it feeds on itself: "Though ye take from a covetous man all his treasure, he has yet one jewel left, ye cannot bereave him of his covetousness." It follows, then, that no amount of *external* policing or surveillance will be of any effect, since the *interior* condition of sinfulness will not have been touched and the sin will "remain entire": "Banish all objects of lust, shut up all youth into the severest discipline that can be exercis'd, . . . ye cannot make them chaste that came not thither so."

How, then, do you make them chaste? The answer, not surprisingly, is by focusing on the true object of correction and reform, the inner constitution of the sinner, and by laboring to alter that constitution so that it will "naturally" express itself in virtuous behavior. Such an alternation, should it ever be achieved, will involve the exchanging of one compulsion for another; where previously the individual, literally in the thrall of covetousness, was compelled to be covetous (covetousness was his essence), now what compels him is whatever principle of desire (e.g., to be chaste) lives in him as a constitutive force. The difference is not between a state of bondage (to sin) and a state of freedom, but between two differing states of bondage; and in either state the possibilities for action will be defined not by some set of external constraints (whose presence or absence will finally be irrelevant) but by those inner constraints of which any action will be the involuntary expression. Milton's name for this condition, in which the individual is at once free of external compulsions and yet bound by the securest of ligaments, is Christian Liberty, which he defines in *The Christian Doctrine* as "that whereby we are loosed . . . from the rule of the law and man"; but he adds that to be so loosed is not to be left free to do anything we like but to be given over to the even stricter rules that now reside within us and, indeed, *are* us:

> So far from a less degree of perfection being exacted from Christians, it is expected of them that they should be more perfect than those who were under the law. . . . The only difference is that Moses imposed the letter, or external law, even on those who are not willing to receive it; whereas Christ writes the inward law of God by his Spirit on the hearts of believers, and leads them as willing followers.[3]

They will be willing followers not at this moment or at that moment but at every moment, since there will be no distance or tension between their own inclinations and the bidding of an *internalized* law. They will not be in that divided state Milton satirizes in the person of the man who, finding the demands of religion and morality too stringent, delegates to some "factor" (hired agent) the "whole managing of his religious affairs":

> he entertains him, gives him gifts, feasts him, lodges him; his religion comes home at night, praies, is liberally supt, and sumptuously laid to sleep, rises, is saluted, and . . . better breakfasted than he whose morning appetite would have gladly fed on green figs between *Bethany* and *Jerusalem,* his Religion walks abroad at eight and leaves his kind entertainer in the shop trading all day without his religion.[4]

This sardonic portrait illustrates the consequences of conceiving of law as an external check on individual desires; the law is experienced only as an alien constraint, and it does not enter into a relationship with those desires that might lead to their reformation. So long as law is a matter of what someone *else* wants you to do, what you yourself want will never be put into question. No genuine inner change occurs, merely the superficial changes that result from the perpetual conflict between public and personal wants. Moreover, the conditions of this conflict are accepted as natural and inevitable, and the possibility of transforming them—of bringing communal rule and individual desire together—is never seriously entertained. The result is a general, if varied, complacency in which everyone is satisfied with the state of his own knowledge and eager to impose that state on everyone else. The status quo is canonized, and the law becomes (ironically) the guardian of "receiv'd opinions"[5] in the name of a liberal tolerance, rather than a means of transcending opinion and ascending to the realm of truth.

For Milton this stasis is the worst product of a law that fails to reach the true source of error, not outward behavior but inward affections. It is a loss, he says, "more than if some enemy at sea should stop up all our havens and ports and creeks," for it "hinders and retards the importation of our richest Merchandize, Truth," and operates to "settle falsehood."[6] As it turns out, falsehood is defined as anything that is settled, a definition that follows from Milton's thinking of Truth not as a property of the world, but as an orientation of being, an orientation that will never be achieved if one remains confined within the partial and local perspectives of custom and tradition. "Truth is compar'd in Scripture to a streaming fountain; if her waters flow not in a perpetuall progression, they sick'n into a muddy pool of conformity and tradition."[7] From this negative definition (negative because it refuses, necessarily, to say what truth is) comes Milton's positive program, "perpetuall progression," keeping the waters stirred up so that stagnation never can occur. In practice this means a continual refusal to be satisfied with any currently persuasive vision of what the truth is. The general rule is, distrust anything that makes a general claim, that claims to be something more than a way station along a road that is still to be traveled: "he who thinks we are to pitch our tent here, and have attain'd the utmost prospect of reformation, that the mortall glasse wherin we contemplate, can shew us, till we come to *beatific* vision, that man by this very opinion declares that he is yet farre short of Truth."[8]

The politics that emerges from this epistemology is (as every schoolchild once knew when *Areopagitica* was required reading) one of tolerance. Given that our visions are now clouded (now we see through a glass darkly), "if it comes to prohibiting there is not ought more likely to be prohibited than truth itself; whose first appearance to our eyes blear'd and dimm'd with prejudice and custom is more unsightly and unplausible than many errors."[9] It therefore behooves us to prohibit nothing, but to welcome each and every voice which together, if in different tune, will form so many "brotherly dissimilitudes"[10] and "neighbouring differences."[11] It is statements like these that explain why Milton has been seen as an honored precursor of a democratic liberalism that centers upon the values of free inquiry and freedom of expression. But, in fact, despite surface similarities, Milton's program is finally the antithesis of that liberalism. The similarity, of course, is in the toleration of differences, but in liberal thought that toleration follows from the severing of the realm of the political from the theological, an act that renders permanently unavailable the transcendent point of view theology assumes and to which it aspires; consequently, *all* one can do is honor the points of view held by individuals and make provision through a political system for their peaceful cohabitation. Difference, then, becomes the bottom line, valued for its own sake and sanctified by being termed "individual freedoms" and "individual rights."

Milton, however, counsels not the managing of difference but its multiplication; and his aim is not to protect difference, in the sacred name of individual rights, but finally to eliminate it. That is why his insistence that we not pitch our tents *here,* on the campgrounds of any orthodoxy, is qualified by a future hope: "till we come to beatific vision." Beatific vision names that state when all visions will be one and indistinguishable from the vision of deity. Difference, then, is only a temporary and regrettable condition, but one, paradoxically, that we must take advantage of if we are to transcend it. That is, since the glasses through which we see are presently, but differently, dark, the danger represented by any one of them—the danger that it will be mistaken for the glass of beatific vision—will be diminished to the degree that we are aware of all the others. It is by encouraging perspectives to proliferate that we minimize the risk of their settling into forms that limit our perception. In order to see further we must always be in the process of unsettling and moving away from the ways of seeing that now offer themselves to us: "The light which we have gain'd, was giv'n us not to be ever staring on, but by it to discover onward things more remote from our knowledge." The entire process is named by Milton "knowledge in the making"[12] and the "constituting of human virtue,"[13] and it will not be completed, he acknowledges, until our "Master's second coming."[14] Meanwhile, we must be ever on guard against the danger of freezing knowledge in its present form and making it into an idolatry; and our vigilance must continuously produce "new positions," new perspectives, which "were they but as the dust and cinders of our feet, . . . they may yet serve to polish and brighten the armoury of truth."[15]

II

Readers of Roberto Unger's work will have recognized in the preceding paragraphs the argument of his *Knowledge and Politics* (1975), a book written before the full emergence of the Critical Legal Studies Movement, of which he is considered a major inspiration. The first half of *Knowledge and Politics* is a critique of what Unger terms "the liberal doctrine," a related set of premises, which, he asserts, "took their classic form in the seventeenth century."[16] Liberal doctrine comes into being with the denial "of the existence of a chain of essences or essential qualities that we could either infer from particular things in the world or perceive face-to-face in their abstract form."[17] This denial creates the "modern conception" of the relationship between nature and perception, in which "it is possible to divide the world in an indefinite number of ways" but not possible to say that any of them describes what the world is really like."[18] In the absence of a "master principle," a transcendent point of view, we cannot "decide in the abstract whether a given classification is justified," for the "only standard is whether the classification serves the particular purpose we had when we made it."[19] Indeed, it is precisely the realm of the abstract, of a perspective not already captured by some partisan vision, that is eliminated in the liberal, secularized, all-too-human world, which now becomes a landscape of ever-proliferating particulars.

But even as modern man is committed by his denial of intelligible essences to this landscape, he is also committed to escaping it, because his practices depend for their justification on the abstract universality he elsewhere denies. He believes at once that "there is no direct appeal to reality for reality is put together by the mind" and that "ultimately one can make a rational choice among conflicting theories [constructs of the mind] about the world."[20] These contradictory beliefs together form what Unger calls the "antinomy of theory and fact,"[21] the irresolvable conflict between two ideas to which modern man pledges allegiance: "the mediation of all facts through theory and the possibility of an independent comparison of theory with fact." Behind this antinomy stands the "radical separation of form and substance, of the universal and the particular, for that separation is the basis of the difference between general ideas . . . which are formal and universal, and the understanding . . . of individual events, which is substantive and particular." In our practices, both scientific and social, we seek and assume the availability of a justification for our particular judgments; but our general conception of the human condition after the demise of intelligible essences—of unmediated knowledge—tells us that particular judgments are all there are.

The psychological form of the antinomy of fact and value is the antinomy of reason (conceived of as a formal universal) and desire. In a liberal world the individual is a bundle of appetites that are arbitrary "in the sense that we cannot determine what we want"; that is, we cannot "use reason to justify their content."[22] The reason is that reason does not have desires; that is what makes it reason. Reason can *point out* desires, describe them, but the moment it acts to *prefer* one desire to another, it has become a desire itself, and is no longer reason, no longer formal and universal. Conversely, desires have no reasons except for the reasons they imply, which are not reasons at all since they spring from desires and cannot legitimately be cited in support of them. Were desire truly to submit itself to reason it would become absorbed by reason and cease to be itself. Reason cannot take serious note of desire without compromising itself; desire cannot defer to reason without denying itself. Desires cannot be the objects of rational choice because choice is the antithesis of desire, but rational choice is nevertheless honored as the only basis of a civilized society, of a society in which desires do not go unchecked. (Of course, in argument and council desires are often urged in the context of "reasons," and one does reject certain courses of desirable action by saying that they are wrong; "but the reason for this is that whenever we act we always have a host of goals other than the one to which the activity of the moment is directed, and we do not allow all our ends to be sacrificed to the achievement of an immediate objective." That is, the preferring of one desire to another follows from a calculation of desire, of what we want *more:* "the priorities among conflicting ends must be settled by the will.")[23]

Liberal politics mediates (and mimes) the antinomy of reason and desire—an antinomy that is the very structure of the liberal self—by dichotomizing human behavior into two opposed and ultimately irreconcilable realms, the public and the private:

Since men are made up of two different elements of reason and will, they move in two worlds precariously bound together. When reasoning, they belong to the public world because knowledge, to the extent it is true, does not vary between persons. When desiring, however, men are private beings because they can never offer others more than a partial [i.e., partisan] justification for their goals.[24]

Obviously, this division merely reproduces in the larger society the split that is constitutive of liberal consciousness, leaving two spheres that show blind faces to one another: in the public sphere desires go unacknowledged (that, at least, is the fiction) except as forces that must be contained, and in the private sphere desires reign uncurbed and a man can do as he likes, trading in the shop of his appetites like Milton's "enlightened" modern, free from the pressure of general censure and constraint. One sphere "assert[s] the priority of the good [the content of desire] over the right"; the other "the priority of the right [of the impersonally just and true] over the good."[25] Pleasure on the one hand and principle on the other triumph in their separate compartments, and human life is forever disunified.

Moreover, any effort at unity is doomed to failure, because "no synthesis of the two seems possible within liberal psychology."[26] This is so because the demands of the two realms do not allow them to interact or cooperate. Cooperation would require, at the very least, recognition of one by the other. But since desire is arbitrary, and springs from personal appetite, it can only recognize the dictates and strictures of reason as the expressions of someone else's desire, and it will reject them as illegitimate impositions. And since reason is by definition neutral—not oriented in this direction or the other—it can only note the existence of desires as items in a purely formal world; it cannot recognize them for what they are, and therefore it cannot say anything about them. To put it another way, the only imperative that reason might direct at desire is "be reasonable," but since reason is by definition "neutral toward the purposes [desires] of specific individuals,"[27] the imperative can never make contact with its object; for there to be contact, the "golden rule" of reasonableness would have to be more than an "empty shell,"[28] would have to be "filled up" by something "concrete," that is, particular; but once that happens, reason is no longer neutral but is all mixed up in the world of purposes from which it must keep its defining distance.

The antinomy of reason and desire is therefore ineradicable, and

it is a fate that falls with terrible force upon those whose moral experience the principles of liberal psychology describe. Its mark on everyday life is the unacceptability, indeed the incomprehensibility, of the two halves of the self to each other. For reason, when it sets itself up as moral judge, the appetites are blind forces of nature at loose within the self. They must be controlled and if necessary suppressed. For the will, the moral commands of reason are despotic laws that sacrifice life to duty. Each part of the self is condemned to war against the other.[29]

This war plays itself out in the alternate claims of the public and private lives. "Public organization strikes the private [desiring] self as a preordained fact in whose making it had no part; private interest . . . has for the public [reasoning] self, the appearance of enslavement to blind instinct and ambition."[30] Thrown back and forth between the two, the self "cannot accept either as a resting place." The result is a politics that has exactly the form Milton critiques in the *Areopagitica:* an external constraint (public morality and law) asserts itself against an inward orientation which can only perceive it as threat and coercion and therefore cannot respond in any constructive—that is, self-reflective—way to its pressures. Consequently, the whole of life becomes an endless succession of momentary adjustments of two contending forces—an unjustified law and an unjustifiable desire—to one another. The best that government can do (and, indeed, this becomes the stated goal of liberal politics) is to guarantee, or *claim* to guarantee, a minimal level of formal procedure—of due process—so as to allow contending desires equal access to the battlefield on which they must endlessly fight. In this dreary landscape the face of things is continually changing, but genuine change of the kind that would provide desire with a justification outside of itself, and reason with a content that was not merely formal and therefore empty, seems forever unavailable.

The great *desideratum,* then, is to find a way out of the liberal antinomies of fact-value, reason-desire, public-private, to bring together in a fruitful cooperation the two halves of a sterile and stagnating antagonism. The second half of *Knowledge and Politics* is concerned to set us on that way, but it begins by first considering and then dismissing one facilely attractive route:

One way to solve the problem of the universal and the particular, and thus the antinomies of liberal thought, would be simply to deny its terms. Instead of assuming the separation of the universal and the particular, we would start off from the premise of their identity. Thus, in a single move, we might stand liberal thought on its head in the hope of escaping from its internal contradictions.[31]

The trouble with this "single move," this version of Hamlet's "thinking makes it so," is that it ignores the important truth the liberal antinomies tell us about our present condition, its distance from the more ideal condition in which the internal contradictions of liberal thought would not be felt. One does not bring about the union of reason and desire simply by declaring them to be unified; all such a declaration accomplishes is the weakening of any impulse to critical analysis and reform, since, if reason and desire are *already* one, all impulses "have become by definition the good"[32] and there is no longer any bite to the "notion that the world might [now] be different from what we think it ought to be." Consequently, we fall into "the sanctification of actuality,"[33] forgetting that our goal should be "the transformation of society."[34] The problematic of the universal and the particular cannot be theorized out of existence; it must be grasped in a way that both acknowledges the inadequacies of which it is the formulation and refuses to acquiesce in those inadequacies as a liberal politics—concerned to protect difference, but without any vision of its transcendence—will always do. "We need a way to make the universal and particular at once the same and different."[35]

That way is found in a recharacterization of the universal and the particular in which the former is expressed by the latter, but never limited by it. That is, the universal is not an empty formal structure, but something that "always exists in a concrete way";[36] but that concrete way does not exhaust the meaning of the universal "or its possible modes of existence."[37] It thus becomes possible to say that the universal and the particular are at once the same and different. They are the same in that one could not have a form independently of the other; the universal needs particulars into which to flow and the particulars acquire their meaning and significance as instantiations of the universal. They are different because the universal is always more than any one of its instantiations, more even than their sum. Indeed, under this conception, the universal is not fixed, but is "the open set of concrete and substantive determinations in which it can appear."[38] Because the set is open, that is, because history brings with it more and more opportunities for concrete determination, the universal is always being changed by each new partial expression of it. The ideal and the actual do not exist in opposition to one another, nor are they merely names for the same static thing; rather they emerge together as a set of possibilities that is always finding a manifestation of itself that it is at the same time always exceeding.

Unger declares that human nature is itself such an open set, a universal filled out by the actions of particular individuals, but never wholly captured in those actions:

> human nature is neither an ideal identity that subsists in its own right [as a purely formal structure] nor a mere collection of persons and culture [just a name for what already is]. Instead, it is a universal that exists through its particular embodiments, always moves beyond any one of them, and changes through their sequence. Each person and each form of social life represents a novel interpretation of humanity, and each new interpretation transforms what humanity is.[39]

What this means is that the nature of human nature is not settled but is always in the process of emerging as persons relate to the world in ways that define both the world and themselves as bearers of human possibility. In the absence of a fixed human nature, of a formal universal, the substantive universal that is human nature is always up for grabs. "All choices," declares Unger, "imply a decision about the kind of person one wants to be"[40] and therefore a decision about the emerging and changing shape of human nature. "Humanity consists in a continuous predicament and in the kinds of relations to nature, to others, and themselves with which persons respond to that predicament."[41]

In social terms the predicament is experienced as the tension between the integrity of the individual and the demands of community. (Duncan Kennedy, one of the leading proponents of Critical Legal Studies, calls this the "essential contradiction.") The individual can only know himself in his relations with others, but insofar as he is defined by those relations, he is in danger of losing his individuality (obviously, this is the liberal antinomy all over again):

> To be an individual one must win the recognition of others. But the greater the conformity to their expectations, the less one is a

distinctive individual. . . . The self is individual and it is social. But the requirements of individuality are in conflict with the demands of sociability in a way that does not seem immediately capable of solution.[42]

That is where liberal thought stops and resigns itself to keeping minimal order, but transformative thought chooses to see this dilemma as an opportunity, "as a circumstance in which others are complementary rather than opposing wills in the sense that to join with them in a community of understandings and purposes increases rather than diminishes one's own individuality."[43] Rather than seeing the other as a representative of a competing vision of what human nature should be, transformative thought sees the other as one of the many instantiations or interpretations of human nature that are necessary to its full emergence. Difference no longer marks conflict between irreconcilable individual wills, but marks rather the various but not opposing paths individual wills follow in their pursuit of a single goal. (The apt comparison is to Milton's "brotherly dissimilitudes.") One therefore welcomes, indeed prizes, perspectives other than one's own as contributions to the end for which everyone works, the end that defines and gives shape to everyone's labors, labors that are therefore at once different and the same.

The model for this generosity toward others that returns as a credit and *addition* to the self, is, not surprisingly, the Christian practice of loving one's neighbor as oneself and for the sake of the God who made both:

> To the religious man, every other person is a particular manifestation of the universal substance in which the soul, including his own soul, consists, and this universal substance is inseparable from its particular embodiments. Such a man cannot prize God or himself without prizing others as the individuals they are.[44]

Such a man is at once partial and many-sided. He is partial because he is situated in a particular historical position; but he is many-sided because he views his actions in that position as in concert with the actions of others whose different situation gives them a vantage point he cannot directly enjoy. The more he is able to see his efforts in this way—as one form of the human nature everyone is trying to express and construct—the larger they are, despite their partiality, for even as they are made, they will be made both for him and for the sake of those others with whom he is a costriver; and at some point the exertions of such a man "have become a gift to the entire species," a gift that is returned to him in the form of an enlargement of the self that he has been willing to lend to a common project.

The presence in the world of such an enlarged and enlarging self is contagious: he "cannot rest, or play, or even dream in peace until he has wakened his fellows from his slumber as he was wakened by others."[45] The slumber is the slumber of partiality as a prison forever separated from the universal; the awakening is to partiality as a participation in and fashioning of the universal. As more and more awakened selves see themselves in this way and act accordingly (differently but in the same spirit), the sense of shared purpose existing through a diversity of practices will result in the emergence of a "community of sympathy," a community marked by "conditions of diminishing domination," for each will see every other as affirming his own nature; furtherance of the other's ends "would mean the advancement of one's own,"[46] and "the conflict between the demands of individuality and of sociability would disappear."[47] At that moment all the other antinomies that fracture liberal thought will disappear too. Reason will be one with desire, because what the individual wants—to be more and more expressive of the essence of human nature—will also be the rule or norm against which he measures himself, and, of course, finds himself still wanting (pun decidedly intended). Fact will be one with value because every thing and action in the world will be seen and engaged with as a manifestation of a controlling aspiration. Public will not be distinguished from private, because the act of the individual will be simultaneously his own and belong to the community that act is even now building. The realm of the extraordinary—of those moments in which one grasps the disparity between what man is and what he could be—will pass over into the realm of the everyday. Indeed, there will no longer be any distinction between them, as the awakened man sees "the task he has set himself . . . before his eyes at every moment and in every circumstance."[48] It is to that task that Unger calls us in remarkably affecting terms, inviting us to be among those "who are able first to anticipate, then to recognize, but finally to embrace perfect being, in imperfect, and fugitive, earthly form."[49]

III

This last sentence, which has the ring of a conclusion, ends Unger's fifth chapter, but there is a sixth chapter, and it draws us back from the glorious promise of the sentence by reminding us of what stands between us and the embracing of perfect being. First, there are the dangers that are the several faces of liberal politics: resignation, utopianism, and idolatry. Resignation is "acquiescence in pure partiality and the abandonment of the universal part of the self as a hopeless dream; the person is completely absorbed in his concrete social position and identifies with it."[50] The same person may come to recognize the universal part of himself but see no connection between it and the necessarily partial nature of his everyday life. He will have fallen prey to utopianism, "the tendency to define the good in such a manner that it cannot be related to the historical situation in which one finds oneself."[51] Or alternatively, he may see all too close a connection between the historical situation in which he finds himself and the realization of the universal; he may think that the universal is already fully actualized in the forms his behavior routinely takes. Like Milton's journeyer, who pitches his tents "here" in the conviction that he has no further to go, he will then be committing idolatry, "mistaking the present situation . . . for the accomplishment of the ideal";[52] he will accept the imperfect as the perfect and remain forever a prisoner of the social and political structures that mirror his complacency.

Although they are distinguishable, resignation, utopianism, and idolatry all have the same effect: they inhibit change and reaffirm the status quo. The resigned man sees no alternative to the imperatives of his own social and political situation, and he devotes himself wholly to those imperatives. The utopian man sees that there exists a mode of being more full and satisfactory than that which he now knows, but believes that his vision of the ideal is wholly discontinuous with the present state of things and that he "has no choice but to worship established power as a mystery [he] cannot grasp and as a fact [he] cannot change."[53] And the idolater, having mistaken "the existing consensus . . . for the final expression of the good,"[54] will naturally regard dissent as evil and change as corruption, and will fall easily into a conservative politics that "is always on the verge of becoming oppression."[55]

Against these dangers Unger poses a politics that is the direct descendant of Milton's, a politics of perpetual distrust and perpetual progression, a politics that "emphasizes the transitory and limited character of all forms of group life and manifestations of human nature."[56] Such a politics "will be committed to the plurality and diversity of groups, and it will prize the conflictual process through which community is created and made universal above the preservation of any one collectivity."[57] It will neither reaffirm the status quo by idealizing it nor celebrate change and disruption for their own sake; rather, it will utilize change and disruption as necessary mechanisms for the continuing of the journey toward a stability that would represent the domination of no one because it would mark the triumph and the emergence into full being of everyone.

Merely to rehearse the promise of such a politics, however, is to raise the question Unger is now obliged to answer, and indeed it is the question with which he opens this final chapter: "How can the ideal be realized in everyday life?"[58] In fact, he has already provided the answer: "one must turn to politics; only politics can make the ideal concrete, concrete in everyday life."[59] But that answer only provokes another question or series of questions. What exactly is the politics that can do this? How does it start? Where does it start? One obvious place to start is the enlargement of democracy, "the progressive replacement of meritocratic by democratic power in the ordinary institutions of society," so that decisions about "what to produce . . . for which objectives to produce and how to produce are increasingly defined as political and . . . collective."[60] Thus public life would be more and more contiguous with private life, as every aspect of daily existence would become a matter of the political choices of fully enfranchised agents in a "democracy of ends." But the questions persist, and again it is Unger who raises them. While the "adoption of the democracy of ends describes a process of [ever-enlarging] choice . . . it does not establish the standards by which individuals engaged in that process ought to choose."[61] Moreover, any attempt to formulate such a standard would be disastrous to the entire enterprise since it "could not lay down . . . principles of choice without . . . lending a spurious authority to the beliefs and practices of a particular society or age."[62] It would seem then that there is a tension between the desire that the individual be fully enfranchised to make choices, and the necessity of some larger or communal sense of purpose whose invocation would assure that the choices made were progressive and cumulative rather than merely ad hoc. Moreover, as Unger is quick to point out, this tension, discovered at the

heart of the democratic ideal to which the entire book has been pointing, "is another aspect of that same conflict between universalism and
particularism encountered before."[63] That conflict, rather than having
been transcended by the notion of a community of ever-enlarging sympathies, is found to inhabit that notion, and, as Milton would have put
it, to be there "writ large." Even as politics is proclaimed as the answer
to the question—"how can the ideal be realized in everyday life?"—the
answer is revealed as fatally flawed, and Unger is forced to acknowledge, late in the game, that the "limits of politics are another side of the
imperfection of all our efforts to achieve the good and to represent it in
a form of social life."[64]

As *Knowledge and Politics* draws to its close, the admissions of failure proliferate:

> The gap between the universal and the partial aspect of personal-
> ity is never directly or completely bridged.[65]
>
> The ideal can never fully be achieved in history.[66]
>
> The ideal of universal community, like the ideal of the self from
> which it derives, is . . . incapable of being realized in history.[67]
>
> Only a person could fully realize the ideal and . . . this person
> cannot be man in history.[68]

Who, then, could it be? The answer is at once surprising and inevitable, and it is the title of the book's last section, "God": "The idea of
a union of immanence and transcendence or of a universal being who
knows and determines all particulars without destroying their particu-
larity is the idea of God."[69] It is knowledge of God and his perfection
that will serve as a "regulative ideal"[70] in relation to which the inadequacies of the present order of things can be measured and transcended.
God, at once universal and the informing spirit of every particular, is
the model of the true community of sympathy. "So completely does He
solve the problem of the abstract and the concrete self that He is eternally everything He might or should be."[71]

Here at last is the solution to every problem and the *dis*solution of
all antinomies, but even as it is offered, it is withdrawn, for it is a resolution that we are incapable of achieving:

> The existence of God and the salvation of men are ideas whose
> truth could only be shown, if they could be shown at all, by God
> through His direct revelation of Himself in history. As a person

who stands above the world and apart from thought, He cannot be known except to the extent that He makes Himself present to us. . . . It is He who must reveal his immanent being, and we who must pray to Him for its showing.[72]

And it is in prayer that the book ends, asking for the revelation that will redeem its failure:

But our days pass, and still we do not know you fully. Why then do you remain silent? Speak, God.[73]

There is more than a little frustration in this plea, and it has been echoed by Unger's readers in the legal community, many of whom feel disappointed and even cheated by a book that advertises (if only in its title) a political agenda, but delivers a lesson that undermines politics by leaving us in the supine posture of supplication. What the book doesn't provide is a *plan,* a set of procedures whose self-conscious implementation would result in the building of the community Unger so powerfully describes. Instead, it leaves us with a renewed sense of the rootedness of the liberal antinomies and with a way of retroactively reading the first half of the book as a religious allegory. The disappearance of intelligible essences, rather than marking a mere shift in philosophical perspective, marks a withdrawal from the world of God, a withdrawal that occurs at the Fall, separating us forever from a truth we continuously but vainly seek. The words are Milton's:

Truth indeed came once into the world with her divine Master, and was a perfect shape, most glorious to look on; but when he ascended . . . then strait arose a wicked race of deceivers, who . . . took the virgin Truth, hewed her lovely form into a thousand peeces.[74]

Those few who wish to restore Truth's lovely form go constantly "up and down gathering up limb by limb" as they can find them. "We have not found them all," says Milton, allowing us for a moment the prospect of a task almost complete, a task within our abilities to accomplish; but he takes that prospect away with these chilling words: "nor ever shall doe, till her Master's second comming; *he* shall bring together every joint and member." It is the movement, in small, of the whole of *Knowledge and Politics,* the indictment of fallen history as the state of being separate from God—of partiality and difference unredeemed by a universal and universalizing vision—followed by a declaration that union with God, the reconciliation of individual actions with divine purpose, is something only He can initiate and achieve. Just as Milton's "nor shall ever doe" is a rebuke to the facile hopes of a reader who expects to be exhorted to specific (and efficacious) acts, so is the entire second half of *Knowledge and Politics* a rebuke to the hopes that Unger has raised (and entertained) of a political remedy for the infirmities that attend fallen consciousness. The final lesson of *Knowledge and Politics*—a lesson that makes a joke of its title—is that redemption is theological, not political, that the union of reason and desire, fact and value, universal and particular, can only be realized in a union with deity in a process of which he must be simultaneously the goal and the way. "I am the way, the truth and the life."

IV

It is a lesson the modern intellectual is ill-equipped to hear and unlikely to applaud, and Unger seems to feel its inadequacy as much as anyone. In effect, he writes "The Critical Legal Studies Movement" to redeem the failed promise of the first half of *Knowledge and Politics,* by offering an "engineering" version of his theological vision. By "engineering" I mean that, rather than beginning with transcendence or requiring its intervention, he builds toward transcendence by identifying some route that is accessible to man in his present condition, by identifying a genuine politics. This is what Unger promises in his first paragraph when he says that the Critical Legal Studies Movement "implies a view of society and informs a practice of politics."[75] This is not the practice of politics as one usually finds it in the dominant legal culture. That practice, which will be the sustained object of Unger's critique, is characterized (as is liberalism in general) by "a belief in the possibility of a method of legal justification that can be clearly contrasted to open-ended disputes about the basic terms of social life, disputes that people call ideological, philosophical, or visionary."[76] This belief cannot survive "historical study," which has "repeatedly shown that every attempt to find the universal legal language . . . revealed the falsehood of the idea."[77] That is to say, whatever has been offered as an alternative to open-ended dispute between interested actors has upon investigation been revealed to be an extension of some interest that is not acknowledging itself, not even to itself. There can finally be no contrast "between the more determinate rationality of legal analysis, and the less determinate rationality of ideo-logical contests."[78] Everything is a matter of ideological contest even if some ideologies succeed in masquerading as the "universal legal lan-guage."

Any such masquerade succeeds only by suppressing the conflict that would ensue if its own ground were contested. In order to avoid that contest the reigning (and always illegitimate) orthodoxy must de-vise ways to account for and accommodate pressures and problems that seem to challenge its hegemony. But as the challenges multiply, the ef-forts to contain them become more frantic. The doctrine that was of-fered "as a canonical form of social life . . . that could never be fun-damentally remade"[79] begins to crack under the strain; as the supposedly bedrock notions are stretched and redefined under the pressure of increas-ingly powerful counterexamples, "the initial conception of a natural form of society becomes weaker: the categories more abstract and in-determinate, the champions more acutely aware of the contentious char-acter of their own claims."[80] And yet they hold on tenaciously, most probably, Unger speculates, in the fear that the abandoning of the claim to generality "would leave nothing standing; the very possibility of le-gal doctrine, and perhaps even of normative argument generally, might be destroyed."[81] The result is a situation in which lip service is paid to a putatively "defensible scheme of human association"[82] at the same time that "an endless series of ad hoc adjustments"[83] empties that scheme of its pretensions to integrity. "It is always possible to find . . . radically inconsistent clues about the range of application of each of the models and indeed about the identity of the models themselves."[84] The claim is to be applying general truths to particular contexts, but in fact the so-called general truths increasingly "fall hostage to context-specific calcu-lations of effect,"[85] "ad hoc qualifications"[86] of principles that leave the principles with no content. It is the worst of all possible worlds: a fro-zen and empty doctrine held in place by a "collection of makeshift apol-ogies"[87] that mask conflict which has no direction because it is never acknowledged. The prevailing orthodoxy threatens us with the choice between it and "the inconclusive contest of political visions";[88] either "resign yourself to some established version of social order, or face the war of all against all." But so long as the established version of order maintains itself by ignoring contest or by adapting shamelessly to con-test's ever-changing shape, the war of all against all is what we really have.

False universals and the war of untransformed particulars—this is what orthodox legal liberal thought offers and where the first two sections of Unger's essay leave us. In section 3, entitled "From Critique to Construction," Unger begins to unfold the positive program that will produce true universals in the form of transformed particulars. That program will be given many names in the course of the essay, and here, in the first few paragraphs of its introduction, it is called "enlarged doctrine," "expanded doctrine," and "deviationist doctrine."[89] By any name, it seeks to open up "the petrified relations between abstract ideals or categories, like freedom of contract or political equality, and the legally regulated practices that are supposed to exemplify them."[90] Only the "casual dogmatism of legal analysis" prevents us from seeing that these abstractions "can receive . . . alternative institutional embodiments" and that therefore the present arrangement of things is neither necessary nor even, when examined critically, plausible. It is just such a critical examination, informed by a general suspicion of the apparently authoritative, that is required; rather than acquiescing in the papering over of the cracks and fissures in the official account of legal doctrine, deviationist doctrine seeks to exaggerate them—"to recognize and develop the disharmonies of the law"[91]—in order to open a window on the "indefinite possibilities of human connection," the many "alternative schemes of human association." The more this is done, the less any one of those schemes will be able to entrench itself, and the larger will be the area of contest, the area in which basic questions about the structure of social life are raised and debated. "In this way no part of the social world can be secluded from destabilizing struggle."[92] "The practice of expanded doctrine begins all over again the fight over the terms of social life."[93]

Obviously, this is the argument of *Knowledge and Politics* all over again: in a world of contesting schemes of human association, none of which has the status of a universal, we must guard against the danger of acquiescing to the claims of any one of them; and we can best do this by exaggerating rather than sublimating their differences, keeping before us the goal of achieving and becoming the universal to which their inadequacies (if only negatively) point. That is, we must prize "the conflictual process through which community is created and made universal above the preservation of any one collectivity."[94] In *Knowledge and Politics* this general statement of a program is unredeemed because we are never told how to move from the prizing of conflict as a cautionary strategy to the utilization of conflict as a way to create the universal. That is, prizing the conflictual process does not lead necessarily to a transcendence of conflict; rather, it would seem to lead to more of the same, to the intensification of the war of all against all. What is required is some principle or lever that will enable us to grasp a foregrounded conflictual process and turn it in a positive direction. What is required is what in *Knowledge and Politics* could only be supplied by God, a starting point. (The naming of God as the starting point short-circuits the development of a politics since it takes agency away from man.) "The Critical Legal Studies Movement" should be understood precisely as an effort to supply that starting point; it will be my contention that the effort repeatedly fails and that Unger only escapes the war of all against all by once again invoking (if only implicitly) the theological intervention that marked his earlier failure.

He begins briskly, with a concise and straightforward outline of a program:

> You start from the conflicts between the available ideals of social life in your own social world or legal tradition and their flawed actualizations in present society. You imagine the actualizations transformed, or you transform them in fact, perhaps only by extending an ideal to some area of social life from which it had previously been excluded. Then you revise the ideal conceptions in the light of their new practical embodiments. You might call this process internal development.

Calling this process "internal development" is no casual gesture. The strong claim is in the word "internal," which suggests that the process generates its own direction. All you need to begin with is the awareness that the foregrounding of conflictual process will have given you, the awareness that the competing ideals of social life do not receive support from the practices we routinely engage in, or, what amounts to the same thing, that those same practices could be understood (by someone sufficiently skilled at rationalization) as supporting any number of ideals. At this point you will have recognized the inadequacy both of the present state of things and of the currently available visions in the name of which that state has been justified.

So far, so good. Then comes the crucial step. "You imagine the actualizations [the present state of things] transformed." But how do you do that? Or more precisely, from where do you do that? Obviously, given Unger's double thesis of the (present) unavailability of a general perspective and the flawed nature of the perspectives we now inhabit, the only position we could possibly occupy is the position of one of those flawed perspectives; and consequently any transformation would have to be imagined from the vantage point of that perspective, as an extension (even as it was a modification) of its partiality. "Transformation" is perhaps too grand a word for this process, which might be better called "change," understood as the passage from one limited (partisan) vision to another with no sense that during the passage the state of being limited will in any way have been relaxed. In short, while I am not denying that something of the sort Unger describes does in fact occur—we do revise our practices in the light of a felt inadequacy— its occurrence will not mean the loosening of limits because the light that provoked it will itself be equally, if differently, limited.

Of course, for the person who has performed the act of revision, the resulting practice will seem larger, more capacious, than the practice he has left behind; but this capaciousness will be evident and palpable only from within the perspective that now becomes his horizon. For another person the new practice will seem not larger at all, but have the aspect of a restriction on the human capacity for growth and self-realization. In the eyes of some, Roe v. Wade represents an extension of the ideal of individual rights (in the form of the right to privacy) "to some area of social life from which it had previously been excluded"; but in the eyes of others the same decision represents a disastrous violation of the same ideal, a setback to the efforts of society to enhance the lives of its members. Moreover, this is a difference of opinion that cannot be adjudicated by some third party, since the perspective from which that party would speak would be no less limited than the perspectives it presumed to judge. Without a mechanism for determining whether a proposed or imagined revision would constitute a step forward rather than a step backward on the journey to a truly transformed society, that journey can never begin, for no claimed beginning would have the authority it would need in order to serve as the uncontroversial basis for the next step. In such a world (the world Unger everywhere acknowledges we live in), the area of conflict can never be enlarged (as his doctrine requires); it can only be reconfigured. And the reason it cannot be enlarged is that the area exempt from conflict, the area bounded by the presently settled convictions of the agent, will always be the same size—the exact size of the agent's necessarily unexamined assumptions—even though its shape and its relationship to the (mutually constitutive) area of the unsettled will change. No matter how often that change occurs, the result will always be a perceiving consciousness for whom some things (facts, theorems, judgments, etc.) are undoubted *and undoubtable,* while others remain a matter of dispute; the members of the two categories will vary, but the structural relationship between them will not, and it will never be possible *absolutely* to diminish the one in the service of the other.

Unger in effect acknowledges as much when he says of the project of "internal development" or "enlarged doctrine" that its "weakness . . . is obviously its dependence on the starting point provided by a particular tradition";[95] that is, the to-be-transformed consciousness begins its task of bootstrapping its way to transcendence while still firmly embedded within a particular, limited point of view. He thinks, however, that this weakness can be overcome with the help of a recent shift in our understanding of our epistemological condition. "To an unprecedented extent," he reports, we now understand "society . . . to be made and imagined rather than merely given."[96] What he is referring to, of course, is the emergence in a number of disciplines of an anti-foundationalist epistemology in which both the facts and structures of our social world (along with the possibilities for action that world is thought to contain) are seen not as naturally or divinely ordained but as the *accomplishments* of interested, situated agents like you and me. Unger's reasoning is that since more and more people have been persuaded to this view of things and therefore know that whatever they take to be certain and unalterable is *in fact* so only within a contingent and revisable construction of the world, those same people should now be "naturally" inclined to regard with suspicion and skepticism any received system of ideas including (indeed, especially) their own. In other words, the hold a "particular tradition" and its "starting point" may have on us will be loosened to the extent that we have become aware of its status as a revisable construction. All we need to do is begin with the assumption (identified by Unger as "crucial") that "no one scheme of human association has conclusive authority," using that insight as a "starting point" with which to counter and critique the starting point of our received traditions.

The trouble is that as a starting point the insight that no one scheme of human association has conclusive authority is empty; as a universal statement all it tells you about any particular scheme of asso-

ciation is that it is not the whole story. But it can't, in the absence of
the whole story, tell you in what way the scheme is deficient; and therefore it can't tell you in what direction to move away from a scheme
that has been the object of an overgeneral indictment. If that scheme is
one to which you are committed—in the strong sense of proceeding
within its assumptions and categories of understanding—the knowledge
that it too must be included in that indictment will not even touch it, first
because "it" is not something graspable by a critical consciousness (it
is, after all, *constitutive* of consciousness), and second because its partiality is known at so abstract a level that there can be no bridge between that knowledge and anything in particular. Nor can it be made
less abstract without losing its identity, for the moment the general
indictment is given a content—the moment it has enough specific bite
to urge you in some particular direction—it will have become a scheme
of association of exactly the kind it urges us to escape. In short, insofar
as the "crucial" assumption generates a program, it can only be a program of directionless suspicion, a program that falls under the criticism
Unger himself makes of agendas that never advance beyond the stage
of negative critique: "freedom to be real, must exist in lasting forms
of life; it cannot exhaust itself in temporary acts of context smashing."[97]

If the effects of context smashing are to be more than temporary,
something must be added to the insight that "none of the social and
mental forms within which we habitually move . . . escapes the quality of being partial and provisional,"[98] and immediately after reiterating
that insight Unger moves to provide that something additional: "But
these mental and social worlds nevertheless differ in the degree as well
as the character of their constraining quality."[99] That is to say, while
all social and mental forms constrain our visions and therefore cause us
to be confined within some or other partial perspective, the constraints
imposed by some forms are looser than others, and therefore it behooves
us to begin by identifying those forms and inhabiting them so as to
afford the most scope possible to man's "most remarkable quality, . . .
the power to overcome and revise, with time, every social or mental
structure in which he moves."[100] As that power is increased, it will then
express itself in an "institutional structure, itself self-revising, that would
provide constant occasions to disrupt any fixed structure of power and
coordination in social life."[101]

The idea is that you build up a community of enlarged sympathies
by taking advantage of those forms of community whose constraints

are sufficiently loose to permit and even to encourage innovative and context-transcending activity. But as an idea it founders on the very difficulty it proposes to remedy: in order for it to work, there must be a way of identifying which structures of constraint are looser—less committed to the limits and norms they declare—than others. Unger, however, gives us no guidance here. He simply declares that "societies differ among themselves in the extent to which they open themselves to self-revision" and adds that if we wish evidence of this difference, "it is enough to compare the liberal democracies themselves to the societies that preceded them."[102] But it is not enough, and indeed if it were, if "schemes of association" were self-evaluating and wore their labels ("conducive to freedom," "tending to the totalitarian") on their faces, they would not constitute the danger that gives urgency to Unger's project; they would not be compelling forms of idolatry. And since they *are* forms of idolatry, that is, forms of belief, they come with their own calibrations of difference in relation to which the "obvious" differences Unger invokes would become matters of contest. That is to say, the attribution of openness and freedom to one social or mental structure relative to others would itself have to be made from *within* one of those structures, and therefore it would not be accepted by someone who was hearing it from within the assumptions of some other structure. Every society believes that its forms are calibrated so as to stimulate and nourish freedom, but freedom is a contested concept, and there is no neutral space in which one can coolly survey societies and decide by which of them it is best embodied. The point can be made by recalling something as crude as the ritual comparisons in the American and Soviet media: the one assures us that Soviet society is closed and permits only a few activities, while in the United States the possibilities are infinite and we are (relatively) free to do what we like; the other responds by observing scornfully that what we are "free" to do is purchase the endless succession of consumer goods produced by a capitalist economy in relation to which we are all slaves whether we know it or not. The example is, as I have already said, crude, but the lesson to be drawn from it is generalizable: the extent to which self-revision or anything else is a feature of some "scheme of association" cannot be determined in the absence of that universal perspective whose (current) unavailability is Unger's first thesis.

But there is an even greater difficulty. Not only is it impossible to determine uncontroversially which of the infinite number of schemes of association are more open to revision than others; the very notion of schemes of association that are more or less constraining is itself incoherent. Here we must be careful, for the point is an important and difficult one. It is important because Unger's project finally rests on a distinction between two limit case types of mental and social structures, or as he later calls them "formative contexts."[103] Some formative contexts, he explains, are especially "open to self-revision"[104] and therefore they do not press their claims with the exclusiveness characteristic of less flexible contexts. At the other end of the scale, standing as the chief obstacle to the achieving of maximum openness and plasticity, are contexts that have become so "entrenched" that they have gained "immunity to challenge and revision in the course of ordinary social activity."[105] These are contexts (or schemes of association) whose hold on us has become so strong that, in the absence of some revolutionary intervention, we will never be moved to look outside them or go beyond them. The doctrine of "internal development" or "destabilization" urges us to activities that will fragment and weaken[106] the frozen demarcations protected by such contexts, so that they will become less and less the prison houses of human possibility and more and more the areas in which human possibility can exercise its capacity for growth.

My response to this urging is to assert that there exist no contexts of either type, because all contexts are equally (if differently) constraining. The assertion may seem counterintuitive, but it can perhaps be rendered less so if we consider one of Unger's concrete recommendations, that we engage "in the systematic remaking of all direct personal connections . . . through their progressive emancipation from a background plan of social division and hierarchy."[107] As long as such a plan is in force, Unger explains, people are confined to "fixed roles . . . according to the position that they hold within a predetermined set of social or gender contrasts," and he urges us to unfreeze these roles by combining them. "For example, people may be enabled and encouraged to combine in a single character qualities that ruling stereotypes assign separately to men and women."[108] Now, of course, many people can and have done exactly that, inspiring articles in the popular press and even motion pictures; and the result certainly has been a change in the way many men and women conceive of their roles. But it is not correct, I think, to describe that change as one in which constraints have been eliminated or even relaxed in a way that contributes to the freeing of the individual from background plans of division and hierarchy. Rather, the shape of the background plan will have been altered, so that its components—those assumptions and distinctions that are for the time being unquestioned and unquestionable—will not be what they were before; but the *category* of the (currently) unquestionable will be as firmly in place as it ever was and will not in any way have been diminished on some absolute scale. In order to put into question the fixity of the qualities assigned by stereotypes to men and women, innumerable other fixities (the distinction between home and workplace, adult and child, workweek and weekend) must remain unchallenged; and were they challenged the challenge could only be intelligible against the background of hierarchies and divisions that could not themselves be challenged because it would be within them that thinking, critical or any other kind, was going on. In short, all contexts have the same (general) shape, a background plan made up of "predetermined contrasts", and an area of "free" inquiry or "open texture" which has exactly the extent and content the background plan allows. Although the structure is a binary one—settled/unsettled—the unsettled is itself configured in a dependent relation to the settled. It follows, then, that no context is looser—more open to revision—than any other; no context is "naturally" suited to be the starting point on the road to liberation.

That's the bad news, but the good news (actually the same news) is that no context is more set—less open to revision—than any other; no context can gain "immunity" to challenge, because challenge—in the form of a background plan, *parts* of which can always be foregrounded—is built into what Unger variously calls "schemes of associations" and "formative contexts." And, indeed, he himself says as much when he speaks of the "transformative possibilities built into the very mechanisms of social stabilization."[109] It is just that he thinks these possibilities—the possibility of turning a critical eye on a previously unexamined "given"—can only be tapped by a special reflective attitude that is developed in conscious opposition to routine ways of thinking and acting, whereas I think that routine ways of thinking and acting can themselves generate the moments in which their transformative possibilities are seized.

Consider as a humble but accessible example the following classroom situation. In the midst of a discussion of a poem, a student raises his hand to offer an observation, and is told by a teacher that while his comment is an interesting one, it isn't literary; it is appropriate to some other discipline, history, or economics, or anthropology. At this point the student will have at least two options: he can acquiesce in the instructor's dismissal of his point, or he can challenge the grounds of that dismissal by questioning the notion of literature by which his observation has been stigmatized as irrelevant. If he takes the latter course there is the possibility (not the inevitability) that the "grounding" definitions and categorical distinctions within which the course had been proceeding will be changed and that at least in one classroom literature will no longer be thought of as an activity performed independently of social and political pressures. Of course, should that possibility be realized, constraints will not have been eliminated or relaxed, but reconfigured, so that other questions will be regarded as obvious, and other concerns will be known in advance to be beside the (newly defined) literary point. (There will still be a background plan, as much in force as ever, but it will not be the same one.)

But, someone might respond, isn't it the case that change of that kind or any other will be more or less likely depending on the structure of the classroom situation? Won't a pedagogical context in which student questions are encouraged and even solicited be more conducive to reconsiderations of basic assumptions than a context in which the instructor's authority is strongly asserted and there is no regular procedure for challenging it? In short, aren't some schemes of association more open to revision than others? The answer to all these questions is no. The difference between a classroom in which participation is routine and a classroom in which a student question would constitute an intervention is not a difference between structures less and more constraining, but a difference between types of structures of constraint. If in one structure there is a pressure to refrain from speaking, in the other there is a pressure to refrain from keeping silent. A student who feels that he must speak (because he knows that silence will be held against him) is not free relative to the student who feels that speaking carries with it the risk of disapproval and penalty; both students are directed in their actions by their understanding of what is and is not an "acceptable" form of behavior in the situation, and the fact that in one situation it is acceptable and indeed *obligatory* to speak doesn't mean that participants in that situation are freer than those who, in another situation, are *allowed* to remain silent. Indeed, it seems that for many students no situation is more threatening and intimidating than one in which they are enjoined from remaining passive. ("Be ye free" is *not* the command of a liberator.)

The point of the example is not to show that the reconsideration
of basic assumptions is impossible, but to demonstrate both that no
particular formative context or scheme of association is "by nature"
the site of reconsideration, and that when reconsideration occurs it will
not be because a special self-reflective stance—a capacity existing apart
from the capacities inherent in ordinary contexts of practice—will have
been assumed, but because someone for some reason (the reasons cannot be cataloged or predicted) has raised a question that an ordinary
context of practice already (implicitly) contains. The power of which
Unger continually speaks, the "power of the self eternally to transcend
the limited imaginative and social worlds that it constructs,"[110] the
power of the individual "to overcome and revise, with time, every social or mental structure in which he moves,"[111] is not a power exercised
in opposition to the sway of contexts, but a power that contexts make
available, a power whose effect is not to transcend the limits of social
and mental structures, but to redraw the lines of structures that will be
no less limiting than they were before. Rather than being the property
of someone characterized by an ability to break contexts, the power of
revision is the power contexts confer on someone who can only exercise it in a context-specific shape. It is not an abstract power, and therefore it cannot be stored in a reservoir from which one can freely draw.
It is not a power that can be cultivated or summoned up at will (you
can't turn it on by throwing a switch marked "critical reflective capacity") because it does not exist apart from the particular conditions
of its possible emergence. In short, the context-breaking power is entirely contextual, and rather than transcending contexts its exercise
will, at the most, re-form (not reform) them.

For it to be otherwise, for there to be the possibility that change
could mark an emancipation from background plans rather than the
exchanging of one for another, both selves and contexts would have
to be reimagined in unimaginable ways. And that is in fact how Unger's argument works, by conceiving of selves and contexts as entities
with the capacity of being without content. Selves that are progressively
emancipated from social divisions, hierarchies, and roles would be selves
with no orientation or angle of habitual vision that inclined them in this
direction rather than that. They would be selves without a core of
assumptions in relation to which the shape of things (physical, mental,
moral) came into immediate and unreflective view. The creation of
such selves is the goal of what Unger calls the "system of destabiliza-

tion rights," the right to "disrupt those forms of division and hierarchy that . . . manage to achieve stability only by distancing themselves from . . . transformative conflicts."[112] It is the right perpetually to unsettle and to be unsettled, and were the condition of being unsettled to become more and more constitutive of the self, the contexts of its activities (such as they might be) would be correspondingly unsettled, characterized (a word in danger of being incoherent) by an openness to revision so total that revisability would be their essence. But of course all of this is a contradiction in terms. Contexts and selves in perpetual movement can have no stability of form, and while that is precisely the state of being (or nonbeing) that Unger desires, it does not correspond to anything that is possible for a finite creature, for a creature defined by his situatedness. Such a creature must always be somewhere (in a context) in order to be something (a self); and if it is never anywhere, if it stands free of all confining hierarchies and roles, it is nothing.

Yet paradoxical though it may seem, nothing is what Unger wants us all to be, and late in the essay he declares as much when he gives his program its final and most revealing name, "negative capability."[113] "Negative capability" is defined as "the practical and spiritual, individual and collective empowerment made possible by the disentrenchment of formative structures,"[114] and we can see exactly what that means by recalling the original context of the term in Keats's praise of Shakespeare:

It struck me what quality went to form a man of achievement, especially in literature, and which Shakespeare possessed so enormously—I mean *Negative Capability,* that is, when a man is capable of being in uncertainties, mysteries, doubts without any irritable reaching after fact and reason. Coleridge, for instance, would let go by a fine isolated verisimilitude . . . from being incapable of remaining content with half knowledge.[115]

In this famous comparison, Coleridge comes off badly because he insists on being certain, on being firmly placed within a perspective that delivers stable facts and is intolerant of doubt. Shakespeare, on the other hand, is capable of entertaining and even multiplying doubts indefinitely and seems not to feel the need to be grounded by an unshifting structure of fact and reason. Generations of Shakespeare critics have enlarged on Keats's observation by saying that what distinguishes the poet is the ability completely to sublimate his own convictions. Whatever position he may have occupied on a particular matter, he manages to project himself sympathetically into the positions occupied by his many and varied characters. He therefore seems, continue the critics, to be all of them and none of them, to be nowhere and everywhere. Or to put it as it has often (and revealingly) been put, he seems to be not a man, but a God.

I say "revealingly" because the vision (and specter) of God is waiting for us at the end of "The Critical Legal Studies Movement" just as it was at the end of *Knowledge and Politics*. You will recall that the whole point of the essay is to come up with a program that does not require God to speak its details and direction. The point is underlined early on when Unger distinguishes between the method of internal development which "pushes by gradual steps toward ever more drastic ways of reimagining society," and "visionary" insight, which "begins with the picture of a reordered human world."[116] Unger attempts to soften the contrast by claiming that the prophet can only be understood because something of what he urges "may be discerned already at work in the anomalies of personal encounter and social practice." But as I have argued here, any discerning of an anomaly will occur from *within* some social practice, and therefore cannot be the beginning of a process by which social practice is transcended altogether. The distinction between the internal and the visionary, between something engineered and something revealed, is sharper than Unger wants it to be, and it is only by blurring it (after having introduced it) that he avoids the realization that without a revelation—without a God who has spoken—internal development can't get started. If negative capability is the "empowerment made possible by the disentrenchment of formative structures," then it is not an empowerment of the kind that Unger requires, because the disentrenchment of one formative structure is always simultaneous with the establishment of another. Whatever "power" the agent acquires he acquires by courtesy of the new structure, and therefore it cannot be a power by which he is emancipated (even partially) from the sway of structure altogether. Truly emancipatory power can only be provided by an agent who is already emancipated, contained and constrained by no structure, capable of entering and exiting from every structure at will.

It is such an agent that Unger hopes to produce by the bootstrapping agendas he variously calls "deviationist doctrine," "internal development," "institutional reconstruction," "expanded doctrine," and "destabilization rights." He hopes, that is, to institute conditions that will promote "the growth of negative capability."[117] But negative capability is not something that can grow. Either you have all of it, or you have none of it. If you are a finite being, and therefore situated, you are wholly situated, and no part of you or your experience is asituational; your every capability is positive, a reflection and extension of the system of belief that bespeaks you and your possibilities, and there is nothing negative (detached, independent, free) to nurture. And if you are not a finite being, if you don't believe anything in particular and therefore don't believe anything at all (since beliefs are by definition particular, products of partial perspectives, a phrase obviously redundant), but straddle all beliefs like the colossus Shakespeare's Caesar seemed for a time to be, you are a god, and growth is beside the point. Despite all his efforts Unger is unable to provide a traversable middle ground, a space in which transcendence has not yet arrived but constraints have in part been relaxed, a space that offers the opportunity of transforming (rather than merely extending) work, a space of *politics,* not of politics as "a disconnected series of trophies with which different factions mark their victories,"[118] but of a politics that "promises to liberate societies from their blind lurching between protracted stagnation and rare and risky revolution,"[119] a politics whose end will make what we know as politics unnecessary. Simply by calling his project "negative capability" Unger acknowledges (if only inadvertently) that he is once again at the impasse he had reached at the end of *Knowledge and Politics,* unable to chart a route by which the ideal of universal community can be realized in history and by historical processes. The capability that is required is at once unimaginable, since our imaginations can only image it in their own form, and unmanufacturable, since to manufacture it you would already have to be in possession of it and in the place—no place and every place—to which it was to bring you; it is a capability that can only be invoked, either forthrightly as Unger does when he cries, "Speak, God," or more obliquely by a phrase ("negative capability") that has no possible realization in everyday life.

The last sentence of "The Critical Legal Studies Movement," like the last sentence of *Knowledge and Politics,* is justly famous. Speaking of the "cold altars" before which the legal academy's shamefaced members insincerely pray, he says of himself and his fellows, "we turned away from those altars and found the mind's opportunity in the heart's revenge."[120] It would seem that the difference between this confident affirmation and the note of passive supplication on which the earlier book ends could not be more marked. But the difference blurs and disappears when we ask what exactly is the heart's revenge? In Unger's terms it is the refusal of the awakened heart to bind itself to the laws of any received system of authority in order that it might expand to accommodate the laws that underwrite the universe. But simply to put it that way (a way fully in harmony with the direction of Unger's thought) is to recall the context in which the manner of that heart's making is prescribed in 2 Corinthians: "Forasmuch as ye are manifestly declared to be the epistle of Christ . . . written not with ink but with the Spirit of the living God; not in tables of stone but in fleshy tables of the heart." It is all here, the opposition of external and inefficacious constraints to the constraints which, because they have been internalized, have joined the universal and particular. But here also is the insistence that this joining can only be effected by an agency more than human, by the Spirit of the living God. Only a God can make gods in his image. The heart's revenge is finally the revenge of human actuality on the aspiration Unger is no closer to achieving than he was when he sent up his prayers to a still silent God.

V

In offering this critique of Unger, I may appear to fall into one of the categories he scorns, "people who implicitly deny the transformability of arrangements whose contingency they also assert."[121] That is, although I agree with Unger when he asserts that no scheme of association has conclusive authority, I deny that this insight can in and of itself loosen the hold of the schemes of association within which we live and move and have our being (although I do not deny that transformation of those schemes can be effected in many ways). My reasoning is simple: the insight that all schemes of association are contingent—rest on an historical rather than a natural authority—does not provide us with a point of leverage on any particular scheme. All it tells us is that any particular scheme, no matter how firmly established, has been put in place by political efforts and that in principle political efforts can always dislodge it. But once that is said, the political efforts still have to be made, and the assertion that they *can* be made is not one of them. That is, you don't challenge the presuppositions of some formative context merely by saying that a challenge is possible. All the work remains to be done, and until it is done, no currently entrenched scheme of association will even tremble, much less be shaken to its foundations.

"Arrangements," then, are not transformed simply by realizing that their transformation is a possibility. The authority of contingent schemes of association is not shaken simply by an awareness of their contingency. Moreover, contingent authority itself cannot be weakened *in general* because particular manifestations of contingent authority have been challenged and set aside. Contingency *itself* is never on trial, only those divisions and hierarchies that follow from the institution of some or other contingent plan; and when those divisions and hierarchies have been abandoned or supplanted it will only be because other divisions and hierarchies, themselves no less contingent, have been instituted in their place. In short, contingency, the fact that every formative context is revisable, is never overcome, even in part; it is merely given a new form in the victory (always temporary) of one partial vision over another. Oppositional activity is not transformative in the sense Unger requires; it is oppositional, a matter of faction warring against faction, interest contending with interest; and when the battle is over, emancipation from the background plan of firmly entrenched assumptions and categories will not have been advanced in the slightest degree.

It would seem that in saying this I will have affirmed Unger's darkest vision, a combination of idolatry and resignation in which the operations of law and other forms of social regulation and management are nothing more than the "context-specific calculations of effect."[122] In such a world, Unger complains, "it will always be possible to find, retrospectively, more or less convincing ways to make a set of distinctions or failures to distinguish look credible."[123] That is to say, the distinctions will only be convincing from within the perspective of some newly victorious context; they will be merely "credible," that is, believable, perspicuous in the light of beliefs; and since beliefs are by definition partial, as distinctions and convictions they will be illegitimate. This is the logic that underlies the entire essay and provides its urgency, but I find the logic incoherent because I can make no sense of the notion of convictions that do not flow from belief. If I am convinced of something it will be because within the assumptions that ground my consciousness I cannot see how it could be otherwise. Independently of such assumptions—or some *angled* opening of the world—I would not be a consciousness and conviction would not be achievable. Moreover, if I *am* a consciousness and I do have a conviction, it makes no sense to say it "looks" credible; it *is* credible, and there is no better, purer kind of credibility to which my conviction might be referred for judgment.

What this means is that no one could occupy the position of false consciousness to which the liberal antimonies have supposedly brought us; none of us is possessed by convictions in which we do not fully believe in or in relation to which we have a reservation rooted in some higher vision. Despite what Unger claims in *Knowledge and Politics,* the contradictions in liberal psychology do not describe anyone's "moral experience";[124] in no one are the "two halves of the self" at war, with a despotic reason struggling to control a blind desire. Rather, desire and reason are always and already joined, for it is from the perspective of some way of conceiving of the world—some partisan vision complete with goals and norms and procedures—that one's sense of the reasonable derives. And since perspectival conceptions of the world are all we have—for finite creatures perspective is unavoidable—there is no more abstract form of reason in relation to which one might feel divided. All of which is to say that one believes what one believes, and therefore one believes that what one believes is true, correct, reasonable. Of course, the structure of one's belief is always challengeable in ways I have described elsewhere, and should the challenge be successful, one will then believe something else, and it will be in relation to that something else that the category of "reason" will take shape.

The result will be the history (both personal and institutional) that Unger disapprovingly characterizes as "an endless series of ad hoc adjustments," a "collection of makeshift apologies," and mere "rhetorical posturing."[125] But these accusations lose their sting when one realizes that what they amount to is a complaint that disputes are settled and problems solved in relation to the norms and urgencies one experiences in particular contexts, and that since in the course of any practice the context of concern will be continually changing, the shape and content of resolution will be changing too. It is only from a point of view uninvolved in the practice (except as a deliberately distanced observer of it) that the succession of outcomes will seem inconsistent. To the participants in the disputes and negotiations that lead to the outcomes, there will be no inconsistency, because the pressures they feel and respond to are the *local* pressures of concrete urgencies rather than the abstract pressure exerted by a demand for transcontextual consistency. Moreover, that abstract pressure cannot properly be exerted on the history of concrete decisions, because it lacks the content that would render its judgments relevant. Not that the abstract pressure lacks content altogether. It has the content of the speculative— that is, philosophical—tradition from which it emerges, a tradition in which one of the primary tasks is to describe the shape and conditions of rationality as they exist independently of any practice or institution whatsoever. But having deliberately removed itself from the concerns and desiderata of practices and institutions, it cannot now with justice propose to judge those practices and institutions and find them inadequate. They are inadequate only with respect to a standard that rejects their urgencies in advance but itself remains empty, and I think that we are more than justified in rejecting that standard (which has nothing to say except "no") and deciding that for all practical purposes— the only kind of purposes there are—it doesn't matter.

When Unger declares that "every thoughtful law student or lawyer has had the disquieting sense of being able to argue too well . . . for too many conflicting solutions," and concludes that "because everything can be defended, nothing can,"[126] he is confusing and conflating two wholly disparate contexts of evaluation. In the one, the context of everyday determinations, defenses are mounted against a background of presently acknowledged relevancies in relation to which different courses of possible (in the sense of thinkable) actions will have different significances. In the other, the context of the classroom or the rhetorical exercise, defenses are mounted in response to a demand that one display a gymnastic skill, the mastery of which is the only relevancy acknowledged. "Everything" can be defended only when the master rule of the context of relevancy is "defend everything"; but that is *never* the master rule in a particular situation, so that the fact that one *could* perform gymnastically if that was what was being required does not mean that one *is* performing gymnastically in any everyday setting. The same argument disarms Unger's complaint that "it is always possible to find in actual legal materials radically inconsistent clues about the range of application of each of the models" of legal reasoning.[127] Of course it is possible, if finding inconsistencies (with respect to no positive vision) is the game you happen to be in; since the only rule in the game is "find inconsistencies," it will always be possible to imagine contextual conditions within which they will emerge. But "actual legal materials" are not the residue of a game in which contextual conditions are imagined; they are the records of what happened *within* contextual conditions the participants experienced and from which they had no distance; and the fact that someone else, at a remove, and at a later time, can appropriate those conditions for philosophical purposes—purposes as special as any other, and no larger or more general than any other—is simply beside the point, or, rather, has a point wholly different from the point that made the materials "legal" in the first place.

This is to say no more than Unger says at the close of *Knowledge and Politics,* and, as usual, he says it better than I could: "the final union of immanence and transcendence is foreign to the earthly life of which philosophy speaks."[128] "The Critical Legal Studies Movement" is an effort to make philosophy speak and speak intelligibly—with content—of a life beyond the earthly and so to provide through social engineering what God withholds so long as he declines to speak. The effort is grand, but it fails, and at the end of the essay God has not yet spoken. This leaves us where we were before the essay began, situated in whatever structure of conviction gives us our world and its indisputable facts, and asserting those facts with a vigor unqualified by philosophical reservation. If this is "rhetorical posturing," so be it. It is all we have and all we shall have until the perfect and whole shape of Truth returns at "her Master's second coming."

19. Critical Self-Consciousness,

Or

Can We Know What We're Doing?

I In an essay entitled "The Construal of Reality," Stephen Toulmin announces as his thesis that "the doctrines of the natural sciences are critical interpretations of their subject matter no less than those of the humanities."[1] He thus puts himself (or seems to put himself) in the line of those who have been persuaded by the anti-foundationalist arguments that have recently become so powerful in philosophy, literary criticism, and elsewhere. Those arguments are as varied as they are complex, but in whatever form they take, their presence is signaled by such assertions as "there are no unmediated facts," "all activity is irremediably interpretive," "there is no such thing as a neutral observation language," "there is no escaping politics," "all descriptions are from a perspective," etc. It is now almost obligatory to genuflect in the direction of these or similar pronouncements, and yet more often than not those who perform these genuflections almost immediately betray the larger insight from which they derive. Toulmin's essay is a particularly powerful case in point, since the proclaiming of that insight *is* his point. As we shall see, however, it is a point that barely survives its introduction.

Toulmin begins by declaring that the "positivist view of scientific argument" (p. 95), in which deductions follow upon pure observation, is untenable since scientists "always approach their investigations with . . . pre-existing questions" and therefore are from the first operating from within some "interpretive standpoint." In short, the proponents of the "objective method" were mistaken because the position of "pure spectator" (so necessary to their program) was a fiction. Apparently, however, it is a mistake they could have avoided by occupying that position less firmly and with reserve. Since they did not, Toulmin complains, the "inherent limits to the scope of this method were not . . .

borne in mind as carefully as they might have been" (p. 96). This seems an innocent enough statement until one realizes that it requires of the "objectivists" the very independence of standpoint whose possibility Toulmin has just denied. It requires, that is, a mind capable of standing to the side of its own ways of thinking in order to critique them. If only they had been more careful, Toulmin seems to be saying, seventeenth-century believers in "objective method" would have inhabited their beliefs in such a way as to not be constrained by them; unfortunately, they did not know what we now know—that "the standpoint of the detached onlooker . . . was no more than an abstraction" (p. 96)—and consequently they were not sufficiently on guard against the influence of their own assumptions. For Toulmin, the upshot of the revolution in scientific and humanistic thought reduces to a simple (and contradictory) caution: remember that your personal convictions are a function of your historical situation and be wary of allowing them to overwhelm your judgment. Accompanying this caution is an equally simple methodological direction: when the scientist is about his proper business, he "must acknowledge and discount his own reactions to and influence on that which he seeks to understand" (p. 97). This does not mean, Toulmin hastens to add, that the scientist should be without interests; after all, the inescapability of interest is one of the lessons the twentieth century has learned; it is just that having learned the lesson we can now bracket our interests and thereby protect ourselves against "any resulting biases and/or prejudices" (p. 106).

The question, of course, is, what enables us to do this? If, as Toulmin himself says, the "posture of pure spectator is no longer available even on the level of . . . theory," how is it that we can suddenly become pure spectators of our own mental operations? If we are already situated in a pregiven structure of interests, how is it that we can simply "discount" those interests as if they had no weight at all? Toulmin has no answers to these questions because it never even occurs to him to ask them, and it doesn't occur to him to ask them because he sees no connection between the anti-objectivism he now embraces and the recommendation that we proceed by setting aside everything that stands between us and objectivity. Or, rather, the connection he sees is one in which, paradoxically, the lesson of anti-foundationist thought—the lesson that we are always and already interpretively situated—becomes a way of escaping its implications. Because we now *know* that we are in a situation (the reasoning goes), we are in a better position to resist its pressures. It is by virtue of this form of "doublethink" (I have called it elsewhere "anti-foundationalist theory hope") that Toulmin can first acknowledge that "all of our scientific explanations and critical readings start from, embody, and imply some interpretive standpoint," and then immediately declare that "the operative question is, which of our positions [i.e., standpoints] are rationally warranted, reasonable or defensible—that is, well-founded rather than groundless opinions" (p. 109). My question is, from what position is this question about our positions to be asked? Either Toulmin means what he has just said and the warranting rationality is itself interpretive, in which case it cannot be used to discriminate between interpretations, or the warranting position exists independently of interpretation, in which case Toulmin's acknowledgment of the inevitability of interpretation is no more than an empty gesture. Either Toulmin is committed to the coherence of his argument and the notion of a rationally warranted choice is problematized, or he affirms the rationality of choice and his argument falls apart in the space between these two sentences. He simply cannot have it both ways, and his dilemma (of which he is wholly unaware) awaits anyone who first acknowledges the essential historicity of all human endeavor but then seeks a space or a moment in which the pressure of that historicity can be escaped.

For Toulmin (as for so many others) that space is named rationality, and the moment is one in which the mind, now armed with an awareness of its tendency to bias, turns its back on bias and moves into what Toulmin calls elsewhere the "courts of rationality," courts in which "all clearheaded men . . . are qualified to act."[2] In these courts the interpretive standpoint of any particular culture or epoch is "trumped," as it were, by an "impartial rational standpoint" which is "neutral as between the local and temporary views of different historico-cultural milieus" (p. 500). In other words, what the clearheaded man is cleared of (or from) is his own head, the repository of the "local and temporary views" that have fallen to him (or to which he has fallen; there is a theological vision lurking here) by virtue of the accidents and limitations of his education, professional training, political affiliations, etc. Once cleared of these views he can then turn an impartial eye on all positions, including his own, and begin to determine which of them "are rationally warranted, reasonable, or defensible."

As a picture of the way the mind operates (when it is at its best), this is decidedly conservative, for it makes progress a matter of *holding on* to something that is everywhere available if we can only keep our eye on it. The courts of rationality are always sitting, and if we could only remain in them we would be less blinded by the partial and delusive lights of local partisan opinion. The ideal situation, then, would be never to leave the precincts of reason's court, but, given human nature, this is an impossible ideal and the best we can do (and Toulmin obviously thinks that it is good enough) is periodically to reenter those precincts by divesting ourselves of any culturally conditioned baggage we have acquired along our historical way. Of course, says Toulmin, we come to any task already informed by interest, but nevertheless, we can "do our best to act in a *dis*interested way" (p. 106).

Again, this seems eminently reasonable (especially as an appeal to reason), and, moreover, it is what we all try to do in a variety of situations, scientific, legal, academic, etc. That is, we say to ourselves "with respect to this matter I am going to put aside my interests, preferences and biases; and consider the evidence and alternatives in an impartial manner." But what this formulation does not acknowledge is the extent to which the specification of what is and is not an "impartial manner" is itself an "interested" act, that is, an act performed within a set of assumptions—concerning what is and is not evidence and what are and are not criteria for judgment—that is, constitutive of and inseparable from some *partial* view of the world. It is not that "acting impartially" is an impossible form of behavior indistinguishable from other forms; it is rather that "acting impartially" is an activity whose shape is a function of a partisan, and therefore potentially challengeable ("you think *that's* evidence?") conception of what such an activity is and should be like; there is certainly a difference between "acting impartially" and acting in the name of one's preferences, but the difference is between different forms of interest-laden behavior—of behavior that is possible and intelligible only within the context of some interested, non-neutral vision—and not between interested behavior and something else. When we act impartially (and again I agree that we can) we do so "by our lights," which means that we act within and as an extension of an interpretive and therefore partial notion of what being impartial means.

This is the strong thesis of anti-foundationalist or interpretivist thought, and it is the only thesis worth taking seriously, the only one that is more than a gesture in the direction of culture and history. It is also the one Toulmin consistently avoids and evades in a manner so naked as to be almost charming: he advocates self-conscious reflection on one's own beliefs as a way to neutralize bias immediately after having asserted the unavailability of the "objective standpoint" that would make such reflection a possible achievement. Of course, he is not unique; there are many whose thought describes the same sequence. Wayne Booth, for example, begins a paragraph by acknowledging that since "every reader carries a load of prejudgments, since in fact he could not read anything without relying on them, one cannot exhort oneself simply to read with an 'open mind.'" This is, from my point of view, exemplary (except perhaps for the equivocation in "relying"), but in the very same paragraph Booth declares that it is possible to protect oneself from one's "prejudgments" by putting on a "true shield" in the form of a "healthy tentativeness about oneself and one's responses."[3] The trick, he says, is "in developing a habit of great skepticism about one's own hypotheses" (p. 225). It would indeed be a trick if it were possible (and in a weak sense, of course, it is possible), but again any skepticism one "developed" would have a content; that is, it would be made up of questions ("are there really no exceptions to this rule whose validity I am assuming?"), tests ("is there anything that would falsify this thesis?"), cautions ("don't rush to premature conclusions on the basis of inadequate evidence"), all of which would presuppose some set of already-in-place distinctions, hierarchies, values, definitions, which could not themselves be the object of "skepticism" because they formed the taken-for-granted background against and within which skepticism acquired its present shape. Skepticism is not a state, but an activity, something one performs, and one can perform it only within—and not outside of—the already structured field that is consciousness; it is a part of that field, and therefore it is a mistake to think that skepticism (or critical self-reflection or critique or self-awareness or provisionality or a healthy tentativeness or anything else in that line) has an independence of other (equally field-specific) operations such that it can act as a check on them. It is a mistake that Owen Fiss (still another who would acknowledge interpretivism and context but would escape their implications) makes when he declares that "'deliberation' is for me a way of thinking" and means that it is a way that protects him from the pressures of other ways by providing him with a space for "reflective moments of decision."[4] Again, my response would be that while such moments are certainly possible (we can and do think in a critical way about what we're doing, whether it be science or literary criticism or lawyering), they are not insulated from, but are a function of, the deeply assumed norms and standards that are the grounds of possibility of *any* moment, including those named "deliberation" or "reflection."

Additional examples could (and later will be) adduced, but I trust that the pattern—in which the force of history and perspective is admitted at one moment only to be discounted in the next—has been established and can now become the subject of analysis. We can begin that analysis by noting that the desire that informs the pattern is not only epistemological, but moral, and the morality is one in which reflection or deliberation or self-consciousness is invoked as a stay against the political. Toulmin's essay was written originally for a conference on the "politics of interpretation," and part of his point is that the political and and social aspects of scientific inquiry must not be confused with the more "determinative factor" of the objects to which such inquiry is directed (p. 99). That is to say, scientists must guard against allowing "their personalities, political views and background to distort their discriminations" (p. 103). In a similar vein, E. D. Hirsch warns against a situation in which "ideology, not truth, determines the results of inquiry"[5] with the result that we are left at the mercy of the "currents of intellectual fashion" (p. 155). Owen Fiss is even more explicit; it is "self-conscious reflection" that makes law possible, for without it judges would feel free to "generate a set of practices that would turn law into politics" (p. 197). In all of these statements, the political stands for the parochial, the interested, the partial, the partisan, the merely historical, in short for everything that turns the inquiring and judging eye away from an abiding rationality that stands ever ready to be consulted as a point of reference. It is finally a static vision, one that puts a premium on not straying beyond certain well-defined limits and this remains true even when the vision is being urged as a way of assuring progress, for the progress that is imagined is one in which every step taken is determined by guidelines and norms known in advance. In short, critical self-consciousness is for these conservative thinkers not a means of self-assertion, but a means of protecting the self from its own inherent limitations and tendencies, and it is thus a secular version of a familiar theological paradigm in which the passionate and carnal will must be submitted to the corrective teaching of an already revealed Word.

II

There is, however, another tradition in which the concept of critical self-consciousness is also prominent but wears another face. It is a tradition on the left, and the assumptions informing it are opposed at almost every point to the assumptions we have been examining (although, as we shall see, they lead finally to the same illegitimate conclusions). First of all, critical self-consciousness on the left, far from being a way of *neutralizing* politics, is a component in a frankly political program; moreover, it is a program which, rather than opposing rationality to interest, begins with the recognition that rationality, at least in its present form, is a structure of interest despite (and, indeed, by virtue of) its claims to the contrary. The program is thus rigorously and relentlessly negative, intent always on exposing or unmasking those arrangements of power that present themselves in reason's garb. As we shall see, the program bears many names—critique, feminism, deconstruction (in some versions), oppositional criticism, critical theory, negative dialectics, reading against the grain, critical legal studies—but whatever it is called, its goal is always as Herbert Marcuse (who calls it dialectic) characterizes it,

> to break down the self-assurance of commonsense, to undermine the sinister confidence in the power and language of facts, to demonstrate that unfreedom is so much at the core of things that the development of their internal contradiction leads necessarily to qualitative change: the explosion and catastrophe of the established state of affairs.[6]

We see at once how different this is from the more backward-looking and protective stance assumed by Toulmin, Booth, Hirsch, and Fiss, for whom the "established state of affairs"—which includes facts not in dispute, standards commonly accepted, traditions of inquiry long honored and followed—stands as a defense against what Booth calls the "depredations" of private or idiosyncratic agendas. In the context of "right" self-conscious practice, what has been established is what can be trusted; facts that have been ratified by public and universally acknowledged procedures (of science and reason) constitute an always-in-place measure of adequacy against which new ideas and proposals must justify themselves. In the world of dialectic or critique, however, it is exactly the reverse, for here we find a philosophy of suspicion, of systematic *dis*trust. "All thinking," says Marcuse, "that does not testify to an awareness of the radical falsity of the established forms of life is faulty thinking" (p. 451); and the chief form of faulty thinking is reason itself, or at least that version of reason that finds its best expression in the (supposedly) pure and interest-free operations of science and technology.

This does not mean that Marcuse abandons reason in favor of the irrational; rather, in concert with the other members of the Frankfurt School, he conceives of reason as a faculty which is true to itself—that is, to its transcendent goal—only when it reflects critically on the conditions of its present exercise. Those conditions include the assumed distinctions, categories, and hierarchies which determine the shape of reason's career at any one moment and in relation to which reason is often claimed to be independent. It is precisely that claim of reason—or, rather, of reason in the form it happens to take at a moment in history—that constitutes the danger; for if reason, or rationality, operates in ignorance of its enabling conditions, of the "givens" that history has put in (temporary) place—then those conditions are rendered invisible, exempt from reason's own scrutiny, and as a result rationality has become rationalization. In Habermas's words,

> this sort of rationality . . . removes the total social framework
> of interests in which strategies are chosen, technologies applied, and
> systems established from the scope of reflection and rational recon-
> struction. . . . That is why, in accordance with this rationality, the
> "rationalization" of the conditions of life is synonymous with the in-
> stitutionalization of a form of domination whose political character
> becomes unrecognizable.[7]

The name of this form of domination is variously "technical reason," "scientific method," and "pure," as opposed to critical, theory, and by any of its names it refers to a discourse and to an activity that is literally unthinkable apart from a set of historically established interests, but which nevertheless presents itself as autonomous and interest-free. The irony is that by insisting on this autonomy unreflective reason becomes a prisoner of the interests it fails to acknowledge. Rather than functioning as a transcendent standard against which currently predominant notions of the true and the real can be judged, reason becomes the unwitting servant of those notions. As a result, says Marcuse, "reason loses its philosophical power and its scientific right to define and project ideas and modes of Being beyond and against those established by the prevailing reality."[8] Potentially an instrument of liberation, reason in this dark scenario becomes the instrument of slavery and those who wield it inadvertently enslave themselves. "In the name of reason," says Adorno, "they turn power over to those who already possess it in the name of mystification. The power of reason today is the blind reason of those who currently hold power."[9]

Those who are thus captive of an unreflecting reason labor under a double delusion: they regard as natural and eternal an order of things that is in fact contingent and transformable; and they regard themselves as freely determining agents whereas, "in fact," as Max Horkheimer puts it, "even in their most complicated calculations they but exemplify the working of an incalculable social mechanism."[10] In short, they are blind to the constituted or constructed character both of the empirical world and of their own consciousnesses, and they are unable to see how either could possibly be changed. It is this double blindness that is to be dispelled by the work of critical theory (or critique or negative dialectic), by an attitude that refuses to accept the naturalness and inevitability either of present social conditions or of the forms of thought within which those conditions are understood. In Horkheimer's words,

> the critical attitude of which we are speaking is wholly distrustful of the rules of conduct with which society as presently constituted provides each of its members. The separation between individual and society in virtue of which the individual accepts as natural the limits prescribed for his activity is relativized in critical theory. The latter considers the overall framework which is conditioned by the blind interaction of individual activities . . . to be a function which originates in human action and therefore is a possible object of planful decision and rational determination of goals. ("Traditional and Critical Theory," p. 207)

The appearance of the word "rational" in this last sentence alerts us to the Janus-like nature of the critical project; on the one hand, the object of its critique is the rationality that accompanies (indeed, is a reflection of) the "overall framework" imposed by those who currently hold power; on the other hand, the project's goal is the establishment, by rational means, of an "overall framework" that is imposed by no one but is the result of planning by freely acting subjectivities who propose and dispose with eyes that have been opened by those same rational means. In a sense, then, rationality is at war with itself, that is, with the content permitted it by the prevailing conditions of empirical reality (so called); it is distrustful of itself, of the forms that it can take given the parameters of thought as they are presently constituted; and yet at the same time it is only within these forms that it knows itself. This is also the situation of those who would enroll in the critical project. Constituted by the society whose limitations they would transcend, they must struggle against horizons that are, *as far as they can see,* their own: "The identification . . . of men of critical mind with their society is marked by tension, and the tension characterizes all the concepts of the critical way of thinking" (p. 208). Men of critical mind "interpret the . . . categories of work, value, and production exactly as they are interpreted in the existing order." In fact, they could not do otherwise and are thus in some respects no different from men of an uncritical mind. What distinguishes them is an unwillingness to accept the categories within which they (like everyone else) think and move; for them, "the critical [as opposed to the unreflective or mindless] acceptance of the categories which rule social life contains simultaneously their condemnation" (p. 208). This condemnation flows from the realization that these categories, however all-encompassing they may seem to be, are neither eternal nor "supra-historical," and that therefore to surrender to them (by living within them uncritically) would be "a sign of contemptible weakness" (p. 210). The weakness is the act (or nonact) of acquiescing in an image of oneself that falls far short of human potential and of the possibilities inherent in a true (not captive or subject) rationality: "Critical thought has a concept of man as in conflict with himself. . . . If activity governed by reason is proper to man, then existent social practice, which forms the individual's life down to its least details, is inhuman" (p. 210). It is most inhuman when it is most convincing, when the false (because partial and partisan) rationality of the current order of things prevents man from moving toward the freedom and autonomy that constitute his true nature.

There is, of course, more to be said about the critical project, and we shall return to it before the conclusion of this chapter, but even this brief summary is enough to make clear the differences between it and the more conservative project of those who, like Toulmin, counsel us to "discount" and set aside our own prejudices and interests. It would be the view of Marcuse, Adorno, Habermas, and Horkheimer that those who follow (or think they follow) Toulmin's counsel deceive themselves, for they merely exchange the bondage of interests frankly and self-consciously acknowledged for the much greater bondage of the interests that have captured the "deep structures" of society's thought. Even as they claim freedom from prejudices, they are slaves to prejudices they cannot see. What is required, if a condition of *true* freedom is to be achieved, is the enlargement or expansion of self-consciousness so that it embraces not only the prejudices that have a perspicuous shape and name, but the underlying and structural prejudices that now reserve for themselves the name of the *un*prejudiced.

The large question, of course, is how is this to be accomplished? For Toulmin, the task is easy; you simply suspend your personal opinions in favor of a calculus that is the respecter of no persons. But this simple resolve is unavailable to the members of the Frankfurt School, for whom what now *passes* for the impersonal calculus is at once the *habitus* of thought and the obligatory object of critique. Another way to put this is to observe that the critical project has two aspects, one negative and the other positive. The negative aspect generates the initial step of its program, "the critical dissolution of objectivism, . . . of the objectivist self-understanding . . . which suppresses the contribution of subjective activity to the preformed objects of possible knowledge."[11] In this stage (which threatens to be interminable) one first seeks out areas of life in which settled facts present themselves as reflections of nature and then exposes their dependence on (and support of) man-made structures of domination and suppression. It is the next (and crucial) stage that presents the difficulty, for it must proceed in ignorance of its goal. That goal is the realization of a society in which communication and perception are no longer distorted by the unexamined—and therefore unchallenged—categories within which life is currently lived; but since those same categories constitute the present horizons of knowledge, we cannot know in advance what it would be like to be free of them. We are, in a strong sense, proceeding in the dark, sure only that we exist in a state of slavery, but barred by that very condition from specifying the shape that our desired liberation will take. While critique in its negative aspect has a concrete and "doable" task—"the dissolution of identifications, the breaking of fixations, and the destruction of projections"[12]—critique in its positive aspect looks very much like a project without content.

It must be said that those who espouse critique are not unaware of the dilemma inherent in the urging of a future whose configurations they cannot know. Horkheimer, for example, acknowledges that while he can easily name his desire—the transformation of "a fragmented society in which material and ideological power operate to maintain privileges" into "an association of free men in which each has the same possibility of self-development"—he can say little about the steps by which that desire could be achieved. "But how many tendencies will actually lead to this association, how many transitional phases have been reached, how desirable and intrinsically valuable individual pre-liminary stages may be, and what their historical importance is in rela-tion to the idea—all this will be made clear only when the idea is brought to realization."[13] But the question that immediately arises is, how do we know that all this will be made clear? How do we know that by exposing a given context as interested and politically repressive we have taken a step toward freedom and not merely stepped into an-other context, no less interested, no less repressive?

The answer given by the critical theorists is at once breathtaking and daring: we know that the critical project will finally succeed by virtue of the fact that we have been able to think of it. That is, the insight that the present order of things is neither natural nor inevitable is itself an indication that the totalizing claims of that order can be resisted; simply by giving voice to the desire for freedom, one initiates the process at the end of which the desire can be realized, even if the exact shape of its future realization cannot be specified: "one and the same subject who wants a new state of affairs, a better reality . . . also brings it forth" ("Traditional and Critical Theory," p. 217). Even though the "harmony between being and thought," between "rational intention and its realization," is now "obscure," its future emergence is assured by the very fact that some men are now striving to achieve it. The hoped-for state in which there will be a relation of identity between a purified rationality and a humanity that finally knows itself has not yet come to pass; but in the struggle to bring it about we experience "a fragmentary reflection of this relation, to the extent that a will which aims at the shaping of society as a whole is already consciously operative in the construction of the theory and practice which will lead to it." (p. 218). That is to say, the condition of unfreedom is breached the moment that we can reflect upon it, for that act of reflection occurs in a space not ruled by the presuppositions of the established reality, and therefore begins the process of over-throwing (by seeing through) that reality and potentially of all the other "realities" imposed upon us by the powers that (presently) be.

Here, then, is the strong—and necessary—claim made by the critical theorists for reflection: it exists in a realm wholly independent of the realms that are the objects of its severe and searching action. "The standards of self-reflection," says Habermas, "are exempted from the singular state of suspension in which those of all other cognitive processes require critical evaluation."[14] Indeed, he continues, these standards (autonomy and responsibility) "possess theoretical certainty"; they can be "apprehended a priori." The man who does not apprehend them "leads an unfree existence because he does not become conscious of his self-reflecting self activity," but for the man who is conscious in the right way, that is, self-conscious, *"Self-reflection is at once intuition and emancipation, comprehension and liberation from dogmatic dependence."*[15] Or, in other words, "ye shall know that the truth is other than it seems, and that knowledge shall set you free."

Of course, this will only work if the moment of self-reflection is in no way dependent on that from which it is to set us free, the presently given world of facts, imperatives, choices, agenda, etc. This is, as I have already said, the strong and necessary claim made by the critical theorists for reflection: it escapes the illegitimate and imposed limitations of the prevailing modes of thought, and by escaping them initiates their overthrow; the realization that one is unfree is itself a step toward freedom. But what if one's very idea of unfreedom, and therefore of freedom, is derived from—in the sense of emerging within—the "prevailing modes of thought"? It would then be the case that reflection would constitute not a *break* from current conditions, but a modification of those conditions in a direction they themselves make possible. Reflection, in short, would not be a radically different (and therefore emancipatory) activity, but an activity like any other, doable and intelligible only within (and by virtue of) a pregiven field of thought and action; and as an activity no different (in kind) from any other, reflection would aim not at universal goals, but at local or community-specific goals; it would then be the case that reflection (so called) would just be a fancy name for persuasion, and that the freedom in whose name it pronounced would be not a transcendent, but a local, particular, and *contestable* concept. How do the proponents of critique know that what they urge is in the service of all mankind and not merely a function that they themselves happen, at the moment, to desire? As Henning Ottman puts it, "The interest shown by a critical theory in doing away with concrete power structures could itself be a child of the times and thereby merely reflect the interest of a particular period and not of a theory of knowledge in general."[16] In the context of an argument that begins by insisting on the inescapability of interest, what, aside from a flat assertion or declaration of faith, supports the claim of the so-called "emancipatory interest" to be different?

Critical theorists have themselves asked this question and, in general, have answered either by identifying some aspect of contemporary experience as a small-scale model of the future state of emancipation or by proposing a method by means of which the universal interest might be nurtured until it emerges fully known. The aspect of contemporary experience most often identified with the project of liberation is art in general and literature in particular. Literature and critique, asserts Marcuse, share a common element, the "search for 'an authentic language,'" that is, for "the language of negation as the Great Refusal to accept the rules of a game in which the dice are loaded."[17] Such a language will be a language of "contradiction," and what it will contradict is the "language of facts" as they are now given. What this negatively liberating language shows is that "reality is other and more than" that which has been "codified" (p. 447). There is general agreement among the partisans of critique, reports David Held, that art generates "emancipatory effects" when by its "very mode of expression it 'opens the established reality' and 'negates reified consciousness.'"[18] Authentic works of art, says Adorno, are characterized by "their . . . rejection of the guilt of a life which blindly and callously reproduces itself, and by their insistence on independence and autonomy, on separation from the prevailing realm of purposes,"[19] and by virtue of that autonomy and separation they stand even now as a "promise of a condition in which freedom were realized." Profoundly at odds with the very conditions of their production, authentic works of art (this time the words are Horkheimer's) "denounce the prevailing forms of communication as instruments of destruction."[20]

But finally all of this amounts to little more than an assertion that a number of equally mysterious (that is, genealogically impossible) activities and agents exist in mutual support. There is, first of all, oppositional (or critical) man, and then there is oppositional language, which in turn makes possible oppositional art, all of which are united by the unexplained and, I would contend, unimaginable capacity of standing apart from "the prevailing realm of purposes." Multiplying impossibilities does not seem to be the way to demonstrate that one of them can be realized. Not that there is no line of reasoning behind this celebration of related negativities. The line is quite clear. (1) What's wrong with the world is that the true nature of things and the true nature of man and the true nature of reason have been obscured and suppressed by the tyranny of ideologically imposed "facts," forms of language, and forms of thought. (2) As a result, perception (of the world and self), communication about what we see, and reasoning about what to do next all occur within a context of massive distortion. (3) That distortion must be removed if we are to see, talk, and reason in ways that are not constricted and enforced in advance. (4) Self-reflection, countercommunicative language, and avant-garde art, because they resist the coercion of the "empirically given reality" and "the prevailing realm of purposes," are first steps in the project of removing distortion and replacing it with a society "whose members' autonomy and responsibility [have] been realized," a society in which communication has "developed into [a] non-authoritarian and universally practiced dialogue."[21] (5) In that society, selves free from ideological constraints will reason freely about alternative courses of action in the light of purposes and goals that belong to no particular party but all of mankind. It all sounds fine until one asks a single question. How, if the tyranny of ideologically imposed "facts" is so complete, if the lines of communication and thought are so wholly in bondage, if as Marcuse puts it, "the established universe of discourse is that of an unfree world,"[22] how, if distortion is everywhere and everywhere controlling (the first thesis, after all, of critical thought), does one even *begin* to get a purchase on that which is *not* distorted?

III

One of the more elaborate and elaborated answers to this question has been given by Habermas in the name of what he calls "Universal Pragmatics." The project of Universal Pragmatics begins with the thesis that even in the most distorted and alienated moments of communication there remains some small residue of or connection with the root purpose of all communication—the assertion and transmission of truth. "Anyone acting communicatively," Habermas asserts, "must in performing any speech action, raise universal validity claims and suppose that they can be vindicated."[23] Thus presupposed in every speech act is the possibility of rational consensus between communicating parties concerning the truth of things in the world. Indeed, "our first sentence expresses unequivocally the intention of universal and unconstrained consensus,"[24] and all subsequent sentences share in the goal of bringing about "an agreement that terminates in the intersubjective mutuality of reciprocal understanding, shared knowledge, mutual trust, and accord with one another."[25] Such an agreement would be marked by a homology between related transparencies, of intention, linguistic form, and true propositions. When agreement between two subjects is genuine, there exists "between the two . . . an accord concerning the rightness of an utterance in relation to a normative background" (p. 3) and "in addition the two can come to an understanding about something in the world, and they can make their intentions understandable to one another."

Such, at any rate, is the case in what Habermas calls the "ideal speech situation," a situation consisting of perfectly symmetrical and reciprocal relationships between participants who neither dominate nor deceive one another. In such a situation,

> the bracketed validity claims of assertions, recommendations, or warnings are the exclusive object of discussion; . . . participants, themes, and contributions are not restricted except with reference to the goal of testing the validity claims in question; . . . no force except that of the better argument is exercised; and . . . as a result, all motives except that of the cooperative search for truth are excluded.[26]

Given such a happy situation, Habermas concludes, we can be sure that "a consensus about a recommendation to accept a norm . . . expresses a 'rational will' in relation to a *common* interest ascertained without *deception.* The interest is common because the constraint-free consensus permits only what *all* can want." That is to say, in the ideal speech situation individual interests become indistinguishable from the interests of humanity because an individual or particular interest is continually being checked against the normative background of a generalized rationality. "The limits of a decisionistic treatment of practical questions are overcome as soon as argumentation is expected to test the generalizability of interests, instead of being resigned to an impenetrable pluralism of apparently ultimate value orientations (or belief-acts or attitudes)" (p. 108).

What strikes one immediately about the "ideal speech situation" is its resemblance to Toulmin's "courts of rationality." Certainly it has the same function; to replace the partial perspective of local interest with the universal perspective of an interest (no interest) that is identified with no one in particular and therefore serves everyone in general. The difference, of course, is that for Toulmin the courts of rationality are readily and unproblematically accessible, while for Habermas rationality, as we are now able to recognize it, is captive to the very interests it should transcend. What this means is that however many times Habermas *describes* the ideal speech situation, it remains little more than the expression of a fervent desire, and we are still without an answer to the question of how that desire is to be achieved.

Habermas attempts to provide such an answer in a lengthy essay entitled, "What Is Universal Pragmatics?," an essay in which he not only rehearses the desideratum of the ideal speech situation, but tells us how it can be brought about. What we must do, he says, is focus on those aspects of communication that are already involved in universal validity claims and exclude or bracket everything else. Since language is the medium in which we know and see, we can purify (and transform) consciousness by purifying language, for "today the problem of language has replaced the traditional problem of consciousness: the transcendental critique of language supersedes that of consciousness."[27] "What raises us out of nature is the only thing whose nature we can know: *language*."[28] And how do we do this? Habermas's answer is complicated and involves a series of operations, but as we shall see, every one of them, rather than solving, merely reinstitutes the problem on which the critical project repeatedly founders, the problem of beginning or taking the first step.

Habermas himself begins many times, first by borrowing from Chomsky the notion of reconstructing from surface phenomena "the universal validity basis of speech" (p. 5). This Habermas further characterizes as "the rational reconstruction of generative structures underlying the production of symbolic formations"; that is, of specific speech acts in empirical situations. Habermas acknowledges the many others who have set for themselves the same goal—the goal of specifying the most basic and abstract level of competence—but he complains that his predecessors "do not generalize radically enough and do not push through the level of accidental contexts to general and unavoidable presuppositions" (p. 8). That is, they do not transcend but remain within the "prevailing realm of purposes" because "they start from the model of the isolated, purposive-rational actor" (p. 12). Having said this, Habermas is now obligated to explain how it is possible to do anything *but* "start from the model of the . . . purposive-rational actor," and, of course, he does not meet that obligation by pointing out that no one else has met it either. He must, if he is going to make good on his claims, show us the way.

He does so, or purports to do so, by performing an act of exclusion: "In what follows," he declares, "I shall take into consideration only consensual speech actions," leaving aside both "strategic" speech action and "the level of argumentative speech" (p. 4). By "consensual speech actions" Habermas means those that occur in "an idealized case of communicative action . . . in which participants share a tradition and their orientations are normatively integrated to such an extent that they start from the same definition of the situation and do not disagree about the claims to validity that they reciprocally raise" (pp. 208–9); and this idealized case is contrasted with cases in which communicative acts are performed for pragmatic or utilitarian reasons (p. 41) and are therefore oriented to local and partisan efforts (p. 41) rather than to the establishment of universal claims of validity. It is in these latter cases that deception, distortion, and competition replace truthfulness as the ruling motivation of speech and conversation. But no sooner has this version of the Habermasian project been articulated than the familiar difficulties, which it does not obviate but renders more urgent, return. First of all, how is one to know that a shared orientation between participants is a reflection of universal validity claims and not of the claims of a local or partisan project whose sway is (at least for the moment) unchallenged? How does one know, that is, whether the pragmatic and strategic components of speech have been set aside and bracketed or have merely been concealed by the force of "presupposed norms" (p. 38). It will do no good to respond by citing, as Habermas does, "clear cases in which the reactions of the subjects converge" (p. 19); for the clarity of those cases may itself be a function of the "epistemic presuppositions" (p. 29) of which they are supposedly independent. And even if it were possible to be sure that you had abstracted away from all "particular situations of use," what then would you be left with? The answer is "nothing." I am not denying that there are clear cases or that they can serve to stabilize discourse, merely observing that the clarity they display is a function of the situations they supposedly transcend. Habermas himself notes with approval the Wittgensteinian dictum "that the meaning of linguistic expressions can be identified only with reference to situations of possible employment" (p. 30), yet he nevertheless persists in positing meanings "determined by formal properties of speech situations in general, and not by particular situations of use." The trouble is that he remains unable to produce any such meanings even though he invokes them as a necessary component of his program. He can only proceed by assuming as already available the very conditions (of freedom from the particular and the perspectival) whose possibility he set out to establish.

He assumes them again when he proposes to begin (again) by disregarding "institutionally bound speech actions" (p. 38)—speech actions intelligible only within pregiven normative contexts—in favor of "institutionally unbound speech actions"—speech actions that are intelligible without reference to any institutional context whatsoever. But, again, it is the *existence* of institutionally unbound speech acts (and therefore of a linguistic space in which critical reflection can occur) that is the question, and the question is begged if it is answered simply by invoking the phrase "institutionally unbound speech acts." The problem is to *find* some, and the only direction Habermas provides is to "start with concrete speech acts embedded in specific contexts and then disregard all aspects these utterances owe to their pragmatic functions" (p. 31). But, of course, this is a direction that needs a direction; it is all well and good to tell us to disregard the context of pragmatic action, but we are ourselves pragmatically situated and any disregarding we managed to do would be no less context-bound than the "functions" that were its object. "Disregard" is finally an empty imperative (exactly like the imperative to "discount" in Toulmin's discourse), not because it is without content, but because it has too much content, because we can never disregard *enough* to be the institutionally unbound speech actors Habermas's project requires. "Disregard," "institutionally unbound speech acts," "consensual speech," "generalized validity claims," "Universal Pragmatics," "the ideal speech situation"—all of these impossible abstractions are offered as if they were supports of one another, but, in fact, they are merely interchangeable expressions of a desire that cannot even be named since every name it receives is intelligible only within the conditions it would escape.

Now it seems to me that the failure of Universal Pragmatics is exemplary in that it can stand in for the failure of the critical project in general. Habermas knows that reflection requires a space in which it can occur, and he knows too that the space of reflection cannot already be occupied by what are to be its objects. He also knows that the space must at some level be a linguistic one; since consciousness operates in and through language, reflection, as a *special* act of consciousness—an act that does not borrow its direction from the "prevailing realm of purposes"—requires a special kind of language, a language not already informed by the motives and strategies of that same realm. His essay (and much else in his work) is a search for that language, and, despite his claims, he never finds it, and therefore he is unable to show that critical self-reflection is something it is possible to do. That is to say what I have already said and what others have said before me: if reflection must occur in a place or moment apart from the "prevailing realm of purposes," and if the first thesis of critical thought is that the "prevailing realm of purposes" covers the field, then reflection can never get off the ground because it is always tethered to the ground from which it claims to set us free.

The point, of course, has been forcefully made by Gadamer who, in his debate with Habermas, argues against the "possibility of methodologically transcending the hermeneutic point of view" because "any attempt to do so is inconsistent with the very conditions of possibility of understanding: the linguisticality and historicity of human existence."[29] In other words (my words), the insight of historicity—of the fashioned or constructed nature of all forms of thought and organization—is too powerful a weapon for those who appropriate it to attack the projects of others; for it turns against them when they attempt to place their own project on a footing that is *different*. As Held puts it, "how can critical theory at once acknowledge its historicality and yet be critical?" (p. 398). The answer is that it can't, which means that critical theory is faced with two unsatisfactory alternatives: either it admits an inability to distinguish between its own agenda and the agenda it repeatedly exposes, admits, in short, that it is, like everything else, merely "interested" and not possessed of a special interest called the emancipatory; or it preserves its specialness by leaving its agenda without content, operating forever at the level of millenarian prophecy, issuing appeals in the name of a generalized human potential, calling for actions that have no particular content, celebrating goals that remain unachievable because they remain unthinkable. In short, left critical theory, despite all that distinguishes it from the conservative pronouncements of a Toulmin or a Hirsch, is finally exactly in the same position, acknowledging as inescapable the condition of historicity, but claiming nevertheless to have escaped it. The only difference is that while the conservative rationalists believe that the escape is easy and requires only the exercise of a firm and vigilant will, the critical theorists believe that the escape awaits us in an as yet unspecified and unspecifiable future and requires a long, arduous, and uncharted journey. But just as Toulmin cannot tell us what it would be like to discount our biases and prejudices, the critical theorists cannot tell us how to take that journey's first step. Like Moses, they are doomed to wander in the desert, but without even a sight of the promised land, for they are without a theology and therefore without any basis whatsoever for their militantly secular faith.

That faith finds a powerful and anguished expression in Adorno's elaboration of "negative dialectics," a technique for discerning the element of "non-identity" in "identifying" forms of thought. "Identitarian thinking"[30] attempts to comprehend the object within its own totalizing system; it "says what something comes under, what it exemplifies or represents," and therefore does not acknowledge what is left over, that about the object to which it is inadequate. It is the "ideology of adequacy"—the claim of our present modes of thought to do justice to the objects they identify, make visible for us—that must be resisted by a form of thinking that uncovers the "secret *telos* of identification," the nonidentity it labors to occlude: "The force that shatters the appearance of identity is the force of [dialectical] thinking" (p. 149); "it is up to dialectical cognition to pursue the inadequacy of thought and thing, to experience it in the thing" (p. 153). It is the (fatal) strength of Adorno's analysis to acknowledge the interminable nature of this pursuit. Nonidentitarian thinking can itself only proceed within the categories whose inadequacy it repeatedly exposes; even as it frees the object from the domination of one totalizing concept, it delivers the object to another. Therefore since it is "at once the impression and the critique of the universal delusive context," dialectics "must now turn even against itself":

The critique of every self-absolutizing particular is a critique of the shadow which absoluteness casts upon the critique; it is a critique of the fact that critique itself, contrary to its own tendency, must remain within the medium of the concept. It destroys the claim of identity by testing and honoring it; therefore it can reach no farther than that claim. (p. 406)

The conclusion is inevitable and Adorno immediately produces it; while "dialectics is the self-consciousness of the objective context of delusion, it does not mean to have escaped from that context" (p. 406). Although negative dialectics would turn us away from the contingent to the absolute, "at the approach of the mind, the absolute flees from the mind; its approach is a mirage" whose illusion must forever be dispelled (p. 407). Dialectics can only be true to its "own tendency" when it refuses to conclude. "The test of the turn to non-identity is its performance; if it remained declarative, it would be revoking itself" (p. 155). That is, if dialectics were to yield anything *positive,* if it were in fact to say something, it would immediately become what it wished to escape. In order to continue to be what it is, it must remain without content, a relentlessly negative operation which rather than bringing us closer to "the transcendent thing is pushing that thing ahead of it, so to speak, and removing it from our consciousness" (p. 407). It is in that endlessly negative motion, in the unwillingness of dialectics "to rest in itself" that Adorno finds hope, but it is a hope that remains without substance, and it is a hope not *for* critical self-consciousness (which is finally a machine for protecting against itself) but for some (unimaginable) force that will burst in upon it. Held contends that while "negative dialectics alone cannot lead to change, . . . it can help break the grip of all congealed systems which would freeze the object" (p. 213), but even this limited claim is disallowed by the rigor of Adorno's formulations in which thought of the most dialectical kind delivers us from the grip of one system only to deposit us in the (equally frozen) grip of another.

IV

I know that this is a conclusion few will welcome. The appeal of critical self-consciousness—of reflection as a critique of the way things are—is enormous, and it is time to take account of that appeal and speak to the fears that are its content. The largest fear is that in the absence of critical self-consciousness or its equivalent there is no hope for change. The reasoning is that since the "prevailing realm of purposes" is entrenched at so deep a level, it is necessary to posit some activity that does not fall within its scope, lest we be left in the miserable condition of being forever bound to the status quo. Indeed, the critical theorists often tell us that the hour is late, and that the forces of oppression are exercising a control so total that it may become invulnerable to the destabilizing thrust of critique. That is why it is so important to nurture the critical impulse wherever it (mysteriously) flowers, in the hope that in time it will work to loosen the hold of the categories of thought through which and by means of which the forces of oppression maintain their hegemony.

Perhaps the most eloquent expression of that hope is found in the work of the legal philosopher Roberto Unger, who also articulates the assumption that must be made if the hope is to have any content. That assumption, quite simply, is that some forms of thought and organization are more open to revision—more responsive to the operation of critique—than others. "Contexts of representation or relationship," says Unger, "differ in the severity of the limits they impose upon our activity,"[31] and "the more entrenched against revision a social plan becomes, the more it enacts and imposes an intolerably restricted picture of our fundamental identity and our opportunities for practical or passionate connection" (p. 25). Through the continual and expanded practice of critique "we can create institutions and conceptions that go ever further in denying . . . immunity to themselves and to the routines they help shape" and by such means, Unger concludes, "we can break through the false necessities that enmesh exchange and production in rigid hierarchies and that hold each individual's experiments in association and self-expression within frozen social forms" (p. 266). Here in more explicit language than any we have yet seen are the key components of the critical scenario, past, present, and future: first, there is a self conceived of as a quantity of energy and vision that can either be left free to discover and nourish its "fundamental identity" or continue to be constrained in its activities by external forces that keep it from realizing its own true nature; second, there are the institutions and conceptions that are complicit with, because they are extensions of, these tyrannous constraints; but, third, even amid these enslaving forces there is always a measure of freedom left somewhere (often in the greatest works of art and in the best impulses of philosophy and religion), and if that measure can be increased by the exercise of critical self-reflection, we can, step by step, transform the material conditions of our existence so that the structures we inhabit are less and less constraining until finally we will have transformed ourselves and realized our true destiny. Moreover, unless we do this we shall remain in the condition of unfreedom inhabited by all of those who live uncritically. Without critical self-reflection, then, there will be no real change.

In its own terms this picture is coherent and powerful, but these terms will not survive a challenge to the thesis on which they rest, that there are degrees of constraint or, more precisely, that there is a continuum on which forms of thought and social organizations can be ranked as they are more or less constraining, more or less free. To this thesis I would oppose the counterintuitive assertion that there is no continuum because the degree of constraint—at least in relation to an ideal condition of freedom—is always the same and always total. By this I do not mean that we are never free to act, but that our freedom is a function of—in the sense of being dependent on—some other structure of constraint without which action of any kind would be impossible. This may seem counterintuitive to those who are accustomed to identify freedom with the *absence* of constraints, but, in fact, such a state, if it could be achieved, would produce not free actions, but *no* actions. An action is only conceivable against a background of alternative paths, a background that is already a constraint in that by marking out some actions as possible it renders unavailable others that might emerge as possibilities against a different background. To imagine a world with no background in place, with no prearticulation of the directions one might take, is to imagine a world where there would be literally nowhere to go, where, since every path would be the same path, the notion of doing this rather than that—of acting freely—would be empty. It follows, then, that it makes no sense to imagine conditions of *no* constraint, and it follows, too, that there can be no continuum which differentiates institutions or structures as being more or less constrained, more or less free, because freedom, in whatever shape it appears, is another name for constraint. Rather than a continuum, what we have is an array, an array of structures of constraint, no one of which is more constraining than any other, and each of which is differently productive of actions that are, in the only sense the word can have, free. Depending on which of those structures one inhabits or by which one is inhabited, things will be very different, including one's sense of what is free and what is constrained, but those differences can never be characterized in the terms that are crucial to the critical project. What the critical theorists call liberation or emancipation is nothing more (or less) than the passing from one structure of constraint to another, a passing that will always be attended by the "discovery of new possibilities," but of possibilities that will be no less (or more) constrained than those that have been left behind.

Of course, by putting the matter this way I raise more questions than I can answer. How does this passing come about? and isn't passing just another word for change? and haven't I left that undeniable fact of life as mysterious as it was when I began? and don't I finally need a category very much like reflection or self-awareness to explain how it occurs? Let me attempt an answer to these questions by way of an example. At this moment I am a member of a committee charged with investigating the status of women in a university. One part of our procedure is to identify departments whose statistical profile with respect to women is out of line with the profile of the discipline as a whole (to say nothing of the profile of the population as a whole). We then send letters to the chairpersons (usually men) of the departments so identified and request a response. Responses, of course, vary, but more often than not they contain two components: (1) a claim that when hiring or promoting, the department looks only to intellectual merit and pays no attention to extrinsic considerations; and (2) a report that the number of woman applicants for the department's advertised positions is typically very small. Now one must assume that such protestations are sincere—these men believe what they say—and therefore one must devise a strategy for bringing them to see that the points they make so complacently depend on assumptions that are challengeable. One must bring them to see, for example, that behind the slogan of intellectual merit lies a structure of exclusionary mechanisms that preselects who will and will not be a candidate for the label of meritorious; that "merit" is always a category whose content is political and contestable; and that the size and nature of an applicant pool is hardly a statistical accident reflecting the perfectly free choice of individuals to refrain from seizing opportunities open to everyone (the fact that relatively few women have applied should not be the end but the beginning of inquiry and explanation).

The question, of course, is "how can one bring them to see?" One part of the answer must be that it is possible that they not be moved at all, that they remain within the circle of beliefs in relation to which the responses they automatically offer are at once obvious and satisfying; and, moreover, if they should be moved, if the strategy of my committee should succeed, it will not be because those beliefs—those assumptions concerning the nature of the academic enterprise and the demands that can properly be made of it—have been discarded or left behind, but because they have been altered in ways that are internal to their constitution. As academics, these department chairmen are prepared to hear, if not necessarily to be persuaded by, arguments that take a certain familiar form. For example, an academic will recognize as legitimate (which is not to say "correct") an argument that would historicize a scale of measurement hitherto regarded as abstract and eternal. He has encountered that kind of argument before, and although he might instinctively resist it, he cannot simply dismiss it (as he might an argument that had no academic pedigree whatsoever) but must counter it with arguments drawn from the same arsenal. It is in the space created by this obligation—an obligation that grows out of the same beliefs it may eventually alter—that movement might occur, although it is not assured; someone for whom the intrinsic (as opposed to historical) nature of merit is a prime article of faith is likely to remain obdurate no matter how much evidence he is offered to the contrary; but on the other hand (or is it the third?) that same someone may reconsider his views on merit and its operations when his own daughter is excluded in ways he finds intolerable, ways that leave him with the choice of either concurring in the negative judgment of his child or rethinking his understanding of the way in which judgment is rendered; he may rethink.

My refusal in the previous paragraph to speak in the language of prediction or of (assured) cause and effect is of course deliberate. It is always a temptation to conceive of persuasion as either too regular or too rational. One simply cannot tell in advance what will work a change in someone's views; and the range of possible change-producing agencies extends far beyond formal argumentation to include family crises, altered financial circumstances, serious illness, professional disappointment, boredom, and so on, ad infinitum. This does not mean, however, that there is nothing one can do except be passively fatalistic; one acts on the basis of calculations that have at least the probability associated with rules of thumb; for example, in this context an appeal to equal access and opportunity is likely to receive a serious and respectful hearing. It is certainly possible that at least some of the chairmen with whom my committee deals will come away from the process with a new understanding of their responsibilities with respect to the recruiting and promoting of women. Let us assume that this has in fact happened. In what terms would one want to characterize this success? The temptation would be to say that it marked the achieving of a heightened or raised consciousness, and that these men had passed from an unreflective state to a state of a new and enlarged awareness. But, in fact, the awareness of the chairmen affected by our arguments would not have been enlarged, but changed. It would not have been enlarged because any gain in awareness is simultaneously a loss: someone who is now able to see merit as a political or social category is now *un*able to see merit as intrinsic; the passing from one point of view to another deprives you of whatever insights and certainties flow from the point of view you have "transcended" (in quotations because it is transcendent only in relation to a new set of constraints). Awareness is not a quantity that can be increased or diminished on an absolute scale; rather, it is a name for what is obvious and perspicuous to us situated as we are within a structure of beliefs. When our beliefs change—when the assumptions within which the possibilities of seeing, saying, and acting emerge are no longer what they were—the category of the obvious and perspicuous—of that of which we are *aware*—will have changed, too; but the change will not be from a state of unreflective slavery to a state of self-awareness, but from one state of self-awareness to another; and neither state will meet the critical theorist's test of existing apart from the "prevailing realm of purposes," for each will precisely be a function of that realm.

In short, one is always aware; one always knows what one is doing, and, when challenged, one can always give reasons of the kind given by the department chairmen to whom my committee wrote. But those reasons are like the reasons given in the catechism; they are reasons for your faith, and they are also reasons that derive from your faith in a circular but not vicious relationship; and when that faith is succeeded by another, a new set of reasons will accompany it, and that set of reasons will be the instantiation of a new awareness. Of course, this is an account from the perspective of neither the one who is newly aware or those who have brought him to his awareness. From *their* perspective words like "emancipation" and "liberation" will seem perfectly accurate, and again the proper vocabulary for describing their experience is theological: the person who comes to believe something that he didn't believe before feels that it is only now that his eyes have been opened; and those who have helped to effect his conversion will say that they have raised or increased his consciousness; but all they will have done—and it is no small thing—is *change* his consciousness; they will have *persuaded* him.

All of which is to say that persuasion and change are one and the same, or rather, that they are names for an act and its result. Once one sees that, one also sees that change cannot be engineered because persuasion is a contingent rather than a formal matter. There exists no certain correlation between the exertions of persuasive pressure (of whatever kind) and the certainty or even the likelihood of success. One can, of course, set out to persuade someone else, but both the career and the success of that effort will be unpredictable; you can never be sure what will work, or if anything will. Will and deliberation are even more irrelevant to what happens on the other side, the side of the persuadee. You cannot direct yourself to be persuaded; you cannot command your mind to change without already having some idea of what steps you might take to effect that change; and if you have such an idea, you will already have taken them. The man who says "I am going to change" and means it is really saying, "I have already changed"; he is simply reporting the conclusion of a process that was marked by none of the reflective self-consciousness with which he now, and retroactively, endows it.

If change cannot be engineered, neither can it be stopped. When Unger urges upon us "a theory that sees transformative possibilities built into the every mechanism of social stabilization,"[32] one wonders why he needs the theory given the fact that transformative possibilities *are* built into every mechanism of social stabilization if only because they are built into the very structure of belief. As I have argued in "Change" (chapter 7), a set of beliefs is not a collection of discrete and static items, but an engine of assimilation, a bundle of related goals, purposes, priorities, hierarchies which is forever transforming the landscape into material for its own project, but which is itself transformed by the very work it does; and this holds too for every form of social organization which, even as it moves to absorb any contingency into the structure of its own assumptions and desires, modifies those assumptions and redefines those desires. Change, in short, cannot be held back on the level either of the individual or of the community. Just as the man who says, "I'm going to change," is really saying, "I have changed," so is the man who says, "I won't change," resisting a change that has already occurred, especially when he says it loudly.

The fact that change can neither be willed nor stopped means that critical self-consciousness is at once impossible and superfluous. It is impossible because there is no action or motion of the self that exists apart from the "prevailing realm of purposes" and therefore no way of achieving distance from that realm; and it is superfluous because the prevailing realm of purposes is, in the very act of elaborating itself, turning itself into something other than it was. The fact that there can be no special act of the will by which its own possibilities are enlarged is rendered harmless by the fact that no special act of the will is required. The failure of critical self-consciousness is a failure without consequences since everything it would achieve—change, the undoing of the status quo, the redistribution of power and authority, the emergence of new forms of action—is already achieved by the ordinary and everyday efforts by which, in innumerable situations, large and small, each of us attempts to alter the beliefs of another.

Indeed, if critical self-consciousness is anything, it is the self-description of a persuasive agenda that dare not speak its name; for if it were to do so and acknowledge itself as a design, it could no longer claim the purity that supposedly marks it off from every other form of coercion and constraint. But would that be such a loss? When Ottman observes that "the interest shown by critical theory in doing away with concrete power structures could itself be a child of the times," he voices a criticism only if acting in the service of local interests is a dereliction of one's moral duty. If, however, that is the only form of action there is, one cannot be faulted for engaging in it; and being "a child of the times" means nothing more (or less) than that you respond to the urgencies of the moment as they are identified by your convictions. If those who presently march under the banner of critical self-consciousness were to put that banner away, they would still be left with whatever projects grounded in whatever senses of outrage brought them to the field in the first place. And this allows me to make a point that the logic of my argument may have tended to obscure. It has been the strategy of that argument to deny the difference between the intellectual left and right at least with respect to the (equally illegitimate) use each makes of the notion of critical self-consciousness; but once that difference is taken away (by the demonstration that critical self-consciousness of either the edenic or utopian variety is not a possible achievement), all the other differences—with respect both to particular issues and general stances of reform or conservation—will remain and mark out genuine alternatives for action. Nothing I have said should be construed as urging quietism or fatalism; the only option this line of reasoning takes away is the option of stepping back from one's beliefs in order to survey or reform them; absent that option, one is in the position one was always in, the position of seeing the world as a field of possibilities to be seized by whatever means your situation recommends. The removal of critical self-consciousness from the list of possible ways of acting does not deprive anyone of anything. It is, as I have already said, a loss entirely without consequences.

There remains, however, the question of the appeal of critical self-consciousness, an appeal that will certainly survive any argument that I or anyone else might make against it. Witness the extraordinary performance by Brian Fay in his recent *Critical Social Science*. In that book, Fay provides a comprehensive analysis of the components of the critical attitude, which, he says, "involves three basic claims about human existence":

> The first is that humans are typically unfree, dominated by conditions which they neither understand nor control. . . . The second is that human life need not be this way. The third is that an increase in knowledge is the way the oppressed can liberate themselves and thereby better their lot.[33]

Liberation in this scenario, Fay explains, is "a state of reflective clarity in which people know which of their wants are genuine, because they know finally who they really are, and a state of collective autonomy in which they have the power to determine rationally and freely the nature and direction of their collective existence" (p. 205). With exemplary rigor and sympathy Fay spends six chapters unfolding the critical program before he turns on it with a force that is increased by the quiet authority he has earned in the course of his exposition. Fay's basic points will be familiar to readers of this chapter: (1) the human condition "is fundamentally historical" and therefore "there are limits in principle to the knowledge which we can have about ourselves" (p. 206). (2) "Persons acquire their identities" not by standing apart from cultural tradition, but by appropriating "a cultural tradition of which, as they become a part, they become a person" (p. 208). (3) Critique requires "creatures . . . who are reflectively clear to themselves," but human beings "cannot be in this sort of situation with respect to themselves—as if their identity and culture were wholly other, to be accepted or rejected as they willed—because every act of self-determination involves working through material appropriated from their [historical] heritage" (p. 208). The conclusion is devastating:

> Critical social science promises to set . . . people free. But the knowledge which it offers, or even the action inspired by this knowledge, is not enough to fulfill this promise. There are serious limits on the ability of critical social science to engender rational social change; in addition, its ideal of freedom as autonomy is inapposite for the beings which comprise its potential audience. (p. 208)

But, then, three pages from the end, Fay asks, "does anything remain of critical social science?" and answers, surprisingly, in the affirmative. Critique can be saved if it will only keep in mind its own limitations; new and improved forms of critical theory will disclaim universalist aspirations and will "build into themselves an explicit recognition of the . . . sorts of limits of which I have spoken." The results, Fay contends, "would be theories which were self-consciously local, particular, situated, experimental . . . theories whose values were not those of rational self-clarity and autonomy, but were something far less grandiose and mundane" (p. 212). But anything so mundane and local would hardly deserve (if that is the word) the name of theory, and, more important, it would not require self-consciousness for its operation. The urgencies and values of situations come along with them "naturally." To be in a situation (as one always is) is already to be equipped with an awareness of possible goals, obstacles, dangers, rewards, alternatives, etc., and nothing is or could be aided by something called "self-consciousness." The phrase "self-consciously local" makes no sense; it either smuggles the (impossible) ideal of reflective clarity and autonomy in through the back door, or it refers to a state of everyday awareness from which, short of sleepwalking, one can hardly fall away. Fay here commits a version of what I have called "anti-foundationalist theory hope" (another name for the critical self-consciousness fallacy). He thinks that situatedness comes in two forms, the garden variety kind experienced by everyone and the "heightened" kind supposedly experienced by those who "know" that they are in a situation and therefore have a special grasp on their situatedness. But either this additional knowledge is not additional at all, but is merely a feature of a particular situation (as when it is a conclusion reached at the end of a philosophical discussion), or it is the asituational knowledge whose unavailability Fay has just proclaimed. In the end, despite the care and patience of a sophisticated, nuanced analysis, Fay's thought describes the same sequence that we met first in the writings of Toulmin.

Why? The answer perhaps lies in the very thesis I have been urging in this and every other chapter, the thesis that being situated not only means that one cannot achieve a distance on one's beliefs, but that one's beliefs do not relax their hold because one "knows" that they are local and not universal. This in turn means that even someone (like me or Fay) who is firmly convinced of the circumstantiality of his convictions will nevertheless experience those convictions as universally, not locally, true. It is therefore not surprising but inevitable that at the end of every argument, even of an argument that says there can be no end, the universalist perspective will reemerge as strongly as ever. In another chapter I say that even though anti-professionalism is an impossible and incoherent stance, it is an ineradicable ingredient of professional activity. I now say that even though the self-reflective clarity of critical self-consciousness cannot be achieved, the experience of having achieved it is inseparable from the experience of conviction. It is *because* history is inescapable that every historical moment—that is, every moment—feels so much like an escape.

Rhetoric

20. Rhetoric

>   . . . up rose
> *Belial,* in act more graceful and humane;
> A fairer person lost not Heav'n; he seem'd
> For dignity compos'd and high exploit:
> But all was false and hollow; though his Tongue
> Dropt Manna, and could make the worse appear
> The better reason, to perplex and dash
> Maturest counsels: for his thoughts were low; . . .
>   . . . yet he pleas'd the ear,
> And with persuasive accent thus began.
> *Paradise Lost,* II, 108–15, 117–18

I For Milton's seventeenth-century readers this passage, introducing one of the more prominent of the fallen angels, would have been immediately recognizable as a brief but trenchant essay on the art and character of the rhetorician. Indeed, in these few lines Milton has managed to gather and restate with great rhetorical force (a paradox of which more later) all of the traditional arguments against rhetoric. Even Belial's gesture of rising is to the (negative) point: he catches the eye even before he begins to speak, just as Satan will in book IX when he too raises himself and moves so that "each part, / Motion, each act won audience ere the tongue" (673–74). That is, he draws attention to his appearance, to his surface, and the suggestion of superficiality (a word to be understood in its literal meaning) extends to the word "act"; that is, that which can be seen. That act is said to be "graceful," the first in a succession of double meanings (one of the stigmatized attributes of rhetorical speech) we find in the passage. Belial is precisely *not* full of grace; that is simply his outward aspect, and the same is true for "humane" and "fairer." The verse's judgment on all of his apparent virtues is delivered in the last two words of line 110—"he seem'd"—

and the shadow of "seeming" falls across the next line which in isolation might "seem" to be high praise. But under the pressure of what precedes it, the assertion of praise undoes itself with every Janus-faced word (the verse now begins to imitate the object of its criticism by displaying a pervasive disjunction between its outer and inner meanings; indicting seeming, it itself repeatedly seems): "compos'd" now carries its pejorative meaning of affected or made-up; "high" at once refers to the favored style of bombastic orators and awaits its ironic and demeaning contrast with the lowness of his thoughts; "dignity" is an etymological joke, for Belial is anything but worthy; in fact, he is just what the next line says he is, "false and hollow," an accusation that repeats one of the perennial antirhetorical topoi, that rhetoric, the art of fine speaking, is all show, grounded in nothing but its own empty pretensions, unsupported by any relation to truth. "There is no need," declares Socrates in Plato's *Gorgias,* "for rhetoric to know the facts at all, for it has hit upon a means of persuasion that enables it to appear in the eyes of the ignorant to know more than those who really know" (459),[1] and in the *Phaedrus* the title figure admits that the "man who plans to be an orator" need not "learn what is really just and true, but only what seems so to the crowd" (260).[2]

This reference to the vulgar popular ear indicates that rhetoric's deficiencies are not only epistemological (sundered from truth and fact) and moral (sundered from true knowledge and sincerity) but social: it panders to the worst in people and moves them to base actions, exactly as Belial is said to do in the next famous run-on statement, "and could make the worse appear / The better reason." This is an explicit reference to a nest of classical sources: the most familiar is Aristotle, *Rhetoric,* II, 1402, 23, condemning the skill of being able to make arguments on either side of a question: "This . . . illustrates what is meant by making the worse argument appear the better. Hence people were right in objecting to the training Protagoras undertook to give them."[3] Socrates makes the same point in the *Phaedrus:* "an orator who knows nothing about good or evil undertakes to persuade a city in the same state of ignorance . . . by recommending evil as though it were good" (260). Behind Belial (or descending from him; the direction of genealogy in *Paradise Lost* is always problematic) is the line of sophists—Protagoras, Hippias, Gorgias, shadowy figures known to us mostly through the writings of Plato where they appear always as relativist foils for the idealistic Socrates. The judgment made on them by a philosophic tradition dominated by Plato is the judgment here made on Belial; their thoughts were low, centered on the suspect skills they taught for hire; the danger they represented is the danger Belial represents: despite the lowness of their thoughts, perhaps *because* of the lowness of their thoughts, they pleased the ear, at least the ear of the promiscuous crowd (there is always just beneath the surface of the antirhetorical stance a powerful and corrosive elitism), and the explanation of their unfortunate success is the power Belial now begins to exercise, the power of "persuasive accent." Encoded in this phrase is a continuing debate about the essence of rhetoric, a debate whose two poles are represented by Gorgias's praise in the *Encomium of Helen* of rhetoric as an irresistible force and the stoic Cato's characterization of the rhetorician as a good man skilled at speaking (*"vir bonus, dicendi peritus"*). The difference is that for Gorgias the skill is detached from any necessary moral center and represents a self-sustaining power ("persuasion allied to words can mould men's minds"), while for Cato the skill is a by-product of a focus on goodness and truth (thus the other of his famous aphorisms, "seize the thing, the words will follow"—*"rem tene, verba sequentur"*—which later flowers in the Renaissance distinction between res et verba.[4] In one position eloquence is the hard-won creation of a special and technical facility, a facility one acquires by mastering a set of complicated—and morally neutral—rules; in the other eloquence is what naturally issues when a man is in close touch with the Truth and allows it to inspire him. Born, it would seem, in a posture of defensiveness, rhetoric has often gravitated toward this latter view in an effort to defuse the charge that it is amoral. Quintilian's formulation (itself gathered from the writings of Cicero) is one that will later be echoed in countless treatises: "no man can speak well who is not good himself" (*"bene dicere non possit nisi bonus,"* Institutes, II, xv, 34). As a defense, however, this declaration has the disadvantage of implying the superfluousness of rhetoric, an implication fully realized in Augustine's *On Christian Doctrine* where eloquence is so much subordinated to wisdom that it disappears as a distinct and separable property. Belial, in contrast, is wholly defined by that property, by his ability to produce "persuasive accents." "Accent" here is a powerfully resonant word, one of whose relevant meanings is "mode of utterance peculiar to an individual, locality or nation" (OED). He who speaks "in accent" speaks from a particular *angled* perspective into which he tries to draw his auditors; he also speaks in the rhythms of song (etymologically, accent means "song added to speech") which as Milton will soon observe *"charms* the sense" (II, 556). "Persuasive accent," then, is almost a redundancy: the two words mean the same thing and what they tell the reader is that he is about to be exposed to a force whose exercise is unconstrained by any sense of responsibility either to the Truth or to the Good. Indeed, so dangerous does Milton consider this force that he feels it necessary to provide a corrective gloss as soon as Belial stops speaking: "Thus *Belial* with words cloth'd in reason's garb / Counsell'd ignoble ease and peaceful sloth" (II, 226–27). Just in case you hadn't noticed.

I have lingered so long over this passage because we can extrapolate from it almost all of the binary oppositions in relation to which rhetoric has received its (largely negative) definition: inner/outer, deep/surface, essential/peripheral, unmediated/mediated, clear/colored, necessary/contingent, straightforward/angled, abiding/fleeting, reason/passion, things/words, realities/illusions, fact/opinion, neutral/partisan. Underlying this list, which is by no means exhaustive, are three basic oppositions: first, between a truth that exists independently of all perspectives and points of view and the many truths that emerge and seem perspicuous when a particular perspective or point of view has been established and is in force; second, an opposition between true knowledge, which is knowledge as it exists apart from any and all systems of belief, and the knowledge, which because it flows from some or other system of belief, is incomplete and partial (in the sense of biased); and third, an opposition between a self or consciousness that is turned outward in an effort to apprehend and attach itself to truth and true knowledge and a self or consciousness that is turned inward in the direction of its own prejudices, which, far from being transcended, continue to inform its every word and action. Each of these oppositions is attached in turn to an opposition between two kinds of language: on the one hand, language that faithfully reflects or reports on matters of fact uncolored by any personal or partisan agenda or desire; and on the other hand, language that is infected by partisan agendas and desires, and therefore colors and distorts the facts which it purports to reflect. It is use of the second kind of language that makes one a rhetorician, while adherence to the first kind makes one a seeker after truth and an objective observer of the way things are. It is this distinction that, as Thomas Kuhn notes, underwrites the claims of science to be a privileged form of discourse because it has recourse to a "neutral observation language,"[5] a language uninflected by any mediating presuppositions or preconceptions; and it is the same distinction that informs Aristotle's observation (*Rhetoric,* III, 1404, 13) that "Nobody uses fine language when teaching geometry." The language of geometry—of formal rules with no substantive content—is contrasted by Aristotle to all those languages that are intended only to "charm the hearer," the languages of manipulation, deception, and self-consciously deployed strategy.

It is this understanding of linguistic possibilities and dangers that generates a succession of efforts to construct a language from which all perspectival bias (a redundant phrase) has been eliminated, efforts that have sometimes taken as a model the notations of mathematics, at other times the operations of logic, and more recently the purely formal calculations of a digital computer. Whether it issues in the elaborate linguistic machines of seventeenth-century "projectors" like Bishop Wilkins (*An Essay Towards a Real Character and a Philosophical Language,* 1668), or in the building (à la Chomsky) of a "competence" model of language abstracted from any particular performance, or in the project of Esperanto or some other artificial language claiming universality,[6] or in the fashioning of a Habermasian "ideal speech situation" in which all assertions express "a 'rational will' in relation to a common interest ascertained without deception,"[7] the impulse behind the effort is always the same: to establish a form of communication that escapes partiality and aids us in first determining and then affirming what is absolutely and objectively true, a form of communication that in its structure and operations is the very antithesis of rhetoric, of passionate partisan discourse.

That desideratum and the fears behind it have received countless articulations, but never have they been articulated with more precision than in these sentences from Bishop Sprat's *History of the Royal Society of London,* 1667:

When I consider the means of *happy living,* and the causes of their *corruption,* I can hardly forbear . . . concluding that *eloquence* ought to be banish'd out of all *civil societies,* as a thing fatal to Peace and good Manners. . . . They [the ornaments of speaking] are in open defiance against *Reason*; professing not to hold much correspondence with that; but with its slaves, the *Passions*: they give the mind a motion too changeable, and bewitching, to consist with *right practice.* Who can behold, without indignation, how many mists and uncertainties, these specious *Tropes* and *Figures* have brought on our Knowledge? How many rewards, which are due to more profitable, and difficult arts, have been snatch'd away by the easie vanity of *fine speaking?* (pp. 111–13)

The terms of banishment are exactly those invoked by Plato against the poets in book X of his *Republic*: Homer, Socrates says, may be "the most poetic of poets and the first of tragedians, but we must know the truth [and] we can admit no poetry into our city save only hymns to the gods and the praises of good men; for if you grant admission to the honeyed Muse . . . pleasure and pain will be lords of your city instead of law and that which shall . . . have approved itself to the general reason as the best" (607a). The "honeyed muse" is precisely what Belial becomes when his tongue drops Manna (113), a quintessentially idolatrous act in which he substitutes his own word for the word sent down to us by God and therefore deprives us of the direction that God's word might have given us. Although the transition from classical to Christian thought is marked by many changes, one thing that does not change is the status of rhetoric in relation to a foundational vision of truth and meaning. Whether the center of that vision is a personalized deity or an abstract geometric reason, rhetoric is the force that pulls us away from that center and into its own world of ever-shifting shapes and shimmering surfaces.

Of course, the allure of surfaces and shapes, of "specious *Tropes* and *Figures*," would not be felt if there were not something already in us that inclined to it. Rhetoric may be a danger that assaults us from without, but its possible success is a function of an *inner* weakness. The entire art, as Aristotle explains regretfully, is predicated on "the defects of our hearers" (*Rhetoric*, III, 1404, 8), on the assumption that members of the audience will be naturally susceptible to the rhetorician's appeal. The anti-rhetorical stance can only be coherent if it posits an *in*coherence at the heart (literally) of the self that is both rhetoric's victim and its source. That self is always presented as divided, as the site of contesting forces; in Christian terms the forces are named the carnal and the spiritual; in secular psychologies the names are passion and reason or the willful and the rational; but whatever the names, the result is a relationship of homology between the inner and outer landscapes, both of which contain a core element of truth and knowledge that is continually threatened by a penumbra of irrationality.[8] If tropes and figures "give the mind a motion too changeable," it is because the principle of change, in the form of the passions, already lives in the mind, and it follows then that banishing eloquence and the poets from your republic will only do half the job. As Milton puts it in the *Areopagitica*, "they are not skillful considerers of human things who imagine to remove sin by removing the matter of sin";[9] policing the outer landscape will be of little effect if the inner landscape remains host to the enemy, to sin, to error, to show.

It is the view of the anti-rhetoricians that this double task of inner and outer regulation can be accomplished by linguistic reform, by the institution of conditions of communication that at once protect discourse from the irrelevancies and contingencies that would compromise its universality and insulate the discoursing mind from those contingencies and irrelevancies it itself harbors. Wilkins proposes to fashion a language that will admit neither *Superfluities*—plural signifiers of a single signified, more than one word for a particular thing—nor *Equivocals*—signifiers doing multiple duty, single words that refer to several things—nor *Metaphor*—a form of speech that interposes itself between the observer and the referent and therefore contributes "to the disguising of it with false appearances" (pp. 17–18). The idea is that such a language, purged of ambiguity, redundancy, and indirection, will be an appropriate instrument for the registering of an independent reality, and that if men will only submit themselves to that language and remain within the structure of its stipulated definitions and exclusions, they will be incapable of formulating and expressing wayward, subjective thoughts and will cease to be a danger either to themselves or to those who hearken to them. In this way, says Wilkins, they will be returned to that original state in which the language spoken was the language God gave Adam, a language in which every word perfectly expressed its referent (on the model of Adam's simultaneously understanding the nature of the animals and conferring upon them their names), a language that in the course of time and "emergencies" has unfortunately "admitted various and *casual alterations*" (p. 19).

In the twentieth century Wilkins's program is echoed point for point (absent the theological scaffolding) by Rudolf Carnap: Carnap would admit into the lexicon only words that can be tied firmly to "protocol" or "observation" sentences, sentences that satisfy certain truth conditions and are therefore verifiable by reference to the facts of the world. The stipulation of this criterion, Carnap asserts, "takes away one's freedom to decide what one wishes to 'mean' by [a] word."[10] The freedom of individual speakers and hearers would be further taken away if the words of a verifiable lexicon were embedded in a grammar that "corresponded exactly to logical syntax," for if that were the case "pseudo-statements could not arise" (p. 68). That is, no one could be misled either by the words of another or by that part of his consciousness inclined to wander from the path of truth; the tendency of language to perform in excess of its proper duty—to report or reflect matters of fact—would be curbed in advance, and the mind's susceptibility to the power of a language unconstrained by its empirical moorings would be neutralized. In short, the danger posed by rhetoric, both to the field of discourse and the discoursing consciousness, would have been eliminated. Of course, there are important differences to be noted between the idealism of Plato, the antienthusiasm of a Restoration bishop, and the logical positivism of a member of the Vienna Circle, but together (and in the company of countless others) they stand on the same side of a quarrel that Plato was already calling "old" in the fifth century before Christ. That quarrel, the quarrel between philosophy and rhetoric, survives every sea change in the history of Western thought, continually presenting us with the (skewed) choice between the plain unvarnished truth straightforwardly presented and the powerful but insidious appeal of "fine language," language that has transgressed the limits of representation and substituted its own forms for the forms of reality.[11]

II

To this point my presentation has been as skewed as this choice, because it has suggested that rhetoric has received only negative characterizations. In fact, there have always been friends of rhetoric, from the sophists to the anti-foundationalists of the present day, and in response to the realist critique they have devised (and repeated) a number of standard defenses. Two of these defenses are offered by Aristotle in the *Rhetoric*. First, he defines rhetoric as a faculty or art whose practice will help us to observe "in any given case the available means of persuasion" (I, 1355, 27) and points out that as a faculty it is not in and of itself inclined away from truth. Of course, bad men may abuse it, but that after all "is a charge which may be made in common against all good things." "What makes a man a 'sophist,'" he declares, "is not his faculty, but his moral purpose" (I, 1355, 17). To the anticipated objection that rhetoric's potential for misuse is a reason for eschewing it, Aristotle replies that it is sometimes a necessary adjunct to the cause of truth, first, because if we leave the art to be cultivated by deceivers, they will lead truth-seekers astray, and, second, because, regrettable though it may be, "before some audiences not even the possession of the exactest knowledge will make it easy for what we say to produce conviction" and on those occasions "we must use, as our modes of persuasion and argument, notions possessed by everybody" (I, 1355, 27). That is, because of the defects of our hearers the truth itself must often be rhetorically dressed so that it will gain acceptance.[12]

Aristotle's second defense is more aggressively positive and responds directly to one of the most damaging characterizations of rhetoric: "We must be able to employ persuasion, just as strict reasoning can be employed, on opposite sides of a question, not in order that we may in practice employ it in both ways (for we must not make people believe what is wrong), but in order that we may see clearly what the facts are" (I, 1355, 28–33). In short, properly used, rhetoric is a heuristic, helping us not to distort the facts, but to discover them; moreover, adds Aristotle, the setting forth of contrary views of a matter will have the beneficial effect of showing us which of those views most accords with the truth because "the underlying facts do not lend themselves equally well to the contrary views." By this argument, as Peter Dixon has pointed out, Aristotle "removes rhetoric from the realm of the haphazard and the fanciful"[13] and rejoins it to that very realm of which it was said to be the great subverter.

But if this is the strength of Aristotle's defense, it is also its weakness, for in making it he reinforces the very assumptions in relation to which rhetoric will always be suspect, assumptions of an independent reality whose outlines can be perceived by a sufficiently clear-eyed observer who can then represent them in a transparent verbal medium. The stronger defense, because it hits at the heart of the opposing tradition, is one that embraces the accusations of that tradition and makes of them a claim. The chief accusation, as we have seen, is that rhetoricians hold "the probable (or likely-seeming, plausible) in more honour than the true" (*Phaedrus,* 267a). The sophist response is to assert that the realm of the probable—of what is likely to be so given particular conditions within some local perspective—is the only relevant realm of consideration for human beings. The argument is contained in two statements attributed famously to Protagoras. The first declares the un-availability (not the unreality) of the gods: "About gods I cannot say either that they are or that they are not."[14] And the second follows necessarily from the absence of godly guidance: "Man is the measure of all things, of the things that are that they are, and of the things that are not that they are not" (quoted in Plato, *Theaetetus*, 152a). What this means, as W. K. C. Guthrie has pointed out, is "that the Sophists recognized only accidental as opposed to essential being, . . . the con-ditional and relative as opposed to the self-existent."[15] This is not to say that the categories of the true and good are abandoned, but that in different contexts they will be filled differently and that there exists no master context (for that could only be occupied by the unavailable gods) from the vantage point of which the differences could be assessed and judged.

The result is to move rhetoric from the disreputable periphery to the necessary center: for if the highest truth for any man is what he believes it to be (*Theaetetus*, 152a), the skill which produces belief and therefore establishes what, in a particular time and particular place, is true, is the skill essential to the building and maintaining of a civi-lized society. In the absence of a revealed truth, rhetoric is that skill, and in teaching it the sophists were teaching "the one thing that mat-tered, how to take care of one's own affairs and the business of the state."[16] The rhetorician is like a physician; it is his job "to diagnose the particular institution and prescribe the best course of action for a man or a state under given conditions"[17] (see Plato, *Theaetetus*, 167b–d, *Protagoras*, 318e–19a); and when Socrates asks Protagoras if he is "promising to make men good citizens," the reply is firm: "That . . . is exactly what I profess to do" (*Protagoras*, 319a). Of course, in this context words like "good" and "best" do not have the meanings a Plato or Socrates would want them to have—good and best in any and all circumstances; rather, they refer to what would appear to be the better of the courses that seem available in what are generally understood to be the circumstantial constraints of a particular situation; but since, ac-cording to the sophist view, particular situations are the only kind there are, circumstantial determinations of what is good are as good as you're going to get.

That is, as I have already said, the strongest of the defenses rhet-oric has received because it challenges the basic premise of the anti-rhetorical stance, the premise that any discourse must be measured against a stable and independent reality. To the accusation that rhetoric deals only with the realms of the probable and contingent and forsakes truth, the sophists and their successors respond that truth itself is a contingent affair and assumes a different shape in the light of differing local urgencies and the convictions associated with them. "Truth was individual and temporary, not universal and lasting, for the truth for any man was . . . what he could be persuaded of."[18] Not only does this make rhetoric—the art of analyzing and presenting local exigencies—a form of discourse no one can afford to ignore, it renders the opposing discourse—formal philosophy—beside the point. This is precisely Isocrates' thesis in his *Antidosis*. Abstract studies like geometry and astronomy, he says, do not have any "useful application either to private or public affairs; . . . after they are learned . . . they do not attend us through life nor do they lend aid in what we do, but are wholly divorced from our necessities."[19] Indeed, he goes so far as to deny to such disciplines the label "philosophy," for "I hold that man to be wise who is able by his powers of conjecture to arrive generally at the best course, and I hold that man to be a philosopher who occupies himself with the studies from which he will most quickly gain that kind of insight" (p. 271). Men who want to do some good in the world, he concludes, "must banish utterly from their interests all vain speculations and all activities which have no bearing on our lives."

What Isocrates does (at least rhetorically) is shift the balance of power between philosophy and rhetoric by putting philosophy on the defensive. This same strategy is pursued after him by Cicero and Quintilian, the most influential of the Roman rhetoricians. In the opening pages of his *De Inventione* Cicero elaborates the myth that will subsequently be invoked in every defense of humanism and belles lettres. There was a time, he says, when "men wandered at large in the field like animals," and there was "as yet no ordered system of religious worship nor of social duties."[20] It was then that a "great and wise" man "assembled and gathered" his uncivilized brothers and "introduced them to every useful and honorable occupation, though they cried out against it at first because of its novelty." Nevertheless, he gained their attention through "reason and eloquence" (*"propter rationem atque orationem"*) and by these means he "transformed them from wild savages into a kind and gentle folk." Nor would it have been possible, Cicero adds, to have "turned men . . . from their habits" if wisdom had been "mute and voiceless"; only "a speech at the same time powerful and entrancing could have induced one who had great physical strength to submit to justice without violence." From that time on, "many cities have been founded, . . . the flames of a multitude of wars have been extinguished, and . . . the strongest alliances and most sacred friendships have been formed not only by the use of reason, but also more easily by the use of eloquence" (I, 1). Whereas in the foundationalist story an original purity (of vision, purpose, procedure) is corrupted when rhetoric's siren song proves too sweet, in Cicero's story (later to be echoed by countless others)[21] all the human virtues, and indeed humanity itself, are wrested by the arts of eloquence from a primitive and violent state of nature. Significantly (and this is a point to which we shall return), both stories are stories of power, rhetoric's power; it is just that in one story that power must be resisted lest civilization fall, while in the other that power brings order and a genuine political process where before there was only the rule of "physical strength."

The contrast between the two stories can hardly be exaggerated because what is at stake is not simply a matter of emphasis or priority (as it seems to be in Aristotle's effort to demonstrate an *alliance* between rhetoric and truth) but a difference in worldviews. The quarrel between rhetorical and foundational thought is itself foundational; its content is a disagreement about the basic constituents of human activity and about the nature of human nature itself. In Richard Lanham's helpful terms, it is a disagreement as to whether we are members of the species *homo seriosus* or *homo rhetoricus*. *Homo seriosus* or Serious Man

> possesses a central self, an irreducible identity. These selves combine into a single, homogeneously real society which constitutes a referent reality for the men living in it. This referent society is in turn contained in a physical nature itself referential, standing "out there" independent of man. Man has invented language to communicate with his fellow man. He communicates facts and concepts about both nature and society. He can also communicate a third category of response, emotions. When he is communicating facts or concepts, success is measured by something we call *clarity*. When he is communicating feelings, success is measured by something we call *sincerity, faithfulness to the self* who is doing the feeling.[22]

Homo rhetoricus or rhetorical man, on the other hand,

> is an actor; his reality public, dramatic. His sense of identity, de-
> pends on the reassurance of daily histrionic reenactment. He is
> thus centered in time and concrete local event. The lowest com-
> mon denominator of his life is a social situation. . . . He assumes
> a natural agility in changing orientations. . . . From birth, al-
> most, he has dwelt not in a single value-structure but in several.
> He is thus committed to no single construction of the world; much
> rather, to prevailing in the game at hand. . . . He accepts the
> present paradigm and explores its resources. Rhetorical man is
> trained not to discover reality but to manipulate it. Reality is
> what is accepted as reality, what is useful. (p. 4)

As rhetorical man manipulates reality, establishing through his words
the imperatives and urgencies to which he and his fellows must respond, he manipulates or fabricates himself, simultaneously conceiving
of and occupying the roles that become first possible and then manda-
tory given the social structure his rhetoric has put in place. By exploring
the available means of persuasion in a particular situation, he tries them
on, and as they begin to suit him, he becomes them.[23] "I hold," says
Isocrates, "that people can become better and worthier if they conceive an ambition to speak well," for in the setting forth of his position the orator "will select from all the actions of men . . . those
examples which are the most illustrious and the most edifying; and ha-
bituating himself to contemplate and appraise such examples, he will feel
their influence not only in the preparation of a given discourse but in all
the actions of his life" (pp. 275, 277). What serious man fears—the in-
vasion of the fortress of essence by the contingent, the protean, and the
unpredictable—is what rhetorical man celebrates and incarnates. In the
philosopher's vision of the world rhetoric (and representation in general) is merely the (disposable) form by which a prior and substantial
content is conveyed; but in the world of *homo rhetoricus* rhetoric is
both form and content, the manner of presentation and what is presented; the "improvising power of the rhetor" is at once all-creating
and the guarantee of the impermanence of its creations: "to make a
thing beautiful or unbeautiful, just or unjust, good or bad is both a
human power and a sign of the insubstantiality of these attributes."[24]
Having been made they can be made again.

Which of these views of human nature is the correct one? The question can only be answered from within one or the other, and the evidence of one party will be regarded by the other either as illusory or as grist for its own mill. When presented with the ever-changing panorama of history, serious man will see variation on a few basic themes; and when confronted with the persistence of essentialist questions and answers, rhetorical man will reply as Lanham does by asserting that serious man is himself a supremely fictional achievement; seriousness is just another style, not the state of having escaped style:

> In a fallen cosmetic world, [plain Jane] is asking *not* to be considered, wants to be overlooked—or perhaps to claim attention by contrast. She is as rhetorical as her made up sister, proclaims as loudly an attitude. Thus the whole range of ornament from zero to 100 is equally rhetorical, equally deep or equally superficial. (p. 30)

That is to say, for rhetorical man the distinctions (between form and content, periphery and core, ephemeral and abiding) invoked by serious man are nothing more than the scaffolding of the theater of seriousness, are themselves instances of what they oppose. And on the other side, if serious man were to hear *that* argument, he would regard it as one more example of rhetorical manipulation and sleight of hand, an outrageous assertion that flies in the face of common sense, the equivalent in debate of "so's your old man." And so it would go, with no prospect of ever reaching accord, an endless round of accusation and counteraccusation in which truth, honesty, and linguistic responsibility are claimed by everyone: "from serious premises, all rhetorical language is suspect; from a rhetorical point of view, transparent language seems dishonest; false to the world."[25]

And so it *has* gone; the history of Western thought could be written as the history of this quarrel. And, indeed, such histories have been written and with predictably different emphases. In one version written many times, the mists of religion, magic, and verbal incantation (all equivalently suspect forms of fantasy) are dispelled by the Enlightenment rediscovery of reason and science; enthusiasm and metaphor alike are curbed by the refinement of method, and the effects of difference (point of view) are bracketed and held in check by a procedural rigor. In another version (told by a line stretching from Vico to Foucault) a carnivalesque world of exuberance and possibility is drastically impoverished by the ascendency of a soulless reason, a brutally narrow perspective that claims to be objective and proceeds in a repressive manner to enforce its claim. It is not my intention here to endorse either history or to offer a third or to argue as some have for a nonhistory of discontinuous *episteme* innocent of either a progressive or lapsarian curve; rather, I only wish to point out that the debate continues to this very day and that its terms are exactly those one finds in the dialogues of Plato and the orations of the sophists.

III

As I write, the fortunes of rhetorical man are on the upswing, as in discipline after discipline there is evidence of what has been called the interpretive turn, the realization (at least for those it seizes) that the givens of any field of activity—including the facts it commands, the procedures it trusts in, and the values it expresses and extends— are socially and politically constructed, are fashioned by man rather than delivered by God or Nature. The most recent (and unlikely) field to experience this revolution, or at least to hear of its possibility, is economics. The key text is Donald McCloskey's *The Rhetoric of Economics* (Wisconsin, 1985), a title that is itself polemical since, as McCloskey points out, mainstream economists don't like to think of themselves as employing a rhetoric; rather, they regard themselves as scientists whose methodology insulates them from the appeal of special interests or points of view. They think, in other words, that the procedures of their discipline will produce "knowledge free from doubt, free from metaphysics, morals and personal conviction" (p. 16). To this, McCloskey responds by declaring (in good sophistic terms) that no such knowledge is available, and that while economic method promises to deliver it, "what it is able to deliver [and] renames as scientific methodology [are] the scientist's and especially the economic scientist's metaphysics, moral, and personal convictions" (p. 16). Impersonal method, then, is both an illusion and a danger (as a kind of rhetoric it masks its rhetorical nature), and as an antidote to it McCloskey offers rhetoric, which he says, deals not with abstract truth, but with the truth that emerges in the context of distinctly human conversations (pp. 28–29). Within those conversations there are always

> particular arguments good or bad. After making them there is no point in asking a last, summarizing question: "Well, is it True?"

> It's whatever it is—persuasive, interesting, useful, and so forth. . . .
> There is no reason to search for a general quality called Truth,
> which answers only the unanswerable question, "What is it in the
> mind of God?" (p. 47)

The answerable questions are always asked within the assumptions of
particular situations, and both question and answer "will always depend on one's audience and the human purposes involved" (p. 150).
The real truth, concludes McCloskey, is that "assertions are made for
purposes of persuading some audience" and that, given the unavailability of a God's-eye view, "this is not a shameful fact," but the bottom
line fact in a rhetorical world.

At the first conference called to consider McCloskey's arguments,
the familiar anti-rhetorical objections were heard again in the land,
and the land might have been fifth-century Athens as well as Welles-
ley, Massachusetts, in 1986. One participant spoke of "the primrose
path to extreme relativism" which proceeds from "Kuhn's conception
of the incommensurability of paradigms" to the "contention that there
are no objective and unambiguous procedures for applying . . . rules
since the meanings of particular actions and terms are entirely . . .
context-dependent." Other voices proclaimed that nothing in McCloskey's position was new (an observation certainly true), that everyone
already knew it, and that at any rate it didn't touch the core of the
economists's practice. Still others invoked a set of related (and familiar) distinctions between empirical and interpretive activities, between demonstration and persuasion, between verifiable procedures and
anarchic irrationalism. Of course, each of these objections had already
been formulated (or reformulated) in those disciplines that had heard
rhetoric's siren song long before it reached the belated ears of economists. The name that everyone always refers to (in praise or blame)
is Thomas Kuhn. His *The Structure of Scientific Revolutions* is arguably the most frequently cited work in the humanities and social sciences in the past twenty-five years, and it is rhetorical through and
through. Kuhn begins by rehearsing and challenging the orthodox
model of scientific inquiry in which independent facts are first collected
by objective methods and then built up into a picture of nature, a picture that he himself either confirms or rejects in the context of controlled experiments. In this model, science is a "cumulative process"
(p. 3) in which each new discovery adds "one more item to the popu-

lation of the scientist's world" (p. 7). The shape of that world—of the scientist's professional activities—is determined by the shapes (of fact and structure) already existing in the larger world of nature, shapes that constrain and guide the scientist's work.

Kuhn challenges this story by introducing the notion of a paradigm, a set of tacit assumptions and beliefs within which research goes on, assumptions which rather than deriving from the observation of facts are determinative of the facts that could possibly be observed. It follows, then, that when observations made within different paradigms conflict, there is no principled (i.e., nonrhetorical) way to adjudicate the dispute. One cannot put the competing accounts to the test of fact, because the specification of fact is precisely what is at issue between them; a fact cited by one party would be seen as a mistake by the other. What this means is that science does not proceed by offering its descriptions to the independent judgment of nature; rather, it proceeds when the proponents of one paradigm are able to present their case in a way that the adherents of other paradigms find compelling. In short, the "motor" by which science moves is not verification or falsification, but persuasion. Indeed, says Kuhn, in the end the force of scientific argument "is *only* that of persuasion" (p. 94). In the case of disagreement, "each party must try, by persuasion, to convert the other" (p. 198), and when one party succeeds there is no higher court to which the outcome might be referred: "there is no standard higher than the assent of the relevant community" (p. 94). "What better criterion," asks Kuhn, "could there be?" (p. 170).

The answer given by those who were horrified by Kuhn's rhetoricization of scientific procedure was predictable: a better criterion would be one that was not captive to a particular paradigm but provided a neutral space in which competing paradigms could be disinterestedly assessed. By denying such a criterion, Kuhn leaves us in a world of epistemological and moral anarchy. The words are Israel Scheffler's:

Independent and public controls are no more, communication has failed, the common universe of things is a delusion, reality itself is made . . . rather than discovered. . . . In place of a community of rational men following objective procedures in the pursuit of truth, we have a set of isolated monads, within each of which belief forms without systematic constraints.[26]

Kuhn and those he has persuaded have, of course, responded to these accusations, but, needless to say, the debate continues in terms readers of this essay could easily imagine; and the debate has been particularly acrimonious because the area of contest—science and its procedures— is so heavily invested in as the one place where the apostles of rhetorical interpretivism would presumably fear to tread.

At one point in his argument Kuhn remarks that in the tradition he is critiquing scientific research is "reputed to proceed" from "raw data" or "brute experience"; but, he points out, if that were truly the mode of proceeding, it would require a "neutral observation language" (p. 125), a language that registers facts without any mediation by paradigm-specific assumptions. The problem is that "philosophical investigation has not yet provided even a hint of what a language able to do that would be like" (p. 127). Even a specially devised language "embodies a host of expectations about nature," expectations that limit in advance what can be described. Just as one cannot (in Kuhn's view) have recourse to neutral facts in order to settle a dispute, so one cannot have recourse to a neutral language in which to report those facts or even to report on the configuration of the dispute. The difference that divides men "is prior to the application of the languages in which it is nevertheless reflected" (p. 201). Whatever reports a particular language (natural or artificial) offers us will be the report on the world as it is seen from within some particular situation; there is no other aperspectival way to see and no language other than a situation-dependent language—an interested, rhetorical language—in which to report.

This same point was being made with all the force of philosophical authority by J. L. Austin in a book published, significantly, in the same year (1962) that saw the publication of *The Structure of Scientific Revolutions*. Austin begins *How to Do Things with Words* by observing that traditionally the center of the philosophy of language has been just the kind of utterance Kuhn declares unavailable, the context-independent statement that offers objective reports on an equally independent world in sentences of the form "He is running" and "Lord Raglan won the battle of Alma" (pp. 47, 142). Such utterances, which Austin calls "constative," are answerable to a requirement of truth and verisimilitude ("the truth of the constative . . . 'he is running' depends on his being running"); the words must match the world, and if they do not they can be criticized as false and inaccurate. There are, however, innumerable utterancees that are not assessable in this way. If, for example, I say to you, "I promise to pay you five dollars" or "Leave the room," it would be odd were you to respond by saying "true" or "false"; rather, you would say to the first "good" or "that's not enough" or "I won't hold my breath" and to the second "yes, sir" or "but I'm expecting a phone call" or "who do you think you are?" These and many other imaginable responses would not be judgments on the truth or accuracy of my utterance but on its appropriateness given our respective positions in some social structure of understanding (domestic, military, economic, etc.). It is only if the circumstances are of a certain kind—that is, if five dollars is a reasonable rather than an insulting amount, if the room I order you to leave is mine not yours—that the utterances will "take" and achieve the meaning of being a promise or a command. Thus the very identity, and therefore the meaning, of this type of utterance—Austin names it "performative"—depends on the context in which it is produced and received. There is no regular—in the sense of reliable and predictable—relationship between the form of the linguistic marks (the words and their order) and their significance. Nothing guarantees that "I promise to pay you five dollars" will be either intended or heard as a promise; in different circumstances it could be received as a threat or a joke (as when I utter it from debtors' prison), and in many circumstances it will be intended as one act and understood as another (as when your opinion of my trustworthiness is much lower than my own). When the criterion of verisimilitude has been replaced by the criterion of appropriateness, meaning becomes radically contextual, potentially as variable as the situated (and shifting) understandings of countless speakers and hearers.

It is, of course, precisely this property of performatives—their force is contingent and cannot be formally constrained—that is responsible for their being consigned by philosophers of language to the category of the "derived" or "parasitic," where, safely tucked away, they are prevented from contaminating the core category of the constative. But it is this act of segregation and quarantining that Austin undoes in the second half of his book when he extends the analysis of performatives to constatives and finds that they too mean differently in the light of differing contextual circumstances. Consider the exemplary constative, "Lord Raglan won the battle of Alma." Is it true, accurate, a faithful report? It depends, says Austin, on the context in which it is uttered and received (pp. 142–43). In a high school textbook it might be accepted as true because of the in-place assumptions as to what, exactly, a battle is, what constitutes winning, what the function of a general is, etc., while in a work of "serious" historical research all of these assumptions may have been replaced by others, with the result that the very notions "battle" and "won" would have a different shape. The properties that supposedly distinguish constatives from performatives—fidelity to preexisting facts, accountability to a criterion of truth—turn out to be as dependent on particular conditions of production and reception as performatives. "True" and "false," Austin concludes, are not names for the possible relationships between freestanding (constative) utterances and an equally freestanding state of affairs; rather, they are situation-specific judgments on the relationship between contextually produced utterances and states of affairs that are themselves no less contextually produced. At the end of the book constatives are "discovered" to be a subset of performatives, and with this discovery the formal core of language disappears entirely and is replaced by a world of utterances vulnerable to the sea change of every circumstance, the world, in short, of rhetorical (situated) man.

This is a conclusion Austin himself resists when he attempts to isolate (and thereby contain) the rhetorical by invoking another distinction between serious and nonserious utterance. Serious utterances are utterances for which the speaker takes responsibility; he means what he says, and therefore you can infer his meaning by considering his words in context. A nonserious utterance is an utterance produced in circumstances that "abrogate" (p. 21) the speaker's responsibility, and therefore one cannot with any confidence—that is, without the hazard of ungrounded conjecture—determine what he means:

> a performative utterance will, for example, be . . . hollow or void if said by an actor on the stage, or if introduced in a poem, or spoken in a soliloquy. . . . Language in such circumstances is in special ways . . . used not seriously, but in ways *parasitic* upon its normal use. . . . All this we are *excluding* from consideration. Our performative utterances . . . are to be understood as issued in ordinary circumstances. (p. 22)

The distinction, then, is between utterances that are, as Austin puts it later, "tethered to their origin" (p. 61), anchored by a palpable intention, and utterances whose origin is hidden by the screen of a theatrical or literary stage setting. This distinction and the passage in which it appears were taken up in 1967 by Jacques Derrida in a famous (and admiring) critique of Austin. Derrida finds Austin working against his own best insights and forgetting what he has just acknowledged, that "infelicity [communication going astray, in an unintended direction] is an ill to which *all* [speech] acts are heir."[27] Despite this acknowledgment, Austin continues to think of infelicity—of those cases in which the tethering origin of utterances is obscure and must be constructed by interpretive conjecture—as special, whereas, in Derrida's view, infelicity is itself the originary state in that any determination of meaning must always proceed within an interpretive construction of a speaker's intention. The origin that supposedly tethers the interpretation of an utterance will always be the product of that interpretation; the special circumstances in which meaning must be inferred through a screen rather than directly are the circumstances of every linguistic transaction. In short, there are no ordinary circumstances, merely those myriad and varied circumstances in which actors embedded in stage settings hazard interpretations of utterances produced by actors embedded in other stage situations. All the world, as Shakespeare says, is a stage, and on that stage "the quality of risk admitted by Austin" is not something one can avoid by sticking close to ordinary language in ordinary circumstances, but is rather "the internal and positive condition" of any act of communication."[28]

In the same publication in which the English translation of Derrida's essay appeared, John Searle, a student of Austin's, replied in terms that make clear the affiliation of this particular debate to the ancient debate whose configurations we have been tracing. Searle's strategy is basically to repeat Austin's points and declare that Derrida has missed them: "Austin's idea is simply this: if we want to know what it is to make a promise we had better not *start* our investigations with promises made by actors on stage . . . because in some fairly obvious way such utterances are not standard cases of promises" (p. 204). But in Derrida's argument, the category of the "obvious" is precisely what is being challenged or "deconstructed." Although it is true that we consider promises uttered in everyday contexts more direct—less etiolated—than promises made on a stage, this (Derrida would say) is only because the stage settings within which everyday life proceeds are so powerfully—that is, rhetorically—in place that they are in effect invisible, and therefore the meanings they make possible are experienced as if they were direct and unmediated by any screens. The "obvious" cannot be opposed to the "staged," as Searle assumes, because it is simply the achievement of a staging that has been particularly successful. One does not escape the rhetorical by fleeing to the protected area of basic communication and common sense because common sense in whatever form it happens to take is always a rhetorical—partial, partisan, interested—construction. This does not mean, Derrida hastens to add, that all rhetorical constructions are equal, just that they are equally rhetorical, equally the effects and extensions of some limited and challengeable point of view. The "citationality"—the condition of being in quotes, of being *in*direct—of an utterance in a play is not the same as the citationality of a philosophical reference or a deposition before a court; it is just that no one of these performatives is more serious—more direct, less mediated, less rhetorical—than any other. Whatever opposition there is takes place within a "general" citationality which "constitutes a violation of the allegedly rigorous purity of every event of discourse or every *speech act*" (p. 192).

Searle points out (p. 205) that in order to achieve a "general theory of speech acts," one must perform acts of exclusion or idealization like Austin's; but it is the possibility of a general theory—of an account that is itself more than an extension of some *particular* context or perspective—that Derrida denies. His is the familiar world of Rhetorical Man, teeming with roles, situations, strategies, interventions, but containing no master role, no situation of situations, no strategy for outflanking all strategies, no intervention in the arena of dispute that does not expand the arena of dispute, no neutral point of rationality from the vantage point of which the "merely rhetorical" can be identified and held in check. That is why deconstructive or post-structuralist thought is supremely rhetorical: it systematically asserts and demonstrates the mediated, constructed, partial, socially constituted nature of all realities, whether they be phenomenal, linguistic, or psychological. To deconstruct a text, says Derrida, is to "work through the structured genealogy of its concepts in the most scrupulous and immanent fashion, but at the same time to determine from a certain external perspective that it cannot name or describe what this history may have concealed or excluded, constituting itself as history through this repression in which it has a stake."[29] The "external perspective" is the perspective from which the analyst knows in advance (by virtue of his commitment to the rhetorical or anti-foundational worldview) that the coherences presented by a text (and an institution or an economy can in this sense be a text) rests on a contradiction it cannot acknowledge, rests on the suppression of the challengeable rhetoricity of its own standpoint, a standpoint that offers itself as if it came from nowhere in particular and simply delivered things as they really (i.e., nonperspectivally) are. A deconstructive reading will surface those contradictions and expose those suppressions and thus "trouble" a unity that is achieved only by covering over all the excluded emphases and interests that might threaten it. These exclusions are part of the text in that the success of its totalizing effort depends on them. Once they are made manifest, the hitherto manifest meaning of the text is undermined—indeed, is shown to have always and already been undermined—as "the rhetorical operations that produce the supposed ground of argument, the key concept or premise," are deprived of the claim to be *un*rhetorical, serious, disinterested.[30]

Nor is this act performed in the service of something beyond rhetoric. Derridean deconstruction does not uncover the operations of rhetoric in order to reach the Truth; rather, it continually uncovers the truth of rhetorical operations, the truth that all operations, including the operation of deconstruction itself, are rhetorical. If, as Paul de Man asserts, "a deconstruction always has for its target to reveal the existence of hidden articulations and fragmentations within assumedly monadic totalities," care must be taken that a new monadic totality is not left as the legacy of the deconstructive gesture. Since the course of a deconstruction is to uncover a "fragmented stage that can be called natural with regard to the system that is being undone," there is always the danger that the "natural" pattern will "substitute *its* relational system for the one it helped to dissolve."[31] The only way to escape this danger is to perform the deconstructive act again and again, submitting each new emerging constellation to the same suspicious scrutiny that brought it to light, and resisting the temptation to put in place of the truths it rhetoricizes the truth that everything is rhetorical. One cannot rest even in the insight that there is no place to rest. "Rhetoric," says de Man, "suspends logic and opens up vertiginous possibilities of referential aberration" (p. 10). But the rhetorical vision is foreclosed on and made into a new absolute if those "vertiginous possibilities" are celebrated as the basis of a new wisdom. The rhetorical beat must by definition go on, endlessly repeating the sequence by which "the lure of solid ground" is succeeded by "the ensuing demystification."[32] When de Man approvingly quotes Nietzsche's identification of truth with "a moving army of metaphors, metonymies and anthropomorphisms," a rhetorical construction whose origin has been (and must be) forgotten, he does not exempt Nietzsche's text from its own corrosive effects. If Nietzsche declares (well in advance of Kuhn and Austin, but well after Gorgias and Protagoras) that "there is no such thing as an unrhetorical, 'natural' language," for "tropes are not something that can be added or subtracted from language at will," the insight must be extended to that very declaration: "A text like *On Truth and Lie,* although it presents itself legitimately as a demystification of literary rhetoric, remains entirely literary, and deceptive itself" (p. 113). The "rhetorical mode," the mode of deconstruction, is a mode of "endless reflection," since it is "unable ever to escape from the rhetorical deceit it announces" (p. 115).

IV

That, however, is just what is wrong with deconstructive practice from the viewpoint of the intellectual left, many of whose members subscribe to Nietzsche's account of truth and reality as rhetorical but find that much of post-structuralist discourse uses that account as a way of escaping into new versions of idealism and formalism. Frank Lentricchia, for example, sees in some of de Man's texts an intention to place "discourse in a realm where it can have no responsibility to historical life" and fears that we are being invited into "the realm of the thoroughly predictable linguistic transcendental," the "rarified region of the undecidable," where every text "speaks synchronically and endlessly the same tale . . . of its own duplicitous self-consciousness."[33] Terry Eagleton's judgment is even harsher. Noting that in the wake of Nietzschean thought, rhetoric, "mocked and berated for centuries by an abrasive rationalism," takes its "terrible belated revenge" by finding itself in every rationalist project, Eagleton complains that many rhetoricians seem content to stop there, satisfied with the "Fool's function of unmasking all power as self-rationalization, all knowledge as a mere fumbling with metaphor."[34] Operating as a "vigorous demystifier of all ideology," rhetoric functions only as a form of thought and ends up by providing "the final ideological rationale for political inertia." In retreat "from market place to study, politics to philology, social practice to semiotics," deconstructive rhetoric turns the emancipatory promise of Nietzschean thought into "a gross failure of ideological nerve," allowing the liberal academic the elitist pleasure of repeatedly exposing "vulgar commercial and political hectorings" (pp. 108–9). In both his study of Benjamin and his influential *Literary Theory: An Introduction,* Eagleton urges a return to the Ciceronian-Isocratic tradition in which the rhetorical arts are inseparable from the practice of a politics, "techniques of persuasion indissociable from the substantive issues and audiences involved," techniques whose employment is "closely determined by the pragmatic situation at hand."[35] In short, he calls for a rhetoric that will do real work and cites as an example the slogan "black is beautiful," which he says is "paradigmatically rhetorical since it employs a figure of equivalence to produce particular discursive and extra-discursive effects without direct regard for truth."[36] That is, someone who says "black is beautiful" is not so much interested in the accuracy of the assertion (it is not constatively intended) as he is in the responses it may provoke—surprise, outrage, urgency, solidarity—responses that may in turn set in motion "practices that are deemed, in the light of a particular set of falsifiable hypotheses, to be desirable."[37]

For Eagleton, the desirable practices are Marxist-socialist and the rhetoric that will help establish them has three tasks:

> First, to participate in the production of works and events which
> . . . so fictionalize the "real" as to intend those effects conducive
> to the victory of socialism. Second, as "critic" to expose the rhetor-
> ical structures by which non-socialist works produce politically
> undesirable effects. . . . Third, to interpret such words where
> possible "against the grain," so as to appropriate from them what-
> ever may be valuable for socialism.[38]

It is, of course, the second of these tasks that presents conceptual and cognitive problems. If all cultural work is, as Eagleton says in the sentence just before this passage, rhetorical, then how does one's own rhetoric escape the inauthenticity it discovers in the rhetoric of others? Eagleton's answer is contained in his assumption of the superiority of the socialist program; any rhetorical work in the service of that program will be justified in advance, while conversely any rhetorical work done in opposition to socialist urgencies will flow from "false consciousness" and will deserve to be exposed. This confidence in his objectives makes Eagleton impatient with those for whom the rhetoricity of all discourse is something to be savored for itself, something to be lovingly and obsessively demonstrated again and again. It is not, he says, "a matter of starting from certain theoretical or methodological problems;

it is a matter of starting from what we want to *do,* and then seeing which methods and theories will best help us to achieve these ends."[39] Theories, in short, are themselves rhetorics whose usefulness is a function of contingent circumstances. It is ends—specific goals in local contexts—that rule the invocation of theories, not theories that determine goals and the means by which they can be reached.

There are those on the left, however, for whom the direction is the other way around, from the theoretical realization of rhetoric's pervasiveness to a vision and a program for implementing it. In their view the discovery (or rediscovery) that all discourse and therefore all knowledge is rhetorical leads or should lead to the adoption of a *method* by which the dangers of rhetoric can be at least mitigated and perhaps extirpated. This method has two stages: the first is a stage of debunking, and it issues from the general suspicion in which all orthodoxies and arrangements of power are held once it is realized that their basis is not reason or nature but the success of some rhetorical/political agenda. Armed with this realization, one proceeds to expose the contingent and therefore challengeable basis of whatever presents itself as natural and inevitable. So far this is precisely the procedure of deconstruction; but whereas deconstructive practice (at least of the Yale variety) seems to produce nothing but the occasion for its endless repetition, some cultural revolutionaries discern in it a more positive residue, the loosening or weakening of the structures of domination and oppression that now hold us captive. The reasoning is that by repeatedly uncovering the historical and ideological basis of established structures (both political and cognitive), one becomes sensitized to the effects of ideology and begins to clear a space in which those effects can be combated; and as that sensitivity grows more acute, the area of combat will become larger until it encompasses the underlying structure of assumptions that confers a spurious legitimacy on the powers that currently be. The claim, in short, is that the radically rhetorical insight of Nietzschean/Derridean thought can do radical political work; becoming aware that everything is rhetorical is the first step in countering the power of rhetoric and liberating us from its force. Only if deeply entrenched ways of thinking and acting are made the objects of suspicion will we be able "even to *imagine* that life could be different and better."

This last sentence is taken from an essay by Robert Gordon entitled "New Developments in Legal Theory."[40] Gordon is writing as a member of the Critical Legal Studies Movement, a group of legal academics who have discovered the rhetorical nature of legal reasoning

and are busily exposing as interested the supposedly disinterested operations of legal procedures. Gordon's pages are replete with the vocabulary of enclosure or prison; we are "locked into" a system of belief we
did not make; we are "demobilized" (that is, rendered less mobile);
we must "break out" (p. 291), we must "unfreeze the world as it
appears to common sense" (p. 289). What will help us to break out,
to unfreeze, is the discovery "that the belief-structures that rule our
lives are not found in nature but are historically contingent," for that
discovery, says Gordon, "is extraordinarily liberating" (p. 289). What it
will liberate are the mental energies that were before prevented by the
"paralysis-inducing" effects of received systems of thought from even
imagining that "life could be different and better." In the words of
Roberto Unger (another prominent member of the movement), if you
start with an awareness of the insight "that no one scheme of human
association has conclusive authority" and come to an understanding of
the "flawed" nature of the schemes now in place, you can then "imagine
the actualizations [i.e., present-day arrangements of things] transformed" and in time "transform them in fact."[41] The result will be a
"cultural-revolutionary practice" that will bring about the "progressive
emancipation from a background plan of social division and hierarchy" (p. 587). To the question, what is the *content* of that emancipation, given a world that is rhetorical through and through, those who
work Gordon's and Unger's side of the street usually reply that emancipation will take the form of a strengthening and enlarging of a capacity
of mind that stands to the side of, and is therefore able to resist, the
appeal of the agenda that would enslave us. That capacity of mind has
received many names, but the one most often proposed is "critical self-
consciousness." Critical self-consciousness is the ability (stifled in some,
developed in others) to discern in any "scheme of association," including those one finds attractive and compelling, the partisan aims it hides
from view; and the claim is that as it performs this negative task, critical self-consciousness participates in the positive task of formulating
schemes of associations (structures of thought and government) that
are in the service not of a particular party but of all mankind.

It need hardly be said that this claim veers back in the direction
of the rationalism and universalism that the critical/deconstructive
project sets out to demystify. That project begins by rejecting the ra-
tionalities of present life as rationalizations and revealing the structure

of reality to be rhetorical, that is, partial; but then it turns around and attempts to use the insight of partiality to build something that is less partial, less hostage to the urgencies of a particular vision and more responsive to the needs of men and women in general. Insofar as this "turn" is taken to its logical conclusion, it ends up reinventing at the conclusion of a rhetorically informed critique the entire array of anti-rhetorical gestures and exclusions. One sees this clearly in the work of Jürgen Habermas, a thinker whose widespread influence is testimony to the durability of the tradition that began (at least) with Plato. Habermas's goal is to bring about something he calls the "ideal speech situation," a situation in which all assertions proceed not from the perspective of individual desires and strategies, but from the perspective of a general rationality upon which all parties are agreed. In such a situation nothing would count except the claims to universal validity of all assertions. "No force except that of the better argument is exercised; and, . . . as a result, all motives except that of the cooperative search for truth are excluded."[42] Of course, in the world we now inhabit there is no such purity of motive; nevertheless, says Habermas, even in the most distorted of communicative situations there remains something of the basic impulse behind all utterance, "the intention of communicating a true [*wahr*] proposition . . . so that the hearer can share the knowledge of the speaker."[43] If we could only eliminate from our discourse performances those intentions that reflect baser goals—the intentions to deceive, to manipulate, to persuade—the ideal speech situation could be approximated.

What stands in our way is the fact that many of our speech acts issue from the perspective of local and historically contingent contexts, and these by definition cannot contribute to the building up of a general rationality. Therefore, it is incumbent upon us to choose and proffer utterances that satisfy (or at least claim and desire to satisfy) *universal* conditions of validity. This is the project Habermas names "Universal Pragmatics" and the name tells its own story. Habermas recognizes, as all modern and postmodern contextualists do, that language is a social and not a purely formal phenomenon, but he thinks that the social/pragmatic aspect of language use is itself "accessible to formal analysis" (p. 6) and that therefore it is possible to construct a universal "communicative competence" (p. 29) parallel to Chomsky's linguistic competence. Sentences produced according to the rules and norms of this communicative competence would be tied not to "particular epistemic presuppositions and changing contexts" (p. 29), but to the unchanging context (the context of contexts) in which one finds the presuppositions underlying the general possibility of successful speech. "A *general* theory of speech acts would . . . describe . . . that fundamental system of rules that adult subjects master to the extent that they can fulfill *the conditions of happy employment of sentences in utterances* no matter to which particular language the sentences may belong and in which accidental contexts the utterances may be embedded" (p. 26). If we can operate on the level of that fundamental system, the distorting potential of "accidental contexts" will be neutralized because we will always have one eye on what is essential, the establishing by rational cooperation of an interpersonal (nonaccidental) truth. Once speakers are oriented to this goal and away from others, oriented toward *general* understanding, they will be incapable of deception and manipulation: "Truthfulness guarantees the transparency of a subjectivity representing itself in language" (p. 57). A company of transparent subjectivities will join together in the fashioning of a transparent truth and of a world in which the will to power has been eliminated.

In his book *Textual Power* (New Haven, 1985), Robert Scholes examines the rationalist epistemology in which a "complete self confronts a solid world, perceiving it directly and accurately, . . . capturing it perfectly in a transparent language" and declares it to be so thoroughly discredited that it now "is lying in ruins around us" (pp. 132–33). Perhaps so, in some circles, but the fact of Habermas's work and of the audience he commands suggests that even now those ruins are collecting themselves and rising again into the familiar antirhetorical structure. It would seem that any announcement of the death of either position will always be premature, slightly behind the institutional news that in some corner of the world supposedly abandoned questions are receiving what at least appear to be new answers. Only recently the *public* fortunes of rationalist-foundationalist thought have taken a favorable turn with the publication of books like Allan Bloom's *The Closing of the American Mind* and E. D. Hirsch's *Cultural Literacy,* both of which (Bloom's more directly) challenge the "new Orthodoxy" of "extreme cultural relativism" and reassert, albeit in different ways, the existence of normative standards. In many quarters these books have been welcomed as a return to the common sense that is necessary if civilization is to avoid the dark night of anarchy. One can expect administrators and legislators to propose reforms (and perhaps even purges) based on Bloom's arguments (the rhetorical force of anti-rhetoricalism is always being revived), and one can expect too a host of voices raised in opposition to what will surely be called the "new positivism." Those voices will include some that have been mentioned here and some others that certainly merit recording but can only be noted in a list that is itself incomplete. The full story of rhetoric's twentieth-century resurgence would boast among its cast of characters: Kenneth Burke, whose "dramatism" anticipates so much of what is considered avant-garde today; Wayne Booth, whose *The Rhetoric of Fiction* was so important in legitimizing the rhetorical analysis of the novel; Mikhail Bakhtin, whose contrast of monologic to dialogic and heteroglossic discourse sums up so many strands in the rhetorical tradition; Roland Barthes, who in the concept of "jouissance" makes a (non) constitutive principle of the tendency of rhetoric to resist closure and extend play; the ethnomethodologists (Harold Garfinkel and company) who discover in every supposedly rule-bound context the operation of a principle (exactly the wrong word) of "ad-hocing"; Chaim Perelman and L. Olbrechts-Tyeca whose *The New Rhetoric: A Treatise on Argumentation* provides a sophisticated modern source book for would-be rhetoricians weary of always citing Aristotle; Barbara Herrnstein Smith who, in the course of espousing an unashamed relativism, directly confronts and argues down the objections of those who fear for their souls (and more) in a world without objective standards; Fredric Jameson and Hayden White who teach us (among other things) that "history . . . is unaccessible to us except in textual form, and that our approach to it and to the Real itself necessarily passes through its prior textualization";[44] reader-oriented critics like Norman Holland, David Bleich, Wolfgang Iser, and H. R. Jauss who, by shifting the emphasis from the text to its reception, open up the act of interpretation to the infinite variability of contextual circumstance; innumerable feminists who relentlessly unmark male hegemonic structures and expose as rhetorical the rational posturings of the legal and political systems; equally innumerable theorists of composition who, under the slogan "process, not product," insist on the rhetorical nature of communication and argue for far-reaching changes in the way writing is taught. The list is already formidable, but it could go on and on, providing support for Scholes's contention that the rival epistemology has been vanquished and for Clifford Geertz's announcement (and he too is a contributor to the shift he reports) that "Something is happening to the way we think about the way we think."[45]

But it would seem, from the evidence marshaled in this essay, that something is always happening to the way we think, and that it is always the same something, a tug-of-war between two views of human life and its possibilities, no one of which can ever gain complete and lasting ascendancy because in the very moment of its triumphant articulation each turns back in the direction of the other. Thus Wayne Booth feels obliged in both *The Rhetoric of Fiction* and *A Rhetoric of Irony* to confine the force of rhetoric by sharply distinguishing its legitimate uses from two extreme-limit cases (the "unreliable narrator" and "unstable irony"); some reader-response critics deconstruct the autonomy and self-sufficiency of the text, but in the process end up privileging the autonomous and self-sufficient subject; some feminists challenge the essentialist claims of "male reason" in the name of a female rationality or nonrationality apparently no less essential; Jameson opens up the narrativity of history in order to proclaim one narrative the true and unifying one. Here one might speak of the return of the repressed (and thereby invoke Freud whose writings and influence would be still another chapter in the story I have not even begun to tell) were it not that the repressed—whether it be the fact of difference or the desire for its elimination—is always so close to the surface that it hardly need be unearthed. What we seem to have is a tale full of sound and fury, and signifying itself, signifying a durability rooted in inconclusiveness, in the impossibility of there being a last word.

In an essay, however, someone must have the last word and I give it to Richard Rorty. Rorty is himself a champion of the antiessentialism that underlies rhetorical thinking; his neo-pragmatism makes common cause with Kuhn and others who would turn us away from the search for transcendental absolutes and commend to us (although it would seem superfluous to do so) the imperatives and goals already informing our practices. It is, however, not the polemicist Rorty whom I call upon to sum up, but the Rorty who is the brisk chronicler of our epistemological condition:

> There . . . are two ways of thinking about various things. . . .
> The first . . . thinks of truth as a vertical relationship between representations and what is represented. The second . . . thinks of truth horizontally—as the culminating reinterpretation of our

predecessors' reinterpretation of their predecessors' reinterpretation. . . . It is the difference between regarding truth, goodness, and beauty as eternal objects which we try to locate and reveal, and regarding them as artifacts whose fundamental design we often have to alter.[46]

It is the difference between serious and rhetorical man. It is the difference that remains.

21. Force

In the opening chapters of his magisterial study, *The Concept of Law,*
H. L. A. Hart emphatically rejects John Austin's view that the essence
of the law is a "situation where one person gives another an order
backed by threats" and thereby "obliges him to comply."[1] Hart objects
that this view fails to distinguish the law and its operations from the
action of a gunman who "orders his victim to hand over his purse, and
threatens to shoot him if he refuses" (p. 6). It is simply counterintuitive, he contends, to assimilate law to this reductive paradigm, and, indeed, "Mere temporary ascendancy of one person over another is naturally thought of as the polar opposite of law, with its relatively enduring
and settled character." "In most legal systems," he adds, "to exercise
such short term coercive power as the gunman has would constitute a
criminal offense" (p. 24). "Coercive power" is the key phrase here, for
it identifies what is for Hart the important distinction between what the
law is and what the gunman does: rather than coercing individuals by
the exercise of mere force, the law binds members of society to a rule
or set of rules that has the character of being general and impartial
(p. 203)—that is, no respecter of persons. Without "the idea of a
rule," Hart declares, "we cannot hope to elucidate even the most elementary forms of law" (p. 78). Of course, as Hart himself sees, the
notion of a rule does not entirely eliminate coercion, since where there
is a rule of law there is necessarily some form of constraint in relation
to which "human conduct is made in some sense non-optional or obligatory" (p. 80). The phrase "in some sense" identifies the difference Hart
would like to establish between legal obligation and the model of the
gunman; while the individual under the law is not wholly free—such
freedom would be incompatible with the very idea of law—the obligations to which he is subject are not merely the effect of arbitrary power

but of a power that is enabled by an independent and authoritative source. That source is the rule of law which, Hart says, operates by "conferring powers . . . on persons qualified in certain ways to legislate by complying with a certain procedure" (p. 75). Notice how much distance there is in this account between the source of power and the object of its exercise. In the gunman scenario the coercion is direct and discrete; in the world of rule the coercing agent stands at the end of a long and articulated chain, beginning with the rule itself, which mandates not an act but a procedure which itself can only be put in motion by persons who meet prestipulated and abstract qualifications (age, education, skills, etc.), and these persons authorize still other persons who must themselves satisfy additional formal requirements. It is from this chain and not from any temporarily ascendant outlaw that the pressure of obligation issues, and the obedience that then follows (if it follows) will be the result not of force and violence, but of a principled process.

Or so it might seem. Could it not be said that procedure rather than doing away with force merely masks it by attenuating it, by placing it behind a screen or series of screens? After all, the crucial question, which returns the original problem to center stage, still has to be asked: Who gets to make the rules? And once that question is answered, another question (it is really the same) waits behind it, who gets to say who gets to make the rules? If the answer to these questions turns out to be something like "whoever seizes the opportunity and makes it stick," then there is finally little to distinguish the rule-centered legal system from the actions of the gunman; this gunman is merely better camouflaged. It is precisely such a danger that Hart spies when, later in the book, he identifies and considers another and more subtle form of imposition and coercion, that exercised by a court when, under the cover of its responsibility to interpret law, it instead *makes* law and thereby demonstrates the truth of Bishop Hoadly's famous observation: "whoever hath an absolute authority to interpret any written or spoken laws it is he who is the lawgiver to all intents and purposes and not the person who first wrote or spake them" (p. 137). As Hart notes, this is simply an older version of what is to us a familar claim: "the law (or the constitution) is what the courts say it is" (p. 138). If this is indeed the case, then the rule of law or, more precisely, the law of rule becomes an illusion, for the rule as a constraint, as a safeguard against casual violence, falls to the daily acts of violence committed by judges who call the tune as they happen to see (and desire) it. Here is a "temporary" ascendancy of one person not only over another, but over many; here is a forceful capture even more sinister than that performed by the gunman because it wears the face of legitimate authority.

The great merit of Hart's analysis is that it makes clear the close relationship—a relationship so close as to be one of identity—between the threat posed to law by force and the threat posed to law by interpretation; if it is the business of law to protect the individual from coercion that is random, unpredictable, and arbitrary, then the individual is no less at risk when he is at the mercy of an interpreting court than when he is at the mercy of an armed assailant. In both cases he is nakedly exposed to an agent who has seized authority and is in the accidental circumstance of being able to get away with it. Of course, there is the difference that in one case a legislature (sometimes democratically elected) intervenes between the would-be coercer and his victim, but that is cold comfort if Bishop Hoadly is right and the interpreter "is he who is the lawgiver to all intents and purposes." If the gunman is the paradigmatic instance of force outside the law, interpretation is the force that resides within the law, and like the gunman it must be regulated and policed lest it subvert the law's claim to enact the dictates of general principles of justice and equity. It is crucial that the law not issue from anyone in particular—even from a justice of the Supreme Court—but from an impersonal source that resists the encroaching desires of particular (interpretive) wills. *The Concept of Law* is an extended search for such a point of resistance, and after having failed to discover it in the writings of his predecessors, Hart announces that he has found it in "the idea of a rule" (p. 78) and, more particularly, in the idea of a "determinate rule" in which, he says, "the life of the law consists" (p. 132). Determinate rules, in contrast to vague or general rules that allow "the applications of variable standards, do *not* require from officials and individuals a fresh judgment from case to case" (p. 132). Indeed, it would be more accurate to say that determinate rules (assuming for the moment that such exist) do not *permit* a fresh judgment from case to case because they are so directing as to leave no room in which the judgment might operate. Determinate, in short, means settled, complete in and of itself, and therefore in no need of further elaboration or addition. Determinate rules perform as barriers or walls on which is written "beyond this point interpretation cannot go."

Given that in Hart's view law is all that stands between us and "the free use of violence" (p. 167), and given too that for him law is thinkable only in terms of determinate rules, it is hardly surprising that he equates the absence of such rules with the advent of chaos: "If it were not possible to communicate general standards of conduct, which multitudes of individuals could understand, without further direction, as requiring from them certain conduct when occasion arose, nothing that we now recognize as law could exist" (p. 121). This single sentence is at once a compendium and an explication of the fears and desires that inform the tradition in which Hart writes; there must be a mode of communication that is general, not tied to the linguistic system of any particular community; once produced, these general communications must be understandable by anyone, no matter what his individual educational or cultural experience; indeed, this understanding must be so immediate as not to be in need of any further elaboration; in fact, its self-sufficiency shall be so perfect that elaboration or direction—otherwise known as interpretation—will constitute an impiety; the content of this unavoidable and self-sufficient understanding will be a set of matching orders; the hearer or reader will be "required," that is, compelled, left without choice, deprived of any opportunity to exercise his creative ingenuity; and unless all of this is the case, unless the framing of such general standards in a fail-safe interpretation-proof mode is a possible achievement, there will be no law.

The point is made even more dramatically by the court in *Cargill Commission Co. v. Swartwood* (198 N.W. 536 [1924]) when it refuses to take into consideration a prior oral agreement entered into by parties who subsequently executed a written contract. In the course of its decision the court invokes the so-called "parol evidence rule" which states that when a written instrument is the complete and final expression of the contracting parties, it cannot be varied or contradicted by oral testimony. Obviously, the intention of the rule is to keep the writing—the palpable evidence of a binding agreement—authoritative by declaring it off-bounds to interpretation. The alternative is so dreadful that the court can only contemplate it in the act of dismissing it:

> Were it otherwise, written contracts would be enforced not according to the plain effect of their language, but pursuant to the story of their negotiation as told by the litigant having at the time being the greater power of persuading the trier of fact. So far as

contracts are concerned the rule of law would give way to the mere notions of men as to who should win law suits. Without that [the parol evidence] rule there would be no assurance of the enforceability of a written contract. If such assurance were removed today from our law, general disaster would result. . . . (p. 538)

It takes one hundred and forty pages for Hart to move from the rejection of force to the identification of force, and its potentially disastrous consequences, with interpretation. The court in Cargill does it in only four sentences, and in steps that can serve as a paradigm for the formalist argument. The "plain effect" of contractual language is opposed to the shifting and variable effects produced by stories powerfully—that is, forcefully—told. On the one hand, a stable and fixed (authoritative) shape; on the other, the many shapes brought into being by the exercise of verbal ingenuity. On the one side, the independent power of self-construing language; on the other, the power generated by the artful distortions of interested agents. If the power of interest is allowed to obscure matters of fact, if the determination of fact turns into a contest of persuasive styles, then the notion of a contract—of an agreement sealed by its verbal representation—goes by the boards; and if that happens, general disaster—the wholesale breakdown of communicative certainty and trust—cannot be far behind.

What the Cargill opinion makes clear is that in the court's view, as in Hart's, the foundations of law are linguistic; the safeguard the law erects in order to repel the depredations of force are made of language, and if they are to perform as safeguards, they must be made of a certain kind of language, language that is capable of making what Hart calls an "authoritative mark" (p. 93). An authoritative mark commands the field in which it operates; it is a mark so complete and self-sufficient in its declaration that no one could mistake it or misread it. An authoritative mark is a determinate mark, and because it is possible to produce such a mark, it is possible to fashion determinate rules, and finally to elaborate a genuine system of law. So long as determinate rules embodied in authoritative marks are available as something to which we can have recourse in the event of disputes, we have "in embryonic form the idea of a legal system," "the germ of the idea of legal validity" (p. 93).

Some of you will have recognized in the vocabulary of "authoritative marks" and "determinate rules" a familiar theory of language. In that theory communication is anchored by something variously called literal language, neutral language, objective language, plain language, scientific language, denotative language, explicit language, etc. By any name, what is referred to is a level of language immune from contextual variation and therefore resistant to interpretation. The problem with this theory is well known: it seems undermined by the variety that is so obviously a feature of interpretive performance; nothing is more common than disputes concerning the meaning of supposedly plain or literal language. In the face of these disputes, in what sense could anything made of language be "determinate"? Hart answers this question by dividing language into two zones; there is at its center a "core of settled meaning" and at its outer edges or "penumbra" a realm of uncertainty and doubt. Disagreements arise in the area of the penumbra where a certain looseness and vagueness results in what he calls "open texture" (p. 120); but disagreements must themselves have a point of reference—something one is disagreeing *about*—and that point of reference is given by the settled core which determines the parameters of any dispute that might occur. Interpreters are thus constrained by the core even as they move with (relative) freedom in the area of the penumbra, and it is because of this "duality of a core of certainty and a penumbra of doubt" (p. 119) that communication is able to occur: "If we are to communicate with each other at all . . . then the words we use . . . must have some standard instance in which no doubts are felt about its application";[2] for then, "when we . . . frame some general rule . . . the language . . . fixes necessary conditions which anything must satisfy if it is to be within its scope, and certain clear examples of what is certainly within its scope may be present in our minds" (p. 125).

The passage, then, is from words with a core of settled meaning to rules with a core of settled meaning, and later, as we shall see, to historical bodies of material (decisions, statutes) whose significance is no less settled. Hart acknowledges that at every level variety and difference exist at the fringe ("nothing can eliminate this . . . penumbra of doubt"), but he insists that the variety is finally controlled and contained by a stability at the center, by the "core," the "germ," the "embryo." By using these words to characterize that which stands between us and the advance of unconstrained interpretation, Hart (inadvertently) alerts us to its fragility. In each of these spatial metaphors the still unmoving point (core, center, germ, embryo) is surrounded by a much larger area (of fringe, penumbra, open texture), and the impression is of an insurgent force always on the verge of overrunning the fortress at the center, of blurring the line that demarcates the variable from the constant, of erasing (by writing over) the authoritative mark. It is Hart's strategy repeatedly to assure us (and himself) that the encroachment of interpretive will can be resisted if only we cling to the "core," but it is a strategy of desperation, and at times Hart himself seems more than half-aware that it has already failed.

The sequence is always the same: he offers a candidate that will fill the position of "authoritative mark"—of something so self-sufficiently clear that it compels agreement and precludes interpretation—but then he so qualifies the status of the "mark" that its authority is put seriously in question. We see this first in his discussion of what he calls "primary rules of obligation" (where primary, of course, is another world like center, embryon, core), rules that place "restrictions on the free use of violence, theft, and deception to which human beings are tempted but which they must, in general, repress, if they are to exist in close proximity with one another" (p. 89). As they first emerge, these rules are "unofficial"; that is, they stem from a shared desire for peace and security rather than from any developed and codified legal apparatus. But even as they are introduced, the primary rules are found to be inadequate, for it is only in a "small community closely knit by ties of kinship, common sentiment, and belief" that they could function successfully. As soon as numbers increase and beliefs diverge—one suspects that the trouble begins when the number reaches two—there will arise "doubts . . . as to what the rules are or as to the precise scope of some given rule." In the absence of an "authoritative text" or of "an official whose declarations . . . are authoritative" there "will be no procedure for settling . . . doubt" (p. 90). At a very early stage, then, a regime of primary rules will be characterized by "uncertainty," and when that happens the rules "will require supplementation."

But if the rules are uncertain and require supplementation, how can they be rules? Hart's project would seem to be compromised even before it gets under way. The entire *point* of rules, after all, is to stand alone and provide a center (core, germ, embryon) to which all parties can turn in the event of disputes. If the rules are incomplete, if one cannot know even what they are without the aid of some supplementary elaboration, then rather than constraining interpretation the rules—so called—provoke it. Hart, however, is not without resources, and he moves to anticipate just an objection by introducing a new line of defense in the form of a set of "secondary rules," which, he says, will provide a "remedy" for the "defects" of the primary rules. Chief among these is the "rule of recognition," a "rule for conclusive identification of the primary rules," a rule that will provide an "affirmative indication" as to whether or not a primary rule put forward by some interest is, in fact, "a rule of the group" (p. 92). In order to perform this function, a rule of recognition must be of "a different kind" (p. 92) than other rules of the system, and much of Hart's discussion is an attempt to specify the difference. He finds it first in the fact that this rule is "inscribed, written down in a list" or "carved on some public monument," but he realizes at once that the fact of the inscription will not be sufficiently distinguishing, since writings can proliferate just as easily as oral sayings or undeclared beliefs. The "crucial step," he declares, is "the acknowledgment of reference to the writing or inscription as *authoritative*" (p. 92), and this happens when the rule of recognition has been "accepted" (pp. 97, 105). But the notions of "acknowledgment" and "acceptance" are obviously and fatally at odds with the requirement that the rule be "ultimate" and "supreme" (pp. 102, 103); for a rule that depends on the acknowledgment and acceptance of those who are to be bound by it can fail in both respects: it could remain unacknowledged—go *un*recognized—and it could be refused, perhaps in favor of other candidates. In order to be a rule of recognition in the strong sense—and that is the only sense that will do the job—the rule must be capable of recognizing or announcing itself and it must *compel* rather than await acceptance. How can a rule be "a supreme criterion of validity" (p. 103) if its own validity can either go unnoticed or become a matter of dispute?

The same difficulty attends Hart's second attempt to claim for the rule of recognition a special, privileged status. Here the claim is that the rule exists "on a different level" (p. 94) from the other rules and from the system whose center or core it is. It is in the nature of the rule, says Hart, that when confronted by it, "we are brought to a stop in inquiries concerning validity: for we have reached a rule which . . . provides criteria for the assessment of the validity of other rules; but is . . . also unlike them in that there is no rule providing criteria for the assessment of its own legal validity" (p. 104); where other rules must "satisfy criteria" in order to be validated, "no such question can arise as to the validity of the very rule . . . which provides the criteria"

(p. 105). But the question has already arisen as soon as acknowledgment and acceptance have been made the criteria for identifying the rule of recognition; for these criteria bring with them precisely what the rule of recognition supposedly eliminates, an area of choice, and choice in turn brings with it the specters of dispute, doubt, and uncertainty, earlier named as the defects of the primary rules, defects which were to have been remedied by the rule of recognition. If that rule can itself go unrecognized or be refused, it is not the end but the beginning of inquiry, and we are no better off than we were before.

Throughout this section of his argument Hart knows that he must firmly demarcate the rule of recognition from the field it must regulate; it cannot, in other words, be a mere item in that field, but must precede it. Indeed, says Hart, "even if it were enacted by statute, this would not reduce it to the level of statute for the legal status of such an enactment necessarily depends on the fact that the rule existed antecedently to and independently of the enactment" (p. 108). The very "assertion that it exists can only be an external matter of fact" (p. 107); that is, its existence is not a matter of inference or interpretation; it is, and must be, self-evident, immediately perspicuous; "it escapes the conventional categories used for describing a legal system, though these are often taken to be exhaustive" (p. 107). But even as he asserts the independence and perspicuity of the rule, Hart gives a disturbing answer to the question of how it is to be identified. Given what is required of this rule, it is a question that should not even be asked, for to ask it is to deprive the rule of the adjectives "supreme" and "ultimate" and to yield the supremacy to the agency contained in the answer. In this case the answer is, to say the least, surprising. If the identification of the rule or recognition "were doubted" (and even to admit this possibility is to lose the game), "it could be established," Hart says, "by reference to actual practice: to the way in which courts identify what is to count as law" (p. 105). But surely this is to put the cart before the horse: Hart's entire argument depends on a rule that stands *apart from* the field of practice, a rule to which practitioners can turn when they are in doubt as to what to do, and a rule to which arbitrators can turn when different practitioners want to do different things. If, however, one can know the rule only by extrapolating from practice, then practice rather than being generated or tested by the rule is the source of the rule; and insofar as practice is itself unsettled—not at all points uniform and stable—there will be not one but many rules and no *independent* mechanism for deciding between them. Once the rule of recognition recedes into practice, it becomes not a matter of fact, but of interpretation, and the way is open to exactly the situation Hart hopes to avoid, the situation in which the law is what the courts say it is; for if one locates the rule by looking "to the way in which courts identify" it, then the actions of the court come first and rule second. In short, the rule of recognition is secondary in a sense much stronger than Hart intends; it is belated in relation to the activity it purports to govern, and that activity, rather than being constrained by the rule, makes and unmakes it in response to the opportunities afforded by power and occasion.

By "that activity" I mean, of course, interpretation, and the failure of the rule of recognition prompts me to formulate a rule of my own: whatever is invoked as a constraint on interpretation will turn out upon further examination to have been the product of interpretation, or, to put it in Hart's terms, although it is always possible to distinguish a settled core from the area of open texture that surrounds it, that core has itself been formed by the very forces it supposedly repels. While the distinction between core and penumbra can always be made at a particular moment, at another moment the *interpretive* conditions within which the distinction is perspicuous can be challenged and dislodged; if that happens, the distinction will not so much disappear as it will take on a new *historical* form, one that is no less precariously in place than its predecessor. The point is one Hart makes himself when he observes that "canons of interpretation"—verbal directions designed to restrict interpretation's scope—"make use of general terms which themselves require interpretation" (p. 123); and once one sees this, one sees too that attaching canons to the canons—putting restrictions on the formulation of restrictions—will not remedy but merely extend the difficulty. No matter how many or what kinds of rules one promulgates, the scope of interpretation will not have been the least whit diminished; for each new attempt to control it will be the occasion for its exercise.

Although Hart both sees and says this, he cannot quite grasp its implications, for he continues to believe that the inability of rules to constrain is only partial and that at the very least they serve to narrow the area in which interpretation can operate. Hart's argument is that a rule framed in the appropriately general terms (e.g., "vehicles are prevented from entering the park") will pick out "standard instances" of its application, and that these instances will constitute a set of "central" or "plain cases" in relation to which other, less clear, cases can be classified. Thus someone "faced with the question whether the rule prohibiting the use of vehicles in the park is applicable to some combination of circumstances in which it appears indeterminate" can proceed by considering "as one does who makes use of a precedent," "whether the present case resembles the plain case 'sufficiently' in 'relevant' respects" (p. 124). The words "sufficiently" and "relevant" indicate Hart's awareness that the agent's discretion remains wide, but still it is a bounded area, marked off by a plain case that at once gives interpretation a direction and holds it in check.

As an account of what people do (line up present cases with clear, paradigm cases), this is impeccable, but as I read it, it is an account not of interpretation subdued, but of interpretation triumphant. The question is not whether there are in fact plain cases—there surely are—but, rather, of what is their plainness a condition and a property? Hart's answer must be that a plain case is inherently plain, plain in and of itself, plain independently of the interpretive activities it can then be said to direct. But it takes only a little reflection to see that the truth is exactly the reverse. A plain case is a case that was once *argued;* that is, its configurations were once in dispute; at a certain point one characterization of its meaning and significance—of its *rule*—was found to be more persuasive than its rivals; and at *that* point the case became settled, became perspicuous, became undoubted, became plain. Plainness, in short, is not a property of the case itself—there is no case itself—but of an interpretive history in the course of which one interpretive agenda—complete with stipulative definitions, assumed distinctions, canons of evidence, etc.—has subdued another. That history is then closed, but it can always be reopened. That is, on some later occasion the settled assumptions within which the case acquired its plain meaning can become unsettled, can become the object of debate rather than the in-place background in the context of which debate occurs; and when that happens, contending arguments or interpretive agendas will once again vie in the field until one of them is regnant and the case acquires a *new* settled and plain meaning. So that while there will always be paradigmatically plain cases—Hart is absolutely right to put them at the center of the adjudicative process—far from providing a stay against the force of interpretation, they will be precisely the result of interpretation's force; for they will have been written and rewritten by interpretive efforts.

Another name for this process is precedent. Hart thinks of precedent as a means of controlling an indeterminate present by reference to an already determined (and therefore determining) past. To quote again the key sentence, the agent who must decide considers "whether the present case resembles the plain case 'sufficiently' in 'relevant' respects." The question that is here elided is what does the plain case resemble; what is *it* like? Hart's answer (which he gives by not giving it) is that the plain case resembles itself, establishes its own configurations in relation to which later cases are either like or unlike it. But resemblance and its opposite—that is, sameness and difference—are not immanent in the object but emerge from the perspective of the differential criteria that inform perception. If I see two poems or two cases as similar, it will be because of the categories (of size, or period, or theme . . .) within which I search; were I to search within different categories (of sameness and difference), the relationship between the two poems or cases would be seen differently, and, moreover, since each is known *in terms* of the relationship between them, the poems and cases would be different, depending on the different categories of difference within which they are seen. What this means is that resemblance (or difference) is always a constructed (i.e., interpretive) phenomenon and therefore it can always be constructed again. In fact, that is what happens in the citing of precedents; the so-called plain case doesn't sit still, silently measuring the distance or closeness between it and the present case. Indeed, the demands are made from either direction, for it is the interests and concerns of the present case that generate the pressure for comparison and dictate its terms; and it is in the light of the interests and concerns flowing from the present case that the "plain case" will then be constituted.

As a result, when the plainness of the settled case is characterized, the very terms of the characterization will have been set by the case that has yet to be settled; rather than the past controlling the present, the present controls the past by providing the perspective from which the two must be brought into line. The truth about precedent, then, is the opposite of the story we tell about it; precedent is the process by which the past gets produced by the present so that it can then be cited as the producer of the present. It is in this way that the law achieves what Ronald Dworkin calls "articulate consistency,"[3] a way of thinking and talking about itself which creates and re-creates the continuity that is so crucial to its largest claim, the claim to have an unchanging center that founds its authority. Articulate consistency is not a fact, but an achievement, something that is forever being wrested out of diverse materials which are then retroactively declared always to have had its shape. The court in *Cargill* fears that if the parol evidence rule is disregarded, the rule of law would give way to the power of those who are able to tell the most persuasive story; but that is already the *whole* of the law, whose collective story is continually being made up and then told both to the lay public and to the agents in the legal system, that is, to the tellers. Again, Hart himself admits as much when he discusses the ways in which courts can slip out of the net of precedent; the chief way is to "distinguish" the earlier case, to find that the scope of its rule is narrower than the concerns of the present case which can then be decided independently of it. All you have to do, Hart explains, is to think up "some legally relevant difference" between the two cases, and, he adds, "the class of such differences can never be exhaustively determined." That is to say, the finding of difference is for all intents and purposes an unconstrained activity, an activity which once knows no natural stopping point, an activity that cannot be stopped. Yet even though Hart makes this point, he fails to see how fatal it is to his general project and continues blithely on, asserting that "notwithstanding these . . . forms of legislative activity" (p. 131) courts are bound by a "vast number" (p. 132) of determinate rules. But his own analysis tells us that the rules are determinate only to the extent that interpreters desire them to be; if the desires of interpreters change, they will always be able to give those rules a new shape and then to declare them determinate even as they are in the process of determining them.

At one point Hart comes very close to saying as much. He is discussing those situations in which it appears that courts are "exercising creative powers which settle the ultimate criteria by which the very laws, which confer on them jurisdiction as judges, must itself be tested" (p. 148). That is, at times courts seem to be themselves constituting the authority (the rule of recognition) they subsequently cite as legitimizing their actions. (Just this account has often been given of the American practice of judicial review.) It may be the case, says Hart, that "when courts settle previously unenvisaged questions concerning the most fundamental constitutional rules, they *get* their authority to decide them accepted after the questions have arisen and the decision has been given" (p. 149). In short, it may be, as I put it at the beginning of this chapter, that authority rests with whoever seizes an opportunity to act and then makes the action stick, that, as Hart observes, "all that succeeds is success" (p. 149). This is a remarkable statement which is perfectly congruent with my argument, not for the denial of "cores" and "centers" and "authoritative marks," but for their status as historical constructions that are in place only so long as a more powerful construction has not yet dislodged them. But even as he moves toward this position, Hart pushes it away by once again invoking the distinction between the settled core and the fringe area of doubt as if it were unproblematical. "[N]ot every rule," Hart points out (correctly), "is open to doubt on all points," and, he adds, "[T]he possibility of courts having authority at any given time to decide these limiting questions concerning the ultimate criteria of validity, depends merely on the fact that, at that time, the application of those criteria to a vast area of law, including the rules which confer that authority, raises no doubt . . ." (p. 149). Hart misses what is almost, and should be, his own point: while it is true that at any one time there are vast areas free of doubt which constitute a core of certainty, that core has been established by the very forces that it now (but only *temporarily*) holds in bounds. It is still the case that what succeeds is success; it is just that one of the things success brings (for a time) are vast areas free of doubt. What must be remembered is that those areas rest on a foundation that is itself doubtful, that is, subject to challenge, and therefore are in no sense (except the local sense of their ascendancy) determinate.

I could go on with this reading of *The Concept of Law,* but it would only reveal further variations on the pattern we have repeatedly seen: a mechanism is proposed with the claim that it will keep force—whether in the form of the gunman or the interpreter—at bay; and in each instance force turns out to be the content of the mechanism designed to control it. No matter how many layers of rules, plain cases, cores of settled meanings, precedents one puts in place, the bottom line remains the ascendancy of one person—or of one set of interests aggressively pursued—over another, and the dream of general rules "judicially applied" (p. 202) remains just that, a dream. It would seem that Richard Rorty is right when he characterizes interpretation as an operation in which the agent—be he a judge or a literary critic—"simply beats the text into a shape which will serve his own purpose" and "makes the text refer to whatever is relevant to that purpose."[4]

Rorty's casually brutal language names the fear in response to which Hart and so many others mount their projects, the fear, first, that nothing stands between the exercise of power and its victims, and, second, that the activities we engage in are finally meaningless. The point has been succinctly put by Wayne Booth: if disagreements are settled by "the most forceful means of persuasion," we are condemned "to a sense of ultimate futility in what we do," and we become successively and perpetually bound "to whichever suitor woos most winningly."[5] The alternative is, of course, to find a stay against the workings of persuasive power, and for most of those who have thought about the question, that stay is some form of rationality, whether it be a logic, a special kind of language, a determinate rule, a monumental text, a neutral procedure. E. D. Hirsch sums up an entire tradition (which begins at least with Plato) when he declares it is "essential to distinguish hypotheses and evidence from the rhetoric used to convey them."[6] It is essential because rhetoric is by definition the forceful presentation of an interested argument—rhetoric is another word for force—and what is desired is a way of neutralizing interest so that the decisions generated by the system will not be the product of any partial or partisan point of view.

It is just such a way that Hart seeks, but even if he were to find it (in some rule or precedent), he would only have done half the job, for the neutralization of interest is an interior as well as an exterior task. The success that rhetoric may have in turning the mind away from purely rational considerations is a function as much of tendencies in the mind as it is of pressuring forces external to the mind; an illegitimate appeal can hardly have an effect if there is nothing to appeal to. (Remember, primary rules are necessary because of the human susceptibility to base actions.) If genuine evidence is to be disentangled from partisan posturing, a corresponding separation must occur in the mind, lest the genuine go unrecognized; as part of its program to protect the individual from force, the law must also control, by neutralizing, the forces that live within the individual, the forces that, if left unchecked, would prompt him to the subversion of the very rules that offer him a world of security and stability. That is why those who, like Hart, argue for a neutral space in the world must also argue for a neutral space in the mind, one free of biases, prejudices, and presuppositions. Thus Stephen Toulmin urges us to "discount" any "biases and prejudices" we may have so that we might act "in a disinterested way,"[7] and in a similar vein, Wayne Booth advises that we develop "a habit of great skepticism about one's own hypothesis" and exercise "a healthy tentativeness about oneself and one's responses."[8] The advice seems sound until one thinks about acting on it. Just how does one distance oneself from oneself? With what part of oneself can one be tentative about oneself?

The answer lies in the assumption by Toulmin and Booth of a *psychological* core that is the equivalent of the cores Hart finds in determinate rules, settled meanings, centrally clear cases, etc.; it is this core of rationality inside us that protects us from the pressure of our own convictions and predispositions. The danger represented by these predispositions, the danger of surrendering to illegitimate appeals, is exactly like the danger represented by the gunman in Hart's scenario. The only difference is that this gunman is in our heads, but that is finally no difference at all, as Terry Eagleton makes clear when he equates being "forced mindlessly" into an action by an "ideological obsession" with the pressure of somebody "holding a gun to my head."[9] It is one thing, Eagleton adds, to be "convinced by the arguments and the evidence" and quite another to hold convictions "because they are convenient . . . or fashionably eccentric." In the first case one is "able to weigh the arguments" and become convinced in a way that is " 'freer' "; in the second, one is the victim of "a spontaneous ideological prejudice" (p. 376). Of course, the source of that prejudice is oneself, and therefore one is, in a curious way, self-victimized. It follows, then, that in order to cease being a victim one must cease being oneself. That at least is the implication of Eagleton's odd phrase "forced mindlessly"; since what you are being forced by in his scenario are the beliefs and predispositions that now fill your mind, in order not to be so forced you would have to empty your mind of everything it contains, so that in Wallace Stevens's words, you would "have a mind of winter."

The problem with this strategy is simply that one cannot follow it; moreover, even if we could somehow follow it, the condition of being free from ideological control would be wholly disabling because there would be nothing either to be free *with* or *for*. There would be nothing to be free *with* because were every preconception, acquired belief, assumed point of view, opinion, bias, and prejudice removed from the mind, there would be nothing left with which to calculate, determine, and decide; and there is nothing to be free *for,* because a mind divested of all direction—a mind not already oriented toward this or that purpose or plan or agenda—could not recognize any reason for going in one direction rather than another or, for that matter, for going in any direction at all. It is often claimed that reason itself is what is left when belief, preconception, and prejudice have been set aside or discounted, but reason cannot operate independently of some content—of some proposition or propositions made up of definitions, distinctions, and criteria already assumed—and that content will reflect some belief or attitude that will inform whatever outcome reason dictates. (This is to say, once again, that the "core" is always and already invaded by the penumbra.) I am aware that in so arguing I am asserting the identity of two entities that are often distinguished and even opposed, reason and belief. Indeed, it is not too much to say that the quest for a way of quarantining the process of law from force depends on that opposition; for if one defines knowledge as that which exists independently of any particular perspective, belief—which is another name for perspective—becomes a bar to its achievement. In this view beliefs are the property of partisan agendas and if one is to resist their appeal, an appeal that amounts to nothing less than coercion, one must distance oneself from them and neutralize their force. It is my contention that this is precisely what one cannot possibly do and still remain a "one," a being with a capacity for action. In short, you can never get away from your beliefs, which means that you can never get away from force, from the pressure exerted by a partial, non-neutral, nonauthoritative, ungrounded point of view.

We see, then, that the two strategies by which force is to be held in check fail in the same way. On the one hand, there is the attempt to erect an *external* barrier—sometimes a determinate rule, or a plain case, or a settled meaning—but in every instance the barrier turns out to be indistinguishable from that which it would hold back; force is already inside the gate because it *is* the gate. On the other hand, there is the attempt to perform an *internal* housecleaning, to remove from the mind the tendencies that correspond to force's appeal; but this turns out to be at once impossible and in a very literal sense *self*-defeating, since a mind so cleansed would have nothing inside it. The ideal of a mind that is insulated from pressure is as unattainable as the ideal of a rule that will be a stay against the assault of interpretive desires; the mind, insofar as it is anything, *is* a structure of pressures, of purposes, urgencies, interests already in place; and the rule, insofar as it is intelligible, is an extension of some interested agenda that cannot be kept out because it is already in. To the extent that the law is compelling, it is compelling in relation to the very prejudices and biases it supposedly neutralizes; the reasons for which we do something or refrain from doing something *are* reasons only by virtue of the preconceptions and predispositions we already have.

The conclusion is inescapable and it is the one I have repeatedly reached: the force of the law is always and already indistinguishable from the forces it would oppose. Or to put the matter another way: *there is always a gun at your head.* Sometimes the gun is, in literal fact, a gun; sometimes it is a reason, an assertion whose weight is inseparable from some already assumed purpose; sometimes it is a desire, the urging of a state of affairs to which you are already predisposed; sometimes it is a need you already feel; sometimes it is a name—country, justice, honor, love, God—whose power you have already internalized. Whatever it is, it will always be a form of coercion, of an imperative whose source is an interest which speaks to the interest in you. And this leads me to a second aphorism: not only is there always a gun at your head; *the gun at your head is your head;* the interests that seek to compel you are appealing and therefore pressuring only to the extent they already live within you, and indeed *are* you. In the end we are always self-compelled, coerced by forces—beliefs, convictions, reasons, desires—from which we cannot move one inch away.

Another way to put this is to say that while there are constraints on the will and therefore on interpretation, those constraints are *internal* to the will and do not provide a point of reference independent of it. By "internal" I mean something directly opposite to what Hart means when he distinguishes between the internal and the external "points of view" with respect to the imperatives of a legal system. In his analysis one operates from the external point of view when one notes, in the manner of an anthropological observer, that "a social group accepts [certain] rules" (p. 99); one operates from the internal point of view when one "uses" those rules in determining one's everyday obligations. The internal agent need not, and characteristically does not, state the rules by which he is guided; his knowledge of them is more integral than that of the mere observer and is expressed in the way he applies them from moment to moment. To this I would object that neither of these "points of view" is genuinely internal. To be sure, they are different: in one the agent specifies the rules without being committed to them, while in the other the agent is committed to the rules but does not (characteristically) specify them. Both agents, however, are in the same (and I would say impossible) relation of *distance* to the rules in the sense that they could be held at arm's length and examined; it is just that for one the examination or noting of the rules is the end point of the activity; while the other goes on to use or apply them. The very words "use" and "apply" make my point, that the rules in Hart's picture are separate from a self that is free to employ them or not; "use" and "apply" signify instrumentality in relation to an independent actor; but what I have been arguing is that the actor is never in such a relation and that the imperatives to which he responds cannot be held at arm's length—cannot, in Eagleton's terms, be "weighed"—because they are constitutive of the actor's every gesture, including the gesture of weighing.

This is the only internal perspective worth the name (and, indeed, the only perspective there is: even the "external" observer does his observing from a vantage point he could not observe because it grounds him; his conclusions are no less internal than the conclusions of a community member, although they are internal to another community), and it is the perspective Hart cannot endorse or even acknowledge because it leaves no room for a "core" or "center" to which the agent's prejudices and desires can be referred for judgment. It is in relation to that core and to the possibility of disinterestedly identifying it that Hart imagines a superior group of citizens who, unlike their less reflective fellows, do not obey the laws out of fear or habit but "appraise" them "critically" (p. 113) and obey them in a more self-consciously rational way. It is this self-consciousness that marks the Hartian internal point of view which is in fact the point of view achieved when the agent has purged himself of whatever is inside him in favor of a standard he prefers to his own. That is to say, Hart's internal point of view is an external point of view in disguise, and, as I have repeatedly demonstrated, it is one that cannot be occupied.

In so saying I may seem to confirm Hart's fear of a world without order or principle, wholly given over to force in the form either of gunmen or of judges unconstrained in their actions or of wills unchecked by any core of rationality. But in fact the implication of my argument is that this fear is unrealizable and is based on an incorrect understanding of what force is and is not. What force is not is "mere" force, force unconnected with any agenda or program. Force is simply a (pejorative) name for the thrust or assertion of some point of view, and in a world where the urging of points of view cannot be referred for adjudication to some independent tribunal, force is just another name for what follows naturally from conviction. That is to say, force wears the aspect of anarchy only if one regards it as an empty blind urge, but if one identifies it as *interest aggressively pursued,* force acquires a content and that content is a complex of goals and purposes, underwritten by a vision, and put into operation by a detailed agenda complete with steps, stages, and directions. Force, in short, is already a repository of everything it supposedly threatens—norms, standards, reasons, and, yes, even rules. One could, of course, object (or complain) that such rules, standards, and reasons are merely local and partisan and provide no mechanism for principled adjudication. But this would be to reinvoke the dream of a principle that was neutral—of a rule of recognition, or a centrally plain case, or a core of settled meaning—and in response I could only offer once again the analyses of the preceding pages in which that neutrality is shown to be unavailable, both in its material and psychological forms. What I am trying to show now is that this state of affairs is in no way disastrous or even disabling; it appears to be disabling only if the alternative to neutrality is unprincipled force; but if the alternative to neutrality is principled force—and it is my argument that there is no other kind—then the unavailability of neutrality simply does not have and *could not have* the consequences Hart fears. The absence of external or independent constraints only means that the constraints inherent in the condition of belief—the condition of having been persuaded to some vision, the condition of not seeking but already occupying a position—are always and inescapably in *force*. The fact that you can never move one inch away from your beliefs means too that you can never move one inch away from norms and principles.

To be sure, this does not solve our practical problems, since we still are faced with the difficulty of adjudicating between beliefs in the absence of a calculus that is not itself a function or extension of belief. It is a difficulty that cannot be removed, but the fact that it cannot be removed does not condemn us to uncertainty and paralysis, but to conflict, to acts of persuasion in which one party attempts to alter the beliefs of another by putting forward arguments that are weighty only in relation to still other beliefs. By definition the career of persuasion is unpredictable and theoretically interminable; there is no guarantee that either party will be victorious, although in some social structures—and the law is certainly one of them—victory is mandated in the form of the obligation to render a decision. But when victory occurs, whether by the surrender of one party to the party of which he now becomes a member or by jurisdictional fiat, it is always provisional; for since it has emerged from argument, from the forceful urging of some partisan point of view, it is always possible, and indeed likely, that what has apparently been settled will become unsettled, and argument will begin again.

Once again we reach a conclusion that seems to realize one of Hart's worst fears, in this case the fear of a legal (?) structure marked by the "mere temporary ascendancy of one person over another" (p. 24). The burden of Hart's complaint falls on "temporary," for which we might substitute, occasional, local, transitory, ad hoc, etc. It is not difficult to see why words like these are distressing; they run contrary to the assumption, so powerful in our legal culture, that what courts and judges do is extend into the present abiding principles of law and morality. (This is the content, for example, of Ronald Dworkin's notion of "law as integrity" and of his distinction between principle and policy.[10]) There are all kinds of good reasons why that assumption continues to inform the story the law tells about itself even as its history enacts quite another story. After all, the law could hardly advertise itself as resting on force (given that word's bad press) and still be accepted as law. Hart is right when he insists that it is the very essence of law to distinguish itself from force; moreover, that distinction is *real* insofar as it refers to a society's understanding of its foundational moorings in relation to the energies that would threaten to dissolve them. My point is that such an understanding, necessary as it is to the constitution of any society or community, is itself an artifact of time, a "mere temporary ascendancy" of one vision or agenda over its rivals, and that when that temporary ascendancy has been succeeded by another, the distinction between law and force will still be in force, but the content and distribution of its terms will be different. It is that succession of differences that makes up the law's history, a history that includes a claim of continuity that is belied by its own events.

Are legal actors then living out a lie, asserting as absolute what they should acknowledge as fragile and transitory? Not at all. Legal actors, like everyone else, live *within* the temporary ascendancies they at once affirm and undo (by endlessly modifying the givens that make action possible), and no analysis of their situation, even the analysis offered here, will remove them from it. That is to say, the acknowledgement that from the long-run point of view law is inseparable from force is itself without force, since no one inhabits the long-run point of view, and in the succession of short runs that make up our lives, the distinction between law and force is unassailable, although one can always assail the form it has presently assumed.

I say this to ward off a conclusion often reached on the left: that a recognition of the temporally contingent nature of our "fundamental" assumptions would lessen their force and make us less likely to surrender to them. But the conclusion is possible only if one makes the mistake (which I have called "anti-foundationalist theory hope") of turning the recognition of contingency into a way of avoiding contingency, as if contingency acknowledged were contingency transcended. You may know *in general* that the structure of your convictions is an historical artifact, but that knowledge does not transport you to a place where those convictions are no longer in force. We remain embedded in history even when we know that it is history we are embedded in, and while that knowledge may be satisfying in relation to alternative stories about our convictions (for example, that they correspond or should correspond to the unchanging nature of things), in relation to the particular convictions (including itself) by which we are now grasped and constituted, it is of no force whatsoever.[11]

22. Withholding the Missing Portion: Psychoanalysis and Rhetoric

I was led to this paper by two moments in the proceedings of the 1958 Style in Language Conference; they are moments in which the topic of persuasion is allowed to surface and then is immediately suppressed. The first such moment coincides with the only substantive mention of Freud at the conference. Roger Brown is discussing the resistance of cognitive psychologists to psychoanalytic procedure in which, it is feared, "anything can mean anything."[1] Brown replies, in apparent defense of psychoanalysis, that one must take into account the fact that its results are often persuasive, and if they are persuasive there must be a good reason. The reason, he suspects, is that psychoanalytic evidence, while not falling obviously into the linear and logical forms with which we are familiar, must nevertheless be speaking to the criteria by which we determine validity, so that at a certain point it must be the case that the accumulation of evidence reaches a level which satisfies those criteria and at that point persuasion occurs. But while Brown's argument acknowledges persuasion, it does so by robbing it of any independent force. Persuasion ceases to be a scandal if it is the programmed consequence of a mechanical calculation. A persuasion so defined is thoroughly domesticated and ceases to be a threat to the formal projects of linguistics and cognitive psychology.

The second moment at which the conference defends itself against the threat of persuasion occurs at the very end, after the last paper, in a discussion between the participants, a discussion one finds, if one finds it at all, in exceedingly small print. There, hidden from view lest it infect the entire volume, is a brief consideration of rhetoric. The topic is introduced by I. A. Richards, who declares that the questions so often debated at the conference, the questions of value and meaning, are finally rhetorical; it is a matter, he says, of the context of discourse and, as

Isocrates observes, good discourse is discourse that works. The response is literally terror. C. E. Osgood protests that if the rhetorical view is accepted, then even advertising can be thought of as good discourse, in fact, as the best discourse; and W. K. Wimsatt adds that if rhetorical standards have any relevance, it is only with reference to productions like "the speeches of Hitler during the last war." Confronted with the choice of standing either with Hitler or with Wimsatt, Richards does the right thing, and in a supremely rhetorical moment withdraws from the defense of rhetoric. "Mr. Wimsatt and I," he says, "are not in disagreement."

I have two epigraphs for this essay. The first is from James Strachey's editor's introduction to his translation of Freud's *Complete Introductory Lectures*. Freud, he says, was "never rhetorical" and was entirely opposed to laying down his view in an authoritarian fashion.[2] The second is a report by the Wolf-Man of what he thought to himself shortly after he met Freud for the first time: "this man is a Jewish swindler, he wants to use me from behind and shit on my head." This paper is dedicated to the proposition that the Wolf-Man got it right.

I

" 'I dreamt that it was night and that I was lying in my bed. . . . Suddenly the window opened of its own accord, and I was terrified to see that some white wolves were sitting on the big walnut tree in front of the window.' "[3] Thus begins Freud's account of the most famous dream in the literature of psychoanalysis, the centerpiece of his most famous case. Freud tells us that although the patient recalled the dream at a "very early stage of the analysis," its "interpretation was a task that dragged on over several years" without notable success (p. 177). The breakthrough, as it is reported, came in an instant and apparently without preparation. "One day the patient began to continue with the interpretation of the dream. He thought that the part of the dream which said . . . 'suddenly the window opened of its own accord' was not completely explained." Immediately and without explanation, the explanation came forth: " 'It must mean: "My eyes suddenly opened." I was asleep, . . . and suddenly woke up, and as I woke up I saw something: the tree with the wolves' " (p. 179). It is important to note that the patient does not say, "Now I remember," but rather, "It *must* mean." His is not an act of recollection but of construction. The question I would ask—and it is a question that will take us far—is simply what is the content of "must"? What compels him to this particular interpretation among all those he might have hit upon? To this Freud's answer is "nothing," at least nothing external to the patient's own efforts. For a long time, Freud tells us, his young charge "remained . . . entrenched behind an attitude of obliging apathy"; he refused, that is, to "take an independent share in the work" (p. 157). It was this "shrinking from a self-sufficient existence" (p. 157) that stood in the way of a progress that could be realized only if he were to come out from behind the fortress of his lethargy, and we are invited to assume that this is what finally happens when he declares "It must mean." Clearly, Freud is here not only characterizing his patient; he is also providing us with a scenario of the analysis in which both his and the patient's roles are carefully specified: the analyst waits patiently for the patient to begin to work on his own, and suddenly "one day" his patience is rewarded.

There is, however, another scenario embedded in this same paragraph, and it is considerably less benign. The sentence in which one finds the phrase "independent share in the work" reads as follows: "It required a long education to persuade and induce him to take an independent share in the work" (p. 157). The sentence is obviously divided against itself, one half proclaiming an independence which in the other half is compromised when it is identified as the product of persuasion and force. That independence is further compromised when Freud reveals the method by which it has been "induced." At the moment when he saw the patient's attachment to him had become strong enough to counterbalance his resistance, Freud announced that "the treatment must be brought to an end at a particular fixed date, no matter how far it had advanced" (p. 157). As it is delivered, the announcement would seem to indicate that Freud does not care whether or not "advancement" will occur, but in fact it is a device for assuring advancement, and for assuring it in a form he will approve.[4] What Freud *says* is "do as you like, it makes no difference to me." What he *means* is, "if you do not do as I like and do it at the time I specify, you will lose the satisfaction of pleasing me to whom I know you to be attached by the strongest of bonds because I forged them." The coercion could not be more obvious, and Freud does not shrink from naming it as an exercise of "inexorable pressure"; yet in the very same sentence he contrives to detach the pressure from the result it produces: "Under the inexorable pressure of the fixed limit [the patient's] resistance . . . gave way, and now in a disproportionately short time the analysis produced all the material which made it possible to clear up his inhibitions and remove his symptoms" (p. 157). Here the analysis is presented as if it were independent of the constraints that father it. At the end of the sentence the clearing up of inhibitions and the removal of symptoms appear as effects without a cause, natural phenomena that simply emerge in the course of their own time—the time, presumably, when the patient suddenly, and of his own accord, exclaims, "It *must* mean."

It is a remarkable sequence, and one that is repeated in a variety of ways in the paragraphs that follow. The pattern is always the same: the claim of independence—for the analysis, for the patient's share, for the "materials"—is made in the context of an account that powerfully subverts it, and then it is made again. Each claim is a disclaimer on the part of the analyst of the control he is everywhere exercising; and his effort to deny his effort extends to a denial that he is exerting any influence on himself: "Readers may . . . rest assured that I myself am only reporting what I came upon as an independent experience, uninfluenced by my expectation" (p. 158). Here there are two claims, one more audacious than the other: the first is that his mental processes function independently of his psychic history (a claim directly at odds with the thesis of this very case); the second is that a similar independence can be achieved by those readers who rest in the assurances he offers. In other words, he counsels submission to himself as a way of being free, and he presents this counsel in the context of an argument for his own disinterestedness. Put yourself in my hands, he says, because my hands are not mine, but merely the instruments of truth.

Of course, this is exactly what an analyst says (not always explicitly) at the beginning of a treatment. In effect, the reader is being put on the couch where he is given the same double message Freud gives to his patient: be independent, rely entirely on me. In rapid succession Freud issues a series of confusing and contradictory directions. First, he tells us, you must "eliminate" your "pre-existing convictions" and consider only the evidence. But within a few sentences we learn that there will be no evidence to consider. "Exhaustive verbatim reports," he declares, "would . . . be of no help at all," and, besides, such reports aren't available anyway since "the technique of the treatment makes it impossible to draw them up" (pp. 158–59). This leaves us at the mercy of what the analyst chooses to tell us, and it would seem that we are simply to exchange his "preexisting convictions" for our own. But no. In a dazzling reversal the reader's independence is reaffirmed when it is revealed that one of his preexisting convictions will be retained, the conviction that psychoanalysis, as Freud practices it, is the true and only way. It is only for such readers, "already . . . convinced by their own clinical experiences" (p. 159), that Freud writes, and because they are convinced those readers will be proof against any attempt, on the part of Freud or anyone else, to convince them. The logic, to say the least, is suspect, but if one accepts it (and we are not given time to do anything else), one will also accept the amazing conclusion that this analysis is not published "in order to produce conviction."

The claim not to be producing conviction is of a piece with the other claims or disclaimers that fill the opening pages. Always they are disclaimers of influence and always their effect is to extend the influence they would disclaim. The inducing of independence undermines it; the denial of a strategy of conviction is itself a strategy of conviction. The text's overt assertions are continually in conflict with the actions it performs, as Freud proclaims the autonomy of a succession of children—the patient, the reader, the analysis—even as he contrives to control them.

The question that arises is one of motive. Why is Freud doing this? Is it simply a matter of a desire for personal power? The text suggests that he would reply in the negative and say that he was only defending the honor of psychoanalysis against what J. O. Wisdom has identified as the oldest charge against it, the charge that it "acts by suggestion," that what the analyst claims to uncover (in the archeological sense of which Freud was so fond) he actually creates by verbal and rhetorical means.[5] Freud is vehement in his rejection of this accusation, declaring at one point that it is "unjust to attribute the results of analysis to the physician's imagination" (p. 231) and confessing at another that he finds it "impossible" even to argue with those who regard the findings of psychoanalysis as "artefacts" (p. 191). These and similar statements would seem to suggest that his motives are not personal but institutional; he speaks not for himself but on behalf of the integrity of a discipline. But since the discipline is one of which he is quite literally the father, his defense of its integrity involves him in the same contradiction that marks his relationship with the patient and the reader: no sooner has he insisted on the independence of psychoanalysis as a science than he feels compelled to specify, and to specify authoritatively, what the nature of that science is; and once he does that he is in the untenable position of insisting on the autonomy of something of which he is unable to let go. It is a position he can only escape by placing himself on an even ground with his opponents; but this is precisely what he cannot bring himself to do, and whenever their arguments surface he responds to them with the paternalism he so vigorously disavows. By rising to the institutional level, Freud only reinscribes the dilemma inherent in his role as analyst and author. He cannot be both liberator and master at the same time; and insofar as that is the task he assigns himself, he becomes the object of his own manipulation, demanding of himself, as he demands of the patient and the reader, that he be active and passive at the same time.

Freud's response to this double bind is to deny it by producing accounts of the analysis in which the actions he is unwilling to acknowledge are performed by others. The first such displacement occurs in the third paragraph of Chapter 1, when he weighs the virtues and defects of competing methodologies. The two possibilities are (1) analyzing a childhood disorder when it first manifests itself in infancy, or (2) waiting until the patient is an "intellectually mature adult" (p. 155). Since Freud is at this very moment engaged in the second practice it is not surprising that he decides in favor of it, but he must find a way to defend it against the objection (which he anticipates) that because of the passage of time what results will be the product of interpretation. He replies by asserting that interpretation will play an even greater part if the child is examined directly because "too many words and thoughts have to be lent" to him. In contrast, when one analyzes an adult, these "limitations" do not obtain, although such analysis "necessitates our taking into account the distortion and refurbishing to which a person's own past is subjected when it is looked back upon" (p. 155). Once one begins to examine it, this is a curious contrast, since it is hard to tell the difference between "lending words" and "refurbishing." What makes the contrast work is the fact that the sentence shifts the burden of "refurbishing" onto the patient. It is a brilliant move which allows Freud to admit interpretation into the scene while identifying it as the work of another, leaving himself the (honorable) work of undoing its effects. In only a few brief sentences he has managed to twice distance himself from the charge of suggestion, first by pushing it off onto the practitioners of a rival method, and second by making it into a property of the illness of which his now innocent labors are to be the cure.

The strategy, then, is to foreground an accusation and to defend against it by turning it back on those who would make it; attribute to others what they would attribute unto you; allow the accusation to surface, but keep pushing it away. In another place it is pushed away before it appears because it is presented as an accusation not against Freud but against his patients, including, presumably, this one. The accusers are his opponents, Jung and Adler, who reject the thesis of infantile neurosis, regarding it as an elaborate rationalization that allows neurotics to avoid confronting their problems by projecting them onto a past for which they can then not be held responsible. "The suporters of this view," says Freud, "assume that the importance of childhood is only held up before our eyes in analysis on account of the inclination of neurotics for expressing their present interests in reminiscences and symbols from the remote past" (p. 192). To these arguments Freud responds with indignation, not on his own behalf, but on behalf of the class of neurotic patients who are impugned and defamed when their motives are reduced to the "self-assertive instinct" of a "will to power" (p. 167). But these are the very motives of which he has been accused, and it is difficult not to see in this ostentatious concern for the reputation of neurotics still another attempt to ward off the charges of manipulation and suggestion. He declares his patients innocent of a willfulness he cannot acknowledge in himself, and he constructs for both the familiar defense of passivity, telling a story in which both he and his patient are the passive instruments of forces over which they have no control. The difference is that in the case of the patient those forces live within him and have their source in the suppressed events of his infantile life, whereas in the case of the analyst the forces to which he submits reside outside him and constitute a reality he does not influence but only registers. Logically these twin defenses contradict one another: one insists that the structures and patterns of psychic history cannot be escaped, the other claims to have escaped them, but the logical inconsistency is a rhetorical triumph as both the patient and the analyst are exonerated from the charge that they have fabricated what they report.

The triumph is complete when that same charge—the charge of rhetorical manipulation—is turned against the proponents of the opposing view. It is they, says Freud, who produce "twisted interpretations," which are, in fact, "high-handed attempts at re-interpretation," that is, blatant exercises of a "will to power" (pp. 155, 167). In this way Freud tars his adversaries with their own brush: after all, it is they not he who make the argument for power, and Freud suggests that what they see in their patients is no more than a projection of their own personal and institutional desires, desires of which he is of course wholly innocent. But even as he thus distances himself from the scene of power, Freud is engaged in establishing (or reestablishing) his power by means that could not be more rhetorical. Whenever he speaks of his opponents he characterizes them in a very particular set of terms: they unthinkingly reject what is new, they resist the unmistakable evidence he brings forward, they cling obstinately to comfortable interpretations and refuse even to examine them. But these are also the terms in which he describes the behavior of infantile neurotics like his patient, whose illness is thereby validated when evidence of it is discovered in the actions of those who would dispute it. That is to say, patient and critic become interchangeable; the only difference is that while Freud's patients have placed themselves under his care and thereby taken the first step in achieving independence from their own resistances, the critics are precisely those who have broken with Freud—they are, in fact, his former pupils—and with their every word they move farther away from him and from the possibility or regaining their health. In the course of this argument the thesis of infantile neurosis is at once defended against its detractors and made into a weapon with which to club them, as the conditions of being an infantile neurotic and of being an opponent of Freud turn out to be one and the same.

It is a master stroke which accomplishes several things at once: whatever Freud's opponents might say about his handling of the present case is discredited in advance, because they are too much like its subject; and, more important, Freud's reader is simultaneously introduced to the opinions of those opponents and inoculated against their effect; for the reader knows that should he hearken to these captious voices, he will identify himself as a neurotic child who "rejected what was new . . . and clung fast to what was old" (p. 221). In effect, the reader is given what appears to be a choice but is in fact an offer he can't refuse: you can either accept what I am about to tell you or you can look forward to being stigmatized as a resistant and recalcitrant infant. Either cast your lot with me or with those bad children who are so sick that they do not even recognize their illness.

II

Those of you who know the text already may have realized that to this point I have been dealing primarily with the very brief first chapter and the opening paragraph of chapter 2, some five pages out of more than one hundred. And yet, in a sense, most of the work—which is the work of denying that there has been or will be any work—has already been done, for although we have yet to hear a single detail either of the patient's history or of his therapy, we are already so much under Freud's influence that when the details do finally appear, they will fall into the place he has prepared for them. In the following pages Freud will repeatedly urge us, in effect, to take up our "independent share" in the work, but that independence has long since been taken from us. The judgment he will soon solicit is a judgment he already controls, and as he begins his narration proper, he increases that control by dictating the terms by which his efforts (or, as he would have it, noneffforts) will be judged. "I am unable," he says, "to give either a purely historical or a purely thematic account of my patient's story; I can write a history neither of the treatment nor of the illness, but I shall find myself obliged to combine the two methods of presentation" (p. 158). A "purely historical" account would be a narrative account tracing out relationships of cause and effect; and by declaring that he is unable to provide it, Freud releases himself from the requirement that in his explanations one thing be shown to follow from another. A "purely thematic" account would be one in which the coherence of events and details was a matter of their relationship to a single master theme; and by declaring that he is unable to provide it, Freud releases himself from the requirement that his explanations go together to form a unified whole. In effect, he neutralizes criticism of his conclusions before they are offered and is in the enviable position of being at once the architect and judge of his own performance.

The crowning (and typical) touch is the word "obliged" ("I shall find myself obliged"), for it allows him to present himself as operating under the severest of constraints just at the moment when he is fashioning the constraints under which and within which both his patient and his reader will labor. What obliges him, it turns out, is the nature of the unconscious, which he tells us is not a linear structure ruled by the law of contradiction but a geological accumulation of forms that never completely disappear and live side by side in an uneasy and unpredictable vacillation: "That there should be an instantaneous and clear-cut displacement of one phase by the next was not in the nature of things or of our patient; on the contrary, the preservation of all that had gone before and the co-existence of the most different sorts of currents were characteristic of him" (p. 204). This picture of the unconscious is offered as though it provided independent support of both his thesis and his procedure; but it *is* his thesis, and it is indistinguishable from the argument it authorizes. That is, the unconscious is not a concept but a rhetorical device, a placeholder which can be given whatever shape the polemical moment requires.[6] If someone were to object to his interpretation of a particular detail, he could point for confirmation to the nature of the unconscious, and if someone were to dispute the nature of the unconscious, he could point to the evidence of his interpretations. All the while he could speak of himself as being "obliged" by constraints that were at once independent *of* him and assured the independence *from* him of his patient and his reader. The rhetorical situation could not be more favorable. Freud can present himself as a disinterested researcher and at the same time work to extend his control until it finally includes everything: the details of the analysis, the behavior of the patient, and the performance of the reader. And he manages to do all of this before the story of the Wolf-Man has even begun to unfold.

I am aware that this is not the usual description of Freud's labors, which have recently been characterized by Peter Brooks as "heroic,"[7] a characterization first offered by Freud in 1938 as he cast a final retrospective look at his most famous case.[8] In Brooks's reading the Wolf-Man's case is a "radically modernist" text, a "structure of indeterminacy" and "undecidability" which "perilously destabilizes belief in explanatory histories as exhaustive accounts whose authority derives from the force of closure" (*RP*, pp. 279, 275, 277). Freud's heroism, according to Brooks, consists precisely in resisting closure, in forgoing the satisfaction of crafting a "coherent, finished, enclosed, and authoritative narrative" (*RP*, p. 277).

This is an attractive thesis, but it has absolutely nothing to do with the text we have been reading, although, as we shall see, Brooks has reasons, and apparently good ones, for thinking as he does. Meanwhile, we can note that Freud's own characterization of his narrative insists precisely on those qualities Brooks would deny to it: completeness, exhaustiveness, authority, and, above all, closure. The requirement that he expects his presentation to meet is forthrightly stated in a footnote as he begins to interpret the wolf dream: "It is always a strict law of dream-interpretation that an explanation must be found for every detail" (p. 186, n. 17). This is the vocabulary not of any "post-modernist narrative" or "structure of indeterminacy," but of a more traditional and familiar genre—one of which we know Freud to have been very fond—the classic story of detection; a genre in which an absolutely omniscient author distributes clues to a master meaning of which he is fully cognizant and toward which the reader moves uncertainly, but always under the direction of a guide who builds the structure of the narrative and the structure of understanding at the same time. As Brooks notes, Freud assumes the stance of the detective in the second chapter, which is a quick survey of "the riddles for which the analysis had to find a solution. What was the origin of the sudden change in the boy's character? What was the significance of his phobia and of his perversities? How did he arrive at his obsessive piety? And how are all these phenomena interrelated?" (p. 163). These questions establish the agenda and anticipate the moment of pleasure and satisfaction, the moment when, with a click and a snap, everything falls into place and no detail is without an explanation, the moment when, as in so many of the stories of Arthur Conan Doyle, the detective reveals the solution and proclaims it to be elementary.

There is, however, a large difference between Freud's detective story and other instances of the genre: in the novels of Conan Doyle or Agatha Christie, author and reader are engaged in a contest in which they are armed with the same weapon, their ability to reason along lines of cause and effect; but these are precisely the lines that Freud has told us he will not pursue, and as a result the reader comes to his task with a double disability—not only must he look to Freud for the material on which his intelligence is to work; he must also be supplied with a way of making that material intelligible. And, of course, it will be Freud who supplies him, and who by supplying him will increase immeasurably the control he already exercises. Not only will he monitor the flow of information and point to the object that is to be understood; he will stipulate the form in which the act of understanding will be allowed to occur.

That is the business of chapter 3, "The Seduction and Its Immediate Consequences." The seduction in question is (or appears to be) the seduction of the Wolf-Man by his sister; but it is less important as an event than as a component in a structure of explanation that will serve as a model for the explanatory acts that will soon follow. The occasion is a succession of dreams "concerned with aggressive actions on the boy's part against his sister or against the governess and with energetic reproofs and punishments on account of them." For a while, Freud reports, a firm interpretation of these dreams seemed unavailable; but then "the explanation came at a single blow, when the patient suddenly called to mind the fact that, when he was still very small, . . . his sister had seduced him into sexual practices" (p. 164). What happens next is a bit of sleight of hand: first of all, the patient's recollection is not the explanation, which therefore does not come at a single blow (at least not at the single blow to which the reader's attention is directed). Rather the explanation emerges as the result of interpretive work done by Freud but never seen by us; the "single blow," in other words, occurs offstage and what we are presented with is its result, offered as if it were self-evident and self-generating. These dreams, Freud says, "were meant to efface the memory of an event which later on seemed offensive to the patient's masculine self-esteem, and they reached this end by putting an imaginary and desirable converse in the place of the historical truth" (p. 164). That is to say, the patient's masculine self-esteem was threatened by the fact that his sister, not he, was the aggressive seducer, and this threat is defended against in the dream material by reversing their respective positions. One critic has objected to this as one of Freud's "apparently arbitrary inversions,"[9] but it is far from arbitrary, for it is a precise and concise direction to both the patient and the reader, providing them with a method for dealing with the material they will soon meet and telling them in advance what will result when that method is applied. Freud says, in effect, if you want to know what something—a dream, a piece of neurotic behavior—means, simply reverse its apparent significance, and what you will find is an attempt to preserve masculine self-esteem against the threat of passivity and femininity. The real seduction in this chapter (which is accomplished at this moment and in a single blow) is the seduction not of the patient by his sister, but of both the patient and the reader by Freud, who will now be able to produce interpretive conclusions in the confidence that they will be accepted as the conclusions of an inevitable and independent logic.

Moreover, in performing this act of seduction, Freud at once redoubles and reverses the behavior he explains: if the patient defends against his passivity by "weaving an imaginative composition" in which he is the aggressor, Freud defends against his own aggression by weaving an imaginative composition in which he is passive; and if it is the case, as Freud will later argue, that the patient is ambivalent and conflicted—at a level below consciousness he wants to be both passive and aggressive—it is no less the case with Freud who wants to be the father of everything that happens in the analysis and at the same time wants the analysis to unfold of its own accord. One is tempted to say that the story Freud tells is doubled by the story of the telling or that his performance mirrors or enacts the content of the analysis; but, in fact, it is the other way around: the content of the analysis mirrors or enacts the drama of the performance, a drama that is already playing itself out long before it has anything outside itself to be "about," and playing itself out in the very terms that are here revealed supposedly for the first time, the terms of the preservation and concealing of masculine self-esteem and aggression. It is a commonplace of psychoanalysis that surface concerns are screens for concerns that are primarily sexual; what I am saying is that in the case of the Wolf-Man (where that commonplace was established historically) the concerns of infantile sexuality are screens for the surface concerns that Freud acknowledges but then apparently sets aside. What Freud presents as mere preliminary material—his prospective discussion of evidence, conviction, and independence—is finally the material that is being worked through, even when the focus was ostensibly shifted elsewhere, to the patient and his infantile prehistory. The real story of the case is the story of persuasion, and we will be able to read it only when we tear our eyes away from the supposedly deeper story of the boy who had a dream.

Both stories receive their fullest telling in chapter 4, which begins as this paper begins: " 'I dreamt that it was night and that I was lying in my bed.' " Here finally is the centerpiece of the case, withheld from the reader for three chapters, and now presented as the chief object of interpretation. But, of course, it appears as an already-interpreted object, even before the first word has been said about it, since we know in advance that whatever configuration emerges need only be reversed for its "true" meaning to be revealed; and, lest we forget what we have been taught, Freud reinforces the lesson with a pointed speculation. "We must naturally expect," he says, "to find that this material reproduces the unknown material of the scene in some distorted form, perhaps even distorted into its opposite" (p. 178). He then reports, as though it were not influenced by his expectations, the moment when the patient takes up his "independent share in the work." When in my dream the window suddenly opens of its own accord, " 'It must mean "my eyes suddenly opened." ' " Indeed, it must, given the interpretive directions he has received, and it is hardly surprising to hear Freud's response: "No objection could be made to this" (p. 179). Indeed, there could be no objection to a meaning he has virtually commanded, and in what follows the pretense that the work is independent is abandoned. "The point," he says, "could be developed further," and he immediately proceeds to develop it, not even bothering to indicate whether the development issues from him or from his patient:

> What, then, if the other factor emphasized by the dreamer were also distorted by means of a transposition or reversal? In that case instead of immobility (the wolves sat there motionless; . . .) the meaning would have to be: the most violent motion. . . . He suddenly woke up, and saw in front of him a scene of violent movement at which he looked with strained attention. (p. 179)

There remains only the final step of determining what the scene of violent motion precisely was, but before taking that step Freud pauses in a way that heightens its drama. "I have now reached the point," he says, "at which I must abandon the support I have hitherto had from the course of the analysis. I am afraid it will also be the point at which the reader's belief will abandon me" (pp. 180–81). Presumably it is because of gestures like this one that Brooks is moved to characterize Freud's text as open and nonauthoritative, but I trust that *my* reader will immediately see this as the gesture of someone who is so confident in his authority that he can increase it by (apparently) questioning it. The tone here is playful as Freud amuses himself by raising as specters two dangers he has already avoided. The first is the danger that might follow were he to abandon the support of the analysis; but that danger cannot be real since what he calls the "course of the analysis" has been entirely determined by him. If he now "abandons" it to strike out on his own, he merely exchanges one rhetorically established support for another. No matter what step he takes next, the support under his feet will be as firm as it ever was. Nor can we take seriously the fear that he will be abandoned by the reader's belief, since that belief—our belief—rather than being independent of his will is by now the child of his will, accepting as evidence only what he certifies. Abandon him? To abandon him at this point would be to abandon the constraints and desires that make us, as readers, what we are. By raising the possibility, Freud only tightens the bonds by which we are attached to him and makes us all the more eager to receive the key revelation at his hands. I give it to you now: "What sprang into activity that night out of the chaos of the dreamer's unconscious memory-traces was the picture of copulation between his parents, copulation in circumstances which were not entirely usual and were especially favourable for observation" (p. 181). The credibility of this revelation is not a function of its probability—we have had many demonstrations of how improbable it is that any such event ever took place—but of its explanatory power. It satisfies the need Freud has created in us to understand, and by understanding to become his partner in the construction of the story. As at so many places in the text, what Freud presents here for our judgment is quite literally irresistible; for resistance would require an independence we have already surrendered. In return for that independence we are given the opportunity to nod in agreement— to say, "It *must* mean"—as Freud, newly constructed primal scene in hand, solves every puzzle the case had seemed to offer. In rapid order he accounts for the patient's fear of wolves, his fantasies of beating and being beaten, his simultaneous identification with and rejection of his father, and his marked castration anxiety:

> His anxiety was a repudiation of the wish for sexual satisfaction from his father—the trend which had put the dream into his head. The form taken by the anxiety, the fear of "being eaten by the wolf," was only the . . . transposition of the wish to be copulated with by his father. . . . His last sexual aim, the passive attitude towards his father, succumbed to repression, and fear of his father appeared in its place in the shape of the wolf phobia.
>
> And the driving force of this repression? . . . it can only have been his narcissistic genital libido, which . . . was fighting against a satisfaction whose attainment seemed to involve the renunciation of that organ. (pp. 189–90)

What we have here is a picture of someone who alternates between passive and aggressive behavior, now assuming the dominant position of the male aggressor, now submitting in feminine fashion to forces that overwhelm him. This we are told is the secret content of the patient's behavior, expressed indirectly in his symptoms and fantasies, and brought triumphantly by Freud to the light of day. But if it is a secret, the drama of its disclosing serves to deflect our attention from a secret deeper still, the secret that has (paradoxically) been on display since the opening paragraphs—the secret that the true story of domination and submission is the story of Freud's performance here and now, the story of a master rhetorician who hides from others and from himself the true nature of his activities. Once more Freud contrives to keep the secret by publishing it, by discovering at the heart of the *patient's* fantasy the very conflicts that he himself has been acting out in his relationships with the patient, the analysis, the reader, and his critics. In all of these relationships he is driven by the obsessions he uncovers, by the continual need to control, to convince, and to seduce in endless vacillation with the equally powerful need to disclaim any traces of influence and to present himself as the passive conduit of forces that exist independently of him. He simply cannot help himself, and even when his double story is fully told, he has recourse to a mechanism that opens it again, not, as Brooks would have it, in order to delay or defeat closure, but in order to *repeat* it, and thereby to be master again.

III

The mechanism is the announcement that he has omitted a detail from the reconstruction of the primal scene. "Lastly," Freud tells us, the boy "interrupted his parents' intercourse in a manner which will be discussed later" (p. 182). This is the missing portion referred to in my title, and by calling attention to it, Freud produces a desire for its restoration, a desire he then periodically inflames by reminding us of the deficiency in our understanding and promising to supply it. "I have hinted," he says in chapter 5, "that my description of the 'primal scene' has remained incomplete because I have reserved for a later moment my account of the way in which the child interrupted his parents' intercourse. I must now add that this method of interruption is the same in every case" (p. 203). Again, he leaves us without the crucial piece of information, and by suggesting that it is even more valuable than we had thought—it is a key not only to this case but to all cases—he intensifies our need for it. Moreover, in a manner entirely characteristic, he then shifts that need onto the patient who is described in the following chapter as "longing for some one who should give him the last pieces of information that were still missing upon the riddle of sexual intercourse" (p. 213). The displacement is transparent: it is of course we who are longing for a piece of information to be given us by a father with whom we will then join. Once again the drama of Freud's rhetorical mastery is at once foregrounded and concealed when it appears, only thinly disguised, as an event in his patient's history.

This technique of open concealment reaches a virtuoso level of performance when, in a gesture of excessive candor, Freud reveals that there is a subject he has "intentionally . . . left on one side" (p. 214). He then introduces as a *new* topic of discussion a term that names the very behavior he has been engaging in all the while, anal eroticism. Of course, as he presents it, it is an aspect only of the patient's behavior, easily discernible, says Freud, in his inability to evacuate spontaneously without the aid of enemas, his habit of "making a mess in his bed" whenever he was forced to share a bedroom with a despised governess, his great fear of dysentery, his fierce piety which alternated with fantasies of Christ defecating, and above all his attitude toward money with which he was sometimes exceedingly liberal and at other times miserly in the extreme. All of this Freud relates to the management of "excretory pleasure," which he says plays "an extraordinarily important part . . . in building up sexual life and mental activity" (p. 215). Of course, he offers his observation with no intention of including himself or his own "mental activity" within its scope. It is an observation about *others,* evidence (if it is evidence at all) only of his perspicuity. "At last," he tells us, "I recognized the importance of the intestinal trouble for my purposes," but as we shall see, he says this without any recognition whatsoever of what his real purposes are. His announced purpose is to find a way of overcoming the patient's resistance. For a long time the analysis was blocked by the Wolf-Man's doubt. He remained skeptical of the efficacy of psychoanalysis, and it seemed that "there was no way of convincing him" until

I promised the patient a complete recovery of his intestinal activity, and by means of this promise made his incredulity manifest. I then had the satisfaction of seeing his doubt dwindle away, as in the course of the work his bowel began, like a hysterically affected organ, to "join in the conversation," and in a few weeks' time recovered its normal functions after their long impairment. (p. 218)

One might describe this remarkable passage as an allegory of persuasion were it not so transparently literal. One persuades, in this account, by emptying the other of his "pre-existing convictions." The patient's doubts, or to speak more affirmatively, his beliefs, are quite literally eliminated; the fragmentary portions that comprise his convictions pass out through his bowel, and he is left an empty vessel, ready to be filled up with whatever new convictions the rhetorician brings forward. (It is no accident that the German word "Klaren" means both to explain and to defecate: one must be emptied out before one can be filled up.) The bowel that is said to "join in the conversation" is in fact the medium of the analyst's ventriloquism; it speaks, but the words are his. So is the satisfaction, as Freud explicitly acknowledges ("I then had the satisfaction"); the managing of "excretory pleasure," the mainspring of the patient's psychic life, is taken over by the analyst, who gives up nothing while forcing the other to give up everything. And even as Freud reveals and revels in his strategy, he conceals it, telling the story of persuasion to a reader who is himself that story's object, and who, no less than the patient, is falling totally under the control of the teller.

All of these stories come together at the moment when the missing portion is finally put into place. "I have already hinted," says Freud (in fact he has already already hinted), "that one portion of the content of the primal scene has been kept back." In the original German the sentence is continued in a relative clause whose literal translation is "which I am now able to offer as a supplement." Strachey makes the clause into an independent unit and renders it "I am now in a position to produce this missing portion" (p. 222). It would seem that this is one of those departures from the text for which the translator has been so often taken to task; but, in fact, Strachey is here being more literal than Freud himself. Rather than departing from the text, he eliminates its coyness and brings us closer to the nature of the act the prose performs, an act to which Strachey alerts us by the insistent physicality of the words "position" and "produce." Just what that position and production are becomes dazzlingly clear when the secret is finally out in the open: "The child . . . interrupted his parents' intercourse by passing a stool" (p. 222). We commit no fallacy of imitative form by pointing out what hardly needs pointing out, that Freud enacts precisely what he reports;[10] the position he is in is the squatting position of defecation, and it is he who, at a crucial juncture and to dramatic effect, passes a stool that he has long held back. What is even more remarkable is that immediately after engaging in this behavior, Freud produces (almost as another piece of stool) an analysis of it. In anal-erotic behavior, he tells us, a person sacrifices or makes a gift of "a portion of his own body which he is ready to part with, but only for the sake of some one he loves" (p. 223). That love, however, is a form of possession or mastery, for in this pregenital phase the "contrast between 'masculine' and 'feminine' plays no part" and "its place is taken by the contrast between 'active' and 'passive.'" "What appears to us as masculine in the activities of this phase . . . turns out to be an expression of an instinct for mastery" (*CIL*, p. 327). In other words, one who is fixed in the anal phase experiences pleasure as control, a control he achieves by the calculated withholding and releasing of feces. What the anal erotic seeks is to capture and absorb the other by the stimulation and gratifying of desire; what he seeks, in short, is power, and he gains it at the moment when his excretions become the focus and even the content of the other's attention. However accurate this is as an account of anal eroticism, it is a perfect account of the act of persuasion, which is, I would argue, the primal act for which the anal erotic is only a metaphor. It is persuasion that Freud has been practicing in this case on a massive scale, and the "instinct for mastery" of which persuasion is the expression finds its fulfillment here when the reader accepts from Freud that piece of deferred information which completes the structure of his own understanding. Once that acceptance has been made, the reader belongs to Freud as much as any lover belongs to the beloved. By giving up a portion of himself Freud is not diminished but enlarged, since what he gets back is the surrender of the reader's will which now becomes an extension of his own. The reader, on his part, receives a moment of pleasure—the pleasure of seeing the pieces of the puzzle finally fitting together—but Freud reserves to himself the much greater pleasure of total mastery. It is a pleasure that is intensely erotic, full of the "sexual excitement" (p. 223) that is said to mark the *patient's* passing of a stool; it is a pleasure that is anal, phallic, and even oral, affording the multiple satisfactions of domination, penetration, and engulfment. It is, in a word, the pleasure of persuasion.

In what remains of his performance Freud savors that pleasure and adds to it by placing it in apparent jeopardy. I refer to the well-known fact that in the four years between the writing and the publishing of this case history Freud added two bracketed passages in which he calls into question precisely what he has been arguing for, the reality of the primal scene. He first wonders if "perhaps what the child observed was not copulation between his parents but copulation between animals, which he then displaced on to his parents" (p. 201). He later considers the possibility that primal scene fantasies may have their source in a "phylogenetic heritage"; when a child's own experience fails him, he "fills in the gaps in individual truth with prehistoric truth; he replaces occurrences in his own life by occurrences in the life of his ancestors" (pp. 238, 239). Brooks finds these speculations "daring" and (as I have already said) "heroic," since in his view they show Freud willing to open up what his text would seem to have closed. But the only thing these later interpolations open up is the opportunity to perform closure once again, and to perform it in conditions that have the appearance of being particularly difficult. What Brooks sees as a breaching of Freud's authority is a confident exercise of that authority which now feels its strength to such an extent that it can allow itself to be challenged with impunity. The challenge comes in the form of alternative accounts of the primal scene's origin, but the question of origin is beside the point once the scene has been made real for both the patient and the reader. This, after all, is the work of the analysis, not to uncover the empirical foundations of the scene but to establish it as an integral part first of the patient's psychic life and then of the reader's understanding of that life. As Freud himself puts it, what is important is the "profound conviction of the reality of these . . . scenes" (p. 195), and once that conviction has been secured, it can tolerate any number of speculations without being shaken. Freud is betting that it has in fact been secured; he is betting that he has been persuasive and that at one level at least the question of the primal scene has been closed. He now closes it again, after having ostentatiously opened it, by saying that although he would "be glad to know whether the primal scene in my present patient's case was a phantasy or a real experience; . . . the answer to this question is not in fact a matter of very great importance" (p. 238). That is why he raises it—so that it can be dismissed as irrelevant by a conviction that now supports itself and is unembarrassed by inquiries into its possible origins. Once that conviction is firmly established it can be cited as confirmation of itself and invoked as a sufficient response to any challenge, including the challenges Freud calls up only so that they can be dramatically defeated.

He does this for the last time in chapter 8 when he declares, "I will make a final attempt at re-interpreting the . . . findings of this

analysis in accordance with the scheme of my opponents" (p. 243).
One might characterize this as a demonstration of openness were it not
so obviously a demonstration of control. Freud is seizing an occasion
to perform a rhetorical feat whose value lies (to borrow a phrase from
gymnastics) in its degree of difficulty. (This is an old rhetorical tradition that goes back at least as far as the exercises of Seneca.) First, he
imagines what Jung and Adler would say if they were presented with
the materials he has now marshaled. He imagines them as "bad"
readers, readers who are unconvinced, and he rehearses their likely
objections. No doubt they would regard the primal scene as the invention of a neurotic who was seeking to rationalize his "flight from the
world" and who was "driven to embark on this long backward course
either because he had come up against some task . . . which he was
too lazy to perform, or because he had every reason to be aware of his
own inferiority and thought he could best protect himself . . . by
elaborating such contrivances as these" (pp. 243, 244). What Freud is
staging here is a moment of scrupulosity very much like some earlier
moments when he presses interpretive suggestions on a resistant patient
and then points to the patient's resistance as a proof of the independence
of the analysis. Here it is we who are (once more) in the position of
the patient as Freud urges on us an interpretive direction and waits for
us to reject it "of our own accord"; but, of course, at this late stage any
rejection we might perform would be dictated not by an independent
judgment, but by a judgment Freud has in large measure shaped. Even
so, he is unwilling to run the risk (really no risk at all) that we might
respond in some errant way, and accordingly he responds for us:

> All this would be very nice, if only the unlucky wretch had not
> had a dream when he was no more than four years old, which
> signalized the beginning of his neurosis . . . and the interpreta-
> tion of which necessitates the assumption of this primal scene. All
> the alleviations which the theories of Jung and Adler seek to
> afford us come to grief, alas, upon such paltry but unimpeachable
> facts as these. (p. 244)

Everything happens so fast in this sequence that we may not notice that
the "unimpeachable fact" which anchors it is the *assumption* of the
primal scene. In most arguments assumptions are what must be proven
out, but in this argument the assumption is offered as proof; what
supports it is not any independent fact, but the polemical fact that

without the assumption the story Freud has so laboriously constructed falls apart. The necessity Freud invokes is a discursive necessity, the necessity of a founding moment in the absence of which an explanation could not be "found for every detail." In effect, Freud says to us, "look, we've worked incredibly hard to put something together; are we now going to entertain doubts about the very assumption that enabled us to succeed?" The primal scene is important because it allows the story of its own discovery to unfold. In that story—the story, basically, of the analysis—the wolf dream comes first and initiates a search for its origin; that search then leads to the "uncovering" of the primal scene, and although it is the last thing to be put in place, it immediately becomes the anchor and the explanation of everything that precedes it.

This is precisely what Freud predicts will happen when early on he describes what it will feel like to look back on a successful analysis. The analyst will recall (as he now recalls)

> how gradually the construction of [the] phantasy . . . came about, and, . . . how independently of the physician's incentive many points in its development proceeded; how, after a certain phase of the treatment, everything seemed to converge upon it, and how later, . . . the most various and remarkable results radiated out from it; how not only the large problems but the smallest peculiarities in the history of the case were cleared up by this single assumption. (p. 196)

In other words, the assumption of the primal scene proves itself by its effects, by its ability to bring order to an apparently heterogeneous mass of fragments and impressions; once order has been brought, there is nothing it does not comprehend, and therefore no vantage point from which it can be meaningfully challenged. Should a challenge be mounted, it can be met as Freud meets it here, with ridicule and incredulity. The investment of work and the yield of that work—certainty, conviction, knowledge—are simply too great to risk losing and comprise a resistance stronger even than the resistance that had to be overcome before they could be accomplished. What Freud is relying on here is not something newly or additionally persuasive, but on the fact that persuasion has occurred, and that having occurred, we will be unwilling and indeed unable to undo it.

It is the definition of a rhetorical object that it is entirely constructed and stands without external support; it is, we are accustomed to say, removed from reality; but we could just as well say that it becomes reality, that insofar as it has been installed at the center of a structure of conviction it acquires the status of that which goes without saying and that against which nothing can be said. It then becomes possible to argue both for and from it at the same time; or, rather, it becomes possible to not argue at all, but merely to point to something that now stands as irrefutable evidence of itself, as something perspicuous, autonomous, and independent, as something that need not be defended or even presented, as something *beyond rhetoric*. That is what Freud does here when the imagined objections to the primal scene are met simply by invoking it as a self-evident and indisputable authority. One might say, then, that at the conclusion of the case history the primal scene emerges triumphant as both the end of the story and its self-authenticating origin; but what is really triumphant is not this particular scene, which after all might well have assumed a quite different shape if the analysis had taken the slightest of turns, but the discursive power of which and by which it has been constructed. The true content of the primal scene is the story of its making. At bottom the primal scene is the scene of persuasion.[11]

IV

Of course, this is not something that Freud knows, or, rather, if he knows it, it is a knowledge that he must compartmentalize lest it paralyze him and render his performance impossible. As we have seen, this compartmentalization often takes the form of displacement, as, time and again, the motives of power and manipulation, seduction and domination, are foregrounded but shifted onto others—the patient, Freud's critics, neurotic children, captious readers. Although the text is filled with accounts of its own workings, they are always disguised as accounts of the workings of other agents; and in this way the truth about itself is at once revealed and concealed. It is concealed not only from those who are the objects of the text's designs, but from the designer, from Freud himself, who displays a marvelous ability to hide from his right hand what his left hand is doing. Perhaps his most virtuoso moment in this "art" occurs late in the case history when the patient is reported as engaging in some "curious behavior." At times, Freud tells us, "he used to threaten me with eating me up and . . . with all kinds of other ill-treatment" (p. 248). Now by the rule of interpretation he himself has laid down, this moment should yield immediately to the principle of reversal and produce the following reading: the aggression the patient threatens is in fact the aggression he fears; it is he who is in danger of being eaten up and it is I who am the devourer. But this is a reading of the situation that Freud cannot bear to contemplate, and he substitutes for it a lame alternative—"all of which was merely an expression of affection" (p. 248). It is an edifying spectacle: the patient, aware at some level that he is being engulfed by the analyst, protests by simulating the analyst's behavior; the analyst in turn looks into a mirror and refuses to recognize what he sees. He is still refusing some years later when he meets the Wolf-Man again and is told by him that "after the end of the treatment he had been seized with a longing to tear himself free from my influence" (p. 262, n. 61). Here one would think is an explicit gloss on the "curious behavior" he had earlier displayed, but Freud makes no connection between the two moments and treats the Wolf-Man's later remark merely as a piece of transference, something left over from the case, a loose end. And what does one do with loose ends, with related but peripheral bits of information? Why, one puts them in a footnote, and that is exactly what Freud does in 1923, once again managing to hide in plain sight the truth he cannot confront. Interestingly enough, it is a truth the patient intuited even before the analysis began; after meeting Freud for the first time he recorded these thoughts: "A Jewish swindler; he wants to use me from behind and shit on my head."

Does this mean that the patient is more aware than the physician? Not at all, for he no less than Freud is caught up in the dialectic of independence and control, knowing at some level what has happened to him but committed at another level to denying it. In his own memoirs that denial emerges as a boast: "in my analysis with Freud I felt myself less as a patient than as a co-worker, the younger comrade of an experienced explorer setting out to study a new, recently discovered land" (p. 140). Here is the voice of someone who believes himself to have taken up his "independent share in the work" and who has written himself into a story that is positively epic. But only a few pages later he tells a quite different story. As the analysis drew to its end, Freud raised the question of the transference and "spoke of the danger of the patient's feeling too close a tie to the therapist" (p. 149). The Wolf-Man then reports with an absolutely straight face that in order to obviate the danger Freud suggested that the patient give him a gift, and thereby lessen "his feeling of gratitude and his consequent dependence on the physician" (pp. 149–50). In other words, the patient is being urged to leave something of himself behind (a piece of stool perhaps?) as a way of *breaking* a tie that threatened to become too close. It seems incredible that he did not see how this device—this soliciting and proffering of a *memento amoris*—could serve only to strengthen a bond that would now not be broken even by a physical separation. It seems even more incredible that he would have chosen as a gift a "female Egyptian figure," which he tells us Freud placed on his desk in the position usually reserved for a photograph of a spouse or a lover. Twenty years later, looking through a magazine, the Wolf-Man spies a picture of Freud at his desk and sees that the figure is still there. It is the first thing he notices in the picture—" 'My' Egyptian immediately struck my eye"—and it is obvious that he interprets it as evidence of Freud's continuing love. He goes so far as to say of the figure that "it symbolized my analysis with Freud" and although he does not gloss the symbolism, its meaning is transparent: he remains forever in the feminine position of submission, a captive work of art displayed as a trophy in the workshop of the analyst. And, indeed, the sentence ends with a recollection that makes sense only as an unacknowledged acknowledgment of the truth about their relationship. He called me, says the Wolf-Man, " 'a piece of psychoanalysis' " (p. 150). The significance of being a piece of psychoanalysis is made apparent when, in what seems to be a random fashion, the Wolf-Man manages in the next few paragraphs to work his way around to a mention of Jung, "whom Freud had always praised highly and whom he had formally designated as his successor." One can only imagine the pleasure with which he then reports that Jung had "broken away" from Freud and "was now going his own way" (p. 151). Going his own way is what the Wolf-Man, in one mood, very much wants to do, and it is what Freud supposedly wants for him; but what they really want is what they get, a lifelong union in the course of which both parties celebrate an independence neither desires. Jung achieves that independence—he breaks the tie—and the price he pays for it is the loss of everything the Wolf-Man cherishes: his inheritance, the Father's approval, his position in psychoanalysis, his place on the desk. It is the Wolf-Man who, by failing to go his own way, succeeds in becoming the perfect rhetorical artifact, a wholly made object who wears his maker's signature like a badge, and who in later years introduced himself by saying "I am the most famous case" and answered the telephone with these words: "Wolf-Man here."

The Wolf-Man, in short, is a piece of language, a textually produced entity whose origins go back no farther than Freud's words. This is what Freud can never admit; indeed, as Ned Lukacher, following Jacques Lacan, has recently put it, it is necessary for Freud to forget "that affect works through and within language and that the object of analysis is therefore the logic of the signifier." At the heart of psychoanalysis and therefore at the heart of the primal scene, Lukacher continues, language must not be allowed in, for "had Freud acknowledged that the . . . force of suggestion worked through the rhythms of language, he would have been deprived of any means with which to defend against it."[12] The defense, as we have seen, is more language, words denying the forces of words, rhetoric disclaiming rhetorical intention. It is a spectacle one finds everywhere in Freud's work, but nowhere more nakedly than in the first of his Introductory Lectures. These lectures were delivered in the winter terms of 1915–16 and 1916–17, some two years after the case of the Wolf-Man was first written up and during the period when Freud was revising it for publication. There is thus a close connection between the two productions, and indeed a case can be made for regarding Lecture 1 as an explicit working out of what remains hidden and disguised in the longer essay.

Especially revealing is Freud's frank acknowledgment of the way he will deal with his audience. "Do not be annoyed," he says, "if I begin by treating you . . . as . . . neurotic patients" (CIL, p. 15). He then describes what such a treatment will be like; it will begin in the assumption that everything the members of the audience know and believe constitutes an obstacle to their understanding. "I will show you," he goes on, "how the whole trend of your previous education and all your habits of thought are inevitably bound to make you into opponents of psycho-analysis, and how much you would have to overcome *in yourselves* in order to get the better of this instinctive opposition" (CIL, pp. 15–16; my emphasis). The cast of characters is smaller here, and the audience must play both its own part and the part of the obstinate critics. Rather than being asked to reject those critics, the listener is asked to reject himself as the necessary source of error and to replace his "habits of thought" with new ones fashioned for him by the words of the analyst. But, Freud cautions, those words will have their effect only if the ear is receptive, and the ear will be receptive only if the hearer turns away from his previous education and surrenders to the speaker. Everything will depend, he announces, "on how much credence you can give to your informant," that is, to me. Freud himself raises the objection that such credence would be supported only "by hearsay"—by words—and replies by asking his listeners to imagine themselves attending a lecture on history. The historian in making his case would refer you to documents, "to the reports given by ancient writers"; but, after all, Freud points out, those documents would prove only that "earlier generations already believed" in the reality of what the historian asserts; in the end you would still be relying on words and on your own belief "that the lecturer had no conceivable motive for assuring you of the reality of something he himself did not think real" (*CIL*, pp. 18, 19). The rhetorical basis of psychoanalysis (and of all knowledge) could hardly be made clearer, but Freud seems determined to drive the point home. In a remarkable paragraph the power of persuasive language is given a due that would seem extravagant to Quintilian or Cicero. "Nothing," he declares, "takes place in a psychoanalytic treatment but an interchange of words," and it is this fact that is always cited by detractors who doubt whether " 'anything can be done about . . . illness by mere talking' " (*CIL*, p. 17). This doubt about talk is met, as it must be, with another piece of talk, with the assertion that it is only by talk—by words—that anything can be done:

> Words were originally magic and to this day words have retained much of their ancient magical power. By words one person can make another blissfully happy or drive him to despair, by words the teacher conveys his knowledge to his pupils, by words the orator carries his audience with him and determines their judgements and decisions. Words provoke affects and are in general the means of . . . influence among men. (*CIL*, p. 17)

It is but a short step from this ringing statement to the conclusion that the basis of argument, and therefore of conviction, is always rhetorical even when a discourse claims to be disinterested and rational. Freud makes this point in the closing paragraphs. The subject is once again the opponents of psychoanalysis who finds its doctrines "repulsive and morally reprehensible" but know that in order to be persuasive they must recast their objections "in intellectual terms." Freud reports that they always succeed, for "it is inherent in human nature . . . to consider a thing untrue if one does not like it" and "it is easy to find arguments against it" (*CIL*, p. 23). But, of course, those arguments will not be truly logical or factual, for they will always "arise from emotional sources" which, after all, are the only sources that human nature knows.

What Freud says next, in the opening sentences of the final substantive paragraph, is, to say the least, surprising: "We, however, Ladies and Gentlemen, can claim that . . . we have had no tendentious aim in view. We have merely wished to give expression to a matter of fact which we believe we have established by our painstaking labours" (*CIL*, pp. 23–24). At the very least we would seem to have a disjunction between Freud's general account of human nature and the claims he makes for his own assertions. The general account says that all knowledge is ultimately rhetorical ("arise[s] from emotional sources"); the claim he makes for his own assertions is that they are not rhetorical but true. How are we to explain this apparent contradiction? As usual, Freud himself gives the answer (although unwittingly) when he says of society in general that it "does not wish to be reminded of [the] precarious portion of its foundations" (*CIL*, p. 23). I would go even further and say that neither society nor any member of society *could* be reminded of that precariousness, for to be so reminded would be to achieve what psychoanalysis itself declares to be unattainable, a distance on one's own concerns and obsessions. The question is whether or not the knowledge (the knowledge rhetoric offers us) that our convictions are unsupported by anything external to themselves will operate to undermine those convictions, and my answer to the question is no.[13] Whenever we are asked to state what we take to be the case about this or that, we will always respond in the context of what seems to us at the time to be indisputably true, even if we know, as a general truth, that everything can be disputed. *One who has learned the lesson of rhetoricity does not thereby escape the condition it names.* The fact that Freud lays bare the rhetorical basis of all convictions does not protect him from the appeal and power of his own. There finally is no contradiction here, only a lack of relationship between a truth one might know about discourse in general—that it is ungrounded—and the particular truths to which one is temporally committed and concerning which one can have no doubts. Once more we come round to the deep point that the case of the Wolf-Man allows us to make: the rhetorical and constructed nature of things does not compromise their reality but constitutes it, and constitutes it in a form that is as invulnerable to challenge as it is unavailable to verification. Like his patient, Freud can only know what he knows within the rhetoric that possesses him, and he cannot be criticized for clinging to that knowledge even when he himself could demonstrate that it is without an extradiscursive foundation. At times in this essay I have spoken as if Freud ought to have been aware that his argument had its sources in his deepest anxieties; but it now should be clear that this is an awareness he could not possibly achieve, since, by the arguments of psychoanalysis itself, every operation of the mind, including the operation we might want to call awareness, issues from those same anxieties. The thesis of psychoanalysis is that one cannot get to the side of the unconscious; the thesis of this essay is that one cannot get to the side of rhetoric.

To say as much is to provide, belatedly, an important corrective to my exposition of Freud's rhetorical mastery. I have spoken at times as if that mastery was absolute, as if the oft repeated claims to be the mere register of forces external to him were nothing more than feints, pieces of strategy. They are surely that, but they are more; they are expressions of an ambivalence in Freud that mirrors the ambivalence he finds in his patient: he wants at the same time to be masculine and feminine, to be at once the generating source of truth and to have the truth impressed upon him by a power whose force he cannot resist. Just as his patient fights in his dream "against the fact" that he "had identified himself with the castrated mother" (p. 191), so Freud fights against the fact or fear that he is not in control of his own performance. In short, another layer of "irony" must be added to my analysis: while it is true that Freud's disclaimer of persuasive power is in the service of a massive effort at persuasion, that effort is itself in the service of an effort to defend against the realization that his power is not his own. Does he provide the missing portion (as he claims to do) and thereby demonstrate his paternity, or is the portion provided for him, completing him just as he boasts to have completed the understanding of his readers? The question cannot be answered because the two accounts and the impulses they embody exist in the case side by side, again mirroring the "constant wavering" Freud discerns in his patient between "the most various and contradictory libidinal cathexes, all of them capable of functioning side by side" (p. 259). One sees this wavering everywhere, but nowhere more clearly than in a note to the conclusion of chapter 8 (p. 244). In rapid alternation Freud presents himself as "holding back" from publication for fear that he has imposed his conclusions on the evidence, and then as being "the first" to recognize the necessity of holding back (he did not hold back from holding back), and finally as being "forced" into publication by the case itself (the position of being first is resigned as soon as it is claimed). He then begins the next chapter with a discussion of his "powers in the act of exposition" (p. 245), powers for whose inadequacy he apologizes, but powers he immediately reinflates by citing as a "mitigating circumstance" the fact that his task has "never before" been attempted. Once again he is "first," but only for an instant before he concludes by embracing, or at least by appearing to embrace, his "own inferiority": "I prefer . . . to put a bold face on it and show that I have not allowed myself to be held back by a sense of my own inferiority." Of course, this is still another reversal: in the act of acknowledging his inferiority he masters it, refusing (heroically) to let it hold him back from assertion, from evacuation, from inscribing himself on the world, from publication. The extraordinary (and intractable) complexity of this gesture is concentrated in the notion of putting on a "bold face." Is this the face of confident masculine assertion beneath which lies the reality of a nature more retiring and feminine? Or is the feminine claim of inferiority a mask—a bold-faced pretense of being not bold—for the aggression it barely conceals? Which is the rhetorical posture and which the stance of "Freud himself"? Neither psychoanalysis nor rhetoric will permit us to answer or even ask this question, and we are left, like the analyst and his patient, in the oxymoronic state of constant wavering.

Notes

Introduction: Going Down the Anti-Formalist Road

1   H. L. A. Hart, *The Concept of Law* (Oxford, 1962), p. 93.
2   Roberto Unger, *Knowledge and Politics* (Boston, 1975), p. 92.
3   W. J. T. Mitchell, ed., *Against Theory* (Chicago, 1985), p. 13.
4   John Searle, *Speech Acts* (Cambridge, Eng., 1969), p. 45.
5   John Milton, "Doctrine and Discipline of Divorce," in J. Max Patrick et al., eds., *Milton's Prose* (New York, 1968), p. 165.
6   Hart, p. 137.
7   See Hart, passim.
8   Kenney Hegland, "Goodbye to Deconstruction," *University of Southern California Law Review* 58 (1985): 213.
9   *Transcript of Proceedings, United States Senate Committee on the Judiciary, Hearing on the Nomination of the Honorable Robert H. Bork,* Washington, D.C., September 19, 1987, pp. 27ff.
10 Paul Brest and Ann Vandenberg, "Politics, Feminism, and the Constitution," *Stanford Law Review* 39 (1987): 659.
11 Catherine MacKinnon, "Feminism, Marxism, Method, and the State: Toward Feminist Jurisprudence," *Signs* 8.4 (Summer 1983): 646.
12 Catherine MacKinnon, "Feminism, Marxism, Method, and the State: An Agenda for Theory," *Signs* 7.3 (Spring 1982): 24.
13 M. F. Belenky, B. M. Clinchy, N. R. Goldberger, and J. M. Tarule, *Women's Ways of Knowing* (New York, 1986), p. 8.
14 Thomas Heller, "Structuralism and Critique," *Stanford Law Review* 36 (1984): 191.
15 Jeffrey Malkan, "'Against Theory': Pragmatism and Deconstruction," *Telos* 71 (1987): 137.
16 Cornel West, "Afterword," in *Post-Analytic Philosophy,* ed. Cornel West and John Rachman (New York, 1985), p. 267.
17 Frank Lentricchia, "The Return of William James," *Cultural Critique* 4 (1986): 29.
18 Hadley Arkes, *First Things: An Inquiry into the First Principles of Morals and Justice* (Princeton, 1986), pp. 132–33.

With the Compliments of the Author:
Reflections on Austin and Derrida

What follows is a carefully circumscribed and limited attempt to explicate for an Anglo-American audience the arguments of Derrida's "Signature Event Context" (*Glyph* 1 [1977]: 172–97) as they relate the project begun by J. L. Austin in *How to Do Things with Words* (Oxford, 1962); all further references to these works, abbreviated "SEC" and *HT,* respectively, will be included in the text. It is also an attempt, as some of my readers will recognize, to assimilate the Derrida of this and related essays to the theory of "interpretive communities" as it is elaborated in my *Is There a Text in This Class? The Authority of Interpretive Communities* (Cambridge, Mass., 1980). Such an effort may appear to be simply one more American domestication of Derridean thought, but it is intended as a counterweight to the more familiar domestication associated with words like "undecidability" and the "abyss." The narrowness of my focus precludes any consideration of Derrida's "Limited Inc." or of the essay by John Searle to which "Limited Inc." is a response. It also precludes a consideration of the other perspectives—psychoanalysis, feminism, sociolinguistics—that have been brought to bear on the issues raised by the Searle-Derrida debate. I refer the reader to the helpful and illuminating analyses of Gayatri Spivak ("Revolutions That as Yet Have No Model," *Diacritics* 8 [Winter 1980]: 29–49); Mary Pratt ("The Ideology of Speech-Act Theory," *Centrum,* n. s. 1, no. 1 [Spring 1981]: 5–18); Samuel Weber ("It," *Glyph* 4 [1978]: 1–31); and Barbara Johnson ("Mallarmé and Austin," *The Critical Difference* [Baltimore, 1980], pp. 52–66). I am indebted to Kenneth Abraham, Michael Fried, and Walter Benn Michaels who worked through these texts with me in a succession of team-taught courses and who have contributed to the result in ways they will immediately recognize. I am grateful for the criticisms and suggestions of Steven Knapp, W. J. T. Mitchell, and Robert Viscusi.

1   Jonathan Culler, *Structuralist Poetics* (Ithaca, N.Y., 1975), p. 133; all further references to this work will be included in the text.

2   John M. Ellis, *The Theory of Literary Criticism: A Logical Analysis* (Berkeley and Los Angeles, 1974), p. 43.

3   Barbara Herrnstein Smith, *On the Margins of Discourse: The Relation of Literature to Language* (Chicago, 1978), pp. 35, 36.

4   Wolfgang Iser, *The Act of Reading* (Baltimore, 1978), pp. 24, 184.

5   Richard Ohmann, "Speech Acts and the Response to Literature" (paper delivered at the December 1976 meeting of the Modern Language Association).

6   John Searle, "The Logical Status of Fictional Discourse," *Expression and Meaning* (Cambridge, Eng., 1979), p. 67; all further references to this work will be included in the text.

7   The argument that the more information one has about a context the more sure will be the interpretation of utterances produced in that context is parallel to the argument that the more words in an utterance (the more

explicit it is), the less likely it is to be misinterpreted or interpreted in a plurality of ways. They are both arguments for a state of saturation (either of words or things) so total that interpretation can find no entering wedge. For a counterargument, see my *Is There a Text in This Class?* pp. 282–83, 311.

8   Of course, it is possible that she could change her mind, but only if he succeeded in changing the belief she now holds about his character. This might happen, for example, if he were to do something he had often promised but failed to do or said something ("I love you") he had been unwilling to say before. The fact that she might be convinced by this or some other piece of behavior does not mean that her belief would have been altered by a direct encounter with unmediated evidence; for that behavior will have the status of evidence only in the context of the particular form her belief takes (it will be belief-specific evidence). If, for example, her belief about his character takes the form of her thinking "he will never do this or say that," then certain pieces of behavior (his doing this or saying that) will count as possible reasons for altering her belief, although those reasons will themselves have their source in belief. Moreover, the force of the behavior as evidence might be felt even if it were only reported to her or conveyed in a letter. Again, the fact of physical proximity is not as decisive or even necessarily relevant.

9   See Derrida, *Of Grammatology*, trans. Gayatri Spivak (Baltimore, 1976), pp. 107–40, for a powerful analysis of the appearance-disappearance of persons within a system.

10 Weber, "It," p. 7.

11 See Johnson, "Mallarmé and Austin," p. 60:

> The performative utterance . . . automatically fictionalizes its utterer when it makes him the mouthpiece of a conventionalized authority. Where else, for example, but at a party *convention* could a presidential candidate be nominated? Behind the fiction of the subject stands the fiction of society. . . . It is, of course, not our intention to nullify all the differences between a poem and, say, a verdict, but only to problematize the assumptions on which such distinctions are based. If people are put to death by a verdict and not by a poem, it is not because the law is not a fiction.

See also Pratt, "Ideology," p. 10:

> "Authorship" is a certain, socially constituted position occupied by a speaking subject and endowed with certain characteristics and certain relationships to other dimensions of that subject. Alternatively, we could say that an implied author exists in all speech acts—an author is implied in a text only in the same way subjects are implied in any speech act they perform.

There is an extended discussion of these matters in my "How to Do Things with Austin and Searle" in *Is There a Text in This Class?*, pp. 197–245; see esp. pp. 231–44.

12   See Derrida, *Of Grammatology,* p. 44: "If 'writing' signifies inscription and especially the durable institution of a sign . . . writing in general covers the entire field of linguistic signs. In that field a certain sort of instituted signifiers may then appear, 'graphic' in the narrow and derivative sense of the word, ordered by a certain relationship with other instituted—hence 'written,' even if they are 'phonic'—signifiers." That is to say, within the field of instituted signifiers, some one sort will occupy the position—within the institution—of 'natural.' See also p. 46: "The rupture of that 'natural attachment' puts in question the idea of naturalness rather than that of attachment. That is why the word 'institution' should not be too quickly interpreted within the classical system of oppositions." That is, the fact that everything is institutional does not mean that there are no distinctions or norms or standards—no "attachments"—only that those attachments, because they are institutional or socially constituted, are not eternal and can therefore change.

13   John Searle, "Reiterating the Differences: A Reply to Derrida," *Glyph* 1 (1977): 198.

14   See John Searle, *The Philosophy of Language* (Oxford, 1971), p. 7.

15   See John Ross, "On Declarative Sentences," in *Readings in English Transformational Grammar,* ed. Roderick Jacobs and Peter Rosenbaum (Lexington, Mass., 1970); Jerrold Katz, *Propositional Structure and Illocutionary Force* (Cambridge, Mass., 1980); and Jerrold Saddock, *Toward a Linguistic Theory of Speech Acts* (New York, 1974).

16   See H. P. Grice, "Logic and Conversation" (delivered as part of the William James Lectures, Harvard University, 1967), and Mary Pratt, *Toward a Speech Act Theory of Literary Discourse* (Bloomington, Ind., 1977).

17   See Kent Bach and Robert M. Harnisch, *Linguistic Communication and Speech Acts* (Cambridge, Mass., 1979).

Why No One's Afraid of Wolfgang Iser

1   Wolfgang Iser, *The Act of Reading: A Theory of Aesthetic Response* (Baltimore: Johns Hopkins University Press, 1978), p. 13.

2   Wayne C. Booth, *A Rhetoric of Irony* (Chicago: University of Chicago Press, 1978), p. 19.

Working on the Chain Gang: Interpretation in Law and Literature

A version of this essay was published in the fall 1982 issue of *Critical Inquiry,* 9 *Critical Inquiry* 201 (1982), along with Ronald Dworkin's essay "Law as Interpretation," 9 *Critical Inquiry* 179 (1982). Both papers grew out of a symposium on politics and interpretation held at the University of Chicago in the fall of 1981. Essays by other participants in that symposium were also published in the same issue.

1 Dworkin, "Law as Interpretation," 60 *Texas Law Review* 527 (1982).
2 Id. at 528.
3 Id. at 542–43.
4 Fish, *Is There a Text in This Class?* (1980).
5 Dworkin, supra note 1, at 541–42 (footnote omitted).
6 Dworkin makes a similar but not exactly parallel point when he acknowledges that the first novelist will have the responsibility of "interpreting the genre in which he sets out to write." Id. at 541 n.6.
7 Id. at 542–43 (emphasis in original).
8 Id. at 544.
9 Id.
10 I am not saying that the present-day case comes first and the history then follows, but that they emerge together in the context of an effort to see them as related embodiments of some legal principle. Indeed, a case could not even be seen as a case if it were not from the very first regarded as an item in a judicial field and therefore as the embodiment of some or other principle. This does not mean, however, that it is to judicial principles that we must look for the anchoring ground of interpretation, for judicial principles cannot be separated from the history to which they give form; one can no more think of a judicial principle apart from a chain of cases than one can think of a chain of cases apart from a judicial principle. No one of the entities that makes up judicial reasoning exists independently, neither the present-day case, nor the chain of which it is to be the continuation, nor the principle of which they are both to be the realizations.
11 Dworkin, supra note 1, at 532.
12 Ian Fleming, *Goldfinger* (1959).
13 One hardly knows where to begin, perhaps simply with the title of David Grossvogel's study, *Mystery and Its Fictions: From Oedipus to Agatha Christie* (1979). The title of Dennis Porter's *The Pursuit of Crime: Art and Ideology in Detective Fiction* (1981) suggests a scope and a thesis somewhat less grand, but Porter does find Christie "working in the tradition of Poe, Collins, and Doyle," id. at 137, and he devotes some very serious pages to a stylistic analysis of the first paragraph of her first novel in the context of V. N. Voloshinov's *Marxism and the Philosophy of Language* (1973). Christie is taken no less seriously by Stephen Knight in *Form and Ideology in Crime Fiction* (1980). Knight speaks without any self-consciousness of Christie as a "major writer" and analyzes her "art" in terms that might well be applied to, say, Henry James: "The rigidity of the time and place structure emphasizes the obscurity of the thematic shape, challenges us all the more urgently to decide it. The dual structure enacts the central drama of the novel, a threat to order that only careful observation can resolve," id. at 126. Knight's book, like Porter's, is replete with references to Lacan, Jameson, Machery, Marx, Freud, and Barthes, and bears all the marks of sophisticated academic criticism. See also in a similarly academic mode, R. Champigny, *What Will Have Happened: A Philosophical and*

Technical Essay on Mystery Stories (1977); J. Palmer, *Thrillers* (1979).
As this essay goes to press, I have received in the mail the most recent issue
of *Poetics Today,* and find Joseph Agassi, a professor of philosophy, discussing the relationship of the novels of Christie, Chandler, Doyle, and
others to the scientific theories of Francis Bacon and Thomas Kuhn. Agassi,
"The Detective Novel and Scientific Method," 3 *Poetics Today* 99–108
(1982). Dworkin, it would seem, could not have chosen a worse example
to support his case.

14 See Dworkin, supra note 1, at 537–39.
15 Id. at 539.
16 Id. at 542.
17 Id. at 540.
18 Id. at 545.
19 Id. at 531.
20 Id. at 528.
21 One must question, too, and for the same reason, Dworkin's distinction between "common-law" cases and cases where there is a statute, at least insofar as it is a distinction between cases whose interpretation is straightforward and cases that must be referred to the background of an institutional
history. In cases where there is a statute for a judge to look at, he must still
look at it, and his look will be as interpretive—as informed by the practices and conventions that define the enterprise—as it would be in a common-law case. That is, a statute no more announces its own meaning than
does the case to which it is to be applied, and therefore cases where statutes
figure are no more or less grounded than cases where no statute exists. In
either circumstance one must interpret from the beginning and in either
circumstance one's interpretation will be at once constrained and enabled
by a general and assumed understanding of the goals, purposes, concerns,
and procedures of the enterprise. See on these and related points two essays
by Kenneth Abraham: "Three Fallacies of Interpretation: A Comment on
Precedent and Judicial Decision," 23 *Arizona Law Review* 771 (1981);
and "Statutory Interpretation and Literary Theory: Some Common Concerns
of an Unlikely Pair," 32 *Rutgers Law Review* 676 (1979).
22 Dworkin, supra note 1, at 542.
23 In its strengths and weaknesses Dworkin's present essay is at once like and
unlike his other writings. I find that in *Taking Rights Seriously* (1977),
Dworkin more than occasionally falls into a way of talking that reinstitutes
the positions against which he is arguing. As an example, I will consider
briefly some moments in the key essay "Hard Cases" (chapter 4 of *Taking
Rights Seriously*). At one point in that essay Dworkin begins a paragraph
by asserting that "institutional history acts not as a constraint on the political judgment of judges but as an ingredient of that judgment." Id. at 87.
The point is that what a judge decides is inseparable from his understanding of the history of past decisions, and it is a point well taken. It is, however, a point that is already being compromised in the second half of this
same sentence: "because institutional history is part of the background that

any plausible judgment about the rights of an individual must accommodate." Id. With the word "accommodate" what had been inseparable suddenly falls apart, for it suggests that rather than having his judgment informed by the history (in the sense that his ways of thinking are constrained by it) the judge takes an independent look at an independent history and decides (in a movement of perfect freedom) to accommodate it; it suggests, in short, that he could have chosen otherwise. The notion of choice, here only implied, is explicitly invoked later in the paragraph when Dworkin discusses the situation in which "a judge chooses between the rule established in precedent and some new rule thought to be fairer." Id. But in accordance with what principle is the choice to be made? Dworkin doesn't tell us, but clearly it is a principle that stands apart from either the body of precedent or the new rule (both of which have been reified), and apart too from the judge himself, who freely chooses to employ it as a way of reconciling two independent entities.

The movement in this paragraph is from an understanding of judgment in which the judge, the context of judgment, and the principles of judgment are mutually constitutive of an understanding in which each has its own identity and can only be integrated by invoking some neutral mechanism or calculus. Later Dworkin slides into the same (mis)understanding when he says of Hercules (his name for an imaginary, all-knowing judge) that in deciding between competing theories he "must turn to the remaining constitutional rules and settled practices under these rules to see which of these two theories provides a smoother fit with the constitutional scheme as a whole." Id. at 106. Here the difficulty (and sleight of hand) resides in the phrase "smoother fit." On what basis is the smoothness of fit determined? Again, Dworkin doesn't tell us, but an answer to the question could take only one of two forms. Either the rules and practices have their own self-evident shape and therefore themselves constrain what does or does not fit with them, or there is some abstract principle by which one can calculate the degree to which a given theory fits smoothly within "the constitutional scheme as a whole." But these alternatives are simply flip sides of the same positivism. If the shape of the constitutive parts is self-evident, then no independent principle is required to decide whether or not they fit together; and by the same reasoning an independent principle of fit will be able to do its job only if the shape of the constituent parts is self-evident. For as soon as the shape of the parts becomes a matter of dispute (as it would for judges who conceived the constitutional rules or the settled practices differently), the judgment of what fits with what will be in dispute as well. In short, the criteria of fitness is no less theoretical than the theories Dworkin would have it decide between, and by claiming an independence for it he once again compromises the coherence of his position.

In general, Dworkin's confusions have the same form: he argues against positivism, but then he has recourse to positivist notions. At one point he observes that Hercules' decision about a "community morality" will sometimes be controversial, especially when the issue concerns "some contested political concept, like fairness or liberality or equality," and the institutional history "is not sufficiently detailed so that it can be justified by only one among different conceptions of that concept." Id. at 127. The language is somewhat vague here, but it would seem that Dworkin is assuming the possibility of a history that *was* "sufficiently detailed": that is, a history so dense (a favorite word of his) that it was open to only one reading of the morality informing it. In relation to such a history Hercules would be in the position of the later novelists in Dworkin's imagined chain, constrained to "admit only one good-faith interpretation." But at that point Hercules would be doing what Dworkin himself says no judge can possibly do, mechanically reading off the meaning of a text that constrained its own interpretation.

I trust that I have said enough to support my contention that the errors I find in the present essay can also be found in Dworkin's earlier work. But I must also say that, at least in the case of "Hard Cases," those errors are less damaging. "Hard Cases" is primarily an argument against "classical theories of adjudication . . . which suppose that a judge follows statutes or precedent until the clear direction of these runs out, after which he is free to strike out on his own." Id. at 118. Dworkin's critique of these theories seems to me powerful and entirely persuasive, and, moreover, in its main lines it does not depend on the general account of interpretation that occasionally and (to my mind) disconcertingly surfaces. In "Law as Interpretation," on the other hand, Dworkin is concerned to elaborate that general account, and in that essay the incidental weaknesses of the earlier work become crucial and even fatal.

Wrong Again

1 Dworkin, "Law as Interpretation," 60 *Texas L. Rev.* 527, 531 (1982).
2 Id.
3 Id.
4 Id.
5 See id. at 532.
6 Id.
7 See id.
8 See Dworkin, "My Reply to Stanley Fish (and Walter Benn Michaels): Please Don't Talk about Objectivity Anymore," in *The Politics of Interpretation,* ed. W. Mitchell (1983), pp. 287, 288–89.
9 *The Living Milton,* ed. F. Kermode (1960), p. 174.
10 C. Ricks, *Milton's Grand Style* (1963).
11 See Dworkin, supra note 8, at 292, 304–6.
12 Dworkin, supra note 1, at 543–44.
13 See id. at 541.
14 Dworkin, supra note 8, at 304.
15 Id. My colleague Walter Dellinger notes that the American media have recently presented a knockdown counterexample to Dworkin's thesis. The

chain-novelists who are the producers of *Dallas,* he reminds me, simply declared that an entire year of script and context was a dream. So much for constraints. Another colleague, Edward Tayler, informs me that the reading of Hamlet as a man of forceful action was in fact for many years the standard reading before the reading Dworkin takes for granted was put into place by new arguments.

16 Id. at 305.
17 Id.
18 Dworkin, supra note 1, at 544.
19 Dworkin, supra note 8, at 306.
20 Id. at 305.
21 Id.
22 Id.
23 See Fish, "Working on the Chain Gang: Interpretation in Law and Literature" chapter 4, pp. 87, 100–102.
24 See Levinson, "Taking Law Seriously: Reflections on 'Thinking Like a Lawyer'" (Book Review), 30 *Stan. L. Rev.,* 1071, 1077, 1099 (1978).
25 Dworkin, supra note 8, at 308.
26 Id. at 307–8.
27 Id. at 307.
28 Id. at 308.
29 Id.
30 Dworkin, supra note 1, at 532.
31 In part, he makes such assumptions because the only alternative he can imagine is the one he mistakenly attributes to me—the "extravagant claim" that "any text allows any interpretation whatsoever." Dworkin, supra note 8, at 302. However extravagant, the claim is certainly not mine, and the reason I disown it is not because it is too obviously and wildly subjective, but because it is through and through positivist. It assumes, first, that there is a text, specifiable in some preinterpretive form, and, second, that someone might say of that text, independently identified, that "it" allows any interpretation whatsoever. Of course, in the position I do hold, as opposed to the position Dworkin *needs* to believe that I hold, the text, while always there, is always an interpreted object; and when the conditions of interpretation change, the text is not merely recharacterized but changed too. It makes no sense, therefore, either to affirm or deny the proposition that a text allows any interpretation whatsoever, because the text as an identity does not survive the sea of changes that a succession of interpretations brings. To be sure, this position gives rise to its own problems, including the problem of explaining the process by which one interpreted object gives way to another (the solution lies in the mechanisms of persuasion as they are operating in a profession at a given time), but it is not open to the objection of making this particular extravagant and absurd claim. The absurdity of the claim, of course, depends precisely on its positivist presupposition (that there is an uninterpreted text), and the fact that Dworkin attributes it to me is another indication of the hold positivism has on him,

despite his frequent protestations to the contrary. So strong is the hold that he can only imagine the position he opposes in a positivist form.

32 See supra text accompanying note 4.
33 Dworkin, supra note 8, at 289.
34 See id. at 289–97.
35 Id. at 292–93.
36 Id. at 292.
37 Fish, supra note 23, at 555.
38 Dworkin, supra note 8, at 289.
39 Id. at 292.
40 Id. at 296.
41 Id.
42 Id. at 297.
43 Id. at 289.
44 See Fish, *Is There a Text in This Class?* (1980).
45 See Dworkin, supra note 8, at 295.
46 Id. at 292.
47 Id. at 295.
48 Id. at 308.
49 Id. at 309.
50 Id. at 308.
51 Id. at 309.
52 Dworkin, supra note 1, at 539.
53 Id.
54 Dworkin, supra note 8, at 310.
55 Id. at 309.
56 See id. at 287.

Fish v. Fiss

1 Fiss, "Objectivity and Interpretation," 34 *Stan. L. Rev.* 739 (1982).
2 Id.
3 Id. at 744.
4 Not that I am accepting this characterization of reader and text; it is just that I am proceeding within the assumptions of Fiss's model so that I can more effectively challenge it in all its aspects.
5 I refer to the distinction, assumed by many historians, between a *text* as something that requires interpretation and a *document* as something that wears its meaning on its face and therefore can be used to stabilize the meaning of a text. My argument, of course, is that there is no such thing as a document in that sense.
6 Fiss, supra note 1, at 744.
7 Id.
8 Id. at 747.

9 Id.
10 Id.
11 Cf. Michaels, "Is There a Politics of Interpretation?," in *The Politics of Interpretation*, 337–39 (W. J. T. Mitchell, ed. 1983) (directing a similar argument at a thesis offered by Ronald Dworkin).
12 It is sometimes the strategy of those who have been forced to acknowledge that all facts are contextual to posit context itself as a new fact or set of facts that can serve as a constraint, but the perception of context is no less contextually determined than the facts that context determines in turn. See, e.g., Fish, "With the Compliments of the Author: Reflections on Austin and Derrida," chapter 2, pp. 37, 52–53.
13 The requirement of explicitness can, in the strong sense, never be met, since it is the requirement that a piece of language declare its own meaning and thus be impervious to the distorting work performed by interpreters. It is my contention that language is always apprehended within a set of interpretive assumptions, and that the form in which a sentence appears is always an interpreted or "read" form, which means that it can always be read again. For the full argument, see Fish, *Is There a Text in This Class?* 281–84 (1980); Fish, supra note 12, at 47–48.
14 T. S. Kuhn, *The Structure of Scientific Revolutions*, 46 (2d ed. 1970).
15 Id. at 191.
16 Id. at 47.
17 I make this point in a more extended way in Fish, "Working on the Chain Gang: Interpretation in Law and Literature," chapter 4.
18 Levinson, "Law as Literature," 60 *Tex. L. Rev.* 373, 392–402 (1982).
19 When I use phrases like "without reflection" and "immediately and obviously" I do not mean to preclude self-conscious deliberation on the part of situated agents; it is just that such deliberations always occur within ways of thinking that are themselves the ground of consciousness, not its object.
20 Fiss, supra note 1, at 762.
21 Fish, supra note 13, at 281–84.
22 Cf. Whitney v. California, 274 U.S. 357, 376 (1927) (Brandeis, J., concurring) ("Men feared witches and burnt women").
23 See, e.g., R. Berger, *Government by Judiciary* (1977).
24 See, e.g., J. H. Ely, *Democracy and Distrust* (1980).
25 See, e.g., L. Tribe, *American Constitutional Law* 452 (1978).
26 On this point see Fish, supra note 13, at 342–49, where a similar argument is made in relation to the practices of literary criticism.
27 Fiss, supra note 1, at 749.
28 Id.
29 Id.
30 Id. at 741.
31 Id. at 757.
32 Id. at 756.
33 Id.
34 Id. at 757.

35   Id.
36   This is a familiar distinction in the literature and is central to the argument of S. Toulmin, *Human Understanding* (1972). For a critique of that argument, see Fish, "Anti-Professionalism," chapter 11.
37   Fiss, supra note 1, at 754.
38   Id. at 759.
39   This may seem to be reinstating the distinction between inside and outside considerations, but any consideration that finds its way into the process of legal inquiry has been recharacterized as a legal consideration and has therefore become "inside."
40   Fiss, supra note 1, at 763.
41   On this point see Fish, supra note 17, at 92–96.
42   Fiss, supra note 1, at 763.
43   Id. at 746.
44   There is a large issue to be considered here, the issue of the consequences of theory in general. It is my position that theory has no consequences, at least on the level claimed for it by its practitioners. Rather than standing in a relationship of precedence and governance to practice, theory is (when it happens to be a feature of an enterprise) a form of practice whose consequences (if there are any) are unpredictable and no different in kind from the consequences of any form of practice. Both those who fear theory and those who identify it with salvation make the mistake of conceiving it as a special kind of activity, one that stands apart from the practices it would ground and direct. If there were a theory so special, it would have nothing to say to practice at all; and, on the other hand, a theory that does speak meaningfully to practice is simply an item in the landscape of practices. See Fish, "Consequences," chapter 14.
45   Fiss, supra note 1, at 750.

Change

1   Walter A. Davis, "The Fisher King: *Wille zur Macht* in Baltimore," in *Critical Inquiry* 10 (June 1984): 668–94.
2   Thomas Kuhn, *The Structure of Scientific Revolutions* (Chicago, 1962), 113.
3   Nelson Goodman, *Ways of Worldmaking* (Indianapolis, 1978), 2–3.
4   Richard Rorty, *Consequences of Pragmatism* (Minneapolis, 1982), xix.
5   Stanley Fish, *Is There a Text in This Class?* (Cambridge, Mass., 1980).
6   Harold Whitehall, "From Linguistics to Criticism," *Kenyon Review* 13 (1951): 713.
7   D. L. Weider, "Telling the Code," in *Ethnomethodology*, ed. Roy Turner (Baltimore, 1974), 161.
8   Ibid., 152.
9   Robert Nisbet, "Introduction: The Problem of Social Change," in *Social Change*, ed. Robert Nisbet (New York, 1972), 1.

10 Jonathan Culler, *On Deconstruction* (Ithaca, N.Y., 1982), 154.
11 *New Literary History* 14 (Spring 1983): 411, 434, 437.
12 Richard Rorty, "The Historiography of Philosophy: Four Genres," in *Philosophy in History,* ed. R. Rorty, J. B. Schneewind, and Quentin Skinner (Cambridge, Eng., 1984), 63.
13 Kuhn, *Structure of Scientific Revolutions,* 171.

No Bias, No Merit: The Case Against Blind Submission

1 William D. Schaefer, "Anonymous Review: A Report from the Executive Director," *MLA Newsletter* 10.2 (1978), p. 4.
2 "Correspondence," *MLA Newsletter* 10.3 (1978), p. 4.
3 Ibid., p. 5.
4 Ibid.
5 Schaefer, p. 5.
6 Raymond Waddington, "The Death of Adam: Vision and Voice in Books XI and XII of *Paradise Lost,*" *Modern Philology* 70 (1972): 9.
7 Schaefer, p. 5.
8 For the topic of professionalism, see B. J. Bledstein, *The Culture of Professionalism* (New York: Norton, 1977); Thomas L. Haskell, *The Emergence of Professional Social Science* (Urbana: University of Illinois Press, 1977); and M. S. Larson, *The Rise of Professionalism* (Berkeley: University of California Press, 1977).
9 John Crowe Ransom, *The World's Body* (Baton Rouge: Louisiana State University Press, 1938), p. 329.
10 Ibid., p. 327.
11 Ibid., p. 335.
12 Ibid., p. 343.
13 Ibid., p. 348.
14 Ibid., p. 343.
15 Ibid., p. 346.
16 D. P. Peters and S. J. Ceci, "Peer-review practices of psychological journals: The fate of published articles, submitted again," *The Behavioral and Brain Sciences: An International Journal of Current Research and Theory with Open Peer Commentary* 5 (1982): 187–255 (with commentary by R. K. Adair, et al.).
17 Ibid., p. 245.
18 Ibid., p. 253.
19 Ibid., p. 196.
20 Ibid., p. 211.
21 Ibid., p. 244.
22 Thomas Kuhn, *The Structure of Scientific Revolutions* (Chicago: University of Chicago Press, 1962), p. 153.
23 Jean Howard, "The New Historicism in Renaissance Studies," *English Literary Renaissance* 16 (1986): 25.

24   Louis Montrose, "Renaissance Literary Studies and the Subject of History," *English Literary Renaissance* 16 (1986): 11–12.

Short People Got No Reason to
Live: Reading Irony

1   *A Rhetoric of Irony* (Chicago and London, 1974), p. 3.
2   Ibid., pp. 5–6. All following (B—oo) quotes refer to this work.
3   Barry Slepian, "The Ironic Intention of Swift's Verses on His Own Death," *Review of English Studies* 14 (1963). All following (S—oo) quotes refer to this article.
4   John Middleton Murry, *Jonathan Swift: A Critical Biography* (London, 1954), p. 459.
5   Marshall Waingrow, *On Swift's Poetry* (Gainesville, Florida, 1978), p. 164. The following (W—oo) quote is from this work.
6   Maynard Mack, *Yale Review* 41 (1951): 83.
7   Robert Uphaus, "Swift's 'Whole Character': The Delaney Poems and 'Verses on the Death of Dr. Swift,'" *Modern Language Quarterly* 34 (1973): 403, 406. The following (U—oo) quote is from this article.
8   This also holds for stable and unstable irony, insofar as the terms mark a distinction between ironies that are decidable and ironies that are not. Both decidability and undecidability are, like irony and literalness, ways of reading. That is, neither exists in the pure form (one constraining interpretation, the other allowing interpretation free rein) that gives Booth's argument its apparent urgency. The distinction between stable and unstable ironies is a real one, but its reality is a function of the availability at a particular historical moment of certain modes of reading; it is thus a conventional distinction that corresponds to conventionally produced entities. As a distinction between essences, however, it cannot be maintained, because the conditions of pure rationality and total interpretive freedom for which its poles stand could never obtain. To put the matter in the form of what is only an apparent paradox: all ironies are stable, even those that point in multiple directions, in that the shape they have (or don't have) will follow from in-place interpretive assumptions; and all ironies are unstable, even those that are sharply pointed, in that they are the product of interpretive assumptions, of ways of reading, and not the property of texts.

Profession Despise Thyself: Fear and
Self-Loathing in Literary Studies

1   See Peter S. Jay, *Baltimore Sun,* September 5, 1982.
2   See Jonathan Yardley, *Washington Post,* November 8, 1982.
3   Richard Ohmann, *English in America: A Radical View of the Profession* (New York, 1976), p. 30.
4   W. Jackson Bate, "The Crisis in English Studies," *Harvard Magazine* 85

(September–October 1982): 49; all further references to this work will be included parenthetically in the text.

5   Donald A. Davie, "Poet: Patriot: Interpreter," *Critical Inquiry* 9 (September 1982): 43.
6   Ibid.
7   Magali Sarfatti Larson, *The Rise of Professionalism: A Sociological Analysis* (Berkeley, 1977), p. 13.
8   Edward W. Said, "Opponents, Audiences, Constituencies, and Community," *Critical Inquiry* 9 (September 1982): 17; all further references to this work will be included parenthetically in the text.

Anti-Professionalism

1   B. Bledstein, *The Culture of Professionalism* (1976).
2   Id. at 334.
3   Id. at 330.
4   M. S. Larson, *The Rise of Professionalism* (1977).
5   Id. at 15.
6   Introduction to *Becoming a Lawyer: A Humanistic Perspective on Legal Education and Professionalism* 2 (E. Dvorkin, J. Himmelstein, and H. Lesnick eds. 1981).
7   Id.
8   Id.
9   R. Levin, *New Readings vs. Old Plays* 196 (1979).
10 Bate, "The Crisis in English Studies," *Harvard Magazine,* September–October 1982, at 85; R. Ohmann, *English in America* (1976); Topf, "Specialization in Literary Criticism," 39 *College English* (1977); Crews, "Deconstructing a Discipline," *University Publishing,* Summer 1980. For a critique, see S. Fish, "Profession Despise Thyself: Fear and Self-Loathing in Literary Studies," chapter 10.
11 Crews, supra note 10, at 2.
12 Id.
13 E. D. Hirsch, *Aims of Interpretation* 155 (1976).
14 Id.
15 Id. at 153.
16 *The Works of Aristotle, Rhetorica* (W. D. Ross ed. 1924).
17 Id. at 1404.
18 E. D. Hirsch, supra note 13, at 152–53.
19 Id. at 152.
20 Id.
21 Id. at 153.
22 Id.
23 Id. at 90.
24 Id. at 13.
25 Id. at 154.
26 Id. at 13.

27   S. Toulmin, *Human Understanding* (1972).

28   Id. at 84.

29   Id. at 97.

30   Id. at 85.

31   Id.

32   Id. at 76.

33   Id.

34   Id. at 267.

35   Id. at 311.

36   Id. at 142.

37   Id. at 311.

38   Id. at 268.

39   Id. at 281, 309.

40   Id. at 117.

41   Id. at 272–73.

42   Id. at 280.

43   Of course, anti-professionalism's voice need not be shrill. All it requires is that there be a sharp distinction between the knowledge provided by professional communities or disciplines, and a better knowledge that would proceed from some acontextual and abiding source. This kind of anti-professionalism informs many of the essays in *The Authority of Experts* (T. Haskell ed. 1984). Haskell, for example, writes in his preface, "[w]hat shapes my belief is as much psychological and sociological as logical." Preface to id. at xi. Like Toulmin, he thinks that he is giving the psychological and the sociological their due, but again, like Toulmin, simply by assuming the distinction between the logical and the sociological, he grants the former a priority that implicitly reduces the status of the latter either to that of a helpmate or an enemy. Other essays in this volume make the same move with varying degrees of self-consciousness. For a particularly egregious example, see id. at 239–40, where Stephen Stitch and Richard Nisbett oppose the rational to the social, the personal, and the historical.

44   S. Toulmin, supra note 27, at 312.

45   Id.

46   Id. at 312–13.

47   Id. at 95.

48   Gordon, "New Developments in Legal Theory," in *The Politics of Law* (D. Kairys ed. 1982).

49   Id. at 284.

50   Kairys, Introduction, in *The Politics of Law* 3 (D. Kairys ed. 1982).

51   Gordon, supra note 48, at 289.

52   Id. at 287.

53   Id. at 288.

54   Id.

55   Id. at 289.

56   Id.

57   Id.

58 Kennedy, "Legal Education as Training for Hierarchy," in *The Politics of Law,* supra note 50, at 47.
59 Id.
60 Id. at 45.
61 Id. at 47 (emphasis added).
62 Gabel and Feinman, "Contract Law as Ideology," in *The Politics of Law,* supra note 50, at 173.
63 R. Ohmann, supra note 10.
64 Id. at 334.
65 Id. at 12.
66 Id. at 16.
67 Id. at 6.
68 Id. at 20.
69 Id.
70 Id. at 17.
71 Id. at 20 (emphasis omitted).
72 Id. at 22 (emphasis omitted).
73 Id. at 30.
74 Id. at 334.
75 J. Donne, "The Ecstasy," at line 76.
76 R. Ohmann, supra note 10, at 48.
77 Id. at 58.
78 Association of Departments of English, *Vacancies in College and University Departments of English for Fall 1971* (1971).
79 Id.
80 R. Ohmann, supra note 10, at 210.
81 Id.
82 Id. at 40.
83 Id. at 211.
84 Id. at 332.
85 Id. at 303.
86 T. Eagleton, *Literary Theory: An Introduction* (1983).
87 Id. at 201.
88 Id. at 205.
89 Id. at 197.
90 Id. at 204.
91 Id.
92 Id. at 201.
93 Id. at 204.
94 Id. at 201.
95 R. Ohmann, supra note 10, at 147.
96 T. Eagleton, supra note 86, at 213.
97 Id. at 214.
98 In what follows I am quoting from the GRIP Report, volume one, second draft (presented on May 6–8, 1983). The GRIP Report is not a publication, but a set of working papers circulated among those associated with the

Group for Research in the Institutionalization and Professionalization of Literary Studies ("GRIP"), sponsored by the Society for Critical Exchange, Inc., and headquartered at the English Department, University of Miami, Oxford, Ohio. The quotation is from Fanto, "Contesting Authority: The Marginal," in the GRIP Report, at 6. Pagination refers to the manuscript pages of individual essays.

99 Fanto, supra note 98, at 17.
100 Id.
101 Id. at 24.
102 Id.
103 Id. at 25.
104 D. Shumway, "Interdisciplinarity and Authority in American Studies," in the GRIP Report, supra note 98, at 16.
105 Id. at 13–14.
106 Id. at 16–17.
107 J. Sosnoski, "The *Magister Implicatus* As An Institutionalized Authority Figure," in the GRIP Report, supra note 98.
108 Id. at 5.
109 Id.
110 Id. at 10.
111 Id. at 12.
112 Id. at 14.
113 Id.
114 Id. at 18.
115 Id. at 53–54.
116 M. S. Larson, supra note 4, at 76.
117 Id. at 221–22 (footnote omitted).
118 Id. at 199.
119 Id. at 229.

Transmuting the Lump: *Paradise Lost*, 1942–1979

1 Raymond B. Waddington, "The Death of Adam: Vision and Voice in Books XI and XII of *Paradise Lost*," *Modern Philology*, 70 (1972): 9–21.
2 *Milton's Poetry: Its Development in Time* (Pittsburgh, Penn., 1979).
3 Quoted in John Shawcross, ed., *Milton: The Critical Heritage* (London, 1970), p. 216.
4 Quoted in C. A. Patrides, ed., *Milton's Epic Poetry* (Baltimore, 1967); from F. R. Leavis, *Revaluation: Tradition and Development in English Poetry* (London, 1936), pp. 42–58; first published in *Scrutiny* 2 (1933).
5 Douglas Bush, *"Paradise Lost" In Our Time* (Ithaca, N.Y., 1945), p. 8.
6 B. A. Wright, *Milton's "Paradise Lost"* (New York, 1962).
7 K. L. Sharma, *Milton Criticism in the Twentieth Century* (New Delhi, 1971), p. 6.
8 C. S. Lewis, *A Preface to "Paradise Lost"* (London, 1942), p. 130.
9 Sir Walter Raleigh, *Milton* (London, 1900).

10 E. N. S. Thompson, "For *Paradise Lost,* XI–XII," *Philological Quarterly* 22 (1943): 376–82.

11 Jonathan Richardson, *Explanatory Notes and Remarks on Milton's "Paradise Lost"* (London, 1734), p. 484.

12 B. A. Rajan, *"Paradise Lost" and the Seventeenth Century Reader* (London, 1947), p. 79.

13 "Milton and the New Criticism," *Sewanee Review* 59 (1951): 3.

14 *The Portable Poe,* ed. Philip Van Doren Stern (New York, 1945), p. 568.

15 Joseph Frank, "Spatial Form in Modern Literature," in Mark Shorer, Josephine Miles, and Gordon MacKenzie, eds., *Criticism: The Foundations of Modern Literary Judgment* (New York, 1948), pp. 379–92; first published in *Sewanee Review* 53 (1945).

16 Northrop Frye, *The Anatomy of Criticism* (Princeton, N.J., 1957), p. 140.

17 Northrop Frye, *The Well-Tempered Critic* (New York, 1963), p. 155.

18 Ernst Cassirer, *An Essay on Man* (New Haven, Conn., 1944), p. 81.

19 "The Archetypes of Literature," in David Lodge, ed., *Twentieth Century Literary Criticism* (London, 1972), p. 429; first published in *Kenyon Review* 13 (1951).

20 "Milton's Counterplot," in Arthur E. Barker, ed., *Milton: Modern Essays in Criticism* (Oxford, 1965), p. 388; first published in *English Literary History* 25 (1958).

21 "The Iconography of Renunciation: The Miltonic Simile," in *Critical Essays on Milton from ELH* (Baltimore, 1969); first published in *English Literary History* 25 (1958).

22 *"Paradise Lost" as Myth* (Cambridge, Mass., 1959).

23 Augustine, *On Christian Doctrine,* ed. and trans. D. W. Robertson (New York, 1958).

24 F. T. Prince, "On the Last Two Books of *Paradise Lost,"* in *Milton's Epic Poetry,* ed. C. A. Patrides (Baltimore, 1967); originally published in *Essays and Studies,* New Series, 11 (1958): 38–52. The paper was even more originally a lecture delivered in 1956.

25 J. B. Broadbent, *Some Graver Subject* (London, 1960), p. 283.

26 John E. Parish, "Milton and God's Curse on the Serpent," *Journal of English and Germanic Philology* 58 (1959): 241.

27 "Milton's Treatment of the Judgment and the Expulsion in *Paradise Lost,"* *Tulane Studies in English* 10 (1960): 77.

28 W. F. McNeir, *Studies in English Renaissance Literature,* in *Louisiana State University Studies: Humanities Series,* no. 12 (1962), 181–96.

29 "Structure and the Symbolism of Vision in Michael's Prophecy, *Paradise Lost* Books XI, XII," *Philological Quarterly* 42 (January 1963): 25.

30 In *Essays in English Literature from the Renaissance to the Victorian Age,* ed. M. MacLure and F. W. Watt (Toronto, 1964): 149–68.

31 "The Conclusion of *Paradise Lost*—A Reconsideration," *College English* 27 (1966): 389.

32 *"Paradise Lost:* The Hill of History," *Huntington Library Quarterly* 31 (1967–68): 43.

33   "Man as a Probationer of Immortality," in *Approaches to Paradise Lost,*
     ed. C. A. Patrides (London, 1968), p. 33.
34   *Literature and History: Theoretical Problems and Russian Case Histories,*
     ed. Gary Saul Morson (Stanford, 1986), 126.
35   "Religion and Ideology: A Political Reading of *Paradise Lost,*" in *Litera-
     ture, Politics and Theory,* ed. Francis Barker, Peter Hulme, Margaret Iver-
     sen, Diana Loxley (London and New York, 1986), 35.

Don't Know Much About the Middle Ages:
Posner on Law and Literature

1   Posner, "Law and Literature: A Relation Reargued," 72 *Virginia Law
     Review* 1351 (1986) [hereinafter cited by page number only].
2   P. 1351.
3   Pp. 1361–62.
4   P. 1362.
5   P. 1363.
6   P. 1364.
7   P. 1367.
8   P. 1364.
9   P. 1362.
10   P. 1360.
11   Pp. 1364–65.
12   P. 1365.
13   Id.
14   P. 1366.
15   Id.
16   P. 1369.
17   P. 1370.
18   Pp. 1370–71.
19   P. 1371.
20   P. 1376.
21   Id.
22   P. 1378.
23   P. 1376.
24   P. 1378.
25   P. 1376.
26   P. 1370 (citation omitted).
27   P. 1371.
28   The argument should surely be familiar to someone who has read cases in
     which the court begins by stating "The issue is, what is chicken?," see
     Frigaliment Importing Co. v. B.N.S. International Sales Corp., 190 F. Supp.
     116, 116 (S.D.N.Y. 1960); or finds that "I guarantee to give you a perfect
     hand" is obviously *not* a guarantee, see Hawkins v. McGee, 84 N.H. 114,
     146 A. 641 (1929); or declares that "a thing which is within the intention

of the makers of a statute is as much within the statute as if it were within the letter," see Riggs v. Palmer, 115 N.Y. 506, 22 N.E. 188, 189 (1889).

29   For literal meaning, see my "Normal Circumstances . . . and Other Special Cases," *Critical Inquiry* 4 (1978): 625–644; and J. Searle, "Literal Meaning," in *Expression and Meaning: Studies in the Theory of Speech Acts* 117 (1979).

30   P. 1351.

31   P. 1371.

32   S. Fish, *Is There a Text in This Class?* (1980), p. 327.

33   I have made this point before in response to Owen Fiss. See "Fish v. Fiss," chapter 6, pp. 120, 137–38.

34   For general discussion of changes in Western cultural understanding of the "literary," see T. Eagleton, *Literary Theory* (1983), pp. 1–53.

35   Pp. 1356–57.

36   P. 1373.

37   P. 1370.

38   P. 1373.

39   P. 1351.

40   P. 1360.

41   "Law as Literature," 60 *Texas Law Review* 1 (1982).

42   P. 1363 n. 45.

43   P. 1379.

44   P. 1357.

45   A. Bloom, *The Closing of the American Mind* (New York, 1987).

46   P. 1367. Again the point hinges on an awareness of historical context. It would have required a cognitive restructuring for Shakespeare and his contemporaries to have seen his plays as "literature," that is, as permanent and stable verbal objects. Rather, they would have regarded a play as something recreated in its every performance. The notion of the Shakespearian text as something sacred, fixed, and publishable is a product of Shakespeare studies. One might say that the decisive gesture is Ben Jonson's: He publishes his own plays in 1616 and therefore makes thinkable the subsequent publication in 1623 of the Shakespeare folio. Posner's mistake is to assume that notions like authorship, property, literature, and text are stable across time and are basic components of any literary culture. For an admirably concise summary, see Orgel, "The Authentic Shakespeare," 21 *Representations* 1 (1988); see also Orgel, "Prospero's Wife," 8 *Representations* 1 (1984); Foucault, "What Is an Author?," in *Textual Strategies* 141 (J. Harari ed. 1979) (discussing historical contingency of concepts of author and literary "work").

47   "What a Wonderful World" (L. Adler, W. Alpert, and S. Cooke) (song lyrics).

Consequences

1   See my *Is There a Text in This Class?: The Authority of Interpretive Communities* (Cambridge, Mass., 1980), p. 370. For a response to the "no consequences" claim, see Mary Louise Pratt, "Interpretive Strategies/Strategic Interpretations: On Anglo-American Reader Response Criticism," *Boundary 2* 11 (Fall–Winter 1982–83): 222.

2   E. D. Hirsch, Jr., *The Aims of Interpretation* (Chicago, 1976), p. 18. I should note here that while I agree in general with Steven Knapp and Walter Benn Michaels on what is and is not a theoretical enterprise, I think them mistaken in their choice of particular examples. Stylistics, narratology, and prosody are, it seems to me, paradigm instances of theory in the strong sense. As I have argued elsewhere (see *Is There a Text in This Class?* chapters 2 and 10), the entire project of stylistics is an effort to produce a taxonomy of observable formal features which can then be correlated in some mechanical or rule-governed way with a set of corresponding significances and/or effects. In short, if stylistics were ever to succeed (and I am certain that it will not), it would be an engine of interpretation, a method, a theory. One sure sign of a theoretical enterprise is the lengths its proponents will go in order to pursue it. It seems to me extremely unlikely that stylisticians would have built their formidable apparatuses and worked out their complex formulations only so as to be able to produce a new reading of James Joyce's "Eveline." The same goes for narratology and for prosody, at least in its transformational or Halle-Keyser version.

3   Hirsch, *The Aims of Interpretation,* p. 18.

4   Cicero *De inventione* 2. 11. 37; and see Raoul Berger, *Government by Judiciary: The Transformation of the Fourteenth Amendment* (Cambridge, Mass., 1977).

5   See John Lyons, *Noam Chomsky,* rev. ed. (New York, 1978), p. 37.

6   Jerrold J. Katz and Thomas G. Bever, "The Fall and Rise of Empiricism," in Bever, Katz, and D. Terrence Langendoen, *An Integrated Theory of Linguistic Ability* (New York, 1976), p. 12; all further references to this work, abbreviated "FRE," will be included in the text.

7   Noam Chomsky, *Aspects of the Theory of Syntax* (Cambridge, Mass., 1965), p. 3; all further references to this work, abbreviated *ATS,* will be included in the text.

8   In the jargon of the trade these are called "performance factors" and belong to the study of utterances as opposed to sentences: "Sentences are abstract objects which are not tied to a particular context, speaker, or time of utterance. Utterances, on the other hand, are datable events, tied to a particular speaker, occasion and context" (Neil Smith and Deirdre Wilson, *Modern Linguistics: The Results of Chomsky's Revolution* [Bloomington, Ind., 1979], p. 45). Utterances are ranked on a scale of "acceptability" according to the conditions—cultural and, therefore, variable—of their production; sentences, on the other hand, are ranked on a scale of grammaticality or well-formedness according to the invariant rules of a formal system. On

this point, see F. R. Palmer, *Semantics: A New Outline* (Cambridge, 1976), p. 8.

9   Judith Greene, *Psycholinguistics: Chomsky and Psychology* (Baltimore, 1972), p. 28.

10 That is, one must begin, as Smith and Wilson observe, by "separating linguistic from non-linguistic knowledge" (*Modern Linguistics,* p. 32), but it is precisely the possibility of that separation that is denied by the argument I am mounting here.

11 See my *Is There a Text in This Class?* pp. 281–92.

12 That is why the history of Chomskian linguistics is a history of counter-examples to what are offered as *the* rules: since rules have been extrapolated from an assumed (if unacknowledged) context, the descriptions they assign will not seem perspicuous to someone who is operating from within *another* assumed (if unacknowledged) context. Of course, any proposed alternative system of rules will be vulnerable to exactly the same challenge.

In a searching and rigorous critique of a draft of this paper, Joseph Graham objects that I misrepresent the Chomsky project in several respects. Echoing some of the arguments in Chomsky's *Rules and Representations* (Woodbridge Lectures, nos. 3, 11, 78 [New York, 1980]), Graham contends, among other things, that the notion of "theory" as it appears in my discussion of Chomsky is far too strong and does not correspond to any claims Chomsky actually makes; that I fail to distinguish between "universal grammar" as an innate biological constraint on the set of possible "core" grammars and one or more of those possible grammars; that I blur the crucial distinction, on which so much depends, between grammatical and pragmatic competence and, thereby, ask more of the grammar than it could ever deliver; and that no theoretical enterprise is "demonstrative" in the sense that I use the word, for all scientific inquiry proceeds on the basis of "abduction or inference to the best explanation." To this I would reply, first, that my account of the Chomsky project and its claims is derived from statements made by Chomsky and some of his more faithful followers and that even if, as Graham says, that theory has been modified and clarified in recent years, the euphoria with which it was received and promoted in its early stages shows that it was for many the basis of what I call foundationalist "theory hope." Moreover, some of the differences between Graham and me stem from the different and opposing traditions in which we stand—he in the tradition of cognitive psychology with its interest in innate properties and inaccessible mental operations, and I in the practice and convention-centered tradition that includes Ludwig Wittgenstein, W. V. Quine, Hilary Putnam, Richard Rorty, and Donald Davidson, in addition to Jacques Derrida, Michel Foucault, and other continental thinkers. Presumably, for example, Graham would hear with equanimity and even with approval Chomsky's suggestion that knowledge and certainty may have little or nothing to do with grounding, justification, reasons, habits, skill, induction, and learning, and everything to do with genetic mechanisms that have yet to be specified, while to my ears the same suggestion sounds counterintuitive and even uninteresting (see Chomsky, *Rules and Representations,* pp. 92–109, 134–36, and 234). To be sure, there is more to be said about these matters, and Graham promises to say them in a series of forthcoming essays, but for the time being I will stick with my present formulations.

13 Rorty, *Consequences of Pragmatism (Essays 1972–1980)* (Minneapolis, 1982), p. 162.

14 Keith Lehrer, *Knowledge* (Oxford, 1974), p. 17.

15 Israel Scheffler, *Science and Subjectivity* (Indianapolis, 1967), p. 19. For similar statements, see Hirsch, *The Aims of Interpretation,* pp. 152–55, and Owen M. Fiss, "Objectivity and Interpretation," *Stanford Law Review* 34 (April 1982): 763.

16 Thomas Grey, "Supplementing the Constitution"; unpublished paper, quoted with permission of the author.

17 Rorty, *Philosophy and the Mirror of Nature* (Princeton, N.J., 1979), p. 3.

18 This is the argument made by Stephen Mailloux in "Truth or Consequences: On Being Against Theory."

19 See Mailloux, pp. 765–66. Mailloux also asserts that theory is a form of practice, but we differ in our conclusions. He concludes that "theory does change practice" and cites as two examples the "theoretical assumptions" that "guide" Edward Said's "practical analyses of Orientalism" and the "New Critical proscriptions against the intentional and affective fallacies" which led critics to avoid "extrinsic approaches" and focus instead on "intrinsic elements in the literary text itself" (Mailloux, pp. 765, 764, 765). To take the second example first, the Wimsatt-Beardsley injunction against taking into account the intentions of the author or the responses of the reader is exactly parallel to the injunction in the legal institution against looking beyond the Constitution itself to supplemental contexts: both make the same impossible recommendations and give the same unfollowable advice. That is, one may *say* "Consider only the text and not its extrinsic circumstances or the accident of its variable effects," but in fact any text one considers will will have come into view only against the contextual—including intentional and affective—circumstances that are supposedly being excluded or bracketed. In short, someone may well think that he is adhering to Wimsatt and Beardsley's theoretical strictures, but the truth is that he could not possibly do so. What he can do is present his argument in terms that make no mention of intention or affect; although that will certainly be a consequence of the pressure exerted by Wimsatt and Beardsley's pronouncements, it will not be a consequence of their theory in the sense of being answerable to its claims and hopes. One cannot, as I have said above, attribute consequences of a theoretical kind to a program that cannot be executed.

The example of Said and *Orientalism* can be assimilated to the discussion of the two legislators who are committed respectively to libertarian and utilitarian principles. It is certainly the case, as Mailloux asserts, that Said's assumptions guide his practice, but assumptions aren't theories, that is, they are not systematic procedures for generating valid conclusions—they are the *assertion* of conclusions which, when put to work as an interpretive "window," will generate or validate themselves. Said's assumption—or conviction, or belief—is that Western discourse, including diplomatic and academic as well as fictional texts, has projected an image of the Orient that has, for all intents and purposes, become its reality. Armed with this assumption, indeed operating as an extension of it, Said proceeds to redescribe texts as instances of a colonialism that does not know itself and is therefore even more powerful and insidious in its effects. But in producing these redescriptions, Said is not consulting a theory but extending a belief: when he urges his redescriptions on others, he is saying "Try on this belief; make it, rather than some other assumption, the content of your perception, and see what you see." It is a recommendation no more theoretical than a recommendation to think of the prefaces to Renaissance plays as part of the texts they introduce; either recommendation, if it is persuasive, will certainly alter practice but only because it will be a *practical* (not theoretical) recommendation, a recommendation to look at it this way rather than that way. To return to a formula used above, the Said example is an instance of something that has consequences but isn't a theory, and the Wimsatt-Beardsley example is an instance of something that is a theory and has consequences but not theoretical ones.

20 For a review and a discussion, see James A. Thomson, "An Endless but Productive Dialogue: Some Reflections on Efforts to Legitimize Judicial Review," *Texas Law Review* 61 (December 1982): 743–64.
21 Ibid., p. 745.

Anti-Foundationalism, Theory Hope, and the Teaching of Composition

1 Noam Chomsky, *Aspects of the Theory of Syntax* (Cambridge: Harvard University Press, 1965), pp. 8, 4.
2 Patricia Bizzel, "Cognition, Convention, and Certainty: What We Need to Know about Writing," *Pretext* 3, no. 3 (1982), p. 215.
3 Richard Lanham, "One, Two, Three," in *Composition and Literature,* ed. W. B. Horner (Chicago: University of Chicago Press, 1983), p. 21.
4 Robert Scholes, *Textual Power: Literary Theory and the Teaching of English* (New Haven: Yale University Press, 1985), p. 132.
5 Ibid., p. 133.
6 Israel Scheffler, *Science and Subjectivity* (Indianapolis: Bobbs-Merrill, 1967), p. 19.
7 Maxine Hairston, "The Winds of Change: Thomas Kuhn and the Revolution in the Teaching of Writing," *College Composition and Communication* 33, no. 1 (February 1982), p. 78.
8 Jacques Derrida, *Of Grammatology* (Baltimore: Johns Hopkins University Press, 1976), p. 9.
9 Kenneth Bruffee, "Liberal Education and the Social Justification of Belief," *Liberal Education* 68, no. 2 (1982), p. 108.
10 Ibid., pp. 108–9.

11   Bizzel, p. 234.
12   Scholes, p. 133.
13   Bizzel, p. 218.
14   E. D. Hirsch, "Reading, Writing, and Cultural Literacy," in *Composition and Literature,* ed. W. B. Horner (Chicago: University of Chicago Press, 1983), p. 145.
15   James A. Reither, "Some Ideas of Michael Polanyi and Some Implications for Teaching Writing," *Pretext* 2 (1981): 38–39.
16   J. Hillis Miller, "Composition and Decomposition: Deconstruction and the Teaching of Writing," in *Composition and Literature,* ed. W. B. Horner (Chicago: University of Chicago Press, 1983), p. 55.
17   Scholes, p. 133.

Still Wrong After All These Years

1   S. Fish, "Working On The Chain Gang," Chapter 4, pp. 93–94.
2   Dworkin, "The Forum of Principle," in *A Matter of Principle* (Cambridge, Mass., 1985), p. 71. Curiously enough, Dworkin reaches this conclusion at the end of a section that begins by declaring—correctly in my view—that "the flight from substance must end in substance" (69). By this very declaration there could not be anything like the forum of principle he then invokes.
3   This essay originally appeared in a special issue of *Law and Philosophy* (vol. 6, no. 3, December, 1987, 401–18). The issue was edited by Jules Coleman and was devoted to the work of Ronald Dworkin. Some of my points are compatible with those made by the other contributors. John Finnis is right on the mark, I think, when he observes that Dworkin's thought continues to exhibit the salient characteristic of liberalism: "it portrays justified politics, and thus law, as neutral about what is truly worthwhile in human life" (378). At the bottom of Dworkin's most complicated arguments one will always find this (doomed) search for a neutral calculus. I also find myself in substantial agreement with Gerald J. Postema's essay, "'Protestant' Interpretation And Social Practices." Postema substitutes for Dworkin's forum of principle in which the rule of integrity works itself out "the world of . . . practice common to its participants" (313). "To learn a social practice," he says, "is to become acquainted through participation with a new common world; it is to enter a world already constituted. One does not bring an understanding (let alone a theory) to the practice; rather, through participation one comes to grasp, tentatively and uncertainly at first, then more securely, then critically, the common meaning of the practice" (313). This is essentially what I intend by the notion of "interpretive community" as elaborated previously in my work. An interpretive community (to use Postema's words) "takes the form of a shared discipline and a thick continuity of experience of the common world of the practice" (318–19).

Dennis Martinez and the Uses of Theory

1 Berkow, "The Old and New Manager," *New York Times,* June 26, 1985, at B13, col. 1.

2 In saying this I am arguing as I often do against the availability of a literal level of language. Meaning is always a function of the interpretive condition of production and reception and never a function of formal linguistic structures. The case against theory and the case against formalism are one and the same. See S. Fish, *Is There a Text in This Class?* (1980), pp. 225–84.

3 At this point, someone might raise what I call the "Charley Lau Objection." Lau, now deceased, was a renowned batting coach who regularly turned .260 hitters into .300 hitters and whose "theories" were widely quoted and praised. How does one explain his success if not by reference to the theory with which he apparently taught so many? Of course, I was not myself privy to the Lau experience, but I am sure that part of that experience involved Lau regularly repeating pieces of his theory to his students. I would contend, however, that such repetition served less as instructions one was to follow than as reminders that something wasn't being done "just right." I would also contend that knowledge of that something was not *produced* by Lau's theory; nor could it be recovered by invoking the theory. Rather the theory operates as a verbal place-marker for a knowledge that develops in the context of a trial-and-error attempt to match an example (e.g., Ted Williams's swing). In other words, the articulation of the theory refers to knowledge acquired independently of it, and it serves as a mnemonic and exhortative device. Listening to theory talk may be a part of the experience of becoming a practitioner but not because theory talk would in any strong sense be generating the practice. See Fish, "Fish v. Fiss," Chapter 6, pp. 120, 123–25.

4 Schön, "Generative Metaphor: A Perspective on Problem-Setting in Social Policy," in *Metaphor and Thought* 254 (A. Ortony ed. 1979).

5 Id. at 257.

6 Id. at 258.

7 Id. at 260.

8 Id. at 259.

9 Id. at 260.

10 Id.

11 Id.

12 Id.

13 This argument, in its broader contours and with slight variations, is traced in Fish, "Consequences," Chapter 14; Knapp and Michaels, "A Reply to Richard Rorty: What is Pragmatism?", 11 *Critical Inquiry* 466 (1985); Knapp and Michaels, "Against Theory," 8 *Critical Inquiry* 732 (1982); and Michaels, "Response to Perry and Simon," 58 *S. Cal. L. Rev.* 673 (1985). Some of these essays are collected in *Against Theory* (W. J. T. Mitchell ed. 1985).

14   This argument is further developed in Fish, supra note 13 at 325–26.
15   See id. at 325 (distinguishing "empirical generalizations" from "theory").
16   Moore, "A Natural Law Theory of Interpretation," 58 *S. Cal. L. Rev.* 277, 283 (1985).
17   R. Dworkin, *Law's Empire* 79 (1986).
18   Unger, "The Critical Legal Studies Movement," 96 *Harv. L. Rev.* 561, 570 (1983).
19   Id.
20   R. Dworkin, supra note 17, at 245.
21   I use right, center, and left to denote places in the intellectual rather than political landscape. It may be the case that in some instances a person's place on the intellectual and political continuums will overlap.
22   For other accounts of judging premised on the belief that theory has consequences, see P. Brest and S. Levinson, *Processes of Contitutional Decision-making* (2nd ed. 1983); R. Wasserstrom, *The Judicial Decision* (1961). These questions continue to be debated. See, e.g., "Colloquy: Does Constitutional Theory Matter?" 65 *Tex. L. Rev.* 766 (1987).
23   Moore, supra note 16.
24   For another application of this analysis, see Fish, supra note 13, at 328–31 (discussing Thomas Grey's argument that theories of constitutional interpretation have consequences for judicial process).
25   Moore, supra note 16, at 287.
26   Id. at 294.
27   See Fish, supra note 13, at 326–27.
28   Moore, supra note 16, at 310. Moore's distinction between beliefs and those of "daily living" is familiar to modern and contemporary philosophy. See D. Hume, *A Treatise of Human Nature* 267–69 (L. Selby-Bigge rev. ed. 1975); Clark, "The Legacy of Skepticism," 69 *J. Phil.* 754 (1972) (distinguishing "plain" from "philosophical" ways of interpreting statements).

Moore makes this point in the context of a familiar anti-foundationalist argument. A conventionalist, he says, cannot coherently and seriously assert the truth of his conventionalist views for to do so would be to assume the very foundationalist stance he is denying. He therefore faces a dilemma: either he asserts his anti-foundationalism strongly and thereby contradicts it (by claiming that something—anti-foundationalism—is foundationally the case) or he clings to his anti-foundationalism and thereby forfeits his claim on our attention (we cannot take anything he says seriously). Moore, supra note 16, at 310–11. The dilemma does not exist. The thesis of anti-foundationalism is not that there are no foundations, but that whatever is taken to be foundational has to be established in the course or argument and debate and does not exist to the side of argument and debate. This thesis includes itself within its own scope, not in any self-contradictory sense, but in the sense that it too must make its way in the face of counterexamples and purportedly "irrefutable" evidence. To put it another way, the assertion that everything is in principle challengeable does not in and of itself constitute a challenge to any assertion. See S. Fish, supra note 2, at 368–70.

29 R. Dworkin, "Hard Cases," in *Taking Rights Seriously* 81, 112 (1977) [hereinafter R. Dworkin, "Hard Cases"].

30 Id. at 88.

31 Id. at 87.

32 Id.

33 Id.

34 R. Dworkin, supra note 17, at 90.

35 Id.

36 R. Dworkin, "Hard Cases," supra note 29, at 109.

37 Dworkin's argument here derives from a venerable tradition (at least as venerable as the Socratic maxim that the unexamined life is not worth living) in which the highest of mental activities involves a self-conscious reflection on one's beliefs and assumptions. It is my thesis that since reflection so defined requires a space free of one's own beliefs and assumptions it is not a possible achievement, and that to the extent that philosophy thinks of that achievement as its goal it will necessarily fail. See Fish, "Critical Self-Consciousness, or Can We Know What We're Doing?," chapter 19.

38 See Fish, "Anti-Professionalism," chapter 11, pp. 215, 243–46 [hereinafter Fish, "Anti-Professionalism"]; "Fish v. Fiss," note 3, at 120–26; and Fish, "Wrong Again," chapter 5, pp. 103, 113–16 [hereinafter Fish, "Wrong Again"].

39 R. Dworkin, "The Model of Rules I," in *Taking Rights Seriously,* supra note 29, at 14.

40 Id. at 40.

41 See R. Dworkin, "How Law Is Like Literature," in *A Matter of Principle* 146, 159 (1985); Dworkin, "My Reply to Stanley Fish (and Walter Benn Michaels): Please Don't Talk About Objectivity Any More," in *The Politics of Interpretation* (W. J. T. Mitchell ed. 1983). For my responses, see Fish, "Working on the Chain Gang," chapter 4; and Fish, "Wrong Again," chapter 5.

42 R. Dworkin, supra note 41, at 159.

43 As Thompson Clark shows, theories which seek to answer "philosophical" questions about what is "really" legitimate (or true, or known) undercut themselves. They demand answers that are entirely detached from practical constraints; and yet it is only from within a constrained practice that asking the questions makes any sense. Clark, supra note 28, at 765.

44 R. Dworkin, "Hard Cases," supra note 29, at 87.

45 Id.

46 R. Dworkin, supra note 17, at 256.

47 Here then is a "consequence" of theory, not however of theory as a blueprint or script for practice, but of theory as an institutional phenomenon that has become so widespread that everyone feels obligated to lard his discourse with theory talk, just as in other contexts practitioners might

feel obligated to lard their discourses with sports talk, or computer talk, or biofeedback talk, or war talk, etc. In short, the consequences of theory are real, but they are political.

48 Of course, one could imagine circumstances in which deciding and telling the story of the decision are simultaneous, not temporally distinct activities. That is, the decisionmaking process may well be one in which a judge "makes up his mind" (a phrase that might be taken literally) by reminding himself of the available forms of argument, and at some point a judge might well say to himself, "I can't go in this direction, because I don't see how I could back it up." Thus, self-presentation (to oneself) might be as much a part of the decisionmaking process as of the presentation of the decision to others. If this were so, the claims of theory would not thereby be revived; rather the claims of rhetoric would be extended, since not only the strategies of self-presentation, but the self that does the presenting would be rhetorically produced.

49 R. Dworkin, "Hard Cases," supra note 29, at 119.

50 Id.

51 R. Dworkin, "Hard Cases," supra note 29, at 16.

52 See Fish, supra note 3, at 138–40 (one need not defend against nihilistic arguments by asserting existence of external constraints "because the necessary constraints are always already in place").

53 33 *Stan. L. Rev.* 591 (1981).

54 Id. at 592.

55 Id.

56 Id.

57 Id. at 592–93.

58 Id. at 672.

59 See Fish, "Wrong Again," supra note 38, at 113–16.

60 Duncan Kennedy and Robert Gordon make this same error. See Fish, "Anti-Professionalism," supra note 38, at 225–31. I call this error, "anti-foundationalist theory hope," the hope that because we now know that our foundations are interpretive rather than natural (given by God or nature), we will regard them with suspicion and shake ourselves loose from their influence. But any such hope rests on the possibility of surveying our interpretive foundations from a vantage point that was not itself interpretive; and the *im*possibility of doing that is the first tenet of anti-foundationalist thought. It follows then that anti-foundationalist thought cannot have the consequences that many hope that it will have, which is to say no more than that anti-foundationalism cannot itself (without contradiction) be made into a foundation. See Fish, supra note 13, at 323–24.

61 Kelman, supra note 53, at 672.

62 This is not entirely true. Readers of Kelman's article might well learn something useful from it. They might learn, for example, how to recharacterize a situation in a way that lessens the responsibility of a client or how to redefine an action so that a client's part in it is detached from any criminal consequences. If it were read in that spirit rather than as a serious call

for the reform of our epistemological practice, the article would take on the dimensions of a rhetorical handbook not unlike those produced by Cicero and other early legal rhetoricians. The classical manuals typically open with two pieces of practical advice. Argue that your client didn't do it; and if that doesn't work, argue that it wasn't a crime. This is the lesson that Kelman teaches even as he laments its effectiveness.

63 P. Goodrich, *Reading the Law* 209 (1986).
64 Kelman, supra note 53, at 611.
65 Id. at 597.
66 Unger, supra note 18, at 572–73.
67 See Clark, supra note 28, at 760.

Unger and Milton

1   Roberto Unger, *Knowledge and Politics* (Boston, 1975), p. 30.
2   John Milton, "Areopagitica," in *Milton's Prose,* ed. J. Max Patrick, et al. (New York, 1968), p. 297.
3   Milton, "The Christian Doctrine," Book I, chapter xxvii.
4   Milton, "Areopagitica," in *Milton's Prose,* pp. 311–12.
5   Ibid., p. 314.
6   Ibid., p. 316.
7   Ibid., p. 310.
8   Ibid., p. 316.
9   Ibid., p. 330.
10 Ibid., p. 322.
11 Ibid., p. 339.
12 Ibid., p. 321.
13 Ibid., p. 288.
14 Ibid., p. 317.
15 Ibid., p. 322.
16 Unger, *Knowledge and Politics,* p. 3.
17 Ibid., p. 32.
18 Ibid., p. 31.
19 Ibid., p. 32.
20 Ibid., p. 33.
21 Ibid.
22 Ibid., p. 42.
23 Ibid., p. 44.
24 Ibid., p. 45.
25 Ibid., p. 53.
26 Ibid., p. 51.
27 Ibid., p. 53.
28 Ibid.
29 Ibid., p. 55.
30 Ibid., p. 60.
31 Ibid., pp. 137–39.

32 Ibid., p. 140.
33 Ibid., p. 139.
34 Ibid., p. 141.
35 Ibid., p. 141.
36 Ibid., p. 143.
37 Ibid.
38 Ibid.
39 Ibid., p. 195.
40 Ibid., p. 204.
41 Ibid., p. 246.
42 Ibid., p. 217.
43 Ibid.
44 Ibid., p. 218.
45 Ibid., p. 224.
46 Ibid., p. 220.
47 Ibid.
48 Ibid., p. 25.
49 Ibid., p. 235.
50 Ibid., p. 223.
51 Ibid., p. 237.
52 Ibid., p. 236.
53 Ibid., p. 237.
54 Ibid., pp. 266–67.
55 Ibid., p. 266.
56 Ibid., p. 267.
57 Ibid.
58 Ibid., p. 236.
59 Ibid., p. 230.
60 Ibid., p. 268.
61 Ibid., p. 269.
62 Ibid.
63 Ibid.
64 Ibid., p. 274.
65 Ibid., p. 226.
66 Ibid., p. 233.
67 Ibid., p. 260.
68 Ibid., p. 293.
69 Ibid., p. 291.
70 Ibid., p. 260.
71 Ibid., p. 293.
72 Ibid.
73 Ibid., p. 295.
74 Milton, "Areopagitica," in *Milton's Prose,* pp. 316–17.
75 Roberto Unger, "The Critical Legal Studies Movement," *Harvard Law Review* 96 (1983): 563.
76 Ibid., p. 564.

77   Ibid., p. 568.
78   Ibid., p. 565.
79   Ibid., p. 576.
80   Ibid.
81   Ibid.
82   Ibid., p. 565.
83   Ibid., p. 572.
84   Ibid.
85   Ibid., p. 566.
86   Ibid., p. 569.
87   Ibid., p. 573.
88   Ibid., p. 577.
89   Ibid., pp. 577–78.
90   Ibid., p. 578.
91   Ibid.
92   Ibid., p. 584.
93   Ibid., p. 583.
94   Unger, *Knowledge and Politics,* p. 267.
95   Unger, "The Critical Legal Studies Movement," p. 580.
96   Ibid., p. 579.
97   Ibid., p. 661.
98   Ibid., p. 585.
99   Ibid.
100 Ibid.
101 Ibid., p. 592.
102 Ibid., p. 586.
103 Ibid., p. 650.
104 Ibid., p. 607.
105 Ibid., p. 650.
106 Ibid., p. 589.
107 Ibid., p. 587.
108 Ibid., p. 588.
109 Ibid., p. 583.
110 Ibid., p. 587.
111 Ibid., p. 585.
112 Ibid., p. 612.
113 Ibid., p. 650.
114 Ibid.
115 December 28, 1817, to "My Dear Brothers."
116 Unger, "The Critical Legal Studies Movement," p. 580.
117 Ibid., p. 650.
118 Ibid., p. 582.
119 Ibid., p. 650.
120 Ibid., p. 675.
121 Ibid., p. 674.
122 Ibid., p. 566.

123   Ibid., p. 570.
124   Unger, *Knowledge and Politics,* p. 45.
125   Unger, "The Critical Legal Studies Movement," p. 572–73.
126   Ibid., p. 570.
127   Ibid., p. 572.
128   Unger, *Knowledge and Politics,* p. 294.

Critical Self-Consciousness, Or Can We Know What We're Doing?

1   Stephen Toulmin, "The Construal of Reality," in *Critical Inquiry,* vol. 9, no. 1 (September 1982): 95.
2   Stephen Toulmin, *Human Understanding* (Princeton, 1972), p. 95.
3   Wayne Booth, *A Rhetoric of Irony* (Chicago, 1975), p. 226.
4   Owen Fiss, "Conventionalism," in *University of Southern California Law Review* 58 (1985): 197.
5   E. D. Hirsch, *The Aims of Interpretation* (Chicago, 1976), p. 149.
6   Herbert Marcuse, "A Note on Dialectic," in *The Essential Frankfurt School Reader,* ed. Andrew Arato and Eike Gebhardt (New York, 1982), p. 447.
7   Jürgen Habermas, *Toward a Rational Society* (Boston, 1970), p. 82.
8   Herbert Marcuse, "On Science and Phenomenology," in *The Essential Frankfurt School Reader,* p. 470.
9   Theodor W. Adorno, "The Sociology of Knowledge and Its Consciousness," in *The Essential Frankfurt School Reader,* p. 465.
10   Max Horkheimer, "Traditional and Critical Theory," in *Critical Theory,* trans. Matthew O'Connell et al. (New York, 1972), p. 207.
11   Jürgen Habermas, *Knowledge and Human Interests* (Boston, 1971), p. 212.
12   Ibid., p. 18.
13   Horkheimer, "Traditional and Critical Theory," p. 220.
14   Habermas, *Knowledge and Human Interests,* p. 314.
15   Ibid., p. 208.
16   Henning Ottman, "Cognitive Interests and Self-Reflection," in *Habermas: Critical Debates,* ed. J. B. Thompson and David Held (Cambridge, Mass., 1982), p. 80.
17   Herbert Marcuse, "A Note on Dialectic," in *The Essential Frankfurt School Reader,* p. 448.
18   David Held, *Introduction to Critical Theory* (Berkeley and Los Angeles, 1980), p. 81.
19   Ibid., p. 83.
20   Horkheimer, *Critical Theory,* p. 279.
21   Jürgen Habermas, *Knowledge and Human Interests,* p. 314.
22   Marcuse, "A Note on Dialectic," in *The Essential Frankfurt School Reader,* p. 449.
23   Jürgen Habermas, "What Is Universal Pragmatics?," in *Communication and the Evolution of Society,* trans. Thomas McCarthy (Boston, 1976), p. 2.

24   Habermas, *Knowledge and Human Interests,* p. 314.
25   Habermas, "What Is Universal Pragmatics?," p. 3.
26   Jürgen Habermas, *Legitimation Crisis* (Boston, 1975), pp. 107–8.
27   Jürgen Habermas, *Zur Logik der Sozialwissenschafter* (Frankfurt, 1970), p. 220.
28   Habermas, *Knowledge and Human Interests,* p. 314.
29   Thomas McCarthy, *The Critical Theory of Jurgen Habermas* (Cambridge, Mass., 1978), p. 193.
30   Theodor Adorno, *Negative Dialectics* (New York, 1973), p. 149.
31   Roberto Unger, *Passion* (New York and London, 1984), p. 10.
32   Roberto Unger, "The Critical Legal Studies Movement," *Harvard Law Review* 96 (1983): 583.
33   Brian Fay, *Critical Social Science* (Ithaca, N.Y., 1987), p. 203.

Rhetoric

1   *Gorgias,* ed. and trans. W. C. Helmbold (Indianapolis, 1952), p. 18.
2   Plato, *Phaedrus,* ed. and trans. W. C. Helmbold and W. G. Rabinowitz (Indianapolis, 1956), p. 46.
3   *The Works of Aristotle,* vol. 11, ed. and trans. W. Rhys Roberts (Oxford, 1946).
4   See A. C. Howell, "*Res et Verba:* Words and Things," in *Seventeenth Century Prose: Modern Essays and Criticism,* ed. S. Fish (Oxford, 1971).
5   Thomas Kuhn, *The Structure of Scientific Revolutions* (Chicago, 1962), p. 125.
6   See Andrew Lange, *The Artificial Language Movement* (Oxford, New York, and London, 1985).
7   Jürgen Habermas, *Legitimation Crisis* (Boston, 1975), p. 108.
8   This is the language of H. L. A. Hart's *The Concept of Law* (Oxford, 1961).
9   John Milton, "Areopagitica," in *Milton's Prose,* ed. J. Max Patrick et al. (New York, 1968), p. 297.
10   Rudolf Carnap, "The Elimination of Metaphysics," in *Logical Positivism,* ed. A. J. Ayer (Glenco, Ill., 1959), p. 63.
11   See on this point George Kennedy, *The Art of Persuasion in Greece* (Princeton, N.J., 1963), p. 23.
12   See John Milton, "Reason of Church Government," in *The Complete Prose Works of John Milton,* ed. D. M. Wolfe et al., vol. 1 (New Haven, Conn., 1953), pp. 817–18.
13   *Rhetoric* (London, 1971), p. 14.
14   *Die Fragmente der Vorsokratiker,* ed. H. Diels and W. Kranz (Berlin, 1960), 371:80, B4.
15   William K. Guthrie, *The Sophists* (Cambridge, 1971), p. 193.
16   Ibid., p. 186.
17   Ibid., p. 187.
18   Ibid., p. 51.

19 Isocrates, "Antidosis," in *Isocrates,* vol. 2, ed. and trans. George Norlin (Cambridge: Harvard University Press, 1962), pp. 275, 277.

20 Cicero, "De Inventione," in *Cicero,* vol. 2, ed. and trans. H. M. Hubbell (Cambridge: Harvard University Press, 1968), I, 2.

21 See, for example, John Lawson, *Lectures Concerning Oratory,* ed. E. N. Claussen and K. R. Wallace (Carbondale and Edwardsville: Southern Illinois University Press, 1972), p. 27.

22 *The Motives of Eloquence* (New Haven, Conn., 1976), p. 1.

23 See Thomas Sloane, *Donne, Milton, and the End of Humanist Rhetoric* Berkeley, Los Angeles, and London, 1985), p. 87: "Rhetoric succeeded in humanism's great desideratum, the artistic creation of adept personhood." See also Stephen Greenblatt, *Renaissance Self-Fashioning* (Chicago, 1980).

24 Nancy Streuver, *The Language of History in the Renaissance* (Princeton, N.J., 1970), pp. 15, 12.

25 Lanham, *Motives,* p. 28.

26 *Science and Subjectivity* (Indianapolis, 1967), p. 19.

27 Jacques Derrida, "Signature Event Context," *Glyph* 1 (1977): 190.

28 Ibid.

29 Jacques Derrida, *Positions* (Chicago: University of Chicago Press, 1981), p. 6.

30 Jonathan Culler, *On Deconstruction* (Ithaca, N.Y., 1982), p. 86.

31 *Allegories of Reading* (New Haven, Conn., 1979), p. 249.

32 William Ray, *Literary Meaning* (Oxford, 1984), p. 195.

33 *After the New Criticism* (Chicago, 1980), pp. 310, 317.

34 *Walter Benjamin or Towards a Revolutionary Criticism* (London, 1981), p. 108.

35 Ibid., p. 104.

36 Ibid., p. 112.

37 Ibid., p. 113.

38 Ibid.

39 *Literary Theory* (Minneapolis, 1983), p. 211.

40 *The Politics of Law* (New York, 1983), p. 287.

41 "The Critical Legal Studies Movement," *Harvard Law Review* 96 (1983): 580.

42 *Legitimation Crisis* (Boston, 1975), pp. 107–8.

43 *Communication and the Evolution of Society* (Boston, 1979), p. 2.

44 *The Political Unconscious* (Ithaca, 1981), p. 35.

45 "Blurred Genres: The Refiguration of Social Thought," *The American Scholar* 49 (Spring 1980).

46 *Consequences of Pragmatism* (Minneapolis, 1982), p. 92.

Force

1 *The Concept of Law* (Oxford, 1962), p. 6.

2 H. L. A. Hart, "Positivism and the Separation of Law and Morals," *Harvard Law Review* 71 (1957–58): 607.

3   Ronald Dworkin, "Hard Cases," in *Taking Rights Seriously* (Cambridge, 1977), p. 88.
4   Richard Rorty, *Consequences of Pragmatism* (Minneapolis, 1982), p. 151.
5   Wayne Booth, *A Rhetoric of Irony* (Chicago and London, 1974), p. 195.
6   E. D. Hirsch, *The Aims of Interpretation* (Chicago, 1976), p. 154.
7   Stephen Toulmin, "The Construal of Reality," in *The Politics of Interpretation*, ed. W. J. T. Mitchell (Chicago, 1982), p. 107.
8   W. Booth, *A Rhetoric of Irony*, p. 226.
9   Terry Eagleton, "Ineluctable Opinions," in *The Politics of Interpretation*, ed. W. J. T. Mitchell (Chicago, 1982), p. 376.
10 See Ronald Dworkin, *Taking Rights Seriously* (Cambridge, Mass., 1977); and Dworkin, *Law's Empire* (London, 1986).
11 This essay was completed before the appearance of Robert N. Moles's *Definition and Rule in Legal Theory* (Oxford and New York, 1987). Professor Moles's emphasis differs from mine (he is interested in rehabilitating John Austin), but many of the points we make are complementary. See especially pages 103 ("Hart's mistake is . . . to suggest that ways of thinking have some autonomous existence independent of the will and desire of their human authors."), 119 ("If the . . . core elements . . . are merely an extrapolation from the practice of the courts, then they are too vague to be helpful."), 156 ("The distinction between a 'literal' and a 'purposive' approach presents us with a false dichotomy."), and 183 (" 'Distortion' is an inevitable feature of knowledge and cannot therefore have the pejorative connotations which may initially be suggested by the use of this word.").

Withholding the Missing Portion: Psychoanalysis and Rhetoric

1   *Style in Language,* ed. Thomas A. Sebeok (Cambridge, Mass., 1960), p. 385. Much of what follows was worked out in a series of team-taught classes with Michael Fried. Although it is always difficult to determine who contributed what in such situations, I think it fair to say that anything unpersuasive or insufficiently nuanced is wholly mine. A very much shorter version of this paper appeared in the *Times Literary Supplement,* August 29, 1986.
2   S. Freud, *The Complete Introductory Lectures on Psychoanalysis,* trans. and ed. James Strachey (New York, 1966), pp. 5–6.
3   *The Wolf-Man By the Wolf-Man,* ed. Muriel Gardner (New York, 1971), p. 177.
4   Freud has been much criticized for this strategy. See on this point Patrick J. Mahony, *Cries of the Wolf Man* (New York, 1984), p. 34; and Robert J. Langs, "Misalliance in the Wolf-man Case," in *Freud and His Patients,* ed. Mark Kanzer and Jules Glenn (New York and London, 1980), pp. 375–80.
5   J. O. Wisdom, "Testing an Interpretation Within a Session," in *Freud: A Collection of Critical Essays,* ed. Richard Wollheim (Garden City, N.Y.,

1974), p. 340. There is, of course, a huge literature focusing on the issues of evidence and testability. For representative positions, see the essays by Boden, Salmon, Gylmour, Alexander, and Mischel in the same collection. H. J. Eysenck articulates the general complaint of hard-core verificationists: "clinical work is often very productive of theories and hypotheses, but weak on proof and verification" (*The Uses and Abuses of Psychology,* Penguin, London, 1959, p. 228). Defenses typically take the form of arguing that verification is indeed available, albeit not always in the (impossibly strict) forms demanded by Freud's critics. Recently the debate has been given renewed life by the publication of Adolf Grünbaum's *The Foundations of Psychoanalysis: A Philosophical Critique* (Berkeley, Los Angeles, and London, 1984). Although Grünbaum disagrees with Karl Popper's contention that psychoanalytic hypotheses are non-falsifiable and therefore unscientific, he argues that psychoanalytic evidence, derived as it is from the clinical practice of free-association, is unavoidably contaminated by "extraneous" influences such as the analyst's selection biases, the patient's sense of what the analyst wants to hear, the untrustworthiness of memory, etc. For a recent review of the literature and the issues, see Marshall Edelson, *Hypothesis and Evidence in Psychoanalysis* (Chicago, 1984). The scientific question becomes a moral one in the work of J. M. Masson who argues (in *The Assault on Truth,* New York, 1984) that Freud's rejection of the seduction theory in favor of fantasy was a turning away from the empirical reality of his patients' suffering, and was prompted by the general unwillingness of a patriarchal society to face the idea of sexual violence in the family. In short, Freud ceased being a truth-seeker and became an apologist. Both Masson and the philosophical critics agree that psychoanalysis will have a serious claim on our attention only if its methods and conclusions rest on some objective foundation; but this is an assumption rejected by another group of analysts who see the "truth" of psychoanalysis as a narrative truth and invoke a standard not of correspondence with empirical facts but of coherence within a discursive structure. See Donald P. Spence, *Narrative Truth and Historical Truth: Meaning and Interpretation in Psychoanalysis* (New York and London, 1982); and vol. 1, nos. 3–4 of the *International Forum for Psychoanalysis,* ed. Joseph Rippen (1984).

6   Cf. Ernest Gellner, *The Psychoanalytic Movement* (London, 1985), p. 48: "The concept of the Unconscious is a means of devaluing all previous certainties. . . . It is not so much a hypothesis as a suspension of all other hypotheses." In other words, as a concept the unconscious validates *anything,* and this "suspension" of "all guidelines" is both its content and the operation (any operation at all) it makes possible.

7   Peter Brooks, *Reading for the Plot* (New York, 1984), p. 277.

8   "Analysis Terminable and Interminable," in *The Complete Psychological Works of Sigmund Freud,* vol. 23 (London, 1964), p. 217.

9   S. Viderman, *Le Celeste et le Sublunaire* (Paris, 1977), p. 287.

10   See on this point Mahony, *Cries of the Wolf Man,* p. 90: "In effect, the analyst and the patient were locked in a quid pro quo of anal retention

and release extending from the clinical setting to the pages of the deferred expository narrative."

11 To say that the primal scene is always a scene of persuasion is to say that it is a scene of closure; a scene marked by the achievement of a seamless coherence in which an explanation has been found for every detail; an explanation whose authority inheres precisely in its power to be wholly convincing, to secure belief. This is not to say that Freud's text cannot be opened, only that it is not his intention to open it. That is certainly the intention of Derrida, Lacan, Brooks, Lukacher, Hertz, and all the other "oppositional" readers who have recently been so busy. It is their project to interrogate the text from an angle that brings to the surface what its operations necessarily exclude; but the undoubted success of that project says nothing about the Freudian text; rather, it says only that if one submits the text to an interpretive pressure different from the interpretive pressure that produced it in the first place, it will become a different text. There is no natural bar to such an exercise (no text in and of itself) which can be repeated ad infinitum; but to repeat it is to prove nothing except that it can be done; once it is done in the service of a thesis *about* the text it becomes a form of closure itself. Either Brooks and his party are demonstrating something about language—that it is infinitely capable of being appropriated—or he is asserting that something is true of *this* text. If he is doing the first, I have no quarrel with him, although at this late date I find the point uninteresting; if he is doing the second, I think that he is just wrong.

12 Ned Lukacher, *Primal Scenes: Literature, Philosophy, Psychoanalysis* (Ithaca, N.Y., 1986), p. 145.

13 For an elaboration of this point, see S. Fish, "Consequences," chapter 14, pp. 323–24 and passim. The issue here is whether or not having realized that we are always and already in a situation, we are now in a better position to operate in the situations we occupy. Those who answer in the affirmative commit what I call anti-foundationalist theory hope, the mistake of thinking that a general awareness of groundlessness leads one to question and distrust the (interpretive) grounds of one's discourse. This distrust could only be performed if one could move to some other (i.e., noninterpretive) grounds from the vantage point of which distrust could be experienced, but that move is precluded by the anti-foundationalist insight itself.

Index

602   Index

Green, Judith, 318
Grey, Thomas, 328–30
Grice, H. P., 7–8, 67
GRIP (Group for Research in the In-
    stitutionalization and Profession-
    alization of Literary Studies), 237–
    42, 571–72 n.98
Grunbaum, Adolf, 592 n.5
Guthrie, W. K. C., 480

Habermas, Jürgen, 443, 450–55, 498–
    99. See also "Universal Pragmatics"
Haley, Alex, 55
Hamlet [character], 104, 107–8, 563
    n.15
Harari, Josué, 341
Harnisch, Robert, 67
Hart, H. L. A., 5, 10, 503–24 passim
Hartman, Geoffrey, 168, 271–72
Harvard English department, 208–10
Hegland, Kenney, 10–11
Heidegger, Martin, 345
Held, David, 449
Heller, Thomas, 25
Hermeneutics: general and local, 316–
    17
Hirsch, E. D., 68, 71–72, 219–20, 310,
    316–17, 319, 353, 441, 499, 517
Historicity: insight of, 455
History, 26, 93–95, 98, 225, 277; Iser
    and, 72, 74; interpretation and, 93–
    95; as constraint, 93, 95; of phi-
    losophy, 157–58; change and, 157–
    58; as persuasion, 250–93 passim;
    question of critical, 288–89; "in-
    ternalist," 289–93; human is con-
    text within which we know, 324; in-
    stitutional, 365–66, 387, 389–90;
    indictment of fallen, 415–16; cannot
    escape from, 438, 456, 467; of
    Western thought as history of
    quarrel between serious and rhetori-
    cal man, 484–85. See also Judges;
    Legal history
Hoadly, Bishop, 9–10, 504–5
Holland, Norman, 500

Horkheimer, Max, 444–45, 447–49
Human nature, 409

Ideation, 80
Ideology, 221, 496
Idolatry, 412, 423, 432
Illusion, 236
Impartiality: as function of partisan
    conception, 438–39
Imperatives: come along with any
    point of view, 12; are historical and
    revisable, 298–300
Incongruities: emerge in context of
    interpretive assumptions and are
    product of interpretation, 182–83
Inconsistencies, 434–35
Independence, 127, 533; constraint
    and, 126–32; Wolf-Man's and
    Jung's from Freud, 548–50
Independent constraints, 12–13
Indeterminacy, 38, 77, 82–84; grad-
    ually increasing, 72–73, 75; distinc-
    tion between determinacy and will
    not hold, 74–75, 78–79, 83–84
Individual, 365; will, 6, 11; community
    and, 83, 409–11, 413; beliefs, in-
    stitutions, and, 240–41
Infantile neurosis, 531–32; as rhetori-
    cal weapon, 532
Infelicity, 44–45, 491
Information, 28, 90
Institution(s), 95; does not respond
    to but creates work to be done, 169–
    72, 179; individuals, beliefs, and,
    240–41
Institutional, 25, 55–56; virtue and
    power, 133–34, interpretive com-
    munities are sets of practices, 153;
    everything is, 242–43, 558 n.12
Institutional history. See History,
    institutional
Institutionalization, 237
Intelligibility, 67; background condi-
    tions of determine or control mean-
    ing and interpretation, 237, 251,
    295, 301–2

Irony(ies) (*Cont.*)
  rests on a structure of assumptions
    and beliefs, 195–96
Irrationality: formalist definition of, 6
Iser, Wolfgang, 39, 68–86 passim,
  500
Isocrates, 481–82, 525–26
Iterability, 47–48, 56–57

Jacoby, Russell, 177
James, Henry, 106
Jameson, Fredric, 292–93, 500–501
Jauss, H. R., 72, 500
Jay, Peter A., 197–203
Johns Hopkins University Press, 37,
  41, 68
Johnson, Samuel, 41
Judges, 10, 111; how constrained, 92–
  93; how constrained by history of
  past decisions, 93, 95, 109–11, 560–
  61 nn.21 and 23; legal decisionmaking and, 94–95; duty to rewrite
  legal history, 94–95; beliefs of and
  legal history, 100–101; self-presentation and, 388–91; as working conception of law, 388; use theory talk,
  389–90. *See also* Judging; Judgment; Judicial reasoning; Law;
  Legal; Legal history
Judging: practice of and theory of,
  378–81, 384–85
Judgment(s), 3, 32, 59, 137, 437, 561
  n.23; belief and, 113, 116; of readers of Freud controlled by him, 533,
  545. *See also* Judges
Judicial reasoning: entities that make
  up inseparable, 559 n.10. *See also*
  Legal reasoning

Katz, Jerrold, 67, 317
Keats, John, 428
Kelman, Mark, 393–97, 584–85 n.62
Kempson, Ruth, 1–3, 8
Kennedy, Duncan, 228–30, 236, 409,
  584 n.60
Kenner, Hugh, 55, 168

King, William, 188–89
Kinte, Kunta, 55–56
Knapp, Steven, 7, 315–16, 319, 321,
  345
Knight, G. Wilson, 252, 257–60
Knowledge, 351, 474; rules for learn-
  ing and tacit, 353–54
Krouse, Michael, 279
Kuhn, Thomas, 125–26, 143, 157, 159,
  176, 345, 474, 486–88

Lacan, Jacques, 550
Language, 6, 40, 48–49, 508, 550;
  philosophy of, 1, 488; theoretical
  model of as goal of linguistics, 3,
  475; ordinary, straightforward, or
  legal and fictional or literary, 38–
  41, 48, 78–79, 81, 301, 303–4, 474;
  purify to purify consciousness, 452–
  54; reform to regulate, 477
Lanham, Richard, 344, 482–83
Larson, Magali Sarfatti, 209, 216,
  243–44
Lau, Charley. *See* "Charley Lau
  Objection"
Law(s), 6, 10, 13, 360, 504, 507, 523;
  rule of replaced by rule of persuasion, 5, 504, 515; resting on grounds
  of force, 10, 523; "principles" as
  constraints on practice of, 13–14;
  meaning of, 87; content of, 130–31;
  literary analysis of interpretation
  and, 306–8; autonomy of academic,
  306–7; "as integrity," 356–71
  passim; conventionalist and pragmatist accounts of, 356–57; is not
  philosophy, 368–69, 397; judges as
  working conceptions of, 388; internalized, 401–2. *See also* Judges;
  Judging; Judgment; Judicial
  reasoning; Legal; Legal history
Law and Economics, 13, 308–9
Lawry, John, 286
Leavis, F. R., 252–54, 256, 266
Left, intellectual, 26–27; defined, 225;
  anti-professionalism and, 225–26;

About the Author

Stanley Fish is Arts and Sciences Professor of English, Professor of Law, and Chair of the Department of English at Duke University. He is the author of *Surprised by Sin: The Reader in Paradise Lost, Self-Consuming Artifacts: The Experience of Seventeenth-Century Literature, The Living Temple: George Herbert and Catechizing,* and *Is There a Text in This Class? The Authority of Interpretive Communities.*